Lecture Notes in Computer Science 13381

More information about this series at https://link.springer.com/bookseries/558

Osvaldo Gervasi · Beniamino Murgante ·
Sanjay Misra · Ana Maria A. C. Rocha ·
Chiara Garau (Eds.)

Computational Science and Its Applications – ICCSA 2022 Workshops

Malaga, Spain, July 4–7, 2022
Proceedings, Part V

 Springer

Editors
Osvaldo Gervasi ⓘ
University of Perugia
Perugia, Italy

Sanjay Misra ⓘ
Østfold University College
Halden, Norway

Chiara Garau ⓘ
University of Cagliari
Cagliari, Italy

Beniamino Murgante ⓘ
University of Basilicata
Potenza, Potenza, Italy

Ana Maria A. C. Rocha ⓘ
University of Minho
Braga, Portugal

ISSN 0302-9743   ISSN 1611-3349   (electronic)
Lecture Notes in Computer Science
ISBN 978-3-031-10547-0   ISBN 978-3-031-10548-7   (eBook)
https://doi.org/10.1007/978-3-031-10548-7

This Springer imprint is published by the registered company Springer Nature Switzerland AG
The registered company address is: Gewerbestrasse 11, 6330 Cham, Switzerland

Preface

These six volumes (LNCS 13377–13382) consist of the peer-reviewed papers from the workshops at the 22nd International Conference on Computational Science and Its Applications (ICCSA 2022), which took place during July 4–7, 2022. The peer-reviewed papers of the main conference tracks are published in a separate set consisting of two volumes (LNCS 13375–13376).

This year, we again decided to organize a hybrid conference, with some of the delegates attending in person and others taking part online. Despite the enormous benefits achieved by the intensive vaccination campaigns in many countries, at the crucial moment of organizing the event, there was no certainty about the evolution of COVID-19. Fortunately, more and more researchers were able to attend the event in person, foreshadowing a slow but gradual exit from the pandemic and the limitations that have weighed so heavily on the lives of all citizens over the past three years.

ICCSA 2022 was another successful event in the International Conference on Computational Science and Its Applications (ICCSA) series. Last year, the conference was held as a hybrid event in Cagliari, Italy, and in 2020 it was organized as virtual event, whilst earlier editions took place in Saint Petersburg, Russia (2019), Melbourne, Australia (2018), Trieste, Italy (2017), Beijing, China (2016), Banff, Canada (2015), Guimaraes, Portugal (2014), Ho Chi Minh City, Vietnam (2013), Salvador, Brazil (2012), Santander, Spain (2011), Fukuoka, Japan (2010), Suwon, South Korea (2009), Perugia, Italy (2008), Kuala Lumpur, Malaysia (2007), Glasgow, UK (2006), Singapore (2005), Assisi, Italy (2004), Montreal, Canada (2003), and (as ICCS) Amsterdam, The Netherlands (2002) and San Francisco, USA (2001).

Computational science is the main pillar of most of the present research, and industrial and commercial applications, and plays a unique role in exploiting ICT innovative technologies. The ICCSA conference series provides a venue to researchers and industry practitioners to discuss new ideas, to share complex problems and their solutions, and to shape new trends in computational science.

Apart from the 52 workshops, ICCSA 2022 also included six main tracks on topics ranging from computational science technologies and application in many fields to specific areas of computational sciences, such as software engineering, security, machine learning and artificial intelligence, and blockchain technologies. For the 52 workshops we have accepted 285 papers. For the main conference tracks we accepted 57 papers and 24 short papers out of 279 submissions (an acceptance rate of 29%). We would like to express our appreciation to the Workshops chairs and co-chairs for their hard work and dedication.

The success of the ICCSA conference series in general, and of ICCSA 2022 in particular, vitally depends on the support of many people: authors, presenters, participants, keynote speakers, workshop chairs, session chairs, organizing committee members, student volunteers, Program Committee members, advisory committee members, international liaison chairs, reviewers, and others in various roles. We take this opportunity to wholehartedly thank them all.

We also wish to thank our publisher, Springer, for their acceptance to publish the proceedings, for sponsoring some of the best papers awards, and for their kind assistance and cooperation during the editing process.

We cordially invite you to visit the ICCSA website https://iccsa.org where you can find all the relevant information about this interesting and exciting event.

July 2022

Osvaldo Gervasi
Beniamino Murgante
Sanjay Misra

Welcome Message from Organizers

The ICCSA 2021 conference in the Mediterranean city of Cagliari provided us with inspiration to offer the ICCSA 2022 conference in the Mediterranean city of Málaga, Spain. The additional considerations due to the COVID-19 pandemic, which necessitated a hybrid conference, also stimulated the idea to use the School of Informatics of the University of Málaga. It has an open structure where we could take lunch and coffee outdoors and the lecture halls have open windows on two sides providing optimal conditions for meeting more safely.

The school is connected to the center of the old town via a metro system, for which we offered cards to the participants. This provided the opportunity to stay in lodgings in the old town close to the beach because, at the end of the day, that is the place to be to exchange ideas with your fellow scientists. The social program allowed us to enjoy the history of Malaga from its founding by the Phoenicians...

In order to provoke as much scientific interaction as possible we organized online sessions that could easily be followed by all participants from their own devices. We tried to ensure that participants from Asia could participate in morning sessions and those from the Americas in evening sessions. On-site sessions could be followed and debated on-site and discussed online using a chat system. To realize this, we relied on the developed technological infrastructure based on open source software, with the addition of streaming channels on YouTube. The implementation of the software infrastructure and the technical coordination of the volunteers were carried out by Damiano Perri and Marco Simonetti. Nine student volunteers from the universities of Málaga, Minho, Almeria, and Helsinki provided technical support and ensured smooth interaction during the conference.

A big thank you goes to all of the participants willing to exchange their ideas during their daytime. Participants of ICCSA 2022 came from 58 countries scattered over many time zones of the globe. Very interesting keynote talks were provided by well-known international scientists who provided us with more ideas to reflect upon, and we are grateful for their insights.

Eligius M. T. Hendrix

Organization

ICCSA 2022 was organized by the University of Malaga (Spain), the University of Perugia (Italy), the University of Cagliari (Italy), the University of Basilicata (Italy), Monash University (Australia), Kyushu Sangyo University (Japan), and the University of Minho, (Portugal).

Honorary General Chairs

Norio Shiratori	Chuo University, Japan
Kenneth C. J. Tan	Sardina Systems, UK

General Chairs

Osvaldo Gervasi	University of Perugia, Italy
Eligius Hendrix	University of Malaga, Italy
Bernady O. Apduhan	Kyushu Sangyo University, Japan

Program Committee Chairs

Beniamino Murgante	University of Basilicata, Italy
Inmaculada Garcia Fernandez	University of Malaga, Spain
Ana Maria A. C. Rocha	University of Minho, Portugal
David Taniar	Monash University, Australia

International Advisory Committee

Jemal Abawajy	Deakin University, Australia
Dharma P. Agarwal	University of Cincinnati, USA
Rajkumar Buyya	Melbourne University, Australia
Claudia Bauzer Medeiros	University of Campinas, Brazil
Manfred M. Fisher	Vienna University of Economics and Business, Austria
Marina L. Gavrilova	University of Calgary, Canada
Sumi Helal	University of Florida, USA, and University of Lancaster, UK
Yee Leung	Chinese University of Hong Kong, China

International Liaison Chairs

Ivan Blečić	University of Cagliari, Italy
Giuseppe Borruso	University of Trieste, Italy

Elise De Donker	Western Michigan University, USA
Maria Irene Falcão	University of Minho, Portugal
Robert C. H. Hsu	Chung Hua University, Taiwan
Tai-Hoon Kim	Beijing Jiaotong University, China
Vladimir Korkhov	St Petersburg University, Russia
Sanjay Misra	Østfold University College, Norway
Takashi Naka	Kyushu Sangyo University, Japan
Rafael D. C. Santos	National Institute for Space Research, Brazil
Maribel Yasmina Santos	University of Minho, Portugal
Elena Stankova	St Petersburg University, Russia

Workshop and Session Organizing Chairs

Beniamino Murgante	University of Basilicata, Italy
Chiara Garau	University of Cagliari, Italy
Sanjay Misra	Ostfold University College, Norway

Award Chair

| Wenny Rahayu | La Trobe University, Australia |

Publicity Committee Chairs

Elmer Dadios	De La Salle University, Philippines
Nataliia Kulabukhova	St Petersburg University, Russia
Daisuke Takahashi	Tsukuba University, Japan
Shangwang Wang	Beijing University of Posts and Telecommunications, China

Local Arrangement Chairs

Eligius Hendrix	University of Malaga, Spain
Inmaculada Garcia Fernandez	University of Malaga, Spain
Salvador Merino Cordoba	University of Malaga, Spain
Pablo Guerrero-García	University of Malaga, Spain

Technology Chairs

| Damiano Perri | University of Florence, Italy |
| Marco Simonetti | University of Florence, Italy |

Program Committee

| Vera Afreixo | University of Aveiro, Portugal |
| Filipe Alvelos | University of Minho, Portugal |

Hartmut Asche	Hasso-Plattner-Institut für Digital Engineering gGmbH, Germany
Ginevra Balletto	University of Cagliari, Italy
Michela Bertolotto	University College Dublin, Ireland
Sandro Bimonte	TSCF, INRAE, France
Rod Blais	University of Calgary, Canada
Ivan Blečić	University of Sassari, Italy
Giuseppe Borruso	University of Trieste, Italy
Ana Cristina Braga	University of Minho, Portugal
Massimo Cafaro	University of Salento, Italy
Yves Caniou	ENS Lyon, France
Ermanno Cardelli	University of Perugia, Italy
José A. Cardoso e Cunha	Universidade Nova de Lisboa, Portugal
Rui Cardoso	University of Beira Interior, Portugal
Leocadio G. Casado	University of Almeria, Spain
Carlo Cattani	University of Salerno, Italy
Mete Celik	Erciyes University, Turkey
Maria Cerreta	University of Naples Federico II, Italy
Hyunseung Choo	Sungkyunkwan University, South Korea
Rachel Chieng-Sing Lee	Sunway University, Malaysia
Min Young Chung	Sungkyunkwan University, South Korea
Florbela Maria da Cruz Domingues Correia	Polytechnic Institute of Viana do Castelo, Portugal
Gilberto Corso Pereira	Federal University of Bahia, Brazil
Alessandro Costantini	INFN, Italy
Carla Dal Sasso Freitas	Universidade Federal do Rio Grande do Sul, Brazil
Pradesh Debba	Council for Scientific and Industrial Research (CSIR), South Africa
Hendrik Decker	Instituto Tecnológico de Informática, Spain
Robertas Damaševičius	Kaunas University of Technology, Lithuania
Frank Devai	London South Bank University, UK
Rodolphe Devillers	Memorial University of Newfoundland, Canada
Joana Matos Dias	University of Coimbra, Portugal
Paolino Di Felice	University of L'Aquila, Italy
Prabu Dorairaj	NetApp, India/USA
M. Noelia Faginas Lago	University of Perugia, Italy
M. Irene Falcao	University of Minho, Portugal
Florbela P. Fernandes	Polytechnic Institute of Bragança, Portugal
Jose-Jesus Fernandez	National Centre for Biotechnology, Spain
Paula Odete Fernandes	Polytechnic Institute of Bragança, Portugal
Adelaide de Fátima Baptista Valente Freitas	University of Aveiro, Portugal
Manuel Carlos Figueiredo	University of Minho, Portugal
Maria Celia Furtado Rocha	Federal University of Bahia, Brazil
Chiara Garau	University of Cagliari, Italy
Paulino Jose Garcia Nieto	University of Oviedo, Spain

Maria Filipa Mourão   Instituto Politécnico de Viana do Castelo, Portugal
Louiza de Macedo Mourelle   State University of Rio de Janeiro, Brazil
Nadia Nedjah   State University of Rio de Janeiro, Brazil
Laszlo Neumann   University of Girona, Spain
Kok-Leong Ong   Deakin University, Australia
Belen Palop   Universidad de Valladolid, Spain
Marcin Paprzycki   Polish Academy of Sciences, Poland
Eric Pardede   La Trobe University, Australia
Kwangjin Park   Wonkwang University, South Korea
Ana Isabel Pereira   Polytechnic Institute of Bragança, Portugal
Massimiliano Petri   University of Pisa, Italy
Telmo Pinto   University of Coimbra, Portugal
Maurizio Pollino   Italian National Agency for New Technologies, Energy
                                  and Sustainable Economic Development, Italy
Alenka Poplin   University of Hamburg, Germany
Vidyasagar Potdar   Curtin University of Technology, Australia
David C. Prosperi   Florida Atlantic University, USA
Wenny Rahayu   La Trobe University, Australia
Jerzy Respondek   Silesian University of Technology, Poland
Humberto Rocha   INESC-Coimbra, Portugal
Jon Rokne   University of Calgary, Canada
Octavio Roncero   CSIC, Spain
Maytham Safar   Kuwait University, Kuwait
Chiara Saracino   A.O. Ospedale Niguarda Ca' Granda, Italy
Marco Paulo Seabra dos   University of Coimbra, Portugal
  Reis
Jie Shen   University of Michigan, USA
Qi Shi   Liverpool John Moores University, UK
Dale Shires   U.S. Army Research Laboratory, USA
Inês Soares   University of Coimbra, Portugal
Elena Stankova   St Petersburg University, Russia
Takuo Suganuma   Tohoku University, Japan
Eufemia Tarantino   Polytechnic Universiy of Bari, Italy
Sergio Tasso   University of Perugia, Italy
Ana Paula Teixeira   University of Trás-os-Montes and Alto Douro, Portugal
M. Filomena Teodoro   Portuguese Naval Academy and University of Lisbon,
                                  Portugal
Parimala Thulasiraman   University of Manitoba, Canada
Carmelo Torre   Polytechnic University of Bari, Italy
Javier Martinez Torres   Centro Universitario de la Defensa Zaragoza, Spain
Giuseppe A. Trunfio   University of Sassari, Italy
Pablo Vanegas   University of Cuenca, Equador
Marco Vizzari   University of Perugia, Italy
Varun Vohra   Merck Inc., USA
Koichi Wada   University of Tsukuba, Japan
Krzysztof Walkowiak   Wroclaw University of Technology, Poland

Zequn Wang	Intelligent Automation Inc, USA
Robert Weibel	University of Zurich, Switzerland
Frank Westad	Norwegian University of Science and Technology, Norway
Roland Wismüller	Universität Siegen, Germany
Mudasser Wyne	National University, USA
Chung-Huang Yang	National Kaohsiung Normal University, Taiwan
Xin-She Yang	National Physical Laboratory, UK
Salim Zabir	France Telecom Japan Co., Japan
Haifeng Zhao	University of California, Davis, USA
Fabiana Zollo	Ca' Foscari University of Venice, Italy
Albert Y. Zomaya	University of Sydney, Australia

Workshop Organizers

International Workshop on Advances in Artificial Intelligence Learning Technologies: Blended Learning, STEM, Computational Thinking and Coding (AAILT 2022)

Alfredo Milani	University of Perugia, Italy
Valentina Franzoni	University of Perugia, Italy
Osvaldo Gervasi	University of Perugia, Italy

International Workshop on Advancements in Applied Machine-Learning and Data Analytics (AAMDA 2022)

Alessandro Costantini	INFN, Italy
Davide Salomoni	INFN, Italy
Doina Cristina Duma	INFN, Italy
Daniele Cesini	INFN, Italy

International Workshop on Advances in Information Systems and Technologies for Emergency Management, Risk Assessment and Mitigation Based on the Resilience (ASTER 2022)

Maurizio Pollino	ENEA, Italy
Marco Vona	University of Basilicata, Italy
Sonia Giovinazzi	ENEA, Italy
Benedetto Manganelli	University of Basilicata, Italy
Beniamino Murgante	University of Basilicata, Italy

International Workshop on Advances in Web Based Learning (AWBL 2022)

Birol Ciloglugil   Ege University, Turkey
Mustafa Inceoglu   Ege University, Turkey

International Workshop on Blockchain and Distributed Ledgers: Technologies and Applications (BDLTA 2022)

Vladimir Korkhov   St Petersburg State University, Russia
Elena Stankova   St Petersburg State University, Russia
Nataliia Kulabukhova   St Petersburg State University, Russia

International Workshop on Bio and Neuro Inspired Computing and Applications (BIONCA 2022)

Nadia Nedjah   State University of Rio De Janeiro, Brazil
Luiza De Macedo Mourelle State University of Rio De Janeiro, Brazil

International Workshop on Configurational Analysis For Cities (CA CITIES 2022)

Claudia Yamu   Oslo Metropolitan University, Norway
Valerio Cutini   Università di Pisa, Italy
Beniamino Murgante   University of Basilicata, Italy
Chiara Garau   Dicaar, University of Cagliari, Italy

International Workshop on Computational and Applied Mathematics (CAM 2022)

Maria Irene Falcão   University of Minho, Portugal
Fernando Miranda   University of Minho, Portugal

International Workshop on Computational and Applied Statistics (CAS 2022)

Ana Cristina Braga   University of Minho, Portugal

International Workshop on Computational Mathematics, Statistics and Information Management (CMSIM 2022)

Maria Filomena Teodoro   University of Lisbon and Portuguese Naval Academy,
                         Portugal

International Workshop on Computational Optimization and Applications (COA 2022)

Ana Maria A. C. Rocha	University of Minho, Portugal
Humberto Rocha	University of Coimbra, Portugal

International Workshop on Computational Astrochemistry (CompAstro 2022)

Marzio Rosi	University of Perugia, Italy
Nadia Balucani	University of Perugia, Italy
Cecilia Ceccarelli	Université Grenoble Alpes, France
Stefano Falcinelli	University of Perugia, Italy

International Workshop on Computational Methods for Porous Geomaterials (CompPor 2022)

Vadim Lisitsa	Sobolev Institute of Mathematics, Russia
Evgeniy Romenski	Sobolev Institute of Mathematics, Russia

International Workshop on Computational Approaches for Smart, Conscious Cities (CASCC 2022)

Andreas Fricke	University of Potsdam, Germany
Juergen Doellner	University of Potsdam, Germany
Salvador Merino	University of Malaga, Spain
Jürgen Bund	Graphics Vision AI Association, Germany/Portugal
Markus Jobst	Federal Office of Metrology and Surveying, Austria
Francisco Guzman	University of Malaga, Spain

International Workshop on Computational Science and HPC (CSHPC 2022)

Elise De Doncker	Western Michigan University, USA
Fukuko Yuasa	High Energy Accelerator Research Organization (KEK), Japan
Hideo Matsufuru	High Energy Accelerator Research Organization (KEK), Japan

International Workshop on Cities, Technologies and Planning (CTP 2022)

Giuseppe Borruso	University of Trieste, Italy
Malgorzata Hanzl	Lodz University of Technology, Poland
Beniamino Murgante	University of Basilicata, Italy

Anastasia Stratigea   National Technical University of Athens, Grece
Ginevra Balletto   University of Cagliari, Italy
Ljiljana Zivkovic   Republic Geodetic Authority, Serbia

International Workshop on Digital Sustainability and Circular Economy (DiSCE 2022)

Giuseppe Borruso   University of Trieste, Italy
Stefano Epifani   Digital Sustainability Institute, Italy
Ginevra Balletto   University of Cagliari, Italy
Luigi Mundula   University of Cagliari, Italy
Alessandra Milesi   University of Cagliari, Italy
Mara Ladu   University of Cagliari, Italy
Stefano De Nicolai   University of Pavia, Italy
Tu Anh Trinh   University of Economics Ho Chi Minh City, Vietnam

International Workshop on Econometrics and Multidimensional Evaluation in Urban Environment (EMEUE 2022)

Carmelo Maria Torre   Polytechnic University of Bari, Italy
Maria Cerreta   University of Naples Federico II, Italy
Pierluigi Morano   Polytechnic University of Bari, Italy
Giuliano Poli   University of Naples Federico II, Italy
Marco Locurcio   Polytechnic University of Bari, Italy
Francesco Tajani   Sapienza University of Rome, Italy

International Workshop on Ethical AI Applications for a Human-Centered Cyber Society (EthicAI 2022)

Valentina Franzoni   University of Perugia, Italy
Alfredo Milani   University of Perugia, Italy

International Workshop on Future Computing System Technologies and Applications (FiSTA 2022)

Bernady Apduhan   Kyushu Sangyo University, Japan
Rafael Santos   INPE, Brazil

International Workshop on Geodesign in Decision Making: Meta Planning and Collaborative Design for Sustainable and Inclusive Development (GDM 2022)

Francesco Scorza   University of Basilicata, Italy
Michele Campagna   University of Cagliari, Italy
Ana Clara Mourão Moura   Federal University of Minas Gerais, Brazil

International Workshop on Geomatics in Agriculture and Forestry: New Advances and Perspectives (GeoForAgr 2022)

Maurizio Pollino   ENEA, Italy
Giuseppe Modica   University of Reggio Calabria, Italy
Marco Vizzari   University of Perugia, Italy

International Workshop on Geographical Analysis, Urban Modeling, Spatial Statistics (Geog-An-Mod 2022)

Giuseppe Borruso   University of Trieste, Italy
Beniamino Murgante   University of Basilicata, Italy
Harmut Asche   Hasso-Plattner-Institut für Digital Engineering gGmbH,
                             Germany

International Workshop on Geomatics for Resource Monitoring and Management (GRMM 2022)

Alessandra Capolupo   Polytechnic of Bari, Italy
Eufemia Tarantino   Polytechnic of Bari, Italy
Enrico Borgogno Mondino   University of Turin, Italy

International Workshop on Information and Knowledge in the Internet of Things (IKIT 2022)

Teresa Guarda   State University of Santa Elena Peninsula, Ecuador
Filipe Portela   University of Minho, Portugal
Maria Fernanda Augusto   Bitrum Research Center, Spain

13th International Symposium on Software Quality (ISSQ 2022)

Sanjay Misra   Østfold University College, Norway

International Workshop on Machine Learning for Space and Earth Observation Data (MALSEOD 2022)

Rafael Santos   INPE, Brazil
Karine Reis Ferreira Gomes   INPE, Brazil

International Workshop on Building Multi-dimensional Models for Assessing Complex Environmental Systems (MES 2022)

Vanessa Assumma   Politecnico di Torino, Italy
Caterina Caprioli   Politecnico di Torino, Italy
Giulia Datola   Politecnico di Torino, Italy

Federico Dell'Anna   Politecnico di Torino, Italy
Marta Dell'Ovo   Politecnico di Milano, Italy

International Workshop on Models and Indicators for Assessing and Measuring the Urban Settlement Development in the View of ZERO Net Land Take by 2050 (MOVEto0 2022)

Lucia Saganeiti   University of L'Aquila, Italy
Lorena Fiorini   University of L'aquila, Italy
Angela Pilogallo   University of Basilicata, Italy
Alessandro Marucci   University of L'Aquila, Italy
Francesco Zullo   University of L'Aquila, Italy

International Workshop on Modelling Post-Covid Cities (MPCC 2022)

Beniamino Murgante   University of Basilicata, Italy
Ginevra Balletto   University of Cagliari, Italy
Giuseppe Borruso   University of Trieste, Italy
Marco Dettori   Università degli Studi di Sassari, Italy
Lucia Saganeiti   University of L'Aquila, Italy

International Workshop on Ecosystem Services: Nature's Contribution to People in Practice. Assessment Frameworks, Models, Mapping, and Implications (NC2P 2022)

Francesco Scorza   University of Basilicata, Italy
Sabrina Lai   University of Cagliari, Italy
Silvia Ronchi   University of Cagliari, Italy
Dani Broitman   Israel Institute of Technology, Israel
Ana Clara Mourão Moura   Federal University of Minas Gerais, Brazil
Corrado Zoppi   University of Cagliari, Italy

International Workshop on New Mobility Choices for Sustainable and Alternative Scenarios (NEWMOB 2022)

Tiziana Campisi   University of Enna Kore, Italy
Socrates Basbas   Aristotle University of Thessaloniki, Greece
Aleksandra Deluka T.   University of Rijeka, Croatia
Alexandros Nikitas   University of Huddersfield, UK
Ioannis Politis   Aristotle University of Thessaloniki, Greece
Georgios Georgiadis   Aristotle University of Thessaloniki, Greece
Irena Ištoka Otković   University of Osijek, Croatia
Sanja Surdonja   University of Rijeka, Croatia

International Workshop on Privacy in the Cloud/Edge/IoT World (PCEIoT 2022)

Michele Mastroianni	University of Campania Luigi Vanvitelli, Italy
Lelio Campanile	University of Campania Luigi Vanvitelli, Italy
Mauro Iacono	University of Campania Luigi Vanvitelli, Italy

International Workshop on Psycho-Social Analysis of Sustainable Mobility in the Pre- and Post-Pandemic Phase (PSYCHE 2022)

Tiziana Campisi	University of Enna Kore, Italy
Socrates Basbas	Aristotle University of Thessaloniki, Greece
Dilum Dissanayake	Newcastle University, UK
Nurten Akgün Tanbay	Bursa Technical University, Turkey
Elena Cocuzza	University of Catania, Italy
Nazam Ali	University of Management and Technology, Pakistan
Vincenza Torrisi	University of Catania, Italy

International Workshop on Processes, Methods and Tools Towards Resilient Cities and Cultural Heritage Prone to SOD and ROD Disasters (RES 2022)

Elena Cantatore	Polytechnic University of Bari, Italy
Alberico Sonnessa	Polytechnic University of Bari, Italy
Dario Esposito	Polytechnic University of Bari, Italy

International Workshop on Scientific Computing Infrastructure (SCI 2022)

Elena Stankova	St Petersburg University, Russia
Vladimir Korkhov	St Petersburg University, Russia

International Workshop on Socio-Economic and Environmental Models for Land Use Management (SEMLUM 2022)

Debora Anelli	Polytechnic University of Bari, Italy
Pierluigi Morano	Polytechnic University of Bari, Italy
Francesco Tajani	Sapienza University of Rome, Italy
Marco Locurcio	Polytechnic University of Bari, Italy
Paola Amoruso	LUM University, Italy

14th International Symposium on Software Engineering Processes and Applications (SEPA 2022)

Sanjay Misra	Østfold University College, Norway

International Workshop on Ports of the Future – Smartness and Sustainability (SmartPorts 2022)

Giuseppe Borruso   University of Trieste, Italy
Gianfranco Fancello   University of Cagliari, Italy
Ginevra Balletto   University of Cagliari, Italy
Patrizia Serra   University of Cagliari, Italy
Maria del Mar Munoz   University of Cadiz, Spain
  Leonisio
Marco Mazzarino   University of Venice, Italy
Marcello Tadini   Università del Piemonte Orientale, Italy

International Workshop on Smart Tourism (SmartTourism 2022)

Giuseppe Borruso   University of Trieste, Italy
Silvia Battino   University of Sassari, Italy
Ainhoa Amaro Garcia   Universidad de Alcalà and Universidad de Las Palmas,
                            Spain
Maria del Mar Munoz   University of Cadiz, Spain
  Leonisio
Carlo Donato   University of Sassari, Italy
Francesca Krasna   University of Trieste, Italy
Ginevra Balletto   University of Cagliari, Italy

International Workshop on Sustainability Performance Assessment: Models, Approaches and Applications Toward Interdisciplinary and Integrated Solutions (SPA 2022)

Francesco Scorza   University of Basilicata, Italy
Sabrina Lai   University of Cagliari, Italy
Jolanta Dvarioniene   Kaunas University of Technology, Lithuania
Iole Cerminara   University of Basilicata, Italy
Georgia Pozoukidou   Aristotle University of Thessaloniki, Greece
Valentin Grecu   Lucian Blaga University of Sibiu, Romania
Corrado Zoppi   University of Cagliari, Italy

International Workshop on Specifics of Smart Cities Development in Europe (SPEED 2022)

Chiara Garau   University of Cagliari, Italy
Katarína Vitálišová   Matej Bel University, Slovakia
Paolo Nesi   University of Florence, Italy
Anna Vanova   Matej Bel University, Slovakia
Kamila Borsekova   Matej Bel University, Slovakia
Paola Zamperlin   University of Pisa, Italy

Federico Cugurullo   Trinity College Dublin, Ireland
Gerardo Carpentieri   University of Naples Federico II, Italy

International Workshop on Smart and Sustainable Island Communities (SSIC 2022)

Chiara Garau   University of Cagliari, Italy
Anastasia Stratigea   National Technical University of Athens, Greece
Paola Zamperlin   University of Pisa, Italy
Francesco Scorza   University of Basilicata, Italy

International Workshop on Theoretical and Computational Chemistry and Its Applications (TCCMA 2022)

Noelia Faginas-Lago   University of Perugia, Italy
Andrea Lombardi   University of Perugia, Italy

International Workshop on Transport Infrastructures for Smart Cities (TISC 2022)

Francesca Maltinti   University of Cagliari, Italy
Mauro Coni   University of Cagliari, Italy
Francesco Pinna   University of Cagliari, Italy
Chiara Garau   University of Cagliari, Italy
Nicoletta Rassu   Univesity of Cagliari, Italy
James Rombi   University of Cagliari, Italy
Benedetto Barabino   University of Brescia, Italy

14th International Workshop on Tools and Techniques in Software Development Process (TTSDP 2022)

Sanjay Misra   Østfold University College, Norway

International Workshop on Urban Form Studies (UForm 2022)

Malgorzata Hanzl   Lodz University of Technology, Poland
Beniamino Murgante   University of Basilicata, Italy
Alessandro Camiz   Özyeğin University, Turkey
Tomasz Bradecki   Silesian University of Technology, Poland

International Workshop on Urban Regeneration: Innovative Tools and Evaluation Model (URITEM 2022)

Fabrizio Battisti   University of Florence, Italy
Laura Ricci   Sapienza University of Rome, Italy
Orazio Campo   Sapienza University of Rome, Italy

International Workshop on Urban Space Accessibility and Mobilities (USAM 2022)

Chiara Garau	University of Cagliari, Italy
Matteo Ignaccolo	University of Catania, Italy
Enrica Papa	University of Westminster, UK
Francesco Pinna	University of Cagliari, Italy
Silvia Rossetti	University of Parma, Italy
Wendy Tan	Wageningen University and Research, The Netherlands
Michela Tiboni	University of Brescia, Italy
Vincenza Torrisi	University of Catania, Italy

International Workshop on Virtual Reality and Augmented Reality and Applications (VRA 2022)

Osvaldo Gervasi	University of Perugia, Italy
Damiano Perri	University of Florence, Italy
Marco Simonetti	University of Florence, Italy
Sergio Tasso	University of Perugia, Italy

International Workshop on Advanced and Computational Methods for Earth Science Applications (WACM4ES 2022)

Luca Piroddi	University of Cagliari, Italy
Sebastiano Damico	University of Malta, Malta

International Workshop on Advanced Mathematics and Computing Methods in Complex Computational Systems (WAMCM 2022)

Yeliz Karaca	UMass Chan Medical School, USA
Dumitru Baleanu	Cankaya University, Turkey
Osvaldo Gervasi	University of Perugia, Italy
Yudong Zhang	University of Leicester, UK
Majaz Moonis	UMass Chan Medical School, USA

Additional Reviewers

Akshat Agrawal	Amity University, Haryana, India
Waseem Ahmad	National Institute of Technology Karnataka, India
Vladimir Alarcon	Universidad Diego Portales, Chile
Oylum Alatlı	Ege University, Turkey
Raffaele Albano	University of Basilicata, Italy
Abraham Alfa	FUT Minna, Nigeria
Diego Altafini	Università di Pisa, Italy
Filipe Alvelos	Universidade do Minho, Portugal

Rogerio Calazan	IEAPM, Brazil
Michele Campagna	University of Cagliari, Italy
Lelio Campanile	Università degli Studi della Campania Luigi Vanvitelli, Italy
Tiziana Campisi	University of Enna Kore, Italy
Antonino Canale	University of Enna Kore, Italy
Elena Cantatore	Polytechnic University of Bari, Italy
Patrizia Capizzi	Univerity of Palermo, Italy
Alessandra Capolupo	Polytechnic University of Bari, Italy
Giacomo Caporusso	Politecnico di Bari, Italy
Caterina Caprioli	Politecnico di Torino, Italy
Gerardo Carpentieri	University of Naples Federico II, Italy
Martina Carra	University of Brescia, Italy
Pedro Carrasqueira	INESC Coimbra, Portugal
Barbara Caselli	Università degli Studi di Parma, Italy
Cecilia Castro	University of Minho, Portugal
Giulio Cavana	Politecnico di Torino, Italy
Iole Cerminara	University of Basilicata, Italy
Maria Cerreta	University of Naples Federico II, Italy
Daniele Cesini	INFN, Italy
Jabed Chowdhury	La Trobe University, Australia
Birol Ciloglugil	Ege University, Turkey
Elena Cocuzza	Univesity of Catania, Italy
Emanuele Colica	University of Malta, Malta
Mauro Coni	University of Cagliari, Italy
Elisete Correia	Universidade de Trás-os-Montes e Alto Douro, Portugal
Florbela Correia	Polytechnic Institute of Viana do Castelo, Portugal
Paulo Cortez	University of Minho, Portugal
Lino Costa	Universidade do Minho, Portugal
Alessandro Costantini	INFN, Italy
Marilena Cozzolino	Università del Molise, Italy
Alfredo Cuzzocrea	University of Calabria, Italy
Sebastiano D'amico	University of Malta, Malta
Gianni D'Angelo	University of Salerno, Italy
Tijana Dabovic	University of Belgrade, Serbia
Hiroshi Daisaka	Hitotsubashi University, Japan
Giulia Datola	Politecnico di Torino, Italy
Regina De Almeida	University of Trás-os-Montes and Alto Douro, Portugal
Maria Stella De Biase	Università della Campania Luigi Vanvitelli, Italy
Elise De Doncker	Western Michigan University, USA
Itamir De Morais Barroca Filho	Federal University of Rio Grande do Norte, Brazil
Samuele De Petris	University of Turin, Italy
Alan De Sá	Marinha do Brasil, Brazil
Alexander Degtyarev	St Petersburg University, Russia

Federico Dell'Anna	Politecnico di Torino, Italy
Marta Dell'Ovo	Politecnico di Milano, Italy
Ahu Dereli Dursun	Istanbul Commerce University, Turkey
Giulia Desogus	University of Cagliari, Italy
Piero Di Bonito	Università degli Studi della Campania, Italia
Paolino Di Felice	University of L'Aquila, Italy
Felicia Di Liddo	Polytechnic University of Bari, Italy
Isabel Dimas	University of Coimbra, Portugal
Doina Cristina Duma	INFN, Italy
Aziz Dursun	Virginia Tech University, USA
Jaroslav Dvořak	Klaipėda University, Lithuania
Dario Esposito	Polytechnic University of Bari, Italy
M. Noelia Faginas-Lago	University of Perugia, Italy
Stefano Falcinelli	University of Perugia, Italy
Falcone Giacomo	University of Reggio Calabria, Italy
Maria Irene Falcão	University of Minho, Portugal
Stefano Federico	CNR-ISAC, Italy
Marcin Feltynowski	University of Lodz, Poland
António Fernandes	Instituto Politécnico de Bragança, Portugal
Florbela Fernandes	Instituto Politécnico de Braganca, Portugal
Paula Odete Fernandes	Instituto Politécnico de Bragança, Portugal
Luis Fernandez-Sanz	University of Alcala, Spain
Luís Ferrás	University of Minho, Portugal
Ângela Ferreira	Instituto Politécnico de Bragança, Portugal
Lorena Fiorini	University of L'Aquila, Italy
Hector Florez	Universidad Distrital Francisco Jose de Caldas, Colombia
Stefano Franco	LUISS Guido Carli, Italy
Valentina Franzoni	Perugia University, Italy
Adelaide Freitas	University of Aveiro, Portugal
Andreas Fricke	Hasso Plattner Institute, Germany
Junpei Fujimoto	KEK, Japan
Federica Gaglione	Università del Sannio, Italy
Andrea Gallo	Università degli Studi di Trieste, Italy
Luciano Galone	University of Malta, Malta
Adam Galuszka	Silesian University of Technology, Poland
Chiara Garau	University of Cagliari, Italy
Ernesto Garcia Para	Universidad del País Vasco, Spain
Aniket A. Gaurav	Østfold University College, Norway
Marina Gavrilova	University of Calgary, Canada
Osvaldo Gervasi	University of Perugia, Italy
Andrea Ghirardi	Università di Brescia, Italy
Andrea Gioia	Politecnico di Bari, Italy
Giacomo Giorgi	Università degli Studi di Perugia, Italy
Stanislav Glubokovskikh	Lawrence Berkeley National Laboratory, USA
A. Manuela Gonçalves	University of Minho, Portugal

Leocadio González Casado   University of Almería, Spain
Angela Gorgoglione   Universidad de la República Uruguay, Uruguay
Yusuke Gotoh   Okayama University, Japan
Daniele Granata   Università degli Studi della Campania, Italy
Christian Grévisse   University of Luxembourg, Luxembourg
Silvana Grillo   University of Cagliari, Italy
Teresa Guarda   State University of Santa Elena Peninsula, Ecuador
Carmen Guida   Università degli Studi di Napoli Federico II, Italy
Kemal Güven Gülen   Namık Kemal University, Turkey
Ipek Guler   Leuven Biostatistics and Statistical Bioinformatics Centre, Belgium
Sevin Gumgum   Izmir University of Economics, Turkey
Martina Halásková   VSB Technical University in Ostrava, Czech Republic
Peter Hegedus   University of Szeged, Hungary
Eligius M. T. Hendrix   Universidad de Málaga, Spain
Mauro Iacono   Università degli Studi della Campania, Italy
Oleg Iakushkin   St Petersburg University, Russia
Matteo Ignaccolo   University of Catania, Italy
Mustafa Inceoglu   Ege University, Turkey
Markus Jobst   Federal Office of Metrology and Surveying, Austria
Issaku Kanamori   RIKEN Center for Computational Science, Japan
Yeliz Karaca   UMass Chan Medical School, USA
Aarti Karande   Sardar Patel Institute of Technology, India
András Kicsi   University of Szeged, Hungary
Vladimir Korkhov   St Petersburg University, Russia
Nataliia Kulabukhova   St Petersburg University, Russia
Claudio Ladisa   Politecnico di Bari, Italy
Mara Ladu   University of Cagliari, Italy
Sabrina Lai   University of Cagliari, Italy
Mark Lajko   University of Szeged, Hungary
Giuseppe Francesco Cesare Lama   University of Napoli Federico II, Italy
Vincenzo Laporta   CNR, Italy
Margherita Lasorella   Politecnico di Bari, Italy
Francesca Leccis   Università di Cagliari, Italy
Federica Leone   University of Cagliari, Italy
Chien-sing Lee   Sunway University, Malaysia
Marco Locurcio   Polytechnic University of Bari, Italy
Francesco Loddo   Henge S.r.l., Italy
Andrea Lombardi   Università di Perugia, Italy
Isabel Lopes   Instituto Politécnico de Bragança, Portugal
Fernando Lopez Gayarre   University of Oviedo, Spain
Vanda Lourenço   Universidade Nova de Lisboa, Portugal
Jing Ma   Luleå University of Technology, Sweden
Helmuth Malonek   University of Aveiro, Portugal
Francesca Maltinti   University of Cagliari, Italy

Jie Shen	University of Michigan, USA
Luneque Silva Junior	Universidade Federal do ABC, Brazil
Carina Silva	Instituto Politécnico de Lisboa, Portugal
Joao Carlos Silva	Polytechnic Institute of Cavado and Ave, Portugal
Ilya Silvestrov	Saudi Aramco, Saudi Arabia
Marco Simonetti	University of Florence, Italy
Maria Joana Soares	University of Minho, Portugal
Michel Soares	Federal University of Sergipe, Brazil
Alberico Sonnessa	Politecnico di Bari, Italy
Lisete Sousa	University of Lisbon, Portugal
Elena Stankova	St Petersburg University, Russia
Jan Stejskal	University of Pardubice, Czech Republic
Silvia Stranieri	University of Naples Federico II, Italy
Anastasia Stratigea	National Technical University of Athens, Greece
Yue Sun	European XFEL GmbH, Germany
Anthony Suppa	Politecnico di Torino, Italy
Kirill Sviatov	Ulyanovsk State Technical University, Russia
David Taniar	Monash University, Australia
Rodrigo Tapia-McClung	Centro de Investigación en Ciencias de Información Geoespacial, Mexico
Eufemia Tarantino	Politecnico di Bari, Italy
Sergio Tasso	University of Perugia, Italy
Vladimir Tcheverda	Institute of Petroleum Geology and Geophysics, SB RAS, Russia
Ana Paula Teixeira	Universidade de Trás-os-Montes e Alto Douro, Portugal
Tengku Adil Tengku Izhar	Universiti Teknologi MARA, Malaysia
Maria Filomena Teodoro	University of Lisbon and Portuguese Naval Academy, Portugal
Yiota Theodora	National Technical University of Athens, Greece
Graça Tomaz	Instituto Politécnico da Guarda, Portugal
Gokchan Tonbul	Atilim University, Turkey
Rosa Claudia Torcasio	CNR-ISAC, Italy
Carmelo Maria Torre	Polytechnic University of Bari, Italy
Vincenza Torrisi	University of Catania, Italy
Vincenzo Totaro	Politecnico di Bari, Italy
Pham Trung	HCMUT, Vietnam
Po-yu Tsai	National Chung Hsing University, Taiwan
Dimitrios Tsoukalas	Centre of Research and Technology Hellas, Greece
Toshihiro Uchibayashi	Kyushu University, Japan
Takahiro Ueda	Seikei University, Japan
Piero Ugliengo	Università degli Studi di Torino, Italy
Gianmarco Vanuzzo	University of Perugia, Italy
Clara Vaz	Instituto Politécnico de Bragança, Portugal
Laura Verde	University of Campania Luigi Vanvitelli, Italy
Katarína Vitálišová	Matej Bel University, Slovakia

Daniel Mark Vitiello	University of Cagliari, Italy
Marco Vizzari	University of Perugia, Italy
Alexander Vodyaho	St. Petersburg State Electrotechnical University "LETI", Russia
Agustinus Borgy Waluyo	Monash University, Australia
Chao Wang	USTC, China
Marcin Wozniak	Silesian University of Technology, Poland
Jitao Yang	Beijing Language and Culture University, China
Fenghui Yao	Tennessee State University, USA
Fukuko Yuasa	KEK, Japan
Paola Zamperlin	University of Pisa, Italy
Michal Žemlička	Charles University, Czech Republic
Nataly Zhukova	ITMO University, Russia
Alcinia Zita Sampaio	University of Lisbon, Portugal
Ljiljana Zivkovic	Republic Geodetic Authority, Serbia
Floriana Zucaro	University of Naples Federico II, Italy
Marco Zucca	Politecnico di Milano, Italy
Camila Zyngier	Ibmec, Belo Horizonte, Brazil

Sponsoring Organizations

ICCSA 2022 would not have been possible without tremendous support of many organizations and institutions, for which all organizers and participants of ICCSA 2022 express their sincere gratitude:

Springer International Publishing AG, Germany (https://www.springer.com)

Computers Open Access Journal (https://www.mdpi.com/journal/computers)

Computation Open Access Journal (https://www.mdpi.com/journal/computation)

University of Malaga, Spain (https://www.uma.es/)

University of Perugia, Italy
(https://www.unipg.it)

University of Basilicata, Italy
(http://www.unibas.it)

Monash University, Australia
(https://www.monash.edu/)

Kyushu Sangyo University, Japan
(https://www.kyusan-u.ac.jp/)

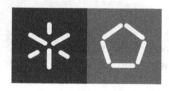

University of Minho, Portugal
(https://www.uminho.pt/)

Universidade do Minho
Escola de Engenharia

Contents – Part V

International Workshop on Smart Tourism (Smart Tourism 2022)

14th International Symposium on Software Engineering Processes and Applications (SEPA 2022)

International Workshop
on Socio-Economic and Environmental
Models for Land Use Management
(SEMLUM 2022)

A Methodological Approach Based on the Choquet Integral for Sustainable Valuations

Francesco Tajani[1] (ID), Francesco Sica[2] (ID), Maria Rosaria Guarini[1] (ID), Pierluigi Morano[3] (ID), and Rossana Ranieri[1 (✉)] (ID)

[1] Department of Architecture and Design, "Sapienza" University of Rome, 00196 Rome, Italy
rossana.ranieri@uniroma1.it
[2] Department of Civil, Environmental and Mechanical Engineering, University of Trento, 38123 Trento, Italy
[3] Department of Civil, Environmental, Land, Building Engineering and Chemistry (DI-CATECh), Polytechnic University of Bari, 70126 Bari, Italy

Abstract. Several methods and operational tools for assessing the sustainability and corresponding aspects can be identified in the current literature. At international level, the use of synthetic indices is clearly established through analytical indicators capable of expressing multiple aspects from an economic, social and environmental perspective. By a literature review, the construction of indices through a multi-criteria approach can be placed in the weights assignment and in construction processes based on the geometric and arithmetic average of values. The allocation of appropriate weights to performance indicators lacks, in particular, an objective methodology and subjective elements linked, e.g., to the decision-makers involved and corresponding interests. This research aims to describe a methodological frame for indices constructing through the multi-criteria approach of the Choquet Integral. The use of Choquet's integral supports the evaluations of multiple aspects of sustainability as monitoring of the relative unbalanced values, and the weights assignment occurs through analytical functions well-established, as the Shapley function.

Keywords: Sustainable index · Choquet integral · Multi-criteria approaches · Territorial investments · 2030 Agenda

1 Introduction

The sustainable assessment of urban networks in changing perspective has become a central issue for the development and implementation of effective planning strategies. In world-wide context, the political agenda has been rating the impacts of sustainable investments on citizens' well-being, environmental quality, economic growth within the decision-systems for territories growing. The well-being "sustainable foot-print" at territorial and urban scale steers to revise the income by integrating multiple aspects, also related to the society and environment [1–4].

In light of this, the use of Gross Domestic Product (GDP) as an effective representative measure of the urban/territorial well-being is becoming less obvious in economic terms too. The limits of GDP are recognized in the inability to distinguish among events that could have positive and negative impacts on well-being – e.g., reconstruction following a natural disaster or war –, so to appear an effective indicator that summarizes a country's economic activity in a comprehensive manner, not in view of environmental impacts, working conditions, health, and human-social capital.

An analysis of the current literature revealed several research focused on alternative quantification of well-being, quality of life, sustainable development and societal progress. Namely, alternative methodological approaches to GDP have been defined [5]. To date (2022), the "Istanbul Declaration" - signed by the European Commission, the Organization of the Islamic Conference, the United Nations, the United Nations Development Program (UNDP) and the World Bank in June 2007, at the end of the 2nd Organization for Economic Co-operation and Development World Forum - has stated that there is the need to go "beyond GDP" for assessing the well-being at scale of territory and city [6–9].

Methodological approaches to measure the progress of a society with relative well-being state are advisable in the reference literature. There is search for methods and tools aimed to integrate financial values with social and environmental items not detected in GDP [10]. With a view to moving beyond the use of GDP as the main performance indicator for expressing the well-being state, alternative composite indices have been proposed to enable the societal welfare declined in the dimensions of the sustainability (economic, social and environmental) [11].

The UNDP implements the Human Development Index (HDI), which considers health, income and education information data [12]. Similarly, the Environmental Performance Index (EPI) is developed based on primarily environmental-natural indicators [13]. Dobrovolskiene et al. (2017) in the specific Lithuanian context, develop a composite index to verify the sustainability of real estate projects [14], and Attardi et al. propose the Land Use Policy Efficiency Index for the assessment of the environmental and social performance of urban and regional planning policies [15]. Many of these are obtained by aggregating weighted averages related to the different dimensions of well-being, in such a way as to express the appropriate weight for each dimension [16–20]. Furthermore, Ravallion proposes an alternative aggregation function based on the generalized aggregation formula of Chakravarty [21, 22], which allows for a more effective weighting of dimensions than geometric mean [23]. On the other hand, further studies analyze the strength of weights by implementing linear programming processes capable of evaluating the accuracy of rankings with alternative weights [24–29]. These works do not consider the potential interaction among dimensions, but focus on the impact of alternative weight allocation among well-being dimensions on ranking accuracy.

In order to attempt to express particular sustainable statement with specific indices of environmental, social and economic nature, the current research work proposes the adoption of a method of aggregation - the Choquet Integral (CI) - capable of considering the synergies among the sustainable dimensions for the construction of evaluation indices [30]. The CI has been developed by Murufushi and Sugeno as a powerful aggregation operator over an established set of elements [31], and it has been used in selection cases, particularly attracting the fuzzy principles. A critical issue encountered in the application of fuzzy measures consists in the exponential complexity in terms of real number for each subset of the criteria and means to evaluate these through appropriate elicitation of interviewed experts or optimization methods [32, 33]. In this sense, Mazziotta and Pareto (2016) propose the structuring of a method to calculate a non-compensatory index, which penalizes the unbalanced values of indicators through the relative standard deviation measurement [34].

In order to capture synergies among dimensions for an index construction, the UNDP moved from the Arithmetic Mean (AM) to the Geometric one (GM) [12]. However, the GM aggregation method doesn't allow to capture the complementarity and synergies among dimensions. A relatively weak performance in one of the dimensions is counted similarly in the composite score obtained. Compared to the UNDP experimentation, the proposed methodological approach develops an alternative and flexible aggregation process able to perceive a set of interactions among the sustainable dimensions, in order to allow different synergies and to detect unbalanced performance among them.

The use and implementation of the CI for obtaining multivariate and composite indices improved in recent years. E.g., Meyer and Pontheire [37] have employed the CI to show that individual preferences could not be effectively described by an additive model (i.e., weighted average aggregation methods) because of com-plementarities and redundancies among analysis dimensions [38–40]. Many of the other authors take advantage of the CI in the optic to assemble indices that allow different interactions among indicators [41–46], namely Campagnolo et al. [47] applied the CI aggregation method to capture interactions across diverse sustainable factors.

1.1 Aim

The research carried out develops a methodology based on the CI, in order to establish a composite index that could be used: *i*) to assess, from a macro-economic point of view, a well-being level of a country and/or its sub-scale; *ii*) to value, from a micro-economic one, the sustainability of territorial investments. The CI is a general methodology that allows interactions across dimensions (economic, environmental, social) while allocating different relative importance to them. This allows to consider if and how balanced (or unbalanced) the accomplishments across dimensions are and to reveal these differences in the composite score [35, 36].

The paper is organized as follows: in Sect. 2, the methodological approach is illustrated; in Sect. 3, a brief discussion about the CI highlights is reported; in Sect. 4, the conclusions of the research are drawn.

2 Methodological Approach

2.1 Overview

The CI aggregation method [30] is able to support multiple decision-making processes thanks to its ability to collect and synthesize different inputs. Figure 1 describes the four steps of the logical protocol that defines the methodology.

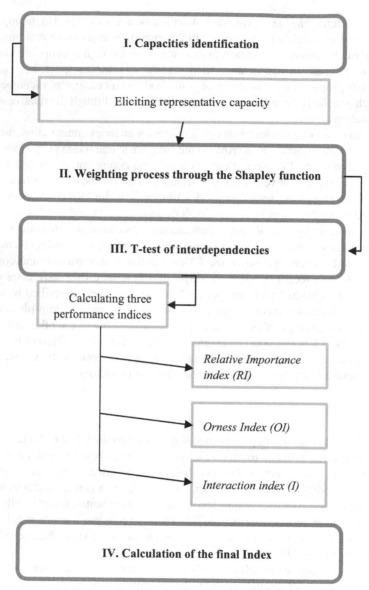

Fig. 1. Logical protocol summary chart for structuring the methodology

Let $\{n_1, n_2, \ldots, n_d\}$ be the values of the dimensions described by a set $T = \{1, 2, 3\}$. The «capacities» are a set of functions where 2T is all possible subsets of the criteria, which assigns a weight from 0 to 1 to each one.

The set function (λ) has to satisfy border and monotonicity conditions as described hereafter:

i. $\lambda (0) = 0; \lambda(T) = 1$;
ii. for any A, B $\subseteq$ T, A $\subseteq$ B $\subseteq$ T $\rightarrow$ $\lambda(A) \leq \lambda(B) \leq \lambda(T)$.

The i) characterizes scenarios in which all dimensions are - respectively - unsatisfactory (i.e., achievements in all dimensions are zero) and satisfactory (i.e., achievements in all dimensions are full). The ii) implies that the value of $\lambda(A)$ signifies the capacity (weight) of dimensions belonging to the subset A in T. This can be interpreted as the weight (importance) that one assigns to the fully satisfactory performances of the dimensions belonging to the subset A, and with fully unsatisfactory performances by the residual dimensions.

Specifically, if a subset has two out of three dimensions, then ({Dimension1, Dimension2}) would signify the weight assigned to the scenario where two-dimension achievements are fully satisfactory, and the other one is fully unsatisfactory.

2.2 Capacities Identification

The CI methodology firstly requires to identify the set of capacities. Though, eliciting representative capacity (monotonic weight sets) for the CI method is quite complex task because of the difficulties in identifying the specific issue to be investigated.

Many identifications methods in the current scientific literature have been elaborated by an optimization problem where restrictions are obtained from the preferences of the decision-makers involved. A review of methods employed for the identification of capacities (i.e. maximum-split, minimum variance, minimum distance, least-squares-based approaches) has been carried out by Grabisch et al. [48]. Other examples to be considered in this phase of the construction of the methodology [49] specify how to elicit capacity by representing decision-makers' preferences. Additionally, Bertin et al. [43] have elicited weights and parameters using a nominal group computer-based technique to reduce the severely disagreeing valuations, to generate an *ex-post* consensus and to mitigate the potential expert-selection bias. The expert elicitation method adapted by Bertin et al. [43] is an effective method to reduce the potential expert-selection bias; however, supposing the most expert selection involves high bias levels, the method adopted may not lessen the potential expert-selection bias, whereas it could increase such bias as the consensus weights are closer to the ones selected by the majority of the experts.

2.3 Weighting Process Within the Choquet Integral

In addition to the need to define capabilities, three important features of the CI must be defined to effectively describe the flexibility of the methodology, in order to include decision-maker preferences in assessments related to multiple aspects of well-being from a sustainable perspective. The CI weighting process is based on the calculation of three different performance indices that allow for consideration of the value of the weight of the assessment domains, specifically indices of: Relative Importance (RI), Orness (OI), Interaction (I). An explanation is given as follows for each index.

Relative Importance Index (RI)
The RI of sustainable dimensions can be assessed using the Shapley value (s_λ) [50] of each dimension, calculated by comparing the weights in every set that includes that dimension against every set that does not include it. Therefore, the overall importance of dimension $i \in T$ can be gained by calculating the average marginal contributions [51, 52] as follows:

$$s_\lambda^{(i)} = \sum_{A \subseteq T/i} \frac{(t-1-a)!a!}{a!} [\lambda(A \cup i) - \lambda(A)]$$

where $t = card(T)$ and $a = card(A)$ represent the cardinality of A and T. Hence, to obtain the importance of a single dimension it is possible to compare the weights assigned to subsets that include the single dimension, with the subsets that do not have the dimension considered. In sustainable perspective, with reference to economic, social and environmental dimensions, this would consist of four comparisons: i) weight attached to a subset that has social dimension only vs. weight attached to an empty subset; ii) weight attached to a subset that includes social and environmental dimensions vs. weight attached to a subset that only includes economic dimension; iii) weight attached to a subset that includes social and economic dimensions vs. weight attached to a subset that only includes environmental dimension; iv) weight attached to a subset that includes all dimensions vs. weight attached to a subset that includes social and economic dimensions.

In terms of the Möbius representation [53] (m) of λ, the Shapley value of dimension i can be expressed as follows:

$$s_\lambda^{(i)} = \sum_{A \subseteq T/i} \frac{1}{a+1} [m(A \cup i)]$$

It is necessary to point out that, the specific importance of the dimensions (i.e., Shapley values) sums to one ($\sum_{i=1}^{d} s_\lambda^{(i)} = 1$), and higher Shapley values represent higher relative importance.

Orness Index (OI)
The CI aggregation also permits to define if the choice of the weights by the decision-maker is optimistic or pessimistic [54]. In other words, the OI determines if a decision-maker assumes that a good performance in one dimension balances another one or not. The OI varies between 0 and 1, and higher (lower) values of this index represent that the decision-maker thinks that the dimensions are substitutes (complements) of each other. In particular, if OI equals to 1, the decision-maker judges a fully compensative situation and, in this case, CI aggregation will be equal to the maximum operator. Otherwise, if OI is equal to 0, then the decision-maker considers a fully non-compensative situation, and the CI corresponds to the minimum operator (i.e., the dimensions are perfect complements),

and the index outcome would be the lowest value amongst the dimensions. The OI is calculated as follows:

$$OI^{(i)} = \frac{1}{a-1} \sum_{A \subseteq T/i} \frac{t-a}{a+1} m(A)$$

where $t = \text{card}(T)$ and $a = \text{card}(A)$ correspond to the cardinality of the subset of T and A.

Interaction Index (I)

The main reason for using the CI to structure a composite index is the ability of CI to consider the interaction and the synergies among sustainable dimensions. Taken the three dimensions of the sustainability of i, j and k, an average Interaction index (I) among the three dimensions i, j and k is determined as follows [55]:

$$I_\lambda^{(ijk)} = \sum_{A \subseteq T/ijk} \frac{(t-a-3)!a!}{(t-1)!} [\lambda(A \cup ijk) - \lambda(A \cup i) - \lambda(A \cup j) - \lambda(A \cup k) - \lambda(T)]$$

where $t = \text{card}(D)$ and $a = \text{card}(A)$ represent, respectively, the cardinality of A and T.

The quantity $I_\lambda^{(ijk)}$ can be explained as a measure of the average marginal interaction among i, j and k. An important property is that $I_\lambda^{(ijk)} \in [-1, 1]$ for all $ijk \subseteq T$. The value 1 (respectively -1) corresponding to maximum complementarity, and not, among i, j and k [56]. In terms of the Möbius (m) representation [53] of $I_\lambda^{(ijk)}$, the interaction index between the three dimensions i, j and k can be rewritten as:

$$I_\lambda^{(ijk)} = \sum_{A \subseteq T/i} \frac{1}{a+1} m(A \cup ijk)$$

3 Highlights of the Choquet Integral for Indices Construction

CI turns out to be an alternative method for defining evaluation indices based on the interaction among the three dimensions of sustainability. The proposed methodological approach takes into account the sustainable dimensions - economic, social and environmental - by means of appropriate performance indicators and brings in itself the functional linkages among the criteria adopted in the evaluation practice, overtaking the weighting attributes to each one. The index achievable by the CI workflow is consequently balanced against the relative weight among the attributes. The development of CI facilitates the solution of the problems of ranking interventions on a territorial scale among different contexts evaluated from the point of view of sustainability. In fact, CI is effective in assessing balanced and unbalanced results across sustainable dimensions, taking care to monitor the different degrees of interaction among them. CI is a generalization of the best known and most widely used weighted average operators (GM, AM), but what distinguishes them as aggregation operators from weighted average operators is their usefulness in the presence of interacting elements. Limits of the proposed methodology could be found in the possible difficulty of immediately replicating the proposed method because of its intricate mathematical structuring.

However, the definition of an evaluation index with the CI method permits to take into account the actual social, economic and environmental imbalances of each territory/context examined. This leads to interesting and significant implications in terms of evaluation of sustainable performance, especially for the identification of political-urban realities to be given priority in terms of investments in order to effectively allocate financial resources among member countries of the same community (e.g. the European Community) and to support the sustainable development of countries with unbalanced realities, with a view to intergenerational equity [57]. Future research developments are aimed at making the IC method as operable as possible to those who need the realization of an evaluation index to be used in decision-making systems of interest, such as those aimed at the selection of investments for sustainable land development. Also, the CI methodological approach applied to different geographical contexts can be effective in fostering the improvement of territorial realities, by considering the existing socio-economic and environmental inequalities, and not only the main performance aspects.

4   Conclusions

In the design and monitoring of policy strategies aimed at increasing global sustainability, it is necessary that decision-makers are supported - at all stages - by tools, techniques and methodologies that enable them to carry out synthetic assessments as quickly as possible. It is also relevant that these tools could capture the complexity of available data and they are able to integrate in a single assessment the many aspects related to the assessment of sustainability, by involving characteristics of economic, social and environmental sustainability. The use of composite indices, based on the aggregation of analytical data, turns out - to date - to be very effective in supporting Public Administrations and politicians in the identification and selection of sustainable project solutions consistent with the objectives expressed in the 17 Sustainability Goals expressed in the 2030 Agenda [58, 59].

In this sense, the adoption of indices constitutes a relevant support for the Public Administrations in the planning of sustainable strategies, as they allow to adequately consider the multiple aspects of sustainability, as well as the effects generated by the intervention in the reference context. In fact, the proposed methodology is particularly effective in considering different degrees of positional interactions among pairs of dimensions related to sustainability. Specifically, CI allows to highlight the preferences of policy-makers and public agencies based on different sets of preferences, including a variety of levels of interaction among pairs of dimensions and different relative importance of the dimensions (considering the logic of the Shapley function). Moreover, the proposed methodology is able to determine the multiple positive interactions among sustainable dimensions. In fact, the definition of an evaluation index with the CI method permits to take into account the effective social, economic, and environmental unbalances of each territory examined. This leads to interesting and significant implications in terms of evaluating the sustainable performance, especially for the identification of the political-urban realities to be prioritized in terms of sustainable investments.

In this perspective, further developments of the application of the proposed methodology to both the Italian and European contexts have already been planned, in order to fully analyze the interactions among the sustainability indicators and to obtain a representative measure of sustainability according to the factors of the urban contexts considered: for example, taking into account the current pandemic contingence, it could be possible to compare the effect of Covid-19 pandemic on the real estate market [60], or the sustainability of the same urban context before and after the Covid-19 pandemic. This will allow to carry out a constant monitoring of the conditions of sustainability of the considered urban contexts, by contributing to the achievement of shared sustainable objectives.

References

1. Fleurbaey, M.: Beyond the GDP: the quest for a measure of social welfare. J. Econ. Literat. **47**(4), 1029–1075 (2009)
2. Fleurbaey, M., Blanchet, D.: Beyond GDP: Measuring Welfare and Assessing Sustainability. Oxford University Press (2013)
3. Sen, A.: Commodities and capabilities. OUP Catalogue (1999)
4. Sen, A.: The Standard of Living: The Tanner Lectures. Cambridge University Press (1987)
5. Giovannini, E., Hall, J., D'ercole, M.M.: Measuring well-being and societal progress. In: Conference Beyond GDP-Measuring progress. true wealth, and the well-being of nations, pp. 19–20. European Parliament, Brussels (2007)
6. Istanbul Declaration. https://ec.europa.eu/environment/beyond_gdp/download/oecd_ista nbul_declaration.pdf. Accessed 12 Dec 2021
7. Beyond GDP. https://ec.europa.eu/environment/beyond_gdp/index_en.html. Accessed 12 Dec 2021
8. Atkinson, A.B., Marlier, E., Wolff, P.: Beyond GDP, measuring well-being and EU-SILC. Income Living Cond. Europe **387** (2010)
9. European Commission: Non solo Pil. Misurare il progresso in un mondo in cambiamento. Comunicazione della Commissione al Consiglio e al Parlamento europeo. https://eur-lex.eur opa.eu/legal-content/EN/TXT/?uri=CELEX%3A52009DC043. Accessed 27 Dec 2021
10. Isabelle, C.: Beyond GDP, Measuring progress, true wealth, and the well-being of nations: Conference Proceedings. n/a (2009)
11. Ness, B., Urbel-Piirsalu, E., Anderberg, S., Olsson, L.: Categorizing tools for sustainability assessment. Ecol. Econ. **60**(3), 498–508 (2007)
12. UNDP: Human Development Report 2010: The Real Wealth of Nations - Pathways to Human Development. http://hdr.undp.org/en/content/human-development-report-2010. Accessed 27 Dec 2021
13. Wendling, Z.A., Emerson, J.W., de Sherbinin, A., Esty, D.C.: Environmental Performance Index. Yale Center for Environmental Law & Policy (2020)
14. Dobrovolskienė, N., Tvaronavičienė, M., Tamošiūnienė, R.: Tackling projects on sustainability: a Lithuanian case study. Entrep. Sustain. Issues (4.4), 477–488 (2017)
15. Attardi, R., Cerreta, M., Sannicandro, V., Torre, C.M.: Non-compensatory composite indicators for the evaluation of urban planning policy: the Land-Use Policy Efficiency Index (LUPEI). Eur. J. Oper. Res. **264**(2), 491–507 (2018)
16. Alkire, S., Santos, M.A.: Measuring acute poverty in the developing world: robustness and scope of the multidimensional poverty index. World Dev. **59**, 251–274 (2014)

17. Decancq, K., Lugo, M.A.: Weights in multidimensional indices of well-being: an overview. Economet. Rev. **32**(1), 7–34 (2013)
18. Pinar, M., Stengos, T., Topaloglou, N.: Measuring human development: a stochastic dominance approach. J. Econ. Growth **18**(1), 69–108 (2013)
19. Pinar, M., Cruciani, C., Giove, S., Sostero, M.: Constructing the FEEM sustainability index: a Choquet integral application. Ecol. Ind. **39**, 189–202 (2014)
20. Ravallion, M.: Troubling tradeoffs in the human development index. J. Dev. Econ. **99**(2), 201–209 (2012)
21. Chakravarty, S.R.: A generalized human development index. Rev. Dev. Econ. **7**(1), 99–114 (2003)
22. Chakravarty, S.R.: A reconsideration of the tradeoffs in the new human development index. J. Econ. Inequal. **9**(3), 471–474 (2011)
23. Pinar, M.: Multidimensional well-being and inequality across the European regions with alternative interactions between the well-being dimensions. Soc. Indic. Res. **144**(1), 31–72 (2019)
24. Athanassoglou, S.: Multidimensional welfare rankings underweight imprecision: a social choice perspective. Soc. Choice Welfare **44**(4), 719–744 (2015)
25. Cherchye, L., Ooghe, E., van Puyenbroeck, T.: Robust human development rankings. J. Econ. Inequal. **6**(4), 287–321 (2008)
26. Foster, J.E., McGillivray, M., Seth, S.: Composite Indices: rank robustness statistical association, and redundancy. Economet. Rev. **32**(1), 35–56 (2013)
27. Pinar, M.: Choquet-integral aggregation method to aggregate social indicators to account for interactions: an application to the human development index. Soc. Indic. Res. **159**(1), 1–53 (2021). https://doi.org/10.1007/s11205-021-02726-3
28. Pinar, M., Stengos, T., Topaloglou, N.: On the construction of a feasible range of multidimensional poverty under benchmark weight uncertainty. Eur. J. Oper. Res. **281**(2), 415–427 (2020)
29. Rogge, N.: On aggregating benefit of the doubt composite indicators. Eur. J. Oper. Res. **264**(1), 364–369 (2018)
30. Choquet, G.: Theory of capacities. Ann. De L'institut Fourier **5**, 131–295 (1953)
31. Murofushi, T., Sugeno, M.: An interpretation of fuzzy measures and the Choquet integral as an integral with respect to a fuzzy measure. Fuzzy Sets Syst. **29**(2), 201–227 (1989)
32. Meng, F., Zhang, Q., Cheng, H.: Approaches to multiple-criteria group decision making based on interval-valued intuitionistic fuzzy Choquet integral with respect to the generalized λ-Shapley index. Knowl. Based Syst. **37**, 237–249 (2003)
33. Labreuche, C., Grabisch, M.: The Choquet integral for the aggregation of interval scales in multicriteria decision making. Fuzzy Sets Syst. **137**(1), 11–26 (2003)
34. Mazziotta, M., Pareto, A.: Methods for constructing non-compensatory composite indices: a comparative study. Forum Soc. Econ. **45**, 213–229 (2016)
35. Grabisch, M.; Marichal, J.L.; Mesiar, R.; Pap, E.: Aggregation Functions. Cambridge University Press (2009)
36. Grabisch, M., Labreuche, C.: A decade of application of the Choquet and Sugeno integrals in multicriteria decision aid. Ann. Oper. Res. **175**(1), 247–286 (2010)
37. Meyer, P., Ponthière, G.: Eliciting preferences on multi-attribute societies with a Choquet Integral. Comput. Econ. **37**(2), 133–168 (2011)
38. Angilella, S., Bottero, M., Corrente, S., Ferretti, V.G., Lami, S., Lami, I.: Non additive robust ordinal regression for urban and territorial planning: an application for siting an urban waste landfill. Ann. Oper. Res. **245**(1), 427–456 (2016)
39. Oppio, A., Bottero, M., Arcidiacono, A.: Assessing urban quality: a proposal for a MCDA evaluation framework. Ann. Oper. Res. , 1–18 (2018). https://doi.org/10.1007/s10479-017-2738-2

40. Gálvez Ruiz, D., Diaz Cuevas, P., Braçe, O., Garrido-Cumbrera, M.: Developing an index to measure sub-municipal level urban sprawl. Soc. Indic. Res. **140**, 929–952 (2018)
41. Carraro, C., Campagnolo, L., Eboli, F., Lanzi, E.; Parrado, R., Portale, E.: Quantifying sustainability: a new approach and world ranking. FEEM **94** (2013)
42. Merad, M., Dechy, N., Serir, L., Grabisch, M., Marcel, F.: Using a multi-criteria decision aid methodology to implement sustainable development principles within an organization. Eur. J. Oper. Res. **224**(3), 603–613 (2013)
43. Bertin, G., Carrino, L., Giove, S.: The Italian regional well-being in a multi-expert non-additive perspective. Soc. Indic. Res. **135**, 15–51 (2018)
44. Bottero, M., Ferretti, V., Figueira, J.R., Greco, S., Roy, B.: Dealing with a multiple criteria environmental problem with interaction effects between criteria through an extension of the ELECTRE III method. Eur. J. Oper. Res. **245**(3), 837–850 (2015)
45. Bottero, M., Ferretti, V., Figueira, J.R., Greco, S., Roy, B.: On the Choquet multiple criteria preference aggregation model: theoretical and practical insights. Eur. J. Oper. Res. **271**(1), 120–140 (2018)
46. Branke, J., Corrente, S., Greco, S., Słowiński, R., Zielniewicz, P.: Using Choquet integral as preference model in interactive evolutionary multiobjective optimization. Eur. J. Oper. Res. **250**(3), 884–901 (2016)
47. Campagnolo, L., Carraro, C., Eboli, F., Farnia, L., Parrado, R., Pierfederici, R.: The Ex-Ante evaluation of achieving sustainable development goals. Soc. Indic. Res. **36**, 73–116 (2016)
48. Grabisch, M., Kojadinovic, I., Meyer, P.: A review of methods for capacity identification in Choquet integral based multi-attribute utility theory applications of the Kappalab R package. Eur. J. Oper. Res. **186**(2), 766–785 (2008)
49. Marichal, J.L., Roubens, M.: Determination of weights of interacting criteria from a reference set. Eur. J. Oper. Res. **124**(3), 641–650 (2000)
50. Shapley, L.S.: A value for n-person games. In: Kuhn, H.W.; Tucker A.W. (eds.) Contributions to the Theory of Games. Princeton University Press (1953)
51. Grabisch, M.: Fuzzy integral in multicriteria decision making. Fuzzy Sets Syst. **69**(3), 279–298 (1995)
52. Grabisch, M.: The application of fuzzy integrals in multicriteria decision making. Eur. J. Oper. Res. **89**(3), 445–456 (1996)
53. Meyer, P., Roubens, M.: On the use of the Choquet integral with fuzzy numbers in multiple criteria decision support. Fuzzy Sets Syst. **157**(7), 927–938 (2006)
54. Marichal, J.L.: Tolerant or intolerant character of interacting criteria in aggregation by the Choquet integral. Eur. J. Oper. Res. **155**(3), 771–791 (2004)
55. Murofushi, T., Soneda, S.: Techniques for reading fuzzy measures (iii): Interaction index. In: 9th Fuzzy System Symposium, pp. 693–696, Japan (1993)
56. Grabisch, M.: K-order additive discrete fuzzy measures and their representation. Fuzzy Sets Syst. **92**(2), 167–189 (1997)
57. Tajani, F., Guarini, M.R., Sica, F., Ranieri, R., Anelli, D.: Multi-criteria analysis and sustainable accounting. defining indices of sustainability under Choquet's integral. Sustainability **14**(5), 2782 (2022)
58. Anelli, D., Sica, F.: The financial feasibility analysis of urban transformation projects: an application of a quick assessment model. In: Bevilacqua, C., Calabrò, F., Della Spina, L. (eds.) International Symposium: New Metropolitan Perspectives, SIST, vol. 178, pp. 462–474, Springer, Cham (2020). https://doi.org/10.1007/978-3-030-48279-4_44

14   F. Tajani et al.

59. Morano, P., Guarini, M.R., Sica, F., Anelli, D.: Ecosystem services and land take. a composite indicator for the assessment of sustainable urban projects. In: International Conference on Computational Science and Its Applications, LNTCS, vol. 12954, pp. 210–225, Springer, Cham (2021). https://doi.org/10.1007/978-3-030-86979-3_16
60. Tajani, F., Liddo, F.D., Guarini, M.R., Ranieri, R., Anelli, D.: An assessment methodology for the evaluation of the impacts of the COVID-19 pandemic on the italian housing market demand. Buildings 11(12), 592 (2021)

An Evaluation Methodology for the Feasibility Analysis of Energy Retrofit Investments

Francesco Tajani[1], Pierluigi Morano[2], Felicia Di Liddo[2], Endriol Doko[3(✉)], and Carmelo Maria Torre[2]

[1] Department of Architecture and Design, "Sapienza" University of Rome, 00196 Rome, Italy
[2] Department of Civil, Environmental, Land, Building Engineering and Chemistry (DICATECh), Polytechnic University of Bari, 70126 Bari, Italy
[3] Department of Civil and Environmental Engineering (DICA), Polytechnic of Milan, 20133 Milan, Italy
endriol.doko@polimi.it

Abstract. Since the current need to renovate the existing residential asset, especially in Italy numerous fiscal measures have been promoted in order to encourage the buildings energy improvement initiatives. Among the incentive policies for the energy requalification, the Italian "Relaunch" Law Decree No. 34/2020 has introduced a fiscal deduction equal to 110% (so-called "Superbonus") that constitutes a relevant financing measure able to support property owners in activating energy retrofit operations. With reference to the issue outlined, the present research aims to develop a methodology for the economic benefits evaluation, by considering the convenience of the subjects involved associated to the energy upgrade interventions using the Superbonus mechanism. The methodology provides for five phases and it is applied with reference to the residential sector and to the three main urban areas into which the Italian city of Bari is divided (central, semicentral and peripheral).

For each urban area, the market value differential between the post-energy intervention situation and ante-energy intervention one is determined, by considering the case "with" the Superbonus incentive and that "without" it. The methodology proposed could represent a valid tool to support the private operators in the determination of the urban areas or, in a more general terms, the cities for which a higher convenience in energy efficiency investments is detected.

Keywords: Energy retrofit · Fiscal incentives · Energy performance · Residential asset · Superbonus · Economic benefits

1 Introduction

The reduction of energy consumption and waste has assumed increasing importance for the European Union (EU): already in 2007, the Union leaders have set a target of decreasing the EU's annual energy consumption by 20% by 2020 [9]. In 2018, a new goal has been defined as part of the 'Clean Energy Package for all Europeans' to limit the energy use at least 32.5% by 2030 [12].

O. Gervasi et al. (Eds.): ICCSA 2022 Workshops, LNCS 13381, pp. 15–26, 2022.
https://doi.org/10.1007/978-3-031-10548-7_2

During the last decades, energy efficiency measures have been increasingly recognized as a tool for i) achieving a sustainable energy supply, ii) reducing green-house gas emissions, iii) improving supply security, iv) reducing the imports costs, v) promoting the EU competitiveness [2].

Within the EU Directive 2018/844 on the energy performance of buildings - so-called EPBD Directive -, all European countries are required to submit to the Commission a long-term renovation strategy in which specific plans for the national building stock refurbishment by 2050 are included [8].

In the context of the National Energy and Climate Plans (NECPs) that determine the national contributions of each Member State towards the binding EU energy-climate targets, over a period of ten-years, the foreseen energy–climate measures and policies to be implemented over this period to reach the proposed national goals are described [6, 10, 14, 29].

With reference to the Italian territory, the Integrated National Plan for Energy and Climate 2030 represents the fundamental tool for improving the country's energy and environmental policy towards decarbonisation. The plan is structured in five action lines, which will develop in an integrated manner: from decarbonisation to energy efficiency and security, passing through the internal energy market, research, innovation and competitiveness development [7, 24].

According to the energy efficiency goals, the strategy for the energy retrofit of the national property assets provides for a saving equal to 9.3 Mtoe/year of final energy by 2030, of which 60% relates to the civil sector [23].

The expected savings could be achieved thanks to new materials and technologies introduction, new construction standards adoption, the building envelope improvement interventions definition and greater diffusion of renewable energy sources. In this sense, the EU Recommendation 2019/786 related to the existing buildings renovation, taking over the EU Energy Efficiency Directive 2012/27, indicates as deep renovations those that involve a modernization able to reduce the building energy consumption by a significant percentage compared to the levels before the interventions, by promoting a very high energy performance [9, 13].

In Italy, the concept of major restructuring has been defined according to the Law 90/2013 and the Ministerial Decree of 26/06/2015 (Minimum Requirements), in which the classification of interventions has been specified - "new construction", "major renovation", "energy requalification" [3, 5, 15, 21].

In accordance with the Ministerial Decree 26/06/2015, firstly, in "new construction" interventions category, the demolition and reconstruction and the expansion of existing buildings (with new air-conditioned gross volume greater than 15% of the existing gross air-conditioned volume or greater than 500 cubic meters) are included, whereas the "important refurbishment" defines the intervention that affects the building envelope with an incidence greater than 25% of the total gross dispersive surface of the building. Furthermore, the major renovations of first-level concern the refurbishment of at least 50% of the envelope and the renovation of the heating and/or cooling plant of the entire building, and the major renovations of second-level are defined as interventions involving more than 25% of the external building surface with or without renovation of the heating and/or cooling plant.

All other energy requalification interventions, despite having an impact on the building energy performance, involve a surface less than or equal to 25% of the total gross dispersant surface of the building and/or consist of new installation or refurbishment of a thermal plant.

By taken into account the consistency of the existing public building stock and the low rate of new constructions, the main goals of the energy retrofit concern the property assets renovation towards nearly Zero Energy Building (nZEB) levels. In particular, for the nZEB construction the local climatic factors to build a housing system model that adapts to winter (heating) and summer (cooling) climatic conditions play a relevant role, by including the assessment of prevailing winds and the influence of external environmental factors on the microclimate: green areas, sun-shine/shading determined by other buildings or natural elements, should be analysed and considered, and the local and natural building materials should be selected in order to sustainable development [17, 22, 28].

From January 1st 2021 in the Italian context the nZEB requirement for all new buildings or for interventions that involve demolition and subsequent reconstruction has been introduced: in this sense, in 2018 the Italian National Agency for New Technologies, Energy and Sustainable Economic Development (ENEA) has developed the National Observatory of the nZEB for the monitoring of the high energy performance buildings construction according to current European and Italian legislation [11, 18].

2 Aim

The present research intends to develop a methodology for the evaluation of the economic benefits, in terms of the convenience of the subjects involved (Public Administrations, private investors, investment funds, banks, real estate lenders, asset management companies), obtained from the implementation of energy retrofit interventions. The operational approach for the assessment of benefits generated by energy improvement interventions on existing buildings is organized into five phases that, starting from the analysis of the reference context to be examined, allow to determine the market value differential between the post-energy and ante-energy intervention situations. The methodology is applied with reference to the residential sector and to the Italian territory and, in particular, to the three main urban areas into which the city of Bari is divided (central, semicentral and peripheral).

For each urban area, the economic benefit, in terms of market value differential between the post-energy intervention situation and ante-energy intervention situation is determined. Furthermore, this differential is calculated with reference to the energy requalification costs, by considering the case "with" and "without" the incentive of the Superbonus.

It should be highlighted that the present work is the first step of a wider and current research line aimed at defining the methodological approach for the evaluation of the economic benefits related to energy retrofit investments. The next research goal will concern the application of the proposed methodology to all the Italian provincial capitals for an overall assessment of the benefits connected to the Superbonus incentive.

The methodological approach defined in the study could be useful for i) the Public Administration, for the monitoring of the influencing market dynamics on the buying decisions and the identification of the most convenient areas for the investments, ii) the private investors, for the elaboration of a summary framework able to support the design phases and for guiding the investment choices towards suitable operations.

The sequence of the Sections contents included in the paper are described below: in Sect. 3 the main questions related to the Italian Superbonus fiscal incentive are specified and the interventions on which the tax measure could be applied are explained. In Sect. 4 the methodology is illustrated and the main steps that constitute the logical procedure to be implemented in order to assess the economic benefits connected to the energy retrofit initiatives are described. In Sect. 5 the case study is presented and the developed methodology is applied to the Italian city of Bari. Finally, in Sect. 6 the conclusions are introduced and the further insights of the research are listed.

3   The Italian Superbonus Incentive

Within the incentives promoted by the Italian government and aimed at improving the existing assets, Superbonus is a tax reduction introduced by the "Relaunch Decree" (Law Decree 34/2020) which raises to 110% the deduction rate of costs incurred for the works associated to the energy retrofit of existing buildings. In particular, all interventions must allow the improvement of two energy labels, by determining the improvement of the energy efficiency of the existing property assets [19].

The bonus constitutes a fiscal deduction that can be transformed into a tax credit equal to the measure of 110% on the value of the costs of the redevelopment works, that can be divided among four annual installments of the same amount, within the limits of the capacity of the annual tax resulting from the tax return [1].

As an alternative to the direct use of the deduction, the fiscal incentive provides for the possibility of opting for an advance contribution in the form of a discount applied by the suppliers of goods or services (so-called "discount on invoice") or for the assignment of the credit corresponding to the tax deduction due.

The Superbonus measure can be applied in case of interventions related to i) thermal insulation, ii) replacement of the winter air conditioning systems and iii) seismic risk reduction. The other costs that are covered by the incentive concern the installation of solar photovoltaic and storage systems, the infrastructure for charging electric vehicles and the interventions aimed at the removal of architectural barriers.

According to the Law No. 234/December 2021 the extension of the tax incentive has been fixed for condominiums and non-profit organizations of social utility to 2025 in the measure of 110% for costs incurred up to 31 December 2023, 70% for the expenses related to 2024 and 65% for the costs paid in 2025, for single-family buildings to 31 December 2023, provided that by 30 June 2022, works are carried out for at least 30% of the total intervention, for the operations on public housing properties developed by IACP or building cooperatives, on the condition that by 30 June 2023, at least 60% of the work has carried out [20].

In the context of the National Recovery and Resilience Plan (NRRP) within the Next Generation EU (NGEU) [26, 27, 30], the component 3 of the "Green Revolution and Ecological Transition" Mission 2 is focused on the energy efficiency and on the private and public buildings renovation. In order to achieve the complete decarbonisation of the civil sector planned for 2050 by Long Term Strategy and the Renovation wave, the NRRP promotes the rapid energetic conversion of the building stock, by favoring the "deep retrofit" and the transformation into nearly zero-energy buildings and by envisaging a combination of economic measures, such as Superbonus incentive, with measures aimed at overcoming the not-economic barriers that reduce the choices of investment in energy redevelopment or that slow down the interventions execution (bureaucratic obstacles, long procedure time, etc.).

4 Methodology

The methodology proposed in the present research intends to provide an operational approach for the assessment of economic benefits generated by energy improvement interventions on existing residential buildings. In particular, the outputs that can be obtained from the implementation of the evaluation protocol concern the market value differential between the post-energy and ante-energy intervention situations.

The five phases in which the methodology is articulated are described in Fig. 1.

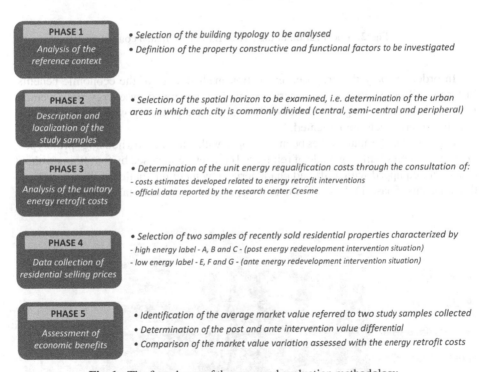

Fig. 1. The five phases of the proposed evaluation methodology

5 Case Study

The case study of the present research concerns the city of Bari (Southern Italy). The localization of the city of Bari in the Italian context is reported in Fig. 2.

Fig. 2. Localization of the city of Bari in the Italian context

In order to apply the proposed evaluation methodology of the economic benefits, in terms of convenience of the operators involved generated by energy improvement interventions on existing residential buildings, the five phases in which the protocol is structured have been implemented.

In particular, the analysis has been developed with reference to a housing "prototype", i.e. a multi-storey building made of reinforced concrete, composed by four floors without basement, equipped with a lift and characterized by medium quality of the finishes and the materials (Phase 1). In Fig. 3 the prototype selected for the analysis is shown.

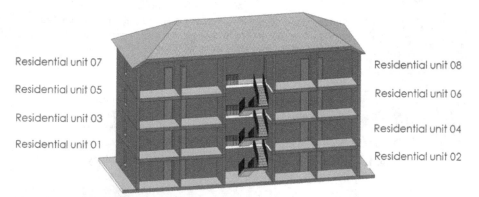

Fig. 3. Building prototype selected for the analysis

Moreover, the spatial horizon considered for the analysis has been defined. In particular, in the research the geographical distribution developed by the Real Estate Market Observatory (OMI) of the Italian Revenue Agency, for the city of Bari has been taken into account (Phase 2) [16]. The urban areas considered are the central, the semicentral, the peripheral one, whereas the suburban and extraurban areas have been excluded as the building scarcely present or mainly for rural use.

In Fig. 4 the distribution of the OMI urban areas in the city of Bari is reported.

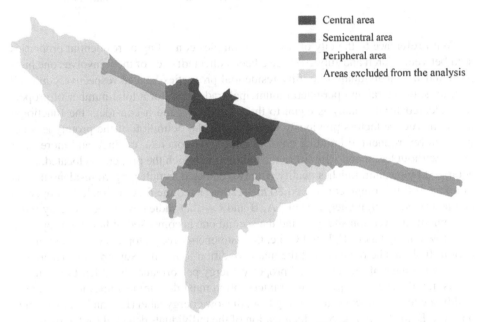

Fig. 4. OMI urban areas in the city of Bari

Furthermore, the Phase 3 of the proposed evaluation methodology has been developed through a comparative methodological approach for the determination of the unit energy requalification costs. Therefore, the data collected from costs estimates developed with reference to interventions aimed at improving the energy performance of buildings located in the Italian territory and the official data reported by the Centro ricerche economiche, sociologiche e di mercato nell'edilizia (Cresme) have been compared [4]. In this sense, the unit redevelopment costs detected by consulting a consistent number of costs estimates relating to energy retrofit initiatives to be implemented or already started on the Italian territory through the Superbonus mechanism have been appropriately adjusted through the building renovation costs reported by Cresme with regards to the "residential renewal" category and the building parameters already defined. In Table 1 the average energy improvement intervention costs from costs estimates and Cresme data recorded for the city of Bari are specified.

Table 1. Unit energy improvement intervention costs considered for the city of Bari

Unit energy requalification costs			
Costs estimates related to energy retrofit interventions in Italy	Average Italian Cresme costs related to the "total" property refurbishment	Cresme data related to the "total" property refurbishment for the city of Bari	Average cost used for the analysis for the city of Bari
408.17 €/m^2	759.16 €/m^2	777.95 €/m^2	418.27 €/m^2

With reference to the city of Bari, two samples consisting of residential properties sold between March and July 2021 have been collected: each of them involves one hundred and fifty individuals - i.e. fifty residential properties located respectively in each central, semicentral and peripheral municipal trade area, for a total number of properties selected for the analysis equal to three hundred - and it considers the functional and constructive factors previously identified for the definition of the prototype – i.e. multi-storey residential building type, in reinforced concrete, of three and more floor levels without basement, with lift in the building in which the property is located, characterized by medium finishes quality. The two detected samples regard residential units of about 100 m^2 (range considered 80 m^2–120 m^2) and the first one include properties characterized by high energy label - A, B and C – that indicates the post-energy redevelopment intervention situation and the second one is composed of housing properties with low energy label - E, F and G, i.e. the ante-energy redevelopment intervention situation. It should be recalled that the main condition to use the Superbonus incentive is the improvement of the residential property energy performance by at least two energy labels, i.e. the energy requalification intervention must determine a relevant upgrade of building energy efficiency, by passing from the low energy label (E, F and G) to the high ones (A, B and C). In Fig. 5 the localization of the individuals detected for the two study samples selected is shown.

The Phase 5 of the assessment methodology developed in the analysis concerns the assessment of the market value differential between the post-energy intervention and ante-energy intervention. In particular, the economic benefits in terms of market value variation has been determined, by considering firstly the energy requalification costs - i.e. considering the situation "without" the incentive of the Superbonus in which the cost of the intervention is borne by the property private owner - and then the situation "with" the mentioned tax measure in which no costs are incurred by the private.

In Table 2 the market value surplus between the post-energy retrofit intervention and ante-energy improvement initiative situations detected for the city of Bari is indicated.

It should be outlined that the present analysis has aimed to assess the effects of the energy efficiency intervention in terms of value differential regardless of the implementation of the Superbonus mechanism and, therefore, to verify the effects of the initiative in absolute terms.

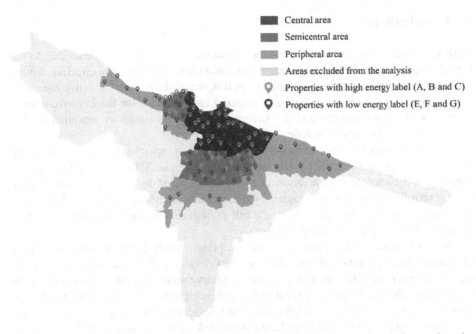

Fig. 5. Localization of the residential properties detected for the two study samples analyzed

In this sense, for each urban area the market value differentials expressed in percentage terms have been calculated without the use of the Superbonus mechanism (first columns of the Table 2) and with the use of the fiscal incentive (second columns of the Table 2). It can be observed that the inclusion of the Superbonus allows an average increase of the economic benefits for the considered urban areas compared to the "without" situation, equal to approximately 75%. The highest growth concerns the peripheral area (equal to +134%), followed by the semicentral area for which the positive variation detected is equal to +53% and, finally, by the central area (+40%).

Table 2. Economic benefits assessed in terms of market value differential between the post-energy retrofit intervention situation and the ante-energy improvement initiative situation detected for the three urban areas of the city of Bari

Economic benefits					
Market value differential between the post-energy intervention and ante-energy intervention					
Without superbonus			With superbonus		
Central	Semicentral	Peripheral	Central	Semicentral	Peripheral
42.20%	43.24%	25.63%	59.25%	66.74%	59.96%

6 Conclusions

With reference to the current contingence associated to the sanitary crisis due to the Covid-19 pandemic, the building stock regeneration is recognized as an effective driving force for the national economic recovery: in this sense, the several incentive measures envisaged allow the implementation of targeted interventions for the improvement of energy performance indices and the saving of significant monetary amounts for the owners of the properties to be redeveloped [25].

In accordance with the relevance of the construction sector in the national economy connected to the sustainability goals fixed by the Agenda 2030 [31], the Superbonus guarantees a complete remuneration of the costs incurred for the mentioned specific energy retrofit intervention typologies, by determining significant benefits in terms of i) the energy consumption reduction, ii) the bill savings, iii) the improvement of building quality, iv) the increase of living comfort.

With reference to the Italian territory, the present study constitutes the first phase of a wider research aimed at assessing the market value differential between the post-energy intervention situation and ante-energy intervention situation – that is one of the main economic benefits deriving from energy redevelopment initiatives. In particular, the present analysis has intended to define a methodological approach capable of supporting the public and private operators in the decision-making processes related to the energy retrofit investments. In this sense, the proposed methodology has been applied with reference to the city of Bari and the residential intended use, but it represents a flexible tool, that could be replicable in any territorial context (national and international) to verify the investment convenience and to identify the urban areas for which a higher sustainability in energy efficiency interventions is detected.

Future developments of the research will concern the implementation of the methodology proposed with reference to other intended uses (commercial, offices, etc.) and to geographical contexts. In particular, with reference to all the Italian provincial capitals and to the main urban areas into which each city is divided, the methodology will allow the identification of the areas of the different Italian cities for which a higher convenience in energy efficiency interventions will be found. Furthermore, the outputs obtained could be represented on geographical maps, able to quickly identify the urban areas of the different Italian provincial capitals for which i) the use of fiscal incentives are required and ii) a higher convenience in carrying out the intervention through the use of the Superbonus incentive is detected. The visualization through maps will support the private operators - entrepreneurs, investors, credit institutions, assets management companies, insurance providers, real estate funds, technical consultants involved in the energy interventions feasibility assessments, etc. - to define the urban areas in which the investment will be financially convenient and the Public Administrations to locate the areas and/or the provincial capitals in which the current Superbonus incentive is necessary, excessive or insufficient and, through a further analysis, to eventually assess the break-even incentive percentages capable of guaranteeing the condition of minimum convenience for the investor.

References

1. Agenzia delle Entrate: Superbonus 110%. https://www.agenziaentrate.gov.it/portale/web/guest/superbonus-110%25. Accessed 10 Sept 2021
2. Agenzia nazionale per le nuove tecnologie, l'energia e lo sviluppo economico sostenibile ENEA: Rapporto Annuale sull'efficienza energetica (October 2020). https://www.enea.it/it/seguici/pubblicazioni/pdf-volumi/2020/raee-2020.pdf. Accessed 11 Feb 2021
3. Bergero, S., Cavalletti, P., Chiari, A.: Energy refurbishment in existing buildings: Thermal bridge correction according to DM 26/06/2015 limit values. In: Energy Procedia, vol. 140, pp. 127–140 (2017)
4. Centro ricerche economiche, sociologiche e di mercato nell'edilizia CRESME. www.cresme.it. Accessed 11 June 2021
5. Corrado, V., Ballarini, I., Dirutigliano, D., Murano, G.: Verification of the new Ministerial Decree about minimum requirements for the energy performance of buildings. In: Energy Procedia, vol. 101, pp. 200–207 (2016)
6. De Paoli, L., Geoffron, P.: Introduction. A critical overview of the European National Energy and Climate Plans. In: Economics and Policy of Energy and the Environment (2019)
7. De Paoli, L.: The Italian draft national energy-climate plan. In: Economics and Policy of Energy and Environment, Franco Angeli, pp. 97–118 (2019)
8. Directive 2018/844/EU of the European Parliament and of the Council of 30 May 2018 amending Directive 2010/31/EU on the energy performance of buildings and Directive 2012/27/EU on energy efficiency, Official Journal of the European Union: Brussels, Belgum (2018). Accessed 25 July 2021
9. Directive 2012/27/EU of the European Parliament and of the Council of 25 October 2012 on energy efficiency, amending Directives 2009/125/EC and 2010/30/EU and repealing Directives 2004/8/EC and 2006/32/EC. Accessed 11 July 2021
10. Economidou, M., et al.: National Energy and Climate Plans for 2021–2030 under the EU Energy Union, EUR 30487 EN, Publications Office of the European Union, Luxembourg (2020)
11. Enea: Osservatorio Nazionale degli Edifici a Energia quasi Zero NZEB. https://www.enea.it/it/efficienza-energetica/osservatorio-nazionale-degli-edifici-a-energia-quasi-zero-nzeb-sempre-piu-numerose-le-adesioni-al-progetto-enea. Accessed 23 June 2021
12. European Commission, Directorate-General for Energy: Clean energy for all Europeans, Publications Office (2019). https://data.europa.eu/doi/https://doi.org/10.2833/21366. Accessed 5 Oct 2021
13. European Commission: Commission recommendation (EU) 2019/786 of 8 May 2019 on building renovation. Official Journal of the European Union (2019)
14. Gabrielli, L., Ruggeri, A.G.: Developing a model for energy retrofit in large building portfolios: Energy assessment, optimization and uncertainty. In: Energy and buildings, vol. 202, p. 109356 (2019)
15. Italian Ministry of Economic Development: Ministerial Decree 26/06/2015. Applicazione Delle Metodologie di Calcolo Delle Prestazioni Energetiche e definizione delle Prescrizioni e dei Requisiti Minimi degli Edifici. Official Journal of the Italian Republic, 15 July 2015 (in Italian). http://www.sviluppoeconomico.gov.it/index.php/it/normativa/decreti-interministeriali/2032966-decreto-interministeriale-26-giugno-2015-applicazione-delle-metodologie-di-calcolo-delle-prestazioni-energetiche-e-definizione-delle-prescrizioni-e-dei-requisiti-minimi-degli-edifici. Accessed 10 Oct 2021
16. Italian Revenue Agency. Real Estate Market Observatory (OMI). Rapporto immobiliare 2019. Il settore residenziale (2019). www.agenziaentrate.gov.it. Accessed 19 July 2021

17. Kurnitski, J., et al.: How to define nearly net zero energy buildings nZEB. Rehva J. **48**(3), 6–12 (2011)
18. Labia, N., et al.: Osservatorio degli edifici a energia quasi zero (nZEB) in Italia–2016–2018. Enea (2019)
19. Law Decree No. 34/2020: Misure urgenti in materia di salute, sostegno al lavoro e all'economia, nonché di politiche sociali connesse all'emergenza epidemiologica da COVID-19. www.gazzettaufficiale.it. Accessed 14 June 2021
20. Law No. 234/2021: State budget for the financial year 2022 and multi-year budget for the three-year period 2022–2024. www.gazzettaufficiale.it. Accessed 5 May 2021
21. Law No. 90/2013: converting into Law Decree No. 63/2013. Transposition of Directive 2010/31/EU on Energy Performance of Buildings. Official Journal of the Italian Republic, general No.181 (2013)
22. Marszal, A.J., et al.: Zero energy building–a review of definitions and calculation methodologies. Energy Build. **43**(4), 971–979 (2011)
23. Ministry of Economic Development, Ministry of the Environment and Protection of Natural Resources and the Sea, Ministry of Infrastructure and Transport: Strategia per la riqualificazione energetica del parco immobiliare nazionale – november, 25 2020 https://www.mise.gov.it/images/stories/documenti/STREPIN_2020_rev_25-11-2020.pdf. Accessed 5 June 2021
24. Ministry of Economic Development, Ministry of the Environment and Protection of Natural Resources and the Sea, Ministry of Infrastructure and Transport: Integrated National Energy and Climate Plan. https://www.mise.gov.it/index.php/it/energia/energia-e-clima-2030. Accessed 20 April 2020
25. Morano, P., Tajani, F., Di Liddo, F., Anelli, D.: A feasibility analysis of the refurbishment investments in the Italian residential market. Sustainability **12**(6), 2503 (2020)
26. National Recovery and Resilience Plan (NRRP). www.mef.gov.it. Accessed 10 July 2021
27. Next Generation EU (NGEU) - Recovery Fund. www.ec.europa.eu.it. Accessed 17 May 2021
28. Official Journal of the European Union: Directive 2010/31/EU of the European Parliament and of the Council of 19 May 2010 on the energy performance of buildings - recast (2010)
29. Roberts, J., Gauthier, C.: Energy communities in the draft National Energy and Climate Plans: encouraging but room for improvements. In: REScoop: Berchem, Belgium (2019)
30. Senato della Repubblica, Camera dei Deputati: Il Piano Nazionale di Ripresa e Resilienza (NRRP) – Schede di lettura. Dossier XVIII Legislatura (2021). www.camera.it. Accessed 14 May 2021
31. United Nations: Agenda 2030 (2015). https://unric.org/it/agenda-2030/. Accessed 12 March 2021

The Cost-Benefit Analysis for the Validation of Next Generation EU Investments: An Application to the Healthcare Sector

Marco Locurcio[1(✉)], Pierluigi Morano[1], Francesco Tajani[2], Felicia Di Liddo[1], and Ilaria Bortone[3]

[1] Department of Civil, Environmental, Land, Building Engineering and Chemistry (DICATECh), Polytechnic University of Bari, 70126 Bari, Italy
marco.locurcio@poliba.it
[2] Department of Architecture and Design, "Sapienza" University of Rome, 00196 Rome, Italy
[3] Institute of Clinical Physiology, National Research Council (IFC-CNR), 56124 Pisa, Italy

Abstract. During the last decades, the public investments have very often determined "white elephants" whose initial costs have increased during construction phase and, at the end of project realization, the necessary financial resources for the operation of the investment have not been available. Starting from these bankruptcy initiatives, different technique for an accurate ex ante planning of the investment costs, and for a detailed analysis of the financial sustainability have been implemented. The Cost-Benefit Analysis is the most used tool for the public investments validation as it is able to verify the financial intervention convenience, and it allows an optimal allocation of available resources in order to guarantee the highest return on investment in the reference area. In this research, the Cost-Benefit Analysis potential and limits have been highlighted through a specific case study.

Keywords: Cost-benefit analysis · Health care sector · NRRP · Willingness to pay · Value of statistical life

1 Introduction

The selection of high quality projects able to meet the changing needs of the community and to determine significant effects on economic growth is a fundamental operation in the definition of urban development strategies. In this context, the Cost-Benefit Analysis (CBA) assumes a key role, being expressly requested for the evaluation of interventions aimed at obtaining co-financing for the "large public projects" – i.e. characterized by a total investment cost higher than € 50 million - included in the operational programs of the European Regional Development Fund (ERDF) and the Cohesion Fund [9, 37].

In general terms, the CBA intends to verify the initiative convenience for the community deriving from the project implementation, in order to orient the urban policies towards an efficient allocation of financial resources. In this way, this analysis constitutes a significant support in the decision-making process for the choice of the investments

O. Gervasi et al. (Eds.): ICCSA 2022 Workshops, LNCS 13381, pp. 27–44, 2022.
https://doi.org/10.1007/978-3-031-10548-7_3

to be carried out [18, 36] taking into account the sustainable territorial development strategies and the priority objectives set by the European Union.

With reference to the Next Generation EU (NGEU) [32], aimed at promoting a "sustainable, uniform, inclusive and equitable recovery" following the crisis caused by the Covid-19 pandemic, in Italy the National Recovery and Resilience Plan (NRRP) [31, 38] establishes an accelerated procedure for the construction of public works on the basis of the technical and economic feasibility project, in order to streamline the bureaucratic procedures related to the design, approval and implementation phases.

The amount of the allocated funds and the timing foreseen for their use of the Resilience and Recovery Facility (period 2021–2026) [10], on the one hand, generate the need to simplify the procedures to speed up the works construction times and, on the other hand, require choices capable of guaranteeing high quality standards of interventions.

In this sense, the NRRP promotes an innovative approach towards the design, construction and management of a public work, paying significant attention to environmental and sustainability goals and, at the same time, making the approval process more efficient through targeted simplification tools. In the context of the guidelines for the drafting of the technical and economic feasibility project to be put out to the awarding of public works contracts of the NRRP and of the National Plan for Complementary Investments (NPC), developed by the Superior Council of Public Works [6], the CBA is recognized as the main methodological tool to support the selection among design alternatives that pursue the preliminary fixed objectives. The document also highlights that, while allowing for the initial use of more "rapid" techniques (multi-criteria analysis [17, 29] and cost-effectiveness analysis), the results obtained must be validated by a CBA, in order to clearly and objectively identify the "best" project solution.

Furthermore, the guidelines recommend a constant monitoring and updating of the data included in the CBA developed for the definition of the selected solution, in accordance with the precise identification of the constructive and functional typologies and a more accurate estimate of the overall intervention costs.

In the mentioned framework, the CBA plays a central role *i)* for forecasting the effects of the project (ex ante analysis), *ii)* for monitoring the evolution of the boundary conditions (in itinere analysis), *iii)* for checking the pursuit of the assessed outputs (ex post analysis).

Within the framework of the structural reforms and investments for the period 2021–2026 envisaged by the NRRP, among the six priority intervention sectors described in the plan, the Mission 6 concerns the health and resilience issue, with the aim of strengthening prevention and health services on territory, of modernizing and digitizing the healthcare system and of guaranteeing equity in access to care. In particular, € 16.63 billion have been allocated for this Mission, i.e. 8.16% of the total amount of € 191.5 billion relating to the Recovery and Resilience Facility (RRF – the main component of NGEU program) to be used through the NRRP implementation. The measure resources are distributed with different shares in two investment lines relating to: *i)* proximity networks, intermediate structures and telemedicine for territorial health care - whose main objectives concern the improvement of the services provided in the territory thanks to the strengthening and creation of territorial facilities (such as Community Homes and Community Hospitals), the consolidation of home care, the development of telemedicals and a more effective integration with all social and health services; *ii)* innovation, research and digitization of the National Health Service - aimed at the renewal and modernization of existing technological and digital structures, at the completion and dissemination of the electronic health record, at a better performance of delivery and monitoring of the essential levels of assistance through more effective information systems.

In general terms, the emergency caused by Covid-19 pandemic has pointed out the need to improve the National Health System (NHS) capacity to provide adequate services, not only to strengthen and reorganize the supplied services, upgrading their quality levels, but also to modernize the technological and digital hospital devices, currently characterized by a significant obsolescence state and frequently lacking in many facilities, also in terms of structural adaptation and safety of hospital buildings.

The present research is part of the framework outlined and it is focuses on the implementation of a CBA on a healthcare building project to be realized through NRRP funds in a city located in Southern Italy. By analyzing the financial and economic effects determined by the intervention with reference to the territorial context and the current temporal horizon, the presented application of the CBA can constitute a vademecum for similar projects: in this sense, the work could effectively support public and private subjects involved in these typologies of investments.

2   Case study

In Italy, the progressive ageing population, the decline in the fertility rate, the negative birth-rate [21] and the consequent increase in the economic and social burden linked to age-related diseases, define the typical framework of the "demographic trap".

This condition could determine extremely relevant effects derived from the impossibility to support the economic weight of assistance with the working population incomes. For this reason, the prevention of pathological aging and the consequent increase in healthy life expectancy are among the fundamental modifiers of the impact of the growth in the socio-economic burden of demographic transition.

Therefore, the case study analysed in the present research concerns the realization of a healthcare building called "Health House 2.0" which aims to overcome the classic idea hospital care, through three different complementary action lines: *i)* optimization of healthcare services; *ii)* creation of a Research, Development and Innovation (RDI) infrastructure; *iii)* the prevention culture spread.

In the following sections, the steps of the CBA - mandatory for the fund request of € 12 million in the context of the NRRP - for the construction of the "Health House 2.0" in a specific area (named "reference area") of the Apulia region in Southern Italy. This fund is required for the property enhancement and the supply and installation of a series of hospital equipment. The project is proposed by a scientific hospitalization institute (the "promoter") and it provides for the involvement of different public partners (universities, local and common healthcare companies) and private ones (companies interested in developing patents).

2.1 Definition of the Intervention Goals

The "Health House 2.0" represents a strategic infrastructure for research, development and innovation:

- to enhance and improve the research activities carried out within the national health system;
- to contribute to the development of the technical, professional, digital and managerial skills of the health system staff;
- to promote the knowledge progress concerning the aging, fragility and functional decline issue, by introducing an infrastructure capable of processing and integrating primary and secondary big data;
- to develop advanced innovative processes and services, such as semi-residential structures for assisted rehabilitation and cognitive-behavioral and physical tele-rehabilitation;
- to strengthen collaboration among research, innovation, education and the business sector in order to generate more employment.

The achievement of mentioned goals translates into the need to implement initiatives aimed at reducing the gap between the national average and the regional data, associated with a series of indicators listed below [20]:

- incidence of total RDI expenditure on GDP (1.47% Italy vs. 0.82% Apulia - 2019);
- RDI employees, units expressed in full-time equivalents per thousand inhabitants (5.96 Italy vs, 2.77 Apulia - 2019);
- companies that have carried out RDI activities in collaboration with external parties out of the total number of companies that perform RDI (0.59% Italy vs. 0.35% Apulia);
- production specialization in high-tech sectors described as the percentage of employees in high-tech manufacturing, knowledge-intensive and high-tech services sectors on the total employment (3.85% Italy vs. 2, 18% Apulia - 2020);
- percentage of elderly people assisted at home compared to the population age at least 65 years old (0.90% Italy vs. 0.60% Apulia);
- percentage of inappropriate hospitalizations in terms of admissions with a high risk of inadequacy beyond 1 day on the total resident population (0.58% Italy vs. 0.65% Apulia for Diagnosis Related Groups (DRG) doctors, 0.29% Italy vs. 0.36% Apulia for DRG - 2019).

2.2 Demand Analysis

Starting from the multiple intervention goals, the demand is articulated on several points of view, summarized below according to the target group:

- *enterprises*: knowledge intensity in the sectors connected to the project, development of new products and participation in the creation of start-ups;
- *researchers, students* and *academics*: increase and diversification of training activities, incentive for public and private investments, creation of partnerships with production companies;

– *population*: increase in the life quality through easier and more targeted access to health services, reduction of the digital divide and social inequalities.

With reference to the *enterprises*, the large team involved in the project and the important equity commitment in terms of newly recruited staff to be paid by the companies (to be allocated to the intervention development), confirm the interest aroused in the regional production system. This empirical observation is validated by the current growth both in the number of researchers employed in RDI activities in collaboration with external parties, and in the companies that have carried out RDI activities using research infrastructures and other RDI services. The described trend effectively represents the current demand from the production sector which plays an increasingly central role in promoting research and its applications.

With regard to the second target group (*researchers*, *students* and *academics*), it should be observed that, despite the low investments in RDI at national and regional level, human capital has grown, supported by the increase in RDI employees and by the Apulian academic system, for which starting from the A.Y. 2016–2017, a constant growth of enrolled students has been recorded. This condition highlights the good scientific level of the local university system and a growing demand for RDI staff.

For the last target group (*population*), a higher difficulty to univocally characterize the demand in terms of load reduction of the fragilty single macro-domains, especially cognitive disorders, functional and lifestyle disability [2] - with particular reference to nutritional balance and dietary habits [41] – has been detected. The "proxy" variables used to characterize this demand are: *i)* the number of elderly people assisted at home; *ii)* the number of high risk inappropriateness hospitalizations.

The combination of these strategies contributes to the implementation of the previously illustrated goals. Compared to the reference area, the number of elderly people to whom home care could be extended is equal to a minimum of 59, if the national average is taken as a referred, to a maximum of 767, if the Bolzano province (the most "performing" area in the Italian context) is considered. However, the subsequent analysis refers to the patients number currently assisted at home (equal to 150 units), in order to consider a prudential scenario for challenging goals. In addition, it should be recalled that the NRRP also aims to promote innovative solutions and instrumental endowments for elderly people to guarantee them an autonomous and independent life and home social assistance services.

In order to define the demand, in terms of reduction in hospitalizations, the "best scenario", that is the shelters number to be prevented at 4 years following the operativity start, has been determined by using two methodologies: the first "bottom up" has concerned the involvement of the local healthcare Entity to specify, for each potentially inappropriate DRG, the number of avoidable hospitalizations; the second "top down" has identified this number as the difference (weighted with respect to the reference area) of the gap existing between the most performing region, i.e. Piedmont, and the Apulia region. The bottom up approach has led to the need to reduce the hospitalizations number by 389 units, the top down approach by 413 units. Prudently, the goal to be achieved implementing the bottom up approach has been selected.

2.3 Options Analysis

The options analysis has been carried out with the support of multi-objective techniques, that are characterized by a high performance in particularly uncertainty contexts; at the end of the analysis, a ranking of the alternative solutions identified by means of a summary numerical indicator has been obtained.

The general goal, previously described, has been divided into four macro-objectives (A, B, C and D) to which a weight (w) has been assigned by the partners involved in relation to the importance compared to the general objective achievement.

A. ($w = 35\%$): to upgrade research quality and products, also increasing the number of graduates connected to smart specialization;
B. ($w = 30\%$): to strengthen collaboration among research, innovation, education and the business sector in order to create new jobs;
C. ($w = 20\%$): to generate a more resilient, inclusive and democratic society, by contributing to greater "Digital Equity" and "Gender Equality";
D. ($w = 15\%$): to improve the life quality of the general population and, in particular, of the elderly one, through a renovation in the social welfare assistance supply.

For each of the four macro-objectives, three options have been identified that differ, depending on the situation, in strategic, technological or location aspects; moreover, an evaluation matrix to identify how the different options pursue the objectives achievement, has been built. For the implementation of this step, the identification of a criteria set (costs, times, revenues, etc.) - each with a different weight, established through the partners involved support - has been developed. For each criterion, a verbal judgment or a general numerical indication - subsequently normalized and included in the 0–1 scale using the MIN-MAX normalizer – has been assigned. Finally, three solutions have been defined and shown in Fig. 1: I. Health House, II. Consortium exclusively composed by regional entities; III. Pool of only public subjects. For these intervention alternatives, a synthetic indicator obtained through the classical aggregative approach of Weighted Sum Model has been calculated. The project one "I" is the preferred solution (synthesis value equal to 0.78) followed by "II" (synthesis value 0.57) and, finally, "III" (synthesis value 0.48). In particular, the solution "I" is more performing compared to the other ones for all objectives except for "C" goal. In the following paragraphs, the analysis is focused on the preferred solution, i.e. on the "Health House 2.0".

2.4 Financial Analysis

For the financial analysis, only incoming and outgoing cash flows have been considered (therefore no amortization or provisions have been included in the analysis) at constant real prices. The VAT has been taken into account as it cannot be recovered by the project promoter. It should be specified that the cash flows have been estimated by using an incremental approach compared to the counterfactual scenario, i.e. that related to the non-realization of the planned project (so-called Business As Usual or "as is" scenario).

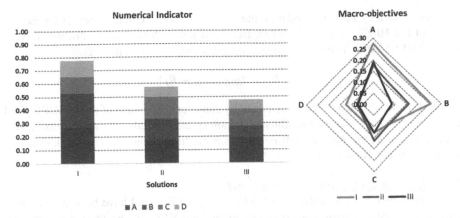

Fig. 1. Outputs obtained by the options analysis

The evaluation data is referred to 06/30/2022, i.e. the presumed date of the fund reception. The analysis has been performed with periods equal to one year, with the exception of the first period considered equal to six months. This differentiation has been explained by indicating that the first semester expenses have been measured in a sufficiently detailed way and correspond to different costs already incurred by the promoter for participating in the procedure. For the subsequent periods the analysis on an annual basis has been developed, as there are not enough elements for a shorter periodization.

The financial analysis has been implemented in the following phases: i. Estimation of the Financial Discount Rate; ii. Calculation of the operating costs; iii. Calculation of the revenues; iv. Analysis of the financial profitability and sustainability.

Phase I: Estimation of the Financial Discount Rate
The project concerns the research and innovation sector, for which the Guide to CBA [9] suggest a time horizon equal to 15–25 years, and the health services context, for which the reference period is set equal to 30 years. Therefore, starting from the previous analysis, a reference period of 29.5 years has been assumed.

The costs and revenues have been actualized using the Financial Discount Rate (FDR) determined by means of the Weighted Average Cost of Capital (WACC): the FDR (equal to the WACC) is the weighted average of the cost of equity (k_E) and debt (k_D) (which corresponds to the public financing in the present case). The WACC mathematic formula is shown in (1):

$$WACC = k_E \cdot E + k_D \cdot D \tag{1}$$

The partners involved in the initiative contribute to the project through an equity commitment connected with the employment of personnel (so-called "contribution in kind") for an amount of approximately € 4.6 million in the first 4.5 project years (E = 19%), whereas the public funds in the same period amounted to a total of € 20 million (D = 81%). The Capital Asset Pricing Model (CAPM) has been applied to estimate k_E, identifying the European $\beta_{HI\&T}$ for the Heathcare Information and Technology (HI&T)

sector published by Prof. Damodaran, the market risk (R_m) equal to Return On Equity (ROE) of the HI&T sector and the risk free R_f equal to the gross yield of the 30-year BTPs on 01/05/2022. The k_E has been assessed through the formula (2):

$$k_E = R_f + \beta_{HI\&T}(R_m - R_f) \qquad (2)$$

The k_D calculation has been carried out by considering the sum of the EURIRS yield at 30 years (03/11/2022) and the adjusted default spread for Italy. The application of this procedure has determined an FDR equal to 4.86%, higher than the rate recommended by the Guide to CBA (equal to 4%) [9].

Phase II: Calculation of the Operating Costs

The investment costs amounted to a total of € 12 million and have been divided into professional costs, construction costs, equipment and VAT. The professional costs will largely occur in the first semester of analysis, whereas the construction costs will arise in 2023 and 2024 and the costs related to the equipment installation will be incurred in 2024. Within the investment costs, theoretically, the value of the property to be transformed should be included, also because it represents a physical asset held by the promoter and by the various project partners, for which a return could be expected as for any other form of (differentiated) invested capital.

However, a reference market of the property has not been detected and is bound to its current intended use; moreover, the cash flows have been determined using the incremental approach, so in the current scenario ("as is") the property performs functions similar to those covered downstream of the enhancement project. For these reasons, the value at year zero has not been considered; to balance this assumption, when determining the residual value, the contribution deriving from the real estate component has been taking into account exclusively in terms of the increase in value associated with its valuation.

Almost all costs of Operation & Maintenance (O&M) will occur starting from 2025 (i.e. at the end of equipment the installation) with the exception of the costs associated with promotional campaigns, training courses that will take place starting from 2024 (year of completion of the building enhancement works).

The equipment maintenance costs have been estimated on the basis of the management contract currently in place between the promoter and a company specializing in the management and maintenance of equipment similar to those of the present project.

The incremental costs of medical and nursing staff employed for the reduction of inappropriate hospitalizations and increase of services are equal to 60% of the corresponding estimated revenues starting from the rates of hospital assistance services. This percentage, proposed by Formez PA (Center for services, assistance, studies and training for the P.A. modernization) [14], considers the fixed management costs (firstly personnel) that are not compressible and associated with each service.

The property management, operation and maintenance costs have been calculated according to the research contribution developed by the Institute of Economic and Social Research (IRES) of Piedmont in 2018 [35], such as (3):

$$p_a = I \cdot \left(\frac{\beta - 1}{\alpha \cdot Vu}\right) \qquad (3)$$

where I is the real estate investment cost, β is a weighting coefficient between useful and operating life with or without maintenance (equal to 3.0), α is the weighting parameter of the useful life to the operating life (equal to 0.8) and Vu is the useful life (equal to 90 years).

To determine the costs associated with the disposal of the abandoned site at the end of the infrastructure life cycle (T), the corresponding parametric value (p) provided by the "Building typology prices" list [4], has been applied to the Gross Building Area (S). Finally, this value has been discounted from the year in which the intervention should be carried out (i.e. in 2113 at the end of the useful life of the property) to the last analysis period (i.e. 2051) through the FDR:

$$T = \frac{p \cdot S}{(1 + FDR)^{62}} \tag{4}$$

The costs to be incurred every 10 years for equipment the replacement is equal to the price incurred at the start of the project, due to the assumption adopted in the analysis for which this is carried out considered real and constant prices.

Phase III: Calculation of the Revenues

The project revenues will start from 2025 through a gradual trend (40% in the 1st year, 60% in the 2nd year, 80% in the 3rd year and 100% from the 4th year), necessary to consider the progressive full implementation of the initiative and the operativity of all aspects. This hypothesis is particularly prudential, especially for revenues related to the health infrastructure that will meet an already existing demand and unsatisfied from the current supply.

Revenues deriving from the consulting services sale and the fees paid for accessing to the laboratories and for the research equipment use have been determined in consultation with the project partners. The reference tariff for the calculation of research services will be assessed with reference to equivalent European centers. In particular, the model proposed by the Center of Advanced Neuro-sciences of the Aalto University in Finland will be taken as a reference: the hourly rate depends on the agreement with the scientific consortium or if the user is a consortium partner. For example, for the use of Nuclear Magnetic Resonance at 3T for the weekdays from 9 to 16, standard rates will be applied that include technical support and auxiliary personnel with the following hourly rates: weekdays € 285 and € 210 for each "off hour" for subjects with a specific agreement, whereas € 427 and € 299 per hour for non-affiliated external parties [1].

Revenues from licenses obtained from the patents marketing have been determined by estimating the costs incurred (or of reproduction): this assumption has led to revenues equal to € 675,000 per patent, in line with the results of the studies carried out by the European Commission [11, 12].

The project intends to activate several masters for a total of 80 students per year (20 places in Public Health, 20 places in Health Data Science, 40 Nutritional Epidemio-logy) and two fellowships for PhDs that will guarantee incomes from the registration fees for a total of € 205,000 per year (2,500 euros for each student).

One of the benefits expected from the project implementation concerns the improvement of health services through three complementary strategies:

- the reduction of 389 inappropriate hospitalizations and emergency department visits in code white (low priority);
- the increase of 4,800 specialist services in one year;
- the activation of remote monitoring services for 150 patients currently assisted at home.

For the reduction of inappropriate hospitalizations, in relation to the year 2021, for the hospitals located in the reference area, the number of accesses to the 43 DRGs with high risk of non-appropriateness in ordinary hospitalization has been analyzed, as defined in the annex 2C of the D.P.C.M. November 29, 2001 [8], and further 55 DRG identified as part of the study carried out by the Ministry of Health [27] have been added.

Within the context outlined, only the DRGs currently provided in the hospitals located in the reference area have been selected. Starting from the data developed by the National Healthcare Institute (partner of the project) for each DRG, an expected reduction in access to 4 years from the intervention completion for a variable percentage from 25 to 60% depending on the specific DRG analyzed, has been assumed, i.e. an equivalent number of missed visits equal to 389 units.

This method represents a prudential approach when compared with the strategies proposed by Formez PA in the context of cost/benefit analyzes of various Health House located in Southern Italy regions [14–16], according to which a reduction equal to 85% in these visits within 4 years from the start of the project has been provided. The corresponding revenues in the "full operatively" period have been assessed by taking into account the expected visits reduction, as already defined, and the fees of acute hospital care services (DRG system) and they are equal to € 386,600 per year.

The increase in diagnostic equipment will allow a growth of at least 20 visits per day which will correspond to an increase in revenues from tariffs of approximately € 3.2 million per year. Currently about 150 patients are assisted at home, and the annual cost for NHS is equal to 4,275 euros/patient, assuming at least 1 weekly visit carried out by a team of 1 medical and 2 nurses within a radius of 15 km for not particularly complex situations. Furthermore, the activation of remote sensing services will determine a lower cost of at least 20%.

The fees paid for the new services envisaged are considered as project revenues in order to assess the financial profitability, as they are incurred for additional services and increases in health services currently provided.

Since the economic life of the initiative works will not completely exhausted at the last year of the time horizon considered, the calculation of the investment residual value has been carried out. This value has been assessed as the sum of two components, that are *a)* the operational component, linked to the residual value of the machinery and to their performance, and *b)* the real estate component connected to the building enhancement investment. With reference to the component *a)*, it should be observed that the hypothesis concerns the machinery replacement since 3 years after the last year of the time horizon (assuming the replacement every 10 years). Therefore the operational component residual value has been determined by anticipating the associated net cash flows at the last year of the time horizon. The residual value (RV) associated with the real estate valuation has been assessed using the formula (5):

$$RV = (1 - D) \cdot I \tag{5}$$

where I is the reconstruction cost equated to the initial investment cost and D is the depreciation coefficient, proposed by the European Union of Accounting Experts [23], determined by applying the mathematical relation (6):

$$D = \frac{\left(\frac{n}{Vu} \cdot 100 + 20\right)^2}{140} - 2,86 \tag{6}$$

where n is the building age in years and Vu is the building useful life in efficiency (considered equal to 90 years).

In overall terms, the residual value is approximately equal to € 6.8 million, of which € 3 million are related to the operating component and € 3.8 million concern the real estate one.

The project provides for a total public funding of € 20 million of which € 12 million are requested in the context of NRRP (which cover the costs for the development of the property and the equipment purchase) and € 8 million are related to national or regional funds previously allocated for the Health House to be used for ordinary activities (maintenance, training, etc.).

Phase IV: Analysis of the Financial Profitability and Sustainability
According to the indications included in the Community Guidelines, the Financial Net Present Value (FNPV) and the corresponding Financial Rate of Return (FRR) have been determined both with respect to the investment in general (FNPV(C) and FRR (C)) – i.e. not considering the specific financing sources - and to the national capital (FNPV(K) and FRR(K)) – i.e. including the financing requested with a negative sign. The results show that the initiative is financially profitable and there are no substantial differences in the profitability of the investment with respect to the two points of view, as the two situations differ exclusively for a different distribution of costs in the early years. In fact, by analyzing the investment in general terms, in the early years there are the cash outflows necessary for the enhancement of the property and the equipment purchase, whereas, by considering the national capital, in the first years the "costs" concern the loans used to cover the investment costs.

The FNPV(C) of the investment is equal to over € 2.9 million which correspond to a FRR(C) equal to 6.7%, higher than the FDR; the FNPV(K) of the national capital is equal to approximately € 2.7 million and the associated FRR(K) is 6.4%.

Despite the good financial performance, the project needs the required public financing as the initiative is not bankable and, therefore, it cannot independently start if not adequately supported.

The project outputs attests the financial sustainability, as the cumulative cash is always greater than zero value and there are not years characterized by cash tensions. This result is strongly influenced by the revenues from the new services performed and by the lower costs incurred thanks to the decrease in improper visits. The optimization of the cash flows by reducing the deficit has not been carried out in order to deal with any critical situations.

2.5 Economic Analysis

The economic analysis has been carried out according to the following steps: *i*. Calculation of the Social Discount Rate; *ii*. Determination and application of the Conversion Factors; *iii*. Evaluation of externalities; *iv*. Estimation of benefits; *v*. Analysis of the economic performance.

Phase I: Calculation of the Social Discount Rate

For the estimation of the Social Discount Rate (SDR), the Community Guidelines suggest a variable reference value between 3% and 5%, from which the variation could be performed through the alternative application of two approaches: the first one is based on the determination of the Social Rate of Return on Private Investments (SRRI) and it consists in considering the return on public investment equal to that obtainable with a private investment without the risk premium, whereas the second one concerns the identification of the Social Rate of Time Preference (SRTP) equivalent to a government bond. In the present project assessment, regardless of the specific approach considered, the same result has been achieved, i.e. the SRRI is equal to the SRTP that is equal to the gross yield of the 30-year BTPs detected on 01/05/2022. By taking into account that this value is lower than 5% recommended by the Community Guidelines for this loan request, as a prudential SDR equal to 5% has been selected.

Phase II: Determination and Application of the Conversion Factors

The costs considered in the economic analysis are those determined in the financial analysis multiplied by the Conversion Factors (CFs). In order to assess the CFs able to pass from the market prices, used in the financial analysis, to the shadow prices, to be applied in the economic analysis, the standard CFs proposed by two official sources [33, 39] have been used. In general, the UVAL has been preferred, as the proposed CFs are differentiated by investment typology and are more recent.

For the determination of the CF to be applied to the costs of healthcare personnel for the transformation from market wages to shadow ones, a relevant modification compared to the values proposed by UVAL and NUVV has been carried out, as they concern the labor. Moreover, the CF to be applied to the costs of healthcare personnel has been determined as the average of the CFs associated with the various profiles, indirectly calculated by applying the following formula (7):

$$CF = (1 - i) \cdot (1 - d) \tag{7}$$

where i is the income tax, i.e. the average IRPEF rate that varies according to salary and, therefore, the specific job position, and d is the unemployment rate of the year 2020 provided by ISTAT for the Southern Italy (differentiated by qualification). The CF of healthcare personnel is higher than labor one, due to the lower unemployment associated with these professional profiles.

Phase III: Evaluation of Externalities

The project generates negative environmental externalities, related to the emission of greenhouse gases.

To estimate the corresponding monetary effects, the equivalent tons of CO_2 generated by investments in construction and machinery, labor and overheads have been firstly determined (applying factors provided by UVAL); subsequently the tons of CO_2 activated have been multiplied by the corresponding unit value (equal to 37 Euro/t-CO_2e) identified by applying the EIB's "Carbon dioxide footprint methodology" [13].

Phase IV: Estimation of Benefits
In general terms, the project involves many regional and national companies, already included in the structuring phase as project partners. Their main benefits concern the incremental shadow profit compared to the "as is" scenario, i.e. the no project situation. The assessment of the increase in profits, and its subsequent correction to take into account market distortions, has been developed starting from the financial analysis revenues, such as the sale of consultancy services, the revenues obtained from the patents marketing and the tariffs for access to laboratories and for the use of research equipment. To these benefits the contribution in kind has been added, i.e. given by the companies involved in terms of personnel included in the project: this approach implicitly considers that the increase in profit will certainly be higher than the investment carried out by companies. Moreover, the approach used is precautionary, as it does not take into account all the benefits associated with the new products development and the existing processes improvement, by avoiding the risk of double counting of the benefits.

The training and research activity plays a central role in the project: in fact, it is planned to activate several masters for a total of 80 students per year (20 units in Public Health, 20 in Health Data Science, 40 Nutritional Epidemiology) and various doctoral schools for a total of 12 doctoral students per year, 10 units of which are directly funded by companies as an equity commitment. In addition, the project focuses on the structuring of data in the health sector and on its systematic management for the benefits of the new knowledge production and its dissemination through scientific publications. The connected unitary benefits can be represented by the marginal social value of scientific publications estimated as the ratio between the gross remuneration of the personnel employed in research activities and the number of publications developed. The researchers involved are mostly PhD students, whose gross annual remuneration is around € 20,000. For the identification of the number of publications potentially carried out in a year by an ordinary PhD student, the threshold value in terms of articles number in 5 years to be presented as a requirement for the National Scientific Qualification for 2nd level Professor has been considered [25] (in relation to the Scientific Disciplinary Sectors interested in the project). Starting from this average value (2.29 publications/year), the value of a publication for an ordinary PhD student has been identified, equal to € 8,750/publication. To apply this value to the project specifications, it has been considered that: i) the researchers employed will also carry out other complementary academic activities for about 10% of their time and ii) the project infrastructure will improve the performance compared to an average researcher, of about 20% in terms of increase in publications. Finally, the benefits per researcher are equal to € 21,600/year which corresponds to an overall benefit of € 259,000/year when fully operational. The approach implemented is precautionary as it does not consider the additional effect resulting from the citations and the consequent increase in the indicators associated with the researcher scientific activity.

In addition to the benefits in scientific publication terms, the positive effect for young researchers and students involved in the project concerned the acquired skills that help in future job collocations, by increasing career prospects has been analyzed. The "proxy" variable used to estimate this benefit is the incremental remuneration for the benefits of PhDs and master's graduates, compared to a "normal" graduate. According to the 2021 reports "Employment condition of research doctors" and "Employment condition of master's graduates" carried out by the AlmaLaurea Interuniversity Consortium [7], the employment rate of PhDs one year after graduation is 88.1%, of master's graduates 86.9%, whereas the second level graduates reach an employment rate of 87.7% 5 years after degree obtainment. Also on the remuneration point of view, the differences are significant: the master's graduate has an average monthly net remuneration equal to € 1,745, the PhD to € 1,728 and the "normal" graduate to € 1,364. The overall benefits, when fully operational, associated with these increases are approximately equal to € 450,000/year. To avoid double counting of these benefits typologies, the fees associated with masters and PhD courses have not been included in the economic analysis. As previously described, the project intends to realize various interventions aimed at reducing mortality and morbidity rates and improving health conditions of the population living in the reference area. These objectives are implemented through a) the reduction of 389 inappropriate hospitalizations and the access to the emergency department visits in code white (low priority), b) an increase of 4,800 specialist services in one year, c) the activation of remote monitoring services for 150 patients currently assisted at home.

The benefits associated with the reduction of 389 accesses have been measured through the monetary amount that the patients would be willing to pay to avoid going to hospital facilities. In this sense, for the benefit monetary quantification, i.e. the Willingness To Pay (WTP), the study developed by Pearce D. [34] has been borrowed. In particular, the analysis has identified the corresponding European average WTP in 2000 at € 490/missed situation, that, revalued in 2022 by means of the consumer price index for families of workers and employees developed by ISTAT [19], is equivalent to € 702/missed situation. This amount implicitly incorporates the costs for avoided mobility and it should be noted that there will be no improvements in terms of increased life expectancy or life quality for the 389 missed accesses, as these patients would have gone to hospital facilities, by obtaining a performance benefit (in terms of decreased mortality and morbidity) similar to that obtained through the project's initiatives. Moreover, it should be pointed out that the corresponding benefits, equal to over 270,000 euros/year, are 80% higher than the financial savings obtained (equal to over 150,000 euros / year).

Furthermore, it is assumed that the 4,800 additional benefits expected to be provided in one year will cause a decrease equal to 25% in the death risk in 10 years, a drop equal to 12.5% of morbidity risk [3] and an increase in quality of life equal to 15 points (measured with surveys based on SF-36 interrupted series analysis on the population living in the intervention area, which will be proposed after the activation of the structure). To estimate the related benefits, the Value of Statistical Life (VSL) has been identified starting from the publication of Miller T.R. [24]. The VSL is equal to approximately € 3.2 million (recalculated in 2022 with respect to the GDP per capita), lower than the approximately € 6.4 million estimated by Viscusi W.K. in 2021 [40] (based on the WTP). As a precaution, the lower amount has been considered. Finally, since these interventions will concern the population over 64 years old, the probability of corresponding mortality has been assessed starting from the mortality tables of ISTAT [22] by reparameterizing the values obtained with respect to the reference area. The "Health House 2.0" project will focus on coronary and cerebrovascular effects: therefore, the relative incidence rates have been identified (based on the Statistical Yearbook of the NHS [26]), and lethality has been reduced by 25%, obtaining a benefit of over € 2.6 million. This monetary amount is 37% higher than the corresponding financial savings of € 1.9 million. The benefits associated with the 150 patients related to the remote sensing have been set equal to the corresponding tariff return corrected for the conversion factor proposed by UVAL, and they have been estimated approximately equal to 460,000 euros/year.

Communities will visit the infrastructure, access the training events and get information about the activities and new publications through the advertising service and the website. The corresponding benefits, that is the marginal social value, is represented by the implicit willingness to pay of visitors, which can be estimated through the travel cost method.

It is assumed that the reference area is composed by the resident population in the Apulia region aged between 15 and 24 years old, and that every year there are about 2,000 entries (equal to 0.5% of the regional population between 15 and 24 years). As suggested by UVAL, the related benefits have been obtained by the sum of the cost per kilometer (equal to € 0.4944/km as indicated in the tables prepared by ACI [5] published in the Official Gazette of 02/03/2022) and the value of the time (assumed equal to 15 €/hour) both for the travel and for the visit (the total duration is assumed to be 2.5 h). The overall benefits have been assessed approximately equal to 290,000 euros per year.

Phase V: Analysis of the Economic Performance
The evaluation carried out has attested good economic performance of the project, as the Economic Net Present Value (ENPV) is equal to approximately € 12.6 million, the Economic Rate of Return (ERR) is equal to 12.0% and the Benefits/Discounted costs (B/C ratio) is equal to 1.3.

3 Conclusions

In the selection phase of the projects to be implemented through the support of EU funding, the importance assumed by the effectiveness of the ex ante evaluation techniques of different project solutions is always growing and strictly connected to an adequate use of the resources allocated by the EU for the realization of successful investments. The systematic and analytical process of comparing benefits and costs deriving from the realization of a project or programme allows to determine the contribution of the project to social well-being. The complexity that intrinsically characterizes urban initiatives and the tools used to decide, design and implement them underlies each intervention to be implemented on the urban territory (urban regeneration, disused property asset enhancement, construction or renovation of transportation infrastructures, recovery and protection of the environment, waste management, etc.), due to the contingent presence of public and private functions to be introduced, the heterogeneity of the subjects involved - Public Administration, private entrepreneurs, landowners, etc. – and of their interests, the scarcity of available financial resources and the different financing sources. From this perspective, each urban transformation initiative requires the definition and the management of several variables which, in different ways, concern the stakeholders involved and affect the overall investment feasibility [28, 30]. In the context of the territorial projects to be implemented, in general, and of the investments financed by the NRRP, assessment tools as the CBA aim to identify the one/s that are suitable of guaranteeing the economic and the financial convenience of the parties, in accordance with the urban and the natural environment identity.

With reference to the valuation of projects within the healthcare sector, the present research has developed a CBA on an initiative to be implemented through NPPR funds in a city situated in Southern Italy, by highlighting the convenience of the intervention for the investor ("financial" point of view) and the community ("economic" point of view). The analysis carried out, disaggregated in all the steps required by an effective CBA, could represent a manual for the evaluation of these typologies of investments, that can be consulted by private and public subjects, in order to appropriately verify the convenience of the initiative and its sustainability for the community, according to the market and socio-economic conditions of the context in which the project will be developed.

References

1. Aalto University: Aalto NeuroImaging (ANI) Infrastructure - Aalto NeuroImaging Rates (2020). https://www.aalto.fi/en/aalto-neuroimaging-ani-infrastructure/aalto-neuroimaging-rates
2. Bortone, I., et al.: Physical and cognitive profiles in motoric cognitive risk syndrome in an older population from Southern Italy. Europ. J. Neurol. **28**(8), pp. 2565–2573 (2021)
3. Castellana, F., et al.: Physical frailty, multimorbidity, and all-cause mortality in an older population from southern italy: Results from the salus in Apulia study. J. Am. Med. Direct. Assoc. **22**(3), 598–605 (2021)
4. Collegio Degli Ingegneri e Architetti di Milano: Prezzi Tipologie Edilizie. DEI Tipografia del Genio Civile. Quine Business Publisher, Milano, Italy (2019)
5. Comunicato di rettifica relativo alle Tabelle nazionali dei costi chilometrici di esercizio di autovetture e motocicli elaborate dall'ACI (22A00702). GU Serie Generale n.28 del 03-02-2022. www.gazzettaufficiale.it
6. Consiglio Superiore dei Lavori Pubblici and Ministero delle Infrastrutture e della mobilità sostenibili: Linee guida per la redazione del progetto di fattibilità tecnica ed economica da porre a base dell'affidamento di contratti pubblici di lavori del PNRR e del PNC, Art. 48, comma 7, del decreto-legge 31 maggio 2021, n. 77, convertito nella legge 29 luglio 2021, n. 108 (2021)
7. Consorzio Interuniversitario AlmaLaurea. Rapporti AlmaLaurea 2021. www.almalaurea.it
8. Decreto del Presidente del Consiglio dei Ministri 29 novembre 2001: Definizione dei livelli essenziali di assistenza. (GU Serie Generale n.33 del 08-02-2002 - Suppl. Ord. n. 26)
9. European Commission, Directorate-General for Regional and Urban policy: Guide to Cost-Benefit Analysis of Investment Projects. Economic appraisal tool for Cohesion Policy 2014–2020 (2014)
10. European Commission: Report from the Commission to the European Parliament and the Council on the implementation of the Recovery and Resilience Facility (2022)
11. European Commission. Directorate General for Research and Innovation: Final Report from the Expert Group on Intellectual Property Valuation (2013)

12. European Commission: The Value of European Patents. Evidence from a Survey of European Inventors. Final Report of the PatVal EU Project (2005)
13. European Investment Bank: The Economic Appraisal of Investment Projects at the EIB (2013). http://www.eib.org/attachments/thematic/economic_appraisal_of_investigation_proj ects_en.pdf
14. Formez PA: Progetto Operativo di Assistenza Tecnica - POAT Salute 2007 – 2013. Analisi Costi E Benefici Casa Della Salute Di Chiaravalle Assistenza tecnica all'applicazione delle Linee Guida regionali: Modello organizzativo e percorso di attuazione delle Case della Salute" (2013)
15. Formez PA: Progetto Operativo di Assistenza Tecnica - POAT Salute 2007 – 2013. Analisi Costi e Benefici Casa della Salute di Siderno. Assistenza tecnica all'applicazione delle Linee Guida regionali: Modello organizzativo e percorso di attuazione delle Case della Salute (2013)
16. Formez PA: Progetto Operativo di Assistenza Tecnica - POAT Salute 2007 – 2013. Analisi Costi e Benefici Casa della Salute di San Marco Argentano. Assistenza tecnica all'applicazione delle Linee Guida regionali: Modello organizzativo e percorso di attuazione delle Case della Salute (2013)
17. Guarini, M. R., D'Addabbo, N., Morano, P., Tajani, F.: Multi-criteria analysis in compound decision processes: the AHP and the architectural competition for the chamber of deputies in Rome (Italy). Buildings 7(2), 38 (2017)
18. Hwang, K.: Cost-benefit analysis: its usage and critiques. J. Public Aff. 16(1), 75–80 (2016)
19. Istituto Nazionale di Statistica - ISTAT: Rivalutazioni e documentazione su prezzi, costi e retribuzioni contrattuali (Rivaluta). https://rivaluta.istat.it/Rivaluta/
20. Istituto Nazionale di Statistica - ISTAT: Indicatori territoriali per le politiche di sviluppo. www.istat.it/it/archivio/16777
21. Istituto Nazionale di Statistica – ISTAT: Rapporto annuale 2021. La situazione del Paese (2021)
22. Istituto Nazionale di Statistica – ISTAT: Tavole Di Mortalità Della Popolazione Residente. https://www.istat.it/it/archivio/7391
23. Manganelli B.: Il deprezzamento defli immobili urbani. In: Principi teorici, approcci metedoloci, profili innovativi nella valutazione, Franco Angeli editore (2011)
24. Miller, T. R.: Variations between countries in values of statistical life. J. Transp. Econ. Policy 169–188 (2000)
25. Ministero dell'Istruzione, dell'Università e della Ricerca (MIUR): Decreto ministeriale n.589 dell' 8 agosto 2018 "Determinazione dei Valori-Soglia degli indicatori di cui agli allegati C, D ed E del D.M. 7 giugno 2016, n. 120". Tabella 1 valori soglia candidati – settori bibliometrici. www.miur.gov.it
26. Ministero della Salute: Annuario Statistico del Servizio Sanitario Nazionale. Anno 2019. https://www.salute.gov.it/portale/documentazione/
27. Ministero della Salute: Progetto Mattoni Sistema Sanitario Nazionale. Proposta metodologica per la modifica DPCM LEA elenco DRG (2006)
28. Morano, P., Guarini, M.R., Tajani, F., Anelli, D.: Sustainable redevelopment: the cost-revenue analysis to support the urban planning decisions. In: Gervasi, O.., Murgante, Beniamino, Misra, Sanjay, Garau, Chiara, Blečić, Ivan, Taniar, David, Apduhan, Bernady O., Rocha, Ana Maria A C., Tarantino, Eufemia, Torre, Carmelo Maria, Karaca, Yeliz (eds.) ICCSA 2020. LNCS, vol. 12251, pp. 968–980. Springer, Cham (2020). https://doi.org/10.1007/978-3-030-58808-3_69
29. Morano, P., Locurcio, M., Tajani, F., Guarini, M.R.: Fuzzy logic and coherence control in multi-criteria evaluation of urban redevelopment projects. Int. J. Bus. Intell. Data Min. 14, 10(1), 73–93 (2015)

30. Morano, P., Tajani, F., Di Liddo, F., Amoruso, P.: The public role for the effectiveness of the territorial enhancement initiatives: a case study on the redevelopment of a building in disuse in an Italian small town. Buildings **11**(3), 87 (2021)
31. National Recovery and Resilience Plan (NRRP). Available online: www.mef.gov.it
32. Next Generation EU (NGEU) - Recovery Fund. www.ec.europa.eu.it
33. Nuclei Regionali di Valutazione e Verifica degli Investimenti Pubblici – NUVV: Studi di fattibilità delle Opere Pubbliche. Guida per la certificazione da parte dei Nuclei regionali di Valutazione e Verifica degli investimenti pubblici (2001)
34. Pearce, D.: Valuing Risks To Life And Health Towards Consistent Transfer Estimates in the European Union and Accession States. Paper prepared for the European Commission (DGXI) Workshop on Valuing Mortality and Valuing Morbidity, Brussels (2000)
35. Perino, G., Sileno, L., Tresalli, G.: Ospedali - Costi teorici di costruzione e di manutenzione 2017. IRES – Istituto di Ricerche Economico-Sociali del Piemonte, No.263 (2018)
36. Priemus, H., Flyvbjerg, B., van Wee, B. (eds.): Decision-Making on Mega-Projects: Cost-Benefit Analysis, Planning and Innovation. Edward Elgar Publishing (2008)
37. Regolamento (UE) No. 1303/2013 del Parlamento Europeo e del Consiglio del 17 dicembre 2013, recante disposizioni comuni sul Fondo europeo di sviluppo regionale, sul Fondo sociale europeo, sul Fondo di coesione, sul Fondo europeo agricolo per lo sviluppo rurale e sul Fondo europeo per gli affari marittimi e la pesca e disposizioni generali sul Fondo europeo di sviluppo regionale, sul Fondo sociale europeo, sul Fondo di coesione e sul Fondo europeo per gli affari marittimi e la pesca, e che abroga il regolamento (CE) n. 1083/2006 del Consiglio
38. Senato della Repubblica, Camera dei Deputati: Il Piano Nazionale di Ripresa e Resilienza (NRRP) – Schede di lettura. Dossier XVIII Legislatura (2021)
39. Unità di Valutazione degli Investimenti Pubblici – UVAL - Gori G., Lattarulo P., Maiolo S., Petrina F., Rosignoli S., Rubino P.: Lo studio di fattibilità nei progetti locali realizzati in forma partenariale: una guida e uno strumento. No. 30 (2014)
40. Viscusi, W.K.: Economic lessons for COVID-19 pandemic policies. Southern Econ. J. **87**(4), 1064–1089 (2021)
41. Zupo, R., et al.: Traditional dietary patterns and risk of mortality in a longitudinal cohort of the salus in apulia study. Nutrients **12**(4), 1070 (2020)

International Workshop on Ports of the Future Smartness and Sustainability (SmartPorts 2022)

Special Economic Zones Planning for Sustainable Ports: General Approach for Administrative Simplifications and a Test Case

Domenica Savia Pellicanò[1(✉)] and Maria Rosaria Trecozzi[2]

[1] Mediterranea University, 89124 Reggio Calabria, Italy
domenica.pellicano@unirc.it
[2] Calabria Region, 88100 Catanzaro, Italy

Abstract. Special Economic Zones (SEZs) are geographical areas with regulatory regime where the enterprises receive incentives, through i.e. tax breaks, and have administrative simplifications, with the aim to increase the enterprises competitiveness, the attraction of direct investments especially by foreign subjects, the new increase in exports, the creation of jobs work and, more generally, the strengthening of the productive fabric by stimulating industrial growth and innovation.

A SEZ implies the implementation of regulatory and administrative simplification actions in order to rationalize the procedures and to make the relationship among administration, citizen and business simpler, transparent and direct.

Calabria Region has approved Strategic Development Plan for SEZ Calabria, that has its center in Gioia Tauro including the port and the industrial area. Gioia Tauro port is specialized in container transhipment operations and it has a great expansion capacity to become a third-generation port also due to the presence of the SEZ.

The paper proposes a general model, a graph, that defines the concept of administrative simplification and introduces a cost function associated with it. The paper presents a general framework of the administrative simplification system developed by Calabria Region for the SEZ. The deepening of this topic is very interesting in relation to its impacts on the economic and social sector of the region and the country.

Keywords: Special Economic Zones · Economic development · Ports · Administrative simplifications

1 Introduction

Special Economic Zones (SEZs) are parts of the territory in which companies are subjected to measures as incentives, tax breaks and regulatory derogation in order *primarily to encourage the formation of capital through the production of goods and services* [1] and for *attracting foreign direct investment, accelerating industrialization and creating jobs* [2]. There are about 4,000 SEZs in the world; in Europe there are about 90 SEZs and Free Zones, 14 of which are established in Poland, which represent some of the most virtuous examples.

The SEZ represents a powerful tool for the development of a region thanks to the presence of adequate financial, fiscal, simplification and bureaucratic support.

There are several interventions that can favor the businesses development and, in general, markets; among these, the cost of labor, infrastructural investments and bureaucratic simplification are of great importance. The latter one is an essential element.

The simplification element is one of the cornerstones of the SEZ which must be increasingly inclusive. It heavily conditions the processes of change in a region because it is very often organized by forms and not by goals. The organizational by form was probably useful during the organization of the unitary state, when it was necessary to unify a lot of microscopic states. Today, proceeding towards goals also becomes a form. And the procedure, the regulation, the paragraph, always prevail over the social need, over the difficulties of the company, over merit.

The different reforms made have removed the managerial responsibility from political executives, giving it to the bureaucracy, without reforming the bureaucracy. The effect has been devastating; it is enough to look at the systematic delays of some regions in spending, delays made up only by means of technical assistance. Bureaucracy that proceeds by forms that are given the responsibility to spend effectively and efficiently puts a strain on the most qualified programs.

Governments in many economies make or maintain regulations that burden entrepreneurs. Whether by intention or ignorance, such regulation limits the ability of entrepreneurs to freely manage a private enterprise. As a result, entrepreneurs resort to informal activities, away from the oversight of regulators and tax collectors, or seek opportunities abroad, or join the ranks of the unemployed.

Simplification therefore represents a goal to be pursued by administrations at different territorial levels; it is a fundamental component of the sustainability of a system [3]. Already in 1987, in the Brundtland report, one of the limits to sustainable development is attributed to the non-predisposition of governments to changes towards integrated and global approaches. *Yet most of the institutions facing those challenges tend to be independent, fragmented, working to relatively narrow mandates with closed decision processes. Those responsible for managing natural resources and protecting the environment are institutionally separated from those responsible for managing the economy. The real world of interlocked economic and ecological systems will not change; the policies and institutions concerned must* [4].

The 2030 Agenda also pays attention to sustainability relating to procedures and the business climate in the following goals and targets [5, 6]:

8. Promote sustained, inclusive and sustainable economic growth, full and productive employment and decent work for all.

- *8.3 Promote development-oriented policies that support productive activities, decent job creation, entrepreneurship, creativity and innovation, and encourage the formalization and growth of micro, small and medium-sized enterprises, including through access to financial services.*

- *8.a Increase Aid for Trade support for developing countries, in particular least developed countries, including through the Enhanced Integrated Framework for Trade-related Technical Assistance to Least Developed Countries.*

10. Reduce inequality within and among countries.

- *10.5 Improve the regulation and monitoring of global financial markets and institutions and strengthen the implementation of such regulations,*

17. Strengthen the means of implementation and revitalize the Global Partnership for Sustainable Development.

- *17.13 Enhance global macroeconomic stability, including through policy coordination and policy coherence.*
- *17.14 Enhance policy coherence for sustainable development.*
- *17.15 Respect each country's policy space and leadership to establish and implement policies for poverty eradication and sustainable development.*

European Commission is in the same direction of the Agenda 2030; in fact, in the Country Report has set the objective 1: A *smarter Europe – innovative and smart industrial transformation* through [7]:

- *enhancing research and innovation capacities and the uptake of advanced technologies*
- *promoting digitisation for citizens, companies and governments*
- *enhancing growth and competitiveness of small and medium sized enterprises.*

At national level, Italy has approved the 2020–2023 Simplification Agenda [8] to relaunch the country after the pandemic crisis, stimulate the ecological and digital transition, promote structural change in the economy, starting from contrast to gender, territorial and generational inequalities. The Agenda is focused on the emergency and on programs to relaunch the economy and employment, providing for interventions that contribute to restarting the country, counting on a simpler, faster public administration that is closer to the citizens. The Agenda implements a program of simplification interventions for the resumption of the epidemiological emergency aimed at pursuing the following objectives: systematic elimination of bureaucratic constraints on recovery; reduction of time and cost of procedures for business activities and for citizens.

Simplification is an objective of the Calabria Regional Transportation Plan, that has 4 main goals: regional economic development, external and internal accessibility, in a general framework of sustainability [9]. The objective 8 specifically regards *Sustainability and streamlining* and the action 8 is related to *Measures for sustainability, simplification and speeding up of procedures, controls and interventions in the regional transport and logistics sector.*

The World Bank has defined an indicator *easy doing business* analyzing aspects of regulation and business practice using specific case studies with standardized hypotheses

[10]. The score defines the strength of the business environment and is assessed on the basis of the performance of an economy. It allows to classify the economy of a country in relation to regulatory performance.

Table 1 reports the top and bottom 20 economies. The European Union ranks in the 45th position with a score of 76.2; Italy is in 67th place with a score of 72.9.

The 20 best performing economies have made around 464 regulatory changes and are aimed at improving the business climate through other reforms. Most of the top 20 economies come from the OECD high income group; vice-versa, the last 20 are mainly regions of sub-Saharan Africa. The top 20 economies have online business establishment processes, electronic tax return platforms and allow online procedures relating to property transfers. In addition, they have solid corporate regulation with a high degree of transparency.

It should be noted that some countries with very low scores have activated numerous regulatory reforms in the business environment; for example, Myanmar has launched a simplification program that has allowed it to move up from the last 20 positions to 165.

It is possible to make an evaluation of the business environment in countries also in relation to the time taken to obtain a license. For example, starting a business in economies ranked in the bottom 50 takes on average almost 6 times longer than in the top 20. Transfer of ownership in the top 20 economies takes less than 2 weeks, compared to about 3 months in the last 50. Getting an electrical connection in an average economy of the top 50 takes twice as long as it takes in an average economy of the top 20; the cost of this connection is 44 times higher if expressed as a share of per capita income.

Table 1. Ease of doing business score (0 = lowest performance to 100 = best performance) [10].

	Economy	Score		Economy	Score
1	New Zealand	86.8	219	Sudan	44.8
2	Singapore	86.2	220	Iraq	44.7
3	Hong Kong SAR, China	85.3	221	Afghanistan	44.1
4	Denmark	85.3	222	Guinea-Bissau	43.2
5	Korea, Rep.	84.0	223	Liberia	43.2
6	United States	84.0	224	Syrian Arab Republic	42.0
7	Georgia	83.7	225	Angola	41.3
8	United Kingdom	83.5	226	Equatorial Guinea	41.1
9	Norway	82.6	227	Haiti	40.7
10	Sweden	82.0	228	Congo, Rep.	39.5
11	North America	81.8	229	Timor-Leste	39.4
12	Lithuania	81.6	230	Chad	36.9
13	Malaysia	81.5	231	Congo, Dem. Rep.	36.2
14	Mauritius	81.5	232	Central African Republic	35.6

(continued)

Table 1. (*continued*)

	Economy	Score		Economy	Score
15	Australia	81.2	233	South Sudan	34.6
16	United Arab Emirates	80.8	234	Libya	32.7
17	North Macedonia	80.7	235	Yemen, Rep.	31.8
18	Estonia	80.6	236	Venezuela, RB	30.2
19	Latvia	80.3	237	Eritrea	21.6
20	Finland	80.2	238	Somalia	20.0

Most economies trade mainly through ports; however, they are very often characterized by the absence of a unitary approach in the management of bureaucratic processes and a total fragmentation of skills, thus causing diseconomies.

In Italy, strategies have been launched to overcome this problem which have not produced any results; the creation of the National Logistics Platform gives only prototypes and studies without any real operational effect.

Many Port System Authorities have been forced to continue investing resources to support the development of their traffic, doing so without any coordination and managing, in some cases, to create valuable ITS systems commonly called Port Community Systems, which have simplified many procedures and supported the action of private operators as well as their own administrations.

EU has proposed a *Digital Economy and Society Index (DESI)* to monitor the digital progress of the member state. Italy ranks 20th among the 27 EU [11].

One of the pillars of the most developed ports in the world is precisely linked to administrative simplification; examples are the ports of Tangier Med, Shenzhen and Dubai. Tangier Med port, one of the main hubs of the Mediterranean for the movement of containers and ships, has a structured Free Zone which has produced a great acceleration in the growth of the area; in the port logistics area and the Free Zone a total of about 600 companies is placed that carries out a total export of over 4 billion euro [12].

The SEZ plays a key-role in this context, especially, for the disadvantaged territories which need to be more supported in order to compete in the world trade where there are countries in which the facilitations and simplifications proposed by the SEZ are unsustainable standards; in this sense, the SEZ is a powerful engine for the socio-economic development of a country.

This prompted the proposal of a SEZ in the Calabria Region, an economically disadvantaged region of southern Italy, a country where the time for export is about 19 days: 11 for documentation, 2 for custom, 6 for transport. The inefficiency linked to the preparation phase of the documentation is evident, which takes up more than half of the total time (for bill of lading, customs declaration, commercial invoice and certificates of technical/health standards, etc.). Not only is the export operation slower than many countries (Netherlands: 6; Cyprus, Germany: 7) but it is also expensive considering $ 1,195 against 577 in Morocco, 613 Egypt, 790 Cyprus [13, 14].

The paper presents the administrative simplifications proposed by Calabria Region for SEZ, of its own competence, in the general approach finalized to increase economic development. The impacts from the SEZ also arise from a special regulatory regime, fiscal benefit, infrastructures and services for the companies already present and for the new one that want to settle down. The SEZ for Calabria can be a source of development in a country where there is a strong delay also due to the bureaucratic machine characterized by many authorities and licenses/permits. On one hand the presence of the port is the minimum requirement for the establishment of the SEZ in Italy, on the other hand the port benefits from it to become a third-generation port [15, 16].

2   General Model

The SEZ can be considered "special" from various points of view, due to the regulatory regime, tax and non-tax benefits, infrastructures and services for businesses [17]. Special regulatory regime is applied by a set of policy instruments that are not generally applicable to the rest of the country. Tax regime, including customs, is applied with capital freedoms, tax incentives, subsidies, and duty or value-added tax, free or deferred. No-tax benefits include the set of administrative simplifications to reduce procedures time. Infrastructures and services are available, starting with efficient transport infrastructures. Then, companies in the SEZ have excellent conditions to grow economically and to attract new investors, contributing to the country economic development.

The general model of the SEZ can be represented as a tree diagram which operates at different levels. In the first level, there are concessions and realizations, on the one hand; the incentives package is on the other side. In turn, these are divided into other links that go to a second level, and so on.

Making a focus on incentives package, the no-tax benefits are given to companies mainly thought simplification of administrative services that allows for a significant reduction in the time and costs required to complete the procedures.

Many countries, especially those with an economic delay, are characterized by a very complex bureaucratic system that forces companies to interface with numerous entities and provide for numerous practices to complete a procedure. In this sense, the simplification proposed by SEZ represents an important tool to solve this problem, to bridge the gap with those countries where simplification is an ordinary guarantee.

To better explain the concept of simplification, it is possible to refer to a graph composed of nodes and links (Fig. 1). The nodes represent the stockholders involved in the process, the links represent the relationships among them, the interconnections. Each company to have an authorization, from the origin to the final node, is forced to cross a multiplicity of nodes (a) which translates into losses in terms of time and costs.

A cost function can be associated to this graph which can be expressed in a simplest form as a linear combination of cost attributes X_{hi} (time, monetary cost, etc.) with coefficients α_i to be calibrated:

$$\sum_{i=1}^{N} a_i \cdot X_{hi} \qquad (1)$$

where N is the number of nodes crossed.

To reduce these costs, it is possible to intervene mainly in two ways. The first one is to eliminate some nodes (b), but it is obvious that this leads to "dangerous" situations; the second one is to group some nodes (c), so that there is a single interface for carrying out different procedures. This is the best solution and is the one provided by the SEZ.

In this sense, simplification does not represent a single administrative action, but it has a scientific basis.

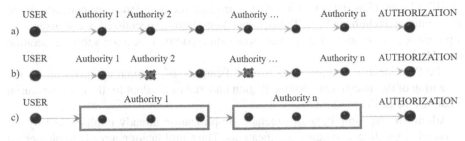

Fig. 1. Graph of administrative procedures

The solution c), in the SEZ areas, is realized by the One Stop Shop (OSS) for Productive Activities which represents the interface between companies and public institutions to deal with all the practices relating to the company opening and management; it allows to have a single public contact for the management of all bureaucratic procedures. The OSS works electronically; so, a practice that requires a lot of requirements can be carried out at the One Stop Shop, that forwards the documents to the entities and offices of destination (Provinces, Municipalities, etc.).

3 A Test Case

In Italy, SEZ program was established with Law Decree no. 91/2017 [17]. A SEZ is defined as a geographically delimited area, uniquely identified, located within the borders of the country, also consisting of areas not territorially adjacent as long as present a functional economic link, and one that includes at least a port area with the characteristics established by the Regulation (EU) no. 1315/2013 for the development of the TEN-T network [18].

New and existing businesses that start a program of business economic activities or of investments incremental in the SEZ, can take advantage of an incentives package by:

- fiscal benefits;
- administrative simplifications.

Subsequently, the Decree of the President of Council of Ministers (DPCM) no. 12/2018 defined the Regulation for the establishment of the SEZ respect to [19]:

- requirements, in terms of business access criteria;
- program characteristics, in terms of definition time and program characteristics

– modalities for the SEZ establishment, including SEZs interregional;
– criteria for the identification and delimitation of the SEZ area;

and general coordination of development objectives.

In March 2018, Calabria Region elaborated and approved the Strategic Development Plan for SEZ [20], according to DPCM no. 12/2018 and Regional Transport Plan [9]. In May 2018, the SEZ Calabria was legally established with another DPCM.

SEZ Calabria has the center in Gioia Tauro area including the core port, one of the main commercial hubs in Italy. Today, Gioia Tauro port is specialized in container transhipment operations and it has a great expansion capacity to become a third-generation port [21–28].

The Plan identifies administrative simplifications, of regional competence, for the realization of the investments that the Region undertakes to adopt for the entrepreneurial initiatives located in the SEZ.

Administrative simplifications include simplification already implemented by the region and executive, and new simplifications. The simplification already implemented and executive are:

- establishment of the Associated OSS of the Gioia Tauro Plain;
- harmonization and digitization of the procedures of the Port Authority;
- territorial marketing.

The Associated OSS of the Gioia Tauro Plain, the SUAP, has the aim to simplify and guarantee the conclusion of procedures quickly and with certainty. The main advantage of SUAP is that the entrepreneur turns to a single office to start or develop a business and receive all the clarifications on the necessary requirements and obligations. SUAP is a tool of public administrations, present by law also in every municipality, and is responsible for all administrative procedures relating to the economic and productive activities of goods and services and for all administrative procedures relating to the construction, expansion, termination, reactivation, localization and relocation of production plants, including the issue of building permits or authorizations. Figure 2 shows a scheme of administrative flow with SUAP.

In 2012, Calabria Region established the SURAP Office for the coordination of the regional network of SUAPs of Municipalities, Local Authorities and other Public Administrations, which constitute the set of users of the regional information system.

SURAP supports the smaller municipal SUAPs that are not equipped in terms of organization and skills. It promotes associative forms to improve the overall efficiency of the municipal SUAPs and the quality of the administrative action of the municipalities themselves, with respect to requests from the business world.

SURAP operates through the CalabriaSUAP telematic platform, that is a multifunctional digital desk that manages administrative procedures with the aim of speeding up the time for their conclusion [29].

In 2016, SURAP promoted the Associated OSS of the Gioia Tauro Plain by the three Municipalities: Gioia Tauro, Rosarno and San Ferdinando. SURAP thus anticipated some of the tools already envisaged for the SEZ establishment, for the integrated development

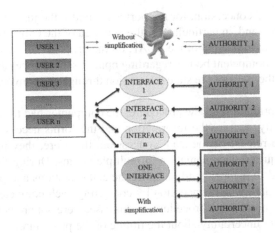

Fig. 2. Scheme of administrative flow with SUAP

of the territory, both in terms of setting up companies in the logistics and manufacturing sector, and in terms of accelerating the procedures for establishment/changing of businesses.

The Associated OSS transmits the necessary impetus for the economic development of the entire territory, with particular reference to the industrial area which falls within the territories of the Municipalities affected by the associated management. It provides a lot of information on activities, such as: location, construction, transformation, restructuring, conversion, extension, transfer, termination and reactivation.

The organizational model chosen for the Associated OSS consists of a "network structure", composed of a central coordination that organizes the service, takes care of the information phase, provides advice and assistance, addresses the most complex problems and deals with relations with external entities. The Associated OSS makes use of the Regional Consortium for the development of Productive Activities (CORAP) technical-organizational structure, in particular for the technical and administrative assistance functions in the verification of the practices presented in the area for industrial settlements as they fall within the area of the SEZ.

Before the adoption of this new procedure, the companies had to submit the request to CORAP, acquire any opinions and/or authorizations or clearances on their own and, after the acquisition of the authorization for the establishment, request the authorizations for the construction of the intervention. at the individual municipal SUAPs.

With the new procedure, the establishment requests within the industrial area (rearport) are presented in electronic format on a special portal. The Associated OSS of Gioia Tauro is responsible for carrying out the entire procedure until the authorization is obtained. It is estimated that the ordinary time of completion of the procedure will be reduced by 50%. The harmonization and digitization of the procedures of the Port Authority is a process initiated by SURAP in collaboration with the Port Authority of Gioia Tauro in relation to the complex procedure for issuing the state concession in the port area. The telematic configuration of this complex procedure allows the insertion and telematic management of applications for the start of entrepreneurial activities, with the request for a state concession, for the port areas under the jurisdiction of the Gioia Tauro Port Authority and, in particular, for the port area of the Gioia Tauro Plain. It also provides that it is the municipal office SUAP, on the proposal of the Port Authority, to involve the various competent bodies regarding opinions, clearances and authorizations to be acquired for the issue of the state concession through the convocation of a service conference.

Before the adoption of this new procedure, the companies had to submit the request to the Port Authority, acquire the information and the forms necessary to present the application for the release of the state concession, therefore, they had to submit the project and the required documentation in multiple copies. During the procedure, the companies also had to independently acquire the authorizations and permits necessary for awarding the state-owned concession by contacting each competent body directly. The terms of the administrative procedure, in this case, were not predictable, leaving the company in absolute uncertainty about the timing of the procedure.

With the new procedure, the Associate OSS of the Gioia Tauro Plain takes care of carrying out the entire procedural process until the concession is obtained. Territorial marketing is another activity launched by SURAP as an online service for the systematic promotion of the future SEZ area aimed at potential international investors. The descriptions make it possible to improve the quality and completeness of information on the entire industrial area of Gioia Tauro and on the regional territory, in terms of infrastructures and services, production and economic opportunities, and settlement opportunities. The contents provide useful information for entrepreneurs to evaluate the opportunity to allocate the activity in the SEZ area, with insights on: production context, territory and environment, transport system and culture and events.

Before the adoption of the new procedure, the companies had to contact the bodies involved (CORAP, Port Authority) for information on the availability of the lots.

With the new procedure, by accessing the portal www.calabriasuap.it, the potential user/investor has the possibility to check online the availability of areas that meet their settlement needs, in terms of surface, cost, existing infrastructures, type of companies already established, name of the contact person to contact.

The new simplifications to be implemented are: Information Desk, Ecologically Equipped Production Areas; further provisions concerning the procedures relating to certain economic activities.

The proposed establishment of a virtual Information Desk aims to provide further support to the productive subjects interested in setting up. The service, dedicated to the SEZ, coordinated to SUAP of Port Authority, has the aim is to contain information and services in a single point to facilitate the process of establishing/strengthening economic activities and attracting investments.

The proposed establishment of Ecologically Equipped Production Areas (APEA) is related to definition of a production area/agglomeration "equipped with the infrastructures and systems necessary to ensure the protection of health, safety and the environment", regulated by low. APEAs represent a regulatory and economic planning tool available to public entities to better guide territorial planning and, at the same time, to ensure that companies that choose to settle there are regulated, sustainable and competitive. APEA is characterized by the presence of common infrastructures and services managed jointly in ways that allow environmental performance higher than the sum of the benefits obtainable from the optimization of the production process of each company. This new perspective, through the activation of the typical advantages of territorial systems of enterprises (clusters), allows to combine the sustainability of production development with the possibility of improving the competitiveness of enterprises.

The proposal to establish further provisions concerning the procedures relating to certain economic activities implies simplifications of the: process; procedures; times.

The simplifications of the process are: identification of the single regional contact person for service conferences; identification of the OSS for the purposes of "administrative concentration"; provision of the substitutive powers of the Region through the SURAP, against the defaulting SUAP; identification of areas of particular interest regional; identification of the competent Authorities for the issuance of the Single Environmental Authorizations and the reorganization of the related procedural process; preparation of agreements to regulate the carrying out in collaboration of activities of common interest with the entities involved in the administrative procedures of interest to the SEZ; preparation of protocols and conventions between the local and state administrations concerned, aimed at regulating simplified procedures and special procedural regimes, as well as intervention proposed at national level to implement the regulation containing rules for simplification and acceleration of the admins operational procedures functional to the SEZ.

The procedural simplifications are: reorganization of the procedural flow for the issuance of similar authorizations; reorganization of the procedural flow for the approval of projects in variant to urban planning instruments; rationalization of the procedural flow for landscape authorizations; reduction of the terms for issuing permits to settle in industrial areas; reduction of investigation costs required in the context of administrative procedures limited to SEZ areas.

The simplifications of the times are: reduction of the time of administrative procedures relating to building permits; reduction of the terms for issuing permits for settlement in industrial areas.

4 Conclusion

A SEZ is a geographical area with regulatory regime and tax and no-tax incentives to attract direct investments especially from foreign subjects, increase in exports and create jobs.

The administrative simplifications are the mainly no-tax incentives, provided by the SEZ, that intervene on the reduction of costs and time to create/manage a business. Simplification is a goal to be pursued by administrations at various territorial levels; it is a fundamental component of the system sustainability according to the goals of the Agenda 2030.

The paper has presented a general model that defines the concept of simplification and has introduced a cost function associated with it. It would be interesting to calibrate the parameters of the cost function considering the average times and monetary costs over each administrative link.

The case study has concerned the administrative simplifications proposed by the Calabria Region, defined in its Strategic Development Plan of the SEZ.

SEZ Calabria has at its center the Gioia Tauro area which includes the port and the rear port with an industrial vocation. On the one hand, the presence of the port is the minimum requirement for the SEZ establishment in Italy, on the other hand, the port benefits from it to become a third-generation port.

Part of simplifications of Calabria is already executive and focuses on the functions of Associated OSS of Gioia Tauro Plain, that allows the investor to have only one interlocutor who implements the practice with a strong reduction in costs. To be implemented is a prototype features and consists in the creation of a virtual Information Desk to strengthen investor support, and of APEA to ensure that companies that choose to establish themselves are competitive in sustainable terms.

References

1. Snehi, Y.: Special economic zones. In: Kaminsky, A.P., Long, R.D. (eds.) India today: an encyclopedia of life in the Republic, vol. 1, Abc-Clio (2011)
2. World bank, Special Economic Zones. http://www.worldbank.org/content/dam/Worldbank/Event/Africa/Investing%20in%20Africa%20Forum/2015/investing-in-africa-forum-special-economic-zones.pdf. Accessed April 2022
3. Russo, F., Pellicanò, D.S.: Planning and sustainable development of urban logistics: From international goals to regional realization. WIT Trans. Ecol. Environ. **238**, 59–72 (2019)
4. World Commission on Environment and Development: Report of the world commission on environment and development: Our common future (1987)
5. United Nations: Transforming our world: the 2030 Agenda for sustainable development (2015)
6. United Nations: Global indicator framework for the sustainable development goals and targets of the 2030 agenda for sustainable development (2018)
7. European Commission: Commission staff working document. Country Report Italy (2019)
8. Governo Italiano: Semplificazione per la ripresa: Agenda 2020–2023 (2020)
9. Regione Calabria: Piano Regionale dei Trasporti (2016)
10. World Bank Group: Doing Business 2020. Comparing Business Regulation in 190 Economies (2020)
11. European Commission: Digital Economy and Society Index (DESI) 2021. Italy (2021)
12. Prete, P.A.P.S., Franca, E.M.: Special Economic Zones Weaknesses (2021)
13. World Bank Group: Doing Business 2014. Understanding Regulations for small and medium-size enterprises (2014)
14. Dipartimento per la Programmazione e il Coordinamento della Politica Economica: Iniziativa di studio sulla portualità italiana (2014)
15. Russo, F., Musolino, G., Assumma, V.: Competition between ro-ro and lo-lo services in short sea shipping market: the case of Mediterranean countries. Res. Transp. Bus. Manag. **2016**(19), 27–33 (2016)
16. Russo, F., Rindone, C.: Container maritime transport on an international scale: data envelopment analysis for transhipment port. WIT Trans. Ecol. Environ. **2011**(150), 831–846 (2011)
17. Governo Italiano: Decreto Legge n. 91/2017. Disposizioni urgenti per la crescita economica nel Mezzogiorno (2017)
18. EU: Regulation (EU) 1315/ 2013 of the European Parliament and of the Council of 11 December 2013 on Union guidelines for the development of the trans-European transport network and repealing Decision No 661/2010/EU (2013)

19. Governo Italiano: Decreto del Presidente del Consiglio dei Ministri n. 12/2018. Regolamento recante istituzione di Zone economiche speciali (ZES) (2018)
20. Regione Calabria: Piano di Sviluppo Strategico Zona Economica Speciale Calabria. (2018)
21. UNCTAD secretariat: Port Marketing and the challenge of the third generation port (1994)
22. Musolino, G., Chilà, G.: Structural factors for a third-generation port: planning general logistics interventions in Gioia Tauro (2021)
23. Russo, F., Chilà, G.: Structural factors for a third-generation port: current state, limits and weakness for Gioia Tauro in the regional transport plan. WIT Trans. Built Environ. **204**, 3–15 (2021)
24. Russo, F., Chilà, G.: Structural factors for of a third-generation port: actions and measures for Gioia Tauro in the regional transport plan. WIT Trans. Built Environ. **204**, 17–30 (2021)
25. Russo, F., Rindone, C.: Structural factors for of a third-generation port: planning interventions for research and development in Gioia Tauro TENT-T node. WIT Trans. Built Environ. **204**, 67–78 (2021)
26. Musolino, G., Trecozzi, M.R.: Structural factors for a third-generation port: planning interventions for agri-food logistics In Gioia Tauro (2022)
27. Musolino, G., Cartisano, A., Fortugno, G.: Structural factors for a third-generation port: planning interventions for mechanical logistics in Gioia Tauro (2022)
28. Russo, F., Panuccio, P., Rindone, C.: Structural factors for a third-generation port: between hinterland regeneration and smart town in Gioia Tauro. WIT Trans. Built Environ. **204**, 79–90 (2022)
29. Regione Calabria: CalabruiaSUAP. https://www.calabriasuap.it/cosa-e-calabriasuap/#:~:text=CalabriaSUAP%2C%20%C3%A8%20uno%20sportello%20digitale,nelle%20quali%20sono%20coinvolte%20pi%C3%B9. Accessed April 2022

Special Economic Zones Planning for Sustainable Ports: Aggregate Economic Impact of Port of Gioia Tauro

Giuseppe Musolino[1]([✉]) [iD], Antonio Cartisano[2], and Giuseppe Fortugno[3]

[1] DIIES, Università Mediterranea di Reggio Calabria, 89100 Reggio Calabria, Italy
giuseppe.musolino@unirc.it
[2] Freelance, Reggio Calabria, Italy
[3] Italferr S.p.A., Rome, Italy

Abstract. Special Economic Zones (SEZ) are a place-based measure to boost the economic growth adopted in several countries all-over the world. SEZs are geographic areas inside a country where tax incentives, favourable land-use policies, employment subsidies, and advantageous financial assistance encourage the settlement of domestic and foreign-invested manufacturing and services for export.

The paper concerns the ex-ante estimation of aggregate economic impact of a SEZ in Calabria region (Italy). SEZ in Calabria was conceived to operate in several existing industrial areas of the region, having its fulcrum around the transhipment hub port of Gioia Tauro, in order to propagate its benefits to the whole region in terms of export and employment. The aggregate economic impacts of the SEZ were quantified through two characteristic variables: exports and employment of industrial firms settled in Calabria. Two development scenarios are defined: a Do-Nothing scenario, in the absence of the SEZ and with the current economic policies operating in Calabria; and a SEZ scenario, assuming a full activation of SEZ (with complete availability of financial resources and decrees for simplification) at the end of 2018.

The comparison of the two scenarios shows relevant direct positive impacts in the SEZ case, both the in terms of export and employment, in the industrial sectors that benefits of the SEZ incentives.

Keywords: Special economic zone · Aggregate economic impacts · Case study · Port of Gioia Tauro

1 Introduction

Programs of governments are driven by the idea that ports development could be a key factor for the (re-)development of local economies. However, today the relations between ports and their own local economy seem to get weaker. Traffic flows increase, but port operations generate weak linkages, so that income and employment multiplier effects not only are less relevant, but they usually spread quite far from the port. Moreover, the presence of the port generates negative externalities at local level, such as pollution and landscape impacts. These negative externalities often make port investments opposed by local communities, which generally push for a different use of soil and environmental resources.

Economic impacts generated by existing port operations and investments may be considered as part of a more general process where a transport system and a spatial economic system interact. The transport system is represented by port infrastructures and services (supply component) and by sea and inland freight (and passenger, if any) flows. The spatial-economic system is represented by several economic actors; among which an important role is played by port stakeholders (demand component). The economic impact of the port stakeholders may be estimated with the support of the so-called economic impact models [1–3].

The paper presents an analysis of the aggregate economic impact generated by the introduction of a Special Economic Zone (SEZ) in the Calabria region, Southern of Italy [4, 5]. The fulcrum of the Calabrian SEZ is represented by the port of Gioia Tauro, whose activities rely both on physical (material) components, such as transport and logistic infrastructures, and on intangible (or immaterial) components, such as the set of SEZ measures [6–9]. The port of Gioia Tauro aims to complete its transition towards a third-generation port, by enhancing the role of the large industrial agglomeration present in its hinterland, destined to industrial, production and service activities [10, 11].

SEZs are geographic areas inside a country where tax incentives, favourable land-use policies, employment subsidies, and advantageous financial assistance encourage domestic and foreign-invested manufacturing and services for export. It was estimated that more than 5000 SEZs had been established worldwide in 2018; and that almost 4000 of them are settled in developing countries. More than 2200 SEZs had been established in China; among these, 570 operate at national-level and 1990 at provincial-level. The greater number of SEZs in China are settled in coastal provinces [12].

The objective of the paper is to quantify the extent of the benefits propagation of the SEZ in the Calabria region, in terms of export and employment. An economic impact model has been applied to ex-ante estimate the aggregate economic impact of the SEZ.

The following part of the paper is articulated into four sections. Section 2 deals with a literature review on port economic impacts studies and models. Section 3 presents the proposed economic impact model concept and specification; and reports the results of the application to the case of SEZ in Calabria region. The last section reports the conclusions and the further developments.

2   Literature Review on Economic Impact Studies

The existing literature on port economic impact studies may be considered as part of the rich literature concerning the impacts of construction and operation of large-scale transport infrastructures on local and national economies. In the case of construction, the aim is the quantification of effects of investments in infrastructure and technology on the local and national economies. In the case of operation, the aim is the definition and quantification of linkages between the operations connected with the existing transport infrastructure and the local and national economies.

Economic impacts of ports on local economies are generally measured as the contribution of the port to the level of some economic variables such as employment, value added, incomes, taxes and duties.

The literature review presented in this section reports some definitions of port economic impact and analyses the existing port impact studies and models.

The major challenge in port impact studies is the identification of the port stakeholders and of the degree of port dependency of these stakeholders with the hinterland area. In general, the total impact of a port on the local economy can be subdivided into direct (or primary) and indirect and induced (or secondary) impacts [13–16].

The *direct impact* is generated by *port-required stakeholders*, which provide transportation, logistics and port services. Transportation services include terminal freight forwarding, and cargo transport by rail and road. Port services include terminal operations, stevedoring, vessel supply, pilotage, towage, launch services, container service and other functions necessary for the handling of freight inside the port.

The *indirect impact* is generated by *port-attracted stakeholders*, which are economically dependent on port-required ones. Port-attracted stakeholders are attracted in the region because of the presence of a port. They would evaluate moving from a port to another port, if facilities and operations in the destination port generate higher value added than the one generated in the current port. These stakeholders can be subdivided into two groups: exporters of commodities and importers of raw or intermediate commodities to be assembled and/or distributed. Value added, employment, and tax revenues associated to such stakeholders are linked to the port because, in the absence of port facilities, they would not locate in the region. It is worth noting that the attractiveness can be 'revealed' (or 'observed'), when it is associated with the actual incoming flows (investments, firms, workers, ….) in a geographical area; or 'perceived', when it refers to how people, perceive a geographical area in which they have a particular interest (see [17–19]).

The *induced impact* is generated by *port-induced stakeholders*, which are economically dependent on the previous ones. Port-induced stakeholders are those ones in the region which have expanded their markets by exporting through the port. For these stakeholders, the presence of the port not only let them reducing transportation costs, but it is also a generator of value added.

There are several port impact studies in literature that attempt to measure the impact of ports on a local and national economy using EIMs. They may be broadly classified into two approaches, according to level of the aggregation of the economy representation: aggregate and disaggregate (at sector level). Among *aggregate approach*, some studies estimate the economic impact of a port by means of aggregated income-expenditure multipliers (see [13–16], and the references included). As far as concerns *disaggregate approach*, studies rely on input-output models [20–25]. These models allow the estimation of the direct, indirect and the induced impacts, through the identification of linkages among the sectors of the economy. Latest developments of input-output models allow to assess the level of embeddedness of a port inside the maritime trade networks and the global supply-chains [26].

Several papers in literature investigated the impact of SEZs on national and regional economies, mainly by means of economic impact models belonging to the aggregate approach. Some papers, among the others, focusing on SEZs establishment process in China, are recalled in the following. Wang [27] specified an aggregate economic impact model, where the outcomes are time-series yearly-based variables that include Foreign Direct Investment (FDI), domestic investment, total factor productivity growth and factor prices. Leong [28] examined the relationship between SEZs, openness and growth at the regional level for both China and India. The specified model structure put in relationship the national and regional GDP to the export, the FDI, the different periods of liberalizations, and the coastal position of the SEZ. Later, Zheng [12] analysed the employment effects of SEZs according to births, relocation, expansion, and death of firms. Firstly, he developed a logit model to predict the probability of having an SEZ for each Chines county, according to several county characteristics working as independent variables: population, population density, local economic structure, and political hierarchy of cities. Secondly, he specified aggregate economic impact models that have time-series employment in new entry firms as outcomes.

3   Aggregated Economic Impact Estimation of SEZ in Calabria

3.1   Economic Impact Model

As long as a port remains a place of transit of goods, the public (or private) governance of a port will adopt measures finalized to improve the performance of transport and to reduce costs. In order to significantly increase the value added generated, the measures adopted by the governance should be aimed to enhance the port hinterland, facilitating the settlement of industrial, production and service activities and the embeddedness of the port in the supply chains. The transition of a port from a centre of cost to a generator of value added determines his membership to the category of third-generation. These ports emerged with the world-wide diffusion of container and the changing requirements of the international trade. From the economic point of view, third-generation ports increase the value added of goods that transit through them, due also to their manipulations.

SEZs constitute the natural evolution of the third-generation ports. As matter of fact, an important element of the main existing SEZs is the physical and functional connection with ports of intercontinental level, located inside the SEZ area. Several measures, such as tax incentives, favourable land-use policies, employment subsidies, and advantageous financial assistance, may be deployed with the introduction of a SEZ.

Given a port a, Eq. (1) certifies that a is a third-generation port if transport costs, C, are lower than added value, AV (C are in absolute value):

$$C_a < AV_a \tag{1}$$

The comparison of economic variables between different ports may be executed according to the criterion of the value added maximization. Given a port a and a port b, Eq. (2) certifies that (third-generation) port b is more competitive than (third-generation) port a:

$$AV_b > AV_a \tag{2}$$

The economic impact model considered in this paper belongs to the aggregate approach, where the outcomes are the export and the employment, considered as a proxy of value added. The outcomes obtained, in both cases, are the following:

- export of firms inside ZES areas and of firms outside the ZES areas;
- employment of firms with foreign capital and of firms with domestic capital.

The models adopted to estimate the above variables rely on models developed in [27] and [28], in terms of specification and calibrated parameters. The infrastructural and economic conditions of the municipalities, and regions, that lie inside the ZESs analysed in [27] and [28], could be compared with the ones existing in Calabria region.

3.2 SEZ and Port of Gioia Tauro

SEZ in Calabria has been conceived to integrate several existing nodal transport infrastructures (ports and airports) and industrial areas of the region in physical and functional terms (Fig. 1). The ports of Calabria included in the SEZ are: Gioia Tauro, Reggio Calabria, Villa S. Giovanni, Crotone, Vibo Valentia, Corigliano Calabro. The industrial areas are: Gioia Tauro-San Ferdinando-Rosarno, Crotone, Vibo Valentia, Schiavonea-Corigliano. The three airports of the region are also included: Lamezia Terme, Reggio Calabria and Crotone.

The centre of the SEZ is the port of Gioia Tauro, which is one of the biggest container transhipment ports of the Mediterranean Sea. The port handled 3,14 million of TEUs in 2020. Some forecasts indicate for 2025 a number of containers handled between 78 and 84 million TEU in the Mediterranean Sea [29, 30]. Mediterranean container ports will increase their traffic in the next years at an annual average of 3.6%.

The port of Gioia Tauro aims to enhance the role of the large industrial agglomeration present in its hinterland (see Fig. 2), destined to industrial, production and service activities; and, therefore to complete the full transition towards a third-generation port. The strategic development plan of SEZ, defined in [4, 5], should support the development and the integration of existing supply chains, to enhance the Gioia Tauro hinterland in order to attract mechanical and agri-food factories, operators, transport and logistics companies, encourage mechanical and agri-food production in the Calabria region for the local and the international markets. A detailed description of the current structural factors and of the development strategies of port of Gioia Tauro is presented in several publications (see [31–37]).

3.3 ZES Scenarios Definition

The aggregate economic impacts of the SEZ were quantified through two characteristic variables:

- export of goods and services produced by firms settled in Calabria operating in the industrial sectors and exported abroad;
- employees in firms settled in Calabria operating in the industrial sector with foreign capital (total or partial) and with domestic capital.

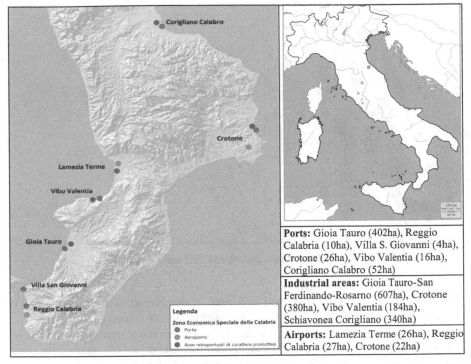

Fig. 1. Map of Calabria region with location of ZES areas (source: [5, 6]).

Two development scenarios have been defined:

- Do-Nothing scenario, in which the two variables are estimated over a period of 2019–2028, starting from the base year 2018, in the absence of the SEZ and with the current economic policies operating in Calabria;
- SEZ scenario, in which the two variables are estimated over a period 2019–2028, starting from the base year 2018, in the hypothesis of a full activation of the SEZ (with complete availability of financial resources and decrees for simplification) at the end of 2018.

3.4 Export

The historical series of exports of firms settled in Calabria operating in the industrial sector for years 2008–2017 was obtained from Italian Institute of Statistics [38].

The Do-Nothing and ZES scenarios were estimated considering two classes of firms:

1. industrial firms currently settled inside SEZ areas, named "Firms inside ZES";
2. industrial firms currently settled outside the SEZ areas, named "Firms outside ZES".

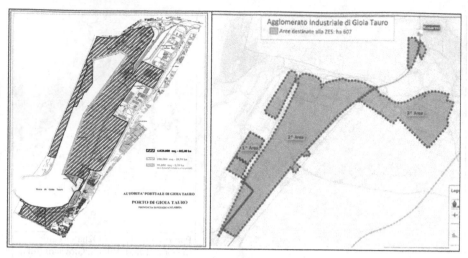

Fig. 2. Port of Gioia Tauro and related ZES area (source: [5, 6])

The two scenarios, Do-Nothing and ZES, and the two classes of firms, "firms inside ZES" and "firms outside ZES", generate four combination of forecasts.

The Do-nothing scenario for "firms inside ZES" was estimated over the period 2019–2028, starting from the base year 2018, assuming a constant rate of change in exports equal to the average of the rate of change in exports in Calabria registered in the years 2009–2017 (+2.0%).

The Do-nothing and ZES scenarios for "firms outside ZES" are identical and have been estimated over the period 2019–2028, starting from the base year 2018, assuming the same constant rate of change in exports as in the previous scenario (+2.0%).

The SEZ scenario for "firms inside ZES" was estimated over the period 2019–2028, starting from the base year 2018, assuming a growth rate equal to the average growth rate of exports observed in some international SEZs in the six years after their activation [27, 28].

Some brief considerations are reported below (see Table 1).

Export in the Do-nothing scenario for "firms inside ZES" increases from 230 M€ in 2017 to 273 M€ at the end of the years considered, while it increases from 209 M€ to 929 M€ in the SEZ scenario. In the Do-Nothing scenario export increases by 60 M€, assuming a growth rate equal to the one observed in the last 8 years. Export increases of four times in the hypothesis of a full activation of the SEZ in 2018, with its effects starting from 2019.

The export of industrial firms settled in Calabria (see 'Firms in Calabria' in Table 1) in the Do-nothing scenario increase from 418 M€ in 2017 to 496 M€ at the end of the reference decade, while it increases from 418 M€ to 1152 M€ in the SEZ scenario.

Table 1. Forecasted export for the four combinations of scenarios and classes of firms defined.

	Scenario	N. firms inside ZES	N. firms outside ZES	N. firms in Calabria
Export 2017 [M€]		230	189	418
Δ year [%]	Do-nothing	0,02	0,02	0,02
	ZES	v.c.(*)	0,02	v.c.(*)
Export 2024 [M€]	Do-nothing	273	223	496
	ZES	929	223	1152

(*)v.c., variable coefficient on year-base (see [27, 28]).

3.5 Employment

Employment in industrial firms located in SEZ areas remained constant around 10,000 units in the three-years 2015–2017 [39].

The employment scenarios Do-Nothing and ZES were estimated considering two classes of companies:

1. industrial firms currently settled in SEZ areas with foreign capital (partial or total), equal to about 12% of the total of firms;
2. industrial firms currently settled in SEZ areas with domestic capital, equal to approximately 88% of the total of firms.

Foreign-capital firms are Italian firms owned by other foreign-based investors, which invest to acquire control or in any case maintain lasting interests, which require some degree of involvement of the investor in the management of the activities.

In particular, the two scenarios (Do-Nothing and SEZ) and the two classes of firms (foreign and domestic capital) generate to four combination of forecasts.

The Do-Nothing scenario for foreign-capital firms was estimated over the decade 2019–2028, starting from the base year 2018, assuming a constant rate of change in employment equal to the average rate of change observed in years 2009–2015 (−1.2%) [39].

The SEZ scenario for foreign-capital firms was estimated for the decade 2019–2028, starting from the base year 2018, assuming a growth rate equal to the average growth rate of FDI observed in some international SEZs in the six years after their activation [27, 28].

The Do-nothing scenario for domestic-capital companies was estimated for the period 2019–2028, starting from the base year 2018, assuming a constant employment growth rate of +2.0%.

The SEZ scenario for domestic-capital companies was estimated for the decade 2019–2028, starting from the base year 2018, assuming a constant employment growth rate of +6.0%.

Some brief considerations are reported below (see Table 2).

Employment of foreign-capital firms settled in SEZ areas in the Do-nothing scenario decreases from 1,315 units in year 2017 to 1,225 units at the end of the decade under consideration, while it increases from 1,315 units to 4,095 units in the SEZ scenario. In the Do-nothing scenario it slightly decreases, if the rates observed in recent years remain unchanged; while it increases three times in the hypothesis of full activation of the SEZ at the end of the base year.

Table 2. Forecasted employment for the combinations of scenarios and classes of firms defined.

	Scenario	N. of foreign-capital firms	N. of domestic-capital firms	N. firms in Calabria
Employment 2017		1315	8798	10113
Δ year [%]	Do-nothing	−0,012	0,02	0,005
	ZES	v.c.(*)	v.c.(*)	v.c.(*)
Employment 2024	Do-nothing	1225	10106	11332
	ZES	4095	13256	17351

(*)v.c., variable coefficient on year-base (see [27, 28]).

Employment of domestic-capital firms settled inside ZES areas in the Do-Nothing scenario increases from 8,798 units in 2017 to 10,106 units at the end of the decade under consideration, while it increases from 8,798 units to 13,256 units in the SEZ scenario. In the SEZ scenario employment grows of about 3,000 units compared to the Do-Nothing scenario. In other words, domestic-capital firms also benefit from the introduction of the SEZ, albeit to lower extent.

The overall employment of firms established in SEZ areas of Calabria increases from 10,113 units in 2017 to 11,332 units in 2028 in the Do-Nothing scenario and to 17,351 units in the SEZ scenario. In the SEZ scenario, employment of industrial firms located in SEZ areas, grows of about 6,000 units compared to the Do-Nothing scenario.

4 Conclusions

SEZs have been widely adopted as a place-based program, in order to attract foreign capitals, boost exports and absorb advanced technology. The impact of SEZs on national and regional economies has been widely studied mainly with aggregated economic impact models.

The paper presented an analysis of the aggregate economic impact generated by the introduction of a Special Economic Zone (SEZ) in the Calabria region, Southern of Italy. The centre of the SEZ is the port of Gioia Tauro, which is one of the most important transhipment container ports in the Mediterranean Sea. The strategic development plan of SEZ, proposed by Regional Government of Calabria in 2018 [4, 5], aimed to the enhancement of the hinterland of the port of Gioia Tauro and of other areas inside Calabria region, by facilitating the settlement of industrial firms, operators, transport and logistics companies. The SEZ should attract firms that actively participate to the process of generating added value, according to the paradigm of the sustainable development of ports [40, 41].

The aggregate economic impacts of the SEZ were quantified through two variables: exports and employment of industrial firms settled in Calabria. Two SEZ scenarios are defined: Do-Nothing scenario, in the absence of the SEZ; and SEZ scenario, assuming a full activation of the SEZ at the end of 2018.

The comparison of the two scenarios shows direct positive impacts in the SEZ case, both the in terms of export and employment, in the industrial sectors that benefit of the SEZ measure.

Future developments of this research regard two directions. Firstly, the criteria for the selection of international ZESs to be used as a reference for the estimation of impacts engendered by the introduction of the ZES in the Calabria region will be further clarified. Secondly, the disaggregated impacts of the SEZs on specific sectors of Calabrian economy, concerning general transport, mechanical and agro-food will be investigated.

References

1. Russo, F., Musolino, G.: A unifying modelling framework to simulate the Spatial Economic Transport Interaction process at urban and national scales. J. Transp. Geogr. **24**, 189–197 (2012)
2. Musolino, G., Cartisano, A., Chilà, G., Fortugno, G., Trecozzi, M.R.: Evaluation of structural factors in a third-generation port: methods and applications. To be published on International Journal of Transport Development and Integration (2022)
3. Russo, F., Rindone, C., Panuccio, P.: External interactions for a third generation port: urban and research developments. To be published on International Journal of Transport Development and Integration (2022)
4. Regione Calabria: Piano Regionale dei Trasporti. Approved with Resolution of the Regional Council No 157 of 2016/12/06 (2016)
5. Regione Calabria: Istituzione Zone Economiche Speciali (ZES). Piano di Sviluppo Strategico della Regione Calabria. Approved with Resolution of the Regional Council No 100 of 2018/03/29 (2018)
6. Panuccio, P., Musolino, D.: Special Economic Zones for sustainable ports: territorial attractiveness and urban planning. The test case of Calabria region. In: 22nd International Conference on Computational Science and its Applications, ICCSA. Malaga, Spain (2022)
7. Pellicanò, D.S., Trecozzi, M.R.: Special Economic Zones for sustainable ports: general approach for administrative simplifications and a test case. In: 22nd International Conference on Computational Science and its Applications, ICCSA. Malaga, Spain (2022)
8. Rindone, C., Cirianni, F.M., Croce, A.I., Delfino, G.: Special Economic Zones for sustainable ports: the role of research and training in the Calabria region. In: 22nd International Conference on Computational Science and its Applications, ICCSA. Malaga, Spain (2022)
9. Russo, F., Chilà, G., Zito, C.: Special Economic Zones for sustainable ports: system of models and case study. In: 22nd International Conference on Computational Science and its Applications, ICCSA. Malaga, Spain (2022)
10. Russo, F., Musolino, G.: Quantitative characteristics for port generations: The Italian case study. Int. J. Transp. Develop. Integ. 4(2), 103–112 (2020)
11. Russo, F., Musolino, G.: Case studies and theoretical approaches in port competition and cooperation. In: Gervasi, O., et al. (eds.) ICCSA 2021. LNCS, vol. 12958, pp. 198–212. Springer, Cham (2021). https://doi.org/10.1007/978-3-030-87016-4_15

12. Zheng, L.: Job creation or job relocation? Identifying the impact of China's special economic zones on local employment and industrial agglomeration. China Econ. Rev. **69**, 101651 (2021)
13. Chang, S.: In defense of port impact studies. Transp. J. **17**, 79–85 (1978)
14. Davis, H.C.: Regional port impact studies: a critique and suggested methodology. Transp. J. **23**, 61–71 (1983)
15. Yochum, G.R., Agarwal, V.B.: Static and Changing port economic impacts. Maritime Policy Manage. **15**(2), 157–171 (1988)
16. De Salvo, J.S.: Measuring the direct impacts of a port. Transp. J. Summer, 33–42 (1994)
17. Musolino, D., Distaso, A., Marcianò, C.: The role of social farming in the socio-economic development of highly marginal regions: an investigation in Calabria. Sustainability **12**(13), 5285 (2020)
18. Musolino, D., Meester, W., Pellenbarg, P.: The mental maps of Italian, German and Dutch entrepreneurs: a comparative perspective. Ann. Reg. Sci. **64**(3), 595–613 (2019). https://doi.org/10.1007/s00168-019-00912-3
19. Musolino, D., Meester, W., Pellenbarg, P.: Stated locational preferences of Italian entrepreneurs: the underlying location factors, Regional Science Policy & Practice (2021)
20. Leontief, W., Strout, A.: Multi-regional input–output analysis. In: Barna, T. (ed.) Structural Interdependence and Economic Development, pp. 119–150. McMillan, London (1963)
21. Cascetta, E., Di Gangi, M., Conigliaro, G.A.: Multi-regional input–output model with elastic trade coefficients for the simulation of freight travel demand in Italy. In: Proceedings of the 24th PTRC Summer Annual Meeting. PTRC, Cambridge (1996)
22. Castro, J.V., Millan, P.C.: Port economic impact: methodologies and application to the port of Santander. Int. J. Transp. Econ. **XXV**(2), 159–179 (1997)
23. Coronado, D., Acosta, M., Cerbán, M.d.M., López, M.d.P.: Economic Impact of the Container Traffic at the Port of Algeciras Bay. Springer (2006)
24. Coppens F., et al.: Economic impact of port activity: a disaggregate analysis. The case of Antwerp. Working paper document n°110. National Bank of Belgium (2007)
25. Danielis, R. (ed.): Il Sistema marittimo portuale del Friuli Venezia Giulia. Aspetti economici, statistici e storici. EUT, Edizioni Università di Trieste (2011)
26. Amador, J., Cabral, S.: Networks of value-added trade. World Econ. **40**, 1291–1313 (2017)
27. Wang, J.: The economic impact of special economic zones: evidence from chinese municipalities. J. Dev. Econ. **101**, 133–147 (2013)
28. Leong, C.K.: Special economic zones and growth in China and India: an empirical investigation. Int. Econ. Econ. Policy **10**(4), 549–567 (2012). https://doi.org/10.1007/s10368-012-0223-6
29. Russo, F., Rindone, C.: Container maritime transport on an international scale: data envelopment analysis for transhipment port. WIT Trans. Ecol. Environ. **2011**(150), 831–846 (2011)
30. Russo, F., Musolino, G., Assumma, V.: Competition between ro-ro and lo-lo services in short sea shipping market: the case of Mediterranean countries. Res. Transp. Bus. Manag. **19**, 27–33 (2016)
31. Russo, F., Chilà, G.: Structural factors for a third-generation port: actions and measures for Gioia Tauro in the regional transport plan. WIT Transactions on the Built Environment, vol. 204, WIT Press, ISSN 1743-3509 (2021)
32. Russo, F., Chilà, G.: Structural factors for a third-generation port: limits and weakness for Gioia Tauro in the regional transport plan, WIT Transactions on the Built Environment, vol. 204, WIT Press, ISSN 1743-3509 (2021)
33. Musolino, G., Chilà, G.: Structural factors for a third-generation port: planning general logistics interventions in Gioia Tauro. WIT Transactions on the Built Environment, vol 204, WIT Press, ISSN 1743-3509 (2021)

34. Russo, F., Panuccio, P., Rindone, C.: Structural factors for a third-generation port: between hinterland regeneration and smart town in Gioia Tauro. WIT Transactions on the Built Environment, vol. 204, WIT Press, ISSN 1743-3509 (2021)
35. Russo, F., Rindone, C.: Structural factors for a third-generation port: planning interventions for research and development in Gioia Tauro TEN-T node. WIT Transactions on the Built Environment, vol. 204, WIT Press, ISSN 1743-3509 (2021)
36. Musolino, G., Trecozzi, M.R.: Structural factors for a third-generation port: planning interventions for agri-food logistics in Gioia Tauro. WIT Transactions on the Built Environment, vol. 204, WIT Press, ISSN 1743-3509 (2021)
37. Musolino, G., Cartisano, A., Fortugno, G.: Structural factors for a third-generation port: planning interventions for mechanical logistics in Gioia Tauro. WIT Transactions on the Built Environment, vol. 204, WIT Press, ISSN 1743-3509 (2021)
38. ISTAT: Export della Regione Calabria (access in Jannuary o 2018) (2018)
39. Banca dati Reprint R&P: Politecnico di Milano - ICE Agenzia. Addetti delle imprese a partecipazione estera insediate in Calabria (access in Jannuary 2018)
40. Ignaccolo, M., Inturri, G., Giuffrida, N., Torrisi, V.: A sustainable framework for the analysis of port systems. Europ. Transp. Int. J. Transp. Econ. Eng. Law **78**, ISSN 1825–3997 (2020)
41. Ignaccolo, M., Inturri, G., Giuffrida, N., Torrisi, V., Cocuzza, E.: Sustainability of freight transport through an integrated approach: the case of the eastern sicily port system. Transp. Res. Procedia **45**, 177–184 (2020)

Special Economic Zones Planning for Sustainable Ports: The Test Case of Territorial Attractiveness and Urban Planning in Calabria Region

Dario A. Musolino[1,2] and Paola Panuccio[3]

[1] Bocconi University, Milan, Italy
[2] Università della Valle d'Aosta, Aosta, Italy
[3] DIIES, Università Mediterranea di Reggio Calabria, 89100 Reggio Calabria, Italy
paola.panuccio@unirc.it

Abstract. The attractiveness of regions and places for investments, tourists, students, talented people, and other economic actors is a relevant issue for regional economic development, due to the increasing importance of flows of firms, resources and people on the global scale. Attractiveness for peripheral regions is even harder, due to their nature of marginal and peripheral locations which causes clear locational disadvantages compared to central locations. Calabria is a case of Italian peripheral region which should raise its attractiveness to increase its level of development, improving several critical location factors, like transport accessibility, which in this region is extremely scarce.

The Special Economic Zone (SEZ) is an opportunity for the development of the territory. The territorial system around the Special Economic Zone must be planned by the strategic urban plan. Only the urban plan determines the integrated quality system between infrastructures, urbanization, territory and landscape. The strategic urban plan for territories with Special Economic Zones converts urban spaces into places of development, maximizes the offer of services and technological innovation and increases the quality of life and well-being of citizens.

Keywords: Special economic zone · Territorial attractiveness · Location factors · Strategic urban plan · Port of Gioia Tauro

1 Introduction

In the age of globalization, attractiveness is a crucial dimension for regional and urban economic development. Nowadays regions, localities and cities on the one hand must be competitive, being able to export and increase their market share in industries where they specialize; on the other hand, they must be attractive for firms, investments, human capital, students, talented people, tourists, etc. if they wish to increase their level of GDP, income and wealth. Therefore, they must also design and implement investment attraction policies, e.g., tax incentives and Special Economic Zones.

O. Gervasi et al. (Eds.): ICCSA 2022 Workshops, LNCS 13381, pp. 72–84, 2022.
https://doi.org/10.1007/978-3-031-10548-7_6

In the case of a remote and marginal region like Calabria attracting firms, investments and people is even harder and more challenging. In fact, this type of regions, due to their geographical location, suffers several locational disadvantages compared to central regions, like a low level of accessibility and the lack of agglomeration effects.

However, at the same time, for these lagging regions, attracting investments and people, designing strategies based on exogenous development, might be a potential game changer. Late studies in fact show that in this type of regions pure endogenous development strategies has usually failed [1]. Studies focused on Southern Italy highlight that regional development policies based on supporting endogenous entrepreneurship realized in the last decades were not able to boost economy significantly [2]. Rather, southern regions suffered from the loss of productive factors (human capital, entrepreneurs, etc.), as for example brain drain demonstrates [3].

The Special Economic Zones (SEZs) are one of the main policies adopted by national and regional governments to attract investments. SEZs create an opportunity for development in lagging regions, not only limitedly to the places where SEZs are settled, but even in the wider surrounding regions, therefore planning is crucial for exploiting the potential effects of SEZs. The strategic urban plan for regions where SEZs is settled, converts urban spaces into places of development, maximizes the offer of services and technological innovation and increases the quality of life and well-being of citizens. The urban regeneration is the support to increase the value of the SEZs.

In this paper we will focus on the analysis of the attractiveness of a Southern Italian region, Calabria, based on the key data about attractiveness at the territorial scale for firms and people, and on the main strategies and plans for improving it, focusing in particular on the SEZ being settled there. As far as we know, case studies on the attractiveness of peripheral and marginal regions, and on the related policies and planning are rare. In this respect, we consider this research contribution rather novel in the current literature.

The structure of the paper is as follows. Section 2 illustrates first the concept of territorial attractiveness. Then, in paragraph 2.1, it presents the main determinants, i.e., location factors, of territorial attractiveness, and in paragraph 2.2 analyses and discusses the case of Calabria, its attractiveness and the (lacking) location factors which might explain why it is so scarcely attractive. Section 3 deals with SEZs Calabria and integrated strategic urban plan for making regions and cities more attractive, focusing on the role of SEZs for territorial and urban regeneration. Lastly, Sect. 4 shortly draws some final conclusions.

2 Territorial Attractiveness

Territorial attractiveness is a complex and multifaceted concept, which lend itself to several interpretations. It can be first intended as 'revealed attractiveness', which is associated with actual incoming flows (investments, workers, talented people, students, etc.) in a geographical area [4]. The existence of these flows reveals its attractiveness. For example, if a region registers a high number of Foreign Direct Investments (FDIs) projects, it means that this region has a high level of 'revealed attractiveness'', at least as concerns foreign investors. But territorial attractiveness can be regarded also as 'perceived attractiveness', when it refers to how people or groups, perceive, see, etc. then evaluate a geographical area in which they have a particular interest [5]. For example, again this can concern entrepreneurs interested in investing in a certain region: if they see it as a potential location of their firms, it means that this region is perceived as attractive for direct investments. Also, it can concern potential migrant workers interested in moving out of their country to search for better job opportunities, tourists planning where to go for holidays, etc. In the case of perceived attractiveness, we do not deal with information about objective phenomena that have occurred (actual flows of people, investments, etc.), but instead we deal with the subjective perception, that is the image of a place.

Territorial attractiveness presents multiple 'facets' also in terms of types of flows that can be attracted. For example, as said above, there might be flows of direct investments (financial resources used to get control of a company), flows of immigrant workers, flows of specific categories of people, such as university students, researchers, talented people (i.e., 'creative class'), flows of tourists, etc. Finally, we should also not forget that territorial attractiveness can be examined at different spatial scales, from the macro-scale (countries) [6] to the micro-scales (regions, provinces, cities, etc.) [7].

2.1 Determinants of Territorial Attractiveness: Location Factors

The revealed and the perceived attractiveness of a region on the one hand is determined by the firms' objectives and strategies (or by the people's socio-demographic characteristics, motivations, attitudes, etc.), as stated by important theoretical approaches, like the neoclassical and behavioral approach; on the other hand, it is explained by the characteristics of the place of destination: said differently, by its location factors (pull factors), as claimed by other approaches, like the institutional theories [8].

Location factors concern all contextual factors (economic, social, cultural, institutional, environmental) in the place of destination which can affect the cost, the productivity and the profitability of firms, and the life of individuals. This is the case for example of traditional factors, like market size, accessibility, human capital, labour costs, trade openness, land, agglomeration and localisation economies, quality and cost of infrastructures and services, scientific and technological assets, etc. But it is also the case of aspects like institutional quality (legal system, bureaucracy, security, political stability, property rights protection, etc.), environmental and cultural assets, quality of life, social cohesion, policy framework (tax policies, labour market regulations, environmental policies, trade policies, etc.) etc. Firms and people, when they decide where to invest or to move, tend to choose locations more favorable in terms of such factors.

The explanatory role of location factors on firm location and individuals' decisions has been highlighted in many studies. For example, the role of traditional factors like market potential, labour costs, trade openness has been investigated in the studies focused on European regions [9, 10]. Several studies also emphasized the importance of institutional quality for attracting FDIs [11, 12]. On the one hand, efficient institutions improve firms' productivity; on the other hand, a good institutional setting means lowering several costs and increasing the level of certainty and security for investors. In fact, due to high sunk costs, FDIs are significantly exposed to uncertainty and insecurity that might stem for example from a weak enforcement of property rights or from the influence of crime organizations [13]. The role of the quality of the institutional environment has been studied also as concerns the attraction of skilled workers [14].

Interestingly, as far as the role of the crime organizations on the territorial attractiveness is concerned, some qualitative studies focused on the perception of found that the Mafia organizations affect remarkably the image of the Southern Italian regions, preventing entrepreneurs from listing them as potential location of their investments [15]. Several authors have investigated the relevance of other location factors to explain firms' location at the regional scale; especially accessibility and agglomeration economies, in particular localization economies (externalities arising from the geographical concentration of firms belonging to the same industry) [16–18]. As concerns accessibility, studies went in depth focusing even on the association between FDIs location and specific modes of transport, i.e., air transport infrastructure and services [19, 20].

Moreover, there is a wide literature that has shown the relevance of policies for investment attraction [21]. This is the case for example of SEZs, which have been created in several countries, and which have been successful in countries like India [22]. Finally, other soft factors, like quality of life, environmental and cultural assets, are extremely relevant in the case of the territorial attractiveness of people, and specific categories such as university students, talented people, and obviously tourists (less, for firms' location). For example, the pioneering studies conducted by Richard Florida on the creative class in the US cities [23] went in depth in the analysis city attractiveness for human capital; but also works focused on universities and student cities, underlined the importance of soft factors in attracting people.

2.2 The Attractiveness of Calabria: Characteristics and Determinants

As illustrated above, territorial attractiveness can be analyzed for both investments and people. Referring to the revealed attractiveness of Calabria, the available official data allow to measure the attractiveness for FDIs and for flows of people, such as migration flows, university students and tourists.

Regarding FDIs, Calabria turns out to be evidently one of the least attractive Italian regions (Table 1). Overall, in fact, in Calabria there are just over 30 companies foreign-owned, equal to 0.22% of the total of Italian companies controlled by foreign investors (about 14,200). In terms of employees, the stock of FDI settled in Calabria has an even lower incidence: is equal to 0.12% of the national total, while in terms of turnover is equal to 0.08%. It is a presence of foreign investors therefore negligible, both in absolute and relative terms. The utilities sector (power, gas, water, waste), to which more than 50% of Calabrian foreign-owned companies belong, and transport (relevant in terms of employees in foreign-owned companies), explains the bulk of the FDI registered in Calabria. Calabria is therefore very unattractive for key macro-sectors of the national economy, such as manufacturing and made in Italy industries (furniture; food; fashion; mechanics). Historical data shows that Calabria over time has become even less attractive: in contrast to the rest of the country, the FDIs stock in Calabria has decreased, in terms of number of projects, employees and turnover.

With regards to the attractiveness for people, it is interesting to consider demographic change first. The population in Calabria has been declining for several years, not only due to a negative natural balance, but also due to the net migration of negative sign. Net

Table 1. Foreign Direct Investments (2011, 2017)

	Firms	%	Employees	%	Turnover (mln €)	%
2017 Calabria	31	0,22	1.618	0,12	481	0,08
Italy	14.253	100	1.350.908	100	615.273	100
2011 Calabria	38	0,31	1.957	0,17	538	0,09
Italy	12.109	100	1.162.265	100	581.596	100

Source: Elaborations on "Banca dati REPRINT, ICE - Politecnico di Milano"

migration is evidently an indicator of the attractiveness for people of a geographical area, referring essentially to transfers of residence caused by the employment opportunities offered by other areas. In 2018 and 2019 net migration in Calabria was negative for 10 thousand units: most of them were transfers of residence to other Italian municipalities, rather than transfers to foreign countries (see demo.istat.it).

Second, it is relevant to analyze the flows of university students, which is a proxy of human capital attraction. Table 2 shows the attractiveness of Calabrian universities universities out of 89 universities in Italy). The index of universities attractiveness, which incorporates not only the attraction of students from outside the region (domestic and foreign students), but also the ability to retain native students, has a negative sign, and is lower than that recorded by most of the southern regions.

Third, taking the tourist movement into consideration (which on the whole captures not only the leisure movement but also the business movement), the poor attractiveness of Calabria is no less. Calabria, in fact, according to Istat (see dati.istat.it), in the period 2017–19 recorded annually about 9 million overnight stays, equal to just over 2% of the number of overnight stays recorded at national level (over 436 million). Of these, stays of foreigners do not exceed 25% of the total, while in Italy they amount to about 50% of the total. Therefore, the ability to attract foreign tourists in Calabria is even lower. Even the analysis of the ratio between overnight stays and resident population shows a territorial attractiveness for tourists significantly lower than the national average.

Table 2. Index of universities attractiveness (2016–18)*

	2016	2017	2018
Calabria	−58,6	−56,6	−53,5
Basilicata	−183,4	−179,3	−176,6
Campania	−10,4	−10,0	−9,8
Apulia	−49,0	−47,6	−42,8
Sicily	−29,9	−30,4	−28,2
Sardinia	−20,3	−19,2	−17,4
Centre	12,7	11,9	9,2
North	11,1	11,0	11,2

*Ratio of net migration of enrolled students to total enrolment students (%).
Source: Istat - Banca dati indicatori territoriali per le politiche di sviluppo

The low attractiveness of this region can be explained by the lack of several of the location factors identified by the relevant literature. First, Calabria is a lagging region in terms of economic development and employment, and is scarcely open to international trade: therefore, it has clear disadvantages as far as traditional location factors are concerned (market size, productivity, trade openness, employment opportunities). The Istat data on GDP per capita, productivity, and export orientation in this respect are clear enough. In 2020, Calabrian GDP per capita was 16.4k euros, compared to the national GDP of 28.8k euros and the southern one of 18.3k euros. In the same year, added value per employee (labor productivity indicator) in Calabria was just above 47k euros, against about 60k euros at national level, and about 50k in the South. Equally significant are the data on the export orientation: in 2018, regional exports, (550mln euros), amounted to 0.1% of national exports and 1.1% of exports from the South.

Second, Calabria appears extremely disadvantaged even regarding other location factors, which, as we have seen above, are also crucial. It has a low level of accessibility, almost at the level of the Mediterranean island regions, as evidenced by the analyses based on the potential global accessibility indicator [24]. The low level of regional accessibility also emerges from other analyses on long distance rail transport [25].

Calabria has no large metropolitan areas able to generate agglomeration effects (the largest city, Reggio Calabria, barely exceeds 170k inhabitants), or in any case cities with quality of life such as to attract specific groups, like talented people or university students. There is also a lack of sector-specific firms' agglomerations (e.g., industrial districts), where investors can potentially benefit from localisation economies. This weakness explain the lack of a large pool of skilled and highly educated labor supply, which can act as an attractor for multinationals looking for pools of skilled workers. Apart from some urban areas (for example, Cosenza) that thanks to the presence of excellent academic institutions have experienced interesting cases of investment attraction [26], Calabria is poorly endowed with human capital. Again Istat (dati.istat.it) shows that only 79% of the Calabrian population aged 20–24 has obtained at least the diploma of higher secondary school (against 83% in Italy, and 80% in the South). In addition, the tertiary education rate of the population aged 30–34 is 20.7%, a value well below the national average, although in line with the southern one.

The institutional quality in Calabria is also low. According to the European Quality of Government Index by the European Commission (EC), including aspects like efficiency of the Public Administration, corruption and crime, the institutional quality of this region in 2017 was low. Calabria ranks 198th out of the 202 European regions in the ranking. In particular, the influence of the Mafia organizations in Calabria is a very serious and dramatic problem [27]. Finally, it is worth reporting the data of the Regional Competitiveness Index by the EC [28], another synthetic indicator that can be interpreted as a measure of territorial attractiveness, since it incorporates several relevant variables. The RCI 2019 states that Calabria ranks 244th in the EU regions ranking.

3 Urban Planning

3.1 Regulatory Framework of the Special Economic Zone in Calabria

The Decree Law of 2017 n.91: 'Urgent provisions for economic growth in the South' defines the SEZ: "*a geographically delimited and clearly identified area, also consisting of areas not territorially adjacent as long as they have a functional economic link, and including at least one port area with the characteristics established by EU regulation n.1315 of 11 December 2013 of the European Parliament and of the Council, connected to the trans-European transport network (TEN-T)* [29].

The Council of the Calabria region with 2015 resolution n. 52 established the SEZ of Calabria, due to the importance at the international scale of the port of Gioia Tauro [30]. The Regional Transport Plan (PRT) approved by the 2016 resolution n.157 outlines the strategic vision for the economic revitalization of Calabria. Action 6 deals with the measures for the development of the Gioia Tauro area in the Euro-Mediterranean and intercontinental contexts, and in particular with the Economic Macronode and the Special Territorial Zone to integrate the areas of the port with those of the retro port [31]. In 2018, the Calabria region finally approved the strategic development plan for the special economic zone, with resolution n. 100 [32].

The article 22 of the urban planning law of the Calabria region for the protection, governance and use of the territory establishes the: 'Particular rules for the logistics hub of Gioia Tauro' [33] and decides that with reference to the Plan National Strategic Port Authority of 2015, the Calabria region can assume, in the Territorial Reference Framework with landscape value, the Special Economic Zone of the Gioia Tauro pole [34].

Urban planning is an opportunity for the protection and regeneration of the territory [35]. An integrated planning process ensures sustainable territorial development. The interaction between urban planning theory, rule, and complex reality, with continuous activity of knowledge, makes objectives and strategies [36], plans the integral sustainable development of the territories [37].

This planning process elaborates a plan that operates on the value of physical integrity and cultural identity [38], ensuring quality of life, social well-being, smart innovation. The integrated territorial urban plan achieves a joint action between all the disciplinary sectors involved in the dynamics of transformation [39]. The territorial system around the SEZ, if provided for by the strategic urban plan, creates an integrated system between infrastructures, services, landscape, giving rise to further advantages to companies located in the SEZ.

The aim of the regulatory framework and its executive tools is to push for a single integrated strategic vision for the entire region. The vision is integrated because it is a connecting element between the institutional policies of the various sectors, but above all because it unifies development projects relating to the various sectors, such as industrial, agricultural, tourism, etc. [34]. In the paradigm of the current strategic sustainable development policies of our territories, the SEZs attract companies that actively participate in the process of generating added value for the places where they locate [40]. Therefore, it is an advantageous opportunity both for firms and for redevelopment of territories [41, 42].

The increase in demand for new employees provokes the response of territories that plan an increasingly incremental offer [43, 44], activating urban regeneration projects.

3.2 Integrated Strategic Urban Plan for the Sustainable Development of the Territory

The establishment of the SEZs close to the main ports of southern Italy is indented as the development opportunity for the territories surrounding them [45]. Urban planning has the tools to incorporate the SEZs into pro-active territories that participate in economic development. SEZs, with the urban support of the territories in which they fall, can produce the effects for which they were established by law. The integrated territorial urban plan, makes decisions and chooses actions [46], so that SEZs, from incentive areas for companies only, become decisive places for the creation of a territorial system suitable for the economic development of the neighboring areas. The strategic urban plan for the sustainable development of the territory sets out the vision for an integrated territorial system, focusing the development on the special area of the SEZ. The strategic urban plan puts into a system, in the planning and decision-making processes, the values and problems that historically represent the limits to development. The strategy is to provide the area with urban planning solutions that, based on multi-sectoral analyzes and assessments, propose decisions for regeneration, smart innovation and sustainable development [47]. The benefits that the SEZs offer to firms must be integrated with the development dynamics of the entire territory, mutually supporting each other. The urban plan equips the territory with material and immaterial infrastructures that become the added value that firms seek for their location. The firms, promote productive activities that increase the demand for employees and thus trigger a true process of economic development. SEZs increase the demand and the territory plans the offers, it is a combined operation, to achieve the best conditions of success. In order to increase demand in the area and trigger the process of economic recovery of the surrounding historically depressed areas, satisfying the existential reason for their settlement, the SEZs must not be configured as closed areas, extraneous to productive vocations and disconnected from their territories [48].

The territorial urban plan sustains the propulsive function of the SEZ for the economic recovery, integrating the special area with the areas outside the port.

3.3 Special Economic Zones as the Key for Territorial Regeneration

Geographical areas economically depressed are often weak in terms of urban quality [49]. SEZs are set up to revive the economy of lagging areas. Experience has shown that only urban redevelopment projects are not sufficient to trigger new processes that generate development and relaunch of the economic and productive sectors [50].

SEZs reverses the action of urban planning; it is proposed as an opportunity for economic recovery and therefore, asks the territory for new offers. These are the economic activities induced by the companies, which ask to satisfy the needs connected to the new infrastructures and to design places where the quality of life is satisfied and where it is possible to benefit from smart services and equipment. The SEZ triggers the processes of territorial regeneration. Convinced that the port and the special area activate sustainable development processes, the focus is on the territorial regeneration, an integrated quality system between the port, urban centers, territory and landscape.

By adopting the methodological approach of the integrated strategic plan, the sustainable regeneration of the entire territorial system on which the SEZ gravitates is proposed [47]. Applying it to the case of the port of Gioia Tauro [51], the vision of the strategic plan of territorial regeneration of the integrated port and retroport system is the new smart town [52].

3.4 Urban Regeneration and New Smart Town

Urban planning deficits can be resolved with territorial rebalancing actions.

Urban regeneration allows territories to be transformed into places of high quality, both environmentally and technologically. The application of smart opportunities allows the creation of new next generation cities, according to an integrated urban planning model.

SEZ must be integrated into the territory because it is its development mover. The strategic urban plan, after completing the analysis and interpretation of the data, decides whether to recover or redevelop the existing one, or whether to plan new smart cities. The demographic data, crossed between the current state and future projections, allow us to evaluate the choices that the strategic plan must take. By adding the share of the population employed in the SEZ, plus the share of the local resident population, we obtain the total number of presences gravitating to the territorial system [53].

$$PoP\ tot = PoP\ sez + PoP\ urban \tag{1}$$

Subsequently, it is necessary to develop further data and calculate the total built-up area, already existing on the territory. By relating the total number of the population (workers + residents) with the built-up areas, an indicator will be obtained that allows us to verify whether what already exists is sufficient, greater, or insufficient. It is necessary to calculate the occupancy index of each inhabitant per square meter, in relation to the quality standards [54].

The qualitative standards are weighted with respect to the functional criteria of quality of life, sustainable development and social well-being. Therefore, if the total population, compared with the existing built areas, expresses a ratio in which the standard index is equal to or higher, it will be necessary to intervene on what already exists.

The recovery or redevelopment choices are entrusted to the plan, so that no more land is consumed. If, conversely, the report indicates that the built surfaces are not sufficient and do not meet the standards, new designs will have to be built. In this case, the plan can choose urban regeneration, adopting the urban planning model of the new towns in smart mode. The vision of the strategic plan of territorial regeneration of the integrated port and retroport system is the new smart town. It will be the scenario chosen if the data relating to the total population, compared with the surfaces already built, do not meet the qualitative standards.

$$SUP\ tot = SUP\ urban\ regeneration + SUP\ new\ town \tag{2}$$

From which it follows that [52]:

$$SUPnew\ town\ =\ SUP\ tot\ -\ SUP\ urban\ regeneration \tag{3}$$

History has given some examples of new towns that have regenerated the territories. The urban model of the new town, built near a production center, has determined a new development model; activated a further question; asked for a new offer to the territory.

This is the original meaning of urban regeneration: the presence of a productive pole (as is the SEZ opportunity for disadvantaged areas) starts up the urban planning process of territorial regeneration. Among all, the original project of Olivetti district, built in Ivrea, Italy [55] and the ENI district in Gela, Italy. They are examples of great interest, for the results obtained in the social and economic productive ambit, as well as in the field of architectural and urban planning.

The latest generation cities are built following the current canons of urban innovation. This new conceptual approach consists of the interaction between the real situation, the vision of the future, the goals of sustainable development and the categories of the smart city. Urban regeneration interventions innovate cities and transform them into the latest generation of cities. Regeneration is essential to increase the quality of life of citizens; moreover, if it is carried out with the principles of integrated urban planning, it will be a regeneration that will give life to smart territories.

4 Conclusions

SEZ based on the port of Gioia Tauro can be the game changer for the Calabrian territorial attractiveness, and therefore for its regional and urban economic development. SEZ can be the appropriate tool for providing and enhancing some of the location factors which are currently lacking in Calabria, and which as seen above are crucial to attract external investors. This is the case of a secure, adequate, and efficient institutional setting, and of an accessible and cheap area, thanks to the location next to sea and nodal infrastructure, land availability and tax breaks. The role of local universities in improving the supply of skilled labor for external companies should also not be overlooked as well. Calabrian urban areas, through proper planning and preparedness, should benefit from the SEZ constitution, and could play on their turn an active role. They can provide a high-quality environment for attracting further human resources and firms, able to boost and increase more regional economic development. Clearly, this research represents a first step of the analysis of a case of attractiveness in peripheral regions based on SEZs. Future research might explore and assess better the effects of SEZ in this region and might focus more on the urban policy and planning tools able to manage the effects and the processes triggered by FDIs attraction.

References

1. Bosworth, G., Atterton, J.: Entrepreneurial in-migration and neo-endogenous rural development. Rural. Sociol. **77**(2), 254–279 (2012)
2. Servidio, G.: Industria meridionale e politiche di incentivazione: storia di un progressivo disimpegno. In: SVIMEZ La dinamica economica del Mezzogiorno, Il Mulino, BO (2015)

3. Vecchione, G.: Migrazioni intellettuali ed effetti economici sul Mezzogiorno d'Italia. REM **3**, 643–662 (2017)
4. Dubini, P.: L'attrattività del sistema Paese. Territori, settori, paese. Il Sole 24 Ore (2006)
5. Meester, W.J.: Locational preferences of entrepreneurs: stated preferences in The Netherlands and Germany. Physica-Verlag, Heidelberg (2004)
6. Lee, K.: The conceptualization of country attractiveness: a review of research. Int. Rev. Adm. Sci. **82**(4), 807–826 (2016)
7. Musolino, D., Meester, W., Pellenbarg, P.: The mental maps of Italian, German and Dutch entrepreneurs: a comparative perspective. Ann. Reg. Sci. **64**(3), 595–613 (2019). https://doi. org/10.1007/s00168-019-00912-3
8. Brouwer, A.E., Mariotti, I., van Ommeren, J.N.: The firm relocation decision: an empirical investigation. Ann. Reg. Sci. **38**(2), 335–347 (2004)
9. Casi, L., Resmini, L.: Evidence on the determinants of foreign direct investment: the case of EU regions. Eastern J. Europ. Stud. **1**(2), 93–118 (2010)
10. Villaverde, J., Maza, A.: The determinants of inward foreign direct investment: Evidence from the European regions. Int. Bus. Rev. **24**, 209–223 (2015)
11. Sabir, S., Rafique, A., Abbas, K.: Institutions and FDI: evidence from developed and developing countries. Finan. Innov. **5**(1), 1–20 (2019). https://doi.org/10.1186/s40854-019-0123-7
12. Peres, M., Ameer, W., Xu, H.: The impact of institutional quality on foreign direct investment inflows: evidence for developed and developing countries. Econ. Res.-Ekonomska Istraživanja **31**(1), 626–644 (2018)
13. Daniele, V., Marani, U.: Organized crime, the quality of local institutions and FDI in Italy: a panel data analysis. Eur. J. Polit. Econ. **27**, 132–142 (2011)
14. Nifo, A., Vecchione, G.: Do institutions play a role in skilled migration? The case of Italy. Reg. Stud. **48**(10), 1628–2164 (2014)
15. Musolino, D.: The mental maps of Italian entrepreneurs: a quali-quantitative approach. J. Cult. Geogr. **35**(2), 251–273 (2018)
16. Bronzini, R.: Industrial Districts, Agglomeration Economies, and FDI in Italy. Urban Economics and Regional Studies eJournal (2003)
17. Chatterjee, S., Mishra, P., Chatterjee, B.: Determinants of inter-state variations in FDI inflows in India. Eurasian J. Bus. Econ. **6**, 93–120 (2013)
18. Musolino, D., Meester, W.J., Pellenbarg, P.H.: Stated locational preferences of Italian entrepreneurs: the underlying location factors. Reg. Sci. Policy Pract. (2021)
19. Strauss-Kahn, V., Vives, X.: Why and where do headquarters move? Region. Sci. Urban Econ. **39**(2) 168–186 (2009)
20. Bannò, M., Redondi, R.: Air connectivity and foreign direct investments: economic effects of the introduction of new routes. Eur. Transp. Res. Rev. **6**(4), 355–363 (2014). https://doi. org/10.1007/s12544-014-0136-2
21. UNCTAD: World Investment Report 2018. Investment and New Industrial Policies. United Nations: Geneva (2018)
22. Chakraborty, T., Gundimeda, H., Kathuria, V.: have the special economic zones succeeded in attracting FDI?. Analysis for India. Theor. Econ. Lett. **7**, 623–642 (2017)
23. Florida, R.: The Rise of the Creative Class: And How It's Transforming Work, Leisure. Community and Everyday Life. Basic Books, New York (2002)
24. S&W Spiekermann & Wegener, Urban and Regional Research: ESPON MATRICES Final Report. 20/05/2014 www.espon.eu
25. Beria, P., Debernardi, A., Ferrara, E.: Measuring the Long-Distance Accessibility of Italian Cities. J. Transp. Geogr. **62**, 66–79 (2017)
26. Guarascio, C.: Opportunità di sviluppo e periferia. L'esperienza del terziario innovativo in una realtà del Mezzogiorno, la Calabria. REM 4/2020, Il Mulino, Bologna (2021)

27. Fondazione Transcrime: Dove operano le mafie in Italia. In: Progetto PON Sicurezza 2007–2013. Gli investimenti delle mafie (2013). http://www.transcrime.it/pubblicazioni/progetto-pon-sicurezza-2007-2013/
28. Annoni, P., Dijkstra, L.: The EU Regional Competitiveness Index 2019. EU (2019)
29. Italian Government: Law of 3 August 2017. http://www.parlamento.it/leggi/htm. Accessed 21 April 2022
30. Regione Calabria: Misure straordinarie per lo sviluppo dell'area di Gioia Tauro – DDL per l'istituzione di una zona economica speciale (ZES) approved with Resolution of the Regional Council N.52 of 2015 (DCR n. 52/2015). http://www.consiglioregionale.calabria.it/DEL10/52_.pdf. Accessed 21 April 2022
31. Regione Calabria: Piano Regionale dei Trasporti 2016. https://www.regione.calabria.it/web site/portaltemplates/view/view.cfm?4582&4582. Accessed 21 April 2022
32. Regione Calabria: Istituzione Zone Economiche Speciali (ZES). Piano di Sviluppo Strategico della Regione Calabria. Approved with Resolution of the Regional Council No 100 of 2018/03/29. Accessed 21 April 2022
33. Regione Calabria: Norme per la tutela, governo ed uso del territorio - Legge Urbanistica della Calabria 30 giugno 2017 n.21. http://www.consiglioregionale.calabria.it/upload/testicoordin ati/2017-21_2017-06-30.pdf. Accessed 21 April 2022
34. Italian Government: Ministero delle Infrastrutture e dei Trasporti. Piano Strategico Nazionale della portualità e della logistica (2015). https://www.confetra.com/wp-content/uploads/PNL. pdf. Accessed 21 April 2022
35. Samonà, G.: L'urbanistica e l'avvenire della città. Universale Laterza, Bari, Italy (1959)
36. Russo, F., Rindone, C., Panuccio, P.: European plans for the smart city: from theories and rules to logistics test case. Eur. Plan. Stud. **24**(9), 1709–1726 (2016)
37. Sustainable Development Goals 2030. https://sustainabledevelopment.un.org, Accessed 22 April 2022
38. Albanese, G.: Il territorio dell'urbanistica. Gangemi Editore, Roma, Italy (1999)
39. Panuccio, P.: Urbanistica e paesaggio. Gangemi Editore, Roma, Italy (2007)
40. Russo, F., Rindone, C.: Structural factors for a third-generation port: planning interventions for research and development in Gioia Tauro, Italy, Ten-T node. WIT Trans.Built Environ. **204**, 67–78 (2021)
41. Russo, F., Chilà, G.: Structural factors for a third-generation port: current state, limits and weakness for Gioia Tauro in the regional transport plan. WIT Trans. Built Environ. **204**, 3–15 (2021)
42. Russo, F., Chilà, G.: Structural factors for of a third-generation port: actions and measures for Gioia Tauro in the regional transport plan. WIT Trans. Built Environ. **204**, 17–30 (2021)
43. Musolino, G., Chilà, G.: Structural factors for a third-generation port: planning transport interventions in Gioia Tauro. WIT Trans. Built Environ. **204**, 31–42 (2021)
44. Musolino, G., Cartisano, A., Fortugno, G.: Structural factors for a third-generation port: planning interventions for mechanical logistics in Gioia Tauro, Italy. WIT Trans. Built Environ. **204**, 55–66 (2021)
45. Musolino, G., Trecozzi, M.R.: Structural factors for a third-generation port: planning interventions for agri-food logistics in Gioia Tauro, Italy. WIT Trans. Built Environ. **204**, 43–52 (2021)
46. Faludi, A.: A Decision-Centred View of Environmental Planning. Pergamon Press, Oxford, UK (1987)
47. Panuccio, P.: Smart planning: from city to territorial system. MDPI Sustain. **11**(24), 7184 (2019). https://doi.org/10.3390/su11247184
48. Zone Economiche Speciali Guida per iniziative nel Mezzogiorno 2019. https://www.pwc.com/it/it/publications/assets/docs/ufficio-studi-ZES.pdf. Accessed 21 April 2022

49. Friedmann, J.: Pianificazione e dominio pubblico: dalla conoscenza all'azione. Edizioni Dedalo, Bari, Italy (1993)
50. Benevolo, L.: Il tracollo dell'urbanistica italiana. Editori Laterza, Bari, Italy (2012)
51. Amaro, O., Tornatora, M.: Idee e Progetti per la Città Metropolitana di Reggio Calabria. Gangemi Editore, Roma, Italy, ISBN 978-88-492-3168-7 (2016)
52. Russo, F., Panuccio, P., Rindone, C.: Structural factors for a third-generation port: between hinterland regeneration and smart town in Gioia Tauro, Italy. WIT Trans. Built Environ. **204**, 79–90 (2021)
53. Russo, F., Panuccio, P., Rindone, C.: External interactions for a third-generation port: urban and research developments. Wessex Institute Journal paper/TDI50175 (2022 in press)
54. Regione Emilia-Romagna: Disciplina regionale sulla tutela e l'uso del territorio - Legge 21 dicembre 2017, n.24. https://territorio.regione.emilia-romagna.it/codice-territorio/pianif-ter ritoriale/legge-regionale-21-dicembre-2017-n-24. Accessed 21 April 2022
55. Olivetti, A., Saibene, A.: City of Man, Community Editions (1960)

Special Economic Zones Planning for Sustainable Ports: The Role of Research and Training in the Calabria Region

Corrado Rindone[1]([✉]) (iD), Francis M. M. Cirianni[2] (iD), Giuseppe Delfino[2] (iD), and Antonello I. Croce[2] (iD)

[1] DIIES, Università Mediterranea di Reggio Calabria, 89100 Reggio Calabria, Italy
corrado.rindone@unirc.it
[2] CSI Ingegneria, 89100 Reggio Calabria, Italy

Abstract. Special Economic Zones (SEZs) play a relevant role for countries to attract foreign investment and increase economic development. A Special Economic Zone (SEZ) can influence production efficiency through various channels. Different factors can contribute to increase the production of value-added other than the one linked with economic activities.

This paper focuses on the possible contribution of research and training for increasing value-added in a SEZ context. Research Centres, and Universities, have to interchange with all productive sectors operating in the Special Economic Zones (SEZs). Systematic connections between research and production are needed. For this reason, in a strategic perspective, a set of actions can be planned and implemented with the aim to activate and consolidate interchanges of knowledge and skills among public administrations and private companies.

The paper studies the role of research and training to realize a SEZ in the Calabria region (Italy). The specific SEZ constitutes an opportunity for the economic development of the existing industrial areas of the region, and particularly the transhipment hub of Gioia Tauro. The Special Economic Zone (SEZ) can support and be a booster for the potentialities of the hub port, in relation with the research centres and universities operating in the area of influence of the SEZ.

Keywords: Special economic zone · Innovation · Research and development · Training · Strategic plan · Logistics · Ports

1 Introduction

Special Economic Zones (SEZs) play a relevant role for countries to attract foreign investment and increase economic development. A SEZ can influence production process and relative efficiency through various ways [1, 2].

In 2019 there were 5,383 SEZs active in 147 countries around the world; three quarters of these are relate to countries characterized by developing economies. The need to realize a SEZ is often linked to the necessity to support sustainable development, especially in depressed areas [3].

© The Author(s), under exclusive license to Springer Nature Switzerland AG 2022
O. Gervasi et al. (Eds.): ICCSA 2022 Workshops, LNCS 13381, pp. 85–97, 2022.
https://doi.org/10.1007/978-3-031-10548-7_7

It is possible to identify different factors that characterise a SEZ. One of the best-known factors is related to special conditions for enterprises defined in terms of simplification of administrative processes and favorable tax regimes [4]. Often, the final aim is to support the increase the production of added value (AV), linked with economic activities [5, 6]. This paper investigates the role of innovation as a way of economic growth in a depressed area. There is a wide variety of innovation incentive policies, such as awarding enterprises' applications for patents and patent-related honors, and awarding cooperation among enterprises, universities and research institutions (see for instance the case of China illustrated by [7]). This paper focuses on the immaterial factors related to research and training aimed to increase AV of the production processes in a port area. Here, AV is related to logistics port function, in a perspective of fourth generation [8, 9]. In this case, policies to encourage innovation are aimed to increase efficiency of port operations [10] and productive processes located in the areas near maritime terminal [8]. These policies result from a planning process that identifies different SEZ structural factors [11] that can produce impacts on the sustainability components [12].

The specific case study is the planning process that configured the SEZ in the Calabria Region, in the south of Italy [13, 14].

The paper, after this introduction, has three sections. Section 2 describes a general framework of a Special Economic Zone strategic planning process; the same section illustrates the role of the research and training (R&T) for port development and a procedure to individuate innovation gaps and interventions aimed to reduce these gaps. According to Sect. 2, Sect. 3 describes the R&T interventions provided to develop the SEZ in the Gioia Tauro port.

2 SEZ Strategic Planning

2.1 The General Framework

Literature individuates structural factors that can be the contents of a strategic plan for defining SEZ configuration. It is possible to individuate the following classes of structural factors [15, 16]:

- material factors, including elements of the territory and relative infrastructures where Special Economic Zones will be located (e.g. transport infrastructures for accessibility);
- immaterial factors, including two sub classes,

  - technologies to support productive processes, from traditional tools to emerging Information and Communication Technologies (ICTs) (e.g. IoT and monitoring tools);
  - research and training to support innovation and increase know-how about productive processes (e.g. methods and models to increase effectiveness and efficiency);

- institutional factors, including rules for introducing special conditions for business operating inside SEZs (e.g. simplification of administrative procedures).

Each factor and their combination have a specific role in order to increase sustainable development in each component (economic, social and environment sustainability). It is possible to express each factor as a quantitative variable of a function for estimating contribution to sustainable development. Note that sustainability constitutes the final goals of SEZ strategic planning process and relative implementations (Fig. 1).

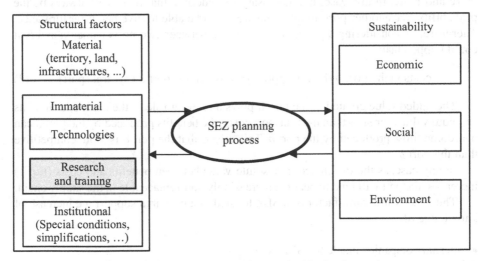

Fig. 1. SEZ planning process for sustainable development

2.2 Research and Training (R&T) Role for Port Development

The paper focuses on the Research and Training structural factor (R&T) inside the Special Economic Zone (SEZ) planning process represented in Fig. 1. The specific context regards a SEZ in a port area with a focus on the role of R&T for developing a port towards the third and fourth generation perspective [15–17].

In general, R&T offers a contribution for increasing regional sustainable development. In the specific case of a SEZ realised in a port area, R&T supports the port's activities, contributing to the increase of the added value (AV). In literature, AV is the measure of the increase in value that occurs in the production and distribution of final goods and services thanks to the intervention of production factors. In the specific maritime transport sector, the AV's generation depends on processes introduced in the supply chain of goods production. Ports play a relevant role in the supply chain and this implies the necessity of knowledge about internal and external activities that characterise all nodes distributed at global level [18]. It requires innovation in the productive processes that generate competition among ports at global level.

For participating to the competition at global level, operators have to optimize all the internal characteristics of the port area, considering almost "adiabatic" compared to the outside territory. Moreover, ports belonging to the third generation interact with the external territory, in order to increase AV.

The potential optimal situation for a third-generation port can be written as:

$$\text{costs (generalized by transport)} < \text{benefits (added value)} \qquad (1)$$

It should be noted that as long as the port remains a place of transit for goods, the management will try to improve the performance of transport, trying to reduce costs more and more. In this case, it is necessary to underline that there will always be the probability that another port, in the same area, will be able to give better performance. Therefore, by considering a potential competition between two ports named a and b, it could happen that:

$$\text{costs in the port } b \text{ (by transport)} < \text{costs in the port } a \text{ (by transport)} \qquad (2)$$

The added value created in the port a plays a relevant role in the competition. If its absolute value is greater than the transport costs, the benefits produced by the port a can overcome those produced by the port b. This means that the port a is more competitive than the port b.

In any case, as the difference in absolute value between benefits and costs (Eq. 1) increases, the port will tend to become increasingly non-replaceable in the supply chain.

The R&T's structural factor of a SEZ located in a port area support the increase of knowledge of:

- internal companies inside the SEZ area;
- business network inside the economic district where the SEZ area is located;
- research centres located in the external territory located in proximity of the SEZ area.

With the other structural factors, R&T contributes to the activation of virtuous processes characterised by mutual interactions among all stakeholders involved in the SEZ planning process. The final aim is to create good conditions for activating innovation processes inside and outside the port. At the medium terms, the expected effect is the increase of the AV in a port of third generation. At long term, SEZ becomes the opportunity to increase sustainable development of the in the entre territory around the port.

For achieving these objectives, literature underlines, from one side, the necessity to increase performances levels in transport operations. For instance, Russo and Chilà [15] analyse the potential effects produced by interventions inside a port area. From other side, it is necessary to improve performance's operations on goods in transit, that increase their added value. Pellicanò and Trecozzi [4] propose a general approach for SEZ planning and for defining administrative simplifications in a SEZ context. An even more important effect derives from the external conditions. It is necessary that the external territory also provides conditions, both material and immaterial, so that the costs of transit decrease and the added value increases [11]. By considering the European and global scales, in many cases the big transport nodes have been created "ex-novo" and are completely free of interactions with the territory: high-speed railway stations, international airports, third generation intercontinental ports. In this context, the immaterial structural factors related to R&T can contribute to increase AV, creating conditions to the achievement of sustainable development. For this reason, it is necessary to consider the interventions connected to the increase in added value connected to manipulation of goods in transit in a port. In particular, this paper focuses on the interventions on R&T aimed to supports activities of economic operators in the SEZ located in a port area. The final aim is to increase knowledge about processes and products related to goods in transit in a port in order to increase the AV. Next section proposes a procedure to individuate innovation gaps and the contexts a R&T interventions programme to fill them, with a specific focus on a port area.

2.3 Innovation Gaps and R&T Interventions

By focusing on a planning process aimed to define SEZ characteristics in a port area, it is necessary to individuate innovation gaps and plan a set of R&T interventions to overcome current limits. A possible procedure to face this issue consists of the following steps:

1. selection of the present and future economic sectors operating in the SEZ area, directly involved in the port activities that potentially increase the AV; the generic sector is indicated with s, belonging to the set of all sectors, S:

$$s_{SEZ} \in S_{SEZ} \tag{3}$$

2. analysis of the existing research centers operating near to SEZ area; the generic center is indicated with r, belonging to the set of all research center, R_{SEZ} operating in the territory near to the SEZ area:

$$r \in R_{SEZ} \tag{4}$$

3. individuation of the centers that can support the development of the port and in particular the economic sectors s_{SEZ}; the generic center is indicated with r_{AV}, belonging to the set R_{AV} that is obtained by the intersection between S_{SEZ} and R_{SEZ}:

$$r_{AV} \in R_{AV} = S_{SEZ} \cap R_{SEZ} \tag{5}$$

4. starting from the identification of the set R_{AV}, individuation of R&T interventions, to support existing research centers and cover the innovation gaps, with the final aim to increase the AV; at long term, the economic sectors s_{SEZ}, supported by the centers r_{AV} produce impacts in all sustainability components.

3 The Case Study: SEZ in the Gioia Tauro Port

3.1 The Strategic Plan of the Calabria Region for SEZ

The Italian government regulated the procedures, conditions and methods for the realization of Special Economic Zone (SEZ) in Italy [19]. According to national legislation, the economic current and future enterprises operating in the SEZ areas will be able to benefit from special conditions, in relation to the incremental nature of investments and business development activities.

According to the national laws, the Calabria Region started the activities for the creation of a Special Economic Zone producing a Strategic Development Plan [14]. The plan identifies specific actions aimed at attracting investors who will be able to operate in the Calabrian SEZ.

The Calabrian SEZ is based on the Gioia Tauro port that is a core node of the TEN-T network. SEZ integrates further area connected to the core port in physical and functional terms. SEZ area are located inside to airports and ports and in the area near the transport terminals (Table 1).

Table 1. SEZ areas: location and surface

SEZ area	Location	Surface (ha)
Ports	**Gioia Tauro**	**402**
	Reggio Calabria	10
	Villa San Giovanni	4
	Crotone	26
	Vibo Valentia	16
	Corigliano Calabro	52
Dry port area	**Gioia Tauro, San Ferdinando, Rosarno**	**607**
	Crotone	380
	Porto Salvo Vibo Valentia	184
	Schiavonea Corigliano	340
Airports	Lamezia Terme	26
	Reggio Calabria	27
	Crotone	22

Source: Strategic Development Plan [14]

This paper focuses on the SEZ areas located in the Gioia Tauro port and dry port areas (Fig. 2).

According to the classification introduced in Sect. 2.1, Gioia Tauro SEZs area presents the following structural factors:

- material factors including facilities available in the port and in the surrounding area, including transport infrastructures.

  - a quay over 3 km long with depths of up to 18 m;
  - a dry port area of 1007 ha;
  - railway and road connections to the TEN-T network;

- immaterial factors including technological connections to telematics networks and a set of programmed financial resources to invest on research and training aimed to support innovation processes and, more in general, to increase the level of knowledge of existing and future economic operators;

- institutional factors including the introduction of special conditions with the introduction of a one-stop shop for productive activities, comprehending simplification of administrative processes.

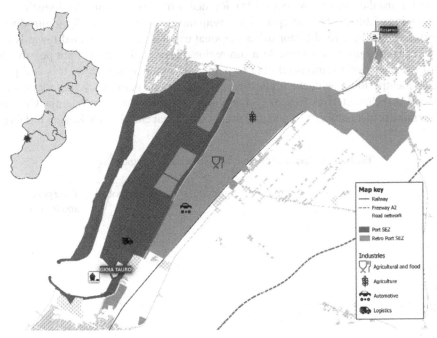

Fig. 2. SEZ in the Gioia Tauro port and in the surrounding area (source elaboration from [14])

Currently the prevailing function of the Gioia Tauro port is the transshipment. The railway gateway has recently been activated and railway connections are being improved, aiming to the European corridors dedicated to the transport of freight (Rail Freight Corridors). This represents an opportunity for the development of the Port of Gioia Tauro. It is necessary to focus on the development of the logistic function promoting economic activities that can increase the added value of goods in transit in the port.

3.2 R&T Investments for Gioia Tauro Port Development

The specific attention of this paper is on the R&T investments defined adopting the procedure illustrated in Sect. 2.3. Each subsection represents a step of the procedure.

3.2.1 Economic Sectors Selection

Calabria SEZ planning and implementation promote existing economic activities and that are intended to be promoted as a result of modeling for the estimation of the impacts expected from the SEZ. From the conducted analyses [5], it emerges that the Calabrian economy is based on small and medium-sized enterprises. There are also some major players operating at the international level with production sites concentrated in the industrial areas of the four provinces of the region. The prevalent economic sectors are manufacturing, with reference to the agri-food sector [20], also correlated to the agriculture sector and the automotive sector [21]. Related activities are transport, logistics and warehousing (Table 2). The enterprises represent the element of the set S_{SEZ} introduced in Sect. 2.3. The agri-food sector drives regional exports, mainly directed towards the countries of the European Union. At a sub-regional level, although it is not possible to identify strong specializations relating to individual production sectors, it is still possible to identify those with the highest relative density of employees and companies: agri-food that characterizes Cosenza; energy that characterizes Vibo Valentia, Crotone and Catanzaro; mechanics, transport and warehousing that characterize Reggio Calabria.

Table 2. Relevant economic sectors in each province (S_{SEZ})

Province	Mechanic/automotive	Agriculture	Agri-Food	Transport and logistics
Cosenza	X	X	X	
Crotone			X	
Catanzaro			X	X
Vibo V.		X	X	
Reggio Cal.	X		X	X

3.2.2 Existing Research Centers

By referring to the province of Reggio Calabria that is the territory where is located the Gioia Tauro port, the set named R_{SEZ} in Sect. 2.3 comprehends the Mediterranea University of Reggio Calabria. The University comprehends six departments, and it develops research in engineering, architecture, agriculture, economics, law and human sciences.

3.2.3 Research Center for Supporting Port's Development

Note that the current expenses on research and development in the Calabria constitute the 0.7% of the total at national level, by considering enterprises, universities, public and private institutions. The great part (near to 60%) is represented by universities (Table 3).

By considering the focus of this paper, and the universities near the SEZ area of the Gioia Tauro (R_{SEZ}), the Mediterranea university of Reggio Calabria has been selected. Inside the Mediterranea university departments, specific laboratories operate developing research themes related to material and services port's activities. Among these, there are a set of laboratories (set intersection R_{AV}) that are working on research's topics of interest for the Gioia Tauro port:

- LAST works in the field of intelligent transportation systems applied in different contexts of sustainable mobility;
- Noel works on research about ocean/marine engineering, focusing on wave modelling related aspects and wave energy harvesting;
- NeuroLab works in the field of remote with applications in the health context.
- FoodTec works on advanced technologies to support food industry;
- ARTS works on research about protocols and applications for advanced telecommunication systems and services;
- LEMMA works on research about of inverse synthesis problems, high-performance antennas and advanced microwave devices design;

LOGICA works on interdisciplinary research related to the development of the Technological District of the Logistics in Gioia Tauro.

Table 3. Expenditure on intra-muros research and development (thousands of euro) Year 2019

Sector		Enterprises (a)	Public institutions (b)	University (c)	Private institutions (d)	Total	
Territory						v.a	%
Calabria	v.a.	56.360	19.942	112.879	746	189.927	0,7%
	%	30%	10%	59%	0%	100%	
Italy	v.a.	16.589.218	3.306.719	5.897.530	466.194	26.259.661	96,7%
	%	63%	13%	22%	2%	100%	

(a) excluding private universities; (b) excluding public universities; (c) public and private; (d) private non-profit. Source: Elaborations from ISTAT [22]

3.2.4 Planned R&T Interventions and Expected Impacts

Research and training represent a main objective of the Regional Transport Plan of the Calabria Region (Objective 1: Training and Research). Furthermore, Objective 6 is dedicated to the "*Gioia Tauro System*". In order to pursue this objective, the plan has set the specific measure "6.9 *Research and operational applications*", which provides for the activation of a research center on transport and logistics to support the main sectors established in the zone.

The objectives, actions and measures of the Regional Transport Plan are strongly connected to the realization of the SEZ in Calabria and in particular in the port and dry port of Gioia Tauro [15]. Specific actions of the strategic plan encourage research and development through research and innovation programs dedicated to universities and businesses. The information desk supports businesses by establishing contacts with University Research Centers and Technological Poles.

The main national and regional planning products provide for the development of Gioia Tauro port a set of interventions [23]: the activation of a research center on transport and logistics; the creation of a Campus for Innovation; the implementation of basic research lines functional to economic activities; the promotion of start-ups and spin-offs, the training and retraining of the workforce and the strengthening of phytosanitary controls. The planned research center should deal with the main operational applications concerning the port and the rear port, contributing to the transformation of the Port of Gioia Tauro into a fourth-generation port. The center could also develop research activities in transport and logistics to support the main sectors established: 1. agri-food, 2. external logistics, 3. manufacturing with particular reference to metal-mechanical, 4. energy, 5. ICT. In order to implement these interventions, it is necessary to promote agreements between enterprises and university departments, having a qualification of excellence recognized by national or international organizations. In this context, it is possible to use the opportunities offered by structural funds of European Commission. The research programs must be based on context analysis and preventive evaluation of the impacts (ex-ante conditionalities/enabling conditions). It is mandatory to verify the correspondence of the actions with the areas provided for by the "Smart specialization strategy for research and innovation of the Calabria Region" (S3 areas). The areas that mostly concern the SEZ of Gioia Tauro are: agriculture 4.0 and agri-food (AA); sustainable construction, energy and climate (EE); ICT, digital technologies and innovative service sector; smart manufacturing (SM); logistics and sustainable mobility (LO).

Table 4, for each economic sector that characterizes the SEZ's area of the Gioia Tauro, reports the corresponding S3 area and research laboratories of the Mediterranea University that could develop university compliant research programmer.

Table 4. Economic sectors in the Gioia Tauro SEZ, S3 areas and reference laboratories

Economic sectors (s_{SEZ})	S3 area	Laboratory (r_{AV})
1. Agri-food	AA	FoodTec
2. Logistics	LO	LAST, LOGICA
3. manufacturing / mechanical	SM	Lemma
4. Energy	EE	Noel
5. ICT	ICT	ARTS

AA: agriculture 4.0 and agri-food; EE: eco-sustainable construction, energy and climate; ICT: digital technologies and innovative service sector; SM: smart manufacturing; LO: logistics and sustainable mobility

The strategic plan for the SEZ specifies investments in R&T. The forecast of the impact of investments in R&T present in the strategic plan highlights the functional economic link between the integrated areas of the SEZ (ports, airports and industrial settlements), and the activities of territorial specialization and those that are intended to be promoted. According to the strategic plan, the activation of the SEZ has an impact on all components of sustainability.

With regard to economic sustainability, one of the main expected impacts is the increase in the AV. The activation of the research centre supports current and expected companies in order to activate the function of regional port that can potentially perform the port of Gioia Tauro in a fourth-generation perspective.

With regard to environmental sustainability, one of the main expected impacts is the increase in green production. An example is the APEA (Ecologically Equipped Production Area), consisting of a set of industrial, craft, commercial and agricultural companies. The APEA is characterized by the integrated management of infrastructures, centralized services and resources to increase sustainable development. Through the collective management of processes and technologies, the aim is to improve the competitiveness and green innovation of production systems and of the settlement as a whole [14].

With regard to social sustainability, one of the impacts expected from the establishment of the SEZ is the retraining of the workforce and the growth of skills through training. In order to pursue objective 1 of the PRT, specific measures are envisaged for the promotion of training in the fields of transport and logistics, in compulsory education, in secondary school and in institutes dealing with education and vocational training. through specialization of the processes of the good school with the activation of specific paths. The activation of paths aimed at increasing knowledge and skills in transport and logistics are aimed at improving the connections of the Calabria Region with the sea system.

4 Conclusive Remarks

Special Economic Zones (SEZs) represent an opportunity to increase economic growth in a depressed area. Different factors can contribute to the growth producing and increase of added value (AV) in the productive processes. Material factors and special conditions offered by a traditional SEZ need a further contribution to pursue sustainable development in all components (economic, social and environment).

In this context, this paper has investigated the role of immaterial factors for incentivizing innovation process, by means of investments on research and training in a SEZ area located in a port.

The paper presents limits connected to the lack of modeling tools for evaluating expected impacts produces by R&T interventions.

Future developments of this research regard two main directions. This first concerns insights about research topics and their expected impacts in relation to port development in a fourth-generation perspectives. The second direction concerns the extension of the case study to entire Calabria region, by considering the other research centers, or the other Italian SEZs, in order to evaluate strengths and weakness of the national planning process.

References

1. Yongjin, W., Guofeng, Z.: Sources of productivity advantages of special economic zones: Agglomeration effect or selection effect?. Econ Res J. (2016)

2. Li, X., Wu, X., Tan, Y.: Impact of special economic zones on firm performance. Res. Int. Bus. Finan. **58** (2021). https://doi.org/10.1016/j.ribaf.2021.101463
3. Zeng, D.Z.: The Dos and Don'ts of Special Economic Zones. International Bank for Reconstruction and Development/The World Bank (2021)
4. Pellicanò, D.S., Trecozzi, M.R.: Special Economic Zones planning for sustainable ports: general approach for administrative simplifications and a test case. In: 22nd International Conference on Computational Science and its Applications, ICCSA. Malaga, Spain (2022)
5. Musolino, D., Distaso, A., Marcianò, C.: The role of social farming in the socio-economic development of highly marginal regions: an investigation in Calabria. Sustainability **12**(13), 5285 (2020)
6. Russo, F., Chilà, G., Zito, C.: Special Economic Zones planning for sustainable ports: system of models and case study. In: 22nd International Conference on Computational Science and its Applications, ICCSA. Malaga, Spain (2022)
7. Wu, M., Liu, C., Huang, J.: The special economic zones and innovation: evidence from China. China Econ. Quar. Int. **1**, 319–330 (2021)
8. Russo, F., Musolino, G.: Quantitative characteristics for port generations: the Italian case study. Int. J. Transp. Develop. Integ. **4**(2), 103–112 (2020)
9. Russo, F., Musolino, G.: Case studies and theoretical approaches in port competition and cooperation. In: Gervasi, O., et al. (eds.) ICCSA 2021. LNCS, vol. 12958, pp. 198–212. Springer, Cham (2021). https://doi.org/10.1007/978-3-030-87016-4_15
10. Russo, F., Musolino, G., Assumma, V.: Competition between ro-ro and lo-lo services in short sea shipping market: the case of Mediterranean countries. Res. Transp. Bus. Manag. **19**, 27–33 (2016)
11. Panuccio, P., Musolino, D.: Special Economic Zones planning for sustainable ports: territorial attractiveness and urban planning. The test case of Calabria region. In: 22nd International Conference on Computational Science and its Applications, ICCSA. Malaga, Spain (2022)
12. Musolino, G., Cartisano, A., Fortugno, G.: Special Economic Zones planning for sustainable ports: aggregate economic impact of port of Gioia Tauro. In: 22nd International Conference on Computational Science and its Applications, ICCSA. Malaga, Spain (2022)
13. Calabria Region: Piano Regionale dei Trasporti. Approved with Resolution of the Regional Council No 157 of 2016/12/06
14. Regione Calabria: Istituzione Zone Economiche Speciali (ZES). Piano di Sviluppo Strategico della Regione Calabria. Approved with Resolution of the Regional Council No 100 of 2018/03/29 (2018)
15. Russo, F., Chilà, G.: Structural factors for of a third-generation port: actions and measures for Gioia Tauro in the regional transport plan. WIT Trans. Built Environ. **204**, 17–30 (2021)
16. Musolino, G., Chilà, G.: Structural factors for a third-generation port: planning transport interventions in Gioia Tauro, Italy. WIT Trans. Built Environ. **204**, 31–42 (2021)
17. Russo, F., Chilà, G.: Structural factors for a third-generation port: current state, limits and weakness for Gioia Tauro in the regional transport plan. WIT Trans. Built Environ. **204**, 3–15 (2021)
18. Russo, F., Panuccio, P., Rindone, C.: Structural factors for a third-generation port: between hinterland regeneration and smart town in Gioia Tauro, Italy. WIT Trans. Built Environ. **204**, 79–90 (2021)
19. Law 3 August 2017, n. 123 Conversione in legge, con modificazioni, del decreto-legge 20 giugno 2017, n. 91, recante disposizioni urgenti per la crescita economica nel Mezzogiorno. (GU Serie Generale n.188 del 12-08-2017)
20. Musolino, G., Trecozzi, M.R.: Structural factors for a third-generation port: planning interventions for agri-food logistics in Gioia Tauro, Italy. WIT Trans. Built Environ. **204**, 43–52 (2021)

21. Musolino, G., Cartisano, A., Fortugno, G.: Structural factors for a third-generation port: planning interventions for mechanical logistics in Gioia Tauro, Italy. WIT Trans. Built Environ. **204**, 55–66 (2021)
22. ISTAT (2022). Expenditure on intra-muros research and development (thousands of euro) Year 2019. http://dati.istat.it/index.aspx?queryid=21942. Accessed May 2022
23. Russo, F., Rindone, C.: Structural factors for a third-generation port: planning interventions for research and development in Gioia Tauro, Italy, Ten-T node. WIT Trans. Built Environ. **204**, 67–78 (2021)

A Study on Ports' Emissions in the Adriatic Sea

Luca Braidotti[1,2(✉)] [iD] and Marco Mazzarino[3] [iD]

[1] Venice International University, Isola di S. Servolo, 30133 Venice, Italy
[2] University of Trieste, Via Valerio 10, 34127 Trieste, Italy
lbraidotti@units.it
[3] Università IUAV di Venezia, Ca' Tron - Santa Croce 1957, 30135 Venezia, Italy

Abstract. Environmental sustainability and energy efficiency are some of the most challenging objectives to be pursued in port areas. In this context, the SUS-PORT project aims to provide its contribution, affecting the Adriatic area. In the initial phase, before applying new technologies/solutions to enhance port sustainability, the baseline status shall be assessed in order to evaluate the impact of tested measures. To this end, a review of the peculiarities of the main ports of the Adriatic Sea (Italian and Croatian), including the evaluation of their carbon footprint should be carried out. The present work reports the results of this phase, focusing on the main statistics of the involved ports and their greenhouse gases inventory at an aggregated level.

Keywords: Greenhous gases · Port · Adriatic Sea

1 Introduction

The improvement of environmental sustainability and energy efficiency in port areas is a very challenging objective, due to the geographical and economical complexity of these areas and the large number of stakeholders and entities contributing to the pollutants emissions. They include port authorities, private companies, dealers, shippers, service providers, shipping companies, etc. In the last decades, increasing attention has been paid to these topics, especially in the European context. This led to a large number of actions devoted to reducing the emissions of pollutants [1, 2] and developing new tools and policies to reduce the environmental impact of navigation [3–5] and port operations [6–8]. In this context, the SUSPORT project aims to provide its contribution. The project involves all the main ports from Italy and Croatia, thus, offering a very useful channel to share past experiences and best practices dealing with port environmental sustainability and the improvement of energy efficiency in port areas. Furthermore, since all relevant ports in terms of traffic and volumes of goods/passengers are engaged, the project enables to analyse globally the environmental impacts of port activities on the whole area: the Adriatic Sea.

In the literature, plenty of works deals with the assessment of port emissions related to a specific aspect [9, 10] or a specific port [11, 12]. However, works focusing on both maritime and terrestrial emissions in a wide geographical area based on a common methodology are still missing. Nevertheless, such kind of studies might be very useful to assess the overall carbon footprint in a region of interest and plan proper cross-border policies to improve port sustainability and energy efficiency. This is one of the goals of the SUSPORT project. In order to to assess the effectiveness of different alternative measures, a comprehensive picture of the existing emissions for the area is required.

To this end, the present work defines the current carbon footprint related to port activities in the Adriatic Region. All the ports involved in the SUSPORT project have been required to provide data to assess the emissions of Green House Gasses (GHG) according to a common methodology which considers both terrestrial and maritime sources. Disaggregate data decomposed by main emission source is then elaborated to get an aggregate picture for the whole geographical region.

2 Methodology

The methodology to assess port emissions refers to the UNI EN ISO 14064 standard, which specifies the equivalent tons of carbon dioxide (t CO2eq) as a unit of measurement for the assessment of greenhouse gas emissions, as established by the Convention on Climate Change (UNFCCC). Based on the aggregation of data collected from each involved port, the processing of the information and the actual emissions calculations have been carried out as prescribed in [13, 14]. In the present study, both terrestrial and maritime emissions have been considered. Terrestrial emissions are related to all the relevant emissions sources on the land-side, whereas maritime emissions are related to all the ships and boats within the port area. In what follows, the considered categories and their assessment methodology are detailed.

2.1 Terrestrial Emissions

In the present work, the following categories have been considered regarding terrestrial emissions in port areas:

- Electric energy: accounting for the overall electricity consumption of all the users inside the port area;
- Heating: accounting for the emissions produced by heating systems of all the buildings/plants inside the port area;
- Service vehicles: emissions related to all the light vehicles used by the port authority or other entities based in the port area;
- Port operational vehicles: emissions related to all the vehicles and systems used inside the port area to move cargo (e.g. wheel loaders, forklifts, excavators, sweepers, cranes, harbour tractors, etc.);
- External vehicles: related to the emissions coming from trucks, coaches, busses, light-duty vehicles and private cars within the port area;
- Railway tractors: related to all the emissions of trains within the port area;
- Others: including the emissions due to power generators or actuators, recharges of air conditioners, consumption of gas not previously entered (Natural gas and LPG for domestic use)

In the following, the adopted methodologies for the assessment of GHG emissions are detailed. Emissions coming from combustion have been evaluated according to:

$$E_{gsc} = AD_{sc} \cdot EF_{gsc} \tag{1}$$

where E are the emissions measured in t CO2eq of the gas g produced by a source s from the fuel c, AD is the activity data (usually, the total consumption of energy required by s while employing c) and EF is the emission factor for g considering s and c. Emission factors have been taken from [13, 14].

Besides, direct emissions of GHG shall be considered too. For instance, leaks of refrigerant gases or gases contained in fire extinguishing systems belong to this category and can be quantified based on the refills carried out in the considered period. The emissions in equivalent t CO2eq are obtained by multiplying the refilled gas quantities by its global warming potential GWP as provided in [15].

Emissions related to electric energy consumption can be computed based on the consumption records and the information and sources employed by energy suppliers. The latter is compulsory to properly convert the electric energy consumption into t CO2eq. If this data is not available, reference has been made to the regional or national energy sources adopted for electric generation.

The calculation of the emissions due to vehicles transited in the port area has been carried out by collecting information on the number of transits from multiple sources and comparing the values obtained to validate them. The number of transits is multiplied by an estimated average route inside the port. In such a case emission factor is measured in kg of greenhouse gas per km and has been taken according to ISO EN 16258: 2013. The obtained emissions are increased by 5.6% to account for stops and manoeuvres [16].

2.2 Maritime Emissions

In the present work, the following categories have been considered regarding maritime emissions in port areas:

- Maritime port services: including all the shipborne emissions coming from port service vessels (tugs, pilot boats, etc.);
- Anchored ships: emissions related to the ships while anchored nearby the port and waiting for access;
- Ships manoeuvring: emissions deriving from the manoeuvring phase of the ships up to their arrival at berth and subsequent inverse departure of the ship;
- Moored ships: the emissions produced during the actual mooring phase of the ship at berth, including waiting and cargo loading and unloading operations (e.g. goods and/or trailers and/or the transit of passengers, etc.).

Usually, freight ships adopt slow-speed 2-stroke main engines directly connected to the shaft line and propeller. These engines usually adopt Heavy Fuel Oil (HFO). In addition, they are equipped with auxiliaries including medium/high-speed 4-stroke engines for electric generation and steam boilers. The auxiliaries often adopt Marine Diesel Oil (MDO). Passenger ships have higher power demand even at berth due to hotel loads. Usually, the main engines of passenger ships are medium-speed 4-stroke engines using HFO or MDO. Most of the recent cruise vessels adopt a diesel-electric propulsion system where electric motors are connected to the shaft lines and electric generation is ensured by medium-speed diesel engines. Finally, small service boats might use lighter fuels, such as diesel, and usually do not emit pollutants while are moored, but only during operation.

The emission factors in kg of GHG per fuel tonne have been taken from IMO (International Maritime Organization) standards for different gases, fuel types and engine speed [17]. Recently, the adoption of Liquefied Natural Gas (LNG) as a marine fuel is also increasing [18]. In the Adriatic Sea, the LNG bunkering facilities are mainly still under development. However, if any LNG fuelled vessel visited the port, the emission factors for LNG have been adopted according to [19].

The emissions factors shall be multiplied by the fuel consumption FC in the port area. If available, the actual fuel consumption in the port area has been used by applying the top-down approach. For instance, for service vessels directly operated by the port authority or a subcontractor, bunkering records provide the most accurate metric to evaluate emissions.

For commercial ships, data regarding actual fuel consumption in a specific port area is usually not available. Hence, it is necessary to estimate the fuel consumption from operations records by applying the bottom-up approach. Starting from data about commercial ship traffic in the port, the hours spent at anchor t_a, moored at berth t_b and in manoeuvring t_m have been determined for each ship entering the port. Moreover, for manoeuvring phases, the actual speed V (measured in knots) and draught T of the vessel shall be also determined or estimated. Moreover, the essential ship data shall be acquired from databases (e.g. IHSF technical specifications), including the installed power (main engine Maximum Continuous Rating MCR), the maximum speed V_{max} and draught at maximum speed T_{max}. If this data is not available, another known condition characterised by a reference engine power P_{ref} at a reference speed V_{ref} and draught T_{ref} can be used instead (mean values related to ship types and deadweight can be assumed [17]). According to [20], reference speed can be taken as the design speed and the reference power as 80% of MCR. Considering a generic ship speed, the actual propulsion engine power can be estimated according to the Admiralty formula:

$$P = P_{ref} \left(\frac{T}{T_{ref}} \right)^{2/3} \left(\frac{V}{V_{ref}} \right)^3 \qquad (2)$$

Then, the fuel consumption FC during the maneouvring phase is given by:

$$FC = c_l \cdot SFOC \cdot P \cdot t_m \cdot 10^{-6} \qquad (3)$$

where $SFOC$ is the specific fuel consumption in g/kWh and c_l is a correction factor taking into account the variation of $SFOC$ at lower engine loads [21]. Reference values for $SFOC$ are given in [17], according to the main engine age.

In all the operation modes (anchor, manoeuvring and moored) the auxiliaries' emissions shall be considered too, including the ones coming from auxiliary engines and auxiliary boilers. The power demand depends upon the operation mode, the ship type and its deadweight. Reference values can be found in Annex 1 of [17]. Then, related fuel consumption can be computed with Eq. (3) assuming unitary correction factor and *SFOC* according to [22].

3 Application on Ports in the Adriatic Region

The methodology has been applied to the major ports of the Adriatic Area in order to map the GHG emissions. In the following, the studied area is briefly described, and then the GHG inventory is presented. All data is related to 2019. Only, Ploce Port Authority used 2020 data.

3.1 The Adriatic Area

Figure 1 shows the ports involved in the present study. They include all the major ports from Italy and Croatia. It is worth noticing that in many cases a single port authority is responsible for multiple ports. It is the case of almost all the Italian port authorities that have been grouped according to the decree n. 169/2016. On the contrary, in Croatia, single port authorities are in charge of single ports. In Tables 1, 2 and 3, the main traffic statistics related to the ports in the project area are reported, including a comparison of figures in Italy, Croatia and the combined cross-border reference values.

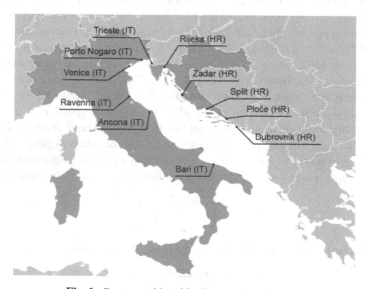

Fig. 1. Ports considered in the cross border study

Table 1. Main traffic statistics for the ports in the project area (Source: Eurostat)

Port	N. Ships	N. Pax Ships	% Pax Ships	N. Fright Ships	% Freight Ships	Total GT (kton)	GT Pax Ships (kton)	% Pax Ships	GT Freight Ships (kton)	% Freight Ships	Mean GT (ton)	Mean GT Pax (ton)	Mean GT Freight (ton)
Dubrovnik	35,031	34,006	97.07%	838	2.39%	33,685	31,832	94.50%	1,845	5.48%	962	936	2,202
Ploce	2,266	43	1.90%	2,214	97.71%	10,734	32	0.30%	10,641	99.13%	4,737	744	4,806
Rijeka	1,672	1,168	69.86%	486	29.07%	16,836	1,864	11.07%	14,930	88.68%	10,069	1,596	30,720
Split	23,145	15,001	64.81%	8,104	35.01%	55,520	20,910	37.66%	34,535	62.20%	2,399	1,394	4,261
Zadar	16,535	8,601	52.02%	7,922	47.91%	30,407	8,634	28.39%	21,772	71.60%	1,839	1,004	2,748
Ancona	2,068	58	2.80%	1,958	94.68%	55,389	3,082	5.56%	52,188	94.22%	26,784	53,138	26,654
Bari	2,764	216	7.81%	2,535	91.71%	59,696	10,211	17.10%	49,423	82.79%	21,598	47,273	19,496
Barletta	362	n.a.	0.00%	362	100.00%	1,641	n.a.	0.00%	1,641	100.00%	4,533	n.a.	4,533
Brindisi	1,833	30	1.64%	1,701	92.80%	33,713	1,903	5.64%	30,786	91.32%	18,392	63,433	18,099
Chioggia	660	2	0.30%	609	92.27%	1,923	1	0.05%	1,892	98.39%	2,914	500	3,107
Monfalcone	702	n.a.	0.00%	541	77.07%	7,573	n.a.	0.00%	7,539	99.55%	10,788	n.a.	13,935
Porto Nogaro	405	n.a.	0.00%	401	99.01%	1,979	n.a.	0.00%	1,927	99.90%	4,763	n.a.	4,805
Ravenna	4,082	15	0.37%	3,348	82.02%	45,515	663	1.46%	43,734	96.09%	11,150	44,200	13,063
Trieste	2,530	55	2.17%	2,308	91.23%	77,355	4,501	5.82%	72,759	94.06%	30,575	81,836	31,525
Venezia	3,903	517	13.25%	3,289	84.27%	85,063	21,978	25.84%	62,972	74.03%	21,794	42,511	19,146
Total	**97,958**	**59,712**	**60.96%**	**36,616**	**37.38%**	**516,979**	**105,611**	**20.43%**	**408,584**	**79.03%**			
Croatia	285,456	171,065	59.93%	112,774	39.51%	380,377	96,207	25.29%	283,776	74.60%	1,333	562	2,516
Italy	472,540	40,517	8.57%	428,079	90.59%	2,865,882	404,595	14.12%	2,455,367	85.68%	6,065	9,986	5,736
Italy + Croatia	757,996	211,582	27.91%	540,853	71.35%	3,246,259	500,802	15.43%	2,739,143	84.38%	4,283	2,367	5,064
% Italy + Croatia	**12.92%**	**28.22%**		**6.77%**		**15.93%**	**21.09%**		**14.92%**				

Table 2. Main statistics for the ports in the project area regarding passenger transport (Source: Eurostat)

Port	N. Cruise ship	N. Other Pax	GT Cruise Ship (kton)	GT Other Pax (kton)	N. Cruise Pax	N. Other Pax	Total N. Pax
Dubrovnik	533	33 473	27 631	4 201	78 000	2 332 000	2 410 000
Ploce	10	33	22	10	0	383 000	383 000
Rijeka	24	1 144	1 488	376	0	114 000	114 000
Split	274	14 727	12 765	8 145	0	4 958 000	4 958 000
Zadar	125	8 476	6 290	2 344	1 000	2 318 000	2 319 000
Ancona	58	n.a.	3 082	n.a.	19 000	1 089 000	1 108 000
Bari	133	83	10 191	20	165 000	1 226 000	1 390 000
Barletta	n.a.	n.a.	n.a.	n.a.	n.a.	n.a.	n.a.
Brindisi	30	n.a.	1 903	n.a.	16 000	504 000	520 000
Chioggia	2	n.a.	1	n.a.	n.a.	n.a.	n.a.
Monfalcone	n.a.	n.a.	n.a.	n.a.	n.a.	n.a.	n.a.
Porto Nogaro	n.a.	n.a.	n.a.	n.a.	n.a.	n.a.	n.a.
Ravenna	15	n.a.	663	n.a.	n.a.	n.a.	n.a.
Trieste	55	n.a.	4 501	n.a.	n.a.	n.a.	n.a.
Venezia	350	167	21 912	66	571 000	283 000	854 000
Total	**1 609**	**58 103**	**90 449**	**15 162**	**850 000**	**13 207 000**	**14 056 000**
Croatia	1 434	169 631	52 143	44 064	79 000	34 063 000	34 142 000
Italy	4 704	35 813	395 354	9 241	5 018 000	81 512 000	86 530 000
Italy + Croatia	6 138	205 444	447 497	53 305	5 097 000	115 575 000	120 672 000
% Italy + Croatia	**26.21%**	**28.28%**	**20.21%**	**28.44%**	**16.68%**	**11.43%**	**11.65%**

Table 3. Main statistics for the ports in the project area regarding freight transport (Source: Eurostat)

Port	GT Liquid Bulk (kton)	GT Dry Bulk (kton)	GT Container Ship (kton)	GT Spec. Carrier (kton)	GT Geng. Cargo (kton)	t of Goods Handled	TEU Handled
Dubrovnik	n.a.	n.a.	n.a.	1	1 844	21 000	n.a.
Ploce	784	1 322	1 240	50	7 245	3 507 000	33 956
Rijeka	16	184	14 099	0	631	3 356 000	287 920
Split	701	478	461	5	32 890	1 942 000	9 430
Zadar	432	81	n.a.	6	21 253	418 000	n.a.
Ancona	75	858	8 510	n.a.	42 745	5 313 000	212 444
Bari	213	1 433	1 433	34	46 310	6 134 000	86 088
Barletta	420	102	n.a.	n.a.	1119	1 084 000	n.a.
Brindisi	4 433	3 243	50	n.a.	23 060	8 583 000	1 654
Chioggia	n.a.	196	9	n.a.	1 687	1 597 000	0
Monfalcone	n.a.	2121	4	2564	2 850	4 489 000	319
Porto Nogaro	n.a.	80	35	n.a.	1 812	1 440 000	n.a.
Ravenna	8 796	13 875	9 569	1 627	9 867	31 348 000	246 983
Trieste	26 866	1 166	24 731	18	19 978	60 333 000	917 866
Venezia	8 972	7 619	18 288	1 056	27 037	27 935 000	547 563
Total	51 708	32 758	78 429	5 361	240 328	157 500 000	2 344 223
Croatia	8 629	3 117	15 800	67	256 163	20 580 000	331 304
Italy	211 868	56 021	377 750	66 117	1 743 611	508 074 000	9 795 968
Italy + Croatia	220 497	59 138	393 550	66 184	1 999 774	528 654 000	10 127 272
% Italy + Croatia	23.45%	55.39%	19.93%	8.10%	12.02%	29.79%	23.15%

In the project area, most of the traffic is composed of freight vessels. In terms of total Gross Tonnage (GT), in 2019, the first port in the area is Venice, followed by Trieste. Considering the number of ships the first port is Dubrovnik, which, however, mostly operates passenger transport (over 90% in terms of both the number of ships and the GT). Rijeka, Split and Zadar show a more balanced split between passenger and freight traffic in terms of the number of ships; however, considering the GT of vessels in all the cases the balance moves towards freight vessels that are characterised, in general, by higher mean GT compared to the passenger vessels in Croatia. On the other hand, considering the Italian ports, the average GT of passenger vessels is usually higher than the freight one.

3.2   Results

Considering the Adriatic Area, which includes all the ports involved in the present study, the aggregate picture of GHG emissions is provided in Table 4. It shall be noted that in most ports, no data about anchoring time was available or it has been grouped with emissions in the mooring phase. Furthermore, the ports of Rijeka and Bari neglect to report the maritime services emissions, whereas the port of Ravenna grouped these emissions in the manoeuvring related emissions. The emissions in the studied area can be decomposed as shown in Figs. 2, 3 and 4.

Table 4. Ports included in the cross border study

Category	Emissions (t CO2eq)	Emissions (%)
Electric energy	20192.1	3.21%
Heating	3230.7	0.51%
Service vehicles	4223.1	0.67%
Operational port vehicles	43519.4	6.93%
External vehicles	32262.1	5.14%
Railway tractors	1875.0	0.30%
Other	1231.0	0.20%
Maritime port services	8800.3	1.40%
Anchored ships	5714.6	0.91%
Ships manoeuvring	93592.4	14.90%
Moored ships	413635.8	65.84%
TOTAL	**628276.4**	**100.00%**

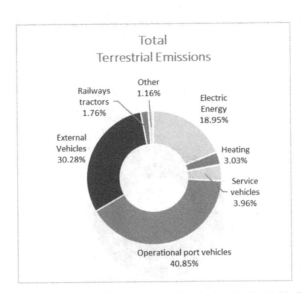

Fig. 2. Decomposition of total terrestrial emissions in the Adriatic Sea

4 Discussion

It is worth noticing that, maritime emissions are the largest contributor (83.04% of the total emissions of GHG) in the studied area. This situation is even more emphasised for passenger ports, such as Dubrovnik, Split or Zadar, where maritime emissions can reach more than 90% of the total. At thee same time, terrestrial emissions are limited to the lighting system, the heating of terminals, a small number of service vehicles and the traffic emissions within the port area.

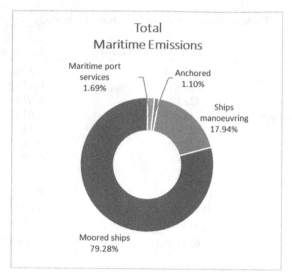

Fig. 3. Decomposition of total maritime emissions in the Adriatic Sea

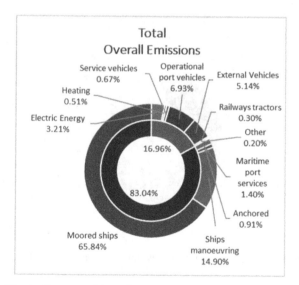

Fig. 4. Decomposition of total emissions in the Adriatic Sea

By decomposing the maritime emissions, the first contribution comes from moored vessels (79.28% of the maritime emissions of GHG), followed by ships manoeuvring (17.94% of the maritime emissions of GHG). The contribution from manoeuvring is strictly dependent on the port access and layout. It reaches the maximum value in the only channel port considered in the present study, e.g., Ravenna (37.04% of the maritime GHG emissions). Emissions from moored and anchored ships relate to the port efficiency, which determines the hotelling and standby time respectively. Besides, no information about anchored ships, i.e. ships waiting to enter the port, was available in several cases. Hence, it is expected that total maritime emissions should be slightly increased in the project area.

Regarding the terrestrial emissions, the main contributors are operational port vehicles (40.85% of the terrestrial emissions of GHG), heavy vehicles entering the port area (30.28% of the terrestrial emissions of GHG) and electric energy (18.95% of the terrestrial emissions of GHG). It is worth noticing that for passenger ports, electric energy consumption represents the main source of terrestrial emissions, reaching, for instance, 90% of terrestrial emissions in the port of Dubrovnik. However, the balance is significantly affected by the port layout and the distances between port access and terminals, which have an impact especially on the external vehicles category.

5 Conclusions

The present work originally elaborated and presented the current status of the Adriatic Area focusing on the GHG emissions in the ports involved in the SUSPORT project. It shall bared in mind that data refers to a pre-pandemic situation, hence, the GHG emissions are not affected by the effects of COVID-19, which caused in many cases a drop in port activities and, consequently, in the related emissions. This is especially true for the passenger ports, that experienced a heavy reduction of calls and passengers (especially the ones related to the cruise sector) in 2020.

Nevertheless, the work provided a portrait of the area carbon footprint that, together with the best practices, will provide a strong baseline to effectively plan the pilot actions that will be implemented during SUSPORT project. From this consolidation process some remarkable conclusions can be drawn. First, most of the emissions in the project area come from the sea-side, and in particular from moored ships. Regarding terrestrial emissions, the situation is different and it depends case by case, thus, a more in-depth analysis is needed. In particular, the distinction between mainly freight or passenger ports might be helpful, along with an analysis of the peculiar geographical characteristics of each specific site. Hence, the specific situation shall be carefully analysed and considered to improve the port sustainability and energy efficiency.

Acknowledgements. This work was entirely financed by "SUSPORT – SUStainable PORTs" Interreg Italy-Croatia 2014–2020 project.

References

1. Mazzarino, M., Braidotti, L., Borruso, G.: A review of best practices to reduce the environmental footprint of port areas in the adriatic region. In: Proceedings of 21st International Conference on Computational Science and Its Applications (ICCSA), pp. 168–173. IEEE, Piscataway (2021)
2. Frederickson, C., Durbin, T., Li, C., Ma, T. et al.: Performance and Activity Characteristics of Zero Emission Battery-Electric Cargo Handling Equipment at a Port Terminal. SAE Technical Paper 2022-01-0576 (2022)

3. Prpić-Oršić, J., Vettor, R., Faltinsen, O.M., Guedes Soares, C.: The influence of route choice and operating conditions on fuel consumption and CO2 emission of ships. J. Mar. Sci. Technol. **21**, 434–457 (2016)

4. Nasso, C., la Monaca, U., Bertagna, S., Braidotti, L., et al.: Integrated design of an eco-friendly wooden passenger craft for inland navigation. Int. Shipbuild. Prog. **66**(1), 35–55 (2019)

5. Bilgili, L.: Comparative assessment of alternative marine fuels in life cycle perspective. Renew. Sustain. Energy Rev. **144**, 110985 (2021)

6. Braidotti, L., Mazzarino, M., Cociancich, M., Bucci, V.: On the automation of ports and logistics chains in the adriatic region. In: Gervasi, O., et al. (eds.) ICCSA 2020. LNCS, vol. 12255, pp. 96–111. Springer, Cham (2020). https://doi.org/10.1007/978-3-030-58820-5_8

7. Kao, S.L., Chung, W.H., Chen, C.W.: AIS-based scenario simulation for the control and improvement of ship emissions in ports. J. Mar. Sci. Eng. **10**, 129 (2022)

8. Kenan, N., Jebali, A., Diabat, A.: The integrated quay crane assignment and scheduling problems with carbon emissions considerations. Comput. Ind. Eng. **165**, 107734 (2022)

9. Zhou, L., Li, M., Cheng, C., Zhou, Z., et al.: Real-time chemical characterization of single ambient particles at a port city in Chinese domestic emission control area - Impacts of ship emissions on urban air quality. Sci. Total Environ. **819**, 153117 (2022)

10. Seyhan, A., Ay, C., Deniz, C.: Evaluating the emission reduction efficiency of automatic mooring system and cold ironing: the case of a port in Izmit Bay. Aust. J. Maritime Ocean Affairs (in press) (2022)

11. Fuentes García, G., Sosa Echeverría, R., Baldasano Recio, J.M., W. Kahl, J.D. et al: Review of top-down method to determine atmospheric emissions in port. Case of Study: Port of Veracruz, Mexico. J. Mar. Sci. Eng. **10**, 96 (2022)

12. Kose, S., Sekban, D.M., Ozkok, M.: Determination of port-induced exhaust gas emission amounts and investigation of environmental impact by creating emission maps: Sample of Trabzon port. Int. J. Sustain. Transp. **16**(3), 258–268 (2022)

13. IPPC: IPPC Guidelines for National Greenhouse Gas Inventories. Institute for Global Environmental Strategies, Kanagawa (2006)

14. EMEP/EEA: Air pollutant emission inventory guidebook 2019. European Environmental Agency, Copenhagen (2019)

15. IPPC: Fifth Assessment Report. Intergovernmental Panel on Climate Change, Geneva (2014)

16. Jääskeläinen, H.: Idling Emissions, DieselNet (2017). https://dieselnet.com/tech/emissions_idle.php. Accessed 21 April 2022

17. IMO: Third IMO Greenhouse Gas Study 2014. International Maritime Organization, London (2014)

18. Le Fevre, C.: A Review of Demand Prospects for LNG as a Marine Fuel. Oxford Institute for Energy Studies (2018)

19. Yaramenka, K., Fridell, E., Åström, S.: Environmental assessment of Sweden-related LNG fleet in the Baltic Sea and the North Sea. Report 369. Swedish environmental research institute (IVL), Stockholm (2019)

20. Jalkanen, J.P., Brink, A., Kalli, J., Pettersson, H., et al.: A modelling system for the exhaust emissions of marine traffic and its application in the Baltic Sea area. J. Atmos. Chem. Phys. **9**, 9209–9223 (2009)

21. Jalkanen, J.P., Johansson, L., Kukkonen, J., Brink, A., et al.: Extension of an assessment model of ship traffic exhaust emissions for particulate matter and carbon monoxide. J. Atmos. Chem. Phys. **12**, 2641–2659 (2012)

22. Cooper, D., Gustafsson, T.: Methodology for calculating emissions from ships: 1. Update of emission factors. Swedish environmental research institute (IVL), Stockholm (Sweden)

The Logistic Carbon Footprint: A Dynamic Calculation Tool for an Indicator of the Sustainability of Logistic Processes with a Case Study on the Port of Trieste

Andrea Gallo[✉]

DEAMS – Department of Economic, Business, Mathematic and Statistics "Bruno de Finetti", University of Trieste, Via A. Valerio, 4/1, 34127 Trieste, Italy
andrea.gallo3@phd.units.it

Abstract. Quantifying the emissions produced along different supply chains is an extremely difficult challenge. However, carbon-based emissions generated by the transport sector have an extremely significant impact on environmental sustainability.

To address these issues, we propose a method for estimating the carbon footprint as an indicator of the environmental sustainability of processes as it represents the total emissions produced within a given process.

Therefore, the first problem we come across is developing a tool for calculating the logistic carbon footprint, which clearly defines the boundaries of application of the model and its scope of application. For this reason, the proposed tool will follow a standardized and uniform approach in order to streamline the calculation processes and make it even more efficient: the sources of emissions related to a supply chain are innumerable, so depending on the different approaches to calculating emissions, they can lead to extremely different results. In order to streamline the calculation process, the main sources of primary emissions and indirect emissions due to the supply of fuel oil have been used in a preponderant manner, and then an adjustment factor that takes into account all factors omitted from the model has been introduced. In this way, the calculation of the carbon footprint has been made uniform, homogeneous, and comparable as well as quantitatively reliable.

Once the method of elaboration of the carbon footprint is framed, we will proceed to use this synthetic indicator for the analysis of environmental sustainability for different logistic processes that consider the Port of Trieste as an intermodal exchange hub for intra-Mediterranean traffic and with destination the main markets of continental Europe, taking into account different modes of transport: road, rail, and maritime transport.

Keywords: Carbon footprint · Logistics · Maritime transport · Sustainability

1 Introduction

The World System is a complex set of delicate balances in relation to each other within which fall the geographical, social, and economic dynamic aspects. The network of

O. Gervasi et al. (Eds.): ICCSA 2022 Workshops, LNCS 13381, pp. 109–123, 2022.
https://doi.org/10.1007/978-3-031-10548-7_9

increasingly dense interconnections on a global scale involves a reduction of physical distances, which is reflected on the intensification of the flow of people, goods, knowledge and capital, through processes and innovations faster and faster.

It is therefore clear that the environmental aspects closely linked to the relationship between human activity and geography, take on an increasingly central role. The two lines that traveled on parallel tracks in terms of economic activity and environmental sustainability, have begun to diverge over the last decades. Hence the need for a careful and concrete assessment of pollutant emissions produced by economic activity, focusing in this case on pollutant emissions from logistics processes.

We can therefore introduce the concept of Carbon Footprint as a synthetic indicator of greenhouse gas emissions generated by a given process, expressed in terms of equivalent CO_2 [1]. This paper proposes to concretely define an approach to the calculation of the logistic carbon footprint, following an innovative approach that is both quantitatively correct and follows a standardized approach, aimed at obtaining comparable estimates of the pollutant emissions [2]. The proposal presented in the following article stems from the ambitious desire not to limit oneself to quantifying the emissions produced in the context of a supply chain, but to define a standardized and uniform calculation tool that can be used regarding two different targets: the first relates to the numerical quantification obtained through an estimate as accurate as possible, and the second relates to the criterion of comparability, using a standardized criterion of evaluation of the greenhouse gases emission as a parameter to take strategical choice [3].

To this aim, the emission factors deriving from intermodal transport will be accurately outlined, then moving on to a concrete evaluation of the pollutants produced by the movement of goods, highlighting not only a quantitative evaluation but also the uniform approach to calculation adopted for an evaluation of the Carbon Footprint to make the proposed effective standardize and comparable.

Calculating the Carbon Footprint is therefore equivalent to carrying out a single issue of the life cycle of a process, that is developing a life cycle study for a single impact category [4]. Every change in the logistics sector of the production chain has a direct effect on greenhouse gas emissions. GHG emissions mainly depend on the energy produced by the combustion of hydrocarbons, which are used in heat engines for various purposes. It is estimated that the logistics sector of transport generates approximately 28% of total greenhouse emissions each year, so in this context the study of the emissions produced by the logistics chain and the policies to limit some of them represent an extremely topical and debated issue [5].

2 Materials and Methods

The Carbon Footprint is a measure to quantify the total greenhouse gas emissions directly associated with a product, an organization, or a service. It represents an indicator for monitoring the effectiveness of environmental management policies through the preparation of what is known as an "emission inventory" [6].

Each of the greenhouse gases considered is weighted for its specific contribution to the increase in the greenhouse effect relative to that of CO_2. We can then define the Global Warming Potential - GWP of greenhouse gas, where GWP indicates the peculiar characteristic of a gas such as the warming power of the atmosphere compared to that of carbon dioxide, which by definition is set equal to 1. The climate-changing power of gas is expressed in terms of equivalent carbon dioxide. The Carbon Footprint is the environmental indicator expressed in terms of equivalent CO_2 that allows measuring the emissions of Greenhouse Gases - GHG associated directly or indirectly with a process, a product, or a service. In particular, the Carbon Footprint is a measure of how much CO_2 a given production and consumption system emits in its entirety. It is therefore a quantitative definition of greenhouse gas emissions and is an increasingly central tool in the management of corporate strategies on the environment and sustainability of economic processes and, in this case, logistics [7].

The normative notions that regulate the Carbon Footprint and allow its reporting are, at an international level, the standards ISO 14064:2006, later updated in 2019 with regard to the Carbon Footprint of a process, and the GHG Protocols proposed by the World Resources Institute (WRI). The objective of these normative references is to create common standards for the measurement and comparable quantification of product or process greenhouse gas emissions.

The ISO 14064 standard divides emission sources into three different categories (Table 1):

Table 1. Emission sources categories – Source: Personal Elaboration, [8]

Direct GHG emissions	This category includes all emissions generated directly by production activities, which are therefore strictly related to the use of fossil fuels: all activities that require thermal or electrical energy are therefore included in this category
Indirect GHG emissions	Emissions deriving from energy consumption: in this case, emissions produced during the production process, but deriving from third-party energy sources that are not relevant, are considered
Other indirect emissions	Includes all emissions not categorized in the two previous areas

The GHG Protocols follow hand in hand what is expressed by the ISO 14064 standard, outlining the three previous different profiles of emissions that will be called 'scope': scope 1: direct emissions, scope 2: indirect emissions, scope 3: other indirect emissions.

Moreover, it is important to underline that in the GHG Protocol emission reports and for the Standards ISO 14064 the drafting of scopes 1 and 2 are mandatory, while scope 3 is optional and not binding [8–10].

2.1 The Logistic Carbon Footprint

We will now introduce the Carbon Footprint for logistic processes: all those operations directly related to the movement of goods from the place of production to the final destination. The idea is to formalize a model capable of defining a standardized approach to calculating the carbon footprint of a logistics chain, articulated through various modal shifts. The core of the logistic chain is represented by maritime transport, the leading sector of international trade, while at the top and the bottom of this process the movement of goods takes place by different means of transport: rail and road. Ports represent the fundamental connection points for these processes [11]. Every year, the logistics sector is responsible for 27% of total greenhouse gas emissions: the study of the carbon footprint of these processes is of primary importance in the reduction of emissions, especially considering the current macroeconomic scenario, increasingly globalized and interconnected [12].

To evaluate the GHG emissions of a logistic chain, we will have to carry out a preliminary analysis of the main ways of transport used, starting from the different categories of ships used in the shipping sector and then focusing our attention on road and rail traffic. We are not going to consider air freight because it is a relative niche sector in terms of volume. After an initial overview of the vehicles, it will be essential to study the heat engine and the energy required in order to define the number of emissions produced. From here, we can proceed to calculate the direct emissions resulting from a logistic process that includes the three modes of transport mentioned above: road, rail, and ship. In this context, we will then go on to calculate the direct and indirect emissions attributable to Scope 1 and Scope 2 of the GHG Protocol for activities carried out in a port environment [6].

The calculation model presented will take into account the main elements of the logistic chain related to the different transport modes. However, to follow a standardized approach to calculation, an adjustment factor of 5% attributable to direct emissions and 2% attributable to indirect emissions will be introduced, taking into account all exogenous factors such as tides, traffic conditions, adverse sea currents, tire wear, etc., as well as relatively negligible emission factors and, also, relatively negligible emission factors such as handling operations in the various intermodal hubs as these operations will be considered within the adjustment factor. It is clear that in the quantification of the logistic carbon footprint many factors can have a slight impact on the quantification of emissions: it is, therefore, necessary to clearly define the boundaries of the model within which to calculate the carbon footprint in order to obtain a model that is qualitatively correct and at the same time applicable to different realities.

Maritime transport is the most important channel for international trade: it is estimated that more than 80% of the global volume of goods, including food, fuel, construction materials, chemicals, and household goods, is transported by sea, with more than 90,000 commercial vessels plying the world's oceans [13, 14].

We will then proceed to analyze the different types of ships categorized based on their cargo capacity to initially analyze consumption and then climate-altering gas emissions [15].

In order to quantify the emissions of the naval segment, we will start from the different types of vessels, taking into account the engine power (expressed in kWh) and assuming an energy efficiency of 70% of the main engines during navigation, while for roadstead and dockside operations the exclusive use of auxiliary engines at 100% energy efficiency is foreseen. This hypothesis will allow us to quantify the average hourly consumption of the different types of ships. Once the consumption produced by the fleet under analysis has been evaluated, it will be possible to convert consumption into the volume of greenhouse gases produced [14].

To calculate the greenhouse gas emissions produced by the maritime segment we will use two different approaches: the first based on the energy used in terms of kWh, able to express the emissions in terms of *g pollutant* /kWh and a second referred to the effective fuel consumption [1].

In order to elaborate a carbon footprint covering the whole logistic chain, the analysis of emissions from road freight transport is essential. In this section, we will define the essential tools for the calculation of greenhouse gas emissions from combustion of heavy-duty trucks. For this reason, estimates will be made on an average sample, considering the most used vehicles for this application [17].

In order to evaluate the diesel consumption of the circulating vehicle fleet, we have used the "Handbook emission factor for road transport (HBEFA)" [15], a Microsoft Access database that shows the emissions and fuel consumption for all categories of circulating vehicles, based on a sample of over 50 thousand different vehicles.

From an elaboration of this information provided the table has been created about the volumes of emissions and average consumption for the circulating fleet, divided by weight [3]. The information provided therefore allows us to calculate in an extremely simple and direct manner the fuel consumption and GHG emissions for each route depending on the type of vehicle used [15].

Concerning the information obtained from the "Handbook emission factor for road transport (HBEFA)", the official estimates made by Isprambiente (Institute for environmental protection and research) report that for every gram of diesel consumed, an average of 3.16 g of carbon dioxide are produced. We can then compare the emission estimates obtained from the HBEFA database against the CO_2 average emissions for the trucks under analysis [1].

The third mode of transport that we will consider for the calculation of emissions from the supply chain is rail transport [26]. The main indicator for calculating energy and emissions from rail transport comes from the energy consumed based on the net weight of the train. For this analysis, the basic assumption is that in almost all situations, locomotives powered by electric motors are used to move goods by rail. As a consequence, direct emissions of greenhouse gases will be insignificant [19].

For this analysis, we will consider different categories of trains, defined according to their load capacity. The average size of freight trains in Europe is 1,000 tons. Freight trains can therefore be divided into different categories according to their maximum load volume.

For the calculation of emissions from the railway sector, we will therefore have to analyze the indirect emissions. This is the set of emissions falls into the producing of energy used to power the electric motors of locomotives [20, 26]. For the railway sector, it is, therefore, possible to estimate the energy consumption in terms of *kWh/t-km* and consequently, the carbon dioxide emissions produced expressed in *kg CO_2/t-km*. It, therefore, becomes necessary to further emphasize how greenhouse gas emissions from locomotives powered by an electric engine are indirect emissions resulting from the "well to wheel" process, thus generated indirectly for the supply of electricity consumed. For the rail transport we will take into account both the direct and indirect factor of adjustment of 5 and 2%, due to reach a more precise estimation [21].

In addition to the direct emissions produced by the engines, the calculation of the Carbon Footprint for the logistics chain also includes indirect emissions: the class of emissions that cannot be directly attributed to the production process under analysis, but which derive from activities connected to it: in particular, for the logistics chain that is the subject of this study, emissions deriving from the production of electrical energy and the supply of essential fuel oil within the transport chain fall within this scope [1]. Generally, these emissions fall within scope 2 of the GHG Protocol, but it is worth remembering that an increasingly significant percentage of the electricity produced and used in the port comes from renewable sources [20].

It will be essential to study the entire life cycle of diesel fuel, from the processes of extraction, processing, refining, storage, and final distribution of the fuel, to evaluate the indirect emissions of a logistics chain, in which the movement of heavy vehicles and therefore the use of fuel oil is of primary importance. Generally, this process is called "From Well to Tank" (WTT) [22]. Focusing on the "Well to Tank" process, the diesel production chain must be considered. The problem to be faced now is to calculate the energy used starting from the extraction of the primary source, oil from the oil well, up to making it available as fuel for the thermal engines used within the supply chain. The emissions of the WTT process will be 645.17 g CO_2 eq/kg of fuel [15].

3 Data

In the previous paragraph, the calculation methodology for structuring the carbon footprint analysis for a chain was proposed.

Therefore, starting from the naval segment, it will be fundamental to subdivide the maritime transport segment starting from the different types of ships used and then quantify consumption as shown in the following tables [14] (Tables 2 and 3):

Table 2. Ships types by category – Soruce: Personal Elaboration, [14]

Ship by category	Class by size	Unit of measurement	Gross weight average (in tons)	Average engine power (in kW)	Average speed (in knots)
Bulk carrier	0–9.999	DWT	3.313	1.687	9,9
	10.000–34.999		28.455	7.112	11,6
	35.000–59.999		54.546	9.548	12,2
	60.000–99.999		81.713	10.989	12,3
	100.000–199.999		198.060	18.997	12,7
	200.000–+		284.595	22.740	12,8

(*continued*)

Table 2. (*continued*)

Ship by category	Class by size	Unit of measurement	Gross weight average (in tons)	Average engine power (in kW)	Average speed (in knots)
Container	0–999	Teus	9.080	6.182	12,7
	1.000–1.999		21.520	13.152	14,5
	2.000–2.9999		37.478	22.640	16,2
	3.000–4.999		58.072	39.328	17,2
	5.000–7.999		81.168	52.556	17,5
	8.0000–11.999		119.058	57.901	17,9
	12.000–14.500		149.023	61.231	17
	14.500–19.9999		178.871	60.202	16,4
	20.000–+		195.615	60.241	16,3
General cargo	0–4.999	DWT	1.913	1.107	8,8
	5.000–9.999		7.534	3.471	10,4
	10.000–+		23.156	7.910	12,2
Oil tankers	0–4.999	DWT	2.781	1.414	8,9
	5.000–9.999		9.005	3.134	9,3
	10.000–19.999		20.338	5.169	9,8
	20.000–59.999		43.467	8.570	11,9
	60.000–79.999		72.401	12.091	12,4
	80.000–119.999		106.477	13.518	11,9
	120.000–199.999		154.878	17.849	12,5
	200.000–+		304.656	26.710	12,9
Ro-Ro	0–4.999	DWT	1.930	1.751	9,2
	5.000–+		11.286	11.526	14,4

Table 3. Ships emission by category – Source: Personal Elaboration, [14]

Ship by category	Class by size	Unit of measurement	Average consumption (tons per day)	
			Main engine consumption	Auxiliary engine consumption
Bulk carrier	0–9.999	DWT	5,5	0,5
	10.000–34.999		17,6	0,5
	35.000–59.999		23,4	0,7

(*continued*)

Table 3. (*continued*)

Ship by category	Class by size	Unit of measurement	Average consumption (tons per day)	
			Main engine consumption	Auxiliary engine consumption
	60.000–99.999		28,8	1,1
	100.000–199.999		42,3	1,1
	200.000–+		56,3	1,1
Container	0–999	Teus	14,4	0,8
	1.000–1.999		26	2,1
	2.000–2.9999		38,5	3
	3.000–4.999		58,7	3,7
	5.000–7.999		79,3	4
	8.0000–11.999		95,6	4,2
	12.000–14.500		107,8	4,2
	14.500–19.9999		109,4	3,9
	20.000–+		108,6	3,7
General cargo	0–4.999	DWT	0,6	0,1
	5.000–9.999		1,7	0,4
	10.000–+		3,6	1,2
Oil tankers	0–4.999	DWT	4,3	0,6
	5.000–9.999		7,1	1
	10.000–19.999		10,8	1,6
	20.000–59.999		22,2	2
	60.000–79.999		31,4	1,9
	80.000–119.999		31,5	2,6
	120.000–199.999		39,4	3,1
	200.000–+		65,2	3,7
Ro-Ro	0–4.999	DWT	3,2	2,4
	5.000–+		7,2	3,7

Based on the information given in the previous tables, we will then consider the emission factors associated with consumption and power demand using the following emissions conversion table [2, 18] (Table 4):

Table 4. Different emission factors for shipping sector - Source: Personal Elaboration, [1, 14]

Emission factor:		gpollutant/gfuel	GWP-100
CO_2	Carbon dioxide	3,114	1
SO_2	Sulfur sulfide	0,05	-
Emission factor:		g/kWh	
N_2O	Nitrogen oxide	0,03	298
CH_4	Methane	0,2	25
CO	Carbon monoxide	1,04	1,8
PM10	Particulate matter	0,01	-

Using this information, it will therefore be possible to quantify the emissions of the shipping segment.

Also, for road transport, we will define an average estimate of consumption and emissions starting from the different categories of vehicles used according to their average weight and taking into analysis only articulated trucks of EURO 4 category or higher, that is meeting certain minimum standards in terms of energy efficiency. In this case, it will be possible to determine the emissions and consumption as follows [16] (Table 5):

Table 5. Rail transport consumption and emissions – Source: Personal Elaboration, [16]

Category	Average speed	Consumption. average		Emission factors				
				CO_2	CH_4	N_2O	NOx	PM
Dimension	km/h	g/km	km/l	g/km				
<7,5	64,74	127,02	6,56	408,6	0,01	0,35	2,15	0,13
7.5–14	64,73	154,14	5,41	494,1	0,01	0,41	3,02	0,13
14–20	64,65	185,66	4,49	559,0	0,01	0,53	3,44	0,13
20–28	64,72	221,46	3,76	691,0	0,01	0,59	3,71	0,13
28–34	64,67	257,56	3,24	795,7	0,01	0,68	4,03	0,13
34–40	64,64	271,32	3,07	808,9	0,01	0,77	4,51	0,14
40–50	64,58	302,93	2,75	953,6	0,01	0,91	5,27	0,14
50–60	64,64	378,01	2,20	1183,2	0,01	1,29	6,58	0,14

Finally, the quantification of emissions about rail transport, which we recall falling into the category of indirect emissions, will be elaborated starting from the following estimates [19, 20, 26] (Table 6):

Table 6. Emissions per rail freight transport – Source: Personal Elaboration, [20, 26]

Type of train	Gross tonne weight train	Energetic consumption (kWh/t-km)	Energetic consumption (kWh/km)	Emissions (gCO$_2$/t-km)	Emissions (kg CO$_2$/km)
Light	500 t	1,1	701,8	22,8	14,5464
Average	1.000 t		1251,8		25,9464
Large	1.500 t		1801,8		37,3464
Extralarge	2.000 t		2351,8		48,7464
Heavy	5.000 t		5651,8		117,1464

Also, for rail transport different types of trainsets will be considered depending on their weight, where it will be possible to quantify the energy consumption in terms of *kWh-t-km* and emissions expressed in *kg CO$_2$-km*.

4   The Case Study: Carbon Footprint Estimate Through the Port of Trieste

In this case study, we are going to quantify the carbon footprint for the handling of a single TEU coming from the Far East, and more specifically from Shanghai with final destination at the Duisburg Freight Village, with a modal shift foreseen in the Port of Trieste where the container will leave for Frankfurt on a freight train, and then face the last step Frankfurt-Duinsburg by road [23].

To evaluate the Carbon Footprint deriving from these processes, we will have to segment the logistic process into three articulated phases:

– First phase: Ship transport from Shanghai to the Port of Trieste, handled through a large container ship, with a maximum capacity of 15,000 Teus and a load factor of 80%, with an average cruising speed of 16.4 knots per hour.
– Second Phase: Transport by rail with origin at the Port of Trieste and with a destination at the railway terminal of Frankfurt am Main, operated by means of a convoy assembled within the boundaries of the Port of Trieste, with a maximum length of 480 m, for a total of 24 wagons capable of carrying up to 48 Teus, with a load factor of 90%.
– Third Phase: Final handling of the container by road, leaving Frankfurt and with final destination Duisburg. We will have to consider in the basic assumptions the use of standard 20 feet containers with an average weight of 20 tons. In this case study we consider the freight village of Duinsburg as final destination by virtue of the agreements between the Trieste and Duisburg freight villages.

We will now go on to quantify the greenhouse gas emissions for each of these phases, starting with shipping [23].

To quantify the emissions deriving from the use of a large container ship for an extremely long route, it will be necessary to first analyze the route followed by the relative transit times and then evaluate the consumption [24, 25] (Table 7).

Table 7. Route Shanghai-Trieste, distance and transit time – Source: Personal Elaboration, [24]

Route Tianjin Xingang - Trieste			
Origin	Destination	Transit Time (hours)	Distance (NM)
Shanghai	Shekou	41	672
Shekou	Singapore	98	1.602
Singapore	Salalah	182	2.985
Salalah	King Abdoullah	72	1.183
King Abdoullah	Port Said	47	771
Port Said	Rjieka	83	1.364
Rjieka	Koper	8	127
Koper	Trieste	1	12
		Transit Time (in hours): 531	Total Distance (in NM) 8.716

To evaluate the emissions produced, it will be necessary to consider the consumption for a container ship with a capacity of 15,000 Teus. Referring to the tables above, the hourly consumption is equal to 4.56 tons of diesel fuel, and at an energy efficiency of 80%, the engines will be able to deliver 48,162 kW/h [14, 15]. Once we know the fuel consumption for the maritime segment of the logistic value chain is close to 2421,36 tons of oil.

The auxiliary engines will be used at 60% of their power for quayside operations: it is assumed that the consumption of auxiliary engines is equal to 0,0978 tons per hour, therefore, assuming that for each port of call 10 h will be necessary to carry out all land-based activities, the consumption at the quay will be equal to 0,978 tons of fuel for each port of call. Considering, therefore, the proposed ocean route from Shanghai to Trieste, we can directly evaluate the total emissions produced by the roadstead activities for the ship under analysis equal to 8,802 tons of diesel fuel, deriving from the unit consumption of 0,978 tons per port of call multiplied by the 9 port calls foreseen by the route in analysis.

Based on this calculation approach, the estimated emissions will be 8301,7 tons of equivalent carbon dioxide, where assuming an 80% load factor, each individual container will be responsible for 691,8 kg of CO_2 equivalent. At this point it will be necessary to consider the adjustment factor of 5% to include in the calculation the neglected factors and the exogenous factors of the process, equal to 34,6 kg. The total emissions produced by the single container for the Shanghai-Trieste route will be equal to 726,4 kg CO_2 equivalent.

We will now calculate the indirect component of emissions from the "from well to the tank" process, where we know that for every kg of diesel consumed, 645.17 g of CO_2 equivalent will be produced, subsequently corrected by an adjustment factor of 2%. Based on this information we can then define the indirect emissions as 158,35 kg of CO_2 equivalent per TEU.

Once the modal shift has been carried out, the container is expected to leave the Port of Trieste by rail with destination Frankfurt. The train assembled in Trieste will have a capacity of 1.018 tons, divided into 48 teus of 20 tons and an electric locomotive weighing 138 tons. This information will be useful to evaluate the estimated consumption of electricity, equal to 1,1 kWh/t-km, and the emissions in terms of CO_2 equivalent equal to 22,8 g CO_2/t-km. This information will be crucial for the evaluation of emissions from rail transport, but first it will be essential to quantify the distance traveled, which for this particular destination is 842 km. Based on the information previously provided, the energy consumption in terms of kilowatt-hours is a total of 942,871.6 or 19,643.16 kWh per single container. At this point it is possible to estimate the emissions based on the emission factor equal to 22.8 g CO_2 equivalent per tonne per kilometer: with this calculation then the consumption in term of kilograms of CO_2 equivalent is 19,543.16, which per single container reaches 407.15 kg of $CO2$ equivalent. Now, we are going to consider the 7% overall adjustment factor for the rail sector as well. The evaluation of this adjustment factor considering all the factors not calculable and considered that are part of this quantification is equal to 28.50, in conclusion, we can therefore state that the emissions for rail transport are equal to 435.65 kg of CO_2 equivalent [19, 20].

For the last step, we will take into account the emissions deriving from the handling of a single container by road from the railway terminal of Frankfurt to the Duisburg Freight Village, for a total distance of 276 km, covered on average in 3 h and 3 min, considering a standard Teu weighing 20 tons handled by an articulated truck capable of carrying up to 40 tons, where the average consumption is estimated to be 221.46 g of diesel per kilometer [16]. We can then quantify with a simple arithmetic calculation the fuel consumption used equally to 60, 99 kg of diesel fuel and consequently direct emissions of 246.5 kg of $CO2$equivalent and indirect emissions of 39.35 kg of CO_2 equivalent. We will finally apply the adjustment factors by which the direct emissions will be 258.83 kg $CO2$ equivalent while the indirect emissions will be 40.13 kg CO_2 equivalent [22].

To conclude, it is, therefore, possible to quantify the total emissions generated by the entire logistics chain for the movement of a single container from Shanghai to Duisburg, evaluated as the sum of the different transport modes (Table 8):

Table 8. Emission for the route Shanghai-Duisburg – Source: Personal Elaboration

Way of transport	Direct emissions	Indirect emissions	Total emissions
Marine vessel	691,8 kg of CO_2	158,35 kg of CO_2	850,15 kg of CO_2
Rail transport	-	-	435,65 kg of CO_2
Road transport	258,83 kg of CO_2	40,13 kg of CO_2	298,96 kg of CO_2
Total emissions	950,6 kg of CO_2	198,48 kg of CO_2	1584,76 kg of CO_2

5 Discussion

The analysis of the carbon footprint cannot disregard two intrinsic components: the evaluation of emissions and their communication. Often, there is a tendency to give greater importance to the first of these two aspects, but it is precisely in the communication of the Carbon Footprint that the importance of defining uniform calculation criteria lies [17]: In fact, the emissions report must not be limited to quantifying in purely numerical terms the volumes of greenhouse gases produced within a process, but must be able to represent a starting point for the strategic and decision-making choices of business processes, thus declining as a comparative advantage, not only in terms of cost-effectiveness due to greater energy efficiency but concerning the reduction of harmful emissions produced [4].

Starting from an assessment of the sources of average emissions for each category of vehicle used in the context of modal transport, a calculation model has been developed that would be able to provide useful information in terms of absolute volumes of emissions and their intensity for each unit moved, following a standardized and uniform approach to quantification, [17] and trying to reduce part of the discretion resulting from the assessment of emissions [15].

It is necessary to point out that there is a problem in the discretionary nature of the quantification of the carbon footprint. In fact, in this sense, delineating the boundaries within which to elaborate a rational analysis of emissions appears extremely complex, and this is why it was decided to define limits for the model, on which to subsequently apply an adjustment factor that would include emissions neglected by the analysis and all exogenous influencing factors. This approach means that the analysis of the Carbon Footprint of the logistics chain includes only the most relevant elements and those closely related to the process. However, all other factors omitted within a single parameter are considered. Therefore, the proposed adjustment factor becomes fundamental in order to concretely define the boundaries of the calculation model for the evaluation of emissions deriving from a logistics chain and to pursue the criteria of comparability and transparency foreseen for the drafting of the Carbon Footprint, since it limits any discretion.

6 Conclusions

This paper aims to combine theoretical and practical information in terms of quantifying carbon footprint emissions for logistics processes. In order to take full advantage of this indicator, it is essential to streamline calculation processes and smooth out the factors that can be included in the quantification of emissions. By defining standardized application criteria for the calculation of the Carbon Footprint, it will take on an even more central role in decision-making processes, allowing rational choices to be made in terms of economic and environmental efficiency and laying the foundations for sustainable development.

The introduction of an adjustment factor for direct and indirect emission sources will make it possible to quantify emissions by analyzing primary emission funds in detail, including exogenous and highly discretionary components in the calculation.[8] However, the importance of the carbon footprint must not be limited to the mere numerical value expressed in the quantity of GHGs produced in the context of a specific production process, but its intrinsic strength is based on the combination of quantification and communication [21]. Generally, the quantitative aspect is the one that catalyzes the attention, but the concept of communicability represents a point of central importance within the concept of Carbon Footprint: it is a clear and direct tool to highlight a specific component of the life cycle of a process, which can represent in a biunivocal way useful information in terms of environmental sustainability, [12] but above all, a performance indicator, thus representing a comparative advantage in terms of attention to environmental issues [2, 7].

References

1. McKinnon, A.: Decarbonizing Logistics: Distributing Goods in Low Carbon World, London, UK, Kogan Page Ltd (2018)
2. Franchetti, J., Apul, D.: Carbon Footprint Analysis Concepts, Methods, Implementation, and Case Studies. CRC Press, New York (2013)
3. Suzanne, G., Lewis, A.: Smart Freight Centre. Global Logistics Emissions Council Framework for Logistics Emissions Accounting and Reporting. Technical report, Amsterdam, Netherlands (2019)
4. Pernigiotti, D.: Carbon Footprint, Calcolare e comunicare l'impatto dei prodotti sul clima – Daniele Pernigiotti, Edizioni Ambiente, Milano (2012)
5. Kouridis, C., Samaras, C., et al.: EMEP European Environment Agency air pollutant emission inventory guidebook (2019)
6. WRI e WBCSD, The Greenhouse Gas Protocol: A Measuring to Manage: A Guide to Designing GHG Accounting and Reporting Programs (2007)
7. Institute of Marine Engineering, Science and Technology (IMarEST), IMO International Maritime Organization: Ship Emissions Tookit, Guide No. 01, Rapid Assessment of ship emissions in the national Context, GleMEEP Project Coordination Unit, London, UK (2018)
8. International Organization for Standardization: ISO 14064-1, "Greenhouse gases - Part 1: Specification with guidance at the organization level for quantification and reporting of greenhouse gas emissions and removals", Geneva, Switzerland (2018)
9. WRI e WBCSD: The Greenhouse Gas Protocol: A Corporate and Reporting Standard – Revised Edition), World Resources Institute and World Business Council for Sustainable Development, Geneva, Switzerland (2016)
10. WRI e WBCSD: The Greenhouse Gas Protocol: Policy and Action Standard, World Resources Institute and World Business Council for Sustainable Development, Geneva, Switzerland (2015)
11. Notteboom, T., Pallis, A., Rodrigue, J.P.: Port Economics, Management and Policy. A Comprehensive Analysis of the Port Industry. Routledge, New York (2021)

12. McKinnon, A.: European Freight Transport Statistics: Limitations, Misinterpretations and Aspirations. Brussels, Belgium (2010)
13. UNCTAD: Review of maritime transport. United Nations Conference on Trade and Development (UNCTAD). Technical report, United Nations Publication, Geneva, Switzerland (2015)
14. Faber, J., et al.: Fourth IMO Greenhous Gas Study, 2020 Full Report – International Maritime Organization (IMO), London, UK (2020)
15. McKinnon, A., Cullinane, S., Browne, M., Whiteing, A., Piecyk, M.: Green Logistics, 3rd edn. Improving the Environmental Sustainability of Logistics, New York, USA, Kogan Page Ltd (2015)
16. Keller, M., Cox, B., Notter, B.: INFRAS: Handbook Emission Factors for Road Transport, Ver. 4.1, Technical report, Bern, Switzerland (2019)
17. Thibault T. for BSR: Clean Cargo Working Group Carbon Emissions Accounting Methodology, The Clean Cargo Working Group Standard Methodology for Credible and Comparable CO_2 Emissions Calculation and Benchmarking in the Ocean Container Shipping Sector. Technical report, Clean Cargo, Paris, France (2015)
18. ISPRA (Istituto Superiore per la Protezione e la Ricerca Ambientale), SINAnet (Rete del Sistema Informativo Nazionale Ambientale), "La banca dati dei fattori di emissione medi del trasporto stradale in Italia" (2015)
19. DB 2008 Deutsche Bahn AG, Bahn-Umwelt-Zentrum: Energy and emission, technical report (2008)
20. EcoTransIt Word, Ecological Transport Information Tool for Worldwide Transportifeu Heidelberg INFRAS Berne IVE Hannover. Technical report (2019)
21. Schmied, M., Freid, C.: Calculating GHG emissions for freight forwarding and logistics services in accordance with EN 16258, Clecat – European Association for forwarding, transport, and customs service (2012)
22. Prussi, M., Yugo, M., De Prada, L., Padella, M., Edwards, R., Lonza, L.: JEC Well-to-Tank report v5, EUR 30269 EN, Publications Office of the European Union, Luxembourg (2020)
23. Midoro, R., Parola, F.: Le strategie delle imprese nello shipping di linea e nella portualità. Franco Angeli, Milano (2013)
24. https://www.msc.com/mkd/our-services/trade-services/east-west-network
25. Vallega, A.: Geografia delle strategie marittime. Dal mondo dei mercanti alla società transindustriale, Milano: Mursia (1997)
26. Alvarez, A.G., Pérez-Martìnez, P.J., Gonzàles-Franco, I.: Energy Consumption and Carbon Dioxide Emissions in Rain and Road freight transport in Spain: A case study of car carriers and bulk petrochemicals, Archivio Digital UPM, Library at the Universidad Politecnica de Madrid (2013)

Investigating the Competitive Factors of Container Ports in the Mediterranean Area: An Experimental Analysis Using DEA and PCA

Gianfranco Fancello⬡, Patrizia Serra(✉) ⬡, Daniel M. Vitiello⬡,
and Valentina Aramu

DICAAR – Department of Civil and Environmental Engineering and Architecture,
University of Cagliari, 09123 Cagliari, Italy
pserra@unica.it

Abstract. In the maritime world scenario, various challenges are affecting Mediterranean container ports, which are trying to keep high their efficiency and their competitiveness through infrastructural and managerial improvements. The identification of the priority actions requires the analysis of the productivity of each port in relation to the use of its resources. This study applies Data Envelopment Analysis (DEA) and Principal Component Analysis (PCA) in order to investigate the potential factors that can affect the efficiency of Mediterranean container ports. These methods use six input variables (yard area, berth depth, number of quay cranes, equipment, berth length and distance of the port from the Suez-Gibraltar axis) and one output variable (port throughput expressed in TEUs). The results can help to highlight the potential factors of success for Mediterranean container ports and to identify future policies and management strategies aimed towards the strengthening of the analyzed context.

Keywords: Data Envelopment Analysis · Principal Component Analysis · Benchmarking · Container port · Mediterranean sea

1 Introduction

Container ports represent the fastest and most immediate access doors to internal markets and constitute crucial nodes of integrated and multimodal supply chains, whose efficiency depends strictly on the efficiency of their ports. To stay competitive, container ports must carry out operations with maximum efficiency to meet the requirements of a continually growing and diversified demand. Not surprisingly, the assessment of port efficiency is among the areas that have attracted much attention in logistics in the last decades [1].

This paper focuses on the specific case of Mediterranean container ports in an attempt to elucidate the most representative factors of their efficiency. The Mediterranean basin has always played a key role in global trading markets due to its key positioning along the main East-West trading routes (known as pendulum routes) and its centrality with respect to both the Atlantic and North European markets, and the Asian and African ones. The unique location of its ports offers network advantages to ocean carriers due to the shortened transit times to major emerging markets, in particular to and from Asia. It is estimated that Mediterranean ports collectively currently handle almost 40% of the world's containerized trade flows [2]. Their future growth trend will depend on several factors, both endogenous and exogenous, which can contribute to determine their success or failure in the market. Some of these factors are mentioned below:

- Mediterranean container ports show different levels of technological advancement [3]. The best Mediterranean container ports are equipped with state-of-the-art handling equipment (for example, super post panamax cranes), often controlled by high performance IT applications. The advent of technology has caused major organizational and technical changes in the port sector. Vertical integration, blockchain and terminal automation are some of the elements that are changing activities in container terminals, and which can constitute distinctive and competitive factors of ports [4]. However, not all Mediterranean ports are able to keep up with these changes in the same way.
- Naval gigantism is another critical factor that affects container trade. In 2013, ships over 10,000 TEU (Twenty equivalent unit) were 14% of the global fleet, 36% at the beginning of 2020 [5]. Naval gigantism directly affects ports, as there are only a few ports properly structured to efficiently manage last generation container ships.
- External commercial strategies can both strengthen or hamper the centrality of the Mediterranean area. From one side, the Belt and Road initiative, for instance, supports the infrastructure of Euro-Asian trade, with particular attention to the port of Piraeus, which aims to become the largest logistics hub in the Mediterranean. On the other side, new alternative routes can pose a threat to Mediterranean ports. For example, the Arctic route has become more plausible given the climate change phenomenon, which has stronger and quicker implications in the Arctic region than elsewhere. The coastal states of the area have begun to take advantage of the sea route that connects the Atlantic and the Pacific Ocean to integrate the conventional trade routes during the summer season. Furthermore, more and more shipping companies decide to use the Cape Route and bypass the Suez Canal, due to slow steaming practice and high fees of the Suez Canal, thus rising interest in African ports [6] at the expense of the ports of the Mediterranean.
- The private sector has been playing an increasing dominant role in the global container market, where few world carriers and global terminal operators control ever-greater market shares. Generally, global enterprises initiate their development plans in the Mediterranean, as they are the decision makers for possible port of calls or the potential buying out of a port's terminal [7].

The effects of the Covid-19 pandemic, which is contributing to transform further the shipping market and the global supply chains, now further complicate this ever-changing market scenario. In such an evolving scenario, Mediterranean ports are required to improve their functionality and productivity to meet new needs and acquire ever-higher market rates [8].

This paper intends to investigate the factors that most affect the efficiency of container ports in the Mediterranean area by applying and combining Data Envelopment Analysis

(DEA) and Principal Component Analysis (PCA). The application considers 35 major Mediterranean container ports characterized in terms of supply (berth length, yard area, number of QCs, depth) and demand variables (TEUs moved in 2019).

The framework of the article is as follows: Sect. 2 presents a brief literature review of the most applied methods used to analyse efficiency of container ports. Section 3 describes the methodology used while Sect. 4 illustrates the selected input and output variables. The results of the analysis are provided and discussed in Sect. 5. Finally, Sect. 6 concludes the paper.

2 Literature Review

In the last decades, there has been a growth of interest in the evaluation of container ports efficiency. Most of the available methodologies are based on Multi-Criteria Decision-Making methods. Table 1, created by adapting to the port area the table proposed by Fancello et al. [9] for road transport, summarizes the main strengths and weaknesses of the most used methods applied to container port efficiency.

Among the available methods for evaluating efficiency, DEA has been chosen for this study because of its following features that, in the authors' opinion, make it very attractive for benchmarking port efficiency:

- Differently from Electre III, DEA does not use any subjective parameter.
- Through the identification of the efficiency frontier, DEA allows to identify not only the most efficient units but also their distance from the inefficient ones.
- DEA can handle multiple inputs and outputs with independent production function specification.
- Some methods, like TOPSIS, use indicators for which the input-output relationship may not be immediate, while DEA results are easily understood.
- PROMETHEE requires obtaining and considering a distribution function, while DEA does not.
- SFA is based on an assumption made a priori for the production function, which may be not appropriate for every port, while DEA provides great flexibility.
- PCA-DEA allows considering the correlation between variables and generates non-discrete positive principal components, thus improving the strength of DEA [19].
- DEA helps decision-making units to remove other sources of inefficiency from the observations.
- DEA allows maximizing profits or minimizing resources by using an input- or an output-oriented approach.
- However, DEA can be also subject to some weaknesses, such as:
- DEA can be sensitive to the presence of an outlying observation that could determine an erroneous efficiency frontier used to measure inefficient DMUs.
- DEA results are sensitive to the choice selection of input and output variables: the number of efficient DMUs on the frontier increases with the number of input and output variables.
- DEA does not consider the correlation between the chosen variables.

Table 1. Most common methods applied to container port performance.

Method	Strengths	Weaknesses	First author	Year	Reference
AHP	Easy to use. Scalable	Possible inconsistencies in the classification criteria. Problems of interdependence between criteria and alternatives	Ismail	2018	[10]
ELECTRE III	Considers uncertainty and vagueness	Not useful for classification purposes. The lowest performance based on certain criteria is not identifiable. Results can be difficult to interpret	Gao	2018	[11]
PROMETHEE	Easy to use. Eliminates scale effects among alternatives	Requires the assignment of weights but does not provide a clear methodology to assign values	Kim	2012	[12]
TOPSIS	Easy to use. Number of steps does not depend on the size of the problem	Does not consider attributes correlation. Difficult to weight attributes	Celik	2009	[13]
HHI	Easy to use. It is not influenced by arbitrary factors	Depends on the size of the sample	Elbayoumi	2016	[14]
SFA	Recognizes the fact that external factors can influence production	Based on an assumption made a priori for the production function	López-Bermúdez	2019	[15]

(continued)

Table 1. (*continued*)

Method	Strengths	Weaknesses	First author	Year	Reference
DEA	Quantifies efficiency. Evaluate the efficiency of alternatives against each other. Can manage multiple inputs and outputs	Assumes that all inputs and outputs are exactly known. Is sensitive to the number of variable measurements. Does not evaluate the correlation between variables	Iyer	2021	[16]
CLUSTERING	Easy to use. Identifies homogeneous groups	Not useful for classification purposes. Results can be difficult to interpret	Fancello Serra	2014 2020	[8] [1]
PCA-DEA	Considers the correlation between variables. Improves the strength of DEA model	Assumes that all inputs and outputs are exactly known. Is sensitive to the number of variable measurements	Venkatasubbaiah Perico	2018 2020	[17] [18]

In order to increase the DEA strength and consider the correlation between variables, DEA has been used together with PCA in different fields, but only rarely it has been applied to container port efficiency. Among the others, Venkatasubbaiah et al. [17] evaluated and analyzed the performance of 28 container terminals in south East Asia using a DEA-PCA hybrid method. The hybrid method was performed implementing PCA to the cross-efficiency matrix obtained through DEA and was used to determine the ultimate cross-efficiency of each DMU. Périco and da Silva [18] applied a hybrid method of BCC-DEA with PCA to evaluate performance of the 24 largest ports in Brazil. They used PCA as a validation method among the chosen variables but applied PCA-DEA considering the initial proposal of variables, as the commonalities of the variables did not allow excluding any. Almost all the documents analyzed apply DEA as a benchmarking technique to compare ports in a geographic area. This paper proposes a decision support tool based on DEA and PCA to define which elements may have the greatest influence on the efficiency of ports in the Mediterranean area.

3 Methodology

3.1 Data Envelopment Analysis

DEA is a performance measurement technique, formulated by Farrell in 1957, that can be used for evaluating the relative efficiency of Decision-Making Units (DMUs). In this application, Mediterranean container ports are identified as the DMUs forming the sample. DEA method is based on a non-parametric approach that leads to the definition of a flexible efficient frontier. The efficiency of each DMU is measured comparing the ratio of outputs (production) to inputs (resources), subject to the condition that the same ratio for all DMUs must be less than or equal to one. The two basic DEA models are:

- the **CCR model** [20], which produces an objective evaluation of efficiency assuming constant returns to scale (CRS);
- the **BCC model** [21], which considers variable returns to scale (VRS) and estimates the pure technical efficiency of the DMUs.

In the first phase of the study, DEA is applied using both CCR and BCC models. Their formulation can be input- or output-oriented. The first approach examines if a DMU wastes inputs in the production phase, while the latter if the outputs are maximized.

CCR Model. The CCR model requires all inputs and outputs to be positive. It is based on CRS, in which all inputs and outputs are driven back to a single virtual input and a single virtual output. Weights must be non-negative and that make the ratio for DMUs greater than 1.

- *Input-oriented*

The goal of the input-oriented model is to verify the efficiency conditions through the minimization of a real variable θ, as described below:

$$min_{(\theta,\lambda)}\theta$$

s.t.

$$\theta x_o - \lambda X \geq 0$$

$$\lambda Y \geq y_o$$

$$\lambda \geq 0$$

where $\lambda = (\lambda_1, \ldots, \lambda_n)^T$ is a transposed non-negative vector of variables.

- Output-oriented

The purpose of the output-oriented model, instead, is to verify the efficiency conditions through the maximization of a real variable τ.

$$max_{(\tau,\mu)}\tau$$

s.t.

$$x_o - \mu X \geq 0$$

$$\tau y_o - \mu Y \leq 0$$

$$\mu \geq 0$$

where $\mu = \lambda\tau$ and $\tau = 1/\theta$.

The input-oriented approach evaluates efficiency in terms of the best reduction of inputs given an observed level of output, while the output-oriented one assesses competitiveness in terms of commercial potential.

BCC Model. The BCC model represents an extension of the CCR model. Its efficient frontier is not a straight line through the origin, as in the case of the CCR model, but a convex function, due to variable returns to scale. The modification is applied, both in CCR and in BCC model, by adding a convexity constraint to the model:

$$e\lambda = 1,$$

where e is a unit row vector.

BCC model estimates the pure technical efficiency of the DMUs. The complexity of the case with multiple inputs or outputs lies in the weighting of the quantitative variables by the calculation of efficiency, as it deals with dimensionally different variables. DEA allows using variable weights obtained from the observations and chosen to maximize the efficiency indices of each DMU relative to any other DMU present in the sample. To be considered optimal, the weights must be non-negative, and the relative efficiency index must be between zero and one.

3.2 Principal Component Analysis

In a second phase of the study, with a view to later applying the DEA by considering several input variables together, PCA is applied to identify the input variables that have the greatest weight in the description of the phenomenon under study. PCA is typically used to reduce the dimensionality of a data set by transforming the set of variables into a smaller one (the so-called principal components - PCs) that still contains most of the information in the original set. The first PC is obtained by projecting the data geometrically on the axis that produces the smallest total projection error, given by the perpendicular distance between the data and their projection, and the greatest variance.

The subsequent PCs are selected similarly, but with the additional requirement of no correlation with the previous PCs. The PCs are ranked by their variances in descending order: the first PC is the one that describes the largest share of variance in the sample. Each PC is expressed as an uncorrelated linear combination of input and output variable, which are multiplied by the corresponding eigenvectors. Each eigenvector, associated with a variable, represents the weight of that variable in determining the i-th PC. The i-th PC will be more influenced by the variables with higher eigenvectors in absolute value. In this study, PCA is used to rank the variables from the most influential to the least influential from a statistical point of view.

4 Data Description

This study considers the 35 main Mediterranean container ports (Fig. 1) in terms of TEUs handled in the last decade. In 2019, the 35 ports, as a whole, handled nearly 60M TEUs.

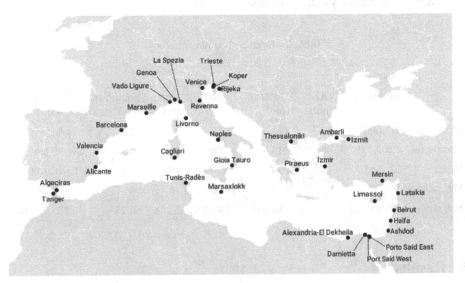

Fig. 1. Geographical location of the 35 container ports (Source: Authors)

The efficiency of a container port may depend on its physical-organizational characteristics and on the correct use of land, infrastructures and equipment. As we have seen previously, DEA requires the definition of input and output variables. Following some literature hints, the input variables can be differentiated in three macro-groups:

• Capital inputs: these variables describe the physical port characteristics, such as yard area, terminal area, storage area, berth length, number of berths, berth depth and others. If well managed, they can represent the effective resources for port activity [4, 6, 17].

- Non-capital inputs: such as labour, number of cranes, number of pieces of equipment, environment, costs, etc. [22, 23].
- Geographic inputs: the port position among global trades is a potential performance factor for container ports as well as their proximity to internal markets and transport networks [24, 25].

The output variables should represent the port production. Therefore, the most used indicator is the annual container throughput, measured in TEUs. In this study, the choice of the input variables was based on the literature reviews about DEA studies on port efficiency provided by Schøyen and Odeck [26], Julien et al. [27], Iyer and Nanyam [16] and Fancello et al. [28]. In detail, three capital inputs, Yard Area (Yard) - m^2, Berth Length (Berth) - m, Maximum Depth (Depth) - m, two non-capital inputs, no. of Quay Cranes (QC), no. of Yard Equipment (Equipment), and one geographic input (Distance) measuring the distance (nm) between each port and the ideal Suez-Gibraltar axis, were chosen as input variables. Port data were collected from official websites of the ports and are updated to 2019. Container throughput in 2019, expressed in terms of TEUs, was identified as the only output variable (Table 2).

Table 2. Input and output variables.

	Inputs						Output
	Yard [m^2]	QC (no.)	Distance [nm]	Berth [m]	Depth [m]	Equipment (no.)	Throughput (TEU)
Minimum	111,000	2	1	515	10	17	54,542
Maximum	1,807,739	40	745	4,790	20	346	5,650,000
Mean	673,562	16	299	1,927	15	130	1,698,748
Median	500,000	14	260	1,520	16	98	1,229,081
Std. dev.	452,487.149	10.854	240.047	1236.302	2.218	90.247	1,575,066.848

5 Results

The application was performed using input- and output-oriented approaches and both CCR and BCC methods. 12 combinations were tested, of which 6 applying an input-oriented approach (IO) and 6 an output-oriented one (OO). Each combination was taken out considering one output variable, fixed for all the combinations (Throughput 2019) and one input variable, changed each time, according to Table 3.

Table 4 provides the scores for each DMU, calculated by applying both CCR and BCC methods using an input-oriented approach. In the case of the CCR model, for each test, only one DMU reaches efficiency, totalizing a unitary score (Algeciras for test 1 and 2; Valencia for test 3 and 4; Haifa for test 5; Port Said East for test 6). In the case of the BCC model instead, more DMUs totalize a score equal to 1.000 in each combination tested. The ports that achieve efficiency are Piraeus (6 times), Algeciras (5), Valencia

Table 3. Combinations of input and output variables.

	Inputs:					
	QC	Berth	Yard	Depth	Equipment	Distance
Output:	Test 1, IO	Test 2, IO	Test 3, IO	Test 4, IO	Test 5, IO	Test 6, IO
Throughput 2019	Test 1, OO	Test 2, OO	Test 3, OO	Test 4, OO	Test 5, OO	Test 6, OO

(4), Port Said East (3), Alicante (2), Haifa (2), Koper (2), Marsaxlokk (1), Rijeka (1), Tanger (1), Thessaloniki (1) and Tunis (1). Algeciras is the best performing port in the combinations that uses QC (test 1) or Berth (test 2) as the input variable while Valencia is the best one when Yard (test 3) or Depth (test 4) variable is considered. The two ports obtain efficiency using both methods.

Table 4. CCR and BCC results: Input-Oriented approach (IO).

DMUs	Test 1		Test 2		Test 3		Test 4		Test 5		Test 6	
	CCR	BCC	CCR	BCC	CCR	BCC	CCR	BCC	CCR	BCC	CCR	BCC
Alexandria.-El Dekheila	0.684	0.736	0.643	0.675	0.572	0.583	0.436	0.902	0.210	0.246	0.011	0.020
Algeciras	**1.000**	**1.000**	**1.000**	**1.000**	0.946	0.946	0.889	0.919	0.461	0.930	0.400	**1.000**
Alicante	0.450	**1.000**	0.185	**1.000**	0.204	0.740	0.038	0.679	0.080	0.415	0.001	0.010
Ambarli	0.431	0.443	0.381	0.388	0.584	0.589	0.588	0.824	0.195	0.276	0.002	0.002
Ashdod	0.527	0.586	0.440	0.471	0.502	0.516	0.282	0.718	0.391	0.391	0.004	0.008
Barcelona	0.605	0.618	0.534	0.542	0.464	0.467	0.630	0.844	0.240	0.353	0.004	0.005
Beirut	0.405	0.459	0.622	0.675	0.512	0.530	0.233	0.659	0.174	0.185	0.002	0.004
Cagliari	0.114	0.286	0.055	0.339	0.068	0.278	0.030	0.594	0.041	0.239	0.001	0.014
Damietta	0.563	0.653	0.410	0.452	0.241	0.251	0.223	0.709	0.137	0.157	0.026	0.077
Genoa	0.397	0.413	0.306	0.314	0.261	0.264	0.549	0.861	0.188	0.255	0.002	0.002
Gioia Tauro	0.579	0.604	0.414	0.426	0.283	0.286	0.438	0.709	0.371	0.497	0.003	0.004
Haifa	0.410	0.456	0.470	0.503	0.502	0.516	0.282	0.718	**1.000**	**1.000**	0.003	0.006
Izmir	0.639	0.839	0.321	0.533	0.472	0.621	0.111	0.586	0.172	0.274	0.000	0.002
Izmit	0.431	0.467	0.378	0.398	0.427	0.436	0.290	0.626	0.459	0.523	0.001	0.002
Koper	0.562	0.665	0.896	**1.000**	0.955	**1.000**	0.207	0.723	0.109	0.132	0.000	0.001
La Spezia	0.524	0.578	0.597	0.636	0.918	0.943	0.321	0.776	0.338	0.354	0.001	0.003
Latakia	0.286	0.463	0.223	0.655	0.090	0.174	0.076	0.719	0.241	0.654	0.000	0.003
Limassol	0.411	0.621	0.271	0.672	0.206	0.353	0.076	0.603	0.075	0.170	0.001	0.005
Livorno	0.320	0.394	0.230	0.303	0.296	0.339	0.190	0.787	0.224	0.303	0.001	0.003
Marsaxlokk	0.717	0.744	0.698	0.714	0.728	0.735	0.500	0.767	0.222	0.304	0.850	**1.000**
Marseille	0.479	0.530	0.241	0.258	0.156	0.160	0.267	0.659	0.312	0.321	0.001	0.003

(continued)

Table 4. (*continued*)

DMUs	Test 1		Test 2		Test 3		Test 4		Test 5		Test 6	
	CCR	BCC	CCR	BCC	CCR	BCC	CCR	BCC	CCR	BCC	CCR	BCC
Mersin	0.730	0.781	0.727	0.759	0.527	0.536	0.384	0.754	0.145	0.175	0.002	0.003
Naples	0.327	0.417	0.326	0.488	0.611	0.754	0.152	0.720	0.061	0.091	0.001	0.004
Piraeus	0.764	**1.000**	0.817	**1.000**	0.921	**1.000**	0.905	**1.000**	0.438	**1.000**	0.007	**1.000**
Port Said East	0.804	0.824	0.742	0.754	0.478	0.481	0.606	0.833	0.701	**1.000**	**1.000**	**1.000**
Port Said West	0.348	0.447	0.387	0.595	0.207	0.260	0.138	0.670	0.100	0.151	0.052	0.250
Ravenna	0.230	0.448	0.181	0.776	0.156	0.444	0.059	0.826	0.064	0.258	0.000	0.001
Rijeka	0.402	0.670	0.270	0.842	0.493	**1.000**	0.067	0.671	0.218	0.630	0.000	0.001
Tanger	0.817	0.819	0.957	0.959	0.615	0.615	0.833	0.893	0.548	**1.000**	0.150	0.350
Thessaloniki	0.592	0.851	0.454	0.988	0.317	0.497	0.117	0.811	0.509	**1.000**	0.000	0.002
Trieste	0.595	0.732	0.571	0.751	0.354	0.405	0.137	0.569	0.293	0.396	0.000	0.001
Tunis	0.301	0.516	0.141	0.466	0.108	0.234	0.094	**1.000**	0.250	0.773	0.001	0.017
Vado Ligure	0.041	0.286	0.026	0.444	0.027	0.306	0.010	0.559	0.025	0.405	0.000	0.003
Valencia	0.717	0.856	0.639	0.729	**1.000**	**1.000**	**1.000**	**1.000**	0.303	0.662	0.010	0.933
Venice	0.391	0.517	0.173	0.292	0.250	0.332	0.161	0.865	0.117	0.189	0.000	0.001

Similarly to Table 4, Table 5 illustrates the results of both CCR and BCC models when an output-oriented approach is used. Apart from the port of Marsaxlokk, all the other ports that achieve efficiency using the input-oriented approach also achieve efficiency when the output-oriented approach is used.

Table 5. CCR and BCC results: Output-Oriented approach (OO).

DMUs	Test 1		Test 2		Test 3		Test 4		Test 5		Test 6	
	CCR	BCC	CCR	BCC	CCR	BCC	CCR	BCC	CCR	BCC	CCR	BCC
Alexandria.-El Dekheila	0.684	0.713	0.643	0.658	0.572	0.576	0.436	0.675	0.210	0.381	0.011	0.348
Algeciras	**1.000**	**1.000**	**1.000**	**1.000**	0.946	0.946	0.889	0.927	0.461	0.970	0.400	**1.000**
Alicante	0.450	**1.000**	0.185	**1.000**	0.204	0.253	0.038	0.051	0.080	0.094	0.001	0.032
Ambarli	0.431	0.554	0.381	0.550	0.584	0.585	0.588	0.609	0.195	0.550	0.002	0.550
Ashdod	0.527	0.550	0.440	0.447	0.502	0.507	0.282	0.318	0.391	0.530	0.004	0.261
Barcelona	0.605	0.638	0.534	0.611	0.464	0.588	0.630	0.652	0.240	0.588	0.004	0.588
Beirut	0.405	0.418	0.622	0.651	0.512	0.519	0.233	0.241	0.174	0.296	0.002	0.220
Cagliari	0.114	0.130	0.055	0.057	0.068	0.069	0.030	0.032	0.041	0.056	0.001	0.029
Damietta	0.563	0.609	0.410	0.421	0.241	0.241	0.223	0.263	0.137	0.241	0.026	0.208

(*continued*)

Table 5. (*continued*)

DMUs	Test 1		Test 2		Test 3		Test 4		Test 5		Test 6	
	CCR	BCC	CCR	BCC	CCR	BCC	CCR	BCC	CCR	BCC	CCR	BCC
Genoa	0.397	0.481	0.306	0.466	0.261	0.466	0.549	0.648	0.188	0.466	0.002	0.466
Gioia Tauro	0.579	0.583	0.414	0.467	0.283	0.447	0.438	0.457	0.371	0.623	0.003	0.448
Haifa	0.410	0.419	0.470	0.479	0.502	0.507	0.282	0.318	**1.000**	**1.000**	0.003	0.257
Izmir	0.639	0.792	0.321	0.337	0.472	0.488	0.111	0.111	0.172	0.232	0.000	0.107
Izmit	0.431	0.436	0.378	0.380	0.427	0.429	0.290	0.308	0.459	0.629	0.001	0.304
Koper	0.562	0.616	0.896	**1.000**	0.955	**1.000**	0.207	0.258	0.109	0.199	0.000	0.170
La Spezia	0.524	0.543	0.597	0.615	0.918	0.941	0.321	0.401	0.338	0.479	0.001	0.264
Latakia	0.286	0.338	0.223	0.240	0.090	0.090	0.076	0.112	0.241	0.249	0.000	0.058
Limassol	0.411	0.510	0.271	0.292	0.206	0.210	0.076	0.082	0.075	0.113	0.001	0.071
Livorno	0.320	0.336	0.230	0.233	0.296	0.299	0.190	0.294	0.224	0.303	0.001	0.140
Marsaxlokk	0.717	0.728	0.698	0.704	0.728	0.731	0.500	0.500	0.222	0.493	0.850	0.850
Marseille	0.479	0.494	0.241	0.270	0.156	0.257	0.267	0.267	0.312	0.449	0.001	0.257
Mersin	0.730	0.762	0.727	0.746	0.527	0.529	0.384	0.420	0.145	0.343	0.002	0.343
Naples	0.327	0.349	0.326	0.340	0.611	0.636	0.152	0.202	0.061	0.129	0.001	0.121
Piraeus	0.764	**1.000**	0.817	**1.000**	0.921	**1.000**	0.905	**1.000**	0.438	**1.000**	0.007	**1.000**
Port Said East	0.804	0.814	0.742	0.746	0.478	0.566	0.606	0.628	0.701	**1.000**	**1.000**	**1.000**
Port Said West	0.348	0.376	0.387	0.409	0.207	0.208	0.138	0.162	0.100	0.166	0.052	0.129
Ravenna	0.230	0.285	0.181	0.199	0.156	0.161	0.059	0.131	0.064	0.086	0.000	0.039
Rijeka	0.402	0.538	0.270	0.300	0.493	**1.000**	0.067	0.087	0.218	0.218	0.000	0.054
Tanger	0.817	0.906	0.957	0.958	0.615	0.850	0.833	0.869	0.548	**1.000**	0.150	0.935
Thessaloniki	0.592	0.792	0.454	0.878	0.317	0.326	0.117	0.224	0.509	**1.000**	0.000	0.079
Trieste	0.595	0.680	0.571	0.617	0.354	0.359	0.137	0.143	0.293	0.369	0.000	0.140
Tunis	0.301	0.373	0.141	0.147	0.108	0.109	0.094	**1.000**	0.250	0.309	0.001	0.054
Vado Ligure	0.041	0.047	0.026	0.027	0.027	0.027	0.010	0.010	0.025	0.030	0.000	0.010
Valencia	0.717	0.963	0.639	0.963	**1.000**	**1.000**	**1.000**	**1.000**	0.303	0.963	0.010	0.996
Venice	0.391	0.437	0.173	0.175	0.250	0.253	0.161	0.357	0.117	0.175	0.000	0.105

Table 6 shows mean values of the IO and OO scores, both for CCR and BCC methods. As regard to the CCR method, the highest average scores are obtained in Test 1, Test 2 and Test 3, using both the IO and OO approach, while, in the case of the BCC, the highest average scores are obtained in Test 1, Test 2 and Test 4 (only for the IO approach). In both methods, the Distance variable assumes very low average values, which indicate that the DMUs are not very efficient with respect to this input variable. While the BCC model produces different results when using input- and output- oriented approaches, the CCR model produces more robust results both in the case of an input or output approach, thus resulting more suitable to evaluate the effectiveness of container ports.

Table 6. Mean values of IO and OO scores, both CCR and BCC methods.

	Test 1		Test 2		Test 3		Test 4		Test 5		Test 6	
	CCR	BCC	CCR	BCC	CCR	BCC	CCR	BCC	CCR	BCC	CCR	BCC
Mean IO	0.503	0.621	0.449	0.623	0.441	0.531	0.323	0.759	0.269	0.449	0.072	0.164
Mean OO	0.503	0.578	0.449	0.525	0.441	0.491	0.323	0.393	0.269	0.449	0.072	0.332

To validate the CCR results, which identify the QC (Test 1), Berth (Test 2) and Yard (Test 3) variables as those that most influence the evaluation of efficiency, it was decided to apply the PCA to verify that the variables identified are the most representative. The eigenvector components are considered as weights of the variables. To do this, six principal components were identified (Table 7).

Table 7. Eigen analysis of the Correlation Matrix.

PCs	PC1	PC2	PC3	PC4	PC5	PC6
Eigenvalue	36.661	0.9611	0.6673	0.5086	0.1516	0.0453
Proportion	0.611	0.160	0.111	0.085	0.025	0.008
Cumulative	0.611	0.771	0.882	0.967	0.992	1.000

The first principal component (PC1) is chosen to minimize the perpendicular distance between the variables and their projection. For this reason, PC1 reaches the greatest eigenvalue and represents 61% of the sample variability. The cumulative value is the cumulative proportion of the sample variability given by consecutive PCs. PC2 cumulative, obtained from the sum of PC1 and PC2 proportion, reaches 0.771, which means having a representativeness of 77% of the sample variability. The eigenvector's components of the PC1 (Table 8) represent the weight of each corresponding variable in determining the PC1. The variables that are correlated the most with PC1 are QC (0.499), Berth (0.492), Yard (0.444) and Equipment (0.417). By increasing the values of QC, Berth, Yard, Equipment and Depth, PC1 enhances its value. PC1 is negatively correlated with Distance variable (−0.149).

Table 8. Principal component PC1 eigenvector.

Variable	QC	Berth	Yard	Equip	Depth	Distance
PC1	0.499	0.492	0.444	0.417	0.340	−0.149

The variables with higher eigenvector's components in absolute value are QC, Berth, and Yard, thus confirming that they are the most significant in the problem at hand.

6 Conclusions

This study applied DEA and PCA for evaluating the factors that most affect the efficiency of 35 major Mediterranean container ports. In a first step, port productivity was assessed on the basis of 12 tests, which differ in the method applied (CCR or BCC), in the approach used (input- or output- oriented approach) and in the input variable used (one variable selected among QC, Berth, Yard, Equipment, Depth, or Distance).

Among the sample, some ports are more affected than others by the method or the approach applied. Few ports, such as Piraeus, are fully efficient - or close to efficiency - in a large number of tests, demonstrating that their capital and non-capital input variables are correctly sized in relation to demand. Other ports, such as Haifa, achieve efficiency only respect to one variable, resulting oversized respect to the others. Furthermore, other ports (e.g. Alicante) achieve high efficiency scores only applying the BCC method, thus comparing them with smaller ports.

In the tests performed by entering QC or Berth or Yard as the input variable, the average score settles around 0.5. This means that, with respect to these parameters, the average efficiency of the sample as a whole is about 50%.

The results obtained using Depth or Equipment as input variables are more sensitive to the approach and to the applied method. In the combinations having Distance as the input variable, the mean scores show that ports are very far from the efficient frontier. This could mean either that the ports are very far from the main route or that the Distance variable is not significant for the assessment of port efficiency. To confirm these results, the PCA was applied. The variables QC, Bert and Yard are the ones characterized by the highest eigenvector's components in absolute value: they can be identified as the most representative of the efficiency of Mediterranean container ports.

The proposed analysis can help highlight the potential success factors for Mediterranean container ports, thus providing decision-makers with useful insights for the implementation of future policies and management strategies aimed at strengthening the Mediterranean port context.

Future studies will have to investigate the correlation of QC, Berth and Yard variables, which are resulted to be the most significant in this study, and apply the DEA-CCR to the combination of two or more input variables. Furthermore, the role of the distance variable when assessing port efficiency should be further investigated.

References

1. Serra, P., Fancello, G.: Performance assessment of alternative SSS networks by combining KPIs and factor-cluster analysis. Eur. Transp. Res. Rev. **12**(1), 1–24 (2020). https://doi.org/10.1186/s12544-020-00449-z
2. UNCTAD: Review of Maritime Transport 2020 (United Nations publication. Sales No. E.20.II.D.31. New York and Geneva) (2020)
3. Serra, P., Fancello, G.: Use of ICT for more efficient port operations: the experience of the EASYLOG project. In: Gervasi, O., et al. (eds.) ICCSA 2020. LNCS, vol. 12255, pp. 3–14. Springer, Cham (2020). https://doi.org/10.1007/978-3-030-58820-5_1
4. Ghiara, H., Tei, A.: Port activity and technical efficiency: determinants and external factors. Marit. Policy Manag. **48**, 1–14 (2021)

5. Alphaliner Monthly Monitor January. Monthly Monitor (2020). www.alphaliner.com
6. Kalgora, B.: Strategic container ports competitiveness analysis in West Africa using data envelopment analysis (DEA) model. Open J. Bus. Manag. **7**(02), 680 (2019)
7. Polyzos, S., Niavis, S.: Evaluating port efficiency in the mediterranean. Int. J. Data Anal. Tech. Strat. **7**(5), 84–100 (2013)
8. Fancello, G., Pani, C., Serra, P., Fadda, P.: Port cooperation policies in the mediterranean basin: an experimental approach using cluster analysis. Transp. Res. Procedia **3**, 700–709 (2014)
9. Fancello, G., Carta, M., Serra, P.: Data Envelopment Analysis for the assessment of road safety in urban road networks: a comparative study using CCR and BCC models. Case Stud. Transp. Policy **8**(3), 736–744 (2020)
10. Ismail, A., Elgazzar, S.: Measuring the Egyptian container ports' efficiency: a FUZZY AHP framework. In: 23rd Annual Conference of the Chartered Institute of Logistics and Transport, Logistics Research Network (LRN) 2018
11. Gao, T., Na, S., Dang, X., Zhang, Y.: Study of the competitiveness of Quanzhou port on the belt and road in China based on a fuzzy-AHP and ELECTRE III model. Sustainability **10**(4), 1253 (2018)
12. Kim, D.J.: A comparison of efficiency with productivity criteria for European container ports. Asian J. Shipp. Logist. **28**(2), 183–202 (2012)
13. Celik, M., Cebi, S., Kahraman, C., Er, I.D.: Application of axiomatic design and TOPSIS methodologies under fuzzy environment for proposing competitive strategies on Turkish container ports in maritime transportation network. Expert Syst. Appl. **36**(3), 4541–4557 (2009)
14. Elbayoumi, O., Dawood, A.: Analysis of the competition of ports in the Middle East container ports using HHI. J. Shipp. Ocean Eng. **6**(6) (2016)
15. López-Bermúdez, B., Freire-Seoane, M.J., González-Laxe, F.: Efficiency and productivity of container terminals in Brazilian ports (2008–2017). Utilities Policy **56**, 82–91 (2019)
16. Iyer, K.C., Nanyam, V.N.: Technical efficiency analysis of container terminals in India. Asian J. Shipp. Logist. **37**(1), 61–72 (2021)
17. Venkatasubbaiah, K., Rao, K.N., Rao, M.M., Challa, S.: Performance evaluation and modelling of container terminals. J. Inst. Eng. India Ser. C **99**(1), 87–96 (2017). https://doi.org/10.1007/s40032-017-0410-x
18. Périco, A.E., Ribeiro da Silva, G.: Port performance in Brazil: a case study using data envelopment analysis. Case Stud. Transp. Policy **8**, 31–38 (2020)
19. Chen, Y., Du, J., David Sherman, H., Zhu, J.: DEA model with shared resources and efficiency decomposition. Eur. J. Oper. Res. **207**(1), 339–349 (2010)
20. Charnes, A., Cooper, W.W., Rhodes, E.: Measuring the efficiency of decision making units. Eur. J. Oper. Res. **2**(6), 429–444 (1978)
21. Banker, R.D., Charnes, A., Cooper, W.: Some models for estimating technical and scale inefficiencies in data envelopment analysis. Manag. Sci. **30**(9), 1078–1092 (1984)
22. Tongzon, J.: Efficiency measurement of selected Australian & other international ports using data envelopment analysis. Transp. Res. Part A: Policy Pract. **35**(2), 107–122 (2001)
23. Barros, C., Athanassiou, M.: Efficiency in European sea ports with DEA: evidence from Greece and Portugal. Marit. Econ. Logist. **6**, 122–140 (2004)
24. Caldeirinha, V.R., Felicio, J.A., Coelho, J.O.A.N.A.: The influence of characterizing factors on port performance, measured by operational, financial and efficiency indicators. Recent Adv. Environ. Energy Syst. Naval Sci. 58–70 (2009)
25. Liu, Z.: The Comparative Performance of Public and Private Enterprises: The Case of British Ports, The London School of Economics and Political Science and University of Bath (1995)

26. Schøyen, H., Odeck, J.: The technical efficiency of Norwegian container ports: a comparison to some Nordic & UK container ports using data envelopment analysis (DEA). Marit. Econ. Logist. **15**(2), 197–221 (2013)
27. Julien, S.A., Cowie, J., Monios, J.: Efficiency, productivity and returns to scale in ports: a comparison of data envelopment analysis and econometric estimation with application to Caribbean Small Island developing states. Marit. Econ. Logist. **22**, 1–26 (2018)
28. Fancello, G., Serra, P., Aramu, V., Vitiello, D.M.: Evaluating the efficiency of Mediterranean container ports using data envelopment analysis. Compet. Regul. Netw. Ind. (2021). https://doi.org/10.1177/17835917211047837

Port Clusters as an Opportunity for Optimizing Small-Scale LNG Distribution Chains: An Application to the Mediterranean Case

Patrizia Serra[1](✉) ⓘ, Simona Mancini[2], Gianfranco Fancello[1] ⓘ, Federico Sollai[3], and Paolo Fadda[1] ⓘ

[1] DICAAR – Department of Civil and Environmental Engineering and Architecture, University of Cagliari, 09123 Cagliari, Italy
pserra@unica.it
[2] University of Palermo, Palermo, Italy
[3] University of Cagliari, 09123 Cagliari, Italy

Abstract. Small-scale LNG logistics chains have become more important for delivering LNG via shipping from large supply terminals to customers via satellite terminals. An ideal application of small-scale LNG logistics chains is in the Mediterranean basin, where the maximum distance between two ports is always less than two thousand miles. Focusing on a Tyrrhenian application case, this study develops a modeling tool capable of defining the optimal configuration for a small-scale LNG distribution network serving a set of Tyrrhenian ports organized as a cluster. The aim is to minimize total network costs, including both port entry costs and travel costs. The problem is modelled as a Vehicle Routing Problem with Draft Limits and Heterogeneous Fleet (VRPDLHF). Different network configurations are being tested to explore the transportation cost savings that could result from systemic and integrated management of LNG supply if ports were organized in a cluster. Computational results show that, by acting as an organized cluster, LNG port depots can potentially leverage their increased bargaining power during negotiations to seek reasonable import prices that can benefit from reduced transportation costs and guaranteed volume of LNG to purchase.

Keywords: Small-scale LNG · Draft limits · Vehicle routing problem · Port coalition

1 Introduction

In the last decades, many nations have faced major challenges related to climate change and environmental preservation. As part of these challenges, many countries have started making substantial efforts to find and adopt cleaner energy solutions [1]. In this regard, natural gas is increasingly in demand as an energy source due to its better environmental performance than conventional energy alternatives.

Natural gas can be traded in two ways: through pipelines or as LNG (Liquefied Natural Gas). Before the development of LNG technology, natural gas transportation

O. Gervasi et al. (Eds.): ICCSA 2022 Workshops, LNCS 13381, pp. 140–155, 2022.
https://doi.org/10.1007/978-3-031-10548-7_11

was limited to gas pipelines [2] with understandable geographic constraints as pipelines are fixed in direction of flow and physically located. The pipeline model typically serves regional markets that involve neighboring countries and are not integrated with the international market. Conversely, the ability to convert natural gas into LNG has made LNG a global commodity that is easily transportable by sea using dedicated ships, thus providing consumers with access to vast natural gas resources around the world and making the world gas market less sensitive to the distance between trading partners [3].

LNG is the cleanest fossil fuel available on a large scale today. In July 2021, the European Commission (EC) presented an ambitious proposal, covering all sectors and all modes of transport, to reduce the EU's carbon emissions by 55% by 2030. For maritime transport, the EC wants to see renewable and low-carbon fuels make up around 6–9% of the bunker fuel mix by 2030 and 86–88% by 2050 [4]. According to the EC, this should be achieved with a combination of electrification, biofuels and other renewable and reduced-carbon fuels, including LNG as a transition fuel.

Traditionally, the LNG supply chains allow supplying large volumes of gas over large distances for which the pipeline delivery model is not viable. More recently, small-scale LNG logistic chains have become more important to deliver LNG by maritime transportation from large supply terminals to customers through satellite terminals [5]. Small-scale LNG supply chains have specific features:

- demands are distributed over short distances (up to few thousand miles)
- ships capacities range from some thousand m^3 up to 50,000 m^3
- ship loads can be split on consecutive receiving ports
- receiving terminals are equipped with storage tanks to be refilled once or a few times a month.

An ideal application of small-scale LNG logistic chains is in the Mediterranean basin, where the maximum distance between two ports is always less than two thousand miles. The ports that make up a small-scale LNG network play a dual role, both as points of use and storage of LNG, and as LNG gateways to the inland areas (which is particularly relevant for areas without methane distribution networks).

Focusing on a Mediterranean application case, this study develops a modeling tool able to define the optimal configuration for a small-scale LNG distribution network serving a set of Tyrrhenian ports.

The proposed modeling tool identifies an optimal small-scale LNG network able to efficiently connect a potential supply port to a set of receiving ports while ensuring minimum transport costs and meeting operational constraints related to draft limits. The latter can prevent ships from entering some ports when they are fully loaded, thus imposing constraints on the sequence of ports visited. Each receiving port is characterized by a demand that must be met in the planning horizon. LNG carriers operating on the network can be chosen from a heterogeneous fleet characterized by different capacities. The problem to be faced consists in selecting how many ships of each type to involve, and providing the route plan for each ship, in compliance with draft constraints. The aim is to minimize total network costs including both port entry costs and travel costs (different for each ship category). The problem is modeled as a Vehicle Routing Problem with Draft Limits and Heterogeneous Fleet (VRPDLHF). Several network configurations are being tested to explore the transport cost savings that could result from systemic and integrated management of LNG supply if ports were organized in coalition. The objective of the application is twofold:

1. define, through the application of an analytical model of network optimization developed ad hoc, the optimal configuration of the distribution network that ensures the lowest transport costs of LNG from a set of alternative supply terminals.
2. explore the potential bargaining margin on the purchase price of LNG that would derive from the reduction of transport costs following an integrated management of the supply system by sea.

The paper is organized as follows. Section 2 introduces the rationale behind the study. Section 3 describes the LNG distribution problem at hand while Sect. 4 proposes its mathematical formalization. Section 5 presents the case study and application data. Section 6 presents the application and its results. Section 7 concludes the paper.

2 The Reference Context

The cost of shipping LNG has always been an important element to consider in the LNG trade [6] and is believed to have a significant impact not only on LNG trade but also on the commercial scale [7]. For a typical LNG value chain, shipping costs are estimated to represent 20 to 30% of the total LNG cost [8]. Importers and exporters generally negotiate to fix the price of the LNG to be included in the commercial contract. LNG contract prices may vary depending on whether LNG is priced Ex-ship or Free-On-Board - FOB [9]. The former reflects downstream prices minus gasification and other costs of the destination terminal and shipping while the latter considers the prices of LNG delivered to the tanker at the export terminal, in this case shipping and insurance are the buyer's responsibility. FOB contracts offer buyers greater flexibility with regards to shipping costs and the ability to take advantage of profit opportunities through arbitrage. Contracts nowadays are increasingly of the FOB type and, together with the greater level of integration of the LNG market [3], they are increasing the opportunity for price arbitrage by decreasing transport costs. Indeed, although LNG is now widely considered a global commodity, there is no clear trend towards a single and uniform gas price [10]. The significant development of the LNG market has inevitably led to a corresponding growth in the level of competition among LNG exporters, which has shifted from regional to global competition [10]. Furthermore, the growing demand for LNG is forcing buyers to seek more LNG suppliers, thus encouraging more competitive relationships between exporters.

While in the past LNG was mainly traded on long-term contracts with a small number of exporters supplying specific regional markets, now a larger share of the volumes is traded on short-term contracts, thus further contributing to the liquidity of the LNG market [11]. The short-term market has two main peculiarities [12]:

– sellers can divert the cargo to alternative buyers (flexibility of supply).

– buyers can look for gas from alternative suppliers (quick response to gas demand).

Given this competitive framework, this study investigates the extent to which the transport cost of LNG can be minimized when ports manage their LNG supply as a coalition rather than individually [13].

However, the economic factor is not the only factor at play. The environmental issue also plays an important role in the management of energy supply and can affect the attractiveness of the transport alternative, as well as the energy source itself. LNG is now extensively recognized as the perfect bridge fuel to a world that uses 100% sustainable energy sometime after 2050 [10]. As for Europe, several factors including, among others, the progressive limitation on CO_2 emissions and obstacles to the development of renewable energy sources, seem to force the EU into an increasing dependence on natural gas. Europe is looking for huge imports of natural gas (in the form of LNG) from overseas and clear and effective policies should be developed to support market growth and market liquidity. In recent years, the EU market has been characterized by a continuous decline in local gas production and the continued diversification of gas imports.

In accordance with the "EU strategy on LNG - COM 2016/49" [14], and the international commitments made at the Paris climate conference, this study proposes a new management strategy for LNG distribution in the Tyrrhenian area that can support the implementation of the European recommendations, and at the same time assisting the areas characterized by limited or absent methanisation networks.

3 Problem Description

The LNG distribution problem under consideration is a routing problem with draft constraints in which a series of ports must be visited by LNG carriers with different capacities and characteristics. Each port is characterized by a demand that must be served within the reference time horizon and by a draft limit which represents the maximum draft with which a ship can safely access the port. Draft limits can prevent ships from entering some ports when fully loaded, thus imposing constraints on the sequence of ports visited.

The required draft of a ship may depend on several factors that determine the minimum depth of water that the ship can navigate safely. Among the most influential factors we can mention the depth of the water, the tide at a particular moment (of particular importance for some ports), and the load on board. The latter varies according to the sequence of ports visited on the route and can, therefore, impose restrictions on the sequence of visits, as well as restrictions on the ports that can be visited within the same route. If the draft of a ship, when approaching a port, is greater than the draft limit allowed by the port, the ship cannot enter it. The same ship will be able to access that port only after having unloaded part of its cargo in other ports and having reduced the draft to a limit that allows safe access. This also implies that some ports with relatively shallow water depths may still be able to accommodate large ships if they occupy a position within the port sequence visit that allows for low loads.

The fleet is made up of different vessels, each characterized in terms of carrying capacity, port costs, unit transport costs and draft values when empty and fully loaded.

The actual draft of a ship at a given time is calculated as the sum of the draft of the empty ship plus a linear function of the load on board at that time. The objective of the problem is to define the optimal configuration of the distribution network that minimizes the total cost of transport over the entire network.

Regarding the related literature, it is possible to find some studies that address the same vehicle routing problem with draft limits investigated in this study, albeit with some differences. Among the closest works we can mention the studies by [15, 16]. In these works, the authors deal with fleet sizing for a maritime routing problem with draft limits but consider a fixed draft for each category of vessels, which does not vary with the percentage of load on the ship. The problem faced has an impact on the fleet sizing but does not affect the sequence of visits within a route. Other papers dealing explicitly with load-dependent draft variations, address single vehicle problems with no choice of vehicle size [17–22].

Differently from the works cited above, this study considers a heterogeneous fleet of vessels to choose from and integrates the fleet sizing problem with draft limits and load-dependent draft variations.

The next section proposes a mathematical formulation of this problem that can be solved with a mixed integer programming solver.

4   Formalization of the Problem: Vehicle Routing Problem with Heterogeneous Fleet and Draft Limits (VRPHFDL)

This study introduces a Vehicle Routing Problem with Heterogeneous Fleet and Draft Limits (VRPHFDL) in which a set of ports I must be served from a depot. Each port is characterized by a demand to be served Q_i, and a draft limit representing the maximum draft of a ship allowed to enter the port. Draft limits can prevent ships to enter some ports when they are fully loaded, thus imposing constraints on the sequence of ports visited. The fleet is composed by a set of heterogeneous ships, S, each characterized in terms of load capacity, Q_s, fixed costs to enter each port i, r_{is}, unitary sailing costs, c_s, and empty and full load draft values. The actual draft of a ship in a given time is calculated as the draft of the empty ship plus a linear function of the load on board at the time. Based on these data, we can compute, for each ship s and port i, the maximum allowed load, for s, to safely access port i, L_{is}. Sailing time among each pair of ports, t_{ij}, is known. The objective of the problem addressed is to minimize the total network cost given by the sum of fixed costs to access ports and the sailing costs.

In the following we provide the mathematical formulation of the newly introduced problem.

Sets	
$I = [1, I_{max}]$	Set of ports
$I0 = [0, I_{max}]$	Set of ports, included the depot
$S = [1, S_{max}]$	Set of ships
Input data	
Q_s	Ship capacity
q_i	Port demand
L_{is}	Maximum loading for ship s to access port i
t_{ij}	Sailing time between port i and j
c_s	Hourly sailing cost for ship s
r_{is}	Access cost for ship s entering port i
Variables	
X_{ijs}	Binary variables taking value 1 if arc ij is traversed by ship s
Y_{is}	Binary variables taking value 1 if port i is served by ship s
l_{is}	Loading of ship s entering port i
u_i	Position of port i in the sequence of visited ports
p_s	Total load for ship s

$$\min \sum_{i \in I0} \sum_{j \in I0} \sum_{s \in S} c_s t_{ijs} X_{ijs} + \sum_{i \in I} \sum_{s \in S} r_{is} Y_{is} \qquad (1)$$

$$\sum_{s \in S} Y_{is} = 1 \qquad \forall\, i \in I \qquad (2)$$

$$\sum_{i \in I} q_i Y_{is} \leq Q_s \qquad \forall\, s \in S \qquad (3)$$

$$\sum_{i \in I0} X_{ijs} = Y_{is} \qquad \forall\, j \in I \;\; \forall s \in S \qquad (4)$$

$$\sum_{i \in I0} X_{ijs} = \sum_{i \in I0} X_{jis} \qquad \forall\, j \in I \;\; \forall s \in S \qquad (5)$$

$$X_{0js} \leq \sum_{j \in I} Y_{js} \qquad \forall\, s \in S \qquad (6)$$

$$X_{0js} \geq \sum_{j \in I} Y_{js}/|I| \qquad \forall\, s \in S \qquad (7)$$

$$u_j \geq u_i + 1 - |I|(1 - \sum_{s \in S} X_{ijs}) \qquad \forall\, i \in I \ \ \forall\, j \in I0 \tag{8}$$

$$l_{js} \geq l_{is} - q_i - Q_s(1 - X_{ijs}) \qquad \forall\, i \in I \ \ \forall\, j \in I0 \ \ \forall\, s \in S \tag{9}$$

$$l_{is} \leq L_{is} \ \ \forall\, i \in I \ \ \forall\, s \in S \tag{10}$$

$$l_{0s} = \sum_{i \in I} q_i Y_{is} \qquad \forall\, s \in S \tag{11}$$

$$X_{ijs} \in \{0, 1\} \quad \forall\, i \in I0 \ \ \forall\, j \in I0 \ \ \forall\, s \in S \tag{12}$$

$$Y_{is} \in \{0, 1\} \qquad \forall\, i \in I \ \ \forall\, s \in S \tag{13}$$

$$u_i \in N^+ \qquad \forall\, i \in I \tag{14}$$

The objective function is reported in (1). Constraints (2) imply that each port is assigned to a ship. Constraints (3) ensure that the maximum load capacity of a ship is never exceeded. If a port is assigned to a ship s it must be visited by that ship exactly once, as stated by Constraints (4) and (5). Each ship must enter and exit the depot once if at least one port has been assigned to it (Constraints (6) and (7)). The position of a port j in the sequence of visits is tracked by Constraints (8), while Constraints (9) track the load of the ship when entering port j. This load must always be lower than the maximum allowed load, as implied by Constraints (10). The load of a ship exiting the depot is equal to the sum of the demands of the ports assigned to it (Constraints (11)). Finally, Constraints (12)–(14) specify variables domain.

5 Case Study and Data

The study considers a small-scale LNG distribution network in the Tyrrhenian area as an application case. The nodes that make up the network are divided into exporting nodes and buyer nodes. The former are the marine terminals used to supply the network while the latter are the marine terminals that acquire the necessary LNG volumes by sea. In particular, the analyzed network includes seven buyer marine terminals and five exporting marine terminals (Fig. 1), the latter to be considered for application purposes as alternative sources of supply.

The network in question constitutes an ideal application of the small-scale distribution scheme, with maximum distances between nodes of less than 1,800 nautical miles (nm). Table 1 shows the complete matrix of the nautical distances for the O/D pairs that make up the network in question.

Table 2 summarizes the main features of the buyer terminals examined in terms of nominal and effective storage capacity, nominal and operational draft. The infrastructural data used in this application are taken from the TDI Rete GNL and SIGNAL projects (Interreg IT-FR Maritime Program 2014–2020) and refer mainly to project data. As

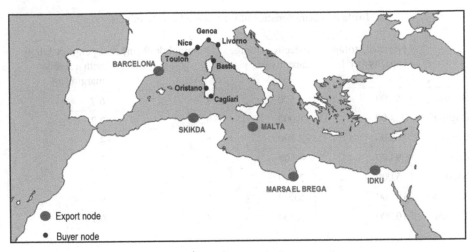

Fig. 1. Analyzed port network. Source: authors

Table 1. Distance matrix [nm].

		Tolone	Genova	Livorno	Bastia	Cagliari	Oristano	Nizza
	Tolone							
	Genova	163						
	Livorno	195	78					
Buyer nodes	Bastia	178	105	61				
	Cagliari	327	349	294	245			
	Oristano	239	304	292	283	142		
	Nizza	82	86	131	126	355	276	
Export nodes	Barcellona	202	352	380	362	370	313	270
	Malta	610	590	532	490	337	491	764
	Skikda	377	460	441	400	174	248	408
	Marsa el Brega	1000	989	895	882	737	1000	985
	Idku	1758	1685	1632	1610	1377	1465	1737

coastal depots operate according to the "50% always full" principle for safety reasons, the effective capacity is calculated as half of the nominal capacity. The operational draft of the terminal is calculated by subtracting a safety margin from its nominal draft. This application assumes a safety margin of 1.3 m which includes net under keel clearance, dredging tolerances, tidal and weather-marine factors [23].

Each import terminal is characterized by an LNG demand to be served. The demand data used in this application are taken from the TDI Rete GNL and SIGNAL projects (Interreg IT-FR Maritime Program 2014–2020) and refers to some forecasts for the year 2025. These demand data are intended as the sum of three components:

Table 2. Characteristics of the marine LNG terminals.

	Nominal storage capacity [m³]	Effective storage capacity [m³]	Nominal draft [m]	Operational draft with a safety margin [m]
Bastia	5,000	2,500	8	6.7
Cagliari	22,000	11,000	8.5	7.2
Genoa	6,600	3,300	5.6	4.3
Livorno	9,000	4,500	9	7.7
Nice	5,000	2,500	7	5.7
Oristano	10,000	5,000	11	9.7
Toulon	10,000	5,000	8	6.7

- maritime demand: it considers the volumes of LNG bunkering required by the maritime propulsion market (pleasure craft, commercial ships, ancillary services, public transport services, police, and coast guard).
- port demand: it considers the energy needs generated within port areas (port handling vehicles, energy systems, etc.) which can be met, at least in theory, by using LNG as a fuel for energy production.
- terrestrial demand: it considers the demand for LNG bunkering and storage services for industrial and private use that comes from the hinterland and retro-port areas.

Since this application considers a monthly time horizon, Table 3 illustrates the monthly LNG demand that characterizes the eight nodes in the network.

Table 3. Monthly LNG demand (m³/month). Year of reference: 2025.

Ports	Monthly LNG demand [m³/month]
Bastia	498
Cagliari	4,842
Genoa	16,062
Livorno	18,255
Nice	794
Oristano	1,014
Toulon	4,524
Sum	*45,989*

It is assumed that the network could be served by five categories of LNG carriers with different capacities. Table 4 summarizes the general characteristics of the five ship categories in terms of carrying capacity, full and empty draft and operating cost per nautical mile. The data relating to the capacity and the draft are taken from the information sheets available on the websites of the main LNG carriers, while the operating cost has been estimated with the support of LNG market experts and is to be considered purely indicative.

Table 4. Characteristics of the LNG carriers.

Category	Capacity [m^3]	Full draft [m]	Empty draft [m]	Operating cost [€/nm]
1	3,000	4.3	3.9	17.6
2	7,500	6	5.5	18.5
3	10,000	6.6	5.9	19.3
4	20,000	7.8	6.8	20.4
5	30,000	8	7.5	21.3

6 Application Results

The optimization model introduced in Scct. 4 is applied to different scenarios in order to identify, for each tested scenario, the configuration of the maritime distribution network that guarantees the lowest transport costs.

The following three different network scenarios are considered:

- Scenario 1: the seven buyer nodes procure themselves autonomously and independently (Business As Usual - BAU procurement scenario). The storage capacity and maximum draft of the seven LNG depots reproduce the state of affairs (Table 2). The optimization model is applied considering the seven nodes separately and assuming that each of them alternatively uses one of the five exporting nodes, for a total of 35 instances. The objective is to calculate the minimum transport cost that would characterize the supply of LNG for each of the seven purchasing nodes analyzed if each of them independently managed their own LNG supplies by sea.
- Scenario 2: the buyer nodes procure themselves in a coordinated way by acting in coalition as an organized pool (Project scenario - coalition procurement scenario). The characteristics of the seven marine depots in terms of storage capacity and maximum draft reproduce the state of affairs (Table 2).
- Scenario 3: the buyer nodes procure themselves in a coordinated way by acting in coalition as an organized pool; the characteristics of the marine depots in terms of storage capacity and draft are improved (Table 5) compared to the current state of affairs (Prospective scenario – coalition procurement scenario with improved offer attributes). The minimum draft is raised to 8 m for all ports, and the capacity of the coastal depots of Livorno and Genoa is set equal to their monthly demand.

Table 5. Improved characteristics of the marine LNG terminals.

	Improved storage capacity [m³]	Improved draft [m]
Bastia	2,500	8
Cagliari	11,000	8
Genoa	16,100	8
Livorno	18,300	8
Nice	2,500	8
Oristano	5,000	9.7
Toulon	5,000	8

6.1 Scenario 1 – BAU Procurement Scenario

Tables 6 shows the transport cost for each of the seven buyer nodes according to the export terminal used. For each buyer node, the most convenient transport option is highlighted in bold. The remaining columns of the table detail:

- the total transport cost of the network for each of the five export nodes (calculated as the sum of the transport costs relating to the seven buyer nodes). The most advantageous network option is highlighted in bold.
- the total number of miles navigated monthly for each network option.
- the cost delta (Δ_{cost}) that characterizes the LNG procurement from each exporting node with respect to the minimum cost network option (shown in the table in bold). Δ_{cost} can be interpreted as the minimum unit discount in terms of €/m³ that should be applied to the purchase price of LNG at export node i so that it can be competitive with respect to the export node serving the minimum cost network.

The Δ_{cost} that characterizes the transport network relating to export port i is calculated as:

$$\Delta cost = \frac{(cost\ of\ network\ i - minimum\ network\ cost)}{cubic\ meters\ transported}$$

6.2 Scenario 2 – Project Scenario

Table 7 summarizes the results relating to the project scenario in which the seven buyer nodes manage their own LNG supplies by sea in coalition, and the characteristics of their marine depots reproduce the state of things. The table follows the same organization seen above. For each of the five export nodes, the table lists the corresponding transport cost falling on each buyer node. The share of the transport cost attributed to each buyer node is calculated by dividing the total transport cost of the network in proportion to the LNG demand of the node. Looking at the results, the transport cost of Genoa remains the same

Table 6. Transport cost of LNG in Scenario 1

	Transport cost of the individual buyer nodes [€/month]							Network cost [€/month]	Distance [nm/month]	Δ_{cost} [€/m^3]
	Bastia	Cagliari	Genova	Livorno	Nizza	Oristano	Tolone			
Barcellona	12742	13690	74342	66180	11018	9504	7474	194951	10832	-
Malta	17248	11862	124608	92231	17283	26893	21472	311598	17312	2.5
Skikda	14080	6125	97152	72668	8730	14362	13270	226387	12578	0.9
Marsa el Brega	31046	25942	208877	153424	35200	34672	35200	524361	29132	7.3
Idku	56672	48470	355872	265864	51568	61142	61882	901470	50082	15.6

as in Scenario 1. The limited draft and capacity of the Genoa depot require six visits per month with a dedicated ship to meet its LNG demand, thus not allowing Genoa to enter a shared route.

Table 7. Transport cost of LNG in Scenario 2

	Transport cost of the individual buyer nodes [€/month]							Network cost [€/month]	Distance [nm/month]	Δ_{cost} [€/m^3]
	Bastia	Cagliari	Genova	Livorno	Nizza	Oristano	Tolone			
Barcellona	587	5707	74342	49635	936	1195	5332	137734	6097	-
Malta	814	7905	124608	69174	1297	1656	7386	212839	9671	2.5
Skikda	597	5800	97152	54501	951	1215	5419	165635	7418	0.9
Marsa el Brega	1333	12953	208877	115068	2125	2713	12102	355171	16112	7.3
Idku	2146	20855	355872	199398	3421	4368	19485	605545	27045	15.6

6.3 Scenario 3 – Prospective Scenario

Table 8 summarizes the results relating to the prospective scenario in which the buyer nodes manage in coalition their LNG supplies, and an enhancement of their supply characteristics (draft and storage capacity) is assumed. The table follows the same organization seen before.

In the prospective scenario that provides for improved infrastructural characteristics in the buyer nodes, the most affordable network option relies on Barcelona, with minimal cost differences compared to the network options served by Malta and Skikda. Given their decentralized geographical position with respect to the study area, Marsa el Brega and Idku are less competitive alternatives.

6.4 Savings in Transport Costs

Table 9 illustrates the percentage savings on transportation costs that would occur when moving from the BAU procurement scenario (Scenario 1) to the project procurement scenario (Scenario 2). The entry into the coalition, whatever the export node used,

Table 8. Transport cost of LNG in Scenario 3

	Transport cost of the individual buyer nodes [€/month]							Network cost [€/month]	Distance [nm/month]	Δ_{cost} [€/m³]
	Bastia	Cagliari	Genova	Livorno	Nizza	Oristano	Tolone			
Barcellona	427	4146	13701	15413	680	868	3874	39109	1866	-
Malta	581	5645	18655	20987	926	1182	5274	53251	2545	0.31
Skikda	467	4536	14988	16861	744	950	4238	42782	2050	0.08
Marsa el Brega	927	9004	29753	33473	1477	1886	8412	84932	4063	1.00
Idku	1563	15186	50182	56455	2491	3181	14188	143244	6863	2.28

involves a significant reduction in costs for all ports, except for Genoa, for which transport costs would remain unchanged. Due to its high demand and infrastructural constraints, Genoa would continue to be served by dedicated ships and to fully bear its procurement cost.

Table 9. Percentage savings on transport costs obtainable in the transition from the BAU scenario to the project scenario

	Savings in transport costs [%]							
	Bastia	Cagliari	Genova	Livorno	Nizza	Oristano	Tolone	Whole network
Barcellona	95	58	0	25	92	87	29	29
Malta	95	33	0	25	92	94	66	32
Skikda	96	5	0	25	89	92	59	27
Marsa el Brega	96	50	0	25	94	92	66	32
Idku	96	57	0	25	93	93	69	33

Table 10 illustrates the percentage savings that would derive from the transition from the BAU procurement scenario to the prospective one with infrastructural upgrading of LNG marine depots (Scenario 3). By bringing the draft of all buyer ports to 8 m and expanding the capacity of the coastal depots of Livorno (from 4,500 to 18,300 m³) and Genoa (from 3,000 to 16,100 m³), it is possible to reduce transport costs by approximately 80%. Thanks to the infrastructural improvements, Genoa could be included in an itinerary that touches various ports of the coalition. Deeper drafts and larger depots would allow all coalition ports to be served using only two LNG carriers, one large and one extra-large. Such a distribution scenario would reduce not only transport costs but also the distances travelled, with environmental benefits in terms of reducing polluting emissions [24].

Table 10. Percentage savings on transport costs obtainable in the transition from the BAU scenario to the prospective scenario with improved infrastructure attributes

	Savings in transport costs [%]							
	Bastia	Cagliari	Genova	Livorno	Nizza	Oristano	Tolone	Whole network
Barcellona	96.6	69.7	81.6	76.7	93.8	90.9	48.2	79.9
Malta	96.6	52.4	85.0	77.2	94.6	95.6	75.4	82.9
Skikda	96.7	25.9	84.56	76.8	91.5	93.4	68.1	81.1
Marsa el Brega	97.0	65.3	85.8	78.2	95.8	94.6	76.1	83.8
Idku	97.2	68.7	85.9	78.8	95.2	94.8	77.1	84.1

7 Conclusion and Implications for Research and Policy

The described application studied to what extent an integrated management of LNG supply between a set of coalition-organized ports could allow a reduction in transport costs. Given a set of Tyrrhenian port depots organized as a cluster, this study identified the network configuration that ensures the minimization of transport costs in compliance with demand and supply requirements. The resulting cost reduction is due to the optimization of the filling coefficients of the ships, to the smaller number of ships to be used for the supply of all the nodes and, clearly, to the reduction in the total number of miles traveled thanks to the optimization of the distribution routes. Significant savings on LNG shipping costs can be achieved by taking advantage of the economies of scale that come from operating as a pool of port depots rather than individually. Acting as an organized cluster, LNG port depots can potentially leverage their stronger bargaining power during negotiations to seek reasonable import prices that can benefit from reduced transportation costs and guaranteed volume of LNG to purchase. Furthermore, the reduction of emissions (due to the reduction of the total distance traveled) and the increase in maritime safety (due to the reduction of traffic) induced by an optimized distribution network, can act as a stimulus for public regulatory bodies in the energy sector. sector for the promotion of similar cluster-based initiatives in support of a more sustainable development of the LNG market. Extensions of the research will concern the economic evaluation of alternative investment scenarios regarding LNG storage infrastructures in the ports analyzed and their effects on the organization of the logistic distribution model.

Acknowledgements. This research was supported by the SIGNAL project (Interreg IT-FR Maritime Program 2014–2020).

References

1. Serra, P., Fancello, G.: Towards the IMO's GHG goals: a critical overview of the perspectives and challenges of the main options for decarbonizing international shipping. Sustainability 12(8), 3220 (2020)
2. Kumar, S., Kwon, H.T., Choi, K.H., Cho, J.H., Lim, W., Moon, I.: Current status and future projections of LNG demand and supplies: a global prospective. Energy Policy 39(7), 4097–4104 (2011)
3. Barnes, R., Bosworth, R.: LNG is linking regional natural gas markets: evidence from the gravity model. Energy Econ. 47, 11–17 (2015)
4. European Commission (2021). https://ec.europa.eu/info/strategy/priorities-2019-2024/eur opean-green-deal/delivering-european-green-deal_en
5. Bittante, A., Pettersson, F., Saxén, H.: A multi-period optimization model for the design of new LNG supply chains. In: Proceedings of the 58th Conference on Simulation and Modelling (SIMS 58) Reykjavik, Iceland, September 25th–27th, 2017, no. 138, pp. 332–342. Linköping University Electronic Press, September 2017
6. Rogers, H.: The LNG Shipping Forecast: Costs Rebounding, Outlook Uncertain. Technical report. The Oxford Institute for Energy Studies (2018)
7. Wood, D.A.: A review and outlook for the global LNG trade. J. Nat. Gas Sci. Eng. 9, 16–27 (2012)
8. Williams, C.: Management 6e. Cengage Learning, 2010 (2010). ISBN 0538745975
9. Maxwell, D., Zhu, Z.: Natural gas prices, LNG transport costs, and the dynamics of LNG imports. Energy Econ. 33(2), 217–226 (2011)
10. Chen, Z., An, H., Gao, X., Li, H., Hao, X.: Competition pattern of the global liquefied natural gas (LNG) trade by network analysis. J. Nat. Gas Sci. Eng. 33, 769–776 (2016)
11. Hartley, P.R.: The future of long-term LNG contracts. Energy J. 36, 209–233 (2015)
12. Wang, S., Notteboom, T.: World LNG shipping: dynamics in markets, ships and terminal projects. Curr. Issues Shipp. Ports Logist. 129–154 (2011)
13. Fancello, G., Serra, P., Mancini, S.: A network design optimization problem for ro-ro freight transport in the Tyrrhenian area. Transp. Probl. 14(4), 63–75 (2019)
14. COM 2016/49, European Commission: Communication from the Commission to the European parliament, the Council, the European economic and social Committee and the Committee of the regions on an EU strategy for liquefied natural gas and gas storage (2016)
15. Bittante, A., Jokinen, R., Pettersson, F., Saxen, H.: Optimization of LNG supply chain. Comput. Aided Chem. Eng. 37, 779–784 (2015)
16. Bittante, A., Pettersson, F., Saxen, H.: Optimization of a smallscale LNG supply chain. Energy 148, 78–89 (2018)
17. Arnesen, M., Gjestvanga, M., Wanga, X., Fagerholt, K., Thuna, K., Rakkeb, J.G.: A traveling salesman problem with pickups and deliveries, time windows and draft limits: case study from chemical shipping. Comput. Oper. Res. 77, 20–31 (2017)
18. Battarra, M., Alves Pessoa, A., Subramanian, A., Uchoa, E.: Exact algorithms for the traveling salesman problem with draft limits. Eur. J. Oper. Res. 235(1), 115–128 (2014)
19. Gelareh, S., Gendron, B., Hanafi, S., Neamatian Monemi, R., Todosijević, R.: The selective traveling salesman problem with draft limits. J. Heuristics 26(3), 339–352 (2019). https://doi.org/10.1007/s10732-019-09406-z
20. Malaguti, E., Martello, S., Santini, A.: The traveling salesman problem with pickups, deliveries, and draft limits. Omega 74, 50–58 (2018)
21. Rakke, J., Christiansen, M., Fagerholt, K., Laporte, G.: The traveling salesman problem with draft limits. Comput. Oper. Res. 39(9), 2161–2167 (2012)

22. Todosijevic, M., Mladenovic, N., abd Hanafi, S., Gendron, B.: A general variable neighborhood search variants for the travelling salesman problem with draft limits. Optim. Lett. **11**(6), 1047–1056 (2017)
23. PIANC. Permanent International Association Navigation Congress (PIANC), Report No. 121-2014, Harbour Approach Channels Design Guidelines (2014)
24. Serra, P., Fadda, P., Fancello, G.: Investigating the potential mitigating role of network design measures for reducing the environmental impact of maritime chains: the Mediterranean case. Case Stud. Transp. Policy **8**(2), 263–280 (2020)

Sea-Rail Intermodal Transport in Italian Gateway Ports: A Sustainable Solution? The Examples of La Spezia and Trieste

Marcello Tadini[1(✉)] and Giuseppe Borruso[2]

[1] DISEI – Department of Economics and Business Studies, University of Piemonte Orientale, Via Perrone, 18, 28100 Novara, Italy
marcello.tadini@uniupo.it

[2] DEAMS – Department of Economic, Business, Mathematic and Statistical Sciences "Bruno de Finetti", University of Trieste, Via A. Valerio, 4/1, 34127 Trieste, Italy
giuseppe.borruso@deams.units.it

Abstract. The paper tackles the issue related to the sea-rail intermodal transport in gateway ports. In recent years there has been a renewed interest in land connections and therefore hinge functions, recalling the logic for which the most competitive ports are those equipped with an articulated and efficient network of internal connections. This attention requires an in-depth study of port intermodality and mutual interactions with the territories served by the port. This paper is focused on rail intermodality for container handling, recognizing the gateway port as a strategic node whose competitiveness increasingly depends on sustainable intermodal transport solutions to and from the hinterland. This is also due to the growing attention to green transport solutions such as rail. After highlighting the distinctive features of gateway ports and their key functions, attention is focused on the main Italian ports that play this role. In particular, this study explores the ports of La Spezia and Trieste due to their aptitude for intermodal rail traffic in relation to the hinterland. In both cases, the share of combined sea-rail transport and the importance of rail transport use in terms of environmental sustainability will be evaluated through an ad hoc tool (EcoTransIT World).

Keywords: Sea-rail transport · Gateway ports · La Spezia port · Trieste port

1 Introduction

Geographical research has long suggested the analysis of the close interaction between the port and its hinterland as a key element to correctly analyze the dynamics of port development. This recommendation has taken up a particularly significant value in the most recent context. In fact, we are witnessing the onset of two phenomena. On the one hand, the clear dichotomy between hub ports and gateways ports has disappeared,

---

The paper is the result of the joint work of the two authors. However, Marcello Tadini wrote Sects. 1, 2, 3, while Giuseppe Borruso wrote Sects. 4, 5, 6.

© The Author(s), under exclusive license to Springer Nature Switzerland AG 2022
O. Gervasi et al. (Eds.): ICCSA 2022 Workshops, LNCS 13381, pp. 156–172, 2022.
https://doi.org/10.1007/978-3-031-10548-7_12

with a reduction in the importance attributed to the pure movement of goods. On the other hand, there has been a renewed interest in land connections and therefore hinge functions, recalling the logic for which the most competitive ports are those equipped with an articulated and efficient network of internal connections. This attention requires an in-depth study of port intermodality and mutual interactions with the territories served by the port.

In terms of port facilities and relationships with the land side, Vigarié [1] devised the model of the so-called "port triptych" in order to represent the spatial relations between the maritime sphere, the port and the continental space. The latter is often referred to as the actual market or geo-economic scope in which the port sells its services [2].

Thanks to the contribution of the geographical research, the concept of gateway emerged to understand the role played by the port in relation to the area in which it is located.

Deepening the work of Bird [3, 4], Vallega [5] emphasizes how it is possible to highlight the nature of the function that the port can assume for the coastal region in which it stands. As concerns the region to which it belongs, the port plays a role as a door through which the region itself maintains relations with the outside. In this case, it is then configured as a gateway. This qualification, however, is not the prerogative of all ports but only of those that perform functions that go beyond the local area (i.e. limited within the coastal region to which they belong), that is, those that define the projection of the port outwards on a national and international scale [5, 6].

The progressive affirmation of containerization has changed the spatial interpretation of the port that has become a strategic intermodal node in the global transport network [6]. This development has determined in parallel on the maritime front the birth of a new type of port called hub, that is, a node that perform transshipment functions. In these ports, the handling of containers takes place from ship to ship and this does not generate land traffic because they are the expression of an organizational method adopted by large shipping companies to optimize global containerized itineraries [7].

The hub port is characterized by an almost total dissociation between the port structure and the territory that hosts it, given that the connections with the terrestrial side are absent or in any case not considered relevant for the development of these nodes [7]. The gateway ports, on the other hand, which can also be defined as hinterland-oriented ports [8], are characterized by an articulated and complex system of relations with the terrestrial context.

Several regional studies have shown that the development of containerization has modified the network of global maritime connections and transformed not only port facilities but also their hinterland, favoring intermodal connection with ports [9–11].

The inland is the area where a port carries out most of its activities; unlike the hinterland, which is a physical space, it is a relational and therefore economic space. Its infrastructure is decisive for the port system of reference [7]. The boundaries of the hinterland vary according to the goods, the dynamics of the global market and, above all, the degree of infrastructure [12].

2 Sea-Rail Intermodality as a Green Solution for Hinterland Connections of Gateway Ports

The development of containerization and intermodal options have pushed ports to prioritize their activities inwards even at great distances [13].

With the continuous growth of unitized load traffic, the mode that is most affected by processes of reorganization of flows between port and territory is precisely the railway one, thanks also to its ability to transport a greater number of containers in a single journey, covering long distances [6].

Through the use of the combined maritime-rail transport, the conditions are created for a higher modal integration between land and sea, with a propulsive role that starts from the port and radiates towards the territory [14]. Thanks to these relationships, the port function finds new possibilities for development towards the hinterland and contributes to the formation of a regional distribution network, which is configured as an organized system characterized by a polycentric structure [15, 16].

Rail connections with internal terminals have become a key factor for the attractiveness of ports as they allow to obtain advantages – distributed over several categories of actors involved along the logistics chain – such as lower urban port traffic, lower transport costs over medium-long distances, higher speed in ports and lower environmental impact [17, 18]. There are also disadvantages such as the need for more detailed transport planning, dependence on economies of scale, higher costs and longer delivery times over short distances. The creation of a well-developed hinterland based on rail connections has the potential to strengthen the maritime transfer segment, increase logistics efficiency and produce a more sustainable global transport chain [19].

Rail-water intermodal transportation is recognized as one of the future transportation methods for being efficient, economical and environmentally friendly. For this reason, the European Union has gradually established a sustainable and collaborative intermodal transport service network with containers as the main cargo-carrying unit and railways as the core. At the same time, the container railway station was built in the main European ports with gateway functions. Railways play an important role in container collection and distribution in the ports [20].

Gateway ports are increasingly becoming multimodal hubs where rail is expected to play a strategic role. Efficient rail operations and links to and from the ports, as well as within the port, are essential to maximize the use of rail as a sustainable transport mode and to comply with the priorities set in the TEN-T legislation [21].

The European Union advocates that railways should take more transportation volumes, which requires an increase in the service level of the multimodal transport chain and in the market share of railway transportation in terms of medium and long-distance freight [20]. However, for combined traffic with an origin or destination in a port, the market segment below 300 km can also be competitive to shift trucks onto the rail. Indeed, many ports have regular rail connections to terminals within a range of 100 km distance and are very important to reduce road congestion and negative externalities in urban areas [21].

3 Italian Gateway Ports and the Case of La Spezia

Currently, in Italy there are about twenty ports that perform gateway functions; the geographical reading of the recent evolution of port traffic shows a particular territorial structure and a tendency to the concentration of these activities.

Using an approach based on port regions, selected using the criteria of the geographical proximity and the functional complementarities, it is possible to identify gateway port systems [6, 7]. In particular, Italy is characterized by two multi-port gateway regions: the first is known as the "Ligurian Range" and is formed by the ports located along the northern Tyrrhenian coast (Savona, Genoa, La Spezia, Marina di Carrara and Livorno); the second one is the so-called "North Adriatic" which includes the ports located in the northern portion of the Adriatic (Koper, Trieste, Monfalcone, Venice and Ravenna) (Fig. 1) [22].

At the national level, the Ligurian Range has emerged for its strategic importance, accounting for over 61% of the domestic gateway traffic in the last six years (Fig. 1). This share is not surprising, given that the ports of the Ligurian Range are nodes connected with a hinterland with many production sites and a large consumer market and constitute the international access/exit points for the territories that support them [23].

Figure 1 also highlights the role of the La Spezia port as the second national gateway port after Genoa (18% of the Italian traffic in the period 2016–2021). For this reason, the case of La Spezia is an interesting area of investigation, considering first of all its marked specialization in containerized traffic that in the last twenty years (2001–2021) has represented 76% (on average) of the total port handling.

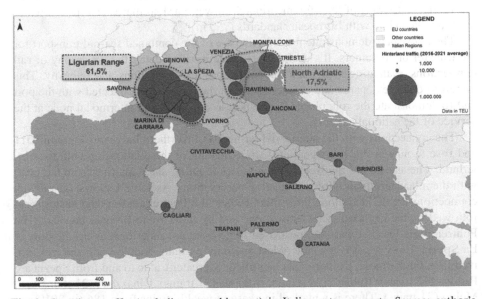

Fig. 1. Container traffic (excluding transshipment) in Italian gateway ports. Source: author's elaboration from [24].

Moreover, this specialization, based mainly on hinterland traffic (on average 88,8% of the total between 2001 and 2021, compared to transshipment movements that account for 11,2%), has led to the development of significant use of railway intermodality in connections with the hinterland.

In this regard, the share of rail transport in the total container hinterland managed in port was significant from 2001 until 2008 (29% on average), considering an amount of average port handling equal to about 920,000 TEUs. The impact of the global crisis of 2009 led to a sharp reduction in the use of rail transport (20.8% in 2010) while starting from 2011 a reversal of the trend took place which, in the face of a marked increase in port container handling (on average 1.2 million TEUs between 2011 and 2021), saw the share of intermodal grow progressively to reach the value of 29.6% in 2020, with an average of 26.6% in the same period [25, 26].

The consistent use of the railway was also possible thanks to the activities of the Santo Stefano Magra backport, which performs functions as a logistics area serving the port. Along the routes that connect the three railway yards of reference of the port (Marittima, Migliarina and Santo Stefano Magra), the management of rail freight maneuvers is unique, with obvious positive effects on handling efficiency [26].

The railway yard of La Spezia Marittima, located inside the port area, in its current configuration is characterized by a bundle of four parallel tracks of limited length to 400–450 m, intended for the composition of trains to be introduced into the network and the decomposition of the convoys before their transfer to the destination ports. La Spezia Marittima has a limited handling capacity (350,000 TEUs/year) repeatedly exceeded in recent years.

Therefore, the further increase in the rail share necessarily requires the improvement (currently underway) of the aforementioned railway yard so that it can have a wider track bundle in line with European standards (750 m).

The above data demonstrate the effective use of the combined sea-rail transport for the transfer of containers. It's useful to examine in more detail the geography of rail connections, evaluating their main directions, origins/destinations and intensity. This allows to define extension and characteristics of the hinterland connected with the port and to demonstrate the role played by the port as a logistic and intermodal node at the service of the national territory.

The connections with the intermodal terminals of Northern Italy were eight in 2011 and rose to nine in 2021, a signal of a strengthening of the relationship with the hinterland. The analysis of the weekly frequencies (coming and departing from the port) with the inland terminals allows interesting observations. As Table 1 shows, the railway connections are divided along three main routes: the Pontremolese is the busiest one, followed by the Ligurian (via Genova) one and by the Tirreno-Brenner corridor. The Pontremolese line is today the most used route by trains entering/leaving the port of La Spezia. However, it is also the oldest and only partially double-track and modernized line. Furthermore, the terminals identified by greater traffic to and from Spezia are Padova (62 trains), Rubiera (34 trains), Bologna (27 trains), Dinazzano (21 trains) and Melzo (21 trains). There is a marked increase in weekly trains from 186 (in 2019 and 2020) to 215 in 2021 as well as a strengthening of relations with Emilia-Romagna and Veneto.

Table 1. The railway relations between the port of La Spezia and inland terminals (trains/week). Source: author's elaboration from [26] (data 2021).

	Via Pontremoli	Via Genova	Via Pisa	Total
Bologna	7	5	15	27
Dinazzano	21	-	-	21
Rubiera	18	4	12	34
Marzaglia	17	-	1	18
Padova	44	17	1	62
Verona	-	5	5	10
Melzo	6	15	-	21
Milano	-	12	-	12
Rivalta Scrivia	-	10	-	10
Total	113	68	34	215

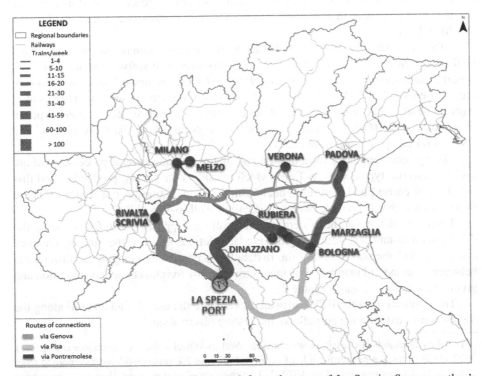

Fig. 2. Routes of container rail traffic to and from the port of La Spezia. Source: author's elaboration from [26] (data 2021).

Figure 2 shows in detail the railway connections for container transport between the port and the hinterland. The traffic flows generated are particularly intense with Emilia Romagna (Rubiera, Bologna, Dinazzano and Marzaglia): 100 trains/week via Pontremoli and via Pisa. The traffic flows with Veneto (Padua in particular) via Pontremoli and via Genova are also relevant (72 trains/week). Less intense are the flows with Lombardy (Melzo, Milano) and Piedmont (Rivalta Scrivia) via Genova. Therefore, in the light of the analysis carried out, it is evident that the port of La Spezia plays a gateway function for the territories of the Po Valley. This freight traffic involves three important TEN-T railway corridors: Mediterranean, Rhine-Alpine and Scandinavian-Mediterranean.

In addition, through these corridors (especially the last two) the port of La Spezia extends its hinterland beyond the Alps, reaching Switzerland, Austria and Germany indirectly, through the railway "relaunches" from the Melzo terminal (managed by the same company that handles most of the containers in La Spezia).

3.1 The Sustainability of the Sea-Rail Intermodal Transport in La Spezia Port

In Sect. 2, the environmental sustainability of rail transport for the relations between the port and its hinterland was highlighted. Therefore, along the routes shown in Fig. 2, the positive impact in terms of emission reduction generated by the railway choice (instead of the more traditional combination with road transport) to reach the destinations was evaluated. In particular, an ad hoc tool was used to carry out this assessment: EcoTransIT World (ETW).

ETW is the most widely used software worldwide to automate the calculation and analysis of energy consumption and freight emissions. The software is accredited by Smart Freight Centre to be in accordance with the GLEC Framework and also meets the requirements of EN 16258 and the GHG protocol (Corporate Standard). The result is worldwide unique because ETW calculates the transport distances, energy consumption, greenhouse gases (GHG) emissions as well as air pollutants (SOx, NOx, NMHC and PM 10) for any global transport chain.

The system boundaries for emission calculation include several processes and are divided into two types: Well-to-Tank (which considers the supply, production and distribution of energy) and Tank-to-Wheel (which considers transport operations). These two types together form the configuration called Well-to-Wheel [28].

Therefore, the use of the aforementioned software appears useful for assessing the different environmental impacts of the modal solutions to reach the nine destinations connected with the port of La Spezia. In detail, it is possible to compare the differences between road and rail in terms of distances travelled by freight, energy consumption and greenhouse gases emissions (Table 2).

The application of the ETW software to compare the use of road and rail along the routes connected with the port allows interesting observations[1].

---

[1] For the calculation of emissions, we consider Well-to-Wheel values and container transport (1 TEU). Besides, for rail traffic, a load factor value of 68.7% was considered as emerged from the 2021 data communicated by ASPMLO. In the case of road sections, the shorter ones have always been considered. For railway, the routes actually served by the operators managing the connections between port and inland terminals shall be considered. For this reason, in some cases the row values do not appear.

First of all, the lower environmental impact of the railway solution is confirmed, which on average emits 24% of the greenhouse gases compared to the road, when the routes are comparable and distances almost the same. Moreover, seven hinterland destinations (Bologna, Rubiera, Marzaglia, Padova, Verona, Melzo, Milano) are connected via alternative rail routes that do not represent the shortest solution in terms of kilometers. These routes are chosen for issues of saturation of shorter lines or issues of availability of tracks for railway operators. However, even these choices allow a significant reduction in emissions that are 65% lower (on average) than those on the road following the shortest route. Similar observations can also be made for energy consumption. On average the energy consumption of rail transport is 64% lower in the case of comparable routes and 50% in the case of alternative rail solutions.

Finally, it is important to underline how the railway advantages in terms of energy consumption and emissions are particularly evident already for short distances (over 160 km) thus making it a competitive solution even on medium-short distances, especially to the extent that the efficiency of the intermodal service allows reduced transport times at low costs.

Table 2. The emission calculation per TEU along routes between the port of La Spezia and inland terminals (differentiated by rail and road). Source: author's elaboration from [28].

	Truck			Train		
	Distance (km)	Energy consumption (megajoule)	GHG emissions (tons)	Distance (km)	Energy consumption (megajoule)	GHG emissions (tons)
Bologna (via Pontremoli)	211	2,143	0.154	215	760	0.037
Bologna (via Pisa, train)	-	-	-	255	902	0.043
Bologna (via Genova, train)	-	-	-	381	1,347	0.065
Dinazzano (via Pontremoli)	170	1,752	0.126	171	706	0.035
Rubiera (via Pontremoli)	164	1,700	0.122	163	577	0.028
Rubiera (via Genova, train)	-	-	-	329	1,164	0.056
Rubiera (via Pisa, train)	-	-	-	303	1,072	0.052
Marzaglia (via Pontremoli)	168	1,709	0.124	166	588	0.031
Marzaglia (via Pisa, train)	-	-	-	299	1,064	0.054
Padova (via Genova, train)	-	-	-	434	1,534	0.074
Padova (via Pontremoli)	322	3,303	0.238	330	1,167	0.056
Padova (via Pisa, train)	-	-	-	376	1,329	0.064
Verona (via Pontremoli, road)	257	2,613	0.190	-	-	-

(continued)

Table 2. (*continued*)

	Truck			Train		
	Distance (km)	Energy consumption (megajoule)	GHG emissions (tons)	Distance (km)	Energy consumption (megajoule)	GHG emissions (tons)
Verona (via Pisa, train)	-	-	-	372	1,314	0.063
Verona (via Genova, train)	-	-	-	369	1,303	0.063
Melzo (via Pontremoli)	225	2,313	0.170	257	902	0.043
Melzo (via Genova, train)	-	-	-	248	875	0.042
Milano (via Pontremoli, road)	223	2,295	0.170	-	-	-
Milano (via Genova, train)	-	-	-	239	843	0.040
Rivalta Scrivia (via Genova)	160	1,697	0.120	155	548	0.027

4 The Port of Trieste

The port of Trieste within the North Adriatic area witnessed interesting dynamics throughout the latest decade, making the most of its historically known and documented – nonetheless little exploited in the recent past - geographical advantages, as its position covered by winds, the natural depths of 18m and an articulated network of rail infrastructure and connections towards a wide hinterland [33], as well as the Free Port regime [30, 34]. After having been part of a gateway in the TEN-T network during the EU Eastwards enlargement, it is playing a crucial role in the connections as the former Corridor V and the Baltic-Adriatic corridor in the new EU's transport policy.

Such dynamics deals particularly with the growth in freight traffic and of the integration with inland logistic nodes and, in parallel, with the further exploitation of national and international rail connections. The overall freight traffic in 2021 saw Trieste ranking first before Genoa with more than 55 million tons[2]. As Port Authority systems, the High Eastern Adriatic Port Authority – with Trieste and Monfalcone – ranks second after the Port Authority of the Western Ligurian Sea – With Genoa and Savona-Vado. The container traffic in Trieste overcame 500,000 TEUs in 2015, and since 2016 it witnessed a period of constant growth, getting close to 800,000 TEUs in 2019 (789,594), then, following the pandemic periods, setting at 757,255 in 2021. The semitrailers and swap bodies traffic was relevant, given the important Ro-Ro[3] ferry flows from Turkey, that bring the equivalent traffic to 1.3 million TEUs.

Still it is interesting to notice how the pure container traffic is split among hinterland and transshipment markets, with shares respectively of 70% and 30%, in a mix of functions between nodal gateway and hub.

---

[2] This despite a drop of 13% as regards as the maximum value recorded in 2019 as a consequence of the pandemic events. Trieste data, however, are distorted by the liquid bulk, still counting for nearly 70% of total traffic.

[3] These benefits of the Free Port regime are not quoted as it happens in other Italian ports.

Nearly the total of hinterland traffic travelled by train. In 2019 nearly 10,000 trains were moved (9.771 precisely), with figures dropping to 8,523 in 2020 following the Covid-19 pandemics slow down, raising again towards 9,000 in 2021. In 2020 more than 400,000 TEUs were moved by train, more than 80% of the hinterland traffic[4].

Central and Eastern Europe (Germany and Austria, followed by Slovakia, Czech Republic, Hungary and Luxemburg), with an articulated network of important connections towards the major Euro-Asiatic traffic routes and flows and with the Northern Range Ports, for a total of 231 weekly connections.

The national connections are mainly linked to the important inland logistic nodes of Padua and Milan, other than, locally, the production systems of Friuli Venezia Giulia Region, with 22 weekly connections, less than 10% of the total.

The port of Trieste is inserted into High Eastern Adriatic Port Authority together with the Port of Monfalcone, and it is integrated with the inland terminal Interporto Trieste, this including the recent free-zone FreeEste, within the port region of Trieste. These latter proximity dry ports are dedicated to warehousing and freight train composition, these latter including RO-LA and similar for the movement of semitrailers, swap bodies, containers and other rolling materials (Fig. 3), before them being sent towards main international destinations.

Table 3. Rail cargo traffic from the Port of Trieste and inland terminals. Source: author's elaboration from [29–31] (data 2020).

O/D National		O/D International	
Padova	10	Karlsruhe (Germania)	14
Pordenone	6	Komarno (Slovacchia)	7
Milano	6	Krefeld (Germania)	4
Total national	**22**	Linz (Austria)	2
		Ludwigshafen (Germania)	28
		Monaco (Germania)	16
O/D International			
Bettembourg (Lux)	24	Ostrava (Repubblica Ceca)	6
Bratislava (Slovacchia)	1	Paskov (Repubblica Ceca)	8
Budapest (Ungheria)	23	Salisburgo (Austria)	2
Burghausen (Germania)	2	Villach (Austria)	8
Colonia (Germania)	48	Wels (Austria)	19
Dunajska (Slovacchia)	7	Wien (Austria)	3
Giengen (Germania)	4	**Total international**	**231**
		Total connections	*253*

---

[4] Data from Port of Trieste; Adriafer.

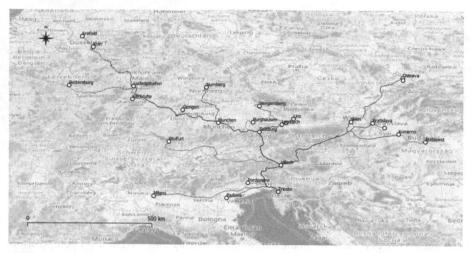

Fig. 3. Rail traffic routes to and from the Port of Trieste. Source: author's elaboration from [29–31].

In the Port of Trieste region, the Port-owned Adriafer company manage shunting operations among inner and regional terminals, as Interporto Trieste and FreeEste node, as well as Interporto of Cervignano, as well as increasing interactions are ongoing with the nodes of Gorizia, Tarvisio and Pordenone. Such a region can be considered as a 'case study' although characterized by a smaller dimension if compared to other international, bigger port systems around the World [32]. The gateway role is further enhanced, particularly considering the land component, by the possible integration with the infrastructure systems of the deep internal regions, bordering the traditional hinterlands. It is worth reminding on one side the historical competition among some ports – as Trieste and Hamburg – and, to-date, an ongoing integration, realized by means of the participation of the company shares among Duisport – Duisburg inland river port – and Interporto Trieste – inland dry terminal. German presence is also represented by the Hamburg port terminal operator holding shares into the new logistic platform in Trieste. These transformations represent a stage of an evolution of the long-distance freight transport systems towards the Euro-Asian traffic routes, also through the Mediterranean gateways.

4.1 The Sustainability of the Sea-Rail Intermodal Transport in Trieste Port

Similarly to the analysis performed in Sect. 3 and Sect. 3.1, an evaluation of the sustainability of rail routes if compared to the equivalent road ones was performed. In particular, routes as in Table 3 and Fig. 4 were examined in terms of their energy absorption (MJ) and greenhouse gases (GHG) emissions. The analysis was performed using the EcoTransIT World (ETW) platform.

As in case of the port of La Spezia, we considered the Well-to-Wheel approach for computing energy consumption and emissions [28]. The calculations were performed considering a loading factor of 77% for the road component and 90% for the train one – this latter figure based on the figures as obtained from the shunting company Adriafer. The comparison was performed considering the national and international rail connections and simulating the equivalent road routes. The case of Trieste is related mainly to the international routes, with just 3 national destinations over a total of 26. Also in this case, we can compare the differences between road and rail in terms of distances travelled by freight, energy consumption and greenhouse gases emissions (Table 4).

Interesting observations can be done after the application of the ETW software over the selected routes. It is worth noting that the positive environmental impacts can be observed at all distances and destinations. The energy consumption of rail cargo compared to the road one spans from 26.77% to 38.04%, while the quota of GHG emissions from 11.83% to a maximum of 24.10%, with a not appreciable relation with the distances travelled, that possibly depending also on the Alpine routes implying covering hills and mountain elevations.

Finally, it is important to underline how the railway distances considered so far span from a minimum of 113 km to a maximum of 1,130 km, thus observing a coverage over short, medium and long distances of rail cargo systems into local-regional and international inland ranges, with considerable benefits in terms of environmental impacts.

Table 4. The emission calculation per TEU along routes between the port of Trieste and inland terminals (differentiated by rail and road). Source: author's elaboration on ETW data [28].

	Truck			Train		
	Distance (km)	Energy consumption (megajoule)	GHG emissions (tons)	Distance (km)	Energy consumption (megajoule)	GHG emissions (tons)
Lambach (Austria)	469	4,894	0.341	464	1,510	0.050
Linz (Austria)	269	2,818	0.199	302	980	0.037
Salisburgo (Austria)	373	3,886	0.272	378	1,226	0.043
Vienna (Austria)	554	5,778	0.400	569	1,849	0.058
Villach (Austria)	186	1,907	0.137	189	609	0.028
Wels (Austria)	488	5,088	0.336	487	1,582	0.048
Wolfurt (Austria)	692	7,131	0.505	673	2,283	0.079
Ostrava (Czech Republic)	843	8,769	0.613	833	2,624	0.099
Paskov (Czech Republic)	849	8,833	0.618	835	2,630	0.099
Burghausen (Germany)	430	4,483	0.315	480	1,436	0.062
Colonia (Germany)	1074	11,023	0.780	1,114	3,677	0.180
Giengen (Germany)	636	6,572	0.460	712	2,256	0.100
Hengersberg (Germany)	518	5,426	0.379	638	1,824	0.066
Karlsruhe (Germany)	794	8,178	0.580	847	2735	0.130
Krefeld (Germany)	1130	11,593	0.830	1,174	3,889	0.190

(continued)

Table 4. (*continued*)

	Truck			Train		
	Distance (km)	Energy consumption (megajoule)	GHG emissions (tons)	Distance (km)	Energy consumption (megajoule)	GHG emissions (tons)
Ludwigshafen (Germany)	838	8,638	0.61	870	2,817	0.130
Monaco (Germany)	508	5,255	0.37	521	1,585	0.066
Norimberga (Germany)	664	6,846	0.48	722	2,295	0.100
Budapest (Hungary)	683	6,942	0.506	783	2,641	0.083
Milano (Italy)	393	4,004	0.288	393	1,268	0.061
Padova (Italy)	180	1,840	0.132	179	569	0.028
Pordenone (Italy)	113	1,158	0.083	126	408	0.020
Bettembourg (Luxemburg)	1007	10,365	0.74	1,091	3,662	0.160
Bratislava (Slovakia)	620	6,471	0.449	616	1,733	0.055
Dunajska (Slovakia)	664	6,953	0.482	648	1,861	0.057
Komarno (Slovakia)	624	6,519	0.458	682	2,155	0.069

5   A Comparison Between Two Rail Ports

Italian North Tyrrhenian Sea and North Adriatic Sea Ports have been fighting an "internal competition" in Italy to attract maritime traffic through the Mediterranean Sea from the Far East, towards the national and European markets. The North Tyrrhenian ports, on one side, have been always winners in terms of freight volumes, movements and dynamicity of port systems, given, in particular, the wider geographic area covered by the range and, in the recent past, by the presence of major urban and industrial systems. These ports granted important services to the old Italian Industrial Triangle – Genoa, Turin, Milan – as well as a connection of these dynamic areas with the European core – Germany and France in particular.

On the other side, the North Adriatic Sea has long been a dead end, because of the presence of several borders – between European Union and Eastern Europe before, and next with the presence of several different states and related borders, including those coming out from the fragmentation of former Yugoslavia – and for the presence of a less dynamic economic system. As a consequence, these ports suffered in terms of minor traffic and port system performances. More recent years, however – with a still pending evaluation over the more recent years as 2020 and 2021, given the effects of the pandemic and post-pandemic periods – witnessed an important increase of performances in the North Adriatic Sea, with particular reference to the Port of Trieste – now in the wider context of the High Eastern Adriatic Port Authority with the Port of Monfalcone.

The changed port dynamics witness an increase of both the Tyrrhenian and Adriatic ports and can be also related to the changed role of ports, with a weakened traditional distinction among pure hubs and gateways as in the late Nineties end the first decade of 21st century. The changes intervened in the international shipping, in terms of container ships dimensions and routes chosen by companies, led changes in the hub ports, with a further consolidation of roles of the bigger ones, and fading of the smaller ones, together with a resizing of minor ones and a reconfiguration towards mixed hub-gateway functions of those better connected with inland infrastructure and networks.

Recent examples of such dynamics can be related, in the Italian case, to the loss of a hub role of a port like Cagliari[5], after the operator's choice of moving its operations on a gateway, continental port as Leghorn. Still, a traditionally pure hub port as Gioia Tauro is expected to enhance the railway connections to allow a higher infrastructure integration with the hinterland and obtain a functional mix of hub and gateway functions, in line with the TEN-T policies and the aim of creating a Third-generation port integrated with its territory [35][6]. Still, we can recall a recent increase of maritime traffic in Taranto after phenomena of congestion in the hub of Malta – Marsaxlokk[7].

While pure hubs are experimenting important transformations, other changes involve gateway ports, whose hub functions are increasing, with a consequent changing role into their land systems. In such a context, in fact, developing pendulum routes in the recent years led to a higher importance of port and their port systems in the mixed movements of freight, as destined to both a hinterland as for transshipment operations, with a number of containers stored on quays ready to be re-embarked on other ships towards other, shorter destinations.

In the case examined the internal connections become particularly important to allow and encourage the sea-rail modal integration and, particularly, to reduce vehicle congestion and carbon footprint moving freight from road to rail. In doing so, and observing the cases of the gateways in Trieste and La Spezia, they appear particularly relevant in reaching this important role. It is interesting to notice a comparison among the rail hinterlands of the two ports. The two ports are specialized in terms of their markets (Fig. 3 and 4). La Spezia is particularly dominant in a context of internal national destinations, well connected to the industrial and production system of Northern Italy, as the classical Industrial Triangle and its more recent evolutions and changes enlarging it towards Northeastern Italy, as the industrial district areas of Veneto and Emilia Romagna regions. Trieste is traditionally connected to international destinations in Central and Eastern Europe, and, from there, towards the Asian markets. It is interesting to notice how a competition among the two ports is quite difficult to detect. Only the important national nodes as Padua and Milan are, in fact, common destinations from the two rail ports, quite a natural one and not the space for a competition on the national markets. A similar consideration is valid for the local markets. A part from the long-distance connections, the two ports serve the macro-regional production system of their territories – Northwestern Italy for

---

[5] https://www.internazionale.it/reportage/monia-melis/2019/07/08/porto-canale-crisi-cagliari.

[6] https://www.uominietrasporti.it/professione/logistica/il-terminal-container-di-gioia-tauro-cresce-e-apre-al-treno/.

[7] https://www.shippingitaly.it/2022/01/01/taranto-nuovo-hub-per-le-navi-di-cma-cgm-dirottate-da-malta-causa-congestione/.

La Spezia and Friuli Venezia Giulia and Eastern Veneto Regions for Trieste – again without a real competition but, likely, a possible integrated cooperation.

In terms of sustainability, although the analysis showed for La Spezia a national range, therefore characterized by a shorter distance range, and for Trieste an international one, advantages from the rail transport in terms of energy consumption and greenhouse gases emissions are visible and quite evident at all scales.

6 Conclusions and Policy Suggestions

We can derive some policy suggestions from the analysis of these local case studies. The two cases are quite different, both in terms of markets, and in terms of connections to the national and international transport systems, and in terms of the dimensions of the overall freight movements. Nonetheless, it is possible to synthetize some common challenges and similar necessities, that can bring interesting suggestions for port systems overall. One consideration needs to be done in the direction of the needs to reinforce the waterfront (quays) – inner harbor connections, both those strictly close, and those located farther in the port region.

The modal shift towards rail, more and more desired at EU level, involves necessarily dedicated spaces for freight train composition – according to the European standard of 750 m – with the need of adequate and fitted for purpose spaces. Also, there is the need for warehousing, handling and shunting. There is the need for a higher functional integration among the strictly port component, facing the sea, and the internal one, creating 'systemic port regions', in which a unique and coordinated management can be proficient in keeping more efficient operations.

Further strategic considerations follow. The current configuration of the maritime transport is based on long-distance maritime and land networks, where gateways are meant both in terms of port regions, therefore not limited to the waterfront, but involving the inland logistic nodes, both as transit and bulk transfer towards farther national and international destinations. This can be seen as an opportunity, but also as a matter of threat. The opportunity lies in the fact that reinforced logistic systems per se can generate local development. Threats can be found in the consideration of long-distance networks, that implies local nodes, as port, becoming just transit points that, in a world becoming more and more IT-based and therefore with an increasing reduction of the human workforce in logistic operations – see the semi-automatic terminals as Savona Vado, or the autonomous guidance transport systems – can potentially reduce the local development effects and a wealth transfer towards other, not necessarily local or national, destinations. Further opportunities can be found in the needs to integrate new forms of manufacturing industrial local development with transport systems, in this intercepting the already existing industrial systems – i.e., the old and new Industrial Triangles – but also enhancing the opportunities offered by reshoring and the development of the Special Economic Zones and Free Zones [36]. From the environmental point of view, rail transport is successful in counting for a limit share of energy consumption and greenhouse gases emissions if compared to container unit (TEU) moved over different distances. Also considering a shorter range - within 200 km from the node of origin – the advantage in terms of reduced consumption and emissions is considerable. Advantages in sustainability can be highlighted when considering longer distances, where rail transport become even more environmentally friendly. In particular, as from the analysis on the two ports, the national destinations – those at a shorter distance – are as well convenient in terms of unitary emissions and consumption. Investments need to be done in order to tackle with the infrastructure limits affecting Italian ports – i.e., rail length, network bottlenecks and turning angle, that currently very often limit the capability of realizing longer block trains that can gain a higher level of efficiency.

References

1. Vigariè, A.: Ports de commerce et vie littorale. Hachette, Paris (1979)
2. Slack, B.: Pawns in the game: ports in global transportation systems. Growth Chang. **24**(4), 379–388 (1993)
3. Bird, J.H.: Seaports as a subset of gateways for regions: a research survey. Prog. Hum. Geogr. **4**(3), 360–370 (1980)
4. Bird, J.H.: Gateways: slow recognition but irresistible rise. Tijdschr. Econ. Soc. Geogr. **74**(3), 196–202 (1983)
5. Vallega, A.: Nodalità e centralità: relais tra teoria regionale e teoria dei trasporti. Studi Marittimi **6**(19–20), 33–35 (1984)
6. Vallega, A.: Geografia delle strategie marittime. Mursia, Milano (1997)
7. Sellari, P.: Geopolitica dei trasporti. Laterza Editori, Bari (2013)
8. Ridolfi, G.: Containerisation in the Mediterranean: between global ocean routeways and feeder services. GeoJournal **48**(1), 29–34 (1999)
9. Hoare, A.G.: British ports and their export hinterlands: a rapidly changing geography. Geogr. Ann. Ser. B Hum. Geogr. **68**(1), 29–40 (1986)
10. van Klink, H.A., van den Berg, G.: Gateways and Intermodalism. J. Transp. Geogr. **6**(1), 1–9 (1998)
11. Guerrero, D.: Deep-sea hinterlands: Some empirical evidence of the spatial impact of containerization. J. Transp. Geogr. **35**, 84–94 (2014)
12. Slack, B.: Globalizzazione e trasporto marittimo: competizione, incertezza, implicazioni per le strategie di sviluppo portuale. In: Soriani, S. (a cura di): Porti, città e territorio costiero. Bologna, Il Mulino, pp. 67–83 (2002)
13. Notteboom, T., Rodrigue, J.-P.: The future of containerization: perspectives from maritime and inland freight distribution. GeoJournal **74**(1), 7–22 (2009)
14. van Klink, H.A.: Towards the Borderless Main Port Rotterdam. An Analysis of Functional, Spatial and Administrative Changes in Port Systems. Tinbergen Institute Research Series n. 104, Rotterdam (1995)
15. Soriani, S.: Riorganizzazione del ciclo di trasporto e spazi di influenza portuale. Dinamiche in atto e poste territoriali in gioco. In: Salgaro, S. (a cura di): Scritti in onore di Roberto Bernardi. Patron Editore, Bologna, pp. 165–177 (2006)
16. Notteboom, T.: The relationship between seaports and the intermodal hinterland in light of global supply chains. International Transport Forum Discussion Paper 2008/10, OECD Publishing, Paris (2008)
17. Roso, V., Woxenius, J., Lumsden, K.: The dry port concept: connecting container seaports with the hinterland. J. Transp. Geogr. **17**, 338–345 (2009)
18. Ignaccolo, M., Inturri, G., Giuffrida, N., Torrisi, V.: A sustainable framework for the analysis of port systems. Eur. Transp. **78**(7), 1–19 (2020)
19. Woxenius, J., Bergqvist, R.: Comparing maritime containers and semi-trailers in the context of hinterland transport by rail. J. Transp. Geogr. **19**, 680–688 (2011)

20. Zhao, J., Zhu, X., Wang, L.: Study on scheme of outbound railway container organization in rail-water intermodal transportation. Sustainability 12(4), 1–18 (2020)
21. European Union Agency for Railways (ERA): Fostering the Railway Sector through the European Green Deal. Report – Part 2 Freight. ERA, Valenciennes (2021)
22. Notteboom, T.: Concentration and the formation of multi-port gateway regions in the European container port system: an update. J. Transp. Geogr. 18(4), 567–583 (2010)
23. Foschi, A.D.: The maritime container transport structure in the Mediterranean and Italy. Discussion Paper n. 24. Dipartimento di Scienze Economiche – Università di Pisa (2003)
24. Assoporti. https://www.assoporti.it/it/autoritasistemaportuale/statistiche/statistiche-annuali-complessive. Accessed 25 Mar 2022
25. Autorità Portuale della Spezia: Statistiche traffico mercantile 2001–2015. http://www.porto.laspezia.it. Accessed 07 Feb 2021
26. Autorità di Sistema Portuale del Mar Ligure Orientale (ASPMLO): Traffico mercantile 2016–2021. https://www.adspmarligureorientale.it/adsp-mar-ligure-orientale/traffici. Accessed 25 Mar 2022
27. Tadini, M.: Intermodalità ferroviaria e assetto territoriale dei porti gateway: il caso di La Spezia. Rivista Geografica Italiana, CXXVIII (4), 104–136 (2021)
28. EcoTransIt World Homepage. http://www.ecotransit.org. Accessed 15 Mar 2022
29. Autorità di Sistema Portuale del Mare Adriatico Orientale – Port of Trieste. Statistiche. https://www.porto.trieste.it/ita/statistiche/stat-anno-2022. Accessed 30 Apr 2022
30. Interporto Trieste. https://www.interportotrieste.it/. Accessed 30 Apr 2022
31. Adriafer, Servizio Di Manovra Dal Porto Alla Ferrovia. https://adriafer.com/wp-content/uploads/2022/01/M53_VER.02.pdf. Accessed 30 Apr 2022
32. Rodrigue, J.P.: The Geography of Transport System. Routledge, New York (2020)
33. Roletto, G.: Il porto di Trieste. Zanichelli, Bologna (1941)
34. Borruso, G., Borruso, G.: Il porto di Trieste: analisi del traffico, impatto economico e prospettive di sviluppo. In: Panaro et al. (ed.): Trasporto marittimo e sviluppo economico. Scenari internazionali, analisi del traffico e prospettive di crescita. SRM, Giannini Editore, Napoli, pp. 235–274 (2012)
35. Russo, F., Panuccio, P., Rindone, C.: Structural factors for a third-generation port: between hinterland regeneration and smart town in Gioia Tauro, Italy. Urban Marit. Transp. XXVII 204, 79 (2021)
36. Pigliucci, M.: Zone economiche speciali nel mezzogiorno d'Italia. Nuova Cultura, Roma (2019)

Strategic Planning for Special Economic Zones to Ports of the Future: System of Models and Test Case

Francesco Russo[1] [ID], Giovanna Chilà[2(✉)], and Clara Zito[3]

[1] DIIES Reggio Calabria University, Feo di Vito, 80125 Reggio Calabria, Italy
[2] Department of Public Works Municipality of Motta San Giovanni (RC), Motta San Giovanni,
Italy
giovannachila@gmail.com
[3] Reggio Calabria, Italy

Abstract. The issue of Special Economic Zones (SEZs) has become increasingly important for underdeveloped European regions. On a world level, the SEZs have allowed the significant development of the territories concerned. The main experiences of SEZs are in the areas of ports. The SEZs became the future of the ports in the underdeveloped regions. It is possible to model some main developments that the SEZ can achieve on the basis of international results. A SEZ has a core node in the area relating to an intercontinental port and can have other nodes located in national ports. A reconstruction of the supply model is then carried out considering all the modalities that allow to connect the different internal nodes to the region and the external macro-nodes. A system of models is proposed to estimate the main impacts of a SEZ. A test case is proposed referring to the TEN-T core node of Gioia Tauro and to the proposed SEZ in the connected areas. It is then modeled the maximum potential increase in employment due to the establishment of the Calabria SEZ, subject to land constraints.

Keywords: Sustainable ports · Special Economic Zone · Port of the future

1 Introduction

The Special Economic Zone (SEZ) has developed in China since the 1980s, with the aim of attracting foreign investment through measures such as incentives, tax breaks and regulatory derogations to favor the development of existing companies and encourage the settlement of new ones, especially foreign ones. The initial SEZ model evolved along different lines in various countries. In the world there are about 4000 SEZs, those in China in Dubai are the best-known examples. In Europe there are about 90, 14 of which are established in Poland, which represent some of the most virtuous examples; there are also examples of SEZs in which significant results have not been achieved. A fundamental element in the most important SEZs worldwide, is the connection with

C. Zito—Independent Researcher.

O. Gervasi et al. (Eds.): ICCSA 2022 Workshops, LNCS 13381, pp. 173–184, 2022.
https://doi.org/10.1007/978-3-031-10548-7_13

ports of an intercontinental level, in this sense the SEZs constitute the natural evolution for the future of third generation ports [1–3]. The first two generations, following the UNCTAD schematization [1], relate to ports connected to cities and to ports connected to large oil plants. The third generation of ports develops from the second half of the twentieth century and reaches maturity in the first 20 years of the twenty-first, and is generated by the container revolution [4–7].

The main challenge of container ports is to be generators of values and not just costs. In fact, while maximizing efficiency for a generic port a, a port b that offers lower costs may be present in the same market [8, 9].

$$cost \ (generalized \ from \ transport) \ b < cost \ (generalized \ from \ transport) \ a$$

If in port a, operating on goods in transit, the value is increased significantly, the following is obtained:

$$cost \ a < benefits \ (value \ added) \ a$$

The expression formalizes the main intervention with which the increase in added value can be introduced in the ports. In this sense, the SEZ is the fundamental element of the ports and allows their future development, on the other hand the ports supplying goods to the SEZs constitute the decisive element for the development of the SEZs. In view of the remarkable results obtained in many contexts by SEZs, the scientific literature is modest regarding the presence of models that allow to evaluate the main impacts of the SEZ such as economic and social outputs, employment of private investments in relation to the main inputs such as available areas and public investments.

The objective of this note is to propose a system of models that allows to estimate ex ante, starting from input variables, the potentially reliable results with the establishment of the SEZ, focusing on the specific models don't present in the literature. After the introduction, in Sect. 2, the set of main objectives that a SEZ should pursue within the goals defined by Agenda 2030 in relation to the development of connected ports is recalled. Section 3 presents the overall system of models that can be implemented to estimate the results obtainable from a SEZ and specifies in particular the models related to the Land Constraints on the available surfaces and to the Economic-functional links between nearby, but not contiguous, areas belonging to a SEZ. A case study is proposed in Sect. 4. The area considered in the study is that of Calabria (IT) and the SEZ is the one that refers to the intercontinental TEN-T [10, 11] port of Gioia Tauro and the other national ports concerned. The port of Gioia has been studied in relation to the transformation into a third-generation port [12–16].

The work can be of particular interest to the technicians of the territorial public administrations and to the technicians of the Port Authorities, to verify the possibilities of development related to the activation of a SEZ.

2 Sustainable Goals and Impact of SEZ

The impacts resulting from the establishment of SEZs can be assessed against the three declinations of sustainability in relation to the 2030 Agenda: economic, social and environmental.

The impacts in terms of economic sustainability of the SEZ mainly concern: export growth; growth in employment levels; growth in foreign capital investments; industrial upgrading and technology transfer; earnings in foreign currency; impacts on the company counts. Compared to the increase in exports, the SEZ can intervene both to accelerate its growth and to diversify the export sectors [17–19]. Tunisia's share of manufacturing exports has more than doubled since 1990. In the Philippines, the share of domestic goods exports increases from 22% in 1995 to 76% in 2003. With regard to the growth in employment levels, the SEZ can be a highly effective tool for job creation. With regard to industrial upgrading and technology transfer, the SEZ can contribute decisively to the improvement of enterprises. Regarding foreign currency earnings, their increase is one of the main expected benefits of the development of the SEZ. With regard to the impacts on the counts, the SEZ transfers to companies the tax policies provided for by the legislation specifically adopted.

Social sustainability should be understood as safety, security and participation. It is necessary to strengthen both the prevention of accidents related to the mobility of citizens and goods (safety) with the consequent reduction of the related social costs, and the protection from criminal acts (security). In line with the indications of the European Union, a qualified target for safety is to eliminate deaths by 2050 with the different intermediate objectives. Participation is declined both as accessibility and reliability of services for all citizens, and passenger rights, and as participation in decisions relating to mobility systems.

Environmental sustainability is divided into different specific objectives related to anthropized and non-anthropized areas. Some issues concern the increase of energy efficiency and environmentally friendly propulsion, the reduction of environmental pollution with particular reference to air quality, the reduction of visual intrusions and noise pollution in urban and non-urban areas.

The environmental sustainability impacts of the SEZ mainly concern: the environmental standards achievable by providing companies with infrastructures and services specifically designed, with the awareness that an effective management of the environment it is a key point for the optimization of the resources committed by investors. It is possible in the SEZ field to develop a prototype area that in Italy is defined by the model of the Ecologically Equipped Production Areas (APEA), L. D. 112/98, art.26.

3   The Proposed System of Models

3.1   The General Framework

This section shows the methodology for estimating the expected impacts of the establishment of a SEZ. The estimation is conducted through an approach based on several models whose scheme is shown in Fig. 1: Aggregated impact (M1); Land Capacity Constraint (M2); Economic - functional link (M3); Factory (M4); Cost (M5); Indirect impact (M6). Figure 1 shows the relationships between the various models, which are framed in a general system, which, through a trial and error procedure, will have as its final output the SEZ Model of the territory considered.

The proposed model structure allows, on the basis of literature data, an estimate aggregate of the impacts deriving from the establishment of the SEZ through the Aggregated Impact Model. The impacts must be verified in relation to the constraints deriving from the surface availability and the socio-economic characteristics of the areas analyzed in the Land Capacity Constraint Model, with a disaggregated approach. The Land model is important because it allows to connect the hypotheses of economic development of companies with the real availability of surface. The economic-functional link between the areas is estimated through Economic Functions Link Model, a gravitational model that includes service level attributes expressed in terms of distances and travel times. The feasibility of the hypotheses with respect to possible settlements and upgrades of companies, based on the available surfaces, and the need for resources is verified with the Factory and Cost models. While the Indirect Impact model allows to estimate the impacts in terms of direct employment and related industries. It is interesting to analyze in detail the Land Constraint (M2) and Economic-functional (M3) models, because there are no models of this type in the literature. The other models studied in the overall system presented have already been developed in the literature. Precisely for the characteristics of innovation, the attention in this note focuses on the M2 and M3 models.

The economic impacts of the SEZ have been quantified through two significant output characteristic variables:

- export of goods and services, produced by companies established in the SEZ operating in the industrial sector that leave the Italian economic territory to be destined for the rest of the world;
- employees in companies established in the SEZ operating in the industrial sector with foreign capital (total or partial) and domestic capital.

3.2 Land Capacity Constraint Model

The Land capacity constraint model estimates the expected impact of the establishment of the SEZ in terms of workforce growth, compared to the capacity constraints resulting from the availability of free areas in industrial agglomerations falling within SEZs.

The impacts of the SEZ must be estimated by considering a reference decade from year 1 to year 10, considering the characteristic variables measured in the base year of activation of the SEZ indicated with year 0:

- d_i density of employees in the industrial agglomerations i of the SEZ;
- $\Delta S_{Ai\_1,10}$ change in the area A_i occupied by new holdings in SEZ areas from the free area in the base year.

The model makes it possible to obtain an estimate according to a bottom-up method and to evaluate the variation generated in the individual industrial agglomerations considered fully integrated between them.

It has the following formulation:

$$\Delta Add_{SEZ\_Total - 1 - 10} = \Sigma_i \Delta Add_{Ai-1,10} = \Sigma_i d_i \cdot \Delta S_{Ai\_1,10} \tag{1}$$

with

- $\Delta Add_{SEZ\_Calabria\text{-}1,10}$ total change in the number of employees;

- $\Delta Add_{Ai\text{-}1,10}$ change in the number of employees in the single agglomeration A_i in the decade considered;
- $\Delta S_{Ai\_1,10}$ change in the area occupied by holdings in the individual agglomeration A_i in the decade considered;
- d_i density of employees in the single agglomeration A_i, estimated on the basis of the current values recorded in the areas considered in the SEZ.

Compared to the change in the area occupied by holdings in the individual agglomeration A_i, model estimates must be made knowing the SEZs surfaces that are free and therefore potentially available for the establishment of new companies. On the basis of the free surfaces, the possible trend scenarios can be constructed; the simplest are:

- low, an increase in the occupied area of 50% of the free area is expected compared to the value of year 0;
- high, it is expected an increase in the occupied area equal to 100% of the free area compared to the value of the year zero.

By combining the assumptions about the density of employees and the variation of occupied area, the overall scenarios are obtained. Equation 1 outputs the reference information. It is necessary to consider two additional elements in the inputs:

1) areas occupied by disused or abandoned warehouses and areas not yet expropriated in industrial areas.
2) strengthening of companies, with an increase in employment capacity and therefore of employees, which does not entail an increase in the areas currently occupied.

The result of the model must be compared with the result of the aggregate impact model. The surface already occupied and affected by regeneration is indicated by $\Delta^r S_{Ai\_0}$.

The increase in use with the inclusion of new employees in companies already operating can be considered in the model expressed by Eq. 1, increasing the d by the factor:

$$\Delta D_d = d_{rif} - d_{act}$$

with
d_{rif} reference density in the scenario considered.
d_{rif}: current density of operating enterprises increasing production and labor requirements.

3.3 Economic - Functional Link

Model 3 "Economic - functional link" must make it possible to estimate the effects deriving from the establishment of the SEZ in the macro-node of the main port of reference and in the economically and functionally integrated area connected to it. A i/o

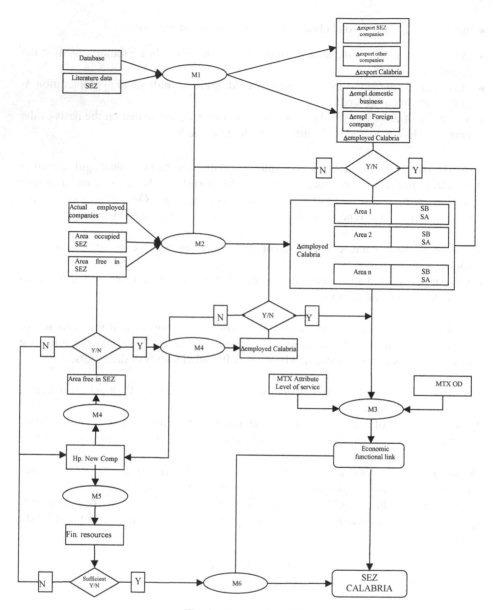

Fig. 1. System of models

model can be considered [20–23], but discontinuity between the areas make difficult the use. An aggregate model is proposed. The hypothesis is that among the areas it is possible to identify hierarchical functional relationships, focused on the core port, starting from the matrix of origin/destination O/D displacements.

It is therefore necessary to first estimate an indicator that allows to evaluate the relationships that exist between the different areas considered in the SEZ under current conditions. It is therefore necessary to estimate a different indicator that allows to evaluate the links between the areas after the first 10 years of activation of the SEZ.

The current indicator is estimated from the flows of vehicles between the areas considered.

Consider:

$d_{od} > 0$ the flow of demand for the users of the pair od.
d the demand vector whose components are the d_{od} demand values for the individual OD pairs
d^* the demand vector to be estimated.
$\hat{d}$ the initial demand vector.
f the flow vector on the network.
$\hat{f}$ the vector of the measured flows.
x the unknown demand vector
$f(x)$ the flow vector obtained by assigning x to the network

The estimation problem can be written as [24, 25]:

$$d^* = argmin_{x \geq 0}\left[z_1(x, \widehat{d}) + z_2(v(x), \widehat{f})\right]$$ (2)

where z_1 is a measure of the distance between the unknown demand x or the a priori question and z_2 is the measure of the distance between the counted flows and those derived from the assignment of $x, \widehat{d}$.

Once the vector d^* including the demand between the areas linked, has been obtained, the indicator of the current economic and functional links between the level I and II areas can be evaluated starting from the percentage of distribution conditioned at the main port h

$$L_{i/h} = (d_{h,i} + d_{i,h})/ \sum_i (d_{h,i} + di, h)$$ (3)

with
$L_{i/h}$ percentage of distribution relative to industrial area i, relative to the hub of the SEZ; $(d_{h,i} + d_{i,h})$ sum of the request for displacement related to the relationships (hub h, generic industrial area i), (generic industrial area i, hub h);

with the summation extended to all level II industrial areas.

The numerical value expressed by Eq. 3 can be further specified by weighing it with the value of the employed.

The establishment of SEZ profoundly changes the economic and functional relations between the areas concerned, with a strong push for integration, for several reasons:

- Sharing administrative simplifications
- Centralization of housekeeper functions in the hub
- Integration of the offer of combined transport services both sea (road + ship) and rail (road + train).

Due to these elements it is possible to evaluate an indicator in the field (0,1).

$$R_{i,j} = k_1 (A_i + A_j)/k2 D_{ij} \qquad (4)$$

Note that the indicator varies in the field (0,1).
A_i attractiveness factor of area i, measured with respect to employees;
A_j attractiveness factor of area j, measured in relation to employees;
D_{ij} disutility between areas i and j, measured in terms of spatial and/or temporal distances;
k_1 and k_2 constant.

Note the matrix of relations, R_{ij} it can be estimating the economic-functional relations, as a percentage of gravitation expressed by:

$$E_{ij/i} = R_{ij}/\Sigma_i R_{ij}$$

with:
E_{ih} percentage of gravitation between area i and area j.
R_{ij} generic element of the matrix of functional links joining the area i and the area j, if search for the link with the hub, it can insert h instead of j.

4   The Study Case of SEZ in Gioia Tauro Port

4.1   Land Capacity Model

The area considered in the study is that of Calabria Region where the first Italian SEZ have been proposed [26–28]. The SEZ is the one that refers to the intercontinental TEN-T [10, 11] port of Gioia Tauro and the other national ports and airport located in the region. To implement the model specific characteristics of Calabria region have been considered [29–33]. The Aggregated Impact model made possible to evaluate the increase in employment in the case studies on the basis of parameters estimated on an international scale.

The Land capacity model makes it possible to verify whether the increase in employment can be constrained by the availability of areas, or if the areas are in excess of potential development. In this phase, it is assumed from the model that the density is homogeneous for all areas and that, in the reference decade, it can assume two possible scenario values, derived from the analysis of the current state:

- $d1 = 10$ add/ha, on the establishment of medium-sized enterprises;
- $d2 = 20$ add/ha, on the establishment of large enterprises.

The change in the area occupied by holdings in the individual agglomeration has been estimated compared to the base year 2018.

Two possible trend developments were considered:

- low, increase of occupied area equal to 50% of the free area compared to the 2018 value, i.e.

$$\Delta S_{Ai\_19,28} = 0,50 \cdot (S_i SA_{i\_18\_AIL})(SCENARIO\ B);$$

- high, increase in the occupied area equal to 100% of the free area compared to the 2018 value, i.e.

$$\Delta S_{Ai\_19,28} = 1,00 \cdot (S_i SA_{i\_18\_AIL})(SCENARIO\ A).$$

Combining the assumptions on the density of employees and the variation of occupied area, 4 possible scenarios were built:

1. *Scenario B_d1*, with 50% occupation of free surfaces and a density of employees equal to 10 add/ha;
2. *Scenario B_d2*, with 50% occupation of free surfaces and a density of employees equal to 20 add/ha;
3. *Scenario A_d1*, with 100% occupation of free surfaces and employee density of 10 add/ha;
4. *Scenario A_d2*, with 100% free surface occupation and employee density of 20 add/ha.

In conclusion, it is estimated that the territorial capacity of the areas destined for the SEZ can generate a variation in employees, in the hypothesis of full employment of the areas and full activation of the SEZ tools, equal to about 5,680 employees. For sparsely dense areas, based on literature data, it is estimated that this value is around 25% of the output generated by the occupation of the available areas. In the hypothesis of scenario A_d2 this value is around 1420 employees. The result of scenario A_d2 is consistent with the aggregate output from Model 1. From the model data, however, it emerges that the total value of 2,476 hectares could prove to be a limit for the plan compared to the potential offered by the SEZ.

4.2 Economic - Functional Link Model

The Economic - functional link model estimates the effects of the SEZ in the port area of Gioia Tauro and in the integrated areas.

The territorial levels in the case study are: at Level I the Gioia Tauro Macronode; at Level II the Integrated Areas relating to other ports and airports.

The OD matrix was derived from the correction model expressed by (2), considering:

- for equivalent vehicles, Istat data [34, 35];
- for heavy-duty vehicles, the daily matrix of equivalent vehicles of the PRT, with the flows of heavy-duty vehicles detected in some type sections.

The relationships between the areas, evaluated with respect to the current OD matrix, with this indicator are not adequately represented, nor can they be considered to be particularly significant, considering the critical issues both infrastructural and functional inherited from decades of absence of regional policies outlined according to an organic approach and consistent with national and community planning and programming.

On the basis of the calculated matrix, the values of the indicator taken from (3) were calculated. The indicator expressed by (4) for all the main modes was then calculated.

The results show, in different measures, how the establishment of the SEZ determines a multiplier effect that translates into a strengthening of the economic-functional link between the level 2 areas and the Gioia Tauro area and between all the areas.

The model applied to the current scenario denotes a framework of different relationships compared to what is obtained from the analysis of the OD matrices, highlighting significant interrelationships between the areas of: Gioia Tauro, Vibo Valentia and Lamezia Terme; Crotone and Corigliano. If it is considered the scenario A_d2 and the area of Gioia Tauro, it is evident that all the areas have an interdependence that stands at least around 10%, with the maximum value of 20% for Lamezia, and with the exception of Corigliano Calabro, which is characterized by an interdependence of around 18% with Lamezia and 15% with Crotone.

5   Conclusions

From the proposed model system and its application to the test case results in various elements that can be summarized. From the Aggregated Impact Model: the total employment in Calabria for companies located in SEZ areas, considering all industrial agglomerations, is estimated at 17,351 units of which 4,095 units in foreign capital companies; 13,256 units in domestic capital companies. The Land Capacity Model shows that the increase in employment in the industrial agglomerations included in the SEZ, based on the estimated current value of employees and available areas, current and potential, is equal to about 7,100 employees, which, added to the current employees, provide a result completely consistent with the Aggregated Impact Model. From the Economic Link Model, it is clear that the increase in employment estimated by the Land Model allows to strengthen the functional economic link with respect to the main pole of Gioia Tauro and to favor the development of functional economic relations also between the II level SEZ areas.

Considering the whole system of models, it appears overall that the employment deriving from the SEZ is about 16,000 employees between direct, indirect and induced. The results obtained in the test case allow to respond positively to the objective of the paper, namely on the feasibility of a system of models that in an aggregate way allows to analyze results that in terms of employment an SEZ can produce. The overall result is valid because it manages to identify a line of research in the available scientific literature.

From the summary of the results obtained and the comparison with the results known for the real implementations of the SEZs, it can be concluded clearly, highlighting the importance of immediately introducing the SEZs in the European areas underdeveloped in order to accelerate social and economic development, in full respect of the environment.

The results also show the importance of the work presented for the technicians who were working to support the strategic direction of the companies that manage the SEZs because they can prepare quantitative analyzes for the development of the different areas, which are part of the single SEZ.

The possibilities for the development of the work go in two directions: on the one hand the development of research, with the study of models in other European realities that have the same delays in development, on the other hand the need to verify the results obtained from the model with those that can soon be obtained in the reality of the SEZ studied. These developments effectively constitute an agenda for future research.

References

1. UNCTAD: Port Marketing and the challenge of the Third Generation Port. Geneva, Switzerland: Trade and Development Board Committee on Shipping ad hoc Inter-government Group of Port Experts (1994)
2. Russo, F., Musolino, G.: Quantitative characteristics for port generations: the Italian case study. Int. J. Transp. Dev. Integr. 4(2), 103–112 (2020)
3. Russo, F., Musolino, G.: Case studies and theoretical approaches in port competition and cooperation. In: Gervasi, O., et al. (eds.) Computational Science and Its Applications – ICCSA 2021. LNCS, vol. 12958, pp. 198–212. Springer, Cham (2021). https://doi.org/10.1007/978-3-030-87016-4_15
4. Coronado, D., Acosta, M., Cerbán, M.M., López, M.P.: Economic Impact of the Container Traffic at the Port of Algeciras Bay. Springer, Heidelberg (2006). https://doi.org/10.1007/3-540-36789-6
5. Coppens, F., et al.: Economic impact of port activity: a disaggregate analysis. the case of Antwerp. Working paper document n° 110. National Bank of Belgium (2007)
6. Mateo-Mantecón, I., Coto-Millán, P., Villaverde-Castro, J., Pesquera-González, M.Á.: Economic impact of a port on the hinterland: application to Santander's port. Int. J. Shipping Transp. Logist. 4(3), 235–249 (2012)
7. Russo, F., Musolino, G., Assumma, V.: Competition between ro-ro and lo-lo services in short sea shipping market: the case of Mediterranean countries. Res. Transp. Bus. Manag. 2016(19), 27–33 (2016)
8. Russo, F., Chilà, G.: Structural factors for a third-generation port: current state, limits and weakness for Gioia Tauro in the regional transport plan. WIT Trans. Built Environ. 2021(204), 3–15 (2021)
9. Russo, F., Chilà, G.: Structural factors for of a third-generation port: actions and measures for Gioia Tauro in the regional transport plan. WIT Trans. Built Environ. 2021(204), 17–30 (2021)
10. Regolamento (UE) n. 1315/2013: Parlamento europeo e Consiglio, 11 dicembre 2013, orientamenti dell'Unione per lo sviluppo della rete transeuropea dei trasporti e che abroga la decisione n. 661/2010/UE. Testo rilevante ai fini del SEE, GU L 348 del 20 dicembre 2013 (2013)
11. Regolamento (UE) n. 1316/2013: Parlamento europeo e Consiglio, 11 dicembre 2013, meccanismo per collegare l'Europa e che modifica il regolamento (UE) n. 913/2010 e che abroga i regolamenti (CE) n. 680/2007 e (CE) n. 67/2010. Testo rilevante ai fini del SEE. (GU L 348 del 20 dicembre 2013), pp. 129–171 (2013)
12. Musolino, G., Chilà, G.: Structural factors for a third-generation port: planning general logistics interventions in Gioia Tauro. WIT Transactions on the Built Environment (2021)

13. Musolino, G., Trecozzi, M.R.: Structural factors for a third-generation port: planning interventions for agri-food logistics in Gioia Tauro. WIT Trans. Built Environ. **204**, 43 (2021)
14. Musolino, G., Cartisano, A., Fortugno, G.: Structural factors for a third-generation port: planning interventions for mechanical logistics in GioiaTauro. WIT Trans. Built Environ. **204**, 67–78 (2021)
15. Russo, F., Rindone, C.: Structural factors for of a third-generation port: planning interventions for research and development in Gioia Tauro TENT-T node. WIT Trans. Built Environ. **2021**(204), 67–78 (2021)
16. Russo, F., Panuccio, P., Rindone, C.: Structural factors for a third-generation port: between hinterland regeneration and smart town in Gioia Tauro. WIT Trans. Built Environ. **2021**(204), 79–90 (2021)
17. Fias: Special economic zones. performance, lessons learned, and implications for zone development, The World Bank Group (2008)
18. Leong, C.K.: Special economic zones and growth in China and India: an empirical investigation. IEEP **10**(4), 549–567 (2012). https://doi.org/10.1007/s10368-012-0223-6
19. Wang, J.: The economic impact of special economic zones: evidence from Chinese municipalities. J. Dev. Econ. **101**(2013), 133–147 (2013)
20. Kochelman, K.M., Ling, J., Zhao, Y., Ruiz-Juri, N.: Tracking land use, transport and industrial production using random utility-based multiregional input–output models: application for Texas trade. J. Transp. Geogr. **13**(3), 275–286 (2005)
21. Leontief, W.: The Structure of American Economy, 2nd edn. Oxford University Press, New York (1941)
22. Leontief, W., Strout, A.: Multi-regional input–output analysis. In: Barna, T. (ed.) Structural Interdependence and Economic Development, pp. 119–150. McMillan, London (1963)
23. Russo, F., Musolino, G.: A unifying modelling framework to simulate the spatial economic transport interaction process at urban and national scales. J. Transp. Geogr. **24**, 189–197 (2012)
24. Cascetta, E.: Transportation Systems Engineering: Theory and Methods, vol. 49. Springer Science & Business Media, New York (2013). https://doi.org/10.1007/978-1-4757-6873-2
25. Russo, F., Vitetta, A.: Reverse assignment: Calibrating link cost functions and updating demand from traffic counts and time measurements. Inverse Probl. Sci. Eng. **19**, 921–950 (2011). https://doi.org/10.1080/17415977.2011.565339
26. Decreto Legge n. 91 del 20 giugno 2017: Disposizioni urgenti per la crescita economica nel Mezzogiorno convertito in legge il 1° agosto 2017 (2017)
27. DGR. n. 294 del 11/08/2015: Misure straordinarie per lo sviluppo dell'area di Gioia Tauro DDL per l'istituzione di una Zona Economica Speciale (2015)
28. Deliberazione n. 52/2015: Misure straordinarie per lo sviluppo dell'Area di Gioia Tauro -DDL per l'istituzione di una zona economica speciale (2015)
29. Piano Regionale dei Trasporti Regione Calabria: DGR n. 503 del 06/12/2016, DCR n.157 del 19/12/2016 e valutato positivamente dalla Commissione UE, Direzione Generale Politica Regionale e Urbana n.1086324 01/03/17 (2016)
30. Pirro F.: L'industria in Calabria. Un profilo di sintesi. STM-MIT (2017)
31. Progetto Strategico Regionale Calabria Competitiva: Interventi per lo sviluppo del sistema produttivo calabrese e la promozione di nuova imprenditorialità DGR n.250/16 (2016)
32. Progetto Strategico Regionale Calabria Impresa.eu: Accesso unico ai servizi e agli strumenti digitali dell'Amministrazione regionale per lo sviluppo imprenditoriale DGR n. 304/16 (2016)
33. Regione Calabria: Dove insediare la tua impresa, servizio online, Calabria SUAP (2018). www.calabriasuap.it/marketing/lotti
34. ISTAT: Censimento generale dell'agricoltura (2010)
35. ISTAT: Censimento dell'industria e dei servizi (2011)

Smart Ports from Theory to Practice: A Review of Sustainability Indicators

Silvia Battino[1]([✉])(iD) and Maria del Mar Muñoz Leonisio[2](iD)

[1] DiSea - University of Sassari, 07100 Sassari, Sardinia, Italy
sbattino@uniss.it
[2] University of Cádiz, 11003 Cádiz, Spain
mar.leonisio@uca.es

Abstract. About 70% of the Earth's surface is covered by water. A "blue planet" whose essential driving force is represented by the ports that ensure the connection also of the most peripheral and insular areas. The activities of ports are configured as an element of economic development and creation of new employment. In Europe, according to the last report of 2020, maritime transport was fundamental to import and export 74% of goods, to generate employment for 1.5 million workers and to move about 420 million passengers.

At the same time, port activities are responsible for several negative externalities that are often not considered in business strategies. In recent decades the port industry has undergone a profound transformation because of different technical, commercial, and legal aspects. The smart port concept is based on the ability of new technologies to transform port services into interactive and dynamic businesses, more efficient and transparent. Its objective is to satisfy the needs of customers and users without forgetting its responsibility to the city and the citizens.

The digitization combined with careful planning and management of port operations allows us to find smart solutions to optimize logistics and environmental impacts, to promote efficiency and to enhance the safety of both seaports and coastal regions involved.

This paper, after a review of the literature on smart port studies, aims to build a matrix of indicators of the sustainability of port ecosystems which will allow the measuring and ranking of ports in its Smart Port category.

Keywords: Seaports · Smartness · Sustainable indicators

1 Introduction

The policies and strategies dedicated to the transport sector are regularly updated by many multidisciplinary contributions that analyze and elaborate solutions to reduce the

This study is developed in the context of "Programma di Sviluppo Dipartimenti di Eccellenza 2018–2022 BES - Benessere Equo Sostenibile", Department of Economics and Business – University of Sassari. This paper is the result of the joint work of the authors. In particular: Sects. 1 and 2 have been written by Silvia Battino and Sects. 3 and 4 by Maria del Mar Muñoz Leonisio.

O. Gervasi et al. (Eds.): ICCSA 2022 Workshops, LNCS 13381, pp. 185–195, 2022.
https://doi.org/10.1007/978-3-031-10548-7_14

negative impacts resulting from the use of transport means (land, air, and sea) and to improve the mobility of people and goods [1].

The concept of sustainable mobility first appeared in Europe in 1992 within the "Green book", which highlighted the impact of transport on the environment and the common strategy to improve the negative effects of the sector on the economic and social life of the Member States. Subsequent documents including the 2030 Agenda (2015), the 7th and 8th Action Programs (2018 and 2021), the European Green Deal (2019) and the Next Generation EU (2021) bring to the attention of all stakeholders the need to implement actions for cohesive and inclusive growth [2]. The plan to reach the goal of climate neutrality in 2050 is ambitious: by this date a 90% reduction in emissions from the transport sector is expected [3]. According to recent statistics, climate neutrality still seems far away. Indeed, this sector has recorded a constant increase in the production of Green House Gases (GHG) from 2013 to 2019: road transport is responsible for 72% of all GHG, followed by aviation (13%) and maritime (14%) [4]. The emissions of the latter two means of transport have increased by more than 50% since 1990. In this panorama of documents and policies, we will focus on the strategy that perceives the future of ports considering the combination of four elements: port operations, environment, energy and safety and security. This combination will allow more efficient and sustainable ports along with improvements in the accessibility and safety.

The remainder of the paper is organized as follows. Section 2 presents a brief re-view of the literature. Section 3 which is divided into three parts explores the key findings on smart port indicators. The first part explains the port model in order to establish responsibility in terms of sustainability. The second part explores the initiatives and regulations that have been implemented in ports to reduce environmental impact and improve port operations. The third part is based on the development of a set of indicators that will allow the comparison of the degree of compliance with smart port objectives.

We summarize our main conclusions and future lines of research in the fourth section.

2   Related Works

The ports have traditionally been defined according to three different classifications: hierarchical, generation and functional. The first classification is based on the hub and spoke system without considering possible horizontal relationships with the hinterland. The second classification (generation) highlights ports in their evolutionary history from a primitive system (e.g., fishing village) to a global hub. This view also considers the development of port-city integrations. Finally, the functional classification emphasizes the regionalization of the port system considering logistics integration as the final step of development [5].

In 1990, the proposal of a theoretical model, carried out during the United Nations. Conference on Trade and Development (UNCTAD), helped to understand the evolution of seaports. The model considers locally adopted strategies, services provided, and information technology to distinguish five generations of ports (Fig. 1) [6–9].

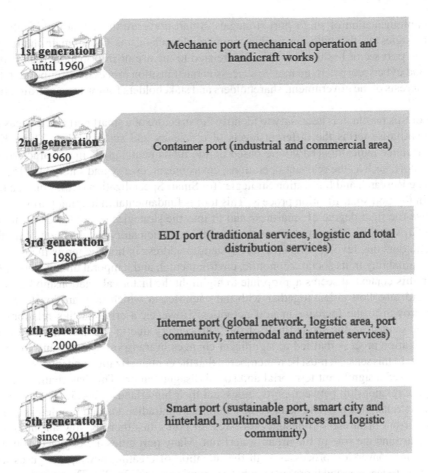

Fig. 1. Evolution of seaport. Source: own elaboration based on [6, 7, 9, 10].

Ports in their evolutionary process have produced numerous changes in various operational areas such as productivity, infrastructure and governance. Also, the adoption of modern technologies and the activation of new business partnerships/strategies have been important. Thus, increasingly sophisticated networks are working to make all port activities sustainable and more interconnected. This trend, accompanied by the evolution of digitization, marks the way for the realization of the Smart Port [11–13]. For a port to reach the definition of smart, it must achieve certain requirements. Among these requirements are the provision of high quality infrastructure; the operational integration with the other port operators and the territories that gravitate towards it; the ability to process significant amounts of data; the achievement of competitive advantages and at the same time having the ability to implement practices that are respectful of the environment and citizenship [8]. The most important ports in the world have taken steps to equip themselves with the most modern and sophisticated technologies to improve their functions in a competitive context and at the same time careful not to cause irreversible negative impacts [14]. However, not all ports start from the same situation regarding the implementation of smart port strategies. Smart ports are those that use intelligent technologies together with sustainable commercial mechanisms. One of main challenges that the port sector has to face is the one related to the use of Information Technology (IT) and cybersecurity. To guarantee success in the transition process, it is important that the interests of the government, shareholders and stakeholders follow the same direction [11, 13].

For this reason, it is necessary to identify the structure of a smart port and to measure in quantitative terms the different levels of efficiency and sustainability. These Key Performance Indicators (KPIs) are based on the fundamental goals that characterize a smart port, such as the relevant operations, environment, energy and safety [14, 15].

The Research and Innovation Strategies for Smart Specialization (RIS3) plays a key role in the port smartification process. This tool is fundamental in helping port systems achieve the right degree of smartness and fit into the strategies of the Green Deal and Blue Growth [16]. This emphasizes the need for a participatory involvement of all the stakeholders that revolve around a port system to address in holistic terms the process of sustainability in its social, economic, environmental, and temporal dimensions [17].

In this context, it seems appropriate to highlight the historical relationship between port and city. Port cities, together with the countries in which they are located, owe their growth to the increase in port activities. However, a crisis in this relationship became evident in the second half of the 20th century due to the acceleration of the globalization process that led to significant changes in transport systems and location choices. In this sense, it must be remembered that the containerization and inter-modality have caused a significant territorial and social disaggregation. This has challenged the complex relationship between ports, cities and their hinterlands [18–25]. The complex city-port relationship is characterized by multiple contradictions and problems arising from current planning and design processes. In port cities there is now an important debate around the role of the urban waterfront. Many port cities are engaged in urban waterfront conversion processes with the intention of creating new spaces, uses and future port scenarios and more sustainable economic growth [26, 27]. The growth of port activities can help revive the city's economy thanks to an increase in the flow of goods, new investments and passenger arrivals, as well as from a tourist perspective linked to cruise tourism. Together with these projects, value-added services will increase and the construction/renovation of road and rail infrastructures will be encouraged, which will also boost the city's economy. Hence the need for sustainable and integrated logistics, which is embodied in the creation of a Smart Tunnel. This is an intelligent platform of logistics services for port cities and is aimed at maximizing the safety and efficiency of the port-retroport corridors. It essentially means increasing the value of the port terminal within supply chain management [28–31].

A digitally-supported network and IT strategy aimed at managing land and sea traffic are helping to maintain the economic viability of the port city. City residents can get around easily and port operations become more efficient. Thus, transportation planning is combined with urban planning promoting the improvement of the quality of life of the port city [32]. The integration between the urban and port system represents the connection between the local and global economy. The application of Data Envelopment Analysis (DEA) on the whole city/port allows to measure and compare the level of sustainable development achieved by the above-mentioned indissoluble pair (port city) [33]. It is to assess and constantly monitor the degree of sustainability of port cities, using, also, methods of classification of different plans and long-term port visions to be compared with a set of social, economic, and environmental KPIs [34]. Finally, it can be said that the study of the economic-territorial organization of a port facilitates the required interventions of territorial planning and economic programming [35].

3   Smart Port Indicators

3.1   Port Organization Model

Globalization and technological developments have not only affected the design and operations of port facilities, but also the organizational and institutional relationships between members of the port community [47, 48]. The characteristics of the demand for port services and the technology of the offer determine the economic structure of the ports and their management. The search for efficiency in maritime transport leads to the introduction of certain mechanisms to encourage internal competition in the provision of port services. Ports face competition between ports and also competition between port terminals. Most of the activity of a port is carried out by private companies that operate in it through licenses, authorizations or concessions granted by the Port Authority (PA). These agreements enable companies to operate in the port under certain conditions of use. The private terminal operator can build and maintain its own buildings, purchase and install its own equipment on port land and hire workers. Port public-private partnerships are considered a very effective tool in the hands of public agencies for port development and performance, while maintaining strategic control over the asset in the long term [36–38]. In fact, landlord port model is the most common organization of the main ports of North America, Europe and Asia. The main strength of a landlord port is that a private operator adapts more quickly to changes in the market than public agencies. It must be taken into account that the survival of private terminals depends on the existence of profits. PAs and the private operators must respond to the demands of society and the ports users.

The management of the PAs should be characterized by a double objective: to make the port attractive for users through a competitive offer of services, and on the other hand to increase the well-being of its citizens [39]. Shareholders consider the financial position and return on investment as well as the reputation of the port in terms of the legal and transparent competitive allocation of port terminals. At the same time, the performance of a high use of information and communication technologies and the use of environmentally friendly procedures, are gaining weight in investors' decisions [40–42].

Table 1 summarizes the configuration of the landlord port model in regard to the ownership and management of resources and commercial activities.

Although the influence of the PA is in many cases indirect, all PAs are called to proceed and operate effectively to implement the Environmental Management System (EMS) of the ports under their jurisdiction. PAs not only have administrative regulations to promote better environmental management but also economic incentive mechanisms

Table 1. Landlord port model. Source: own elaboration.

Administrative management of the port space Enabling private operators through licenses, concessions or authorizations	PORT AUTHORITY
Organization of the activity Management, surveillance and control of port activity	
General services Cleaning of common areas, cleaning of floats, etc	
Basic Infrastructure: shelter dikes, dredging Complementary Infrastructure: development of docks, berths, roads, service networks	PRIVATE PORT OPERATORS
Superstructure: Loading, unloading, handling and storage equipment	
Port services (provided by licence) Handling of merchandise, passenger services, technical nautical services and reception of ship waste	
Commercial services (provided by concession) Storage, activities of added value to the merchandise, etc.	

such as discounts on activity rates or extensions to the concession term for those operators who comply with Good Practice agreements.

3.2 Smart Port Initiatives

The increase in social and economic demands is causing that ports around the world to incorporate initiatives to reduce environmental impact and improve port operations. In this context, the Good Practice Guides developed by the Spanish State Ports aim to provide a common frame of reference. These guides provide initiatives to promote better environmental performance of operations within the entire port system. Two guides are currently available:

– Guide to good practices in the implementation of environmental management systems. It provides recommendations for implementing environmental management systems in port companies. The purpose of these recommendations is to adapt the management systems to operations in the port and to the needs for verifying the good practice agreements.
– Guide to good practices in the handling of solid bulk. This guide provides recommendations on both good practices in operations and in the provision of equipment. The objective is to help control the environmental impacts linked to the handling of solid bulk through a wide variety of operating schemes.

There are some international regulations related to the prevention of marine pollution and greenhouse gas emissions. Some of them are the protocols of the International

Convention for the Prevention of Marine Pollution from Ships (MARPOL) 73/78/97. The Eco-Management and Audit Scheme (EMAS) is a tool developed by the European Union that recognizes those organizations that have implemented an EMS.

In addition, the European Sea Port Organization (ESPO) supports environmental protection in European ports and emphasizes the importance of adopting programs that include actions to control and monitor green practices. The Environmental Product Declaration (EPD) is a comprehensive, internationally harmonized report created by a product manufacturer that documents the ways in which a product, throughout its lifecycle, affects the environment.

In the social sphere, ISO 45001 standard recognizes the organization's commitment to corporate responsibility and the development of a preventive culture in the organization.

ISO 50001, an international standard for energy management systems, specifies the requirements for designing, applying, maintaining and enhancing an Energy management system.

In addition to the risks inherent to the activity itself, ports are exposed to threats of terrorist attacks and cyber security. International Ship and Port Facility Security (ISPS) code is a set of measures to enhance the security of ships and port facilities.

These are only some of the most popular guides and recommendations, but the transition to smart port is an ever-evolving process.

3.3 Smart Port Indicators

The smart definition finds application in all human activities, from production and management activities to mobility of people and goods. The use of indicators is aimed at monitoring the operational, managerial, and environmental performance of seaports. For this reason, academic research needs a continuous confrontation with maritime transport professionals to ascertain, choose, estimate, and confirm plausible, achievable, and feasible indicators for the sector [43]. The involvement of multiple actors in the determination of Port Sustainability Indicators (PSI) seems to be becoming more attractive and decisive. In fact, the scientific work carried out thanks to the confrontation with the experts of the PAs is associated with the experiential points of view of local political/administrative powers, of companies that manage other transport systems (air, rail, and road) and, finally, of citizens. The involvement of citizens in the process, who may lack specific knowledge but "gravitate" to or "live" in the port, highlights a decision-making approach with social implications [44].

A smart port is based on the implementation of behavior strategies that can be classified into four main activity domains: Operations, Environment, Energy and Safety and security [14]. Recent research [45, 46] has determined a rank of smartness achieved by the most important (10) Spanish ports, both for each of the four pillars considered (economic operational, social, institutional political, natural environment).

Based on the related Works and previously mentioned guidelines and standards management system (SMS) we have established a set of performance indicators that will allow ports to be classified within the Smart category. Smart port performance indicators are defined on measurable and realistic objectives. Each PA establishes its own objectives regarding the transition to smart ports through the implementation of the best available practices and their own resources. Table 2 shows a matrix of Smart Port KPIs classified into four categories and a brief description.

Table 2. Smart port key performance indicators. Source: own elaboration.

Description			Key performance indicators
Smart port operations	Operational	Operational efficiency	Total cargo moved in relation to seaport equipment
	Economics	Economic efficiency	Investments and returns
	Political & Institutional	Management transparency Private operators (%) Quality private services SMS	Open data system Concession area Index Number of private operators with discounts for the quality of their services ISO 9001
	Social	Health & Safety. SMS Labor inclusion and equality in the workforce	ISO 45001 Number of female workers of total workers Gender diversity in the Board of Administration
	Mobility	Optimize the mobility of heavy vehicles Boost rail traffic	Existence of railway tracks inside the port
Environment	Water quality Water consumption management Noise pollution		EPD ISO 14001 EMAS III
Energy	Renewable energy production Energy management systems		Use of renewable (wind energy, solar power) ISO 50001
Safety and security	Actions to improve cybersecurity		ISPS

We have established four categories of measures related to easily identifiable indicators. These measures are not the only ones possible nor do they exclude the possibility of adding other alternatives. It is important to mention the fact that this is voluntary behavior on the part of the PAs. This analysis will permit us to investigate which are the most accepted and applied indicators.

The objective pursued is to monitor the implementation of KPIs and at the same time detect which of the dimensions of smart port requirements are not met. The comparison between ports will allow the establishment a smart port ranking.

4 Conclusions and Future Lines of Research

Smart port is a broad concept that encompasses different organizations and requires a long-term commitment. Although the term is relatively recent, the interest shown by researchers reveals the importance of the topic throughout the world. National governments and PAs are interested in the implementation of good practices that combine economic growth and social responsibility.

In this work, three relevant topics have been observed. First, the ability of seaports to evolve under the sustainability and smart paradigm principles was presented. Second, the port city relationship is analyzed through the evolution of technology and global networks and the ports´ contribution to the creation of incomes in their hinterland. Third, possible mechanisms are studied to reduce the undesirable output of port activity. The best way to improve harmony between the port and its citizens is the implementation of transparent management that incorporates the requirements of all stakeholders. At the same time, studies and researches seem to confirm that implementing smart strategies improves both the operational efficiency and port city relationships. Taking into account that some practices are mandatory, the true scope of the smart port category is in the implementation of voluntary actions. This behavior will lead the way for other ports in the future.

The first step for the design of quantifiable SMIs consists in the identification of responsible behaviors within each port environment. In this sense, this work is a starting point to measure the reality of progress in the implementation of smart development goals. The second step of this research will consist of the application of KPIs to Spanish and Italian ports to check the level of commitment of their PAs. Additionally, it should be interesting in the future to contrast the use of KPIs and port economic or operational performance.

References

1. Holden, E., Gilpin, G., Banister, D.: Sustainable mobility at Thirty. Sustainability **11**(1965), 1–14 (2019)
2. Madau, C., Battino, S.: Trasporti e innovazione per "ripensare" gli spazi. L'approccio smart della Regione Sardegna. In: Dini, F., Martellozzo, F., Randelli, F., Romei, P. (eds.) Oltre la globalizzazione – Feedback, Società di Studi Geografici. Memorie geografiche NS 19, pp. 67–73 (2021)
3. Di Marco, L.: Obiettivi di sviluppo sostenibile e politiche europee. Le sfide del futuro dell'Europa. Quaderni dell'ASviS. **5**, 1–156 (2021)
4. European Environment Agency: Greenhouse gas emissions from transport in Europe (2021). https://www.eea.europa.eu/ims/greenhouse-gas-emissions-from-transport
5. Kanellopoulos, J., Mininel, S., Daems, F., Nikolopoulou, A.: Port of the future challenges, enablers and barriers. In: COREALIS Consortium 2018–2021 (2021)
6. UNCTAD: Port Marketing and the Challenge of the Third Generation Port. Trade and Development Board Committee on Shipping ad hoc Intergovernmental Group of Port Experts (1994)
7. UNCTAD: The Fourth Generation Port. UNCTAD Ports Newsletter **19**, 9–12 (1999)
8. Karaś, A.: Smart porto ad a key to the future development of modern ports. TransNav **14**(1), 27–31 (2020)

9. Kaliszewski, A.: Fifth and sixth generation ports (5gp, 6gp) evolution of economic and social roles of ports. Retrieved **5**, 1–31 (2018)
10. Flynn, M., Lee, P., Notteboom, T.: The next step on the port generations ladder: customer-centric and community ports. In: Notteboom, T. (ed.) Current Issues in Shipping, pp. 497–510. Ports and Logistics, University Press Antwerp, Brussels (2011)
11. Jović M., Kavran N., Aksentijević S., Tijan E.: the transition of Croatian seaports into smart ports. In: MIPRO 2019, 20–24 May, Opatija - Croatia, pp. 1.386–1.390 (2019)
12. Hossain T., Adams M., Walker T.R.: Sustainability initiatives in Canadian ports. Marine Policy **106**, 11 (2019). (103519)
13. (de la) Peña Zarzuelo, I.: Cybersecurity in ports and maritime industry: reasons for raising awareness on this issue. Transp. Policy **100**, 1–4 (2021)
14. Molavi A., LKaras G. J, Race B.: A framework for building a smart port and smart port index. Int. J. Sustain. Transp. **14**(9), 686–700 (2020)
15. Makkawan, K., Muangpan, T.: A conceptual model of smart port performance and smart port indicators in Thailand. J. Int. Logist. Trade **19**(3), 133–146 (2021)
16. Meyer, C.: Integration of baltic small and medium-sized ports in regional innovation strategies on smart specialisation (RIS3). J. Open Innov. Technol. Mark. Complex **7**(3), 184, 16 (2021). https://doi.org/10.3390/joitmc7030184
17. Lozano, R., Carpenter, A., Sammalisto, K.: Analysing organisational change management in seaports: stakeholder perception, communication, drivers for, and barriers to sustainability at the Port of Gävle. In: Carpenter, A., Lozano, R. (eds.) European Port Cities in Transition. SS, pp. 205–224. Springer, Cham (2020). https://doi.org/10.1007/978-3-030-36464-9_12
18. Vallega, A.: Nodalité et centralité face à la multimodalité. Élements pour un relais entre théorie régionale et théorie des transports. In: Muscara, C., Poli, C. (eds.) Transport Geography Facing Geography, pp. 69–88. Dipartimento di Pianificazione Urbanistica e Territoriale, Rome (1983)
19. Vallega, A.: Cityports, coastal zones and sustainable development. In: Hoyle, B.S. (ed.) City-ports, coastal zones and regional change, pp. 295–306. Jhon Wiley & Sons Ltd., Hoboken (1996)
20. Hoyle, B.S.: The port-city interface: Trends. Problems and examples. Geoforum **29**(4), 429–435 (1989)
21. Hoyle, B.S. (ed.): Cityports, Coastal Zones and Regional Change. John Wiley & Sons Ltd., Hoboken (1996)
22. Hoyle, B.S., Pinder, D.A.: European Port Cities in Transition. Belhavwen Press, London (1992)
23. Musso E.: Città portuali: l'economia e il territorio. FrancoAngeli, Milano (1996)
24. Ducruet, C.: Approche comparée du développement des villes-ports à l'échelle mondiale: problèmes conceptuels et méthodologiques. Les Cahiers scientifiques du transport AFITL **48**, 59–79 (2005)
25. Ducruet, C.: The port city in multidisciplinary analysis. In: Alemany, J., Bruttomesso, R. (eds.). The Port City in the XXIst Century: New Challenges in the Relationship Between Port and City, pp. 32–48. RETE, Venezia (2011)
26. Giovinazzi, O.: Citta' portuali e waterfront urbani: costruire scenari di trasformazione in contesti di conflitto. Méditerranée: Revue géographique des pays méditerranées **111**, 69–74 (2008)
27. Gras, P.: Storia dei porti. Declino e rinascita delle città portuali, pp. 1940–2010. Odoya, Bologna (2013)
28. Carbone, V., Martino, M.: The changing role of ports in supply-chain management: an empirical analysis. Marit. Policy Manag. **30**(4), 305–320 (2003)
29. Shan, J., Yu, M., Lee, C.Y.: An empirical investigation of the seaport's economic impact: evidence from major ports in China. Transp. Res. Part E **69**, 41–53 (2014)

30. Mazzarino, M., Battino, S.: Lo sviluppo di servizi di trasporto innovativi a supporto della mobilità dei crocieristici: una valutazione di fattibilità strategica per il porto di Ragusa (Dubrovnik). Boll. della Soc. Geogr. Ital. **2**(2), 29–48 (2019)

31. Amaro García A., Battino S.: Turismo de cruceros en Las Palmas de Gran Canaria (España): reflexiones territoriales. In: Parreño Castellano J.M., Moreno Medina, C.J. (eds.) La reconfiguración capitalista de los espacios urbanos: transformaciones y desigualdades, pp. 19–39. ULPGC editores, Las Palmas de Gran Canaria (2021)

32. Gurzhiy, A., Kalyazina, S., Maydanova, S., Marchenko, R.: Port and city integration: transportation aspect. Transp. Res. Proc. **54**, 890–899 (2021)

33. Chen, C., Lam, J.S.L.: Sustainability and interactivity between cities and ports: a two-stage data envelopment analysis (DEA) approach. Marit. Policy Manage. **45**(7), 944–961 (2018)

34. Schipper, C.A., Vreugdenhil, H., de Jong, M.P.C.: A sustainability assessment of ports and port-city plans: comparing ambitions with achievements. Transp. Res. Part D **57**, 84–111 (2017)

35. Carpenter, A., Lozano, R. (eds.): European Port Cities in Transition. SS, Springer, Cham (2020). https://doi.org/10.1007/978-3-030-36464-9

36. Vining, A.R., Boardman, A.E.: The potential role of public–private partnerships in the upgrade of port infrastructure: normative and positive considerations. Maritime Policy Manage. **35**(6), 551–569 (2008)

37. Siemonsma, H., Van Nus, W., Uyttendaele, P.: Awarding of Port PPP contracts: the added value of a competitive dialogue procedure. Marit. Policy Manage. **39**(1), 63–78 (2012). https://doi.org/10.1080/03088839.2011.642314

38. Panayides, P.M., Parola, F., Lam, J.: The effect of institutional factors on public–private partnership success in ports. Transp. Res. Part A: Policy Pract. **71**(C), 110–127 (2015)

39. Musso, E., Benacchio, M., Ferrari, C.: Ports and employment in port cities. UME **1**(4), 283–311 (2000)

40. Ferretti, M., Schiavone, F.: Internet of Things and business processes redesign in seaports: the case of Hamburg. Bus. Process Manag. J. **22**, 271–284 (2016). https://doi.org/10.1108/BPMJ-05-2015-0079

41. Botti, A., Monda, A., Pellicano, M., Torre, C.: The re-conceptualization of the port supply chain as a smart port service system: the case of the port of Salerno. Systems **5**, 35 (2017). https://doi.org/10.3390/systems5020035

42. Yang, Y., Zhong, M., Yao, H., Yu, F., Fu, X., Postolache, O.: Internet of things for smart ports: technologies and challenges. IEEE Instrum. Meas. Mag. **21**, 34–43 (2018). https://doi.org/10.1109/MIM.2018.8278808

43. Puig, M., Wooldridge, C., Darbra, R.M.: Identification and selection of environmental performance indicators for sustainable port development. Mar. Pollut. Bull. **81**(1), 124–130 (2014)

44. Shiau, T.A., Chuang, C.C.: Social construction of port sustainability indicators: a case study of Keelung Port. Marit. Policy Manage. **41**(1), 1–17 (2015)

45. Rodrigo, G.A., González-Cancelas, N., Molina, S.B., Camarero, O.A.: Preparation of a smart port indicator and calculation of a ranking for the Spanish port system. Logistics **4**(9), 1–22 (2020)

46. Rodrigo, G.A., González-Cancelas, N., Molina, S.B., Camarero, O.A.: Smart ports: ranking of Spanish port system. World Sci. News **144**, 1–12 (2020)

47. Haezendonck, E., Dooms, M., Verbeke, A.: A new governance perspective on port–hinterland relationships: The Port Hinterland Impact (PHI) matrix. Maritime Econ. Logist. **16**, 229–249 (2014). https://doi.org/10.1057/mel.2014.10

48. González-Laxe, F., Martín-Bermúdez, F., Martín-Palmero, F., Novo-Corti, I.: Sustainability at Spanish ports specialized in liquid bulk: evolution in times of crisis 2010–2015. Marit. Policy Manage. **46**(4), 491–507 (2019)

Not Only Waterfront. The Port-City Relations Between Peripheries and Inner Harbors

Ginevra Balletto[1], Giuseppe Borruso[2(✉)], and Tiziana Campisi[3]

[1] DICAAR – Department of Civil and Environmental Engineering and Architecture, University of Cagliari, Via Marengo 2, 09123 Cagliari, Italy
balleto@unica.it

[2] DEMS – Department of Economic, Business, Mathematic and Statistical Sciences "Bruno de Finetti", University of Trieste, Via A. Valerio, 4/1, 34127 Trieste, Italy
giuseppe.borruso@deams.units.it

[3] Faculty of Engineering and Architecture, University of Enna Kore, Cittadella Universitaria, 94100 Enna, Italy
tiziana.campisi@unikore.it

Abstract. The paper tackles the issue related to the sea-rail intermodal transport Important but often conflictual relations have for long times related cities and their ports. In particular, the mutual evolutions of cities and ports drew very often the attention on waterfronts and on the older port areas and facilities that are abandoned or converted to urban uses and functions. There is little attention, on the contrary, towards the new areas becoming important for ports, as the inner harbors, that host increasingly important operations that are vital for linking ports and their hinterlands in order to free quays for freight handling on the seaside. These operations include, among others, warehousing, modal shift, block-train assembly. Similarly, cities are living a complex relation among their centres, the focus of policies and attention by policymakers, and their where, on the contrary there is a general lack of services and communities suffering for deprivation and little access. These areas, furthermore, become more and more the ideal location for transport and port-related activities and facilities, among them, ideally, disused commercial and industrial sites. Such transport and logistic-related activities, however, not always are inserted into urban and transport plans, but also very often being carried on by privately-owned companies. The paper is focused on the definition of a method for highlighting the inner relations between peripheries, semi-peripheries and inner harbors, proposing a methodological analytical framework for spatially-locating the spatial pressures and potential for development. The research started from the local cases of Cagliari, Catania and Trieste as starting points for the observation of these phenomena, to extract analytical and research points for further evolutions on national and international cases.

Keywords: Port-City relation · Peripheries · Inner harbors

The paper is the result of the joint work of the three authors. However, Ginevra Balletto wrote Sects. 1.1, 2.1; Giuseppe Borruso wrote Sects. 2.3, 3.2, 4 and 5; Tiziana Campisi wrote Sects. 1.2, 2.2 and 3.1.

1 Introduction

1.1 The Port City Relation

The problems and stresses that characterised the contemporary cities are mainly caused by natural and health factors - similarly to what happened in the past - linked to climate change and the recent COVID-19 pandemic crisis.

A number of studies have described the urban shocks that have affected cities in the last decade and they have defined strategies, actions and tools useful for the realization of a post-pandemic, climate-proof city [1, 2]. In several areas of many Mediterranean cities, as those object of the present paper, like, particularly, Catania, but also, in different and less evident ways, like Cagliari and Trieste, changes are taking place, involving in particular the former port areas as waterfronts, as well as other old industrialized areas.

The waterfront, in particular, generally identifies the area of a city close to the sea - or a lake - in particular the area bordered by a port, dockyard, arsenal or other commercial or industrial maritime activities. It does not therefore correspond to the waterfront, which may instead be a road or other scenic route running along the seashore [3]. These urban spaces are the object of a series of interventions aimed at increasing accessibility and public use, but also of urban-port reconversion processes and transformation projects on the waterfronts.

The port-city relationship, in its complexity, lays at the heart of a set of contradictions and problems in contemporary planning, starting from its scalar dimension, to funding and the most suitable planning tools. Several studies have conducted research on the transformation of port cities and urban waterfronts in Italy, to demonstrate that the relationship between the city and the port cannot be conceived as a problem of homogeneity, but rather of diversity.

This derives from the fact that political choices, projects and resources are often not defined with the same degree of interest and importance [4, 5]. On the basis of these concepts, this paper therefore describes the most recent evolution in particular of three Italian ports (Trieste, Cagliari and Catania). The work highlights the evolution of the inner port areas and at the same time underlines the criticalities that local administrators will have to solve to make them more usable and to improve the port-city relationship.

1.2 The Development of Inner Harbors

In Italy, the policy related to the development of waterfront areas focuses on the redevelopment of the port-city and the urban area immediately behind it that has non-merchant functions. It is particularly important and aims at improving the landscape, trying to reduce the environmental impact and increasing the economic resources, attracting tourist activities and flows (museums, refreshment and conference centres, etc.).

In general, the term "inner harbor" refers to an intermodal terminal for goods, which is generally located in a place that is close to a seaport. In this area there is also an intermodal area including both road and rail modes, and often other areas with sorting and distribution functions [6, 7]. The main function is the decongestion of port areas by storing goods a few - or even hundreds - of kilometers away from the port itself.

The hinterland is connected to the port through a series of rail services that are as regular and frequent as possible - dedicated services. This ensures efficient management of the entire transport cycle, including handling, storage and warehousing, and intermodal break of bulk. The port project is a dynamic infrastructural, transport and production project that produces impacts in terms of landscape/environment [8].

In order to mitigate the negative impacts new opportunities for tourism development and new challenges have to be taken into account to produce more and more energy from renewable sources - i.e. Rotterdam.

In addition, the port and the surrounding areas should become the privileged interface of land transport networks, improving intermodal connections and becoming a place of commercial exchange with a strong potential for growth and tourist attraction. [9]. In Europe, medium-sized and medium-small port cities are characterized by a particularly complex situation caused by the fragmentation of development choices but also by the presence of different authorities that are not always cohesive, by the reduced availability of resources.

Crisis conditions can also slow down, or make unfavorable, regeneration proposals based on integrated port-city development models [10]. Medium-sized port cities have great potential for urban regeneration in the interface areas between port and urban entities.

2 Port - City Relations Among Peripheries and Inner Harbors

2.1 The Case of Cagliari

In Italy the port-city system has specific features that do not emerge in other cases. Specifically, they are part of urban systems and have developed operational relationships with logistics hubs and the environment and the urban layout. However, despite the centrality and functionality, especially in southern Italy, ports are experiencing roles resulting from the multitude of entities that have a decisive role in functional reorganization (Region, Municipalities, Port System Authorities, etc.). This is what is happening in the port system of Cagliari (freight and passengers). The port system of Cagliari consists of two main areas: the historic or old port, which extends over 5,800 m of quay and has a vocation for commercial traffic, Ro-Ro, passenger and cruise ships (with a dedicated terminal), and the canal port, which extends over 1,600 m and offers five berths for transshipment and Ro-Ro traffic. To the west of Porto Canale, in the locality of Sarroch - Porto Foxi, there are petrochemical - oil docks with moorings for seventeen ships, a service of one of the most important national refineries (Fig. 1).

The recovery and revitalization of the land-sea interface constitutes the most ambitious objective for Cagliari in the context of an urban planning aimed at defining structures that ensure a renewed and solid link between the city and its sea. The completion of the Porto Canale outpost (2022), the redevelopment project of the Via Roma (2022), the drafting of a new Municipal Urban Plan (2022) constitute some of the significant events for the city: the possibility of using the new port In fact, while it opens up numerous perspectives for the reorganization of port functions, it also offers a unique opportunity aimed at the reuse and redevelopment of the city-port up to graft into the main historic districts.

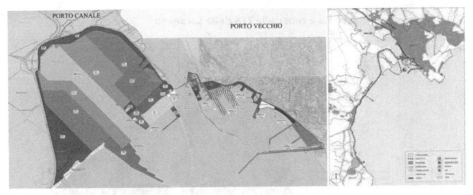

Fig. 1. Cagliari Old Port and Channel Port. Source: author's elaboration from [11].

The entire seafront of Cagliari extends for about 12 km from the Santa Gilla pond in Sant'Elia with the new marina under construction (2022). The seafront, with singular places of historical and environmental value that alternate with abandoned spaces or spaces intended for port or industrial activities, is involved overall in the transformation and redevelopment process, animated by multiple public actors. The design theme of the city-port interface can be summarized as a redefinition of the relationship between the "historical" city and the seafront, with the aim of integrating the sea-city. The goal that everyone agrees is given by the connections of long and short, fast and slow networks.

The complex network of relationships between the parts and elements of the waterfront and the city offers a progressive redevelopment of empty spaces and abandoned sites, responding to the needs of the metropolitan city.

The interface is thus configured to give rise to the different types of relationship between the urban and port systems. Furthermore, in December 2021 the ZES (Special Economic Zones) of Sardinia (7 + 7 years) were approved with the aim of promoting economic production opportunities facilitated by a more advantageous tax and customs system (Fig. 2).

However, the port system of Cagliari, goods in particular, is affected by the lack of railway infrastructures that oblige any movement of goods and passengers by road in road infrastructures, including those of urban relevance.

2.2 The Case of Catania

The port of Catania is currently defined by many activities, ship-related and otherwise. The port and its back harbor are part of the special economic zones (ZES) of Eastern Sicily [12]. The Port of Catania is defined as a first generation port through the UNC-TAD classification [13] as are the ports of Taranto and Ravenna; these ports have a strong interaction with their cities [14]. Currently, the port of Catania covers an area of approximately 470,000 square metres.

It is located in the centre of the Mediterranean Sea; to the east, a breakwater encloses it, 1860 m long, with an end section of approximately 40 m.

To the south it is bordered by another quay about 420 m long. There is also a new port (to the northeast), polygonal in shape, delimited by two small piers to the east and

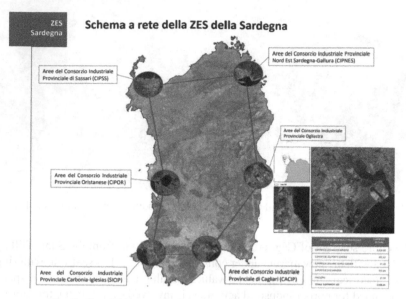

Fig. 2. Special Economic Zones (SEZ). Focus on Cagliari [11].

west. The old port is located to the west of the new one. It serves as a quay for fishing and motor fishing boats. The location and connections to the road and motorway network as well as to the regional airport and airport network have made the port a key player in the regional economy (Fig. 3).

In particular, in 2018, the port recorded the presence of approximately 99,157 ferry passengers and 123,985 cruise passengers; these results have made the port of Catania one of the main passenger ports in Sicily [15, 16]. Cargo traffic is located in the southern area of the port, in the Nuova Darsena commercial dock.

The Northern area of the port is instead characterised by a mixed use of areas and infrastructures, due to the significant and continuous commercial growth registered recently.

Unfortunately, in the areas surrounding the port there is a negative interference of vehicular flows (i.e. private and goods) with pedestrian flows and there is also a lack of dedicated spaces and reserved paths for pedestrian and bicycle mobility.

In order to minimise interference with congested urban traffic, the access and exit of heavy vehicles is allowed through the gate called Faro Biscari, located to the south and connected to a motorway structure. The Dusmet gate is dedicated to pedestrians and private vehicles.

Although several redevelopment proposals have been planned, the conditions of marginality and degradation that characterise the portion between the Faro Porta Biscari and Porta Dusmet gates remain [17].

The Port Committee, contrary to art. 4, paragraph 4, letter c of Law 84/94, did not consider it opportune to deepen the problem of promiscuity by strengthening the road system and trying to solve the problem of congestion with a view to a future modification of transport and communication modes. This action, while solving the problem, also

Fig. 3. The Port and city of Catania (author's elaboration over Google Earth).

increases the conflict between the city and the port. In 2016, a project was signed by the competent authorities for the construction of a very long cycle-pedestrian promenade of about two kilometres with lighting and benches, the creation of a sports area and also a saltwater swimming pool. To date, this project has not yet started, with only the beginning of some of the work to reunite the "Civita" district with the port of Catania.

2.3 The Case of Trieste

The port of Trieste is located near the northeastern border of Italy with Slovenia, and at the crossroads of the main international routes between the Mediterranean and central Europe. It occupies about 2.3 million square meters, around 1.8 million square meters of free zones. The quays cover a total length of 12 km with 58 operational moorings, and maximum depths of up to 18 m (container terminal - Pier VII in particular), and served by a total length of 70 km of railway tracks (Fig. 4).

The Port of Trieste presents itself as a unique case on the national scene, especially for the international Free Port regime, sanctioned after the end of the Second World War, and after the long definition of the northeastern border of Italy. This regime, recently regulated in order to adapt to the transformation of national ports within the Port System Authorities, provides in particular for customs relief, and port development as a transit hub and for the development of local economic activity. In particular, the free points of the port of Trieste are considered as a duty-free territory, with consequences, in particular, linked to simplifications in terms of introduction of goods, storage, processing, deferred payments, as well as relative to the possibility of on-site processing while maintaining the origin, or, on the contrary, according to certain conditions, acquiring the 'made in'. The facilitation of transit functions is also guaranteed by free rail access, with the opening of access for all rail carriers to free points, and the exemption of fixed rights on the movement of vehicles, with the liberalization of the transport of goods in transit. The strong development of the Port of Trieste as the first Italian railway port, as well as the most connected to an international hinterland, and the strong presence of traffic, especially Ro-Ro, are elements that can certainly be connected to this regulatory situation which, in perspective, can orient the port and local economic development towards the definition of free zones [18, 19].

Fig. 4. The Port and city of Trieste (author's elaboration over Google Earth).

The evolution that has taken place in recent years, starting from January 2016, has led to a potential changing and changed relationship between the port and neighboring areas or areas linked to the urban context. From that moment, in fact, the free zone regime, up to that moment unchangeable in its locations, was able to be 'moved' and assigned to areas where it could more readily and fully be exploited: in particular, from the Punto Franco Vecchio, a large part, in fact, of port structures dating back to the Austro-Hungarian period, the area of which is now destined for a 'traditional' redevelopment as an urban waterfront, towards other locations, such as the new FreeEste logistics center, part of Interporto Trieste (Fig. 5).

Precisely the logistic nodes external to the port, albeit at its service, such as the Fernetti dry port and its free zone FreeEste are the testimony of a process of organization of a port region in a broader perspective than the traditional relationship 'city-port' , in which new spaces are involved in operations connected to handling, and in which new relationships arise with portions of territory once touched in a different way by transport operations.

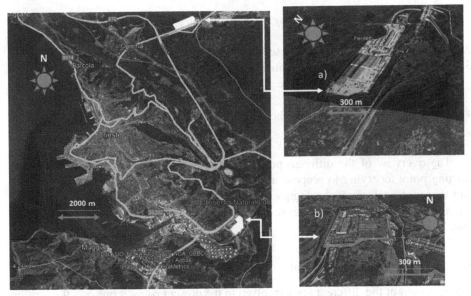

Fig. 5. Trieste and its main inland logistic nodes (North: Interporto Trieste - Fernetti; South: Interporto Trieste - FreeEste/Free zone)

3   Not Only Waterfront - A Methodological Proposal

3.1   Not Only Waterfront

It is necessary to integrate these spaces into urban systems (physical, economical, social and cultural) and at the same time to attract inhabitants by proposing that they use these spaces for socialising.

While the waterfront concept represents a boundary at different levels (e.g. between land and sea), it is also possible to define an environment with a multi-layered historical, economic, social and cultural characterisation. Considering the increasing separation between port and city, it is necessary to maintain this link and to reassure that the presence of the port is still an asset for the city and not the other way around.

Ports are complex systems but some portions of them could be more easily integrated into the context by technology, for example. A balance must be found between the positive and negative effects that port activities generate, as this balance is often the key to the tension between port and city. It is necessary to experiment with new projects and organisations that support hybrid spaces between ports and cities.

Another important issue is the reconstruction and re-functionalisation of the imaginary port-city area, based on citizen participation processes, where people can talk about and recover a sense of belonging to the port as 'their' own port.

There are no universal solutions. Although ports are very often similar, each one presents different problems in the port-city relationship. At a general level, it is possible to emphasise certain strategies in terms of urban planning:

1. It is essential to open up planning processes to the public, particularly those relating to the port-city interface;
2. Improve the management of these areas;
3. It is necessary to identify negative port externalities affecting local inhabit-ants, which vary from case to case (e.g. smoke reduction in some cases, traffic or noise pollution in others);
4. Reuse resources generated by the port, which would otherwise be wasted, such as heat or energy.

The overview of the different ports involved in the present paper represents the starting point for trying to propose a methodological framework for a more punctual and thorough analysis of the complex set of relations among the urban areas, in their articulated framework of centres, semi peripheries and peripheries, and the port and port-related activities.

3.2 A Methodological Proposal

The overview of the different ports involved in the present paper represents the starting point for trying to propose a methodological framework for a more punctual and thorough analysis of the complex set of relations among the urban areas, in their articulated framework of centres, semi peripheries and peripheries, and the port and port-related activities.

The descriptive overview so far briefly introduced, should be integrated by a different set of analysis, that implies the organization of the different planning tools, together with the de-facto, spontaneous organization of the industrial and logistic players, in space. On one side there is the need to organize and analyse the approved, adopted or in progress planning tools in terms of their capacity to tackle together the aspects related to the different land uses at urban and peri-urban levels, therefore observing the effects on urban and port centres. If we can observe that strictly urban and port planning tools are generally coordinated and interrelated, this is not always true when we consider transport and industrial planning tools, as well as when we consider the 'spontaneous' behavior of de-facto logistic operators, whose location in space can be non-structured and referred to traditional standard industrial and retail locations, but with logistic-like impacts in space. This, in particular, needs to be appropriately surveyed and investigated.

The proposed matrix, that can provide in perspective a useful tool for evaluating the urban-port performances [20, 21], as well as a planning instrument for an overall harmonization of the set of the planning tools.

Different sets of procedures need therefore to be put in action in order to fill the matrix as proposed.

1. Desk research on the approved (AP), adopted (AD) or in progress (IP) planning tools;

2. Desk/cartographic/field research on the major urban/industrial/transport areas involved
3. Field survey on the existing logistic and logistic-related activities on the territory;
4. Overlay of the different levels of information (Table 1).

Table 1. A matrix for estimating the city-port relations' impact over different areas and according to structured and non-structured tools (Source: Authors' elaboration).

Urban & port areas/Planning tools (AP-AD-IP)	Urban planning	Port planning	Transport planning	Industrial planning	De facto planning
Central area					
Semi-periphery					
Periphery					
Port area					

Such a framework should be useful for 'filling the gap' among the different sets of knowledge over the logistic needs and characters of city-port regions, in order to propose tools for better exploiting their evolution towards a smart port region concept.

4 Discussion

The port - city relation holds historical origins and is related, with particular reference to the oldest urban areas, to the same birth, development and evolution of cities itself, with a very tight and strong link [22–28]. The transformations occurred in time modified the relations among the two subjects: ports on one side changed their roles - so as cities - servicing not only the cities they were located in, but more and more oriented towards a wider hinterland, regional and often national or international, with changed links, often weaker, with the cities themselves and their neighboring territories.

The port-city relation passed through several evolutions and in the post-industrial - or trans-industrial - stage it faced a particular attention towards waterfronts and a renewed interest towards their conversion to urban uses. In such sense, the typical case studies involved Genoa with its Old Port and its urban redevelopment in the Nineties of the past century and, almost potentially and only partially, Trieste, where, currently, the urban redevelopment has been only partial so far, considering also the gigantic dimension of the buildings' volumes and surfaces involved, whose conversion and redevelopment is challenging and still to be defined and properly ignited.

In such a situation, cities and ports today coexist in their differentiated functions, often in the waterfront where such a mix is more evident. As a matter of example, we can recall the pedestrian function coupled with mobility and free time, together with the port one, related mainly to passengers' traffic, as the urban public transport and transit systems, ferry - Pax and/or Ro-Pax -, cruise ships.

The changed - and changing - functions and relations as played by ports, as nodes of a wider set of links with the hinterland and other maritime destinations, as well as areas for handling, managing, storing and warehousing freights, other than as break of bulk and transshipment to other transport means, and of local and regional distributions, produce, as a consequence, a shift of the spaces connected to port functions and activities, towards the inner areas of the port region, actually connecting and competing with urban uses and functions for land use.

In such a sense, new "geographies of marginality" are being drawn, with a city - port relation that does not deal any more with traditional places, that can be defined as central within the different urban areas, but with those in peripheral or marginal areas, often localized also in different municipalities to those strictly urban and hosting the port itself.

5 Conclusions

The coordination among the different planning levels - urban plan and port plan - is foreseen in the Italian planning framework, and, particularly for the areas having concurrent and mixed use, different is the case of the other new planned logistic areas and their interaction with urban activities.

Important changes are ongoing, both related to urban logistics and to the locations becoming necessary from the widespread diffusion and importance of the last mile in the door-to-door urban distribution, and with reference to the new inner harbor spaces, where logistic functions supporting port activities are mixed and confused with the urban ones, often without a proper coordination. Inner-harbor industrial and logistic zones often coordinate with ports themselves - and this is, as a matter of example, what the Port of Trieste is doing, via the coordination of the Industrial Zone Board and inland terminals, while a lower attention is for private activities related to logistic and distribution, often related, or referable to greyfields conversion from industrial and/or commercial uses to logistic ones, with an impact non always foreseen or foreseeable on activities and urban functions.

In conclusion and in perspective, therefore, in addition to greater coordination between the plan initiatives already in place at the urban and logistical-port level, it becomes possible and necessary to map the logistical and distribution nodes, whether linked to the already existing and planned dedicated infrastructures, both those managed by private operators, also for micro-distribution and storage functions, in order to be able to evaluate the development areas of these activities more precisely and highlight possible interactions and criticalities in urban interactions, including periphery and margin.

References

1. Moraci, F., Errigo, M.F., Fazia, C., Campisi, T., Castelli, F.: Cities under pressure: strategies and tools to face climate change and pandemic. Sustainability **12**(18), 7743 (2020)
2. Mitchell, D., Barth, B., Ho, S., Sait, M.S., McEvoy, D.: The benefits of fit-for-purpose land administration for urban community resilience in a time of climate change and COVID-19 pandemic. Land **10**(6), 563 (2021)

3. Giovinazzi, O., Rodrigues-Malta, R.: Port cities and urban waterfronts: constructing scenarios of transformation in the context of conflict. Mediterranee. Revue geographique des pays mediterraneens. **111** (2008)
4. Kajava, M.: I porti del Mediterraneo. Introduzione. Il Mediterraneo e la storia III Documentando città portuali-Documenting Port Cities. Atti del Convegno Internazionale Capri, 9–11 maggio 2019 (2021)
5. Mazzeo, P., Paderni, S.: Il Porto di Messina tra passato e presente: storia, paesaggio, cartografia e territorio. Bollettino dell'Associazione Italiana di Cartografia
6. Fazia, C., Errigo, M.F.: Il paesaggio costiero portuale: nuove opportunità turistiche e sfide per un'energia pulita. TRIA **10**(2), 57–74 (2017)
7. Fonti, L.: (Ed.). Porti-città-territori. Processi di riqualificazione e sviluppo, vol. 56. Alinea Editrice (2010)
8. Gastaldi, F., Camerin, F.: Percorsi di riorganizzazione dei waterfront: i casi di Savona e La Spezia. TRIA **10**(2), 23–36 (2017)
9. Calace, F., Paparusso, O.G., Angelastro, C.: La costa metropolitana e la costruzione di una visione comune: alcuni indizi dal caso Bari. TERRITORIO **93**, 99–106 (2020)
10. Carta, M., Lino, B., Ronsivalle, D.: Re-cyclical Urbanism. Visioni. paradigmi e progetti per la metamorfosi circolare. LIST Laboratorio Internazionale Editoriale (2016)
11. Autorità di Sistema Portuale del Mare di Sardegna. Cagliari. http://www.adspmaredisarde gna.it/cagliari/. Accessed 01 May 2022
12. Manti, E.: Zone Economiche Speciali. Settori di intervento, aree produttive e poli logistici per una politica industriale nel Mezzogiorno. Rivista economica del Mezzogiorno, **33**(3–4), 921–962 (2019)
13. Taylor, I., Smith, K.: United Nations Conference on Trade and Development (UNCTAD). Routledge, Milton Park (2007)
14. Russo, F., Musolino, G.: Quantitative characteristics for port generations: the Italian case study. Int. J. Transp. Dev. Integr. **4**(2), 103–112 (2020)
15. Ignaccolo, M., Inturri, G., Giuffrida, N., Torrisi, V., Cocuzza, E.: Sustainability of freight transport through an integrated approach: the case of the eastern Sicily port system. Transp. Res. Proc. **45**, 177–184 (2020). https://doi.org/10.1016/j.trpro.2020.03.005
16. Port System Authority of the Eastern Sicilian Sea: Traffici Portuali 2018 Porto di Catania (2018). https://www.adspmaresiciliaorientale.it/wpcontent/uploads/2019/04/Traffici-por tuali2018-Portodi-Cantania-1.pdf. Accessed 05 Jan 2020
17. Giuffrida, N., Cocuzza, E., Ignaccolo, M., Inturri, G.: A comprehensive index to evaluate non-motorized accessibility to port-cities. Int. J. Sustain. Dev. Planning **15**(5), 743–749 (2020)
18. Roletto, G.: Il porto di Trieste. Zanichelli, Bologna (1941)
19. Borruso, G., Borruso, G.: Il porto di Trieste: analisi del traffico, impatto economico e prospettive di sviluppo. Panaro et al. (edited by): Trasporto marittimo e sviluppo economico. Scenari internazionali, analisi del traffico e prospettive di crescita. SRM, Giannini Editore, Napoli, pp. 235–274 (2012)
20. Balletto, G., Borruso, G., Donato, C.: City dashboards and the Achilles' heel of smart cities: putting governance in action and in space. In: Gervasi, O., et al. (eds.) Computational Science and Its Applications – ICCSA 2018. LNCS, vol. 10962, pp. 654–668. Springer, Cham (2018). https://doi.org/10.1007/978-3-319-95168-3_44
21. Borruso, G., Balletto, G., Milesi, A., Ladu, M.: Cartography and security. port security: trends and perspectives. In: Gervasi, O., et al. (eds.) Computational Science and Its Applications – ICCSA 2021. LNCS, vol. 12958, pp. 252–261. Springer, Cham (2021). https://doi.org/10.1007/978-3-030-87016-4_19
22. Vigariè, A.: Ports de commerce et vie littorale. Hachette, Paris (1979)
23. Slack, B.: Pawns in the game: ports in global transportation systems. Growth Chang. **24**(4), 379–388 (1993)

24. Vallega, A.: Nodalità e centralità: relais tra teoria regionale e teoria dei trasporti. Studi Marittimi **6**(19–20), 33–35 (1984)
25. Vallega, A.: Geografia delle strategie marittime. Mursia, Milano (1997)
26. Rodrigue, J.P.: The Geography of Transport System. Routledge, New York (2020)
27. Notteboom, T.: The relationship between seaports and the intermodal hinterland in light of global supply chains. International Transport Forum Discussion Paper 2008/10, OECD Publishing, Paris (2008)
28. Sellari, P.: Geopolitica dei trasporti. Laterza Editori, Bari (2013)

International Workshop on Smart Tourism (Smart Tourism 2022)

Rural Tourism and Walkability. Compare Sardinia and Gran Canaria Models

Silvia Battino[1]([✉]), Ginevra Balletto[2], Alessandra Milesi[2], and Ainhoa Amaro García[3]

[1] Department of Economics and Business, University of Sassari, Sassari, Sardinia, Italy
sbattino@uniss.it
[2] Department of Civil, Environmental Engineering and Architecture, University of Cagliari, Cagliari, Sardinia, Italy
balletto@unica.it, alessandra.milesi@gmail.com
[3] Instituto Universitario de Turismo y Desarrollo Económico y Sostenible, University of Las Palmas de Gran Canaria, Canary Islands, Las Palmas de Gran Canaria, Spain
ainhoa.amaro.garcia@gmail.com

Abstract. The tourism crisis following the Covid-19 pandemic has caused many communities to rethink and review tourism. In fact, in European countries, many destinations are now focused on more inclusive and sustainable measures rather than over tourism, so they have invested in sustainability to create tourist-friendly places. The rural areas, in particular, are affected by a demand motivated by a longing for discovery and authenticity, and they seem to be working towards a multi-scalar planning: walkability and digitalization stand out as fundamental choices to meet the needs of tourists and residents. In this context, the paper aims, after a preliminary review of the literature on rural areas' walkability, to highlight the relationship between rural walkability and tourism through the analysis and comparison of two rural paths: the Mining Path of Santa Barbara (Sardinia, Italy) and the Path of Saint James (Gran Canaria, Spain). It represents virtuous examples of fruition and enhancement of the insular landscape, promoting a place-based approach for a sustainable and cohesive local development.

Keywords: Walkability tourism · Rural tourism · Undertourism · Sustainable tourism

1 Introduction

The regeneration of territories and a new use of spaces in different destinations. This is the topic widely debated among researchers and institutions in the light of the economic and social crisis due to the Covid-19 pandemic. Tourism is the economic sector that has suffered the greatest losses when different countries have been forced to suspend their internal and cross-border relations. The high restrictions and general insecurity

---

This paper is the result of the joint work of the authors. In particular: Sects. 1 and 2 have been written by Silvia Battino, Sect. 3.1 by Alessandra Milesi, Sect. 3.1 by Ainhoa Amaro García, Sect. 4 by all authors and Sect. 5 by Ginevra Balletto.

O. Gervasi et al. (Eds.): ICCSA 2022 Workshops, LNCS 13381, pp. 211–221, 2022.
https://doi.org/10.1007/978-3-031-10548-7_16

discouraged travel, but fueled the desire for escape and leisure by motivating potential travellers to seek places with a strong identity and outdoor experiences with more contact with nature [1, 2]. In this way, following the European policies moving for decades to improve territorial balances and achieve the objectives of sustainability and cohesion, several destinations have developed local development strategies combining tourism, walkability and sustainable mobility [3]. More attention is focused on the revitalization of internal rural areas, that is spaces with low population and economic attractiveness, even in the presence of significant landscape resources [4]. In these areas, the place-based governance approach is highlighted through initiatives and measures aimed at designing new geographical configurations based on the valorization of resources to increase territories' attractiveness and competitiveness. The rural tourism activity must be initiated with a participative project by transforming the condition of peripherality through the creation of identity networks [5, 6].

The paper, after a review of the literature on the relationship between rural tourism and walkability, aims to analyze two rural tourism paths in the islands of Gran Canaria (Spain) and Sardinia (Italy) organized with a structured offer of resources and services for a sustainable fruition of the internal areas. The paper is composed, in addition to the Introduction, by four other paragraphs: Sect. 2. Related works, Sect. 3. Rural tourism paths: models in Sardinia and Gran Canaria, Sect. 3.1 The Path of Santa Barbara (Sardinia – Italy) and Sect. 3.2 The Path of Saint James (Gran Canaria – Spain), Sect. 4. Highlights of the two paths and Sect. 5. Conclusions.

2 Related Works

Rural tourism can be considered as a real strategy for the development of internal areas. According to their own needs and peculiarities, each territory activates different forms of rural tourism: agritourism, cultural and natural itineraries, eno-gastronomic tourism, albergo diffuso are some examples. The rural realities embracing this tourist practice try to achieve the objectives of sustainability to create multifunctional places where the conservation and enhancement of resources is combined with the growth of economic and social value of the territory. In its broadest meaning, we can consider it as an experiential tourism that allows tourists to experience the rural landscape [7–9]. The tourist demand for a greater contact with the identity of places is expressed in several studies and rural tourism practices can represent an opportunity to improve the quality of travel of tourists and the quality of life of destinations [10–12]. This slow philosophy of travel, combined with increased accessibility and walkability of sites (pedestrian and bicycle paths, use of public transport), brings environmental, social and economic benefits [1, 3, 13]. Indeed, improving the walkability of spaces helps to make resources more attractive both physically and emotionally. Achieving this goal requires enhancing spatial connectivity by creating integrated pathways in which hospitality and mobility make safe and sustainable "crossings" for residents and tourists [14, 15]. Walkability, in its first meaning, relates to multiple studies that focus on sustainable city living. Indeed, it is combined with "pedestrian well-being", whereby users of urban spaces can move easily and safely [16–19]. In the context of urban zoning, the assessment of the level of efficient and effective walkability can be measured and verified on indicators such as, for example, traffic safety, crime/security, connectivity, suitability and accessibility [17, 20–22]. Likewise, it is necessary to remember that the decision to move by foot is not to be attributed only to the degree of quality of organization of the "built" environment, but must also be related to individual peculiarities, including age, gender, ethnicity and income. Although the planning of routes and spaces for walking has essentially involved cities, it also seems to be of interest in rural areas. Some academic contributions support the idea that rural walks allow a conscious fruition of the rural world [18, 23–25].

3 Rural Tourism Paths Models

3.1 The *Path of Santa Barbara* (Sardinia – Italy)

Sardinia is the second largest island in Italy and its resident population at 31 December 2021 was 1,590,044 (ISTAT, 2022). In addition to these, 16.5 million tourists (summer 2021) who have visited the Island for vacations dedicated mainly to the beach market [26]. In order to deseasonalize and diversify tourist flows, an integrated cultural tourism destination is proposed on the island. The richness of the cultural heritage is also manifested through the religious paths: 33% of the island's monumental heritage consists of churches or religious buildings. This heritage has been organized by the Region of Sardinia since 2012 with the institution of the "Register of Sardinian Paths and Religious and Spiritual Tourist Routes". The Register currently identifies eight paths that, for the areas involved, represent an opportunity for recovery and valorization of marginal landscapes [27]. The Santa Barbara path in Sulcis-Iglesiente is one of these itineraries. The path is also the only route included in the "Atlas of the Italian Paths" and, besides the religious value, it promotes a slow tourism closely linked to the conservation-promotion of the mining and natural heritage. In fact, the path of Santa Barbara is part of an area affected by important mining activities active until the 90s and today included in the geo-mineral park of Sardinia. This park, officially instituted in October 2001 to safeguard and enhance the architectural and landscape heritage, covers an area of 3,500 hectares, involves 90 municipalities and represents an atypical case among national parks due to the discontinuity of mineral deposits located in different regions of Sardinia.

The Santa Barbara Mining path has a ring route, passable in clockwise, crossing 25 municipalities, with a total length of about 500 km, 75% of which takes place on paths, mule tracks, cart tracks and driveways. It is divided into 30 stages of varying difficulty and lengths, which can be covered on foot, by bicycle or horse. The mining-landscape crossed can be defined in '*transition*', that is, which changes over time due to both the geomorphological characteristics of the site and the mining activity that has affected the territory over time. The tourist offer is linked to the uniqueness of the context, involving different types of users, such as: pilgrims, tourists and sportsmen. The context is rich in natural and anthropogenic elements (landfills, mine muds and abandoned buildings), characterised by a complex geological heritage and of industrial archaeology - mineral deposits, excavations and mine dumps and buildings - as well as by archeological sites - domus de janas, nuraghi, sacred wells, etc. - and natural heritage (beaches, cliffs, lagoons, etc.) [18, 28–30] (Fig. 1).

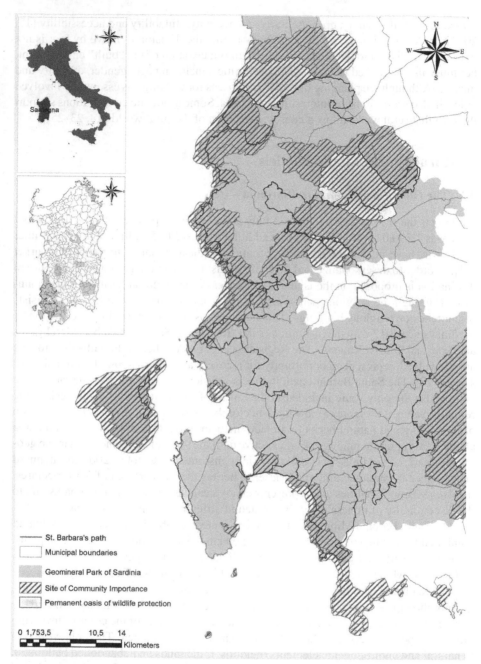

Fig. 1. St. Barbara path (Sardinia, Italy). Territorial framework within the Geomineral Historic and Environmental Park of Sardinia and with natural sites.

3.2   The *Path of Saint James* (Gran Canaria – Spain)

In terms of extension, Gran Canaria is the third largest of the eight islands that make up the Canarian archipelago, and its resident population as of December 31, 2021 was 852,688 [31] (ISTAC 2022). In addition to these, there are 1,789,513 tourists who have elected the Island for vacations dedicated mainly to the beach market [32] (Tourism Gran Canaria, 2021). Gran Canaria is known as a sun and beach destination which means that the numbers of tourists who visited the islands has been always high. In fact, in the pre-pandemic era, in 2019, 4,267,382 visited Gran Canaria and in 2018 the rate was similar with 4,509,829 visitors [33] (ISTAC 2020). Consequently, tourism is, indeed, centred on the combination of sun and sea. However, over the last few years the mass tourism of sun and beach has been questioned due to their negative impacts on the local economy and on the environment. One of the conclusions that local administration and management staff have obtained was to rethink the tourism model of the Canary islands providing and adopting sustainable development strategies. In other words, to diversify the offer through the valorization of landscape resources and the more active involvement of rural areas. These areas, subject to depopulation and other criticalities typical of internal areas [5], hold most of the environmental (natural monuments, special and integral reserves, natural and rural parks) and cultural (archaeological sites, museums, monuments, real estate) attractions. The actions carried out to motivate alternative tourists are highlighted in the form of experiential itineraries where nature, villages and local production firms describe the territory's identity [34].

The St. James' Path is one of these routes, which crosses the island from Maspalomas (South) to Gáldar (North). This route is proposed as a trip to the interior of the island, highlighting the landscape, flora, fauna, gastronomy, historical and ethnographic heritage and the rich island network of trails and paths, through which you can get to know the authentic essence of the island, a long-distance route that crosses the island from south to north through the peaks of the island. The history of the Path came from a religious story in which a ship was surprised in the middle of a storm in the south of Gran Canaria. On board, there were Galician sailors, who were devotees of Apostle Santiago, so in the middle of the storm they started to pray for their lives. If they survived, they promised to take the figure of the saint to the highest in the seen earth [35].

Nowadays, there are cultural, ethnographic and historical values involved. Usually the path consists of three stages for a total of 66 km and takes about 23 h to complete: Maspalomas-Tunte (28 km), Tunte-Cruz de Tejeda (17 km) and Cruz de Tejeda-Gáldar (21 km). There are eight municipalities directly involved and they include Tejeda, Artenara, Vallesco, Moya, Gáldar, San Bartolomé de Tirajana, Vega de San Mateo and Santa Maria de Guía (Fig. 2). A large part of this trail was used by the ancient inhabitants of the island as a communication route from the south to the north and, later, it came to be used by herders who practised transhumance, -that is, the seasonal migration of livestock in search of better pastures-, and by pilgrims. The path begins in the south of the island, in the Maspalomas dunes, to enter the centre through the Caldera de Tirajana, winding its walls to reach the Tejeda caldera and descend through the agro-pastoral landscapes of the North of Gran Canaria, next to the most recent volcanoes of the island. As a reference to the destination of the road, another volcanic cone emerges, the Mountain of Gáldar, visible from the midlands and the entire north coast of the island, so that in addition to

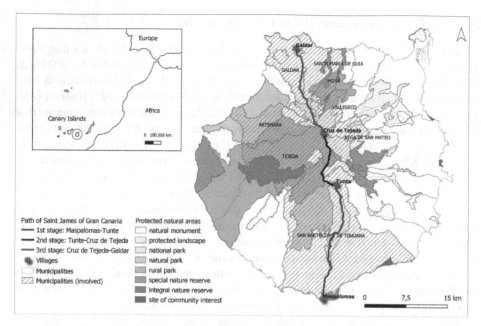

Fig. 2. St. James path and protected areas in Gran Canaria (Spain).

the values described, entering its different stages is considered as an authentic "Route Between Volcanoes" that takes us back to the volcanic origin of the island [35]. The type of track is 38% hiking trail, 31% rural road and 31% paved road. Tourists and pilgrims, in addition to satisfying their religious needs, are able to enjoy a naturalistic and cultural experience. The path crosses between volcanoes and, among the many natural and cultural resources, we would like to remember two of them in particular: Montañas Sagradas and Risco Caído, which have been declared UNESCO World Heritage Sites in 2019. The Cultural Landscape of Risco Caído and the Sacred Mountain Areas of Gran Canaria is, like all cultural landscapes, the product of a specific geography and its interaction with its inhabitants. The mountainous centre of Gran Canaria, extraordinary in its geomorphology and biogeography, is also extraordinary due to the fact that two radically different cultures have occupied it continuously for more than 1,500 years. A pre-Hispanic occupation by populations from the Amazing (Berber) cultural orbit of North Africa who probably arrived in Gran Canaria around the turn of the era, was succeeded after the Castilian conquest of the island at the end of the 15th century by a European civilization in the dawn of the Modern Age. Current Canarian society is heir to both [35].

4 Highlights of the Two Paths

The comparison between the two methods has the purpose of highlighting any point of contact and/or elements-characteristics that could allow an improvement for both, also through the identification of the relative strengths and weaknesses. From the comparison you can put it as both paths are of religious origin with an important sporting propensity. They develop in landscapes with a strong natural geological value and mining production. The methodological approach underlying the project has two different systems: Santa Barbara circular path and Santiago de Compostela linear path that join points of interest.

The two paths have good accessibility and all related information is widely disseminated on the web social media. Most of the paths develop in the original tracks, with no or almost no interference from vehicular traffic (Fig. 3).

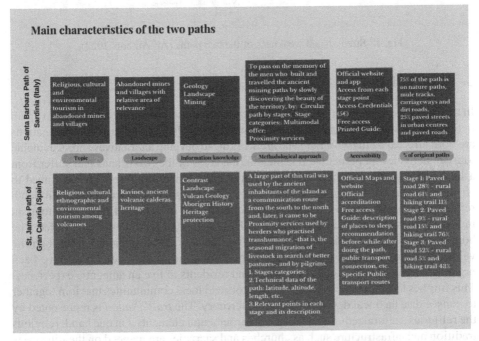

Fig. 3. Main characteristics of the two paths (All Authors 2022).

The strengths and weaknesses can instead be shown in the Fig. 4.

Finally, from the comparison it emerges that in the two paths there is a pre-eminent natural environmental dimension over the anthropic one, the latter characterized by both ancient archaeology and industrial. Precisely in this sense, the environmental dimension has stimulated the use of trails for sporting and leisure purposes, gradually contrasting both with over tourism and with xenophilic tourism. The trails therefore lead both towards slow tourism and proximity [36].

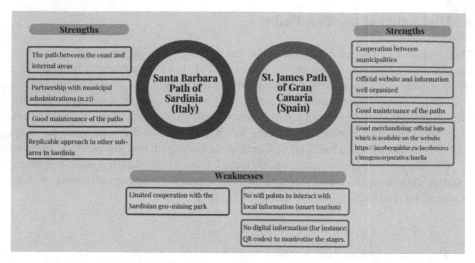

Fig. 4. Strength and weakness of the two paths (All Authors 2022).

5   Conclusions

In this paper the focus lied on two island religious-cultural itineraries: Santa Barbara path in Sardinia and St. James path in Gran Canaria (Canary Islands, Spain). The destinations are both affected by mass tourism and are working to develop alternatives and sustainable tourism activities. In particular, it is the internal areas of the two islands that suffer from a lack of the traditional circuits of the tourist offer. Therefore, it outlines the need to change the current tourism model and stressed the importance of "making an in-depth reflection", so it seems to conclude that the main axis of action of these new tourism models is to "work around Diversification, Dispersion and Differentiation". In fact, the both areas analyzed in this article are moving towards the differentiation through the valorization and promotion of their identity. Furthermore, these resources have been organized as an itinerary to allow tourists and residents to live an authentic experience. This implies the daily involvement of operators and local communities that join together to consolidate the local development of the territory. The *trait d'union* is represented by the religious, cultural, ethnographic and environmental elements. On one hand, religious tradition and infrastructure such as churches and sacristies are mapped on the itineraries as the most relevant points of interest in order to provide visitors with local history and culture. On the other hand, landscapes through these internal areas give tourists the opportunity to interact directly with nature. Offering an alternative to sun and beach mass tourism. Taking into account this, it seems that rural tourism is a perfect solution to promote the socio-economic and territorial development of the areas that organize its offer. The two paths are an example of a structured rural offer that has become a territorial regeneration catalyst. According to the principles of sustainable planning, both paths satisfy the requirement of accessibility because they are easily accessible and walkable by different users. These users have the possibility to combine walking with other alternatives and slow mobility (especially cycling and horseback riding) and to enjoy along the trail of different landscape peculiarities (natural and cultural heritage).

The synergies created between the different local actors of the municipalities involved have allowed them to organize an integrated system of accommodation and services to support the paths. Finally, it is also essential to focus on the virtuous activation of smart systems. This would make it possible to correct weaknesses and satisfy the European mission for greater territorial cohesion.

References

1. Brundu, B., Battino, S., Manca, I.: The sustainable tourism organization of rural spaces. The Island of Sardinia in the era of "staycation". In: Proceedings of ICC2021 - 30th International Cartographic Conference, pp. 14–18. Florence, Italy (2021)
2. Sharma, D.G., Thomas, A., Paul, J.: Reviving tourism industry post-COVID.19: a resili-ence-based framework. Tour. Manage. Perspect. **37**, 100786, 1–10 (2021)
3. Balletto, G., Ladu, M., Milesi, A., Battino, S., Borruso, G.: Walkability, digital technolo-gies and internal area tourism. In: AAVV (eds.), SUPTM 2022 1st Conference on Future Challenges in Sustainable Urban Planning & Territorial Management, pp. 1–4. MDPI, Svizzera (2022)
4. Union, E.: Methodological Manual on Territorial Typologies/2018 Edition. Publications Office of the European Union, Luxembourg (2019)
5. Battino, S., Balletto, G., Borruso, G., Donato, C.: Internal areas and smart tourism. Promoting territories in Sardinia Island. In: Gervasi, O., et al. (eds.) Computational Science and Its Applications – ICCSA 2018. LNCS, vol. 10964, pp. 44–57. Springer, Cham (2018). https://doi.org/10.1007/978-3-319-95174-4_4
6. Prezioso, M.: Green economy e capitale territoriale. Dalla ricerca geografico economica proposta di metodi, indicatori, strumenti. Patron Editore, Bologna (2016)
7. Ana, I. M.: Ecotourism, agrotourism and rural tourism in the European Union. Cactus Tour. J. **15**(2), 6–14 (2017)
8. Bambi, G., Iacobelli, S., Rossi, G., Pellegrini P., Barbari, M.: Rural tourism to promote territories along the ancient roads of communication: case study of the rediscovery of the St. Francis's ways between Florence and La Verna. Eur. Countries. **11**, 462–474 (2019)
9. Cucari, N., Wankowicz, E., Esposito de Falco, S.: Rural tourism and Albergo diffuso: a case study for sustainable land-use. Land Use Policy. **82**, 105–119 (2019)
10. Stankov, U., Filimonau, V., Vujicic, M.D.: A mindful shift: an opportunity for mind-fulness-driven tourism in a post-pandemic world. Tour. Geogr. **22**(3), 1–10 (2020)
11. Zhu, H., Deng, F.: How to influence rural tourism intention by risk knowledge during COVID-19 containment in China: mediating role of risk perception and attitude. Int. J. Environ. Res. Publ. Health **17**(10), 1–23 (2020)
12. Rosalina, P.D., Dupre, K., Wang, Y.: Rural tourism: a systematic literature review on definitions and challenges. J. Hosp. Tour. Manag. **47**, 134–149 (2021)
13. Wieckowski, M.: Will the Consequences of Covid-19 trigger a redefining of the role of transport in the development of sustainable tourism? Sustainability **13**(1887), 1–15 (2021)
14. Blecic, I., Canu, D., Cecchini, A., Congiu, T., Fancello, G.: Walkability and street intersections in rural-urban fringes: a decision aiding evaluation procedure. Sustainability **9**(883), 1–19 (2017)
15. Hall, M.C., Ram, Y.: Measuring the relationship between tourism and walkability? Walk score and English tourist attractions. J. Sustain. Tour. **27**(2), 223–240 (2019)
16. Gehl, J., Gemzoe, L.: Winning back public space. In: Tolley, R. (eds.), Sustainable Transport, Planning for Walking and Cycling in Urban Environments. Woodhead, Cambridge (2003)

17. Kelly, C.E., Tight, M.R., Hodgson, F.C., Page, M.W.: A comparison of three methods for assessing the walkability of the pedestrian environment. J. Transp. Geogr. **19**(6), 1500–1508 (2011)

18. Balletto, G., Milesi, A., Ladu, M., Borruso, G.: A dashboard for supporting slow tourism in green infrastructures. A methodological proposal in Sardinia (Italy). Sustainability **12**(9), 3579 (2020)

19. Balletto, G., Ladu, M., Milesi, A., Camerin, F., Borruso, G.: Walkable City and military enclaves. Analysis and decision-making approach to support the proximity connection in urban regeneration. Sustainability **14**(1), 457, 1–16 (2022)

20. Moura, F., Cambra, P., Goncalves, A.B.: Measuring walkability for distinct pedestrian groups with a participatory assessment method: a case study in Lisbon. Landsc. Urban Plan. **187**, 282–296 (2017)

21. Su, S., Zhou, H., Xu, M., Ru, H., Wang, W., Weng, M.: Auditing street walkability and associated social inequalities for planning implications. J. Transp. Geogr. **74**, 62–76 (2019)

22. Ladu, M., Balletto, G., Borruso, G.: Sport and smart communities. Assessing the sporting attractiveness and community perceptions of Cagliari (Sardinia, Italy). In: Misra, S., et al. (eds.) Computational Science and Its Applications – ICCSA 2019. LNCS, vol. 11624, pp. 200–215. Springer, Cham (2019). https://doi.org/10.1007/978-3-030-24311-1_14

23. Frost, S., et al.: Effects of the built environment on physical activity of adults living in rural settings. Am J Health Promot. **24**(4), 267–283 (2010)

24. Kegler, M.C., Alcantara, I., Haardörfer, R., Gemma, A., Ballard, D., Gazmararian, J.: Rural neighbourhood walkability: implications for assessment. J. Phys. Act. Health **12**(Suppl. 1), 40–45 (2015)

25. Fonseca, F., Ribeiro, P., Jabbari, M., Petrova, E., Papageorgiou, G., Conticelli, E., Tondelli, S., Ramos, R.: Smart Pedestrian Network: an integrated conceptual model for im-proving walkability. In: Pereira, P., Ribeiro, R., Oliveira, I., Novais, P. (eds.) Society with Future: Smart and Liveable Cities. SC4Life 2019. Lecture Notes of the Institute for Computer Sciences, Social Informatics and Telecommunications Engineering, vol. 318, pp. 1–18. Springer, Cham (2019).

26. https://www.sardegnaturismo.it/it. Accessed 30 Mar 2022

27. Nocco, S.: I "Cammini di Sardegna e gli itinerari turistico-religiosi e dello Spirito": un'opportunità di sviluppo per le aree interne della Sardegna? RiMe - Rivista dell'Istituto di Storia dell'Europa Mediterranea **7**(III), 209–237 (2020)

28. Balletto, G., Borruso, G., Milesi, A., Ladu, M., Mundula, L.: Ancient mining paths and slow tourism. assessments and challenges in Sardinia (Italy). In: Gervasi, O., et al. (eds.) Computational Science and Its Applications – ICCSA 2021. LNCS, vol. 12958, pp. 275–287. Springer, Cham (2021). https://doi.org/10.1007/978-3-030-87016-4_21

29. Balletto, G., Milesi, A., Battino, S., Borruso, G., Mundula, L.: Slow Tourism and smart community. The case of Sulcis-Iglesiente (Sardinia -Italy). In: Misra, S., et al. (eds.) Computational Science and Its Applications – ICCSA 2019. LNCS, vol. 11624, pp. 184–199. Springer, Cham (2019). https://doi.org/10.1007/978-3-030-24311-1_13

30. Balletto, G., Borruso, G., Ladu, M., Milesi, A.: Smart and slow tourism. Evaluation and challenges in Sardinia (Italy). In: La Rosa, D., Privitera, R. (eds). International Conference Innovation in Urban and Regional Planning. INPUT 2021. Lecture Notes in Civil Engineering. LNCS, vol. 242, pp. 175–182. Springer, Cham (2021). https://doi.org/10.1007/978-3-030-96985-1_20

31. ISTAC: Cifras Oficiales de Población (2022). http://www.gobiernodecanarias.org/istac/estadisticas/demografia/poblacion/cifraspadronales/E30245A.html. Accessed 25 Mar 2022

32. Tourism Gran Canaria: Gran Canaria Tourism is nearest to pre pandemic tourist statistics (2021). https://www.grancanaria.com/turismo/es/area-profesional/noticias/noticia/?tx_ttnews%5Btt_news%5D=922&cHash=01add03151da6c7c8915fbc60bc2b0ca. Accessed 25 Mar 2022
33. ISTAC: Estadística de Movimientos Turísticos en Frontera de Canarias (2020). http://www.gobiernodecanarias.org/istac/estadisticas/sectorservicios/hosteleriayturismo/demanda/E16028B.html. Accessed 25 Mar 2022
34. Battino, S., Lampreu, S.: The role of the sharing economy for a sustainable and innovative development of rural areas: a case study in Sardinia (Italy). Sustainability **11**(3004), 1–20 (2019)
35. Galdar, J.: Canarian Government (2022). https://jacobeogaldar.es/patrimoniomundialunesco. Accessed 5 Apr 2022
36. Palumbo, M.E., Mundula, L., Balletto, G., Bazzato, E., Marignani, M.: Environmental dimension into strategic planning. The case of metropolitan city of Cagliari. In: Gervasi, O., et al. (eds.) Computational Science and Its Applications – ICCSA 2020. LNCS, vol. 12255, pp. 456–471. Springer, Cham (2020). https://doi.org/10.1007/978-3-030-58820-5_34

Game-Based e-Tourism-e-Health Using SQL

Chze-Yee Lim(✉) 🆔 and Chien-Sing Lee 🆔

Department of Computing and Information Systems, Sunway University, 47500 Petaling Jaya, Selangor, Malaysia
jjameslim98@gmail.com, chiensingl@sunway.edu.my

Abstract. AR games such as Pokemon Go, Jurassic World Alive and other games encourage us to venture out in the real open world to also see the beauty of it. However, tourism has come almost to a virtual stop during the first year of the COVID-19 pandemic and recovery is slow. We present a tile-based experience-sharing *PixoMap*, which incorporates some aspects of smart tourism. For user requirements gathering, we first compare factors that make popular games such as Pokemon Go, Minecraft, and the Sims popular. Findings indicate that people enjoy collecting objects, such as monsters or cards, freedom and creativity, escape and sometimes nostalgia. Our *PixoMap* game allows players to virtually browse an area in the map, and choose a tile. Each tile contains memories (*Memors*)/experiences/stories. Users can read others' experiences and share their own experiences, play a minigame to earn in-game currency, to change his/her 2D avatar or change the tile's color or optionally, to own the tile. Alpha user feedback confirms and refines our design. Heuristic evaluation and user experience feedback at the end of the study, are positive and encouraging.

Keywords: e-Tourism · e-Health · SQL · Minigames

1 Introduction

In 2020 and for 2–3 years to come, tourism is put into a tight spot due to the pandemic. Malaysian tourism did not escape the drastic drop in revenues (Fig. 1).

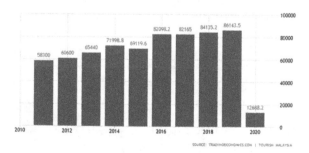

Fig. 1. Malaysian tourism revenues

O. Gervasi et al. (Eds.): ICCSA 2022 Workshops, LNCS 13381, pp. 222–235, 2022.
https://doi.org/10.1007/978-3-031-10548-7_17

We would like to propose smart tourism-cum-e-health, using games. The benefits in playing games are known: education, cognitive stimulation, and enjoyment. Edmonds and Smith (2017) find that games can be beneficial to learning online, enhanced by location-based learning, mobile learning, digital storytelling and gamification. Wang and Hsieh (2018) add that games provide a means to work towards, and achieve dreams virtually. Moreover, games can provide a channel for players to escape reality, de-stress, and to learn (Cairns et. al., 2019).

Balakrishnan and Griffiths (2018) also find that a challenging game contributes most to a game being addictive, followed by "friends and family," then "entertainment". However, an increase in challenge leads to an increase in cognitive load. This will affect the enjoyment of the game. Hence, is challenge suitable for all ages? If challenge is more difficult for those who do not play games or play less games, then can cognitive training help reduce cognitive load?

Toril et al. (2014) find that older adults who participate in cognitive training via video games evidence positive effects. However, Sala et. al.'s(2018) meta-analysis study questions these benefits, as findings from other literature, indicate that cognitive training improves performance, only if the tasks are pre-trained. Furthermore, there is a lack of evidence in skill generalization across domains (far transfer). Hence, they investigate the psychology of expertise (what makes a person an expert), and a series of reviews on meta-analytic studies, via three random-effect meta-analytic models.

The first meta-analysis investigates the degree of correlation between video game skill and cognitive ability; the second, differences in video game players and nonplayers' cognitive ability; and the third, the effects of video game training on participants' cognitive ability. They find small or no overall effect sizes in all three studies. The more positive finding, is a weak correlation between overall cognitive ability and video game skill. Hence, they suggest that playing video games and enhanced cognitive ability are not causally related, and that video game training does not enhance cognitive ability.

Bediou et. al.'s (2018) meta-analysis on the effects of action video games on perceptual, attentional, and cognitive skills, shed further light. They first formulate cognitive profiles from the habitual actions of video game players via cross-sectional studies. Findings indicate a positive average effect of approximately, half a standard deviation ($g = 0.55$). Subsequently, they utilize long-term intervention studies, to investigate the potential of causally introducing changes in cognition by playing action video games. Findings are even more promising, with a smaller average effect of $g = 0.34$. Findings further reveal that action video game play greatly increases top-down attention and spatial cognition – promising for perception studies. Hence, they find that not all video games are similar in its effect on cognition.

From the above, we surmise that by itself, any game remains a game, unless the player has the ability to recognize patterns and to derive inferences. Thus, for those who are not experts, there is a learning curve, and as with any learning process, cognitive ability usually increases, with scaffolding. In non-structured games for seniors (Lee & Hughes, 2019), improved performance is due to freedom of expression, and varied alternatives in problem-solving. Hence, for cognitive stimulation/training, we need to generate germane load first, to tradeoff intrinsic and extraneous cognitive loads. The assumption is that strategy games involve more modelling and alternatives, than speed games. This is positive in terms of motivation and morale. In the past, Lee and Ling (2020) find that students benefit more on cognitive training via strategy games compared to speed games.

1.1 Problem

Due to the pandemic in 2020 and 2021, physically travelling from one destination to another is highly discouraged, due to the virus itself having an increased chance of spreading when there are crowds. There are efforts to develop software/systems, which allow users to take pictures of themselves at a virtual preferred location of interest. There are also efforts to bring tourism to zoom or Youtube or 360.

Lee and Wong (2017) have attempted to develop community engagement in Smart Cities. In this paper, we look towards digital games, because they are popular and because there are multiple benefits. We look towards digital games, because they are popular and because there are multiple benefits. Hence, the first problem is to find out what makes these games popular, in order to develop tourism games, which can help intro-duce/promote a place and sustain visits to the game/place. Soukup (2020) note that the players' physical locations can create a cognitive map that directs, and focuses move-ments within a geographical space. They regard *Pokemon Go* as such a cognitive map, which can simplify and focus movements in urban spaces. The question that arises is, how can we use this for smart tourism-e-health?

There were some dangers to playing Pokemon Go as reported in Wagner-Greene et al. (2017), in places with heavy traffic. Hence, we adapt the cognitive map, to tiles. We were inspired by Reddit's "pixel-art". An example would be from a sub-reddit called "r/place" (Fig. 2). It was popular 4 years ago, as an April Fools' experiment. Users were to choose a pixel (and color) in the canvas, and create their own collective Art. If a certain part of a map is fully filled up with the cumulative effort of the playerbase, players can opt to disrupt the artwork of the other players, by taking over and changing the tiles' color.

Fig. 2. The final product of "r/place"

Wang and Hsieh (2018) point out that a location can have a positive bond with the memories of the players. However, perceived crowding can damage the enjoyment of the game. The next research question is, how can we address perceived crowding?

1.2 Objectives

Our objectives are:

1) to allow players to virtually browse an area in a real-world map, and choose a tile. The tiles contain memories, experiences and stories, shared by those who came to the tile before the player. These memories are called *Memors*. Users can read others' experiences and share their own experiences, within that area via the menu panel. Each of the tiles also contain a specific minigame, which every player can play to earn in-game currency called "gold". Gold is used to claim ownership of the tiles and to change the player's 2D avatar. Owners of the tile are also allowed to choose from 14 colors, to color the tile they own on the map. Hence, the main gameplay is to conquer tiles in order to color and/or put in *Memors* within the chosen tile. This would incorporate the experiences of a player within a single tile. By representing the real-life location in a tile, the tile becomes a virtual communication/review/recommendation space for smart tourism. Augmented Reality (AR) is a possible future venture.

2) to avoid overcrowding as highlighted by Wang and Hsieh (2018), we implement SQL. MySQL is required in multiplayer games, such as World of Warcraft MMORPGs. For *Pixomap*, SQL is used to scan a player and tile, and data manipulation. Such player data includes the player's ID, name, amount of gold and etc., while the map tiles' data are the tile's ID, the owner of the tile, the *Memors* and etc.

3) to enable repurposing of this system for e-health as well, as the note-taking/sharing of experiences/playing the mini-games can reduce cognitive load, be a part of cognitive training, as well as de-stressing.

2 Related Work

2.1 Game Genre

To identify the relevant game genre, which would fit our objectives, we identify possible relevant examples within the following game genres: action games (shooters), simulation and builder games, MMORPGs and collecting games (card and monsters). These are presented in Table 1.

Table 1. Game genre

Action games (shooter)	Simulation and builder games	MMORPGs	Collecting games (card, monsters.)
Call of Duty: Modern Warfare	The Sims	World-of-Warcraft	Pokémon
Warframe	Spore	RuneScape	Jurassic World Alive
Counterstrike-Global Offensive	Zoo Tycoon	Ragnarök Online	Magic-The-Gathering
Halo: Combat Evolved	Minecraft	Elder Scrolls Online	Yu-Gi-Oh!

2.2 Factors Which Made Life Simulation and Collecting Games Popular

Subsequently, we compare factors, which contribute to the games' popularity (Table 2), and similarity among these factors (Table 3).

Table 2. Factors which contributed to their popularity

Games			
Game 1: Pokémon Go	Game 2: Yu-Gi-Oh!	Game 3: Minecraft	Game 4: The Sims

Factors which popularized them			
Enjoyment in collecting monsters [16, 24, 25, 30]		Freedom of creativity and playing within the constraints of the game [17, 29]	
Enjoyment in battling opponents with the Pokémon and taking over the gym or in Yu-Gi-Oh!, the cards [25]		Life simulation and escapism [15, 23]	
Nostalgia/Word-of-Mouth/established brand	Potential investment - prices of some physical cards may skyrocket [30]	Ability to roleplay [15, 26, 27]	
Recognition and Approval [28, 30]		Diverse gameplay [18]	

Table 3. Similarity in factors, which popularized the games

	Games				
Factors, which made them popular	Pokémon Go	Minecraft	The Sims	Yu-Gi-Oh!	*PixoMap*
Collecting	■			■	■
World-building and customizing /Simulation		■	■		■
Role-Play		■	■		
Battling	■			■	■
Competitive	■	■		■	■
Exploration	■			■	

2.3 Scope

There are multiple game genres, such as action games, simulation and builder games and etc. From the above literature reviewed, we choose object customization (the tiles), collection (take over) and exploration of different places, which the players not have visited within that city/area.

3 Methodology

The incremental agile methodology is applied, with distributed processing in mind, due to *PixoMap*'s storytelling nature. As stated above, the main focus of the game is how players interact with each tile, and how they creatively utilize and manage them. With XAMPP in this project, it will also be a multiplayer game that is server-based. The SQL-side of the game will only handle the player and tile's data. The game's engine will be Unity, php. SQL operators applied are:

- The Arithmetic (e.g. +, *, | | for in-game currency calculations);
- Comparison (e.g. =, >, < to check whether the player has the conditions they are required fulfilled before performing an action or compare if the player's ID matches with a conquered tile, e.g. when purchasing an item);
- Logical Operators (e.g. NOT, AND, OR to determine whether the condition or values are true or false, e.g. whether the player is the tile's owner or if the tile is taken).

The UI design is via the *Clip Studio Paint* software, while some parts of the game that requires pixelated designs is via a free web-based tool *Piskel*. Users can hold left click and drag to pan or WASD to navigate. The middle mouse wheel is to zoom in/out.

The user requirements gathering/confirmation questionnaire is designed mainly based on *PixoMap*'s proposed functional requirements, with Davis' (1989) Technology Acceptance Model in mind. Beta testing user survey results are based mainly on Davis' (1989) Technology Acceptance Model, supported by Nielsen's (1994/2000) heuristic evaluation questionnaire and Schrepp et. al.'s (2017) user experience questionnaire.

4 System Description

4.1 Game Genre

PixoMap is an ARG that uses tile-based elements and mechanics based on the real-world map. Players visit each tile, share their experiences/memory of the location of the tile, and unlock various rewards that they can use, e.g. to colour the chosen tiles. This can lead to artistic pieces, if the user(s) decides to capture the tiles surrounding it, and creatively colour them. Not only that, each tile would have a different minigame, where users can also play for more gold. Players can *optionally* take over the tile, and change the player's avatar.

4.2 Design

Use Case. The *PixoMap* use case diagram (Fig. 3), indicates the primary actor (the player), and tasks that he/she can carry out in *PixoMap*.

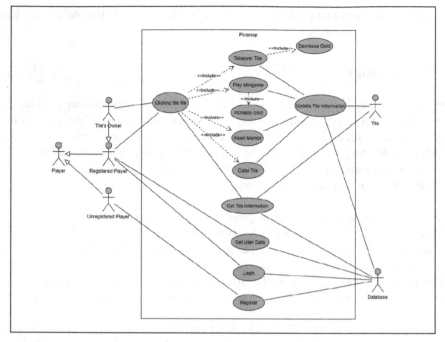

Fig. 3. *PixoMap's* use case diagram

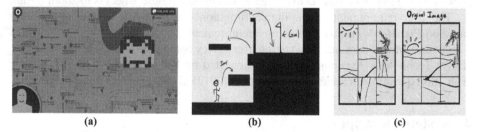

(a)   (b)   (c)

Fig. 4. a. Proposed *PixoMap* UI, gameplay. **b, c.** Sample minigames

PixoMap UI and Gameplay. Figure 4a presents the proposed PixoMap UI and gameplay. Figures 4b, c present sample minigames. Minigames would be from the Internet since this is just a capstone project and there is a time constraint.

4.3 User Requirements Gathering/confirmation and Refinement of System Design/functional Requirements

To confirm the functional requirements derived from related work, and our own hypotheses and ideas, we carried out a user survey. The survey covered 2 sections: demographics, and perception towards the design of the main gameplay, perception towards the design of *Memors*, perception towards the potential of *PixoMap*, as a means to express their own creativity and perception towards the design of the minigames.

Participants' Age Group and Their Experiences with Video Games. Most of the participants (83.3%) are aged between 19–23, and 16.7% are slightly older, i.e., 24–55 years of age (Fig. 5). Majority of the players have played video games for many years, i.e., 5–9 years (30%), and 10 years and above (36.7%) (Fig. 5b).

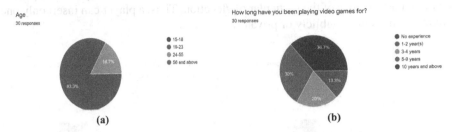

(a)   (b)

Fig. 5. a. Participants' age. **b.** Participants' gaming experience

Gameplay. From the alpha user feedback, we find that perception towards *PixoMap* is mixed, but more inclined towards positive, for players mainly within the 19–23 age bracket. Most of them (36.7%) have more than 10 and 30% 5–9 years of experience playing games. Hence, expectations are higher. Furthermore, this majority prefer competitive games and taking over objects (Figs. 6a, b). Between collecting items and in-game currency, 90% of the respondents prefer the former (Figs. 6c, d). To discourage tile ownership, we increase the amount of gold required to 600 gold, instead of 40, and increase the merit of playing a minigame to 200 gold, instead of 20.

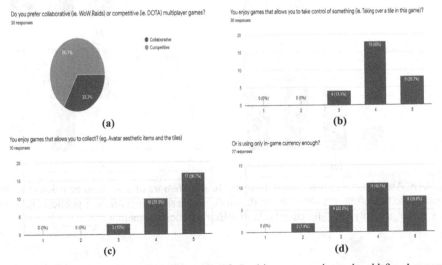

Fig. 6. a. Should it be collaborative/competitive? **b.** Is object conquering enjoyable? **c.** Are games with collectibles fun? **d.** Is in-game currency fun enough?

Memors. Majority (86.6%, 99.3%) of the respondents think that *PixoMap* and *Memors* can help smart tourism by attracting players to the location of the tile (Figs. 7a, b, c). Hence, a 2-grid system, where one is used to interact with the grid, while the other is to display the colours of the tiles, is implemented. However, 63.3% are not sure whether to share *Memors* publicly (Figs. 7d, e), but 93.3% agree that *PixoMap* will help them remember past memory of the particular tile/location. Thus, a player can insert only one *Memor* in a tile, either publicly or privately.

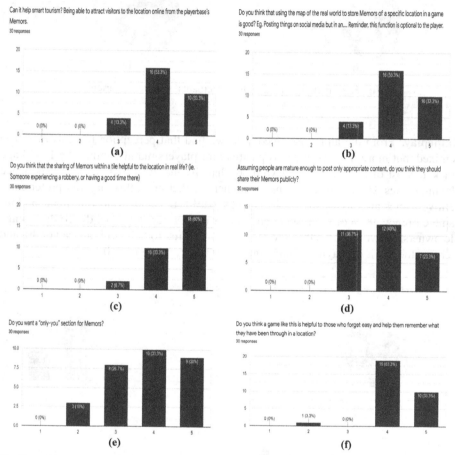

Fig. 7. **a.** Are there benefits to Smart Tourism? **b.** Are *Memors* of a location beneficial? **c.** Will *Memors* also be useful for future visitors? **d.** Should people share their *Memors* publicly? **e.** Would users prefer an "Only-You" function? **f.** Is *PixoMap* beneficial to memory?

Creativity and Minigames. As for creativity, 76.7% are positive about possibilities for creative expression (Fig. 8a). Furthermore, 73.3% think that minigames are fun (Fig. 8b). The respondents are also split about whether the minigame should be random (46.7%) or specific to a tile (53.3%) (Fig. 8c). Hence, we infer that some respondents play to win, whereas some, play for fun and look forward to a preferred minigame. Moreover, 83.3% think that avatars should be developed, only if they are customizable (Figs. 8d, e), as part of identity.

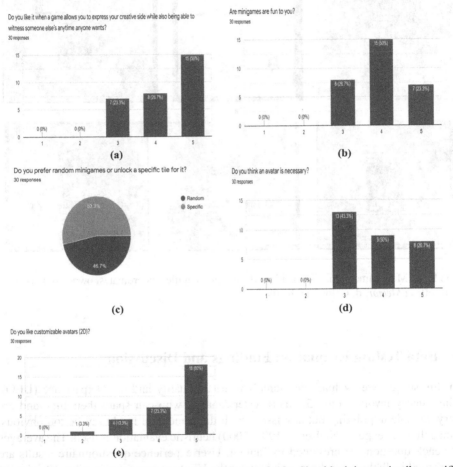

Fig. 8. **a.** Sharing creativity of players **b.** Are minigames fun? **c.** Should minigames be tile-specific or random? **d.** Demand for an avatar **e.** Customizable 2D avatars

5 Development

Based on the above user requirements gathering/confirmation of our proposed design, the camera views, a 2-grid system is introduced, and the point system, and number of *Memors* per person per tile are revised. The final prototype is presented in Figs. 9a–d below.

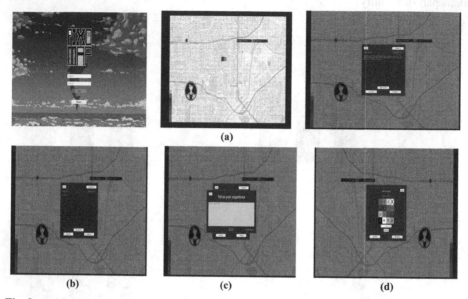

(a)

(b)   (c)   (d)

Fig. 9. a. Main game scene. **b.** Opening *Memor* (getting tile's coordinates, owner and *Memor*). **c.** Inserting *Memor*. **d.** Colouring the tile

6 Beta Testing Evaluation Findings and Discussion

In this survey, we evaluate the game's heuristic quality and user experience (UEQ). This survey involves only 5 expert testers/gamers who can spare their time and are very capable in pointing out any issues with the game, that might not be too obvious. Since they are experts, Nielsen's (1994; 2000) heuristic evaluation is used. The averages for each question are presented in Table 4. User experience questionnaire results are presented in Table 5. Further breakdown of the UEQ are presented in Figs. 10a–d.

We find that players are mostly positive about *PixoMap*. They find it clear and easy to use (ease of use in TAM, easy in UEQ), inventive (100%) and moderately leading edge (60%). These reflect system quality in TAM. Other promising aspects are the liveliness/action progression of each tile, it being an ARG, with actual relation to the real world, and challenging (take-over) games. These contribute to the interesting factor in the UEQ. As such, 60% would recommend *PixoMap* to their friends. Comments gathered indicate requests for more minigames, and more multi-tile selection. We conjecture, the authenticity of the in-currency game may also be a key motivator, similar to Shoppee's.

Table 4. Heuristic evaluation results

No.	Construct	Avg.
1	Match between system and the real-world	0.84
2	Consistency and standards	0.84
3	Recognition and efficiency of use	0.84
4	Visibility of system status	0.80
5	User control and freedom	0.80
6	Flexibility and efficiency of use	0.76
7	Aesthetic and minimalist design	0.76
8	Help users recognize, diagnose, recover from errors	0.76
9	Help and documentation	0.72
10	Error prevention	0.64

Table 5. UEQ results

No.	Construct	Avg.
1	Complicated/easy	0.88
2	Conventional/inventive	0.88
3	Not interesting/interesting	0.84
4	Obstructive/supportive	0.80
5	Inefficient/efficient	0.80
6	Confusing/clear	0.76
7	Usual/leading edge	0.76
8	Boring/exciting	0.68

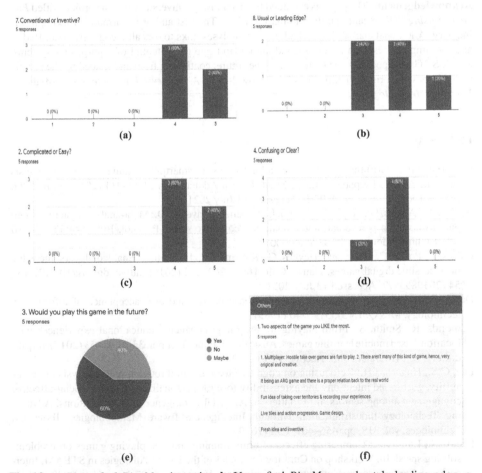

Fig. 10. a. Users find *PixoMap* inventive. **b.** Users find *PixoMap* moderately leading edge. **c.** Users find *PixoMap* easy. **d.** Users find *PixoMap* sufficiently clear. **e.** Possibilty of returning to *PixoMap*/playing in the future. **f.** What players like about *PixoMap*

7   Conclusion

The literature review has highlighted the significance of memorability, collectibles, freedom and creativity, escape and sometimes nostalgia in games. *PixoMap* can be used for e-tourism and e-health. Since it can be made public/private, it can serve as a notebook of memories and experiences of different places of visits and interest (private). Reading of others' experiences other than reviews available at other websites, and earning authentic in-game currency, to being a part of a larger community of gamers or artists, can help sustain interest. Incorporating SQL has prevented perceived sense of over-crowding. With the tile as thumbnail, it may enable users/players to link to the places of interests, receive recommendations, and collect specific rewards as well. We hope that *PixoMap* will lead to more cross-SDG platforms, lean in design, but beneficial to diverse stakeholders. We also acknowledge that images may serve better than text in the sharing of experiences.

Acknowledgement. The paper is extended from a Sunway University capstone project, titled *Fun Games using SQL*, meant mainly for smart tourism. The first author is currently working in the industry. Additional elaboration and additional analyses/links to e-health, cognitive load, Reddit and e-commerce research by the second author, indicate the potential of repurposing systems, across SDGs and possibly, the metaverse in the future; continuing from and funded by the second author's past Fulbright Visiting Scholar Fellowship on *A Framework for Interactive Media in Emerging Technologies*.

References

Balakrishnan, J., Griffiths, M.: Perceived addictiveness of smartphone games: a content analysis of game reviews by players. Int. J. Ment. Health Addict. **17**(4), 922–934 (2018). https://doi.org/10.1007/s11469-018-9897-5. Accessed 13 July 2021

Bediou, B., Adams, D., Mayer, R., Tipton, E., Green, C., Bavelier, D.: Meta-analysis of action video game impact on perceptual, attentional, and cognitive skills. Psychol. Bull. **144**(1), 77–110 (2018). https://doi.org/10.1037/bul0000130

Cairns, P., Power, C., Barlet, M., Haynes, G., Kaufman, C., Beeston, J.: Enabled players: the value of accessible digital games. Games Cult. **16**(2), 262–282 (2019). https://doi.org/10.1177/1555412019893877. Accessed 13 July 2021

Davis, F.D.: Perceived usefulness, perceived ease of use, and user acceptance of information technology. MIS Q. **13**(3), 319–340 (1989)

Edmonds, R., Smith, S.: From playing to designing: enhancing educational experiences with location-based mobile learning games. Australas. J. Educ. Technol. **33**(6), 41–53 (2017). https://doi.org/10.14742/ajet.3583. Accessed 13 July 2021

Lee, C.S., Hughes, J.H.: Refocusing on cognitive load design through a meta-analysis on learnability, goal-based intentions and extensibility towards personalized cognitive-social-affective engagement among seniors. In: Frontiers in Artificial Intelligence and Applications, Advancing Technology Industrialization Through Intelligent Software Methodologies, Tools and Techniques, vol. 318, pp. 456–469, IOS (2019)

Lee, C.S., Ling, Y.L.: Comparing effects of brain-training and role-playing games on problem-solving speed. In: Workshop on Curating Examples of the Use of Analogies in STEAM, International Conference on Computers in Education, Vietnam, 23–27 November 2020, vol. 2, pp. 607–616 (2020)

Lee, C.S., Ooi, E.H.: Design to encourage reframing and transformations through digital storytelling and analogical thinking. Int. J. Adv. Trends Comput. Sci. Eng. **9**(13), 64–70 (2020)

Lee, C. S., Wong, K. D.: Developing community-based engagement in smart cities: A design-computational thinking approach. In: IEEE International Conference on Industrial Engineering and Engineering Management, pp. 832–836. Singapore (2017)

Nielsen, J.:. Designing web usability: The practice of simplicity. Indianapolis. In: New Riders Publishing (2000)

Nielsen, J.: 10 Usability Heuristics for User Interface Design (1994, 2020). https://www.nngroup.com/articles/ten-usability-heuristics

Reddit Pixel Art. https://www.reddit.com/r/place/comments/639htx

Sala, G., Tatlidil, K., Gobet, F.: Video game training does not enhance cognitive ability: a comprehensive meta-analytic investigation. Psychol. Bull. **144**(2), 111–139 (2018). https://doi.org/10.1037/bul0000139

Soukup, C.: Pokémon Go as a cognitive map: simplifying and focusing movement in postmodern urban spaces. Explor. Media Ecol. **19**(2), 179–194 (2020). https://doi.org/10.1386/eme_00034_1. Accessed 13 July 2021

Schrepp, M., Hinderks, A., Thomaschewski, J.: Design and evaluation of a short version of the user experience questionnaire (UEQ-S). Int. J. Interact. Multimed. Artif. Intell. **4**(6), 103–108 (2017)

Toril, P., Reales, J., Ballesteros, S.: Video game training enhances cognition of older adults: a meta-analytic study. Psychol. Aging **29**(3), 706–716 (2014). https://doi.org/10.1037/a0037507

Wagner-Greene, V.R., Wotring, A.J., Castor, T., Kruger, J., Mortemore, S., Dake, J.A.: Pokémon GO: healthy or harmful? Am. J. Public Health **107**(1), 35–36 (2017). https://doi.org/10.2105/AJPH.2016.303548

Wang, S., Hsieh, C.: Ubiquitous Pokémon Go: human–environment relationships and the location-based augmented reality game. Environ. Behav. **52**(7), 695–725 (2018). https://doi.org/10.1177/0013916518817878. Accessed 13 July 2021

14th International Symposium on Software Engineering Processes and Applications (SEPA 2022)

Image Gradient Based Iris Recognition for Distantly Acquired Face Images Using Distance Classifiers

Arnab Mukherjee[1], Kazi Shah Nawaz Ripon[2]([⊠]), Lasker Ershad Ali[1]([⊠]),
Md. Zahidul Islam[1], and G. M. Mamun-Al-Imran[1]

[1] Khulna University, Khulna, Bangladesh
ershad@math.ku.ac.bd
[2] Østfold University College, Halden, Norway
ksripon@hiof.no

Abstract. This paper presents an iris recognition framework to recognize irises from distantly acquired face images using image gradient-based feature extraction and K-Nearest Neighbor with various distance classifiers. The work herein applies the gradient local auto-correlation descriptor to extract discriminative features from the iris images and to reduce feature dimensionality by optimizing some parameters. Several distance metrics are applied in the iris classification stage to reduce computational complexity and build the classification models. The proposed framework effectively handles the noisy artefacts, rotation, occlusion, and illumination variation challenges. The experiments are carried out on a publicly accessible CASIA-V4 distance database to ascertain the effectiveness of distant iris recognition and to compare the efficacy of several existing distant classifiers. The experimental results justify that distance metrics influence the recognition outcomes of the classifier significantly, and the recognition performance of the Correlation distance metric is better than the other distance classifiers for iris gradient features.

Keywords: Iris recognition · Image gradient feature · Distance classifier · Local auto correlation feature descriptor · Distance metrics

1 Introduction

Iris recognition is one of the most automatic systems for recognizing or confirming an individual's identity swiftly, uniquely and reliably without the need for bearing or reminiscing anything, unlike conventional methods. Most security fields still follow the knowledge or token-based methods for individual identification. But those traditional methods, like username, password, personal identification numbers (PINs), credit cards, identification cards, and even passports, are susceptible to losing, conjecturing by a third party, forgetting, or damaging [23]. Recently, several studies have demonstrated that biometric technique is a promising solution for maximum security because biometric traits cannot be

O. Gervasi et al. (Eds.): ICCSA 2022 Workshops, LNCS 13381, pp. 239–252, 2022.
https://doi.org/10.1007/978-3-031-10548-7_18

faked, borrowed, forgotten, stolen and guessed easily [4,19]. The main advantage of the biometric traits is that these are not forged practically [20]. Usually, biometrics are categorized into two groups: physiological and behavioural traits. Physiological traits include iris, facial thermo-grams, fingerprints, palm-prints, hand geometry, eyes, retina DNA, etc. In contrast, behavioural traits include gait, voice recording, human action, signature, handwriting, keystroke, rhythms, and the like [12].

The iris is regarded as the most reliable biometrics for human identification among various physiological traits. As the human iris is the only internal and external visible organ with its exclusive structure, it is highly protected from varied environmental conditions [8]. The construction of iris patterns is not related to genetic factors but somewhat arbitrary. Even a person's left and right irises are different due to a high degree of randomness and uniqueness of iris texture, and the irises of identical twins have no similarity [27]. Having rings, freckles, ridges, furrows, crypts, and zigzag patterns within the iris region are the causes of complexity in iris patterns. Also, the iris trait ensures a high degree of stability over a person's lifetime [7,8,12,20,23,27]. These desirable properties has motivated the researchers to consider the iris as the most secure and reliable biometric for high-security surveillance.

It is challenging to ensure the reliability of an automated system of identifying persons using the iris recognition system. This is because the eye images are captured in a controlled environment and a less controlled environment [20]. In a less controlled environment, the images are acquired at a longer distance from the subject, whereas the images are taken at short distances in a controlled environment. Under different imaging conditions, the distantly acquired iris images have motion blurs, occlusions owing to shadows, eyelashes and eyelids, lighting reflections, and other artefacts. These issues degrade the image quality significantly and cannot illustrate iris textures clearly in less controlled environments.

The iris recognition system still has various challenges like robust segmentation, appropriate feature extraction for distantly acquired noisy images, the computational complexity of classification, etc. Considering these challenges, this work focuses on developing an effective iris recognition framework by employing image gradient features, more specifically, local auto-correlation feature descriptor (GLAC) and distance classifiers. The novelty of the proposed framework is that the descriptor retrieves more informative features with lower dimensionality from the iris images of defocusing, motion blur, poor contrast and non-uniform illumination etc. Further, this work investigates the effectiveness of several existing distant classifiers within the K-Nearest Neighbor (K-NN)–based classifier. Experimental results suggest that the distance classifiers have the lowest noise implications and can enhance recognition accuracy and reduce the computational complexity of the iris recognition algorithm.

The remainder of this paper is organized as follows. Section 2 discusses iris recognition affiliated works briefly. Section 3 describes the Iris recognition framework, feature extraction strategy, and classification. Section 4 presents experimental measurement, results, and discussion. Finally, Sect. 5 concludes the paper.

2   Related Work

There is extensive literature on human identification, but the relevant papers on distant iris recognition are mentioned herein. John Daugman presented the first successful automated prototype of an iris recognition system using a 2D Gabor wavelet filter with hamming distance in 1994 [7]. Wildes et al. approached another prototype system employing Laplacian of Gaussian filter (LGF) with phase quantization at multiple scales and matched the binary features with normalized correlation [27]. Boles et al. considered the iris texture a zero-crossing of 1D dyadic wavelet filters for encoding iris patterns and recognized binary iris codes using Euclidean or Hamming distance [6]. Mukherjee et al. provided a comparative study on various distance measures by employing different types of mother wavelets on distance database in [18]. Noh et al. introduced a wavelet decomposition-based iris recognition system in [24]. Monro et al. encoded iris features using discrete cosine transform [17]. All these earlier attempts have focused on wavelet-based iris recognition systems with close distance images requiring equal high-quality iris textures and performing well under ideal imaging conditions. Moreover, the existing wavelet descriptors cannot retrieve multi-directional information. A contourlet transform to extract the intrinsic geometrical structures of iris patterns was proposed in [5] to address the drawback of wavelets. However, their recognition rate substantially decreases with increasing the number of subjects.

In 2017, Mahesh et al. provided a survey for the present scenario related to iris recognition works. Their survey included various practical techniques for iris image preprocessing, image segmentation, feature encoding, and iris classification, which were published from 2010 to 2015 [16]. Considering the need for remote human identification automatically, Fancourt et al. proposed the first distant image-based iris recognition at up to 10 m from the subject [11]. Hollingsworth et al. developed the best iris shift bit code using the fragile bit method, which worked effectively for distant iris images [13]. Dong et al. introduced a personalized weight map technique for iris matching [9]. Later, Tan and Kumar merged the fragile bit and personalized weight map techniques using the weighted sum method for classification [26]. Ali et al. established a composite feature descriptor including Log Gabor wavelet (LG), GLAC, Contourlet transformed (CT) and convolutional neural network (CNN) to enhance the recognition performance [2]. The feature-level fusion proposed in this work provides a promising solution for distance-based challenges. The same authors later provided an LG wavelet-based contourlet transform to overcome wavelet and contourlet transform limitations [3]. The feature descriptor retrieves two-dimensional singularities and spatial information more effectively in various directions than LG wavelet or contourlet transform. Still, it increases computational complexity in classification due to having high dimensionality for feature level fusion. In 2020, Tan and Domingo introduced an iris segmentation technique using a deep convolutional neural network [25]. The authors comprise encoder and decoder modules to enhance the iris segmentation performance for remotely captured iris or face images. However, the complete iris recognition framework is absent in their work.

Still, most of the existing iris recognition systems cannot provide any satisfactory outcome through their frameworks on varying levels of illumination, noisy and visible distant images. The work herein adopts the GLAC feature descriptor and distance-based classifier to overcome these shortcomings, which have robustness against low contrast and local illumination changes in the iris images.

3   Methodology

Figure 1 presents the block diagram for the proposed iris recognition framework. It includes the following key steps: eye image pre-processing, annular iris segmentation, iris feature extraction, classification, and iris recognition. The main contribution of the proposed framework is its computational simplicity due to the low order of local auto-correlation. Further, the investigation demonstrates that the Correlation distance metric may be employed instead of the usual Euclidean or Hamming distance for image patch matching, classification problems, object recognition, etc.

3.1   Image Pre-processing

During the acquisition process, the distant images suffer from non-uniform illumination, occlusions, and other noises. These artefacts present some difficulties in the iris segmentation and recognition stage. Thus, this work adopts a *Single Scale Retinex* (SSR) algorithm [3] to reduce the effect of uncontrolled light

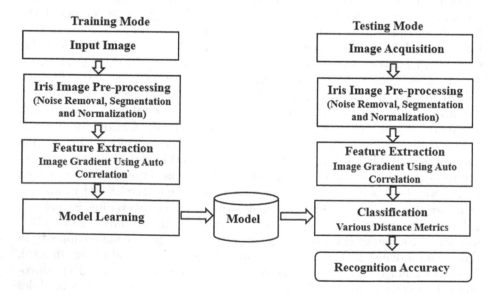

Fig. 1. The block diagram of the proposed iris recognition framework.

sources and improve the images' low contrast and sharpness. The general mathematical form of the algorithm is given by

$$R(u,v) = log\frac{Im(u,v)}{G_\tau * Im(u,v)} \qquad (1)$$

where, $Im(u,v)$ is a grey scale eye image, $G_\tau(u,v) = Cexp[-(u^2+u^2)/\tau^2]$ is a low pass Gaussian filter with standard deviation τ, and $*$ is the convolutional operator.

3.2 Iris Segmentation

A robust and efficient segmentation algorithm can significantly enhance the distant iris recognition performance. The work herein utilizes a *Random Walker* (RW) algorithm to obtain coarse iris segmentation through a set of post-processing operations as detailed in [3]. It provides the iris texture and corresponding binary iris mask. The proposed framework also applies a circular model to localize approximately the boundaries of pupillary and limbic as the binary masks cannot inform details about the boundaries. The segmentation phase is finished after eliminating the occlusion noises, for example, eyelids, eyelashes and shadow.

3.3 Iris Normalization

As mentioned earlier, iris sizes vary from person to person, even both person's irises. These occur by the dilation and contraction of the pupil with variations in illumination. Such elastic distortions of iris texture influence the recognition results. So, it is expedient to compensate for those distortions to extract more accurate features. To account for the issues, the proposed framework applies the *Daugman's Rubber Sheet Model* [7] to normalize the segmented iris by constructing a remapping from Cartesian to dimensionless polar coordinates. The complete iris pre-processing steps are presented sequentially in Fig. 2.

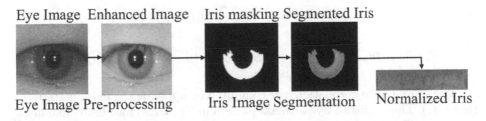

Fig. 2. The schema of eye image pre-processing to iris normalization.

3.4   Gradient Feature Extraction

The gradient local auto-correlation (GLAC) feature descriptor is a relatively newer feature descriptor for iris recognition. This shift-invariant descriptor was proposed by Kobayashi and Otsu [14] as a root extension scale Invariant and feature transform (SIFT) or histogram of oriented gradients (HOG). If $Im(u,v)$ be a 2-dimensional iris image region with a position vector $p = (u,v)^t$ on Im, the image gradients $(\frac{\partial G}{\partial u}, \frac{\partial G}{\partial v})$ are computed with any gradient filters, like Sobel, Prewitt, Roberts filter, and one-dimensional derivatives $[-1,0,1]$ and $[-1,0,1]^T$. At the point $Im(u,v)$, the gradient norm and oriented vector can be expressed as $m = |\Delta G(u,v)| = \sqrt{(\frac{\partial G}{\partial u})^2 + (\frac{\partial G}{\partial v})^2}$ and $\theta = \tan^{-1}(\frac{\partial G}{\partial v}/\frac{\partial G}{\partial u})$, respectively [16]. The oriented angle θ is coded into D-orientational bins by casting weighted votes to the closest bins. The orientational bins construct a D-dimensional gradient oriented G-O vector with g. In other words, the vector is a sparse vector of $g \in R^D$, and the G-O vectors are sparsely defined in terms of their norms and oriented angles. With the gradient norm m and G-O vector g, the Nth order gradient auto-correlation function around the local neighbors is given by

$$R(d_0, d_1, d_2 \ldots\ldots\ldots d_N, f_0, f_1, f_2, \ldots\ldots, f_N) = \int_{Im} \omega[m(p), m(p+f_1), \ldots\ldots, m(p+f_N)]$$

$$g_{d_0}(p)g_{d_1}(p+f_1)\ldots\ldots g_{d_N}(p+f_N)dp \tag{2}$$

where, the displacement vectors $f_1, f_2, f_3 \ldots\ldots f_N$ are known as shifting vectors with respect to the location vector from the reference point $p(u,v)$ of each pixel in Im, and $m(p)$ is the norm of p. The scalar function $\omega(.)$ is used as the weights of auto-correlation, which is derived from norm m functions and g_d is the dth element of g.

There have two types of gradient correlations in Eq. 2: (i) orientational correlations obtained from the products of the element values g_{d_i} and (ii) spatial correlations attained from displacement vectors f_i. Equation 2 can be taken in various forms by changing the values of N, f_i and ω. According to the suggestion in [2], the experiments in this work considers $N \in \{0,1\}$, $f_{1x,y} \in \{\pm\Delta p, 0\}$ and $\omega(.) = min$. The formulation of 0th and 1st order GLAC features are as follows:

$$F_0 : R_{N=0}(d_0) = \sum_{p \in Im} m(p)g_{d_0}(p) \tag{3}$$

$$F_1 : R_{N=1}(d_0, d_1, f_1) = \sum_{p \in Im} min[m(p), m(p+f_1)]g_{d_0}(p)g_{d_1}(p+f_1) \tag{4}$$

The spatial auto-correlations are computed by applying the mask patterns of $(p, p+f_1)$. There exists only one mask pattern in Eq. 3, and four individual mask patterns in Eq. 4 for computing the auto-correlations by avoiding duplicates that arise from shifts. The mask patterns to compute the element values of G-O vector pairs are mentioned in Algorithm 1.

Finally, all the elements for the 1st order are multiplied and summed over the image region. Although the GLAC feature dimension vector (concerning

F_0 and F_1 in $D + 4D^2$) is large, its feature vector computation is not so high because of the sparseness G-O vector g. Since the sparseness of$g$ is independent of orientational bins D, the computational cost is also invariant to the number of D.

Algorithm 1: Basic Algorithm of GLAC Computation

Pre-processing: The gradient norm m and G-O vector g are computed from the image gradients;

0th **Order GLAC:** In Eq. (3), summation is taken to two non-zero elements of the G-O vector g with weight $m(p)$ only at each pixel g;

1st **Order GLAC:** In Eq. (4), summation are taken by multiplying the non-zero elements of $g(p)$ and $g(p + f_1)$ with weight of $min[m(p), m(p + f_1)]$ for each mask pattern at p. Only four times multiplication requires for this operation;

3.5   Classification

K-Nearest Neighbor (K-NN) is a distance-based supervised classifier that assigns a label to classify the test iris image based on the majority vote of its K-nearest neighbours, which are closest to the test image. If $u = (u_1, u_2, u_3, ..., u_n)$ and $v = (v_1, v_2, v_3, ..., v_n) \in R^n$ be two feature vectors in a multi-dimensional feature space, then the distance metrics tested in this work – Euclidean (Eucl), standardized Euclidean (Steu), Minkowski (Min), city block (City), Chebychev (Cheb), cosine (Cos), correlation (Cor), Hamming (Ham) and Spearman (Spr), can be defined as follows:

$$D_{Eucl}(u, v) = \sqrt{\sum_{i=1}^{n}(u_i - v_i)^2} \tag{5}$$

$$D_{Steu}(u, v) = \sqrt{\sum_{i=1}^{n}(u_i - v_i)^2 / s^2} \tag{6}$$

where, s_i is the standard deviation of the u_i and v_i over the feature sets.

$$D_{Min}(u, v) = \sqrt[r]{\sum_{i=1}^{n}|u_i - v_i|^r} \tag{7}$$

$$D_{City}(u, v) = \sum_{i=1}^{n}|u_i - v_i| \tag{8}$$

$$D_{Cheb}(u, v) = \max_i |u_i - v_i|, \tag{9}$$

$$D_{Spr}(u, v) = 1 - \frac{\sum_{i=1}^{n}(u_i' - \overline{u_i'})(v_i' - \overline{v_i'})}{\sqrt{\sum_{i=1}^{n}(u_i' - \overline{u_i'})^2 \sum_{i=1}^{n}(v_i' - \overline{v_i'})^2}} \tag{10}$$

where, u_i' is the tied rank of u_i and $\overline{u}' = \frac{1}{n}\sum_{i=1}^{n} u_i'$; and v_i' is the tied rank of v_i and $\overline{v}' = \frac{1}{n}\sum_{i=1}^{n} v_i'$

$$D_{Cos}(u,v) = 1 - \frac{\sum_{i=1}^{n} u_i v_i}{\sqrt{\sum_{i=1}^{n} u_i^2 \sum_{i=1}^{n} v_i^2}} \tag{11}$$

$$D_{Cor}(u,v) = 1 - \frac{\sum_{i=1}^{n}(u_i - \overline{u_i})(v_i - \overline{v_i})}{\sqrt{\sum_{i=1}^{n}(u_i - \overline{u_i})^2 \sum_{i=1}^{n}(v_i - \overline{v_i})^2}} \tag{12}$$

$$D_{Ham}(u,v) = \frac{1}{n}\sum_{i=1}^{n}(u_i \neq v_i) \tag{13}$$

4 Experiments and Results

The experiments are carried out on the CASIA-V4 distance database – the largest open-source database for distantly acquired facial images [1]. The Chinese Academy of Science's Institute of Automation (CASIA) has released this database for secure biometrics recognition. The complete database is made up of 2,567 facial images with 142 subjects, including regular and more complicated images in most subjects. A Near-Infrared camera acquires the facial images in less controlled environments at 3 meters distance from the subject.

For the experiments in this work, firstly, the eye images are isolated from the whole facial images and are obtained 5,134 images, including left and right eye images. It was not possible to isolate all the eye images correctly from the facial images due to containing eyes with glasses, reflections, hair, or other noise factors. This work does not consider the regular images of the first 14 subjects to enhance the reliability of the proposed system. From each of the remaining 128 subjects, a total of 3,041 randomly chosen images are selected as training images. Similarly, 712 images are selected as test images. The experiments are implemented using MATLAB R2018a (Intel core i5) and python 3.7.

The proposed framework applies the GLAC descriptor to extract informative iris features by customizing some parameters. All the features are normalized, adopting the min-max normalization technique in the data pre-processing stage [3]. All the training images are employed to train the classifier and test images for classification. As mentioned earlier, distance metrics are used to build the K-NN classification models. The average precision, recall, F_1-measure values from the confusion matrix are computed for each distance metric and other gradient feature descriptors to evaluate and compare the classification performance, as shown in Table 1.

Table 1. Performance of distance metrics on GLAC features.

Distance metrics	Avg. precision	Avg. recall	F1-measure	Accuracy (%)
Euclidean distance	0.9124	0.8956	0.8918	89.59
Minkowski distance	0.9124	0.8956	0.8917	89.59
City block distance	0.9151	0.8992	0.8961	90.02
Chebychev distance	0.6595	0.6380	0.6210	63.99
Spearman distance	0.9169	0.9153	0.9059	91.56
Cosine distance	0.9015	0.9019	0.8908	90.02
Correlation distance	**0.9139**	**0.9175**	**0.9073**	**91.84**
Standardized Euclidean distance	0.8625	0.8373	0.8306	84.24
Hamming distance	0.9105	0.8942	0.8868	89.45

4.1 Performance Study

The recognition performance is analyzed sequentially by changing parameter values. The key parameters are: (i) Roberts cross operator; (ii) 17 Orientation bins over $[0°, 180°)$ (unsigned gradients); (iii) Spatial interval $\Delta p = 5$ with 1st order auto correlation; (iv) 4×5 Spatial bins and L_2-Hys block normalization.

Initially, all the gradient orientated vectors are computed across the iris image by convolving with gradient operators such as Roberts, one-dimensional derivatives $[-1, 0, 1]$, Prewitt, and Sobel operators. Figure 3 presents the comparative results. The performance of Roberts's operator is more compact and effective than other operators, whereas the Prewitt operator is least effective, as illustrated in Fig. 3. Finally, the gradient orientations are quantized into 17 bins and follow the min-weighted function to suppress the noisy effect on surrounding auto-correlations. The orientation bins are equally spread over $[0°, 180°)$ (unsigned gradients) or $[0°, 360°)$ (signed gradients). The unsigned gradient always performs better than the signed gradient for auto-correlations of orientations, as depicted in Fig. 4.

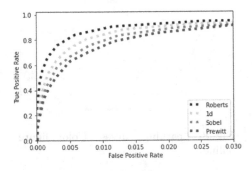

Fig. 3. ROC curves for gradient operators

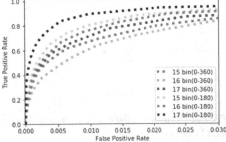

Fig. 4. ROC curves for different orientation bins

From Fig. 3 and Fig. 4, it can be observed that the auto-correlations of orientations depend on spatial interval Δp, which is highly correlated with the scale of images that would be recognized. The order of gradient auto-correlation also influences the GLAC configuration and increases feature dimensionality with higher running time. Although small spatial intervals work better with local auto-correlations, the spatial interval performs well in the case of 1st order component with the Roberts filter, as shown in Fig. 5.

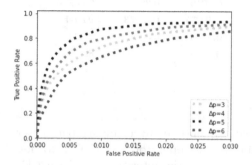

Fig. 5. ROC curves for special intervals

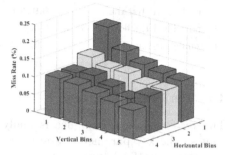

Fig. 6. Block diagram for special bins

The coarser spatial binning is adopted for the high dimensionality of gradient features, equally spaced over the normalized iris image. Among the spatial bins, the performance of spatial bins is the most effective as the spatial binning increases discriminative power by reducing shift-invariance. The spatial bins 3×4 also result in a good performance but not as good as spatial bins 4×5, as illustrated in Fig. 6.

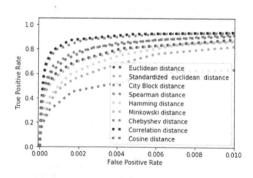

Fig. 7. Various distance metrics based ROC curves

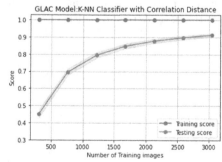

Fig. 8. Learning curves (Color figure online)

Figure 7 shows the performance comparisons for the distance matrices. As shown in this figure, the Correlation distance is the most compact and effective metric for the K-NN classifier among the distance metrics for image gradient features. The values mentioned in Table 1 also confirms this. As shown in the figure and Table, the Correlation distance metric slightly improves performance by around 2.25%, compared to the most widely used Euclidean distance metric. And, the performance of Chebychev distance is always the least effective. Figure 7 shows that Euclidean and Minkowski distance metrics perform equally well. In contrast, the accuracies of city block and cosine distance metrics are almost the same, but the performance of city block distance is significantly better than cosine distance. The Chebychev and standardized Euclidean distance metrics perform at the cost of a much longer run time.

In addition, the parameter tuning during the experiments implies that the image gradient features are not uniformly distributed and have more non-linearity between training and test features. It indicates that most subjects have noisy, complicated eye images with light reflection. The proposed framework could not recognize iris features accurately in those subjects. In addition, the parameter tuning during the experiments implies that the image gradient features are not uniformly distributed and have more non-linearity between training and test features.

Table 2. Accuracies achieved by different gradient features based iris recognition approaches.

Feature descriptor	Avg. precision	Avg. recall	F1-measure	Accuracy (%)
EOH	0.7784	0.7786	0.7595	77.95
HOG	0.9012	0.8899	0.8761	89.03
GLBP	0.9171	0.8949	0.8901	89.87
STACOG	0.7399	0.7113	0.6953	71.17
GLAC	**0.9139**	**0.9175**	**0.9073**	**91.84**

Table 2 presents the performance comparisons of the proposed feature descriptor (GLAC) against the state-of-the-art gradient and standard histogram-based feature descriptors, namely space-time auto-correlation of gradients (STACOG), edge orientation histograms (EOH), rotational invariant gradient local binary pattern (GLBP) and histogram of oriented gradients (HOG). As shown in the Table, the proposed gradient feature descriptor achieves the highest recognition rate of 91.84%, reducing longer running time.

Figure 8 plots the learning curves of the K-NN model with Correlation distance that employs the gradient auto-correlation features. The boldface line for the test scores refers to the mean scores, and the shaded region surrounding the line denotes the range of its standard deviation. The red and cyan colour curves indicate the training and testing scores. It is visible from Fig. 8 that the learning curve converses at a good score, which suggests that the GLAC model is not under-fitting. It is also noticeable that the training scores are always high along with the iterations, and the testing scores will be enhanced by increasing the training images.

Table 3. Performance evaluation with competitive methods.

Research methods	Accuracy (%)
Symlet Wavelet and Spearman distance [18]	78.38
Local Binary Pattern and Euclidean distance [22]	84.88
Gray Level Co-Occurrence Matrix and Euclidean distance [10]	85.00
Contourlet Transform and Hamming distance [5]	86.40
Laplacian of Gaussian filters and Normalized correlation [27]	86.49
Convolutional Neural Network and Euclidean distance [2]	86.94
Principal Component Analysis and City block distance [21]	90.00
Monogenic Log Gabor filter and normalized Hamming distance [15]	90.43
Gradient Local Auto-correlation and Correlation distance (Proposed)	**91.84**

Table 3 compares the overall recognition accuracy of the proposed GLAC descriptor against the existing competing approaches. It should be mentioned that it is not feasible to directly compare the achieved results of the proposed framework with those of the existing models. This is because the proposed framework has adopted different strategies in iris segmentation, feature extraction and classification on various types of databases with different distributions. For example, the accuracies obtained in [5] are 86.40% for 100 subjects, 92.50% for 60 subjects and 96.50% for 20 subjects on CASIA-V1 iris database. Only the approach proposed in [2] and [3] experimented on a distantly acquired complicated database with a large number of images and subjects similar to this work. In [2], the authors reported several achieved values for efficiency using different feature fusion techniques. Among those values, there is a reported efficiency of 98.17%. However, this efficiency is not directly comparable to the efficiency achieved in this work. This is because the reported efficiency of 98.17% in [2] is based not only on the iris, like our approach, but also on the contextual eye, including the sclera, eyelid, pupil, eyelash, etc. The value (86.94%) mentioned in Table 3 for [2] is the efficiency acquired by using the actual iris and Euclidean distance-based method (K-NN), which is comparable to this work.

Several distance-based human identification techniques using only eye images are available in the existing literature. However, most of them are not completely based on iris texture. For example, the approach presented in [20] is a deep feature-based eye recognition for human identification. In addition, the experiments in this work include multiple noisy sources, occlusions and more complicated images with specular or light reflection in each subject. However, the comparative evaluations against earlier approaches identify that the proposed framework is highly effective and robust for remote human identification in the perspective of image conditions, as compared with other gradient and distance-based approaches.

5   Conclusion

This paper proposes a robust iris recognition framework for distant iris images in less controlled environments. The experimental results suggest that the proposed framework works effectively on local image gradients with spatial and oriented auto-correlations. The comparisons with the existing approaches also indicate that it performs better under varying imaging conditions than other gradient-oriented approaches. This work also investigates the performances of several existing distant classifiers. The results justify that the recognition rate of the K-NN classifier is improved slightly by choosing distance metrics depending on feature properties and image conditions. Further, this work studies the influence of various parameter settings and finds the optimal parameters for reliable performance. In future, it is essential to overrate the iris pre-processing stage for accurate iris segmentation by mitigating the influence of noisy artefacts such as non-uniform illumination, eyelash, and eyelid. A further natural extension is to employ feature fusion, selection and robust classifiers to overcome the inter-class ambiguities and enhance the overall recognition performance for the iris images acquired using visible or near-infrared illumination.

References

1. Biometrics ideal test CASIA iris image database (2011). http://biometrics.idealtest.org/. Accessed 28 Apr 2022
2. Ali, L.E., Luo, J., Ma, J.: Iris recognition from distant images based on multiple feature descriptors and classifiers. In: 2016 IEEE 13th International Conference on Signal Processing (ICSP), pp. 1357–1362. IEEE (2016)
3. Ali, L.E., Luo, J., Ma, J.: Effective iris recognition for distant images using log-Gabor wavelet based contourlet transform features. In: Huang, D.-S., Bevilacqua, V., Premaratne, P., Gupta, P. (eds.) ICIC 2017. LNCS, vol. 10361, pp. 293–303. Springer, Cham (2017). https://doi.org/10.1007/978-3-319-63309-1_27
4. Arora, S., Bhatia, M.: Challenges and opportunities in biometric security: a survey. Inf. Secur. J. Glob. Perspect. **31**(1), 28–48 (2022)
5. Azizi, A., Pourreza, H.R.: A new method for iris recognition based on contourlet transform and non linear approximation coefficients. In: Huang, D.-S., Jo, K.-H., Lee, H.-H., Kang, H.-J., Bevilacqua, V. (eds.) ICIC 2009. LNCS, vol. 5754, pp. 307–316. Springer, Heidelberg (2009). https://doi.org/10.1007/978-3-642-04070-2_35
6. Boles, W.W., Boashash, B.: A human identification technique using images of the iris and wavelet transform. IEEE Trans. Sig. Process. **46**(4), 1185–1188 (1998)
7. Daugman, J.: How iris recognition works. In: The Essential Guide to Image Processing, pp. 715–739. Elsevier (2009)
8. Daugman, J.: Information theory and the iriscode. IEEE Trans. Inf. Forensics Secur. **11**(2), 400–409 (2015)
9. Dong, W., Sun, Z., Tan, T.: Iris matching based on personalized weight map. IEEE Trans. Pattern Anal. Mach. Intell. **33**(9), 1744–1757 (2010)
10. Emrullah, A.: Extraction of texture features from local iris areas by GLCM and iris recognition system based on KNN. Eur. J. Tech. (EJT) **6**(1), 44–52 (2016)

11. Fancourt, C., et al.: Iris recognition at a distance. In: Kanade, T., Jain, A., Ratha, N.K. (eds.) AVBPA 2005. LNCS, vol. 3546, pp. 1–13. Springer, Heidelberg (2005). https://doi.org/10.1007/11527923_1

12. Hamouchene, I., Aouat, S.: Efficient approach for iris recognition. SIViP 10(7), 1361–1367 (2016). https://doi.org/10.1007/s11760-016-0900-y

13. Hollingsworth, K.P., Bowyer, K.W., Flynn, P.J.: The best bits in an iris code. IEEE Trans. Pattern Anal. Mach. Intell. 31(6), 964–973 (2008)

14. Kobayashi, T., Otsu, N.: Image feature extraction using gradient local auto-correlations. In: Forsyth, D., Torr, P., Zisserman, A. (eds.) ECCV 2008. LNCS, vol. 5302, pp. 346–358. Springer, Heidelberg (2008). https://doi.org/10.1007/978-3-540-88682-2_27

15. Kumar, A., Chan, T.S., Tan, C.W.: Human identification from at-a-distance face images using sparse representation of local iris features. In: 2012 5th IAPR International Conference on Biometrics (ICB), pp. 303–309. IEEE (2012)

16. Mahesh, K.K., Kishore, P., Kailash, J.K.: Survey on iris image analysis. Indian J. Sci. Technol. 10(9), 1–15 (2017)

17. Monro, D.M., Rakshit, S., Zhang, D.: DCT-based iris recognition. IEEE Trans. Pattern Anal. Mach. Intell. 29(4), 586–595 (2007)

18. Mukherjee, A., Islam, M.Z., Mamun-Al-Imran, G., Ali, L.E.: Iris recognition using wavelet features and various distance based classification. In: 2021 International Conference on Electronics, Communications and Information Technology (ICECIT), pp. 1–4. IEEE (2021)

19. Ngo, D.C.L., Teoh, A.B.J., Hu, J.: Biometric Security. Cambridge Scholars Publishing, Cambridge (2015)

20. Ripon, K.S.N., Ali, L.E., Siddique, N., Ma, J.: Convolutional neural network based eye recognition from distantly acquired face images for human identification. In: 2019 International Joint Conference on Neural Networks (IJCNN), pp. 1–8. IEEE (2019)

21. Sari, Y., Alkaff, M., Pramunendar, R.A.: Iris recognition based on distance similarity and PCA. In: AIP Conference Proceedings, vol. 1977, p. 020044. AIP Publishing LLC (2018)

22. Sarode, N.S., Patil, A., Nssdam, P.: Iris recognition using LBP with classifiers-KNN and NB. Int. J. Sci. Res. 4(1), 1904–1908 (2015)

23. Savoj, M., Monadjemi, S.A.: Iris localization using circle and fuzzy circle detection method. World Acad. Sci. Eng. Technol. (61), 2 (2012)

24. Seung-In, N., Bae, K., Park, Y., Kim, J.: A novel method to extract features for iris recognition system. In: Kittler, J., Nixon, M.S. (eds.) AVBPA 2003. LNCS, vol. 2688, pp. 862–868. Springer, Heidelberg (2003). https://doi.org/10.1007/3-540-44887-X_100

25. Tan, C.W., Domingo, S.T.: Accurate iris segmentation for at-a-distance acquired iris/face images under less constrained environment. In: Proceedings of the 2020 International Conference on Pattern Recognition and Intelligent Systems, pp. 1–5 (2020)

26. Tan, C.W., Kumar, A.: Accurate iris recognition at a distance using stabilized iris encoding and Zernike moments phase features. IEEE Trans. Image Process. 23(9), 3962–3974 (2014)

27. Wildes, R.P.: Iris recognition: an emerging biometric technology. Proc. IEEE 85(9), 1348–1363 (1997)

E-Payment Continuance Usage: The Roles of Perceived Trust and Perceived Security

Thanh D. Nguyen(✉) ⓘ and Quynh N. T. Tran

Banking University of Ho Chi Minh City, Ho Chi Minh City, Vietnam
thanhnd@buh.edu.vn

Abstract. E-payment is an important concept of the core e-commerce elements; it has become one of the essential success factors for financial and business services. This work elaborates the roles of perceived trust and perceived security on continuance usage of e-payment through collecting data from students who have used e-payment for e-commerce in Vietnam. The maximum likelihood of structural equation modelling is analyzed on a total sample of convenient of 210 customers. Research findings demonstrate that perceived trust and perceived security have significant roles in the model of e-payment adoption. The model amounts to 26% of continuance usage of e-payment.

Keywords: Continuance usage · e-payment · Perceived security · Perceived trust

1 Introduction

E-payment has gained recognition and is deployed worldwide [16]. The habit of cash payment is the biggest impediment for the e-payment development. Besides, in e-commerce, customers and consumers are still reluctant to use non-cash payments. E-payment brings convenience, efficiency, and risk reduction because there is no longer have to bear the cost of handling the amount of cash held and reach more customers. E-payment allows customers to make e-transactions anywhere and anytime. Besides, customers can directly deal with manufacturers, bypassing intermediaries so they can buy goods in a convenient solution [18]. E-commerce in Vietnam is booming at over 25% per year [35]. Notwithstanding, according to market research by Q&Me [36], the number of e-payment transactions is quite low, accounting for 20% of payments, although up to 70% of the population uses the Internet, according to We Are Social [30], the habit of paying cash is the biggest obstacle to the development of e-payments in Vietnam. Customers are still reluctant to use e-payment when participating in e-commerce. There are many theoretical models of IT adoption such as TAM [6], TAM2 [37], TAM3 [38], and UTAUT [28], UTAUT [39] – these are typical theories for measuring the behavioral intention of information systems and actual use by users. There are several IT adoption theories, which are based on the users' use intention and actual usage of information systems. Although there are many works related to e-payment continuance usage (e.g., Bhattacherjee [4], Limayem et al. [16], Ventakesh et al. [29]), m-learning [34], e-commerce [40], not many related works in Vietnam.

© The Author(s), under exclusive license to Springer Nature Switzerland AG 2022
O. Gervasi et al. (Eds.): ICCSA 2022 Workshops, LNCS 13381, pp. 253–264, 2022.
https://doi.org/10.1007/978-3-031-10548-7_19

This work objective examines the roles of perceived trust and perceived security on e-payment continuance usage, which tests impact factors on continuance usage of e-payment for customers. The data was collected from students who used e-payments in Vietnam. The analysis of the maximum likelihood (ML) of structural equation modelling (SEM) for testing the model. Interestingly, research findings are accommodating information to corporations in expanding the e-payment system for e-commerce and adding scientific to the theory of continuance usage. Therefore, the rest of the paper is structured as follows: in the next section, related works and research models show the definition of e-payment and the model reviews of literature and theoretical framework, including hypotheses. The following section presents research methods. Then, analysis results and result discussion. Finally, the conclusion is in Sect. 5.

2   Related Works and Research Model

2.1   E-payment

The trade presto expansion through technological and e-commerce progress are the elements that led to the rapid development of e-payment and resulted in the constantly evolving payment services [25]. According to Abrazhevich [1, p. 3], *e-payment is defined as online transactions are conducted via the Internet.* Whereby there are a variety e-payment of types, e.g., e-wallet, e-cash, debit/credit cards, digital accumulating balances, digital checking payments, and online stored value [13, 24]. The e-payment systems stakeholders include customers, merchants, consumer banks, merchant banks, payment instrument issuers, and payment service providers [14].

2.2   Advantages and Disadvantages of E-Payment

- **Advantages**
  For Economy. E-payment has numerous positive positive aspects to the economy [9]. It guarantees the price and guarantees quality. E-payment reduces the quantum of cash in rotation and brings profitable benefits. E-payment gradationally eliminates the use of cash, limiting illegal conditioning, thereby adding translucency and law enforcement capacity. *For Organization.* E-payment costs are another benefit for utmost providers, businesses and merchandisers–this cost is accessible [33]. *For Customer.* E-payment systems are veritably accessible–the most significant benefit of electronic payments is to reuse their deals. It allows customers to make their electronic payments anytime and anywhere [33]. Either, it can increase the benefit of cashless payment without using retail payment. Inversely important, the e-payment systems can commit to the quality of e-commerce services to serve the requirements of customers [9]. Consequently, every sale is translated, making coverage more accessible and effective.
- **Disadvantages**
  Fee. Some e-payment system merchandisers bear customers or merchandisers to pay a service figure [22]. In addition, one of the disadvantages of electronic payments is the rejection of freights, as there's no transactional information about electronic payments, so customers may have a grueling time agitating these costs [26]. Hence, customers

should know how to cover themselves against charges for indecorous processing of electronic payment systems, videlicet. *Missed Mistake.* The goods arrive with an error paid for and ordered in the e-shop [26], so they can not be used, and customers have run out of plutocrat [22]. *Online security.* e-payment systems warrant authentication – the biggest problem of electronic payments [22]. In the meantime, there are no results to corroborate or corroborate who has entered electronic payment information systems, which are not culprits.

2.3 Related Works

- **IT Adoption**
  The Reasoned Action (TRA) theory aimed to explain the relationship from attitudes to behaviours within the action of a human. Planned Behavior (TPB) recommended a new component of perceived behavioural control. Davis et al. [6] built the Technology Acceptance Model (TAM), which is based on the foundational theories of TPB and TRA, with the two new factors of usefulness and perceived ease of use. TAM2 of Venkatesh and Davis [37] and TAM3 of Venkatesh and Bala [38] are extended models of TAM. Besides, Unified Theory of Acceptance and Use of Technology (UTAUT) is proposed by Venkatesh et al. [28]. Then, Venkatesh et al. [29] added facilitating conditions, effort expectancy, social influence, and a key of perceived trust to introduce the information systems continuance intention theory. UTAUT2 of Venkatesh et al. [39] is an extended model of UTAUT. These theories of UTAUTs and TAMs are the celebrated information systems models with the most cited in the global.

- **Perceived Risk**
  Perceived risk theory explains the behavior of users in the face of risks [3]. Negative antecedents can emphasize stoner conduct and lead to a significantly established conception in consumer behavior, videlicet perceived risk [3]. Meanwhile, perceived risk is a natural generality of the sense of unreliability regarding possible use negatively affiliated with a service or product [7]. Perceived risk has been divided into two confines perceived risk in the electronic sale and perceived risk with a service or product [20]. In which, the perceived risk in the electronic transaction is a possible threat of deals that druggies may face when using e-commerce [20].

- **Perceived Trust**
  Perceived trust is one of the two critical challenges of electronic payment systems [2]. In addition, perceived trust is the private belief in good faith that one party will fulfill its scores according to the prospects of the stakeholders [21]. Trust also comes from reputation, and reputation is belief in the trading terrain. Numerous authors have studied both perceived risk and perceived trust in e-services [7], e-commerce [21], e-banking [8], m-learning [34], and they have proven that perceived risk and trust are the most salient rudiments in electronic payment. When making a comparison between traditional payment and electronic payment systems, the confidence in electronic payments will be advanced if further consumers prefer to use electronic payment channels [32].

2.4 Research Model

From the theoretical basis of IT adoption (e.g., TRA, TAM, UTAUT), the theories of perceived security, and perceived trust, and the previous studies, it proposes the roles of perceived security and perceived trust on e-payment continuance usage for measuring the relationships between the factors of a structure model (Fig. 1). All concepts are performed as below:

- *Technical Protections (TEP).* Specific technical mechanism series are used to stabilize e-payment transactions safety on the Internet and have now been developing [13]. Furthermore, Chellappa and Pavlou [5] emphasized that the factors of technical protections, such as integrity, and stability, including privacy, have a positive impact on perceived trust and perceived security.
- *Transaction Procedures (TRP).* There are steps users must take to perform a service [13]. There are three procedures in transaction procedures: (1) providing customers with many separate steps toward the e-payment completion; (2) authenticating each participant before the making of the transaction; and (3) sending messages of acceptance to each attendance after the e-payment consummation [11].
- *Security Statements (SES).* Which are statements made by enterprises providing e-payment services on security [13]. Security statements are possible to influence the perceived trust and perceived security of customers in e-payment [21], by reassuring and informing consumers regarding the e-payment transaction security.
- *Personal Past Experience (PPE).* That is a level of familiarity with a certain amount of knowledge [31]. Personal past experience leads to faster than e-payment adoption [22]. Meanwhile, Hackbarth et al. [10] interest that users are more convenient to use technology when users have advanced underwent.

The related works showed the positive effect of the factors of transaction procedures, technical protections, personal past experience, and security statements on the perceived trust and the perceived security as Kim et al. [13], Linck et al. [17], Oney et al. [19]. Hence, under the e-payment system, these hypotheses are proposed:

- *H1:* Transaction procedures (TRP) has a positive impact on perceived security (PES) in e-payment continuance usage.
- *H2:* Transaction procedures (TRP) has a negative impact on perceived trust (TRU) in e-payment continuance usage.
- *H3:* Technical protections (TEP) has a positive impact on perceived security (PES) in e-payment continuance usage.
- *H4:* Technical protections (TEP) has a negative impact on perceived trust (TRU) in e-payment continuance usage.
- *H5:* Security statements (SES) has a negative impact on perceived security (PES) in e-payment continuance usage.
- *H6:* Security statements (SES) has a positive impact on perceived trust (TRU) in e-payment continuance usage.
- *H7:* Personal past experience (PPE) has a negative impact on perceived security (PES) in e-payment continuance usage.
- *H8:* Personal past experience (PPE) has a positive impact on perceived trust (TRU) in e-payment continuance usage.

- *Perceived Security (PES).* That is the customers' subjective evaluation of the security of the online system [13]. In this study, perceived security is understood as the degree of security customers' evaluation e-payment transactions and services. Kalakota and Whinston [12] confirmed that the resistance and technical strengthening of the online system against the attacks on security are two important factors that impact online system security.
- *Perceived Trust (TRU).* That is the belief that customers with online services will proceed under the expectations of customers and consumers [27]. Perceived trust is identified as one of the most critical elements, impacting online customer usage, and with trust higher levels are more than slantwise to use [21]. In this study, perceived trust is understood as the willingness to use e-payment despite potential risks.
- *E-payment Continuance Usage (ECU).* It performs behavioral patterns reflecting e-payment continued usage, which mentions to post-adoption behavior form [16]. For the viability of long-term of the e-payment system and the rearmost success depending on the continuous use more than the first time use [4].

    Furthermore, the factor of perceived security [23] and the factor of perceived trust [29] also have a negative effect on e-payment continuance usage. Contrastly, perceived security has a negative impact on e-payment continuance usage in Shao and Zhang [23], and perceived trust has a positive impact on e-payment continuance usage in Venkatesh et al. [29]. Thus, under the e-payment system, these hypotheses are proposed:

    - *H9:* Perceived security (PEC) has a negative impact on e-payment continuance usage (ECU).
    - *H10:* Perceived trust (TRU) has a positive impact on e-payment continuance usage (ECU).

3   Research Method

There are two phases in this work: the first phase is the qualitative method used for the preliminary research, and the second is the quantitative method used for a formal analysis. Firstly, from the literature review and the related research, which construct a scale with a draft. Then, the banking system and e-payment experts are discussed, which ensures the scale contents accuracy. Next, a measurement scale in the formal research uses the revision scale. A questionnaire with 7–point Likert: strongly disagree (1) – disagree (2) – somewhat disagree (3) – undecided (4) – somewhat agree (5) – agree (6) – strongly agree (7), which measures the indicators assessment levels. Convenient sampling method use for data collection, based on the survey accessibility. The survey is sent to students who have used e-payment of all kinds in Vietnam via Google docs by sending it directly to their e-mail and Facebook lists. Finally, collection data are analyzed by the method of the maximum likelihood (ML) of the structural equation modelling (SEM) by AMOS and SPSS. In this study, there are 210 valid samples out of 290 samples (80 invalid samples) of 27 items in the scale of the measurement which are used for analysis, as detailed in Table 1.

Table 1 Measurement scales and analysis results

Talent	Indicator	EFA loading	CFA loading
Transaction procedures	TRP1: E-payment system always calls for the user name and password when log-in	0.821	0.584
	TRP2: There are various measures to authenticate	0.867	0.932
	TRP3: There is a step to verify payment before the finalization of the actual payment	0.881	0.939
Technical protections	TEP2: Personal information has not been released to other third parties	0.852	0.877
	TEP3: The payment amount or transaction data displayed is always accurate	0.854	0.842
	TEP4: E-payment transaction data transferred over the Internet is securely protected	0.853	0.843
	TEP5: Payment services are always available at any time in a day	0.859	0.830
	TEP6: Temporary or sudden errors rarely occur during e-payment transactions	0.815	0.809
Security statements	SES2: The site provides security statements	0.868	0.905
	SES3: It is easy to find security statements	0.908	0.919
	SES4: Every concern can be easily found in a help section	0.898	0.916
	SES5: Security statements are drafted in an easily understandable way	0.878	0.920
Personal past experience	PPE1: Having experience of e-payment	0.945	0.976
	PPE2: Getting many benefits from e-payment	0.936	0.947
	PPE3: Starting using e-payment considerably a long time ago	0.942	0.963
Perceived security	PES1: Believing e-payment as secure	0.898	0.881
	PES2: Believing the information relating e-payment transactions as secure	0.876	0.850
	PES3: The information provided is helpful for secure payment transactions	0.849	0.859
Perceived trust	TRU1: Believing each participant. such as seller and buyer, involved in e-payment	0.869	0.915
	TRU2: Believing the security mechanisms of e-payment	0.901	0.931
	TRU3: Believing e-payment services	0.903	0.939

(continued)

Table 1 (*continued*)

Talent	Indicator	EFA loading	CFA loading
E-payment continuance usage	ECU1: Using e-payment more often than others	0.836	0.857
	ECU2: Using currently and will continue to use e-payment	0.862	0.964
	ECU3: Believing e-payment use will increase	0.851	0.899

4 Research Result

4.1 Data Description

Gender. They include 54.3% of males and 46.7% of females. *Education.* They incude students account for 76.7%, 10.0% vocational training, college and associate degree are 8.6% and 4.7%. *Study Year.* They take junior students amount to 36.7%, 30.5% sophomore, 19.1% senior, and 13.7% freshman. *Expense a Month.* They take 42.9% for spending about VND 2.5–3 million, VND 2–2.5 million amounts to 32.4%, VND 1.5–2 million, over 3 million and below 1.5 million are 11%, 9%, and 4.7%, respectively. *Total Amount of an E-order.* It is 70% of VND 0.1–0.5 million, 22.4% of below VND 0.1 million, and 7.6% of over VND 0.5 million. *Types of Goods.* Books and stationery are 57.1%, 33.1%, 32.9%, and 31.7% for e-devices and accessories, home appliances, and health and beauty, respectively. *Numbers of E-payments.* 41% of 4–6 times, 1–3 times, and 7–10 times are 31.5% and 22.3%, over 10 times is 5.2%. *E-payment Type.* e-wallet is 63.3%, 33.8% for ATM transfer, and 16.7% for e-banking. *Bank Account.* State-owned banks represent 45.6%, joint-stock commercial banks are 38.9%, and 15.5% for the other banks. *E-wallet Account.* 78.2% use *MoMo*, other e-wallets, *Zalo pay* and *Moca* are 14.5%, 12.8% and 9.0%, respectively.

4.2 Exploratory Factor Analysis and Confirmatory Factor Analysis

The first exploratory factor analysis (EFA) has enucleated seven factors from 27 items. The variables combine into seven groups of elements in the rotated component matrix as in the theory: transaction procedures, perceived trust, perceived security, security statements, technical protections, personal past experience, and e-payment continuance usage. The factor loading of all items in EFA range between 0.588 and 0.940 (Table 1). Notwithstanding, the total variance extracted (TVA) = 82.66% could explain the data difference of 82.66%. Therefore, the measurement scale can be used for the next analysis: the confirmatory factor analysis and the structural equation modelling.

The first confirmatory factor analysis (CFA) continues to eliminate three observational variables, including TEP1 of *technical protections* factor, SES1 and SES6 of *security statements* factor, whereas the factor loading of CFA < 0.50. Next, the second CFA with 24 items manifests that the measurement scale the indexes: $\chi^2/dF = 1,775$; TLI = 0.946; CFI = 0.963; RMSEA = 0.041; GFI = 0.902, which can be accepted.

Table 2 Data and coefficients of square correlation

	Mean	S.D.	TRP	TEP	SES	PPE	TRU	PES	ECU
TRP	4.467	1.480	0.835*						
TEP	2.996	1.073	0.020	0.840*					
SES	5.492	1.050	0.034	0.091	0.915*				
PPE	5.098	1.277	0.013	0.078	0.040	0.962*			
TRU	5.075	1.421	0.019	0.081	0.091	0.047	0.928*		
PES	3.402	1.496	0.040	0.006	0.005	0.005	0.093	0.863*	
ECU	5.498	0.996	0.043	0.045	0.049	0.097	0.087	0.037	0.908*

AVE: Average Variance Extracted; S.D.: Std. Deviation

Thus, the data assort with the measurement model. The factor loading of all items in CFA range from 0.584 to 0.976 (Table 1). Another side, these factors composite reliability (CR): transaction procedures, perceived trust, perceived security, security statements, technical protections, personal past experience, and e-payment continuance usage range between 0.869 and 0.974 (> 0.5), as detailed in Table 2.

Moreover, the values of average variance extracted (AVE) are from 0,835 to 0.926, as indicated in Table 1. Thus, the convergence value is gained from the measurement scale. Furthermore, the square correlation coefficient (r^2) is smaller than the AVE value for each factor, respectively. Hence, the measurement scale is an outstanding value.

4.3 Structural Equation Modelling

The maximum likelihood (ML) of the structural equation modelling (SEM) accommodates that the indexes of scale: $\chi^2/dF = 1,959$; TLI = 0,945; CFI = 0,953; RMSEA = 0,048; GFI = 0,901, can be accepted. Accordingly, the data in the theoretical model is a well-proportioned fit. Meanwhile, antecedent factors – *transaction procedures* and *technical protections* have a positive impact on *perceived security*. There is a negative relationship from *security statements* to *perceived security* with γ coefficient = −0.098 (p > 0.05), the relationships from *perceived security* to the other factors are statistically significant (p < 0.05), except for *personal past experience* (p = 0.734). Thus, hypotheses *H1*, *H2*, and *H3* are supported, while hypotheses *H5* and *H7* are rejected. Likewise, *personal past experience* and *security statements* have the positive impact on *perceived trust* with γ coefficient = 0.399 (p < 0.001) and 0.347 (p < 0.001), respectively.

However, the relationship between *transaction procedures* and *perceived trust* is not statistically significant (p > 0.05). Hence, hypotheses *H6* and *H8* are accepted, while hypothesis *H4* is rejected. Furthermore, intermediate factors – the negative path from *perceived security* to *e-payment continuance usage* is statistically significant (p < 0.001), so hypothesis H09 is accepted. Furthermore, the data accept the positive path from *perceived trust* to *e-payment continuance usage* with γ coefficients = 0.370 (p < 0.001). Thus, hypothesis H10 is accepted. Pleasantly, the relationships of all paths with continuance usage of e-payment are strongly accepted (Table 3).

Table 3 SEM and hypotheses testing results

H	Path	Beta	SE	p	Result
H1	PES ← TRP	0,249	0.102	0.002	Supported
H2	TRU ← TRP	−0.172	0.093	0.012	Supported
H3	PES ← TEP	0.383	0.098	***	Supported
H4	TRU ← TEP	−0.108	0.089	0.102	Rejected
H5	PES ← SES	−0.098	0.105	0.203	Rejected
H6	TRU ← SES	0.347	0.099	***	Supported
H7	PES ← PPE	0.024	0.076	0.734	Rejected
H8	TRU ← PPE	0.399	0.072	***	Supported
H9	ECU ← PES	−0.307	0.049	***	Supported
H10	ECU ← TRU	0.370	0.046	***	Supported

*** *p-value < 0.001; S.E.: Standard Error*

4.4 Result Discussion

The research results demonstrated that the perceived security negative and the positive perceived trust influence on the continuance usage of e-payment are comparatively large, with $\gamma = 0.370$ and -0.307. The relationships from antecedents of transaction procedures and technical protections to the factor of perceived security are positive, and the path from transaction procedures to perceived trust is negative (Fig. 1).

The relationships between antecedents such as security statements and personal past experience and the factor of perceived security are harmful and not statistically significant, but the path from security statements and personal past experience to perceived trust is positive. One explanation of this notion could be that the security statements issued can not convince the users that e-payment is free from risk. In addition, the customer care services of some enterprises are considered to be relatively poor in the event of an incident, due to failure to handle or delay in handling queries. This result indicated that personal past experience and security enunciations have a positive impact on perceived trust as in Kim et al. [13], Oney et al. [19].

Practically, there are seven out of 10 hypotheses are supported. Especially, the structural equation modelling also manifested that antecedent factors of personal past experience, technical protections, security statements, and transaction procedures, and intermediate factors of perceived security and perceived trust may be explained 26% ($R^2 = 0.26$) the outcome factor – e-payment continuance usage. This finding is comparable with Limayem et al. [16] amounted to 26% of continuance usage.

4.5 Theoretical and Practical Implication

Research results expropriated the theoretical basis for the theories of IT adoption, such as TAM or UTAUT, the theories of perceived security, and perceived trust. Besides, the

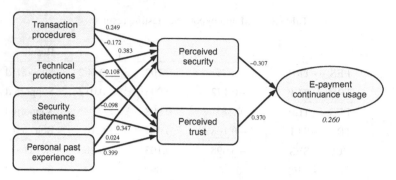

Fig. 1. Research model and testing results

research results also indicated several factors that can take the important role in influencing on e-payment continuance usage. Perceived trust impact most on continuance usage in e-payment usage contexts. Thus, web commerce sites, online payment method providers and web browser developers should encourage customers to have more experience to use their system. Hands-on experience gained through use and training may help reduce the uncertainty and create favorable user perceptions. Moreover, security statements should be written simply and understandably. Security statements should also be placed markedly, thus, customers can easily find them.

Especially, perceived security affects negatively on e-payment continuance usage. Hence, better technical protections should be implemented to foster e-payment system security. In fact, web commerce sites, online payment method providers and web browsers have become more aware of the importance of security. They have been investing in the latest and modern technology to ensure the security of e-payment transactions. In addition, transaction procedures is also an important factor when evaluating about the security of e-payment system. They should pay attention to improve the website interface as well as e-payment application, hence, customers can feel comfortable during the payment transactions.

5 Conclusion

The work results illustrated that antecedent factors measurement scale, intermediate factors, and continuance usage of e-payment is evidenced by reliability. The exploratory factor analysis and the confirmatory factor analysis of all items manifested that all factor loading of items loaded high-value concerns. Therefore, the scale of the measurement is indicated convergence and distinguishing value. Especially, the maximum likelihood of the structural equation modelling accommodated these relationships among constructs, including transaction procedures, perceived trust, perceived security, security statements, technical protections, personal past experience, and e-payment continuance usage. Interestingly, transaction procedures play an essential role in increasing the perceived security, while security statements and personal past experience have been the principal roles of rising perceived trust. The results investigated the roles of multifarious beliefs in anticipating continuance usage of e-payment, so furnishing support for inflating beliefs set in the e-payment context. Generally, the study findings fertilize the phenomenon understanding of continuance usage. Future studies may be possible to add more elements, such as personal or social related factors, to the model. It is also possible to expand more subjects in the study, students and office workers.

Acknowledgment. We would like to say acknowledge to three blind reviewers for their helpful comments on this research. We also would like to say thank for these comments and supports of Prof. Sanjay Misra on this work.

References

1. Abrazhevich, D.: Electronic Payment Systems: A User-Centered Perspective and Interaction Design. Technische Universiteit Eindhoven (2004)
2. Aladwani, A.M.: Online banking: a field study of drivers, development challenges, and expectations. Int. J. Inf. Manag. **21**(3), 213–225 (2001)
3. Bauer, R.A.: Consumer behavior as risk taking. In: AMA Proceeding, Chicago (1960)
4. Bhattacherjee, A.: Understanding information systems continuance: an expectation-confirmation model. MIS Q. **25**(3), 351–370 (2001)
5. Chellappa, R.K., Pavlou, P.A.: Perceived information security, financial liability and consumer trust in electronic commerce transactions. Logist. Inf. Manag. **15**(5), 358–368 (2002)
6. Davis, F.D., Bagozzi, R.P., Warshaw, P.R.: User acceptance of computer technology: a comparison of two theoretical models. Manage. Sci. **35**, 982–1003 (1989)
7. Featherman, M., Pavlou, P.: Predicting e-services adoption: a perceived risk facets perspective. Int. J. Hum. Comput. Stud. **59**(4), 451–474 (2003)
8. Gao, L., Waechter, K.A.: Examining the role of initial trust in user adoption of mobile payment services: an empirical investigation. Inf. Syst. Front. **19**(3), 525–548 (2015). https://doi.org/10.1007/s10796-015-9611-0
9. Gefen, D., Karahanna, E., Straub, D.: Trust and TAM in online shopping: an integrated model. MIS Q. **27**(1), 51–90 (2003)
10. Hackbarth, G., Grover, V., Mun, Y.Y.: Computer playfulness and anxiety: positive and negative mediators of the system experience effect on perceived ease of use. Inf. Manag. **40**, 221–232 (2003)
11. Hwang, R.J., Li, J.F., Hsiao, Y.K.: A wireless-based authentication and anonymous channels for GSM system. J. Comput. **17**, 31–36 (2006)
12. Kalakota, R., Whinston, A.B.: Electronic Commerce: A Manager's Guide. Addison-Wesley, Boston (1997)
13. Kim, C., Tao, W., Shin, N., Kim, K.S.: An empirical study of customers' perceptions of security and trust in e-payment systems. Electron. Commer. Res. Appl. **9**, 84–95 (2010)
14. Laudon, K., Traver, C.: E-Commerce: Business Technology Society. Pearson (2021)
15. Liao, C., Liu, C.C., Chen, K.: Examining the impact of privacy, trust and risk perceptions beyond monetary transactions: an integrated model. Electron. Commer. Res. Appl. **10**, 702–715 (2011)
16. Limayem, M., Hirt, S.G., Cheung, C.M.: How habit limits the predictive power of intention: the case of information systems continuance. MIS Q. **31**(4), 705–737 (2007)
17. Linck, K., Pousttchi, K., Wiedemann, D.G.: Security issues in mobile payment from the customer viewpoint. In: ECIS Proceedings, p. 62 (2006)
18. Nguyen, T.D., Huynh, P.A.: The roles of perceived risk and trust on e-payment adoption. In: Anh, L.H., Dong, L.S., Kreinovich, V., Thach, N.N. (eds.) ECONVN 2018. SCI, vol. 760, pp. 926–940. Springer, Cham (2018). https://doi.org/10.1007/978-3-319-73150-6_68

19. Oney, E., Guven, G.O., Rizvi, W.H.: The determinants of electronic payment systems usage from consumers' perspective. Econ. Res.-Ekonomska Istraživanja **30**, 394–415 (2017)
20. Park, J., Lee, D., Ahn, J.: Risk-focused e-commerce adoption model: a cross-country study. J. Glob. Inf. Technol. Manag. **7**, 6–30 (2004)
21. Pavlou, P.A.: Consumer acceptance of electronic commerce: integrating trust and risk with the technology acceptance model. Int. J. Electron. Commer. **7**, 101–134 (2003)
22. Rahman, S.: Introduction to E-commerce technology in business. GRIN (2014)
23. Shao, Z., Zhang, L.: What promotes customers' trust in the mobile payment platform: an empirical study of alipay in China. In: CONF-IRM Proceedings, p. 45 (2018)
24. Shon, T.H., Swatman, P.M.: Identifying effectiveness criteria for Internet payment systems. Internet Res. **8**(3), 202–218 (1998)
25. Suwunniponth, W.: Customers' intention to use electronic payment system for purchasing. Image **3**, 39994 (2015)
26. Swick, N.K.: Benefits & risks of electronic payment systems (2010). https://thatcreditunion blog.wordpress.com
27. Tsiakis, T., Sthephanides, G.: The concept of security and trust in electronic payments. Comput. Secur. **24**, 10–15 (2005)
28. Venkatesh, V., Morris, M.G., Davis, G.B., Davis, F.D.: User acceptance of information technology: toward a unified view. MIS Q. **27**(3), 425–478 (2003)
29. Venkatesh, V., Thong, J.Y., Chan, F.K., Hu, P.J.H., Brown, S.A.: Extending the two-stage information systems continuance model: incorporating UTAUT predictors and the role of context. Inf. Syst. J. **21**, 527–555 (2011)
30. We are social. Digital 2020 Vietnam report (2021)
31. Wu, J.H., Wang, S.C.: What drives mobile commerce?: An empirical evaluation of the revised technology acceptance model. Inf. Manag. **42**, 719–729 (2005)
32. Yang, Q., Pang, C., Liu, L., Yen, D., Tarn, J.: Exploring consumer perceived risk and trust for online payments: an empirical study in China's younger generation. Comput. Hum. Behav. **50**, 9–24 (2015)
33. Yaokumah, W., Kumah, P., Okai, E.: Demographic influences on e-payment services. Int. J. Econ. Bus. Res. **13**(1), 44–65 (2017)
34. Shaba, M., Roland, A., Simon, J., Misra, S., Ayeni, F.: A real-time sentimental analysis on e-commerce sites in Nigeria using machine learning. In: Shaba, M., Roland, A., Simon, J., Misra, S., Ayeni, F. (eds.) HIS 2021. LNNS, vol. 420, pp. 452–462. Springer, Cham (2022). https://doi.org/10.1007/978-3-030-96305-7_42
35. Vietnam E-commerce Association: Vietnam e-commerce (2021)
36. Q&Me: Vietnam e-commerce report, Ho Chi Minh City (2018)
37. Venkatesh, V., Davis, F.D.: A theoretical extension of the technology acceptance model: four longitudinal field studies. Manag. Sci. **46**, 186–204 (2000)
38. Venkatesh, V., Bala, H.: Technology acceptance model 3 and a research agenda on interventions. Decis. Sci. **39**, 273–315 (2008)
39. Venkatesh, V., Thong, J., Xu, X.: Consumer acceptance and use of information technology: extending the unified theory of acceptance and use of technology. MIS Q. **36**(1), 157–178 (2012)
40. Afolabi, A.O., Oluwatobi, S., Emebo, O., Misra, S., Garg, L.: Evaluation of the merits and demerits associated with a diy web-based platform for e-commerce entrepreneurs. In: Garg, L., et al. (eds.) ISMS 2020. LNNS, vol. 303, pp. 214–227. Springer, Cham (2022). https://doi.org/10.1007/978-3-030-86223-7_19

Trustworthy Machine Learning Approaches for Cyberattack Detection: A Review

Blessing Guembe[1,3](✉) (iD), Ambrose Azeta[2,3] (iD), Sanjay Misra[2,3] (iD),
and Ravin Ahuja[3,4] (iD)

[1] Department of Computer and Information Sciences, Covenant University, Ota, Ogun, Nigeria
blessingodede@gmail.com
[2] Department of Computer Science, Namibia University of Science and Technology,
Windhoek, Namibia
aazeta@nust.na
[3] Department of Computer Science and Communication, Ostfold University College,
Halden, Norway
[4] Delhi Skills and Entrepreneurship University, Delhi, India

Abstract. In recent years, machine learning techniques have been utilized in sensitive areas such as health, medical diagnosis, facial recognition, cybersecurity, etc. With this exponential growth comes potential large-scale ethical, safety, and social ramifications. With this enhanced ubiquity and sensitivity, concerns about ethics, trust, transparency, and accountability inevitably arise. Given the threat of sophisticated cyberattacks, it's critical to establish cybersecurity trustworthy concepts and to develop methodologies and concepts for a wide range of explainable machine cybersecurity models that will assure reliable threat identification and detection, more research is needed. This survey examines a variety of explainable machine learning techniques that can be used to implement a reliable cybersecurity infrastructure in the cybersecurity domain. The main aim of this study is to execute an in-depth review and identification of existing explainable machine learning algorithms for cyberattack detection. This study employed the seven-step survey model to determine the research domain, implement search queries, and compile all retrieved articles from digital databases. This research looks at the literature on trustworthy machine learning algorithms for detecting cyberattacks. An extensive search of electronic databases such as ArXiv, Semantic Scholar, IEEE Xplore, Wiley Library, Scopus, Google Scholar, ACM, and Springer was carried out to find relevant literature in the subject domain. From 2016 to 2022, this study looked at white papers, conference papers, and journals. Only 25 research papers were chosen for this research paper describing trustworthy cybersecurity and explainable AI cybersecurity after we retrieved 800 articles from web databases. The study reveals that the decision tree technique outperforms other state-of-the-art machine learning models in terms of transparency and interpretability. Finally, this research suggests that incorporating explainable into machine learning cybersecurity models will help uncover the root causes of defensive failures, making it easier for cybersecurity experts to enhance both cybersecurity infrastructures and development, rather than just model results, policy, and management.

Keywords: Machine learning · Trustworthiness · Trustworthy cybersecurity

© The Author(s), under exclusive license to Springer Nature Switzerland AG 2022
O. Gervasi et al. (Eds.): ICCSA 2022 Workshops, LNCS 13381, pp. 265–278, 2022.
https://doi.org/10.1007/978-3-031-10548-7_20

1   Introduction

Machine learning has seen considerable industrial use in recent years, with machine learning systems displaying superhuman ability in a variety of activities. However, increased model complexity has often resulted in increased performance, making such systems into black-box techniques, and generating ambiguity about how they function and, eventually, how they draw conclusions [1]. This inconsistency has made it difficult for machine learning techniques to be implemented in sensitive yet vital fields, such as cybersecurity and medical diagnosis, where their benefit may be enormous. Since machine learning algorithms are being more widely used in practical systems, any discrimination or unfairness propagated by those models could have a direct impact on human lives [2]. Machine learning trustworthiness and fairness is a sub-domain of machine learning interpretability that evaluates machine learning algorithms in terms of fairness, discrimination, accountability, and discrimination. It is difficult to trust systems whose outcomes are difficult to explain, especially in domains like healthcare and cybersecurity, where ethical and equitable questions have inevitably developed. The need for trustworthy, fair, robust, high-performing models for real-world applications such as cybersecurity defense models prompted the revival of explainable machine learning, a field devoted to the understanding and interpretation of machine behavior that had fallen out of favor in recent years due to most research focusing on the predictive power of algorithms rather than the understanding of machine behavior [2].

Cybersecurity experts are constantly developing sophisticated cybersecurity infrastructures that depend on a variety of components, such as technology, processes, and people to scale and operate efficiently [3]. In the cybersecurity domain, where so many decisions are critical to organizational breakdown, a lack of interpretability in machine learning models might decrease trust in those systems. The ability to Incorporate trustworthiness in cybersecurity infrastructure is completely based on the relationship between these components, consisting of people and technology, organizations and people, and groups and people. These trusting components can deploy cybersecurity infrastructures that organizations, businesses, governments, and individuals can rely on to detect, prevent, and protect cyberspace against sophisticated cyberattacks [4, 5].

The lack of explainability in internal data representations and the decision-making process of machine learning systems are one of the most challenging problems in increasing the acceptance of machine learning systems, especially in critical domains such as cybersecurity, finance, medicine, etc. For instance, people tend to blindly accept the outcomes of machine learning models in critical domains such as cybersecurity, object recognition, chatbots, and games, therefore permitting the possibility of false positives, but this method of accepting machine learning and deep learning outcomes should not be tolerated when it comes to sensitive decision-making domains such as medicine, finance, or cybersecurity, where important assets or human lives are priority [6]. Given the high demand for ethical AI, individuals are generally hesitant to accept technology that is not explicitly explainable, intractable, or trustworthy. It's natural to believe that focusing solely on model performance will make the models increasingly inscrutable. As a result, model performance and transparency are mutually exclusive. Improvements in a model's explainability, understanding, and trustworthiness, on the other hand, might lead to the correction of false positives and deficiencies [7].

When building a machine learning model, it is important to consider explainability and interpretability as a design driver to ensure impartiality in decision making (i.e., to detect anomalous behavior and automatically correct for bias in the training dataset, provide robustness by highlighting potential anomalies and adversaries that could change the prediction and decision logic, and ensure that only relevant features infer the result) [7, 8]. In response, it is important to make machine learning cybersecurity models to be trustworthy. Explainable machine learning enables the development and deployment of moral philosophical and moral AI models that are completed based on philosophical and ethical solutions [9]. Given the sophistication and unpredictable nature of cybersecurity threats, understanding the reasoning driving their outputs has become increasingly desirable. Explainability approaches in machine learning focus on giving users a comparable degree of knowledge, allowing them to make knowledgeable decisions about whether to adopt a model decision. In practice, explainability techniques usually yield a new interpretable model that basically duplicates the behavior of a black-box model, or they offer some statistical information or a graphic to show roughly how the model uses inputs. When interpretations are direct accounts of model behavior and structure, explanations are comprehensible generalizations [2].

Despite the exponential growth of trustworthy machine learning algorithms, there is still an immature and undeveloped area, hampered by a lack of formality and a lack of widely accepted terminology. As a result, even though many reliable machine learning approaches and scholarly articles have been produced, they hardly constitute a vital part of trustworthy machine learning algorithms for combating cyberattacks. Hence, the embedding of explainable machine learning in cybersecurity models will eliminate the bias attached to traditional machine learning black-box models. The purpose of this review is to act as a reference source for both researchers and industry experts by offering an in-depth review of existing methods, as well as a synopsis of the best use cases for reviewed techniques and connections to their strengths and weakness in implementing a trustworthy machine learning cyberattack detection model. The main contribution of this study is to provide an in-depth review and identification of existing explainable machine learning algorithms for cyberattack detection.

In this research, we first discuss the background of explainable and trustworthy machine learning, followed by a description of the research questions and their justifications. We also discussed the search strategy and criteria for selecting the relevant articles to archive the research objective. The responses to the study questions were thoroughly reviewed, and finally, the future research directions were also discussed.

1.1 Research Methodology

In this study, we adopted the seven steps survey model. Figure 1 represents a synopsis of designing the seven-step survey model utilized in this study. The purpose of this research was to find a collection of studies on trustworthy machine learning models in cybersecurity, and the impact of explainable machine learning in the cybersecurity domain. To archive this, the study identifies relevant articles in the explainable machine learning domain with respect to trustworthy cybersecurity. The authors formulated the research questions presented in this study and explain the concept behind the research questions.

1.2   Identification of Studies and Search Criteria

We obtained the adopted articles from the following databases: ArXiv, Semantic Scholar, IEEE Xplore, Wiley Library, Scopus, Google Scholar, ACM, and Springer. For each of these databases, we utilized the same search query to retrieve the adopted literature. The search query comprises keywords and synonyms such as ("Trustworthy machine learning algorithms" OR "explainable machine learning algorithms in cybersecurity" OR "impact of explainable machine learning in cybersecurity") OR ("explainable machine learning in cybersecurity" OR "explainable machine learning approach in cybersecurity" OR "trustworthy machine learning cybersecurity models").

1.3   Research Questions

The research presented in this study is intended to review the concept of trustworthy machine learning algorithms in cyberattack detection to ensure ethics, interpretability, and fairness in machine learning cybersecurity detection models. The formulated research questions alongside the concept behind each research question are summarized in Table 1 which also forms the basis of our search criteria.

Table 1. Research questions

Research questions	Justification of research questions
RQ1: What are the trustworthy machine learning techniques?	To identify and analyze existing trustworthy machine learning algorithms
RQ2: What is the most efficient machine learning to implement an explainable cybersecurity model?	To identify and analyze the different machine learning models in implementing trustworthy cybersecurity models
RQ3: What are the impacts of explainable machine learning in the cybersecurity domain?	To identify the impacts of explainable machine learning in cybersecurity

The selected papers were entered into a data extraction spreadsheet in Microsoft Excel 2020. The following information was extracted from the studies: author(s), year, AI technique, explainable technique, types of cybersecurity attacks, and data sources.

2 Eligibility Criteria

The inclusion, exclusive, and quality selection requirement was utilized to screen the required articles for this study. The adopted papers for this study were obtained using the selection criteria.

2.1 Exclusive Criteria

This eligibility technique involves evaluating the retrieved articles based on the following criteria:

- The same literature from a different source
- Articles with the same topic and authors
- Articles that do not address the research questions
- Articles that do not discuss trustworthy machine learning models in cybersecurity, and explainable machine learning applications in cybersecurity.

2.2 Inclusion Criteria

This inclusion screening technique involves evaluating the retrieved articles based on the following criteria:

- Articles that are relevant to trustworthy machine learning cybersecurity models
- Journals, symposiums, white papers, methodologies, and conference papers that addressed trustworthy machine learning techniques in the cybersecurity domain.
- Comparative studies of trustworthy machine learning techniques in combating cyberattacks.

2.3 Quality Criteria

The downloaded papers were screened based on the following quality criteria:

- Do the articles provide relevant answers to either of the research questions?
- Do the articles emphasize explainable machine learning algorithms in cyberattack detection?
- Do the papers discuss the positive impacts of explainable machine learning algorithms in detecting cyberattacks?
- Does the research methodology in the papers appear to be adequately disclosed?

3 Selected Articles

We utilized the search criteria to perform a search query on the databases. The search result was retrieved in the bibliography reference CSV file. A total of 760 articles were retrieved from the databases and 40 articles were retrieved from other sources. From the 800 retrieved articles, 320 articles consist of duplicated articles. The eligibility criteria were applied in the remaining 480 articles as earlier mentioned. The exclusion and inclusion screening techniques were applied in the title, abstract, and keywords which screened out a total of 281 articles. This means that a total of 199 articles are related to our study area but do not necessarily address all the required selection criteria. The titles, abstracts, and keywords were studied to identify relevant literature that discussed the research questions. After the successful completion of this phase, 199 articles were retrieved. The skimming and scanning reading approach was used to study the returned 25 research articles which involve careful study of the methodologies, headings, sub-sections, theoretical framework, and conceptual framework. After the successful completion of this phase, 174 didn't meet the selection criteria. In this paper, we select only papers that investigated trustworthy and explainable cybersecurity machine learning models, and comparative studies of explainable machine learning in cybersecurity. Figure 2 illustrates the selected year of publication. Figure 3 depicts the distribution of the selected articles based on publication year, while Fig. 3 shows the number of retrieved articles based on publication outlets.

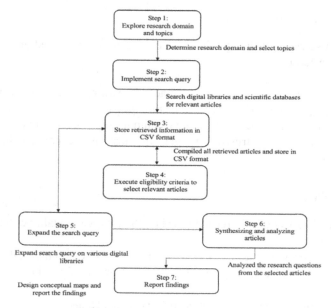

Fig. 1. Seven-step survey model

The results in Fig. 3 demonstrate that 2019 and 2020 had the most publications (7), respectively, followed by 2018 (6). While the number of selected publications (1) is lowest in 2016.

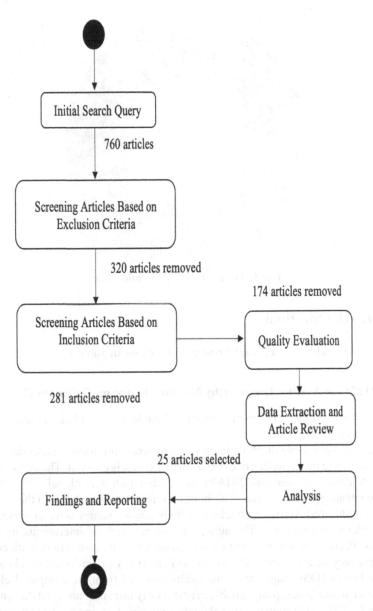

Fig. 2. Mapping of the search and selection procedure

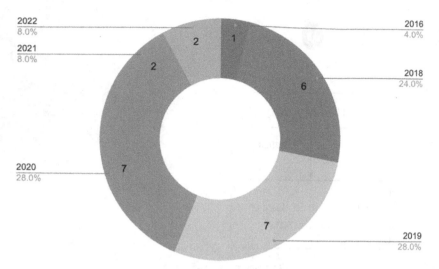

Fig. 3. Distribution of publication year

4   Research Questions

This section provides answers to the research questions in Table 1.

4.1   RQ1: What Are the Trustworthy Machine Learning Techniques?

This subsection discusses the trustworthy machine learning techniques utilized in the cybersecurity domain.

In [10] an explainable machine learning framework in intrusion Detection Systems (IDSs) to optimize the decisions of cybersecurity experts is evolved. The authors utilized SHapley Additive exPlanations (SHAP), in collaboration with global and local explanations to enhance specific inputs. The important features extracted, and the correlation between the different types of attacks and their feature values were provided by the global explanation technique. The authors also compared the interpretations between the one-vs-all classifier and the multiclass classifier. The proposed framework enhanced the transparency of any IDSs and can help cybersecurity practitioners obtain a quality understanding of IDSs judgment. 'The results obtained from the compared classifiers can play a vital role in designing reliable cybersecurity infrastructure, and design reliable structures for IDSs. [11] evolved an explainable machine learning model to enhance trust management in IDSs. The authors asserted that existing studies only demonstrated the performance accuracy of different machine learning classification techniques to enhance trust in IDSs without consideration for explainable machine learning models. Hence, the authors evolved an XAI machine learning model using a decision tree to enhance the trust management of IDSs. The authors utilized the decision tree technique because it is easy to read, and the decision tree technique is like a human expert decision-making process in terms of splitting the choice into various smaller sub-choices in IDSs. [12] evolved an adversarial approach for XAI in IDSs to trigger explanations for inaccurate classifications produced by data-driven IDSs. The authors obtained the minimum qualification required to adequately classify a set of misclassified samples using the adversarial technique. The most relevant features that interpret the reason for the misclassification were visualized using the magnitude of the qualifications. The result shows the explanations generated by the model efficiently describe the reason behind the misclassifications with the interpretation that matches the cybersecurity practitioner's knowledge. Variable importance techniques, also known as feature importance, estimate the statistical impact of each feature on a model's performance to generate explanations [2, 13]. A machine learning cybersecurity implementation pipeline can utilize feature importance to determine whether a model is learning correctly and whether the features contributing to the predictions are trustworthy. Global explanations are provided by feature importance techniques. Mean decrease in impunity, permutation importance, and conditional feature importance are examples of feature important techniques. When a single feature is randomly shuffled, permutation importance evaluates how much black-box models predicted accuracy suffers [2]. Permutation importance works by retesting a model multiple times, each time with the values of a separate feature mixed up randomly. When each feature is shuffled, this technique measures prediction performance. If rearranging the values of a feature has no effect on predictive performance, the feature is not contributing significantly to the model's performance. Permutation importance also provides simple explanations that are generally easily understandable [2]. The heuristic technique of permutation importance seeks to correct the feature importance bias by normalizing feature importance measures. The method attempts to estimate the parameters of a feature based on the premise that its random relevance follows some probability distribution. This is accomplished by permuting the output array of predictions periodically and then assessing the importance distribution for each feature on the non-permuted output. The adjusted measure of feature importance is proxied by the computed p-value [1]. The permutation importance technique has the advantage of being computationally efficient because they do not require constant retraining of models. However, in circumstances where a model uses strongly correlated features, permutation importance can provide incorrect outcomes. In such circumstances, conditional variable importance can be used, however, it has the disadvantage of being less computationally efficient.

Surrogate techniques, such as short decision trees or logistic regression models, explain a black-box machine learning technique by generating a new interpretable model based on the black-box model's prediction. The purpose of training with the black-box model is to get the new interpretable model as close as possible to the black-box model. The interpretable model can be used to acquire a basic concept of how the black-box model operates by users looking for an explanation [14]. To explain relationships between a machine learning prediction outcome and a set of variables of interest, visualization methods for black-box interpretations can be employed. Malicious patterns can be explained using these techniques [15].

Rule-based learning refers to any model that develops rules to describe the data from which it intends to learn [4]. The simplistic conditional if-then rules or more complicated combinations of simple rules may be used to create their knowledge. Fuzzy rule-based systems, which are connected to this general family of models, are built for a larger variety of actions, enabling the formulation of vocally defined rules across imprecise domains. Firstly, they enable more intelligible models since they function in linguistic terms. Second, in scenarios with varying degrees of uncertainty, they outperform standard rule systems. Rule-based models are transparent models that may be used to explain complicated models by establishing rules that explain their outcomes [4]. Rule-based models are great models in terms of interpretability across domains. They are good for understanding and describing other models due to their seamless and natural interaction with human behavior. A rule wrapper may be deemed to include enough information about a model to explain its behavior to a non-expert if a particular degree of coverage is achieved, without compromising the ability to utilize the derived rules as an independent prediction mode [4]. Hence, this technique is efficient for ensuring trustworthy cyberattack detection.

4.2 RQ2: What Is the Most Efficient Machine Learning to Implement an Explainable Cybersecurity Model?

Only a few explainable machine learning models have been utilized in literature to archive trustworthy cybersecurity. In this section, the study identifies and analyzes the different machine learning models utilized in literature in terms of explainability in the cybersecurity domain. [11] compared the decision tree technique with other state-of-the-art machine learning techniques to ascertain their performance. The result shows that the decision tree technique outperformed other state-of-the-art techniques in terms of marginal improvement. The performance accuracy, recall, F1score, and precision of the decision tree algorithm outperformed other state-of-the-art techniques in terms of explainability. The authors asserted that the decision tree technique is easy to evaluate, and it is computationally cheaper than other supervised learning techniques. Among the supervised learning approaches, a decision tree is nonparametric. It makes decisions using a tree-like technique and shows the probability of event occurrences. This technique includes a conditional control statement and provides straightforward and interpretable decision rules. Unlike other supervised models, it allows you to observe and interpret the data logic. The decision tree technique assesses the importance of features, generates explainable rules for threat detection, and achieves comparable performance with state-of-the-art techniques in terms of accuracy [11]. SVM is a compelling technique, and it is also computationally expensive, and non-interpretable. The missing value in the dataset does not affect the process of development and deployment in the decision tree technique which is a competitive advantage over other state-of-the-art machine learning techniques. Another advantage of the decision tree is that it does not need to be normally distributed. However, there may be a chance of overfitting if the model encounter noise in the dataset. Hence, the decision tree technique might perform inadequately in the testing set but perform better in the testing set. Another drawback of the decision tree technique is that categorical features with a different number of levels, and information gained in the technique is biased in favor of those features with more levels. This action might influence prediction performance, but the decision tree technique is considered the most efficient technique in terms of interpretability and trustworthiness [16].

4.3 R3: What Are the Impacts of Explainable Machine Learning in the Cybersecurity Domain

In this subsection, the study impact of explainable machine learning algorithms in the cybersecurity domain. The transparency, fairness, and trustworthiness of explainable machine learning cybersecurity models are becoming increasingly important. These models can be utilized to eliminate the risk of making cybersecurity decisions that are unethical, unjustifiable, and difficult to explain to users and cybersecurity experts. The misclassification of cyberattacks can cause serious damage to any organization and create vulnerability to organizations' sensitive resources [11]. Explainable machine learning plays a crucial role in ensuring trust management and understanding the impact of malicious data to detect any system infiltration. The focus on explainable cybersecurity detection machine learning models in recent times, which is very important in enhancing practical deployment of machine learning cybersecurity infrastructures can enhance their design and empower their implementation because interpretability and fairness can strengthen the robustness of cybersecurity models. This draws cybersecurity experts' attention to possible adversaries that could negatively influence or manipulate machine learning predictive models. Explainable machine learning models are also capable of ensuring the trust of cybersecurity models through offering meaningful variable inference and model reasoning causality. Explainable machine learning models can also help ensure impartiality in the decision-making process, for instance, to detect and correct biases such as imbalanced datasets in the training set [11, 17, 18]. A lot of research using black-box techniques based on the KDD original dataset has reported high-performance accuracy for malicious threat detection. Detecting malicious threats is essential but understanding and explaining how they are detected, and their decision-making process is a critical issue. Black-box machine learning techniques are very complicated and complex to understand, and it is sometimes very convoluted how they derive their conclusion. This makes them complicated I am making sensitive decisions such as malicious threat detection. It is essential that the decision-making process of machine learning in the cybersecurity domain need to be understood. Threat intelligent experts have a right to the details and decision logic of cyberattack detection models [19–23].

Explainability techniques aim to overcome the concerns of black-box machine learning models, which have long been a major roadblock to machine learning adoption in sensitive areas such as cybersecurity. Explainability can improve the robustness of cybersecurity infrastructures by highlighting possible adversaries that could alter the predictions. Explainability ensures that only contextual accurate variables deduce the outcome (i.e., in the reasoning method, there must be an underlying truthful causality).

Cyberattacks can be easily interpreted if they are explained as rules. Simple interpreted rules, such as If, then statements, are an example. Also, the explanation should be able to explain which network features are infringed, which sections of the target of the attack, and which parts of the security regulations are violated. Explainable machine learning address cybersecurity transparency requirements, and there is some indication that it can improve trustworthiness in cybersecurity systems. Hence, explainable machine learning is necessary for proving fairness, trustworthiness, and reliable interpretation of the outcome of machine learning cyberattack detection models [11, 19, 24, 25].

5   Conclusion

The contribution of this study is to execute an in-depth review and identification of existing explainable machine learning algorithms for cyberattack detection. Existing explainable machine learning techniques for defending against cyberattacks were identified using this selected article identified in this study. Machine learning takes decisions by analyzing vast volumes of data using a dynamic system to find potentially hidden patterns and weak signals. Despite the accuracy and excellent performance of machine learning cybersecurity detection models, their rising complexities are huge setbacks when users are involved, as these models cannot provide any explanation or information about the logic for their outcome. Interpretability in machine learning-based cybersecurity solutions has become critical for increasing confidence in machine learning-based cybersecurity infrastructures. Cybersecurity infrastructures are sensitive programs that can be attacked maliciously. However, understanding how a cybersecurity system makes decisions is important for establishing confidence, resolving issues of justice, and debugging a model to ensure trustworthy cybersecurity. This paper investigates the explainable machine learning techniques that can be utilized to enhance trustworthiness in cyberattack detection. In this study, extensive literature and state-of-the-art explainable machine learning techniques were reviewed. The impacts of trustworthy machine learning techniques were also reviewed to ascertain the best machine learning model in terms of interpretability in the cybersecurity domain. The study reveals that the decision tree technique outperforms other state-of-the-art machine learning models in terms of transparency and interpretability. Finally, this research suggests that incorporating explainable into machine learning cybersecurity models will help uncover the root causes of defensive failures, making it easier for cybersecurity experts to enhance both cybersecurity infrastructures and development, rather than just model results, policy, and management.

The number of research on trustworthy and explainable machine learning techniques in combating cyberattacks that have been published in recent years has highlighted the potential for improvement by considering the advantages and enhancements that these techniques can bring to existing machine learning frameworks in combating cyberattacks, but it has also exposed their flaws, weaknesses, and how much performance they lack. In any case, we anticipate that explainable machine learning still has many untapped potential areas to examine in combating cyberattacks in the future. In the future, we consider implementing a trustworthy federated learning framework for combating fraudulent credit card transactions.

References

1. Linardatos, P., Papastefanopoulos, V., Kotsiantis, S.: Explainable AI: a review of machine learning interpretability methods. Entropy **23**(1), 18 (2020). https://doi.org/10.3390/e23 010018
2. Petch, J., Di, S., Nelson, W.: Opening the black box: the promise and limitations of explainable machine learning in cardiology. Can. J. Cardiol. **38**(2), 204–213 (2022). https://doi.org/10. 1016/j.cjca.2021.09.004
3. Pienta, D., Tams, S., Thatcher, J.: Can trust be trusted in cybersecurity? In: Proceedings of the 53rd Hawaii International Conference on System Sciences (2020). https://doi.org/10.24251/ hicss.2020.522

4. Arrieta, A.B., et al.: Explainable artificial intelligence (XAI): concepts, taxonomies, opportunities and challenges toward responsible AI. Inf. Fusion **82**, 82–115 (2020). https://doi.org/10.1016/j.inffus.2019.12.012
5. Perarasi, T., Vidhya, S., Leeban Moses, M., Ramya, P.: Malicious vehicles identifying and trust management algorithm for enhance the security in 5G-VANET. In: Second International Conference on Inventive Research in Computing Applications (ICIRCA) (2020). https://doi.org/10.1109/icirca48905.2020.9183184
6. Nassar, M., Salah, K., Rehman, M., Svetinovic, D.: Blockchain for explainable and trustworthy artificial intelligence. Wires Data Min. Knowl. Discov. **10**(1), e1340 (2019). https://doi.org/10.1002/widm.1340
7. Dosilovic, F., Brcic, M., Hlupic, N.: Explainable artificial intelligence: a survey. In: 41st International Convention on Information and Communication Technology, Electronics and Microelectronics (MIPRO) (2018). https://doi.org/10.23919/mipro.2018.8400040
8. Zhu, J., Liapis, A., Risi, S., Bidarra, R., Youngblood, G.: Explainable AI for designers: a human-centered perspective on mixed-initiative co-creation. In: 2018 IEEE Conference on Computational Intelligence and Games (CIG) (2018). https://doi.org/10.1109/cig.2018.8490433
9. Keeling, G.: Why trolley problems matter for the ethics of automated vehicles. Sci. Eng. Ethics **26**(1), 293–307 (2019). https://doi.org/10.1007/s11948-019-00096-1
10. Wang, M., Zheng, K., Yang, Y., Wang, X.: An explainable machine learning framework for intrusion detection systems. IEEE Access **8**, 73127–73141 (2020). https://doi.org/10.1109/access.2020.2988359
11. Mahbooba, B., Timilsina, M., Sahal, R., Serrano, M.: Explainable artificial intelligence (XAI) to enhance trust management in intrusion detection systems using decision tree model. Complexity **2021**, 1–11 (2021). https://doi.org/10.1155/2021/6634811
12. Marino, D., Wickramasinghe, C., Manic, M.: An adversarial approach for explainable AI in intrusion detection systems. In: IECON 44th Annual Conference of the IEEE Industrial Electronics Society (2018). https://doi.org/10.1109/iecon.2018.8591457
13. Daghistani, T., Elshawi, R., Sakr, S., Ahmed, A., Al-Thwayee, A., Al-Mallah, M.: Predictors of in-hospital length of stay among cardiac patients: a machine learning approach. Int. J. Cardiol. **288**, 140–147 (2019). https://doi.org/10.1016/j.ijcard.2019.01.046
14. Jones, Y., Deligianni, F., Dalton, J.: Improving ECG classification interpretability using saliency maps. In: IEEE 20th International Conference on Bioinformatics and Bioengineering (BIBE) (2020). https://doi.org/10.1109/bibe50027.2020.00114
15. Elshawi, R., Al-Mallah, M., Sakr, S.: On the interpretability of machine learning-based model for predicting hypertension. BMC Med. Inform. Decis. Making **19**(1) (2019). doi: https://doi.org/10.1186/s12911-019-0874-0
16. Gilpin, L., Bau, D., Yuan, B., Bajwa, A., Specter, M., Kagal, L.: Explaining explanations: an overview of interpretability of machine learning. In: IEEE 5th International Conference on Data Science and Advanced Analytics (DSAA) (2018). https://doi.org/10.1109/dsaa.2018.00018
17. Carvalho, D., Pereira, E., Cardoso, J.: Machine learning interpretability: a survey on methods and metrics. Electronics **8**(8), 832 (2019). https://doi.org/10.3390/electronics8080832
18. Guo, W.: Explainable artificial intelligence for 6G: improving trust between human and machine. IEEE Commun. Mag. **58**(6), 39–45 (2020). https://doi.org/10.1109/mcom.001.2000050
19. Wu, M., Hughes, M.C., Parbhoo, S., Zazzi, M., Roth, V., Doshi-Velez, F.: Beyond sparsity: tree regularization of deep models for interpretability. In: Proceedings of AAAI Conference on Artificial Intelligence, New Orleans, LA, USA (2018)
20. Zahavy, T., Zrihem, N., Mannor, S.: Graying the black box: understanding DQNs (2022). https://doi.org/10.48550/arXiv.1602.02658. Accessed 12 May 2021

21. Luong, N., et al.: Applications of deep reinforcement learning in communications and networking: a survey. IEEE Commun. Surv. Tutor. **21**(4), 3133–3174 (2019). https://doi.org/10.1109/comst.2019.2916583
22. Huawei: AI Security White Paper (2018). https://www-file.huawei.com/-/media/corporate/pdf/trust-center/ai-securitywhitepaper.pdf. Accessed 2 Jan 2021
23. Gunning, D.: DARPA's explainable artificial intelligence (XAI) program. In: Proceedings of the 24th International Conference on Intelligent User Interfaces (2019). https://doi.org/10.1145/3301275.3308446
24. Castelvecchi, D.: Can we open the black box of AI? Nature **538**(7623), 20–23 (2016). https://doi.org/10.1038/538020a
25. Sarhan, M., Layeghy, S., Portmann, M.: Evaluating standard feature sets towards increased generalisability and explainability of ML-based network intrusion detection (2021). https://doi.org/10.48550/arXiv.2104.07183. Accesssed 9 Jan 2022

Comparing Effectiveness of Machine Learning Methods for Diagnosis of Deep Vein Thrombosis

Ruslan Sorano[(✉)][iD], Lars V. Magnusson[iD], and Khurshid Abbas[iD]

Østfold University College, Halden, Norway
{ruslans,lars.v.magnusson,khurshid.abbas}@hiof.no

Abstract. This paper presents the results of a comparative study of machine learning techniques when predicting deep vein thrombosis. We used the Ri-Schedule dataset with Electronic Health Records of suspected thrombotic patients for training and validation. A total of 1653 samples and 59 predictors were included in this study.

We have compared 20 standard machine learning algorithms and identified the best-performing ones: Random Forest, XGBoost, Gradient-Boosting and HistGradientBoosting classifiers. After hyper-parameter optimization, the best overall accuracy of 0.91 was shown by Gradient-Boosting classifier using only 15 of the original variables.

We have also tuned the algorithms for maximum sensitivity. The best specificity was offered by Random Forests. At maximum sensitivity of 1.0 and specificity of 0.41, the Random Forest model was able to identify 23% additional negative cases over the screening practice in use today.

These results suggest that machine learning could offer practical value in real-life implementations if combined with traditional methods for ruling out deep vein thrombosis.

Keywords: Deep vein thrombosis · DVT · VTE · Machine learning

1 Introduction

Deep vein thrombosis (DVT) is a common medical disorder that is caused by a blood clot, also called a thrombus, forming in any section of the venous system. The disease can quickly become lethal if a thrombus dislodges from the location where it coagulated and enters the blood circulation system, obstructing the blood flow at other locations. This often results in pulmonary embolism (PE), when a thrombus blocks a lung artery, affecting the oxygen supply to the cells in the whole body. Timely diagnosis of DVT and PE, commonly known as venous thromboembolism (VTE), is vital to prevent patient's disability or death.

The most common tools for VTE pre-testing are risk assessment models, including Wells [33] and Revised Geneva [22].

These integer-based scoring systems are time and cost-efficient, but their results can be inaccurate. More invasive and expensive clinical testing, such as compression ultrasound (CUS) or computed tomography (CT) is often required to get a conclusive diagnosis.

In the past two decades, the growing volumes of Electronic Health Records (EHR) and other digital patient data have enabled the extensive application of machine learning (ML) techniques in all areas of medicine, including prediction and diagnosis of DVT and PE. However, the comparative study of the performance of ML algorithms on patient data from the Norwegian healthcare system has not been previously performed.

1.1 Research Objectives and Questions

The data used in this research was collected by Østfold Hospital Trust during the Rivaroxaban for Scheduled Work-up of Deep Vein Thrombosis Study, or Ri-Schedule study [17]. The Ri-Schedule dataset has 1653 suspected DVT patient records registered by a Norwegian regional hospital. Neither this dataset nor its combination of features were previously used in any machine learning based predictions of deep vein thrombosis.

The primary objective of this study was to compare the predictive abilities of a larger number of ML algorithms on the Ri-Schedule dataset.

We would also like to see how ML-based method can compare in performance with the traditional DVT classification model currently used as a standard solution.

To achieve these objectives, we have defined the following research questions:

RQ1: How do state-of-the-art ML algorithms compare in accuracy on the Ri-Schedule dataset?
RQ2: How do state-of-the-art ML algorithms compare in terms of specificity when maximizing sensitivity?
RQ3: To what degree can machine learning models improve existing diagnostic procedures?

In order to answer these questions, we will compare a wide selection of modern machine learning techniques, and we will ensure that we evaluate the techniques fairly.

2 Related Work

Ma et al. [25] trained the XGBoost classification model using a dataset comprising 70 features and 9213 patients, 1165 of which were VTE positive. The model's predictive abilities were found to be comparable to or better than traditional assessment methods.

Wang et al. [32] utilized the ML approach to assess the risk of VTE using the clinical EHR of 376 patients with 22 risk factor variables. The number of samples with positive and negative outcomes was evenly balanced with 188 labels of each class. Nine classification algorithms, including RF, GBDT, LR, KNN, SVM, NB, XGBoost, EBM and EBM-inter, were trained and their performance was compared with each other and with Padua risk assessment model. The ML model performance was also validated on a holdout set including EHRs for 42 patients with and 1537 without VTE. RF was shown to be the best performing model, but its sensitivity results were inferior to those of Padua model.

Nafee et al. [26] developed two ensemble learning algorithms by combining estimates across multiple ML models to predict VTE in acutely ill patients. The ensemble models were built with 39 candidate ML methods in five families of models, such as generalized additive models, elastic net, extreme gradient boosting, RF and Bayesian logistic regression. The dataset comprised 6459 samples, including 6052 with negative and 407 positive DVT outcome. The first ensemble model was trained using 68 predictors, the second model used a subset of 16 variables, identified to have association with VTE. The experiments have shown that ML-based solution outperformed the traditional risk score model in predicting VTE from randomized clinical trial data.

In their recent research, Luo et al. [24] trained XGBoost, SVM, GLM and RF machine learning models to predict DVT based on the records for 518 patients, including 189 with confirmed DVT diagnoses. Among the four classification models, GLM and SVM showed the largest ROC AUC, which was used as the primary performance metric.

These studies were conducted used limited amount of techniques, and dataset sizes were either in the range of several thousand or a few hundred samples. To the best of our knowledge, there isn't a comparative study of ML-based DVT prediction on a dataset from the Norwegian healthcare system.

3   The Setup of the Comparative Study

This section describes the framework for Ri-Schedule dataset preparation and comparison of the performance of classification methods in the prediction of DVT. Figure 1 illustrates the general design of the research methodology framework.

3.1   Data Source

The electronic medical records were collected by Østfold Hospital Trust during the Rivaroxaban for Scheduled Work-up of Deep Vein Thrombosis Study (Ri-Schedule study). The study included patients with suspected DVT referred to the Emergency Department of Østfold Hospital, Norway, between February 2015 and November 2018. The other inclusion criteria were age not younger than 18 years old, agreement to sign written consent and no recent prior enrollment in the study.

The original Ri-Schedule dataset contains 1800 patient records, with 195 attributes per record. The dataset contains both numerical and categorical data. The data includes personal characteristics (age, gender, weight, height), clinical symptoms, risk factors, vital signs, laboratory test results, limb measurements, information from the follow-up visits, prescribed medication and diagnostic outcomes.

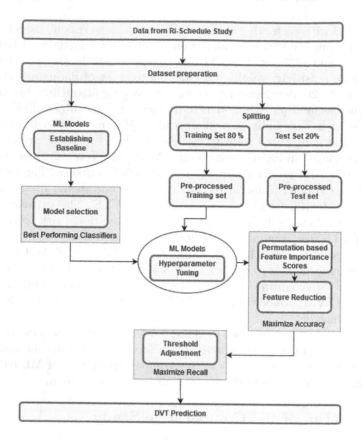

Fig. 1. Framework design for DVT prediction on Ri-Schedule dataset.

Target Variable. The labels are in binary format, representing positive or negative DVT diagnosis. The ground truth values were determined during the Ri-Schedule study based on D-dimer [20] attribute values and confirmed with the compression ultrasonography (CUS) test.

3.2   Dataset Preparation

Here we describe how we have prepared the data for machine learning analysis.

Duplicates. Each data sample in Ri-Schedule dataset contains an identification number that is unique to a patient. Some of the records appear to be duplicate entries, referring to the same patient ID. These duplicate entries were compared with each other to find out if they had identical medical data. We kept the latest entry for each patient ID, which contained the most complete or up-to-date information. After removing duplicate records, the dataset contained 1653 samples. The target attribute had 1342 negative and 311 positive values.

Feature Selection. We removed some of the attributes from the original dataset due to the following factors: (a) irrelevance to this research, (b) highly sparse data, (c) follow-up information for positively diagnosed patients, (d) conflicting data values, such as Wells risk scores from three different examiners. The two variables containing circumference measurements of left and right knees were replaced with a new variable containing absolute values of the difference in these measurements. This transformation makes sense, as an individual measurement of a limb does not present predictive value for diagnosing DVT. The non-zero difference between the two values, however, may indicate a swollen limb, which is one of the possible signs of a blood clot. The same procedure was applied to the pairs of measurements for left and right ankles. After removing empty, sparse or irrelevant features, the dataset contained 1653 samples and 59 independent variables.

Categorical Data. We converted categorical features to dummy variables. This transformation creates a binary representation of predictor categories and replaces the variable with $k - 1$ binary features, where k is number of original categories. The number of predictors increased to 197 as we converted categorical features to dummy variables.

Missing Values and Outliers. The Ri-Schedule dataset contains a large number of missing values. Discarding the samples with incomplete data is not a feasible option due to the relatively small dataset size. Extreme values confirmed as valid by medical experts were kept unchanged. Those of erroneous or accidental nature were removed from the dataset. We replace missing, invalid and extreme outlier values using univariate imputation of means, medians or modes, depending on each attribute's nature and valid range. As a general rule, the missing or invalid values were imputed with means when the predictor values were real numbers. The modes were imputed into columns containing binary values. Some of the features contained limited sets of integer values; these columns were imputed with medians.

Processed Dataset. The final class distribution is unbalanced, with a negative to positive label ratio of 0.81:0.19. We adjust class weights using the balanced mode of the relevant hyper-parameter provided in algorithm implementation.

The transformed dataset is randomly split into training (80%) and test (20%) sets. We maintained the same distribution of classes using labels for stratified sampling. After splitting, the training and test sets contained 1322 and 331 samples, respectively. The negative to positive ratios in training and test subsets remained approximately the same 0.81:0.19.

The value magnitudes in different independent variables within the dataset vary greatly. We use standardization to transform features to a common value range [0, 1].

3.3 Data Analysis

Performance Metrics. We use overall classification accuracy for training and selecting the best models. We also used balanced accuracy, sensitivity, precision, specificity, f1-score, f2-score, ROC AUC (Receiver Operator Curve – Area Under Curve), PRC AUC (Precision-Recall Curve – Area Under Curve) for finding the final results.

Machine Learning Methods. Twenty classification methods from different families of ML algorithms were selected to compare their performance in classifying DVT using the Ri-Schedule dataset. The following classification models were used: AdaBoost (AB) [29], Bagging Classifier (BC) [4], Decision Tree (DT) [7], Extra Tree Classifier (ET) [7], Extra Trees Classifier (ETs) [5], GaussianNB (GNB) [8], GaussianProcess (GP) [35], Gradient Boosting (GB) [15], HistGradient Boosting (HGB) [21], K-Neighbors Classifier (KN) [27], Linear Discriminant Analysis (LDA) [14], Linear SVC (LSVC) [2], Logistic Regression (LR) [19], MLP Classifier (MLP) [1], Passive Aggressive Classifier (PA) [12], Quadratic Discriminant Analysis (QDA) [30], Random Forest (RF) [6], Ridge Classifier (RC) [18], SGD Classifier (SGD) [28], SVM Classifier (SVC) [11] and XGBoost Classifier (XGB) [9]. Nineteen models were used from the Scikit-learn package, one from the XGBoost package. Each model was initialized with default parameters, trained and validated on the entire dataset using 10-fold stratified split and cross-validation. This procedure was repeated 5 times, and the average accuracy across all training-validation cycles was calculated. The models that showed top 4 accuracy results were selected for further parameter optimization.

Hyper-parameter Tuning. The hyper-parameter search was implemented on the training dataset using grid search with stratified 5-fold cross-validation. The classification accuracy metric was chosen as the primary metric for predictive performance evaluation of models at this stage of our experiments.

The best performing model was then fit and validated on the training set using five rounds of 10-fold stratified split and cross-validation. The mean and standard deviation of the cross-validation results were reported for accuracy, balanced accuracy, recall, precision, specificity, f1- and f2-scores, ROC AUC and PRC AUC.

Feature Importance. We inspected feature importance for our fitted estimators using the model agnostic permutation technique. We fitted models on the training set and then estimated how important each feature is for a particular model.

Individual features were permuted one at a time, and the model performance was estimated on the holdout test set. The model performance metrics reflect the loss of relationship between the permuted feature and the output variable so that we can arrange and output the predictors in the order of their importance for each trained classifier. The procedure is repeated ten times, and the mean and standard deviation of the importance scores are reported.

In the next step we created N subsets of training and test datasets, containing top n most importance features for an estimator, n varied from 1 to N, where N is number of independent variables with non-zero importance scores. The mode was then refitted on each training subset and evaluated on a test subset. The final model and corresponding data subset were selected based on the results of classification metrics. The feature names and their importance scores were then reported for each classifier.

Threshold Adjustment. In the medical domain the tolerance for false negatives is often much lower than for false positives. In the case of DVT prediction, it is more acceptable to send a patient to an extra CUS testing to confirm a negative result, than to discharge a patient with thrombosis who was falsely identified as negative. We explored different values for classification decision thresholds to find the value that gives predictions with zero number of false negatives. In the case of an imbalanced dataset, it is expected that the default cut-off value for the binary classification threshold of 0.5 does not deliver satisfactory results. We iterated over decision thresholds, trying all values from 1.0 to 0.0 with the step of 0.01, and we recorded the cut-off point when the recall reaches 100%. When we did not find an optimal classification decision threshold value that gives a perfect recall score, we registered threshold as equal to zero. In the next step, we counted the number of patients correctly identified as negative and whose D-dimer value is above or equal to the default cut-off point of $0.5 \lg mL^{-1}$ [16]. The ratio of this number to the total number of patients sent to CUS with a D-dimer $\geq 0.5 \lg mL^{-1}$ gives us the estimated savings in CUS testings that our models can propose.

3.4 Hardware and Software

Our project was developed in Python 3.8.10. The machine learning component was implemented in Scikit-learn v.1.0, XGBoost v.1.4.2. The experiments were run on HPC with $\times 2$ AMD EPYC 7551 32-Core CPUs with 2 threads per core. Operating system Ubuntu 20.04.1.

4 Results

This section presents the results of our comparative study.

4.1 Baseline Results

In the baseline performance test, the top result was shown by HistGradient-Boosting Classifier, followed closely by Random Forest, and XGBoost and Gradient-Boosting classifier sharing the third place. The summary is presented in Table 1.

4.2 Results After Hyper-parameter Tuning

The four selected algorithms that showed the best baseline results were optimized using hyper-parameter tuning.

Table 1. Baseline performance metrics on complete dataset. Averaged results with standard deviation shown after 5 rounds of 10-fold stratified split and cross-validation.

Model	Accuracy	Recall	Precision	Specificity
AB	0.853 (0.025)	0.498 (0.109)	0.652 (0.094)	0.936 (0.026)
BC	0.858 (0.020)	0.431 (0.089)	0.707 (0.082)	0.959 (0.019)
DT	0.813 (0.030)	0.520 (0.103)	0.505 (0.093)	0.879 (0.030)
ET	0.772 (0.036)	0.356 (0.091)	0.383 (0.061)	0.860 (0.036)
ETs	0.852 (0.015)	0.260 (0.083)	0.847 (0.118)	0.989 (0.009)
GNB	0.244 (0.016)	0.943 (0.038)	0.192 (0.006)	0.081 (0.021)
GP	0.833 (0.011)	0.127 (0.055)	0.899 (0.217)	0.997 (0.005)
GB	0.863 (0.021)	0.460 (0.104)	0.715 (0.086)	0.956 (0.018)
HGB	0.865 (0.020)	0.468 (0.099)	0.718 (0.083)	0.956 (0.017)
KN	0.815 (0.018)	0.159 (0.062)	0.530 (0.144)	0.967 (0.014)
LDA	0.856 (0.019)	0.371 (0.081)	0.740 (0.100)	0.969 (0.016)
LSVC	0.860 (0.017)	0.392 (0.077)	0.752 (0.095)	0.968 (0.017)
LR	0.861 (0.018)	0.344 (0.082)	0.814 (0.115)	0.980 (0.013)
MLP	0.850 (0.023)	0.441 (0.097)	0.659 (0.096)	0.941 (0.027)
PA	0.813 (0.111)	0.571 (0.256)	0.658 (0.226)	0.844 (0.250)
QDA	0.261 (0.024)	0.896 (0.046)	0.190 (0.008)	0.114 (0.033)
RF	0.864 (0.015)	0.329 (0.079)	0.866 (0.101)	0.988 (0.010)
RC	0.858 (0.016)	0.317 (0.081)	0.822 (0.105)	0.983 (0.012)
SGD	0.851 (0.030)	0.476 (0.173)	0.702 (0.133)	0.944 (0.087)
SVC	0.788 (0.031)	0.595 (0.094)	0.454 (0.062)	0.833 (0.031)
XGB	0.863 (0.021)	0.481 (0.099)	0.704 (0.091)	0.951 (0.021)

HistGradient Boosting Classifier and Gradient Boosting Classifier slightly improved overall accuracy, while the other two estimators showed small decline compared to baseline results. XGB, GB and RF showed higher recall values and f-scores after hyper-parameter optimization step. Table 2 presents the average results for classification metrics for each model's performance after this stage. HGB had largest ROC AUC and PRC AUC, see Fig. 2.

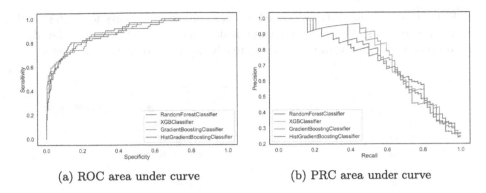

(a) ROC area under curve   (b) PRC area under curve

Fig. 2. Averaged ROC and PRC curves generated with four top performing models during training with 5 rounds of 10-fold stratified split and cross-validation.

Table 2. Model performance metrics after hyper-parameter tuning on training data. Averaged results with standard deviation shown after 5 rounds of 10-fold stratified split and cross-validation.

	RF	HGB	GB	XGB
Accuracy	0.862 (0.022)	0.867 (0.019)	0.865 (0.02)	0.859 (0.023)
Balanced accuracy	0.701 (0.051)	0.711 (0.039)	0.715 (0.042)	0.735 (0.045)
Recall	0.444 (0.103)	0.462 (0.08)	0.474 (0.087)	0.537 (0.088)
Precision	0.720 (0.095)	0.742 (0.088)	0.720 (0.085)	0.657 (0.081)
Specificity	0.959 (0.018)	0.961 (0.019)	0.955 (0.019)	0.934 (0.021)
f1-score	0.542 (0.094)	0.564 (0.071)	0.566 (0.074)	0.587 (0.075)
f2-score	0.478 (0.100)	0.497 (0.077)	0.506 (0.082)	0.555 (0.082)
ROC AUC	0.848 (0.038)	0.859 (0.034)	0.846 (0.038)	0.852 (0.038)
PRC AUC	0.647 (0.078)	0.653 (0.07)	0.639 (0.072)	0.651 (0.074)

4.3 Results of Permutation-Based Feature Importance Scoring

We further optimized the tuned models by investigating permutation-based feature importance scores. GB reached the accuracy of 0.91, using only 15 features for both training and predicting.

The other three models reached a classification accuracy of around 0.90. RF needed 31 predictors to reach the accuracy of 0.90 while HGB used only 12, reaching a marginally lower accuracy of 0.897. XGB showed the highest values for recall, f2-score and both ROC AUC and PRC AUC, while GB had heist precision and f1-score results. Table 3 shows the complete results for accuracy, balanced accuracy, recall, precision, specificity, f1- and f2-scores, ROC and PRC areas under curve.

Figure 3 shows the features ranged by their importance scores for each model. D-dimer value was the most significant feature for all models, while the other top 5 most important variables varied greatly between different ML models.

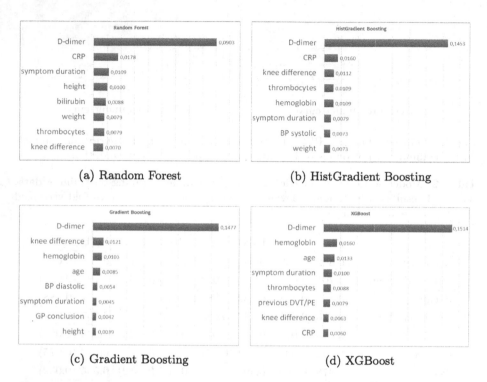

(a) Random Forest   (b) HistGradient Boosting

(c) Gradient Boosting   (d) XGBoost

Fig. 3. Permutation-based feature importance. The top 8 features with names and scores shown for each algorithm.

4.4   Results of Threshold Adjustment

We attempted to optimize classification decision thresholds for each model to find the value that gives us perfect recall. At this stage, Random Forest showed the highest specificity of 0.405 when reaching a maximum recall of 1.0 at the classification threshold level of 0.14. The ratio of predicted negatives to all negatives for the samples with a D-dimer value over 0.5 was approximately 23%. XGBoost and HGBC had specificities, ratios and thresholds of 0.04/16%/0.04 and 0.03/6%/0.03 accordingly. GradientBoosting model did not have a discrimination threshold giving 100% recall. Table 4 presents recorded threshold values, selected performance metrics, the number of correctly predicted negatives for samples with D-dimer 0.5 or higher, and their proportion in the total amount of cases requiring further diagnostic confirmation.

Table 3. Model performance metrics after permutation-based feature importance scoring and feature reduction on validation data.

	RF	HGB	GB	XGB
Number of features	31	12	15	18
Accuracy	0.900	0.897	0.909	0.903
Balanced accuracy	0.790	0.776	0.814	0.816
Recall	0.613	0.581	0.661	0.677
Precision	0.809	0.818	0.820	0.778
Specificity	0.967	0.970	0.967	0.955
f1-score	0.697	0.679	0.733	0.724
f2-score	0.644	0.616	0.688	0.695
ROC AUC	0.90	0.89	0.89	0.91
PRC AUC	0.77	0.73	0.77	0.80

Table 4. Results of threshold adjustment. The 3 algorithms that has reached perfect recall of 1.0 are RF, HGB and XGB. Gradient Boosting did not have a threshold which could give a perfect recall.

	RF	HGB	XGB
Threshold	0.14	0.03	0.04
Accuracy	0.517	0.411	0.468
Precision	0.279	0.241	0.261
Specificity	0.405	0.275	0.346
True negatives (D-dimer $\geq$ 0.5)	41 (23%)	11 (6%)	28 (16%)

5   Discussion

This study explored the predictive abilities of ML classification algorithms on the Ri-Schedule dataset of patients with suspected deep vein thrombosis.

All four models that performed best on our dataset rely on tree-based ensemble ML algorithms for binary classification. These results confirm that ensemble methods such as Random Forest and gradient boosting algorithms perform well on high-dimensional data with non-linear relationships, such as the Ri-Schedule dataset. Similar trends were reported in the studies of ML method classification performance on VTE related datasets [31,32,36].

Removing redundant features based on their insignificant or zero importance score improved all observed classification metrics for all four models. The results indicate that many features in the Ri-Schedule dataset either do not contribute to the identification of DVT or introduce noise that potentially reduces prediction accuracy. The sparse data content of the input variables and their irrelevance to blood clotting condition could be the two reasons for low or near-zero feature importance for DVT prediction.

Ranging features by their permutation-based importance allowed us to identify the D-dimer variable as having the highest score for all models across all experiments. This finding confirms its high predictive value in ruling out DVT [3,16]. It is interesting to see that apart from the D-dimer assay value, the ML models identified a limited number of features in the Ri-Schedule dataset that can also contribute to the DVT prediction accuracy. The frequently seen variables among the highest scored features were values for hemoglobin, c-reactive protein, thrombocytes, height, weight, symptom duration and knee measurements. To the best of our knowledge, the combination of these variables is not routinely used as biomarkers for the diagnosis of DVT or PE [10,23].

The standard approach to identifying DVT in patients is to start with prediction rule validation and screen with D-dimer assay [34]. This simple model identifies samples with a D-dimer value below 0.5 as negative and excludes them from further examinations. Those with D-dimer equal to or above 0.5 are subject to more resource- and time-consuming procedures. This model applied to the Ri-Schedule test dataset would yield an overall accuracy of only 0.468 with a recall of 1.0 and specificity of 0.346. We have observed that the RF model, tuned for maximum recall, had reached higher specificity of 0.405 and higher overall accuracy than the D-dimer model. However, the RF model had several false positives for samples with D-dimer values below 0.5.

The D-dimer based model's most important advantage is that it can safely exclude all cases with the D-dimer below the standard cut-off value. At the same time, the D-dimer model produces zero false negatives, which is crucial for correct diagnoses of a potentially lethal health condition. Combining the D-dimer model with the tuned RF model can ensure that no patient with DVT is falsely identified as healthy and reduce the number of patients sent to further examinations. First, the negative cases are ruled out based on the D-dimer cut-off value of 0.5. Then, the RF model with the new classification discrimination threshold is applied to exclude healthy patients from unnecessary examinations.

In the next iteration of this research, we should collect more data for further validation and model optimization. A new set of features could help identify other markers that could contribute to better class discrimination in the future study of DVT prediction on Ri-Schedule data. Another approach that could increase classification accuracy is using an age-adjusted D-dimer for ruling out VTE. This method can especially prove more efficient with older patients [13].

6   Conclusion

This work is the first comparative analysis of the performance of ML algorithms in identifying DVT among patients whose EHRs were collected by Østfold Hospital Trust, Norway.

The tree-based ensemble algorithms classified DVT from previously unseen data with a higher level of accuracy than other ML methods.

Random Forests achieved the highest specificity while reaching a perfect recall score.

The findings in this study confirm the importance of the D-dimer variable for diagnosing DVT. Furthermore, the results of our experiments suggest that the proposed combination of the standard D-dimer model and ML-based prediction can exclude a larger number of negative cases than by using the D-dimer based method alone. This proposed approach can have practical application in medicine and help save time and resources in real-life scenarios.

References

1. Bishop, C.M., et al.: Neural Networks for Pattern Recognition. Oxford University Press, Oxford (1995)
2. Bordes, A., Bottou, L., Gallinari, P.: SGD-QN: careful quasi-newton stochastic gradient descent. J. Mach. Learn. Res. **10**, 1737–1754 (2009)
3. Božič, M., Blinc, A., Stegnar, M.: D-dimer, other markers of haemostasis activation and soluble adhesion molecules in patients with different clinical probabilities of deep vein thrombosis. Thromb. Res. **108**(2), 107–114 (2002). https://doi.org/10.1016/S0049-3848(03)00007-0
4. Breiman, L.: Bagging predictors. Mach. Learn. **24**(2), 123–140 (1996). https://doi.org/10.1007/BF00058655
5. Breiman, L.: Rejoinder: arcing classifiers. Ann. Stat. **26**(3), 841–849 (1998). http://www.jstor.org/stable/120059
6. Breiman, L.: Random forests. Mach. Learn. **45**(1), 5–32 (2001). https://doi.org/10.1023/A:1010933404324
7. Breiman, L., Friedman, J.H., Olshen, R.A., Stone, C.J.: Classification and Regression Trees. Routledge, New York (2017)
8. Chan, T., Golub, G., LeVeque, R.: Technical report STAN-CS-79-773, Department of Computer Science (1979)
9. Chen, T., Guestrin, C.: XGBoost: a scalable tree boosting system. In: Proceedings of the 22nd ACM SIGKDD International Conference on Knowledge Discovery and Data Mining, pp. 785–794 (2016)
10. Coleman, D.M., Wakefield, T.W.: Biomarkers for the diagnosis of deep vein thrombosis. Expert Opin. Med. Diagn. **6**(4), 253–257 (2012)
11. Cortes, C., Vapnik, V.: Support-vector networks. Mach. Learn. **20**(3), 273–297 (1995). https://doi.org/10.1007/BF00994018
12. Crammer, K., Dekel, O., Keshet, J., Shalev-Shwartz, S., Singer, Y.: Online passive aggressive algorithms (2006)
13. Douma, R.A., et al.: Using an age-dependent D-dimer cut-off value increases the number of older patients in whom deep vein thrombosis can be safely excluded. Haematologica **97**(10), 1507 (2012)
14. Fisher, R.A.: The use of multiple measurements in taxonomic problems. Ann. Eugen. **7**(2), 179–188 (1936)
15. Friedman, J.H.: Greedy function approximation: a gradient boosting machine. Ann. Stat. **29**(5), 1189–1232 (2001). https://doi.org/10.1214/aos/1013203451
16. Fronas, S.G., et al.: Safety of D-dimer testing as a stand-alone test for the exclusion of deep vein thrombosis as compared with other strategies. J. Thromb. Haemost. **16**(12), 2471–2481 (2018). https://doi.org/10.1111/jth.14314

17. Fronas, S.G., et al.: Safety and feasibility of rivaroxaban in deferred workup of patients with suspected deep vein thrombosis. Blood Adv. **4**(11), 2468–2476 (2020). https://doi.org/10.1182/bloodadvances.2020001556
18. Hoerl, A.E., Kennard, R.W.: Ridge regression: biased estimation for nonorthogonal problems. Technometrics **12**(1), 55–67 (1970). https://doi.org/10.1080/00401706.1970.10488634
19. Hosmer, D.W., Jr., Lemeshow, S., Sturdivant, R.X.: Applied Logistic Regression, vol. 398. Wiley, Hoboken (2013)
20. Johnson, E.D., Schell, J.C., Rodgers, G.M.: The D-dimer assay. Am. J. Hematol. **94**(7), 833–839 (2019)
21. Ke, G., et al.: LightGBM: a highly efficient gradient boosting decision tree. In: Guyon, I., et al. (eds.) Advances in Neural Information Processing Systems, vol. 30. Curran Associates, Inc. (2017). https://proceedings.neurips.cc/paper/2017/file/6449f44a102fde848669bdd9eb6b76fa-Paper.pdf
22. Le Gal, G., et al.: Prediction of pulmonary embolism in the emergency department: the revised Geneva score. Ann. Intern. Med. **144**(3), 165–171 (2006). https://doi.org/10.7326/0003-4819-144-3-200602070-00004
23. Lippi, G., Cervellin, G., Franchini, M., Favaloro, E.J.: Biochemical markers for the diagnosis of venous thromboembolism: the past, present and future. J. Thromb. Thrombolysis **30**(4), 459–471 (2010). https://doi.org/10.1007/s11239-010-0460-x
24. Luo, L., Kou, R., Feng, Y., Xiang, J., Zhu, W.: Cost-effective machine learning based clinical pre-test probability strategy for DVT diagnosis in neurological intensive care unit. Clin. Appl. Thromb. Hemost. **27** (2021). https://doi.org/10.1177/10760296211008650
25. Ma, H., et al.: A novel hierarchical machine learning model for hospital-acquired venous thromboembolism risk assessment among multiple-departments. J. Biomed. Inform. **122**, 103892 (2021). https://doi.org/10.1016/j.jbi.2021.103892
26. Nafee, T., et al.: Machine learning to predict venous thrombosis in acutely ill medical patients. Res. Pract. Thromb. Haemost. **4**(2), 230–237 (2020). https://doi.org/10.1002/rth2.12292
27. Peterson, L.E.: K-nearest neighbor. Scholarpedia **4**(2), 1883 (2009)
28. Ruder, S.: An overview of gradient descent optimization algorithms. arXiv preprint arXiv:1609.04747 (2016)
29. Schapire, R.E.: Explaining AdaBoost. In: Schölkopf, B., Luo, Z., Vovk, V. (eds.) Empirical Inference, pp. 37–52. Springer, Heidelberg (2013). https://doi.org/10.1007/978-3-642-41136-6_5
30. Tharwat, A.: Linear vs quadratic discriminant analysis classifier: a tutorial. Int. J. Appl. Pattern Recogn. **3**(2), 145–180 (2016)
31. Wang, K.Y., et al.: Using predictive modeling and supervised machine learning to identify patients at risk for venous thromboembolism following posterior lumbar fusion. Glob. Spine J. (2021). https://doi.org/10.1177/21925682211019361
32. Wang, X., Yang, Y.Q., Liu, S.H., Hong, X.Y., Sun, X.F., Shi, J.H.: Comparing different venous thromboembolism risk assessment machine learning models in Chinese patients. J. Eval. Clin. Pract. **26**(1), 26–34 (2020). https://doi.org/10.1111/jep.13324
33. Wells, P.S., et al.: Value of assessment of pretest probability of deep-vein thrombosis in clinical management. The Lancet **350**(9094), 1795–1798 (1997). https://doi.org/10.1016/S0140-6736(97)08140-3
34. Wilbur, J., Shian, B.: Diagnosis of deep venous thrombosis and pulmonary embolism. Am. Fam. Physician **86**(10), 913–919 (2012)

35. Williams, C.K., Rasmussen, C.E.: Gaussian Processes for Machine Learning, vol. 2. MIT Press, Cambridge (2006)
36. Xue, B., et al.: Use of machine learning to develop and evaluate models using preoperative and intraoperative data to identify risks of postoperative complications. JAMA Netw. Open **4**(3), e212240 (2021). https://doi.org/10.1001/jamanetworkopen.2021.2240

A Predictive Model for the Detection of Clients Suspicious Behavior

Marcelo Leon[1]($\boxtimes$) (iD), Fidel Shagñay[2] (iD), Claudia Rivas[1] (iD),
and Fabricio Echeverria[1] (iD)

[1] Universidad Ecotec, Guayaquil, Ecuador
marceloleon11@hotmail.com
[2] Universidad Central del Ecuador, Quito, Ecuador

Abstract. The purpose of this work is to identify the suspicious behavior of the clients of a financial institution. Financial institutions use rule-based systems to detect unusual transactions. These systems focus on individual transactions or simple transaction patterns. Due to this, the need arises to detect suspicious behavior using machine learning since many of the machine learning algorithms are designed to capture complex patterns. Descriptive analysis and predictive analysis are used to detect suspicious behavior. Within the descriptive analysis, outliers are sought in transactional movements. For the predictive analysis, we start from a set of alerts with the label of whether or not they were reported by the Compliance Unit. As a result of the descriptive model, a set of customers that have behaved in an unusual way is obtained and as a result of the predictive model, the alerts that should be reported are predicted. It is concluded that the techniques: descriptive analysis, descriptive analysis and the rule-based system can complement each other, since they focus on different aspects of the identification of unusual transactions and should not be considered as exclusive alternatives.

Keywords: Rules-based systems · Machine learning · Predictive analysis · Transactional movements · Alerts

1 Introduction

Financial institutions use rule-based computer systems to detect unusual or out-of-the-ordinary transactions; these systems use rules to detect unusual transactions. These systems focus on individual transactions or simple transaction patterns and can be breached simply by knowing the thresholds, so they may not be sufficient to detect complicated transaction patterns [1].

The present work is focused on detecting suspicious behavior by applying machine learning algorithms [2]. In addition, rule-based systems focus on individual transactions or simple transaction patterns, so they may not be sufficient to detect complicated transaction patterns.

With the development of high-speed computing, machine learning can analyze large amounts of data quickly. Many machine learning algorithms are designed to capture

O. Gervasi et al. (Eds.): ICCSA 2022 Workshops, LNCS 13381, pp. 294–312, 2022.
https://doi.org/10.1007/978-3-031-10548-7_22

complex patterns such as nonlinear relationships between a dependent variable and explanatory variables, where linear rules fall short [3, 4].

A challenge in modelling suspicious behavior is that they are rare events. The rarity of an event refers to the situation where the events of interest are few relative to non-events. These events are infrequent, but their effects can be just as detrimental. Because of their rare occurrence, the information associated with the events tends to be masked by the dominant non-events, which imposes challenges for the model to effectively classify the various signals in the data and accurately separate the two types of events. Because of these problems, models can perform sub optimally in discriminating events from non-events when events are rare [5].

For the construction of the models, the transaction database of a financial institution in Ecuador was used. For the descriptive model, a cluster analysis is applied to find unusual transactional behavior that deviates from normal behavior. For the predictive model, different machine learning algorithms such as random forests, extreme gradient boosting, support vector machine and stacking classifier are applied.

The relevance of this work lies in the use of statistical methods for the detection of suspicious behavior that serve as a tool for the Compliance Unit to locate unusual transactions.

In order to identify suspicious behavior, the transactional movements made by natural customers registered in the financial institution's database are analyzed. The transactions analyzed are those registered in the period February 2019 to September 2019 in the savings account, credit portfolio and fixed-term investment modules. As the financial institution has branches in some provinces of Ecuador, the geographical scope is nationwide.

The financial institution currently uses a rule-based system to detect unusual transactions. The rules are basically conditions with thresholds defined by the Compliance Unit. These systems focus on individual transactions and can be breached simply by knowledge of the thresholds, so they may not be sufficient to detect complicated transaction patterns. Due to these drawbacks, the use of statistical methods for the detection of unusual behavior of the financial institution's customers is proposed. The study does not cover the analysis of credit card transactions and transactional movements of legal clients.

2 Methodology

This paper uses applied research as it developed a descriptive model and a predictive model to identify suspicious behavior of customers of a financial institution.

For the descriptive model, the unsupervised learning technique and a cluster analysis were used to find transactional behavior that deviates from normal behavior or, in other words, to detect unusual behavior [6].

For the predictive model, the supervised learning technique was used in which the alerts that were reported by the compliance unit were labelled [7]. Once the alerts were labelled, several machine learning algorithms were applied and the models with the best performance were used in a meta-classifier. The benefit of the meta classifier is that it can leverage the capabilities of a variety of well-performing models in a classification task and make predictions that perform better than any individual model. The level of research employed was classificatory and predictive. Classificatory because it seeks to establish unusual customer behavior according to their transactional movements. Predictive because it seeks to define whether or not an alert will be reported based on the characteristics of the alert and the customer.

For the descriptive model, the data available correspond to the transactional movements recorded between February 2019 and September 2019 for the Savings Accounts, Credit Portfolio, Clients and Fixed-Term Investments modules. As the financial institution has branches in some provinces of Ecuador, the geographical scope is nationwide.

For the predictive model, the data available are the records of alerts generated between February 2019 and September 2019 for alerts such as Customers with Multiple Transfers Received, Customers with Frequent Deposits of Fixed Term Deposits, among others. As the alert records are generated from transactional movements, the geographical scope was also nationwide. The study will not cover the movements of the credit card module.

The target population is only the customers who transact in the different modules of the transactional system, which as of February 2019 are around 70,000 and generate around 1,600,000 transactions per month.

Regarding the registration of alerts between February 2019 and September 2019, there are around 6,700 of which 90 are reported by the compliance unit.

The method and approach used was quantitative because it requires statistical analysis, a cluster analysis was performed to identify unusual transnationality and for the predictive analysis different machine learning algorithms were applied to find patterns to determine whether an alert is reported or not.

The temporal dimension of the study is cross-sectional as it took place at a specific time. For the descriptive and predictive model, transactions in a given month are considered.

3 Modeling

This section describes the development of the descriptive and predictive models.

3.1 Data Exploration

We proceed to explore the data used to build the models. The variables considered for the transactional movements of savings accounts and the verification of missing values are presented in Table 1.1.

It is observed that the variables "CodeDocReserved", "CauseCode", "Description" have many missing values so they are removed from the data structure.

The variables considered for the transactional credit flows and the missing value check are presented in Table 1.2. It is noted that there are no missing values in the data structure.

The variables considered from the transactional flows of fixed-term investments and the missing value check are illustrated in Table 1.3. It is observed that the variable "CodeDocReserved" has many missing values so it is removed from the data structure.

The variables considered from the transactional alert records and the missing value check are presented in Table 1. It is observed that the variable "Alert" has many missing values and is therefore removed from the data structure.

Table 1. Missing values: (1.1) in savings accounts, (1.2) in appropriations, (1.3) in fixed-term investments, (1.4) in alert records.

Variables (1.1)	Variables (1.2)	Variables (1.3)	Variables (1.4)
CodeTransaction	CodeTransaction	CodeTransaction	Registration
CodeAccount	InvestmentCode	InvestmentCode	Code
Date	TransactionType	TransactionType	CodeAlert
Hour	CashValue	CashValue	Alert (317)
TransactionType	ValueCheck	ValueCheck	Client Code
TotalAmout	Date	Date	Description
CashValue	DateHour	DateHour	Date
ValueCheck	CodeDocument	CodeDocument	Time
BalanceAccount	CodeDocReserved (1782)	CodeDocReserved (1782)	Total Value
CodeDocument	Posted	Posted	Office Code
CodeDocReserved	Reversed	Reversed	RiskLevel
(1369637)	CodeOfficeOrigin	CodeOfficeOrigin	Condition
ReservedIndicator	CodigoOficinaDestination	CodigoOficinaDestination	CodePhase
CheckNumber	UserCode	UserCode	phases
UserCode	RetentionValue	RetentionValue	UAF List
CodeOfficeOriigin	ValueCheck	ValueCheck	PepList
CodigoOficinaDestination	Channel	Channel	
PostedIndicator			
CauseCode (2045223)			
Description (768202)			
TypeMovement			
Channel			
PaymentMethod			

3.2 Modern Descriptive Model

Descriptive analysis or unsupervised learning aims to find unusual anomalous behavior that deviates from average behavior [8]. This norm can be defined in several ways. It can be defined as the behavior of the average customer at a snapshot in time, or as the average behavior of a given customer over a particular time period, or as a combination of both. When used in the detection of suspicious behavior, unsupervised learning is often referred to as anomaly detection, as it aims to find anomalous and therefore suspicious observations. In the literature, anomalies are commonly described as outliers or exceptions [9, 10].

In the construction of the descriptive model we proceed to create a table of customers who have transacted in a given cut-off, in this case for the month of February 2019. This table is constructed on the basis of the transactional movements of savings accounts and customer tables.

The data structure is analyzed by the variable "CodeProfession", the aim is to examine homogeneous groups as it indicates about peer group analysis [11]. The professions with the highest concentration of clients, it can be observed that the profession with code 28 has 17.649 clients which represents about 25%. And the professions with the lowest concentration of clients, are 58, 42, and 38 with only one client each. These professions are grouped into a single set based on a threshold (the threshold can be defined based on a number of clients e.g. 500 or based on a percentage e.g. 0.5%.) (Table 2).

Table 2. Professions with: (4.1) the highest concentration of clients, (4.2) the lowest concentration of clients.

Index	Code profession	Customer number	Percentage	Index	Code profession	Customer number	Percentage
0	28	17649	25.5095	72	36	3	0.00433614
1	81	8497	12.2814	73	66	2	0.00289076
2	82	8076	11.6729	74	63	2	0.00289076
3	80	4310	6.22958	75	44	2	0.00289076
4	88	3969	5.73671	76	43	2	0.00289076
5	26	3605	5.21059	77	35	2	0.00289076
6	79	3397	4.90995	78	27	2	0.00289076
7	78	2209	3.19284	79	58	1	0.00144538
8	03	1461	2.11170	80	42	1	0.00144538
9	16	1387	2.00474	81	38	1	0.00144538
10	64	1290	1.86454				

The resulting profession codes are: p26, c0, p65, p77, p74, p80, p78, p79, p81, p71, p73, p70, p72, p19, p82, p03, p17, p16, p08, p28, p75, p18, p83, p64, p29, p88, p21. Codes starting with the letter "p" are the codes of professions that are above the threshold and codes starting with the letter "c" are the product of the cluster analysis (professions below the threshold).

The outliers are then analysed for each profession based on customer transactionality ("TransactionValue" = Total Transaction Value in a given month, "TransactionFrequency" = Number of Transactions in a given month) using the One-ClassSVM algorithm. Once the outliers in the transnationality have been identified, we proceed to perform a cluster analysis using the KMeans technique with these records marked as outliers. Prior to the cluster analysis, binary variables are generated for the categorical variables and quantitative variables are scaled by the theme of scales [12, 13].

Records containing the cluster with the maximum transaction value are defined as high risk and medium risk in the opposite case. This analysis is carried out for each profession code and the result is stored in a data structure. After analyzing all the occupational codes, the variable "Label" is defined according to the level of risk (1: if the risk level is high or medium, 0: for low risk level) (Table 3).

Table 3. Initial data structure with the 2 generated variables (risk, label).

Province	Age	Risk	Label
17	69	Low	0
17	83	Low	0
10	82	Low	0
17	76	Low	0
17	73	Low	0
17	75	Low	0
17	70	Low	0
17	66	Medium	1
17	67	Low	0
17	67	Low	0
17	81	Low	0
17	69	Low	0

Once the label has been defined, a probability for flagging a customer with anomalous behavior is calculated using logistic regression. Table 4 illustrates the grouping of the data by the variable "Label". The data are not balanced, the customers with anomalous behavior represent 4.18% and those without anomalous behavior represent 95.82%, so we proceed to sub-sample the majority class to obtain balanced data.

Table 4. Grouping of data by the variable label.

Index	Label	Quantity	Percentage
0	0	66796	95.8171
1	1	2916	4.1829

The subsampling with the sampling strategy parameter equal to 1, means that the number of records of the minority class will be equal to the records of the majority class.

A logistic regression is then applied and the variable "Probability" is generated, which indicates the probability that a customer has an anomalous behavior (Table 5).

Table 5. Data structure with variable Probability.

Risk	Label	Probability
High	1	1
High	1	0.999815
High	1	1
High	1	0.999921
High	1	0.999999
High	1	1
High	1	0.999828
Low	0	0.530792
Low	0	0.433696
Low	0	0.350096

3.3 Model Predictive

In predictive analytics, the goal is to build an analytical model that predicts a target metric of interest. The target metric is typically used to drive the learning process during an optimization procedure. For the construction of the predictive model, the first task is to define the target measure or variable, which is defined on the basis of the status of the alerts [14–18].

The data structure of the predictive model was created joining the tables AlertRegister, Customer and CustomerNatural. Then, the target variable is defined on the basis of the alert statuses. Table 6 shows the different statuses of the alert records. Based on its analysis, the compliance officer determines whether the alert is reported, which is why the target variable is defined as one if the alert is reported and zero if it is not (status other than reported).

Table 6. Registration status alerts.

Code	State
1	Entered
2	Official analysis
3	Analisys agency
4	Reported
5	Not reported
6	Reopened
7	To discharge
8	Expired

Figure 1 illustrates the percentages representing the statuses of the alert records. The status "Reported" represents 1.2% of the total number of records.

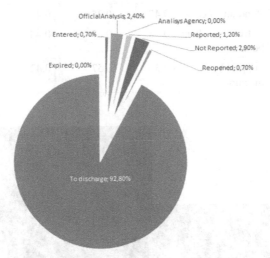

OfficialAnalysis; 2,40%   Analisys Agency; 0,00%

Entered; 0,70%   Reported; 1,20%

Not Reported; 2,90%

Expired; 0,00%   Reopened; 0,70%

To discharge; 92,80%

Fig. 1. Percentage of alert registration statuses.

Alerts with status "Entered", "Official Analysis", "Agency Analysis", "Reopened", "Expired" are deleted as these alert records have not been analyzed. The creation of the variable "Reported" was made with a value of 1 if it is reported and 0 otherwise.

The number of records with a value of one in the variable "Reported" is 81, representing 1.2% of the total. As the data are unbalanced, the techniques of under sampling and oversampling are used. The training and test partitions are defined. For this case 70% (4512) of records will be destined for model training and 30% (1934) for model testing.

To imbalance in the training partition (0:4457, 1:55), first the minority class is oversampled (with the sampling strategy parameter equal to 10%, the minority class will be 10% of the majority class), then the majority class is under sampled (with the sampling strategy parameter equal to 100% the minority class will be 100% of the majority class).

This combination of oversampling and under sampling is used because using each technique individually, the model does not perform well and when combining the two techniques the performance of the model improves.

Several models were built with different algorithms, obtaining better performance with the Random Forest, Extreme Gradient Boosting and Support Vector Machine algorithms [19–22]. The confusion matrix metrics of the three models are presented in Table 7. As the data are unbalanced, the metrics considered to evaluate the performance are: accuracy, sensitivity and F1 score.

Once the optimal parameters of the three models have been found, the Stacking Classifier method is used to combine the three classification models and thus utilize the strength of each individual estimator using its output as input to a final estimator. Figure 2 illustrates the combination of the three models.

Table 7. Metrics of the RF, XGB and SVM models.

Model	Accuracy	Sensitivity	F1 score
Random forests	0.47	0.35	0.40
Extreme gradient boosting	0.38	0.67	0.48
Support vector machine	0.33	0.57	0.42

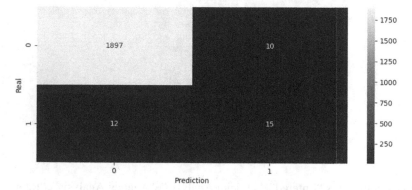

Fig. 2. Confusion matrix of the final model.

The metrics with class 0 (alert was not reported) are good with a sensitivity accuracy and f1 score of 99% one could conclude that it is a very good model, but the metrics for class 1 (alert was reported) should be reviewed because the data is unbalanced and the model was designed to detect alerts that will be reported (Fig. 3).

```
In [89]: print(classification_report(y_true=y_real,y_pred=y_pred))
                precision    recall  f1-score   support

            0       0.99      0.99      0.99      1907
            1       0.60      0.56      0.58        27

    accuracy                           0.99      1934
   macro avg       0.80      0.78      0.79      1934
weighted avg       0.99      0.99      0.99      1934
```

Fig. 3. Final model classification report.

Be positive when the alert is reported and negative when the alert is not reported. In the following, the accuracy, sensitivity and f1 score can be interpreted as:

– Accuracy (with a value of 60%) indicates how many of the cases that the model predicts as positive are actually positive. The accuracy takes into account false positives (type I error) i.e. when the model predicts that the alert is reported when it is not actually reported.

- Sensitivity (with a value of 56%) indicates how many of the cases that are actually positive the model can capture or predict as positive. Sensitivity takes into account false negatives (type II error), i.e. when the model predicts that the alert is not reported when it is actually reported.
- The f1 score which can be interpreted as a weighted average of accuracy and sensitivity has a value of 58% is improved by the f1 scores obtained from the individual models (40%, 48% and 42%).

As false negatives (12) are higher than false positives (10) the accuracy is higher than the sensitivity. Table 8 shows the calculation of the metrics of the confusion matrix of the final model.

Table 8. Metrics of the confusion matrix of the final model.

Metric	Calculation	Value
Accuracy	(VN + VP)/(VN + VP + FN + FP) = (VN + VP + FN + FP)/(VN + VP + FN + FP) = (1897 + 15)/(1897 + 15 + 12 + 10)	98.86%
Accuracy	VP/(VP + FP) = 15/(15 + 10)	60.00%
Sensitivity	VP/(VP + FN) = 15/(15 + 12)	55.55%
F1 score	2 * (Accuracy * Sensitivity)/(Accuracy + Sensitivity)	57.69%
Error rate	(FN + FP)/(VN + VP + FN + FP) = (FN + FP)/(VN + VP + FN + FP) = (12 + 10)/(1897 + 15 + 12 + 10)	1.14%
Specificity	VN/(VN + FP) = 1897/(1897 + 10)	99.47%

4   Discussion of Results

This section presents the results obtained from the descriptive and predictive model. For the presentation of the results, an analytical web application was created in Python with Dash and the application was published on the IIS (Internet Information Services) web server [18, 23–25].

Dash is an open source framework for creating data visualization interfaces. Released in 2017 as a Python library, it has grown to include implementations for R and Julia. Dash helps data scientists create analytical web applications without requiring advanced web development skills [23].

4.1 Descriptive Model

The descriptive model was run for the months of February 2019 to September 2019, where the anomalies for the different months were obtained. Figure 4 shows the anomalies detected for the month of February 2019.

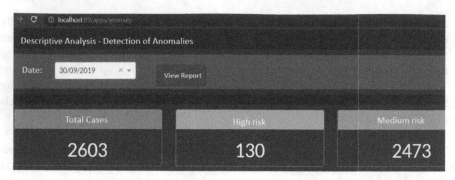

Fig. 4. Final model classification report (web application - Python dash).

Anomalies are categorized with a medium and high risk level. Giving the compliance officer an additional tool to detect unusual transactions. These anomalies do not necessarily represent observations linked to money laundering; these observations require extensive follow-up and validation by the Compliance Officer. Table 9 shows the results of the model for the different months.

Table 9. Anomalies detected (descriptive model - results).

Date	Total cases (anomalies)	High risk	Medium risk
September 2019	2603	130	2473
August 2019	2663	146	2517
July 2019	2686	150	2536
June 2019	2474	189	2285
May 2019	2506	277	2229
April 2019	2705	205	
March 2019	2742	218	2200
February 2019	2630		2433

Since the transaction variable province is available, this variable is used to present the anomalies on a map of the provinces of Ecuador in GeoJSON format. Geographic JSON (or GeoJSON) is an open format for encoding simple geospatial datasets using the JSON (JavaScript Object Notation) standard. Figure 5 illustrates the anomalies by the different provinces of Ecuador, as the financial institution has a greater presence in the provinces of Pichincha and Guayas, where the greatest volume of transactions and therefore the greatest number of anomalies are concentrated.

For September 2019 there are 2603 anomalies of which 1150 correspond to the province of Pichincha.

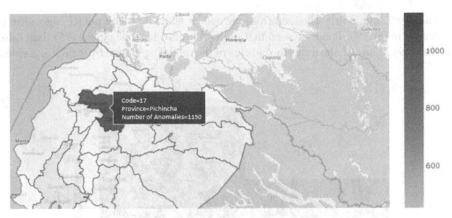

Fig. 5. Anomalies by province.

Figure 6 shows the volume of transactions in millions of dollars and the number of anomalies for the months of February 2019 to September 2019.

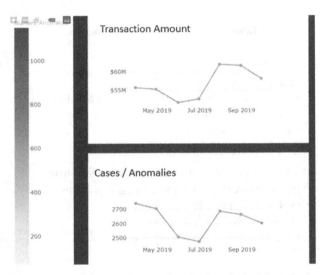

Fig. 6. Transactions and anomalies (Python dash elaboration).

4.2 Predictive Model

The classification metrics of the 3 models generated (Random Forests, Extreme Gradient Boosting, Support Vector Machine) and the final model (Stacking Classifier) are presented below.

Because the data are unbalanced the metrics considered to evaluate the models are: accuracy, sensitivity and f1 score.

The confusion matrix obtained from the model generated with the RF algorithm is illustrated in Fig. 50. It can be seen that there are more false negatives (15) than false positives (9). Table 10 illustrates the metrics of the model generated by the RF algorithm (Fig. 7).

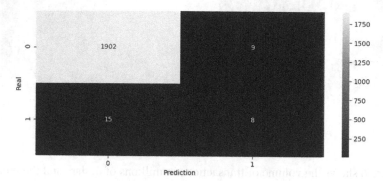

Fig. 7. RF confusion matrix.

Table 10. RF confusion matrix metrics.

Metric	Calculation	Value
Accuracy	(VN + VP)/(VN + VP + FN + FP) = (VN + VP + FN + FP)/(VN + VP + FN + FP) = (1902 + 8)/(1902 + 8 + 15 + 9)	98.76%
Accuracy	VP/(VP + FP) = 8/(8 + 9)	47.05%
Sensitivity	VP/(VP + FN) = 8/(8 + 15)	34.78%
F1 Score	2 * (Accuracy * Sensitivity)/(Accuracy + Sensitivity)	40.00%
Error rate	(FN + FP)/(VN + VP + FN + FP) = (FN + FP)/ (VN + VP + FN + FP) = (15 + 9)/(1902 + 8 + 15 + 9)	1.24%
Specificity	VN/(VN + FP) = 1902/(1902 + 8)	99.58%

Because there are more false negatives than false positives the sensitivity is lower than the accuracy. The sensitivity with a value of 34.78 is not very good and indicates that of the cases that are actually positive how many cases the model can capture or predict as positive. The f1 score can be interpreted as a weighted average of the precision and the sensitivity represents a value of 40.00.

The confusion matrix obtained from the model generated with the XGB algorithm is illustrated in Fig. 8. It can be seen that there are more false positives (33) than false negatives (10). Table 11 illustrates the metrics of the model generated by the XGB.

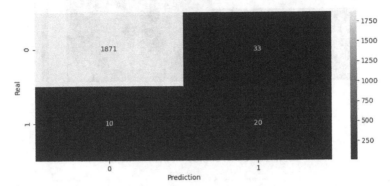

Fig. 8. XGB confusion matrix.

Table 11. XGB confusion matrix metrics.

Metric	Calculation	Value
Accuracy	(VN + VP)/(VN + VP + FN + FP) = (VN + VP + FN + FP)/(VN + VP + FN + FP) = (1871 + 70)/(1871 + 70 + 10 + 33)	97,83%
Accuracy	VP/(VP + FP) = 20/(20 + 33)	37,73%
Sensitivity	VP/(VP + FN) = 20/(20 + 10)	66,66%
F1 Score	2 * (Accuracy * Sensitivity)/(Accuracy + Sensitivity)	48,19%
Specificity	VN/(VN + FP) = 1871/(1871 + 33)	98,26%

Because there are more false positives than false negatives the precision is lower than the sensitivity. The precision with a value of 37.73 is not very good and indicates that of the cases that the model predicts as positive how many are actually positive. The f1 score which can be interpreted as a weighted average of the precision and sensitivity represents a value of 48,19.

The confusion matrix obtained from the model generated with the support vector machine algorithm is illustrated in Fig. 9. It can be seen that there are more false positives (34) than false negatives (13).

Table 12 illustrates the metrics of the model generated by the Support Vector Machine algorithm.

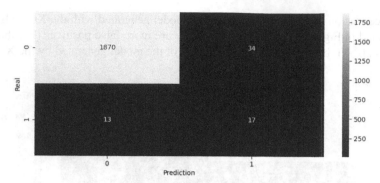

Fig. 9. SVM confusion matrix.

Table 12. SVM confusion matrix metrics.

Metric	Calculation	Value
Accuracy	(VN + VP)/(VN + VP + FN + FP) = (VN + VP + FN + FP)/(VN + VP + FN + FP) = (1870 + 17)/(1870 + 17 + 13 + 34)	97,57%
Accuracy	VP/(VP + FP) = 17/(17 + 34)	33,33%
Sensitivity	VP/(VP + FN) = 17/(17 + 13)	56,66%
F1 Score	2 * (Accuracy * Sensitivity)/(Accuracy + Sensitivity)	41,98%
Error rate	FN + FP)/(VN + VP + FN + FP) = (VN + VP + FN + FP) = (FN + FP)/(VN + VP + FN + FP) = (13 + 34)/(1870 + 17 + 13 + 34)	2,43%
Specificity	VN/(VN + FP) = 1870/(1870 + 34)	98,21%

Because there are more false positives than false negatives the precision is lower than the sensitivity. The precision with a value of 33.73 is not as good and indicates that of the cases that the model predicts as positive how many are actually positive. The f1 score which can be interpreted as a weighted average of the precision and sensitivity represents a value of 41.98.

The confusion matrix obtained from the model generated with the stacking classifier method is presented in Fig. 56. It can be seen that the difference between false positives (10) and false negatives (12) is not very marked (Fig. 10).

Table 13 illustrates the metrics of the model generated with the stacking classifier method.

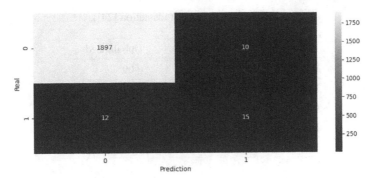

Fig. 10. SC confusion matrix.

Table 13. SC confusion matrix metrics.

Metric	Calculation	Value
Accuracy	(VN + VP)/(VN + VP + FN + FP) = (VN + VP + FN + FP)/(VN + VP + FN + FP) = (1897 + 15)/(1897 + 15 + 12 + 10)	98,86%
Accuracy	VP/(VP + FP) = 15/(15 + 10)	60,00%
Sensitivity	VP/(VP + FN) = 15/(15 + 12)	55,55%
F1 Score	2 * (Accuracy * Sensitivity)/(Accuracy + Sensitivity)	57,69%
Error rate	(FN + FP)/(VN + VP + FN + FP) = (FN + FP)/ (VN + VP + FN + FP) = (12 + 10)/(1897 + 15 + 12 + 10)	1,14%
Specificity	VN/(VN + FP) = 1897/(1897 + 10)	99,47%

Because the difference between false positives and false negatives is not very marked, the accuracy is somewhat equated with the sensitivity. The f1 score which can be interpreted as a weighted average of accuracy and sensitivity represents a value of 57.69 which is higher than the individual models. As the data are not balanced, the precision-sensitivity curve is used instead of the ROC curve as the ROC curve may be optimistic under severe class imbalance, especially when the number of examples in the minority class is small.

To easily measure the success of a classification model based on AUC, Gorunescu [24] presents different ranges for interpreting the AUC of the accuracy-sensitivity curve (Table 14).

Figure 11 illustrates the accuracy - sensitivity curve of the final model.

Table 14. AUC ranges (adaptation [24]).

Interpretation	Balanced	Unbalanced
Random	0.50	0.09
Malo	0.74	0.23
Good	0.84	0.51
Excellent	0.98	0.90
Perfect	1.00	1.00

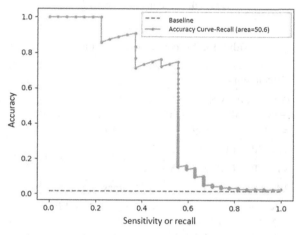

Fig. 11. Accuracy-sensitivity curve of the final model.

According to the AUC rank table and with an AUC of 50.6 it can be said that the final model using the stacking classifier method is relatively good.

5 Conclusions

The descriptive model that was built aims to find unusual anomalous customer behavior that deviates from normal behavior or, in other words, to detect anomalies, so customer transnationality was analyzed for each profession to find anomalies. This resulted in records marked as anomalies with a medium or high level of risk. The anomalies detected do not necessarily represent observations linked to money laundering. Therefore, the use of unsupervised learning for the detection of unusual transactions requires extensive follow-up and validation of the suspicious observations identified.

For the development of the predictive model, the main drawback is that the data are unbalanced, i.e. the events of interest are few in relation to the other events, when applying different algorithms to obtain the model, the performance of the models generated is sub-optimal, so the techniques of under sampling (eliminates or combines records of the majority class) and oversampling (creates new synthetic records of the minority class) are used, and oversampling (creating new synthetic records from the minority class). Using the two techniques in combination yields more effective results than using the two techniques in isolation, so we first oversampled and then under sampled the training partition.

Several models were built with different algorithms, obtaining acceptable performance with the RandomForest, Extreme Gradient Boosting and Support Vector Machine algorithms. To improve the confusion matrix metrics of these three models, the Stacking Classifier method was applied to create a final model and the f1 score of the individual models was improved. It can be concluded that multiple algorithms can capture different parts of the input data space and as such complement each other's deficiencies.

Based on the results obtained, the hypothesis is somewhat rejected as the descriptive, predictive and rule-based system analysis techniques can complement each other as they focus on different aspects of the identification of unusual transactions and should not be considered as exclusive alternatives. An effective suspicious behavior detection system will make use of and combine these different tools, which have different capabilities and limitations, and will therefore reinforce each other when applied in a combined configuration.

References

1. Adewumi, A.O., Akinyelu, A.A.: A survey of machine-learning and nature-inspired based credit card fraud detection techniques. Int. J. Syst. Assur. Eng. Manag. **8**(2), 937–953 (2017). https://doi.org/10.1007/s13198-016-0551-y
2. Sharif, O., Hoque, M.M., Kayes, A.S.M., Nowrozy, R., Sarker, I.H.: Detecting suspicious texts using machine learning techniques. Appl. Sci. **10**(18), 1–23 (2020)
3. Clarke, B., Fokoue, E., Zhang, H.H.: Principles and Theory for Data Mining and Machine Learning. Springer, New York (2009). https://doi.org/10.1007/978-0-387-98135-2
4. Flach, P.: Machine Learning: The Art and Science of Algorithms that Make Sense of Data. Cambridge University Press, Cambridge (2012)
5. Ross, I.: Exposing Fraud: Skills, Process and Practicalities. Wiley, Hoboken (2016)
6. Danenas, P.: Intelligent financial fraud detection and analysis: a survey of recent patents. Recent Patents Comput. Sci. **8**(1), 13–23 (2015)
7. More, R., Awati, C., Shirgave, S., Deshmukh, R., Patil, S.: Credit card fraud detection using supervised learning approach. Int. J. Sci. Technol. Res. **9**, 216–219 (2021)
8. Bolton, R.J., Hand, D.J.: Statistical fraud detection: a review. Stat. Sci. **17**(3), 235–255 (2020)
9. Young, M.R.: Financial Fraud Prevention and Detection: Governance and Effective Practices. Wiley, Hoboken (2014)
10. Spann, D.D.: Fraud Analytics: Strategies and Methods for Detection and Prevention. Wiley, Hoboken (2013)
11. Baesens, B., Vlasselaer, V.V., Verbeke, W.: Fraud Analytics Using Descriptive, Predictive, and Social Network Techniques: A Guide to Data Science for Fraud Detection. Wiley, Hoboken (2015)
12. Witten, I.H., Frank, E.: Data Mining: Practical Machine Learning Tools and Techniques. Morgan Kaufmann, Burlington (2005)
13. Swamynathan, M.: Mastering Machine Learning with Python in Six Steps: A Practical Implementation Guide to Predictive Data Analytics Using Python. Apress, New York (2017)
14. Shmueli, G., Bruce, P.C., Gedeck, P., Patel, N.R.: Data Mining for Business Analytics: Concepts, Techniques and Applications in Python. Wiley, Hoboken (2020)

15. Vona, L.W.: Fraud Data Analytics Methodology: The Fraud Scenario Approach to Uncovering Fraud in Core Business Systems. Wiley, Hoboken (2017)
16. Géron, A.: Hands-On Machine Learning with Scikit-Learn, Keras, and TensorFlow: Concepts, Tools, and Techniques to Build Intelligent Systems. O'Reilly Media, Sebastopol (2019)
17. Bowles, M.: Machine Learning in Python: Essential Techniques for Predictive Analysis. Wiley, Hoboken (2015)
18. Julian, D.: Designing Machine Learning Systems with Python: Design Efficient Machine Learning Systems that Give You More Accurate Results. Packt, Birmingham (2016)
19. Breiman, L.: Random forests. Mach. Learn. **45**, 5–32 (2001). https://doi.org/10.1023/A:101 0933404324
20. Cutler, A., Cutler, D.R., Stevens, J.R.: Random forests. In: Zhang, C., Ma, Y. (eds.) Ensemble Machine Learning. Springer, Boston (2012). https://doi.org/10.1007/978-1-4419-9326-7_5
21. Carmona, P., Climent, F., Momparler, A.: Predicting failure in the US banking sector: an extreme gradient boosting approach. Int. Rev. Econ. Finance **61**, 304–323 (2019)
22. Cervantes, J., Garcia-Lamont, F., Rodríguez-Mazahua, L., Lopez, A.: A comprehensive survey on support vector machine classification: applications, challenges and trends. Neurocomputing **408**, 189–215 (2020)
23. Dabbas, E.: Interactive Dashboards and Data Apps with Plotly and Dash: Harness the Power of a Fully Fledged Frontend Web Framework in Python - no JavaScript Required. Packt, Birmingham (2021)
24. Döble, M., Großmann, T.: Data Visualization with Python: Create an Impact with Meaningful Data Insights Using Interactive and Engaging Visuals. Packt, Birmingham (2019)
25. Layton, R.: Learning Data Mining with Python: Harness the Power of Python to Analyze Data and Create Insightful Predictive Models. Packt, Birmingham (2015)
26. Belorkar, A., Guntuku, S.C., Hora, S., Kumar, A.: Interactive Data Visualization with Python Second Edition: Present Your Data as an Effective and Compelling Story. Packt, Birmingham (2020)
27. Gorunescu, F.: Data Mining: Concepts, Models and Techniques. Springer, Heidelberg (2011). https://doi.org/10.1007/978-3-642-19721-5

Autoclassify Software Defects Using Orthogonal Defect Classification

Sushil Kumar[1]($\boxtimes$), Meera Sharma[2], S. K. Muttoo[3], and V. B. Singh[4]

[1] Shyam Lal College, University of Delhi, Delhi, India
kumar.sk106@gmail.com
[2] Swami Shraddhanand College, University of Delhi, Delhi, India
meerasharma@ss.du.ac.in
[3] Department of Computer Science, University of Delhi, Delhi, India
[4] School of computer and systems sciences, JNU, New Delhi, India
vbsingh@mail.jnu.ac.in

Abstract. Software systems have become an integral part of all the organizations. These systems are performing many critical operations. A defect in these systems affects the product quality and the software development process. Prediction of the impact category of these defects helps in improving defect management process as well as taking correct decisions to fix defects. Orthogonal defect classification is a popular model for classifying defects and it provides an in-depth analysis of the defects. In this study, we proposed an auto classify approach to classify the defects into impact categories as defined by Orthogonal Defect Classification (ODC). Bag of words, term frequency-inverse document frequency and word embedding have been used to represent the textual data into numeric vectors. For experimental work, we have used 4,096 reports form three NoSQL databases. We have trained and tested the proposed autoclassify approach using Support Vector Machine (SVM) and Random Forest Classifier (RFC). We achieved maximum accuracy 94% and 85.99% using SVM and RFC respectively.

Keywords: Orthogonal defect classification · Bag of words · Term frequency inverse document frequency · Word embedding

1 Introduction

Business organizations are using software to record and maintain data about their employees, products and various operations such as financial and database management. Predicting the impact of these defects can help us to save cost and time in software development as well as in improving software defect prediction and classification models. ODC [1, 2] is a well-defined framework for analysing and classifying defects during software development. It is a systematic approach that provides a valuable feedback method for assessing the different phases of the software development. ODC can be applied in any phase to capture the semantic of each defect quickly. It characterizes the defects into eight attributes by knowing cause and its effect on the quality of software product. The ODC attributes include defect type, impact, trigger, activity, target, source,

O. Gervasi et al. (Eds.): ICCSA 2022 Workshops, LNCS 13381, pp. 313–322, 2022.
https://doi.org/10.1007/978-3-031-10548-7_23

qualifier and age. Defect type denotes change made to solve or correct a problem. The change can be in a function, condition and assignment. Impact refers to an experience of a user when the defect was surfaced. Impact can be capability, reliability, usability etc. Activity refers to the action performed when a defect was disclosed. Code inspection and function test are the actions fall under the activity attribute. Target refers to the object of the correction i.e., the build scripts or package. Trigger is a condition which makes a defect to occur. Qualifier describes the code point before a correction was made. Source refers to the origin of the defect i.e., the location of the defect where it was initially occurred. Age refers to the occurrence of a defect to the correction of another defect.

ODC is a systematic approach which helps in prioritizing the defects and assigning defects to the experts. It also enables managers to take correct decisions after they know the category of the defect. It helps in improving software defect prediction techniques. The systematic classification of software failures allows us to know the impacts on the software product quality. ODC further divides the impact attribute into 13 categories to understand the nature of impact. Impact category includes usability, performance, capability, installability, documentation, capacity, migration, serviceability, standards, integrity/security, serviceability, and reliability.

Bridge and Miller [3] presented a methodology that successfully applied the ODC to classify the defects found in Motorola GSM division. They successfully applied the orthogonal defect classification to software development group. Zheng et al. [4] applied ODC to analyse the software defects by adopting defect type attributes with the development process.

The limitation of the ODC is the manual classification of defect reports which is a time taking process and involves high cost. This process of manual classification becomes a complex task when the number of defect reports increases. Hence, there is a need to automate this process. Therefore, we propose an autoclassify classification approach to automate the process of defect classification based on ODC impact attributes.

The important highlights of the proposed autoclassify approach are:

- Defect reports classification using textual description of the defect;
- Model the classification approach into a multiclass text classification;
- Bag of words, term frequency inverse document frequency and GloVe word embedding were employed;
- 4,096 defect reports from Hbase, MongoDb and cassandra;
- Synthetic Minority Over Sampling Technique (SMOTE) for balancing the data distribution among ODC impact categories;
- The proposed approach evaluate the performance of SVM and RFC;
- SVM and RFC classify the defects with accuracy of 94% and 85.99% respectively.

The remainder of the paper is divided into six parts. ODC based related work has been introduced in Sect. 2. Proposed approach and results are discussed in Sects. 3 and 4 respectively. Section 5 presents the threats to validity of the work and finally work is concluded in the last section.

2   Related Work

ODC defect type and impact have been widely used in literature to classify the defect reports. Some proposed studies have used a single attribute such as impact or type while others have focused on multiple ODC attributes. A common problem is that the defects are manually classified by the experts or researchers in the field which is very tedious and time consuming process. Hence, there is a need to automate the process of classification. A classification approach has been introduced in literature, which classifies defects automatically by grouping ODC defect types in categories like non-functional, control and data flow and structural [5]. The categories Algorithm/Method, Assignment/Initialization, Checking, Timing/Serialization are grouped into control and flow. Function/Class/Object, Interface/O-O Messages and Relationship are grouped into Structural. Remaining defect types are grouped as non-functional. Total 500 defect reports were collected and labeled manually. The proposed approach achieves an average accuracy of 77.8% using support vector machine. The authors used the expert's experience to label the defects and evaluate the performance on minimal labeled data.

In another study [6] an active semi supervised approach has been proposed to minimize the effort of manual labeling. Out of 500 defect reports, only 50 defect reports were manually labeled. The proposed approach achieved a weighted precision, recall, f-measure and area under curve (AUC) score of 65.1%, 66.9%, 62.3% and 71% respectively.

In [7], authors suggested a method for automatically classifying software bugs based on attributes retrieved from the Abstract Syntax Tree (AST) of the source code. The approach was assessed by labeling the 1,174 defect reports into four categories, Computational, Control or Logic, Data and Interface. The experimental results show the highest accuracy, precision and recall of 79%, 75% and 73% respectively. With minimum number of classes, the classification task seems to be easy as compared to the eight ODC attributes and their sub-attributes.

An Auto ODC technique to classify the software defects according to ODC defect impact attribute has been presented in [8]. The technique combines ODC expertise with domain knowledge. The authors also proposed an annotation framework to assign a category with justification.

In [9], the authors presented a software defect classification approach using crowd labeling for 1,444 defect reports from two datasets compendium and Mozilla, and labeled according to ODC defect impact by set of 5 annotators having no expertise in the field. The authors used 4 out of 14 impact categories to train the classifier.

Recently, in [10] authors presented an automatic classification of software defects using supervised machine learning algorithms. For experimental work, Authors collect and manually labels the 4,096 defect reports according to all ODC attributes. As opposed to the previous work, we have generated a new word embedding along with pre trained embedding GloVe by Stanford. Similar work [11] discusses the effectiveness of word embedding techniques to envisage the intensity of defect in the software product. Similarly authors [12] presented a bug severity assessment to predict the forecity of the bug reports in the context of cross project. The previous research has employed multiple ODC defect attributes to automate the process of defect classification. Moreover, the exiting works use the Tf-Idf or Bag of Words (BoW) model to represent the words in numerical vectors. In this work, we generate numerical vectors for defect corpus using GloVe word embedding [13]. Word embedding represents the similar words into similar vector representation and hence able to capture the semantic of the words. Recently word embedding techniques have been used in [14–17].

3 Proposed Approach

The proposed approach can be viewed as a 5 step process from collecting dataset to get the results shown in Fig. 1.

Step 1: Collecting the dataset
We have collected a dataset consisting of 4,096 defect reports from http://odc.dei.uc.pt/. The dataset contains software defect reports from Hbase, Cassandra and MongoDB. The defects are labeled by the researchers by considering the six orthogonal defect attributes, namely defect type, Trigger, Activity, Impact, Target and Qualifier. For this study, we use the impact attribute that is further divided into following categories- Capability, Usability, Installability, Maintenance, Integrity/Security, Documentation, Serviceability, Performance, Reliability and Requirements.

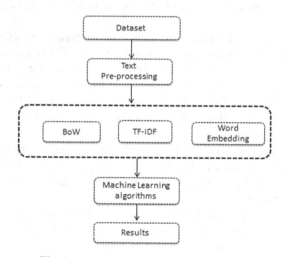

Fig. 1. Overview of the proposed approach

Step 2: Text Preprocessing
The dataset contains two fields summary and impact categories. Each defect report contains a textual description about the defect. For example, a defect report with summary *"misspelled columsort attribute* results *deleted commit logs db files"* has been labeled with *"Reliability"* category. We preprocess the text by applying text mining techniques such as removing punctuation and stop words, converting into lowercase and tokenize the text. Stop words were removed using stop word provided in NLTK library. Finally, we get the cleaned and tokenized text.

Step 3: Text to numbers
We have used three schemes- Tf-Idf, GloVe word embedding and BoW, to construct the numeric vector from tokenized corpus. In bag of words, a binary vector is created for each word in each report. If a word is present in the report, it is assigned 1 otherwise 0. Bag of words is a count based method.

Tf-Idf is frequency based method which specifies the importance of a word in a report. Tf refers to the term frequency and calculated using Eq. (1). The inverse document frequency is calculated using Eq. (2). Finally, Tf-Idf is the product of Tf and Idf score as shown in (3).

$$Tf_{i,j} = \frac{\#times \ a \ word \ i \ appear \ in \ a \ document \ j}{\#total \ document} \tag{1}$$

$$Idf_i = log\frac{\#total \ document}{\#document \ containing i} \tag{2}$$

$$TfIdf = Tf \times Idf \tag{3}$$

Word embedding is a process to represent the text into word vectors of fixed size. The idea behind word embedding is that words having similar meaning have similar representation. We use GloVe word embedding in this work. GloVe word embedding model [13] is based on the word occurrences. We downloaded the GloVe pre trained word2vec model from http://nlp.stanford.edu/data/glove.6B.zip. It contains 1.2 million word embedding. Pre trained GloVe word embedding is used in many classification tasks [18, 19]. It has been used recently for text classification [25–28].

Step 4: Machine learning algorithms
In this work, we have used two classifiers SVM and RFC. SVM [20, 21] is most widely used supervised classification algorithm. SVM is a binary classifier that separates two classes by finding the optimal hyper plane by minimizing the cost function between the feature points using Eq. (4) and (5).

$$min\frac{1}{2}\left\|w^2\right\| + C\sum \xi_i \tag{4}$$

$$s.t \ y_i\left(w^T x_i + b\right) \geq 1 - \xi_i \tag{5}$$

where C is the parameter between margin and error. ξ_i represents the measure of training. But it can be extended to a multiclass classification problem by using the combination of several binary support vector machine classifiers. Many methods exist for modeling a multiclass problem into a series of n binary sub problems. For this study, we have used one against all approach (OAA) in which the ith classifier is trained to differentiate the examples belong to i^{th} class from rest of the examples. Because of the variety of kernel functions utilized, SVM can handle the high volume data. SVM has been utilized in variety of investigations.

A set of random trees is used in the Random Forest classifier (RFC) [22]. It selects the features at random to create distinct trees. The bagging method [23] is proposed in which, distinct trees are trained parallelly depending on the supplied information.

Bootstrapping aggregation guarantees that each tree in the random forest is distinct lowering the classifier's variance. RFC can accurately classify massive amounts of data. Because of its random character, it is less prone to over fitting. In comparison to other algorithms, RFC yields more consistent results.

Step 5: Results
The classification performance is presented using four evaluation metrics, namely accuracy, precision, recall and F1 score.

4 Experimental Setup

This section presents the dataset details and performance evaluation.

4.1 Dataset

For the experimental work, we used the same dataset as used in [10]. The dataset is publically available and it is verified by the two researchers. The agreement between these researchers is calculated using kohen kappa agreement. For the impact ODC attribute, the kohen kappa value is 82% which is almost perfect. The dataset details are outlined in Table 1. The impact attribute is further divided into 13 categories. In this study, we have used only 6 categories- capability, integrity/security, performance, reliability, requirements and serviceability. The rest of the categories have assigned to very few reports.

Table 1. Dataset details

Defect impact	#Reports
Capability	2,165
Integrity/Security	87
Performance	199
Reliability	988
Requirements	227
Serviceability	156

Comments, title and description are the part of the defect report which helps in defect report classification manually into orthogonal defect classification impact attributes. Researchers have assigned the capability category to 50% of the data. The defect impact categories are varying proportionally and lead to an imbalance problem. To tackle this, we use Synthetic Minority Over Sampling Technique (SMOTE) [24] for balancing the data distribution for the defect impact categories.

4.2 Evaluation Metric

We evaluated the efficiency of our proposed approach using four metrics like F1 score, precision, accuracy and recall. A confusion matrix consisting of actual and predicted values is used to calculate these four metrics: accuracy, Precision, Recall and F1 score are calculated as follows;

$$Accuracy = \frac{tp_c + tn_c}{tp_c + fp_c + tn_c + fn_c} \tag{6}$$

$$Precision = \frac{tp_c}{tp_c + fp_c} \tag{7}$$

$$Recall = \frac{tp_c}{tp_c + fn_c} \tag{8}$$

$$F1 = 2 * \frac{Precision_i * recall_i}{Prcision_i * recall_i} \tag{9}$$

where tp_c and tn_c represents the true positive and true negative which is the number of instances correctly and not correctly respectively classified as class c; while they belong to some other classes. fp_c represents the false positive which is the number of instances correctly not classified as c; tp_c represents the true negative which is the number of instances assigned to some other classes while they belong to class c.

5 Results

We evaluated the performance of two classifiers SVM and RFC by learning features using three methods BoW, Tf-Idf and GloVe word embedding. The results obtained by these classifiers in terms of accuracy, precision, recall and F1 are presented in Table 2. In Bag of words method, each defect report is represented as numerical vector consists of total count i.e. the number of times a word present in a particular defect report. A total of 23,530 unique words are present in the defect corpus and forms a feature matrix where row represent the defect reports while columns are the unique words. The proposed approach achieves accuracy of 64.03% for RFC and 62.15% for SVM. Tf-Idf is a frequency based method to convert text into numeric vectors. The Tf-Idf score is inversely proportional to the occurrence of a word in the document. Our approach achieves an accuracy of 85.99% and 94% for RFC and SVM. We have used GloVe pre trained word embedding to get the real valued vectors of fixed dimension. The dimension for each vector is taken as 300. We downloaded the GloVe word embedding from http://nlp.stanford.edu/data/glove.6B.zip. We fed our defect corpus to GloVe to generate the numerical vectors for the words present in the corpus. Using these vectors, RFC and SVM are able to achieve 72.26% and 81.43% accuracy. There are some tunable parameters associated with classifiers to get the optimum results. GridSearchCV is used to search the best parameter for both the classifiers- RFC and SVM. For RFC, we search for the number of trees. The number of trees for all the experiments varies from 128 to 1,024. For SVM, we search for C and for C = 1 we get the highest accuracy, precision, recall and F1 score. We carried out all the experimental work in Python.

Table 2. Accuracy, precision recall and F1 (%)

Method	Classifier	Accuracy	Precision	Recall	F1
BoW	RFC	64.03	60.28	58.81	54.61
	SVM	62.15	59.64	54.09	52.82
TF-IDF	RFC	85.99	86.21	85.20	82.68
	SVM	94	95.08	93.99	93.85
GloVe	RFC	72.26	71	62.24	60.11
	SVM	81.43	79.67	74.56	71.38

6 Threats to Validity

In terms of external threats, an obvious threat is the training from word vectors which is generated for the thousands of defect reports. But the word vectors can be further improved. The distribution of the classes in the datasets is not uniform. The chance of biased learning is high. We attempted to eliminate the bias. The external threat is also concerned about the size of defect reports and brief description of each defect is also a concern to the external threat. In the future, this hazard can be mitigated in the future by using a larger dataset to provide more accurate results. In terms of construct validity, the issues in defect repositories such as defect duplication must be addressed. Only description of defect is extracted for all the three datasets Cassandra, Hbase and MongoDB. Moreover the dataset is transformed into 6-class classification problem due to the assignment of remaining classes to fewer defect reports. However more techniques should be adopted, to deal with multiclass imbalance problem. The internal validity is related with how the examined systems are represented and how well the classifiers function on the combined datasets. However, they differ for every combination of the datasets. That may be due to the discriminant ability of textual description of the defect. It can also be affected by the word embedding produced by pre trained word embedding model. As a result, machine learning algorithms must react to different contexts.

7 Conclusion

We present an autoclassify approach to automate the defect classification into impact categories as defined by ODC. For evaluating the efficiency of the proposed approach, we test the performance of support vector machine and random forest in terms of accuracy, precision, recall and F1 score on 4,096 defect reports collected from Hbase, MongoDb and Cassandra. We model the autoclassify approach as multiclass text classification problem. We represent the text into numeric vectors using pre trained word embedding GloVe, Term Frequency Inverse Document Frequency and Bag of Words. Word embedding is generated for the defect corpus using GloVe. SVM and RFC achieves highest accuracy 94% and 85.99% while learning form the frequency based method i.e. Tf-Idf. However the proposed approach can be further improved on large number of defect reports. In future, we will also evaluate the performance of proposed approach on other machine learning classifiers including Naïve Bayes and XGboost.

References

1. Chillarege, R., et al.: Orthongonal defect classification-a concept for in-process measurements. IEEE Trans. Software Eng. **18**(11), 943–956 (1992)
2. Chillarege, R.: Orthogonal defect classification. In: Lyu, M.R. (ed.) Handbook of Software Reliability Engineering, pp. 359–399. IEEE CS Press, Los Alamitos (1996)
3. Bridge, N., Miller, C.: Orthogonal defect classification using defect data to improve software development. Softw. Qual. **3**(1), 1–8 (1998)
4. Zheng, J., Williams, L.: Nagappan, N., Snipes, W., Hudepohl, J. P., Vouk, M. A.: On the value of static analysis for fault detection in software. IEEE Trans. Softw. Eng. **32**(4), 240–253 (2006)
5. Thung, F., Lo, D. Jiang, L.: Automatic defect categorization. In 19th Working Conference on Reverse Engineering, pp. 205–214. IEEE (2012)
6. Thung, F., Le, X.B.D., Lo, D.: Active semi-supervised defect categorization. In: IEEE 23rd International Conference on Program Comprehension, pp. 60–70. IEEE (2015)
7. Liu, C., Zhao, Y., Yang, Y., Lu, H., Zhou, Y., Xu, B.: An AST-based approach to classifying defects. In: IEEE International Conference on Software Quality, Reliability and Security-Companion, pp. 14–21. IEEE (2015)
8. Huang, L., et al.: AutoODC: automated generation of orthogonal defect classifications. Autom. Softw. Eng. **22**(1), 3–46 (2015)
9. Hernández-González, J., Rodriguez, D., Inza, I., Harrison, R., Lozano, J.A.: Learning to classify software defects from crowds: a novel approach. Appl. Soft Comput. **62**, 579–591 (2018)
10. Lopes, F., Agnelo, J., Teixeira, C.A., Laranjeiro, N., Bernardino, J.: Automating orthogonal defect classification using machine learning algorithms. Futur. Gener. Comput. Syst. **102**, 932–947 (2020)
11. Kumar, L., Kumar, M., Murthy, L.B., Misra, S., Kocher, V. Padmanabhuni, S.: An empirical study on application of word embedding techniques for prediction of software defect severity level. In:16th Conference on Computer Science and Intelligence Systems (FedCSIS), pp. 477–484. IEEE (2021)
12. Singh, V.B., Misra, S., Sharma, M.: Defect severity assessment in cross project context and identifying training candidates. J. Inf. Knowl. Manag. **16**(01), 1750005 (2002)
13. Pennington, J., Socher, R., Manning, C.D.: Glove: global vectors for word representation. EMNLP **14**, 1532–1543 (2014)
14. Sangwan, N., Bhatnagar, V.: Optimized text classification using deep learning. In: Goar, V., Kuri, M., Kumar, R., Senjyu, T. (eds.) Advances in Information Communication Technology and Computing. LNNS, vol. 135, pp. 293–302. Springer, Singapore (2021). https://doi.org/10.1007/978-981-15-5421-6_30
15. Sivakumar, S., Rajalakshmi, R.: Analysis of sentiment on movie reviews using word embedding self-attentive LSTM. Int. J. Amb. Comput. Intell. **12**(2), 33–52 (2021)
16. Bayer, M., Kaufhold, M., Reuter, C: A survey on data augmentation for text classification. arXiv preprint arXiv:2107.03158 (2021)
17. Rahimi, Z., Homayounpour, M.M.: TensSent: a tensor based sentimental word embedding method. Appl. Intell. **51**(8), 6056–6071 (2021). https://doi.org/10.1007/s10489-020-02163-8
18. Lu, X., et al.: MKPM: Multi keyword-pair matching for natural language sentences. Appl. Intell. **52**(2), 1878–1892 (2021). https://doi.org/10.1007/s10489-021-02306-5
19. Yue, C., Cao, H., Xu, G., Dong, Y.: Collaborative attention neural network for multi-domain sentiment classification. Appl. Intell. **51**(6), 3174–3188 (2020). https://doi.org/10.1007/s10489-020-02021-7
20. Cortes, C., Vapnik, V.: Support-vector networks. Mach. Learn. **20**(3), 273–297 (1995)

21. Duan, K.B., Keerthi, S.S.: Which is the best multiclass SVM method? An empirical study. In: Oza, N.C., Polikar, R., Kittler, J., Roli, F. (eds.) MCS 2005. LNCS, vol. 3541, pp. 278–285. Springer, Heidelberg (2005). https://doi.org/10.1007/11494683_28
22. Breiman, L.: Random Forests. Mach Learn. **45**, 5–32 (2001)
23. Breiman, L.: Bagging predictors. Mach. Learn. **24**(2), 123–140 (1996)
24. Chawla, N.V., Bowyer, K.W., Hall, L.O., Kegelmeyer, W.P.: SMOTE: synthetic minority over-sampling technique. J. Artif. Intell. Res. **16**, 321–357 (2002)
25. Asudani, D. S., Nagwani, N.K., Singh, P.: Exploring the effectiveness of word embedding based deep learning model for improving email classification. Data Technol. Appl. **56**(1) (2022). https://doi.org/10.1108/dta-07-2021-0191. ISSN: 2514:9288
26. Hossain, T., Mauni, H.Z., Rab, R.: Reducing the effect of imbalance in text classification using SVD and GloVe with ensemble and deep learning. Comput. Inform. **41**(1), 98–115 (2022)
27. Ebrahimi, F., Tushev, M., Mahmoud, A.: Classifying mobile applications using word embeddings. ACM Trans. Softw. Eng. Methodol. (TOSEM) **31**(2), 1–30 (2021)
28. Kirelli, Y., Özdemir, Ş. Sentiment classification performance analysis based on glove word embedding. Sakarya Univ. J. Sci. **25**(3), 639–646 (2021)

Traffic Control System Development Based on Computer Vision

Diogo Eugênio da Silva Cortez, Itamir de Morais Barroca Filho(✉),
Everson Mizael Cortez Silva, and Gustavo Girão

Digital Metropolis Institute, Federal University of Rio Grande do Norte Natal, Lagoa Nova,
Natal, Brazil
{itamir.filho,girao}@imd.ufrn.br
http://www.imd.ufrn.br, http://www.ufrn.br

Abstract. In 2020, the number of Brazil inhabitants was approximately 212 millions, whereas the number of vehicles jumped from 104 to 107 millions. It is observed, therefore, that there is 1 vehicle for every 2 inhabitants. That same year, the population in urban areas went to 80%. Managing traffic in big cities is becoming a huge challenge. Traffic lights operating with Fixed Time Signal to control vehicle flux are no longer efficient in all traffic scenarios. Technological advances in Computer Vision, moving objects detection and classification techniques and the demanding of little computer power to manage these tasks allowed the development of TEOP, a CV-based traffic control system. This low cost solution was implemented to advance the Fixed Time Signal system, cameras and logical network infrastructure already in use in Brazilian cities, transforming regular traffic lights into smart traffic lights (STL). An application was developed and installed in a computer to capture images of traffic, count vehicles and calculate time needed for them to pass through. Raspberry controlled traffic lights. In comparison to regular traffic lights, STLs improved traffic flow by 33%, allowing a wait of just 4 s in cases where there is no vehicle flow at the competing traffic light and reducing the crossing time of 46 vehicles from 152 to 116 s when there were 12 vehicles on the competing side, a significant gain. It was also capable of reporting traffic jams and creating a database that could be used for decision-taking by agencies responsible for each route.

Keywords: Smart traffic management system · OpenCV · YOLO-Tiny · SSD · MobileNetV2

1 Introduction

According to 2020 data shown in [1] the vehicle fleet in Brazil and some of its states such as Rio Grande do Norte reaches approximately half the number of their respective populations. Most of these vehicles are registered in the metropolitan regions of the state.

The disorderly growth of urban areas, that are now housing 80% of Brazilians, was accompanied by continuous growth in vehicles as well. Excess traffic on streets are not only harmful, however, to life quality but also implies financial losses [2].

© The Author(s), under exclusive license to Springer Nature Switzerland AG 2022
O. Gervasi et al. (Eds.): ICCSA 2022 Workshops, LNCS 13381, pp. 323–339, 2022.
https://doi.org/10.1007/978-3-031-10548-7_24

The traffic light was first implemented in London, 1968, as a response to increasing traffic accident occurrences at the time. It remains the main traffic regulator to this date [3]. According [4] a traffic efficient system, including better time management for traffic lights, could reduce pollution in urban areas. In many parts of the world, vehicle traffic is the main cause for air pollution [5]. This happens because of the increase in gas usage when there is deficiency in traffic light programming.

Smart Traffic Lights (STLs) can use sensors or cameras to calculate the density of vehicles that go through it. With data in hands, it is possible to adequate light time and in turn provide better traffic flux. It is also possible to adjust dates, times and other parameters. Traffic connectivity with the traffic control unit allows configuration and monitoring of traffic light networks.

If adjusted according to the route's demands, smart traffic lights employ better traffic scenarios, while also being adaptable to other positive scenarios [6].

According to [7] one efficient traffic light control solution is the car flux automatic detection. According to literature review made by these authors, smart traffic lights are one of the most propelled nowadays to optimize traffic systems, but its high cost prevents mass implementation, especially in small towns.

According to [17] two and a half million dollars were spent on equipment and infrastructure for the installation of 88 traffic lights, an average of twenty six thousand dollars per traffic light.

Nowadays, many states and cities have high quality camera monitoring systems to help provide safety and control traffic [8]. In many cases, the systems have optic fiber infrastructure and/or wireless technology to allow high-definition image transferring.

The smart traffic light is highly recommended because it is able to improve traffic flow, according to the data collected by the sources mentioned above, so it is recommended to use the solution proposed in this work together with the implementation of the green wave to avoid excess traffic. traffic at adjacent traffic lights.

As it is a strategic issue of great relevance to cities, it is recommended to implement information security policies together with the solution proposed in this work. According to [10], it is not only present in hardware and software implementation, but information security in organizational units must also include infrastructure, logistics and human resources.

According to literature revision made by the authors, the majority of papers analyzed suggest traffic light control based on density of vehicles that traffic under it. Some of these studies found gaps that could make them unfeasible since they rely on camera images or the internet to generate time management and controlling traffic lights. Part of these papers shows the traffic light could freeze in the last time setting made, providing red light for an undetermined time. In other cases, traffic control systems would not allow broader parameter settings.

This paper intends to create a smart traffic control system using Computer Vision (CV). In order to do that, the traffic light and CV control algorithm will work on a PC computer, traffic lights will be controlled (turned on and off) through a single board unit with Raspberry Pi 3. Computer Vision would then count vehicles crossing the traffic light; in these instances, data collected is used to identify traffic jams. Besides, the system would also have redundancy for fixed time mode for instances where camera issues are identified. Other aspects of this solution are its low implementation costs, since it relies on already-installed traffic systems, cameras and other logic network infrastructure on multiple Brazilian cities, low energy usage and high efficiency. More differentials of the proposed system allow more than 50 adjustments to be configured for each traffic light allowing to customize each intersection to obtain maximum fluidity and improvements in vehicle counting, in addition to adapting working independently of cameras and the Internet, as it detects problems on these items and changes its working mode automatically.

This article was organized in the following structure: the second section presents the related works, the third section describes the methodology used and, in Fig. 3, shows the simplified operation of the algorithm used, the fourth section presents the tests, the fifth section presents the limitations found and finally, the contributions and future works are arranged in the sixth section.

2 Related Works

In order to improve traffic flow, according to literature revision, many analyzed studies suggest controlling traffic lights based on how many vehicles go through it. According to [9], who proposed traffic light control based on vehicle density, this technique allowed a 35% improvement in traffic flux when compared to pre-existing Fixed Time System traffic lights. Some works on the topic will be listed below:

In works of [11], they proposed a Distributed Traffic Control System. In this system, each traffic light has one camera pointed at each direction of the road. Employed were two techniques to count objects: the first one called border detection technique, used to count just vehicles, and the second, YOLO, would classify them. All systems were implemented using a Raspberry Pi 3. With the goal of verifying which techniques would come closer to real counting of objects in roads, a comparison was made between them. Towards the end of testing, border detection technique showed mistakes and remained distant from the quantity of objects passing through. On the other hand, YOLO showed closer results to what was expected. Authors say that Distributed Traffic Control System will give successful results, avoiding major delays and lowering traffic time.

On the other hand [12], proposed a Traffic Vigil System for Vehicle Counting. This system has each traffic light equipped with a camera pointed at each road direction. Background subtraction, detection and tracking through blobs were used to detect and count objects on the road. The system was implemented in a type PC computer, and experimental results showed that it could provide real-time useful information for traffic vigilance. This paper does not inform us if the traffic lights control is in use.

The proposal of [13], was a solution for real-time monitoring, tracking and counting of vehicles in the city of Jelgava, Latvia. This system has each traffic light equipped with a camera pointed at each road direction. Background subtraction, detection and tracking through blobs were used to detect and count objects on the road. The paper does not specify which hardware was used to count objects. Traffic light control is not the goal of this paper and, according to its authors, the system shows good performance and acceptable precision. In parts of the test, precision reached a 97% hits level for regular traffic conditions. Tests also showed that this system proved to be inadequate for traffic jam days.

The work of [14], proposes an ARM-based real-time Traffic Classification System. In this system, each traffic light is equipped with a camera pointed at each road direction. It suggests linking a single board computer based on ARM Cortex-A8 to each camera that will process images, count objects and send data to a remote server. The counting algorithm was Harris' border detection. Experiments showed that the proposed system could process real-time images four times quicker than other OpenCV-based implementations. Traffic light control was not the aim of this paper.

Whereas [15], proposed a System to detect Physical Characteristics of Objects in Traffic. However, the study does not inform how many cameras were used in this system. A PC computer was used to process images. Traffic light control was not the aim for this study. Tensorflow was also used to train learning models. Java and OpenCV were used to classify objects. Success rate in detecting size and object color was below 70%, although object classification rate was above 90%.

At last [16], proposed an Intelligent Control System for Traffic Intersections. In this study, Raspberry Pi 3 was used to capture and process traffic images., as well as controlling traffic lights. The entirety of this study works based on Raspberry Pi 3 B+. The Tensorflow with SSD and MobileNetV2 were used in model training and object detection. Developers made bench tests in small scale and according to these tests, the system functioned as expected, reducing waiting time in traffic for a minimum.

3 Methodology

After completing the bibliographic review, it was noted that there are numerous works with solutions to improve traffic flow based on the CV. Despite that, there are gaps that need filling, such as the traffic lights relying exclusively on data generated by camera images to work or, exclusive internet dependence to receive data and control traffic lights. In these instances, the traffic light might be disrupted; it can freeze in its last generated time setting, with the time of 0, 1 or 2 s for the red light, meaning the traffic light would always be red until the problem is solved. This issue was resolved in two steps: first, monitoring the health of cameras and internet was implemented in order to detect problems in these items. Second, if camera or internet problems are identified, the traffic light returns to work at fixed times until the problem is resolved.

During the planning of the system suggested by this work, it was observed that there are numerous possibilities for configuring the operating parameters of a traffic light. According to our bibliographical review, analyzed papers implemented a small part of these parameters, making it impossible for users to have access and alter them.

Therefore, the development of the Traffic Engineering Operations Center (TEOP) was proposed, which would create, set and manage traffic lights through WEB – smart traffic lights or fixed time signal traffic lights, which operate controlling vehicles using a predefined time stamp. Besides registration and system setting of a city's traffic light, TEOP can also work as an interface for the traffic light's state. By warning the Traffic Controller (TC) about the situation of each traffic light that comprises this system, either informing if they are working properly or if there is a communication problem between them or the cameras, or if there is congestion and their classification. TEOP will allow the Traffic Controller access to more than 50 traffic light configuration patterns, some examples of traffic light customization are: creating regions of interest (ROI), vehicle count line, size of detectable vehicles, fixed light time settings, time (in seconds) for each vehicle to pass the intersection, operation that can be legacy mode (fixed time operation), Photo mode (counting vehicles waiting for the green light to turn on and calculating the time for their passage) or Photo with Video mode (which allows counting the vehicles that manage to pass the intersection pointing out traffic jams depending on the number of vehicles that can pass), among dozens of other parameters.

And it will also allow the TC to train their own models using images from objects that usually pass through the traffic lights.

3.1 Selected Computer Vision Techniques

Every image processing, whether through detection or object classification, will work using the OpenCV 4 framework, which will load network classification settings for multiple objects through YOLOv3-Tiny, YOLOv4-Tiny and MobileNetV2. Alternatively, it will execute the detection algorithm by removing image background, MOG2. Algorithm that will work inside this framework is described as follows: MOG2 – according to [13], this algorithm detects motion based on background removal and shows great performance and acceptable precision, reaching 97% hits. YOLOv3, YOLOv4 – these algorithms detect and classify objects. According to [11], tests made with different condition images gave us an average precision around 91%. MobileNetV2 with SSDLite – just like YOLO, this algorithm detects and classify objects, and according to [16], MobileNetV2 with SSDLite is 20 times more efficient and 10 times smaller than YOLOv2, and using COCO dataset, with success rate comparable between them. For this work, the success rate is given by the number of vehicles correctly counted.

Aiming at providing hardware variety, the proposed solution allows the user to choose between CV technologies for live video according to their reality, between MOG2, MobileNetV2 with SSDLite, YOLOv3-Tiny and YOLOv4-Tiny.

3.2 Used Hardware

The computer model used in tests was the Dell 7050 notebook. This model was equipped with an Intel Core i5 7300HQ 2.5 GHz processor with integrated video and dedicated video Nvidia GTX 1050, 16 GB RAM and SSD A2000 PCIe NVMe. Besides the computer, which executes image capturing and processing and then controls the traffic lights, Raspberry Pi 3 was also used to serve as intermediate between the computer and traffic lights, and will execute commands to turn on and off traffic lights using times stamps calculated by the computer.

3.3 System Operation

Figure 1 shows the visual diagram with the working system. Circle number 1 identifies the system composed by the server that allows TEOP, web register system and traffic lights management. Circle number 2 highlights, organized in gray rectangles, some functions available on TEOP for users, such as traffic light register, operation mode selection, traffic light state follow up, network follow up and congestion follow up. It will also be possible to open and accompany calls to resolve traffic light issues, and the user could train the model using images from objects that traffic through the traffic light in question. Circle 3 shows the computer with the image processing algorithm and traffic light control, using the network to connect and capture images from the camera on circle 3a, which receives the images, processes them and obtains vehicle quantity while waiting for the traffic light to turn green. With this number, it calculates the time to open the traffic light and sends this information to Raspberry Pi 3, identified in circle 4, that will turn on and off lights according to information sent to the computer.

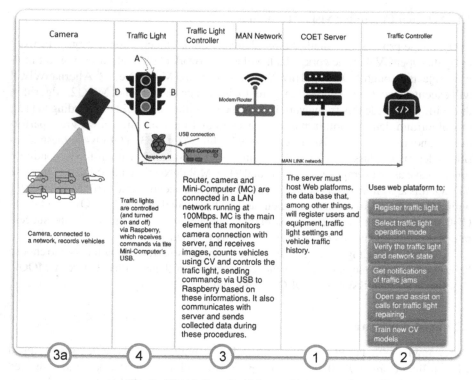

Fig. 1. Visual diagram of the working system

3.4 Preparation of Images Used in Training

In this work, models trained by the developers of YOLOv3-Tiny, YOLOv4-Tiny and MobileNetV2 were used, containing 80, 80 and 90 types of objects respectively. These models were used by the authors to create new models with six types of objects found in traffic, such as: people, bicycles, cars, motorcycles, buses and trucks. The objective was to compare models provided by developers with models trained by the authors and verify if there is any advantage or disadvantage in using a smaller number of objects.

The COCO 2014 database with more than 80 thousand images was used, and the author developed a tool separating the first 1 thousand objects of each of the six types mentioned. Later, the tool edited text documents referring to selected images and removed objects that would not be used. At this moment, there were 1 thousand objects of each class that were used in a percentage of 70% for training, 20% for tests and 10% for validation.

3.5 Model Training

After selecting the images, the learning transfer from YOLOv3-Tiny and YOLOv4-Tiny, which are simpler versions with fewer parameters of YOLO (recommended for CV on mobile and embedded devices), to the customized models used in the project, was carried out.

Then, the same procedure was performed using the MobileNetV2 algorithm. In this case, it was necessary to convert images to the Tensorflow TFRecord format. Training information is displayed in the Table 1 below:

Table 1. Information on utilized models.

Source	Algorithm	Classes	Dataset	Images per class	Training Time	mAP%	Training loss	Validation loss	Iterations
Devs.	yolov3-tiny	80	-	-	-	50%		-	-
Devs.	yolov4-tiny	80	COCO 2017	-	-	50%		-	-
Authors	yolov3-tiny	6	COCO 2014	1.000	9h 14min	52%	C:0.0%	-	12.000
Authors	yolov4-tiny	6	COCO 2014	1.000	7h 50min	70%	C:0.0%	-	12.000
Devs.	SSD MobileNetV2	90	COCO 2018	-	-	-	-	-	-
Authors	SSD MobileNetV2	6	COCO 2014	1.000	7h 38min	50% : 95%	0.6%	0.5%	30.000

TEOP also allows its users to train their own models, implementing even more options in the system. Available algorithms in the training function are YOLOv3-tiny, YOLOv4-tiny and MobileNetV2 with SSD. The user has an option for using images of objects captured in the traffic light using the capture tool available in the Computer Vision Improvement screen, as shown on Fig. 2:

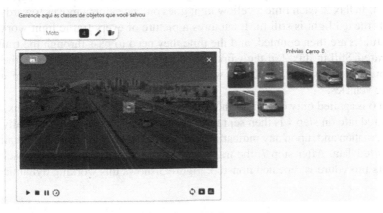

Fig. 2. Object capture image tool.

Figure 3 shows the workflow of the traffic light control algorithm that will be executed on a PC computer, installed next to the traffic light that will process the images, as mentioned in 3.2, calculate the time required for the crossing of vehicles, using the formula described in 3.6, and send the information to turn the traffic lights on and off, via USB connection, to the Raspberry Pi. This dynamic was divided into two streams: 1 and 2. They start equally and differentiate from step three. The algorithm is described below:

After the algorithm starts (step 1), the system asks which method will be used to load traffic light settings and starting times of Fixed Time Signal traffic lights. By pressing letter L, settings and times will be loaded in a text file already downloaded and saved in a local folder. If pressed M, the user will type times manually and settings will be loaded from a local file. If chosen A key, regular predefined times already in the algorithm and its settings will be loaded from the local file. If the S key is chosen, times and settings will be loaded on the server.

Afterwards, the algorithm goes to step 2. It is important to point out that each time it reaches this step, the algorithm researches in its database new settings. This allows the traffic controller to make real-time settings such as modifying regions of interest, real-time vehicle counting lines and even fixed time signals in traffic lights.

In step 3, the traffic light functioning mode is loaded. If it is a Fixed Time Signal traffic light, flux 1 starts and the traffic light will work with predefined times repetitively until a new model is selected. This mode is identical to what regular traffic lights operate, with advantages such as the possibility of changing time signals according to controllers demands, as well as problem monitoring in the traffic light, camera and network connection.

Step 4, connection tests with server and camera are made. From the server side, every 30 s a test will also verify if traffic lights are accessible. If found any issues, a call will be automatically opened informing the possible issue found. In flux 1 tests are made and information is kept in variables until reach step 7, where everything is sent to the server. In flux 2, if success is obtained with camera testing, it follows Picture Mode (PM) or Picture and Video Mode (PVM). If not, fixed times chosen in step one are loaded and PM and PVM will wait until the problem is solved.

On step 5, the traffic light starts working by lighting in the loaded time signals. In flux 1, it will work repetitively with pre-programmed times until another working mode is chosen. In flux 2, each time a yellow light goes on, the camera moves towards an area in which the red light is still lit. It captures a picture of every traffic light working this way. Vehicles are then counted, and the time they need to pass through the traffic light is generated. Still in flux 2, if the working mode is picture and video mode, the camera will capture pictures of traffic lights with green lights on, and the algorithm will start counting vehicles.

Step 6 is applied only on flux 2, and it repeats the step 5 routine for this flux. On step 7, collected info on step 4 is then sent to the server. The server will periodically consult this information and, upon any indication of error, it will open a call automatically based on collected data. After step 7, the traffic light finishes its cycle and goes back to step two. This procedure is repeated nonstop. Figure 3 shows this working dynamic.

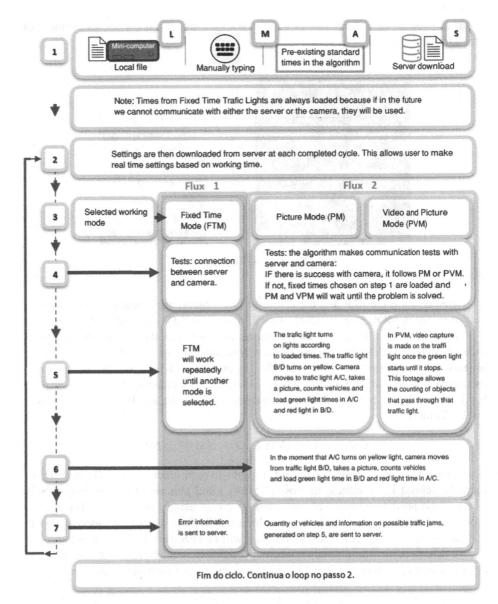

Fig. 3. Fluxogram showing the simplified working of the traffic light control algorithm

3.6 Object Count and Error Correction on Object Counting

Object counting, whether in photos or video, is done only in the region of interest (ROI) selected by the user via the web in the traffic light general settings screen. Exclusively in the case of video mode, after selecting the ROI and on the same screen of the Web system, the user selects a counting line that has the trigger function, performing the count as soon as the vehicle makes contact with the line. Figure 4 shows example of video mode counting.

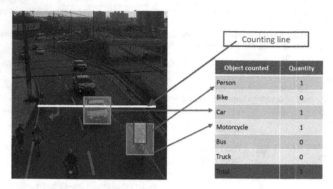

Fig. 4. Counting line

After creating the ROI and the counting line, objects are counted through motion detection, using MOG2, or object classification with YOLO-Tiny and MobileNetV2.

The counting can happen in two moments depending on the traffic light operation mode, if in Photo mode, the image capture will be done before the traffic light opens, the objects will be counted through YOLOv3-Tiny or YOLOv4-Tiny, which can be chosen by the user on the traffic light general settings screen. After counting the vehicles waiting for the traffic light to turn green, the time that sets the traffic light will be calculated based on the formula:

$$\text{Green light} = (\text{VWTLG} * \text{NSDVC})/\text{NC}$$

Where, vehicles waiting for the traffic light to turn green (VWTLG), number of seconds defined for a vehicle to cross (NSDVC) and number of carriageways (NC). There is no need to correct vehicle counting errors using Photo mode. The second moment, where there is a need to count vehicles, is in Photo with Live Video mode - in this case - the counting correction techniques will be necessary and shown below.

At this moment, some issues might happen, such as multiple counts of the same object or lack of counting. Table 2 below shows the rate of multiple reads:

Table 2. Multiple read errors

Modelo	Objetos detectados Dia	Taxa acertos (%)	Deixou de contar	Erro de leituras múltiplas	Observações
MOG2 Téc. 1	53	49,23	33	21	Resolução da detecção: 1280x720
Yolov3 80 Classes	63	90,77	6	4	
Yolov3 6 Classes	65	93,85	4	4	
Yolov4 80 Classes	65	96,92	2	2	Resolução da detecção: 416x416
Yolov4 6 Classes	66	96,92	2	3	
SSD Mobilenetv2 90 Classes	62	93,85	4	1	
SSD Mobilenetv2 6 Classes	25	38,46	40		Resolução da detecção: 300x300

To solve the multiple count problem, each object was given a unique ID that allowed its tracking. The idea is for the ID to remain the same until the object disappears from view, but usually the applied technique will not work as expected in most cases, but did resolve the issue – with a success rate higher than 90%.

To resolve the issue of missing object count, a margin of error has been added to the count line. This meant adding more vertical pixels to the count line. Users can choose pixel quantity using the general traffic light settings screen. If the object is within this interval, it will be counted. After performing tests, it was found that this margin of error should not be large, to avoid multiple counts, and should not be too small, otherwise it will not count some objects.

4 Tests

This work does not intend to reach high levels of object classification. This can happen, however, depending on several factors analyzed in this section that can lead to further improvements. The main goal here is to count traffic objects and try to come closer to the real life number of objects. Therefore, it was not taken into account whether the classified objects correspond to the real objects. The traffic light studied in this work works based on the number of vehicles that pass through it, in this sense it is extremely important to obtain results closer to reality to optimize the work of the traffic light, thus achieving its objective of increasing traffic flow. In addition, it is of great importance to keep the system running for as long as possible through problem detection and alerting techniques, as well as follow-up of call openings.

4.1 Test General Settings

All tests were performed on a DELL 7050 notebook that was in the role of the mini computer processing the images and sending the commands to the Raspberry Pi to control the traffic lights. Notebook settings were detailed in Sect. 3, item 3.2. Tests with MOG2 were done using native video resolution; Tests with YOLO-Tiny had a resolution of 416×416 and tests with SSD MobileNetV2 had a resolution of 300×300. When necessary, the analyzed image was resized, making it larger or smaller, according to the resolution previously described for each algorithm. For example, if the original image was 240p and YOLO was chosen, the image was resized to 416×416.

As the video tests and photos were stored inside the notebook, the frames were limited to 25 fps because the videos were recorded in this setting. This limited the algorithm functioning but did not affect object detection. Tests used images captured at around 3pm. Tests that analyzed pictures were made with YOLO-Tiny since this algorithm is responsible for counting vehicles on pictures. The developer trained models based on algorithms YOLO-Tiny and MobileNetV2, these models names are: YOLOv3 6 classes, YOLOv4 6 classes and SSD MobileNetV2 6 Classes. These models were trained using only object classes found in traffic. This was detailed in Sect. 3, item 3.4. Preparation of images used in training.

For the execution of the tests, the CV algorithm was chosen via the Web platform. The application used was the traffic light control and in it the functions of counting frames per second (FPS) and showing the images of vehicles at the traffic light were temporarily enabled. In this sense, it was possible to count the vehicles and the FPS for each algorithm used.

4.2 On Detecting Objects in Pictures

During the tests carried out on photos, it was observed that the model trained by the authors, based on YOLOv4-tiny, obtained better results than expected in relation to the others, reaching 90% hits in detectable objects eligible (by the authors) in photos in 360p resolution as shown in Table 3. This mode, named Yolov4 6 classes, classified twice as many objects than other algorithms, as shown on Table 4. It was also the best at analyzing resolutions.

Table 3. Test 2 results with 360p pictures

Model	Object Detected Day	Success Rate (%)
Yolov3 80 Classes	6	60
Yolov3 6 Classes	5	50
Yolov4 80 Classes	7	70
Yolov4 6 Classes	9	90

Table 4. Test 1 results with 360p pictures

Model	Object Detected Day	Success Rate (%)
Yolov3 80 Classes	2	40
Yolov3 6 Classes	1	20
Yolov4 80 Classes	2	40
Yolov4 6 Classes	4	80

The model trained by the author, named Yolov3 6 Classes, had the lowest hits among others tested, despite utilizing the same image quantities and same settings as Yolov4-Tiny. This shows that Yolov4-Tiny improved its learning and detection in contrast to its previous version.

4.3 On Detecting Objects in Videos

During the video tests, it was observed that the model trained by the authors, based on YOLOv4-tiny, was better than the others, reaching 92% hits in eligible detectable objects (by the developer). Table 5 has more in-depth data. This model, named Yolov4 6 classes, classified approximately 28% more than YOLOv3 80 Classes and 67% more than YOLOv3 6 Classes, as shown on Table 5.

SSD MobileNetV2 had the worst results on video 1, but on video 2 it was among those with the best classification rate, as shown in Table 6. It obtained better speed among object classification algorithms evaluated.

Video 1 had the worst classification rate due to vehicle-camera distance, which highlights that distance and recording angle influence object detection.

Average object detection through MOG2 was above 90% on video 1, but had the biggest multiple reading rate, reaching 9%.

Generally, object classification algorithms such as YOLO-Tiny and MobileNetV2 had a great classification rate among all video image resolutions, reaching hits levels of 96% with lower multiple reading objects rate.

4.4 On Mean Average Precision (mAP) and their Relation with Resolution and Image Attribution

It was clear that during tests, the relation between object classification, by either YOLO-Tiny or MobileNetV2, is proportional to picture quality and resolution. The bigger the image resolution, both photo and video, and better the image quality attributes such as bits per second rate (kbps) when it comes to video, the better the object classification rate. Under 240p resolution, most algorithms could not detect any object.

On specific videos, the fact they have 25 frames per second gives the algorithm more chances to try to classify objects, and the problem related in the previous paragraph is not as big. However, it reflects object classification error rates. Motorcycles are rarely classified as motorcycles, and in these cases, they were classified either as cars or as people when it was possible to detect either the motorcycle or the person.

Table 5. Test 1 result executed in 720p vídeo resolution

Model	Average FPS	Success Rate (%)	Observations
MOG2 Téc. 1	21,44	90,20	Detected resolution: 1280x720
Yolov3 80 Classes	15,7	64,71	Detected resolution: 416x416
Yolov3 6 Classes	16,88	25,49	
Yolov4 80 Classes	13,83	78,43	
Yolov4 6 Classes	14,78	92,16	
SSD Mobilenetv2 90 Classes	21,21	41,18	Detected resolution: 300x300
SSD Mobilenetv2 6 Classes	28,11	3,92	

Table 6. Test 2 result executed in 720p vídeo resolution

Model	Average FPS	Success Rate (%)	Observations
MOG2 Téc. 1	18,95	49,23	Detected resolution: 1280x720
Yolov3 80 Classes	15,84	90,77	Detected resolution: 416x416
Yolov3 6 Classes	16,33	93,85	
Yolov4 80 Classes	14,29	96,92	
Yolov4 6 Classes	14,75	96,92	
SSD Mobilenetv2 90 Classes	20,26	93,85	Detected resolution: 300x300
SSD Mobilenetv2 6 Classes	27,03	38,46	

4.5 On Analyzed Techniques Performance

The techniques used to count objects in this article have been divided into two steps. First step: working through MOG2, does movement detection and will always have a bigger success rate than the second category that does detection and identifies kinds of objects. Due to rapid MOG2 processing, it was necessary to create a delay mechanism to maintain the frame rate in 25 fps, otherwise the video would be too fast and rapidly perpass 150 and 200 fms, making video analysis and algorithm counting almost unviable.

In the second step, where algorithms are able to classify objects, video tests showed that MobileNetV2 was overall faster, obtaining better frame rates and easily reaching 25% advantage over YOLOv4-Tiny, despite the fact YOLO-Tiny versions used bigger video resolution than MobileNetV2, as shown in item 4.1. However, YOLOv4-Tiny version was better than MobileNetV2 since it identified more objects in all tests. YOLOv3-Tiny also shared the same advantage over MobileNetV2 in mostly all tests.

4.6 Test Results After System Implementations

Below are the results of a test done to quantify the maximum time a vehicle waits for a traffic light to open when the other road is empty. Next, the traffic light efficiency test in Smart mode will be described:

Waiting Time Test

The traffic light general settings screen gives us the option to set up a minimum time the traffic light with less than a four seconds timer will get. It is possible, in this instance, that the traffic controller enters a value such as zero so that the green light in that traffic-less traffic light does not light, prioritizing the traffic light that has traffic. This solution might cause an issue where all traffic lights get values lower than four seconds. In this scenario, traffic lights would get red lights constantly until vehicles start arriving. A complementary mechanism would verify if the master traffic light has a timer with less than four seconds, and if that is the case, it will receive 8 s while the other gets the minimum time chosen by the traffic controller.

After tests carried out with this mechanism, it was proved that the waiting time of vehicles arriving at the main traffic light is equal to the time given to the yellow traffic light of the other traffic lights where there is no flow of vehicles. The maximum waiting time for those arriving at non-main traffic lights is 8 s plus yellow traffic light time, at times when there are no vehicles at main traffic lights, this solves one of the main problems of fixed time traffic lights that commonly turn on the traffic light green for 1, 2, 3 or more minutes, even when there is no traffic.

Traffic Flux Test

The main purpose of our work is to control the traffic light according to how many vehicles are waiting for the green light. To validate the proposal, some tests were carried out using photos with vehicles waiting for the green light of the traffic light. The solution proposed by this work was made for two-time traffic lights and the following test was performed on a cross-shaped road, where the first time was identified as A-C and the second as B-D (in Table 7), with two lanes on each way. For simplicity, the yellow light time and the minimum time given for the red light, mentioned in item 4.5, when there is no flow of vehicles, were not considered. Table 7 shows the test results:

Table 7. Comparison between fixed time semaphore and smart semaphore

Item	Traffic light	Vehicles waiting for the green light	Estimated average time for a vehicle to cross	N. of lanes per lane	Total time for crossing all vehicles	Fixed Time Semaphore set to 60s (FTS)	Smart Traffic light
		(N. vehicle	x seconds)	/ lanes	= time + FTS	Flow: 30 vehicles per minute	
1	A-C	46			92s + 60s	152s	60s + 24s + 32s = 116s
	B-D	12			24s + 60s	84s	84s
2	A-C	60			120s + 60s	180s	60s + 20s + 60s = 140s
	B-D	10			20s + 60s	80s	80s
3	A-C	40	4s	2	80s + 60s	140s	80s
	B-D	0			0s	0s	0s
4	A-C	8			16s	16s	16s
	B-D	60			120s + 60s	180s	60s + 16s + 60s = 130s
5	A-C	14			28s	28s	28s
	B-D	50			100s + 60s	160s	60s + 28s + 40s = 128s

Table 7 shows the comparison between the fixed-time traffic light (FTTL) and the smart traffic light (Si) proposed by this work. Item 1 shows that Si was more efficient and managed to provide flow to the 46 vehicles using 36 s less than the FTTL. In item 4, the time savings were even greater, being 50 s compared to the FTTL.

In item 3, in addition to the gain in relation to time, there was also 1 cycle less of the traffic light opening since B-D did not open, when the algorithm verified that there were no vehicles waiting for the green light, the traffic light did not open. In this case, there was a gain of 60 s by Si in relation to the functioning of the FTTL.

Examples with three opening and closing cycles were used in these tests. They prove that the smart traffic light promotes considerable time savings, reaching an improvement of 33% in relation to the fixed time traffic light, as mentioned in item 3. In general terms, the results were within the expected reaching close to 35%, results obtained by (KANUNGO, SHARMA and SINGLA, 2014).

5   Limitations

Considering this paper intends to propose a solution based on working traffic lights, camera and network in Brazil, where they use a single PTZ camera, the functioning mode was a bit limited. With a single camera, it is not possible to simultaneously observe traffic in every road to compare and see which has more traffic in order to prioritize it. This could make the algorithm more efficient and simple. Another limitation imposed by a single camera was that once the red light is on, if there were multiple cameras it would be possible to record the flow of vehicles under all traffic lights. However, it was only possible to choose one side with the green light, and that was the one that had the most vehicles counted before the green light came on.

Regarding the evaluation of the system, it is necessary to do more case studies to bring more data about the benefits, problems and challenges of using the proposed solution. The system evaluation limited itself in previously recorded video and picture analysis since it was not possible to use traffic lights in a real environment.

6   Contributions and Future Works

Because of the work presented in this paper, the following contributions are numbered:

1) The development of an intelligent traffic control system based on computer vision was proposed. With this system it is expected to easily promote the implementation of intelligent traffic lights for local and remote operation, improve the flow of traffic and detect problems quickly and automatically. Currently, multiple cities rely on conductors and citizens to report issues, causing delays on repairing processes.
2) Enable the implementation of a smart traffic lights control system by using camera and network infrastructure that is already in use by states and cities, drastically reducing implementation costs in comparison to other marketing proposals.
3) The web platform, TEOP, responsible for controlling the system and traffic light control algorithm, will be available to download.
4) Allowing temporary traffic light use in the following instances:

Mobile traffic lights to meet temporary events demands;

Viability tests while installing new traffic lights and;

Temporary substitution in places where traffic lights are necessary, but there were problems that shortly made the fixed time traffic light stop working.

Regarding future work, there is still room for implementations and improvements to reach more efficient results.

1. Implementing the green wave to allow vehicles to go through a bigger adjacent traffic lights number, keeping a constant medium velocity and avoiding encounters with a red light. This is the more interesting scenario to work with a smart traffic light to avoid jams on traffic lights located immediately after the smart traffic light.
2. Considering that the system includes regular Brazilian traffic lights, it is possible to expand the search to adapt the control algorithm to other types of traffic lights so that it can operate in more models.
3. To make the traffic flow even more efficient, it is recommended to implement a new functionality using the data obtained by the PVM, which counts the vehicles under the green traffic light. Based on this data, it is possible to predict opening and closing times, suggesting times for the traffic light to work more and more accurately.
4. Regarding improvement on detection and counting, there is still space to improve mean Average Precision (mAP) on vehicle classification and MOG2. This will make the system work more efficiently and, besides, it can lower multiple detection error rates and uncounted vehicles. Tests in other climate conditions created by the user, based on objects captured by the traffic light camera, could verify if there are any improvements on object detection using this approach.
5. For the system to be fully functional in a production environment, it is necessary to interconnect the PC computer with the Raspberry so that the Raspberry can execute the commands, coming from the PC, to turn the traffic lights on and off. Following this path, it is also necessary to allow communication between the traffic light control algorithm and the PTZ camera using the ONVIF protocol, which is standard. It works by sending out commands as codes to connected cameras, allowing the moving of cameras to traffic lights that will open, in turn leading to system improvement.
6. Another improvement indicated for future work is the creation of a model based on the set of images generated in the traffic light. It is possible that the models created using these photos achieve a better average hits than those achieved in this work.

References

1. IBGE. Frota de veículos no Brasil (2020). https://cidades.ibge.gov.br/brasil/pesquisa/22/28120?ano=2020. Acesso em 12 ago. 2020 (BAUZA; GONZALVES; SANCHEZ-SORIANO, 2010)
2. Krauss, M.: Automação de sistema semafórico. 67 f. Trabalho de Conclusão de Curso (Tecnologia em Automação Industrial). - Universidade Tecnológica Federal do Paraná. UFTPR, Curitiba (2014)
3. Martins, J.A.: Transporte, Uso do Solo e Autossustentabilidade: Teoria e Prática para a Previsão de Impactos sobre a Qualidade do Ar. 1996, 250f. Tese (Engenharia de Transportes). UFRJ, Rio de Janeiro (1996)

4. Silva, G.C.: Tráfego, monóxido de carbono e ruído em áreas urbanas: o caso de Florianópolis. 1998. 126 f. Dissertação (Engenharia Civil). UFSC, Florianópolis (1998)
5. G1. Distrito Federal. Semáforos inteligentes devem ser implantados em fevereiro no DF, diz Detran. G1, Distrito Federal, 08 November 2017. https://g1.globo.com/distrito-federal/noticia/semaforos-inteligentes-devem-ser-implantados-em-fevereiro-no-df-diz-detran.ghtml. Acesso em 29 maio. 2021
6. Castro, F.S., et al.: Identificação e Rastreamento de veículos utilizando fluxo ótico. Colloquium Exactarum 7(2), 73–88 (2015)
7. Valente, J.: Aumento do monitoramento traz debate sobre modernização e privacidade. Agência Brasil. Brasília, 12 September 2019. https://agenciabrasil.ebc.com.br/geral/noticia/2019-09/aumento-do-monitoramento-traz-debate-sobre-modernizacao-e-privacidade. Acesso em 01 maio 2021
8. Kanungo, A., Sharma, A., Singla, C.: Smart traffic lights switching and traffic density calculation using video processing. In: Recent Advances in Engineering and Computational Sciences (RAECS), pp. 1–6 (2014)
9. Marciano, J.L.P.: Segurança da informação: uma abordagem social. 212 f. Tese (Doutorado em Ciência da Informação)-Universidade de Brasília (2006)
10. Bhatnagar, S., Bhatnagar, Y.: Distributed Trafic Control System (2019)
11. Ardhapure, M.R., et al.: Smart traffic signal management (2018)
12. Komasilovs, V., et al.: Traffic Monitoring System Development in Jelgava City, Latvia. VEHITS (2018)
13. The, P.N., et al.: Real time ARM-based traffic Level of Service classification system. In: 2016 13th International Conference on Electrical Engineering/Electronics, Computer, Telecommunications and Information Technology (ECTI-CON). IEEE (2016)
14. Altundogan, T.G., Karakose, M.: Image processing and deep neural image classification based physical feature determiner for traffic stakeholders. In: 2019 7th International Istanbul Smart Grids and Cities Congress and Fair (ICSG). IEEE (2019)
15. Cismaru, S.-I., et al.: Experimental study regarding an intelligent control system for traffic light intersections. In: 2020 International Symposium on Power Electronics, Electrical Drives, Automation and Motion (SPEEDAM). IEEE (2020)
16. Sandler, M., et al.: MobileNetV2: Inverted Residuals and Linear Bottlenecks, 13 January 2018
17. Aquino, C.: Dos Barris à Paralela: 88 Smart traffic lights will reduce traffic time. Correio 24 horas. Salvador, 08 may 2017. https://www.correio24horas.com.br/noticia/nid/dos-barris-a-paralela-88-semaforos-inteligentes-vao-diminuir-tempo-no-transito/. Acesso em 31 May 2021

Cerebrospinal Fluid Containers Navigator. A Systematic Literature Review

Yésica Rodríguez[1], Alejandra Huérfano[1], Fernando Yepes-Calderon[2,4], J. Gordon McComb[3], and Hector Florez[1(✉)] 🔴

[1] Universidad Distrital Francisco Jose de Caldas, Bogota, Colombia
{ytrodrigueza,fahuerfanov}@correo.udistrital.edu.co,
haflorezf@udistrital.edu.co
[2] SBP LLC - RnD Department, 604, Fort Pierce, Fl 34950, USA
fernando.yepes@strategicbp.net
[3] Children's Hospital Los Angeles, 1300 N Vermont Ave 1006, Los Angeles, CA 90027, USA
gmccomb@chla.usc.edu
[4] GYM Group SA - Departamento I+R, Cra 78A No. 6-58, Cali, Colombia
fernando@gym-group.org

Abstract. Robotics is used successfully in medicine. Mechanical gadgets assist the most intricate procedures, providing precision, error correction, stereotactic positioning, subtle controlling, and in-place visualization, among other benefits. However, few applications are designed to perform continuously embedded within the human body. Implants such as the peacemaker that works permanently inside the patient involve high risk. However, the risk is acceptable given the benefit that peacemakers provide when working correctly. The current proposal envisages a similar scenario. One in ten babies in America develops hydrocephalus. The abnormality is more incident in premature babies, but term babies are also subject to malady. Even adults develop a sort of hydrocephalus that keeps intracranial pressure at normal levels. Hydrocephalus quickly escalates from mild to severe due to cerebrospinal fluid circuit issues (CSF) issues. The only mechanism to alleviate the pressure within the CSF containers is to release the fluid progressively. Such as purpose requires opening the skull and locating a discharging device – diverting shunt – that goes through the brain mass and reaches the ventricles. This invasive gadget grants a way out to liquid but is not always infallible. The shunt often fails, and reiteratively opening the skull is the method to pursue. Shunted patients with more the 100 brain surgeries have motivated the campaign no-more-brain-surgeries promoted by the Hydrocephalus Association (https://www.hydroassoc.org/join-us-as-we-say-nomorebs/).

This document registers a revision on immersive robotics and sensors that allow us to create a submergible device capable of exploring 3D printed macro models of the CSF containers. This first approach will serve as a testing land to understand fluid mechanics, navigability, and blockage removal techniques from inside a model mimicking the brain in healthy and abnormal conditions. Once this is accomplished, we intend to

O. Gervasi et al. (Eds.): ICCSA 2022 Workshops, LNCS 13381, pp. 340–351, 2022.
https://doi.org/10.1007/978-3-031-10548-7_25

miniaturize the device and check the feasibility of a medical application that controls cerebrospinal fluid abnormalities while avoiding recurrent surgery.

Keywords: CSF · Hydrocephalus · Shunting · Submersible robots · Brain pressure · CSF analysis · Medical imaging

1   Introduction

The inclusion of technology in medicine has optimized the resources and empowered physicians' decision criteria to benefit the patients. Initially, the tech-based gadgets played an assisting role that speeds up processes and granted healthcare providers leading insights that favored verdicts' accuracy [4]. Soon, the technology became more intrusive that machines now perform specific procedures where high precision is crucial [14], or the reproducibility of human operators is highly compromised [7].

The technology to study and intervene in the brain has been thoroughly tested and commercialized. Devices to visualize the anatomy are prolific and have made the radiology departments the busiest units in hospitals and clinics. Imaging systems are not intrusive but are limited to diagnosing static representations of the structure inside the skull. At the same time, dynamics remain mostly hidden even with sophisticated tools such as diffusion and functional MRI [1].

Some other technology interfaces the brain to recover sensor capabilities [5], and specialized research is venturing into the recovery of motor functions using electromyography to provide signaling to a human part that has lost motion or to a robotic prosthesis [10]. Interfacing the brain through electromyography is not directly touching the brain. However, its implementation requires a learning process that will modify neuronal interaction, which enlights the complexity of the organ.

The most intrusive medically approved devices working on the brain are the ventriculoperitoneal shunt (VPS) valves used to release pressure created by the accumulation of cerebrospinal fluid namely hydrocephalus [9]. The original device was a passive tube surgically implanted in the brain ventricles. Modern valves are also intrusive but can regulate the fluid using closed-loop controls and communicate with external devices for monitoring purposes [13].

The insertion of a VPS is the most common treatment for hydrocephalus, with approximately 30,000 procedures performed annually in the USA. Complications in adults can range from 17% to 33%, leading to hospital readmissions for treating complications that increase hospital costs by 50 million dollars per year [7].

Although the technological advances in shunting valves, the abnormality yields 750 new cases per 100,000 live births worldwide, and some HC patients may have more than a hundred surgeries in their life span.

The hydrocephalus association annually releases grants to study the HC precursors and supports research to alleviate an old problem with no solution. Our research aims to explore the phenomena associated with the HC abnormality from the inside by creating a 3D replica of the CSF space and navigating that structure while gathering data that presents consistent information to understand HC genesis. We also envisaged the possibility of taking the CSF navigator inside the brain after miniaturization, where this active device might localize blocking particles and dissolve them safely.

This systematic literature review investigates edging technology in submersible robots, buoyancy, propulsion, visibility in watery environments, wireless video transmission, autonomous displacement, light-based boundary detection, and remote control.

This paper is structured as follows. Section presents the SLR methodology used in this research. Section 3 presents the results of the research that allowed us to solve the research questions. Section 4 discusses the method and results presented in the previous sections. Section 5 proposes future works based on this research. Finally, Sect. 6 concludes the paper.

2   Materials and Methods

This paper applies the guidelines proposed by professor Barbara Kitchenham in her article: *Procedures for Performing Systematic Reviews* [6]. The guide focuses on how to perform a Systematic Literature Review (SLR) with referential coherence and selectiveness. It consists of 3 parts:

1. Planning. We state the justification, needs, and search strategy of the SLR.
2. Execution. We perform document search, quality filtering selection, and extraction of relevant information.
3. Reporting. We consolidate the information, discuss usability and integration possibilities, and postulate guidelines for further work.

2.1   Research Questions

This study is based on the following research questions:

- RQ1. Which is the best micro-robot design to achieve stability, buoyancy control, and harmless navigability in a waterly-closed environment?
- RQ2. How to displace a submergible robot while optimizing hardware?
- RQ3. How can a robot communicate with the outside while immersed in a fluid?
- RQ4. What are the sequelae in patients who suffer hydrocephalus secondary to shunting procedures?

Search Strategy. Kitchenham [6] suggests identifying relevant aspects in regards to population, intervention, outcome, and experimental design of the gathered data.

- **Population.** The population refers to a specific group of people who suffer hydrocephalus. So, the keywords are `non-invasive hydrocephalus treatment` or `CSF circuit` or `hydrocephalus` or `Complications after shunt` or `Shunt procedure`.
- **Intervention.** The technologies that address the specific approach are robotics; in particular, soft robotics. Also, submersible robots, buoyancy, displacement, the propulsion strategies and hydrophobic materials. Also biomimicry suggest to solve complex problems by mimicing designs adopted in the nature. Then, the keywords are `soft robotics` or `submersible robot` or `micro robot bio-mimicry` or `hydrophobic materials` or `submerged nanobots` or `buoyancy underwater`.
- **Outcome.** The relevant outcomes are associated with moving devices inside the fluid, autonomous microrobots, and reliable communication inside a fluid. Therefore, the keywords are `kinetics underwater` or `communication underwater` or `robot navigability`.
- **Experimental design.** A stage of development that we partially accomplished in this delivery. Device creation and records of operation will be detailed in the next delivery of the project.

Selected Journals and Conferences. The research articles were found in the following digital databases: Scopus, IEEE Xplore, Springer Link, Oxford, and Science Direct. We filtered the search for a range of time between 2011 to 2020, as shown in Table 1.

2.2 Study Selection Criteria

We employed inclusion and exclusion criteria in the selection process. Refer to complementary information for more details. The inclusion and exclusion criteria derive from the research questions.

The inclusion criteria are as follows:

- **IC1:** Submersible micro-bots capable of realizing underwater manipulation or monitoring their surroundings
- **IC2:** The submersible robot's design has its mechanical structure and electronic system isolated from surrounding fluid or covered by hydrophobic materials
- **IC3:** Studies that show the shunt procedure's effects and the complications in patients with hydrocephalus

The exclusion criteria are as follows:

- **EC1:** Submersible robots using a external structure or propeller for its locomotion

Table 1. Search process documentation

Database	Years covered by search	Search strategy
Scopus	2011–2020	TITLE-ABS-KEY((“buoyancy”) AND ((“underwater”) OR (“soft robotics”) OR (“submersible robot”)) AND (LIMIT-TO(SUBJAREA, “ENGI”)))
Science Direct	2017–2020	((“circuit CSF”) AND ((“Hydrocephalus”) OR (“Complications after shunt”) OR (“Shunt procedure”) OR (“non-invasive hydrocephalus treatment”)) AND ((“hydrophobic materials”) OR (“robot navigability”)))
IEEE Xplore	2016–2020	((“robot navigability”) AND ((“buoyancy underwater”) OR (“submersible robot”) OR (“communication underwater”))) AND (“microrobot”)
Springer Link	2015–2019	((“micro robot bio-mimicry”) AND ((“kinetics underwater”) OR (“communication underwater”)) AND ((“submerged nanobots”) OR (“Submersible robot”)))
Oxford	2000–2020	((“circuit CSF”) AND ((“Hydrocephalus”) OR (“Complications after shunt”) OR (“Shunt procedure”)))

- **EC2:** Non-submersible robots
- **EC3:** Informative articles related to hydrocephalus without measurement data

2.3 Study Quality Assessment

After filtering with the inclusion and exclusion criteria, a total of 29 articles remained on the list. 13 articles passed a second selection phase from the original list, where we took care of duplicate or similar content as presented in Table 2. In addition, we classified the pre-selected articles into the needed modules as shown in Table 3.

Table 2. Pre-selected articles

Database	Retrieved	Duplicated	Pre-selected
Scopus	12	2	5
Science Direct	5	1	2
IEEE Xplore	8	1	2
Springer Link	3	0	3
Oxford	1	0	1
Total	**29**	**4**	**13**

Table 3. Definition of study designs modules

Module	Basic type	Definition
Treatment's effect	Secondary studies	A quantitative study in which shunting procedure effects in patients suffering hydrocephalus can be visualized based on results data
Communication	Experiment	An experiment testing submersible robot communication. Pertinent and substantial data are extracted from the submerged system
Motion	Prototype	A submersible robot prototype capable of generating its motion using the surrounded fluid and avoid any filtration that could damage internal mechanics
Structure's design	Observation prototype experiment	A study comparing robots' physical structure's prototypes from which the best physical design could be inferred. In addition, an experiment in which the robot does not harm or change in any way the environment where navigability takes place

2.4 Data Extraction

Important information was extracted from pre-selected articles as follows.

- Title, authors, journal or conference, publication details (year, country, reference)
- Article database where it was found
- Topic area
- Problem trying to solve
- Objectives
- Methods (used to provide a solution)
- Results

2.5 Data Synthesis and Quality Verification

We synthesized the pertinent data after classifying the articles in operative-wise modules obtaining the results presented in Table 4. This table exposes verification criteria (VC) that enlighten the source classification.

After applying the quality criteria, we have selected those documents that meet the requirements of the study. Table 5 presents the number of selected works by the database. In addition, Table 6 summarizes the journals or conferences of selected articles, their Scopus h-index, and their country.

3 Results

3.1 Shunting Sequelae

According to the literature review conducted by Hebb and Cusimano [4], 38% of shunted patients presented complications after valve implantation, 22% underwent additional surgery, and 6% developed a permanent deficit or died. Among the most insidious reasons for the post-surgical complication, non-hemorrhagic stroke was suffered by 5 out of 37 individuals. At the same time, the deadly postoperative cerebellar hematoma was present in out of 9 patients.

An alternative option to the invasive shunting is the CSF puncture; in that procedure, specialists drain 40 to 50 mL from the lumbar cistern to alleviate intracranial pressure. Using this alternative, according to the results shown in the literature review done by Hebb and Cusimano, patients who had controlled and continuous drainage avoided unnecessary surgery in the future [4]. Nevertheless, since CSF production is continuous, the puncture is not a long-lasting solution.

3.2 Robotics

Biomimetics is the science that studies the behaviors or characteristics existing in nature, aiming to mimic designs and functions that could solve problems in diverse fields. An example is the biomimetic robots is proposed by Wissman et al. [14]. The authors built a cupule that provides fishes – and the robot as well – with rheotaxis. This property characterizes how a body interacts with a current of a fluid. The rheotaxis will yield a value around zero (static in fluid) depending on the body moving along with (negative) or against (positive) the current. The measuring cupule is 5 mm in height and has a sensitivity of 0.5 pF (capacitance vs. tip deviation). The transducers are embedded metal plates in a soft silicone body located inside the body cupule [14].

Table 4. Quality criteria per module

Module	Quality criteria
Treatment's effect	**VC1.** Does the study contains quantitative information related to people who were treated with a shunting procedure?
	VC2. Is it mentioned in an explicit way which one are the consequences after receiving a shunting treatment?
	VC3. Does the article consider more than 1 person to conclude secondary effects after received a hydrocephalus treatment?
Communication	**VC1.** Is there a communication immersed in a fluid?
	VC2. Does the article mention at least one communication technique?
	VC3. Is it shown experimental communication results?
Motion	**VC1.** Is there a submersible robot using the external fluid to its locomotion?
	VC2. Does the article show experimental results which justify the motion way?
	VC3. How were isolated the internal structure?
Structure's design	**VC1.** Is there safe navigability that avoids crashing or damage its external environment?
	VC2. Does the article mention which material the robot is?
	VC3. Does the article justify why the robot's shape?

Table 5. Selected articles

Database	Pre-selected	Selected
Scopus	5	4
IEEE Xplore	2	1
SpringerLink	3	2
ScienceDirect	2	1
Oxford	1	1
Total	**13**	**9**

Table 6. Selected journals and conferences

Name	h-index	Country
Neurosurgery	198	United States
Chemical Engineering Journal	223	Netherlands
Journal of Marine Science and Engineering	22	Switzerland
Scientific Reports	213	United Kingdom
IEEE Int. Conference on Robotics and Biomimetics, ROBIO 2016	12	United States
Microsystem Technologies	63	Germany
Journal of Intelligent and Robotic Systems: Theory and Applications	77	Netherlands
Sensors	172	Switzerland
Neurologic Clinics	82	United Kingdom
Science Robotics	50	United States
Total	**1112**	**Worldwide**

Soft robotics is a subfield of robotics where the materials of the robots built are as similar as possible to those found in a living organism. The uses it has are varied, such as prosthetics, medical monitoring, and motion tracking. For the mentioned cupule, resistive and capacitive sensors are used due to their usefulness in soft robotics, these are built using conductive particles embedded in the rubber.

A robotic system incorporates six thrusters grouped by two that keep track of displacements in three axes providing the robot with an accurate localization in floating devices. The system does not need external references and represents the most sophisticated proposal regarding navigation among the reviewed material.

3.3 Detecting Obstructions

There are different types of ways to detect obstruction in the aquatic environment such as:

1. Lateral line system. It is a sensory organ of some marine animals. Fishes employ it to detect the movement and vibrations of the surrounding water, avoid collisions, orient themselves about water currents, and locate their prey.
2. Reconfigurable AUV. Yue et al. [16] refer to underwater intervention with autonomous management through performing a search and manipulation under the sea.

3.4   Buoyancy

Finding suitable materials is crucial since the robot must repel water when navigating; nonetheless, the system should control liquid absorption/rejection and immersion deepness. Superhydrophobic coatings have diverse applications such as corrosion protection, water separation in aquatic devices, and submersible robots. Suyambulingam et al. [12] present a superhydrophobic coating is developed using porous Zinc Oxide (ZnO) and copper stearate (CuSA2) nanoparticles, using an economical sputtering method. The authors assert that any surface with surface energy lower than 0.07 Nm1 will float and get repelled from the surface, which is the primary reason for hydrophobicity. Thus, ZnO, and CuSA2 material was used to make a superhydrophobic spray coating with porous particles in a single step. The ZnO/CuSA2 coating has a high WCA level of 161, indicating its high hydrophobic effect. It floats for approximately four months and has a high loading capacity, almost 333 times its weight.

SUR II is a circular autonomous ROV (Remotely Operated Vehicle). The system uses water jet propulsion for its displacement and employs thrusters to assert direction. The SUR II produces little noise as it implements a Kalman filter for data gathering. The SUR II design features a circular structure that provides robustness and maneuverability beyond the specification of any other shape. The invertors accomplished displacement through an equilateral triangle that distributes water to propellants, which produces a more efficient operation; however, it requires more complex algorithms. [15]. The authors fabricated the supporting parts in polylactic acid for 3D printing, making the case biocompatible and light. Additionally, the material is collected from renewable sources; therefore, it has a lower cost than other suitable hydrophobic and low-density materials. The case consists of two hemispherical hulls that protect the electronics. These hemispheres are light, so a few air interchanges achieve the robot's buoyancy. The hemispheres are secured with 10 mm screws, and these are attached to the box, making the height of the air box adjustable.

In the center of the robot platform, the authors created air chambers to aid buoyancy. In [16], the system uses electrolysis on the surrounding water to obtain hydrogen and oxygen gas and direct it to the air chambers. The authors justified their work based on Archimedes' Law: "Archimedes' Law: $FB = \rho g V$ where g is the gravity $g = 9.81 \, \text{m/s}^2$; V is volume of the hydrogen and oxygen which is collected by the grooves; ρ is the fluid's density – $\rho = 1.0 \, \text{g/cm}^3$ for water –. If we ignore the compression of the gas, the maximum of V_{max} is equal to the volume of the grooves. $Vmax = 2Vgr = 2 \times 20 \times 5 \times 6 = 1200 \, \text{mm}$ and the maximum buoyancy force $FBmax = 11.8 \, \text{mN}$".

Sun et al. [11] present two AUV prototypes. The first design has oil capsules placed within the case, while the capsules reside out of the main body in the second version. The designs have different hydrodynamics, and thus, their energy management and durability are different. The researchers submitted the designs to inertia and viscosity; the first design is frictionless. In the second version, the friction is present with variable intensity depending on the fluid type. The Authors concluded that prototype number one was more resistant than prototype two.

There is another type of autonomous vehicle found in the literature. Capocci et al. [2] introduces an ROV design consisting of a general box shape and a flotation section at the top. The thrusters and equipment are purposely located below the main structure to assert stability and separate the center of gravity and the flotation center vertically. Such as design reduces noise produced by fluctuations in the water and rocking.

Christianson et al. [3] introduce a submersible robot with neutral buoyancy that reduces the energy required for displacement by introducing air in laterally located chambers. The robot's speed is low compared to others of the same kind; however, the DEA is not opaque and does not require electrical membranes. The device is also provided with an arm that creates resistance to free movement.

4   Discussion

The study of submersible robots forced us to consider different modules, as shown in the previous section. The design selection will define the subsystems that better suit the purpose of the current work. Multipurpose designs are attractive since energy consumption remains an unattended challenge. Therefore, robots with multifunctional modules – meaning no real distinction between buoyancy, propulsion, sensor, and mechanical systems – will be prioritized. Bulky types of frames were found to be disadvantageous due to dragging. The drag coefficient in non-hollow objects is equivalent to the cross-sectional area. The fluid passing rapidly over bulky objects causes a turbulent flow regime [2], which is not desirable if thinking that this device may navigate in biological containers. The literature suggests spherical objects with a drag coefficient below 0.4 [15].

The inspection ROVs have in common the thrusters to move, which is essential to maneuver underwater or maintain their position; these thrusters vary according to the specifications, such as DC motors with brushes, brushless, coupled by magnetism, or driven by tires (in amphibious designs). The medium class ROVs have hydrodynamics developed to improve their movement underwater; they have a square internal structure divided into an upper buoyancy block and the thrusters and equipment below. Such as disposition yields better stability by distributing the center of gravity and buoyancy in the vertical axis. [2]. These devices are primarily spherical, and a center airbox achieves buoyancy [3,15].

Movement depends on the surface's texture, and the resistance of the material in contact with the surrounding liquid [14]. A spherical-shaped robot can use three vectorized thrusters in the three axes X, Y, and Z, through 3 spaces that allow the entry and exit of water. A triangular base is used to feed the thrusters connected to 2 servomotors to move horizontally and vertically [8,15].

Communication is essential to recovering information collected by a robot. Coarse wavelength division multiplexing (CWDM) devices enable data transfer from several channels for sonar, cameras, navigation, control, and other sensors. Some research prototypes feature fiber optics for communication; nevertheless, twisted pair cable is the most common and preferred [2]. Bioluminescence is also an option for communications in liquid environments. In robotics, optical communication can be of help when radio waves cannot be used or are not favorable [3].

Finally, the coating is essential. According to the literature, polymer materials have the benefits of low weight, no degradation in water, and low-cost [2]. Alternatives mention zinc oxide (ZnO) and Cation efflux system protein CuSA2 to make superhydrophobic spray coatings on porous surfaces [12].

5   Future Work

This SLR aims to settle the bases for building a lower-risk solution that provides better insights into hydrocephalus mechanisms. We propose a micro-robot with a spherical design preventing damage to the sounding structures. The device will use hydraulic flows generated by single-engine instrumentation inside the micro-robot. The envisaged structure has several advantages, such as placing an air chamber in the center that allows better buoyancy and stability. The structure will allocate an IP camera with the capacity of sending frames – single or streaming – wirelessly. Light-based echolocation prevents collisions with the required speed and enables the reconstruction of boundaries in those regions where the camera does not have enough resolution.

6   Conclusions

Shunting complications include subdural hemorrhage or effusion, infection, seizures, focal neurological deficits, shunt malfunction, and death. For these reasons, further work is proposed based on this systematic literature review. A micro-robot that inspects CSF containers is envisaged. Firstly, to learn about the abnormality genesis in a synthetic macrostructure that serves for more reliable simulations. Secondly, with a possibility to navigate inside the skull after miniaturization and when complex issues about energy supply are overpassed. According to the SLR, robots with a spherical shape and buoyancy control are the best option for energy-saving displacement and unharmed navigability strategies. During this review, we also discovered that liquid filtration and internal damage could be overcome by using hydrophobic materials that are also biocompatible.

References

1. Bandettini, P.A., Jesmanowicz, A., Wong, E.C., Hyde, J.S.: Processing strategies for time-course data sets in functional MRI of the human brain. Magn. Reson. Med. **30**(2), 161–173 (1993)
2. Capocci, R., Dooly, G., Omerdić, E., Coleman, J., Newe, T., Toal, D.: Inspection-class remotely operated vehicles-a review. J. Mar. Sci. Eng. **5**(1), 13 (2017)
3. Christianson, C., Goldberg, N.N., Deheyn, D.D., Cai, S., Tolley, M.T.: Translucent soft robots driven by frameless fluid electrode dielectric elastomer actuators. Sc. Robot. **3**(17), eaat1893 (2018)
4. Hebb, A.O., Cusimano, M.D.: Idiopathic normal pressure hydrocephalus: a systematic review of diagnosis and outcome. Neurosurgery **49**(5), 1166–1186 (2001)
5. Johnson, B.W., Crain, S., Thornton, R., Tesan, G., Reid, M.: Measurement of brain function in pre-school children using a custom sized whole-head meg sensor array. Clin. Neurophysiol. **121**(3), 340–349 (2010)
6. Kitchenham, B.: Procedures for performing systematic reviews. Keele UK Keele Univ. **33**(2004), 1–26 (2004)
7. Merkler, A.E., Ch'ang, J., Parker, W.E., Murthy, S.B., Kamel, H.: The rate of complications after ventriculoperitoneal shunt surgery. World Neurosurg. **98**, 654–658 (2017)
8. Phillips, B.T., et al.: A dexterous, glove-based teleoperable low-power soft robotic arm for delicate deep-sea biological exploration. Sci. Rep. **8**(1), 1–9 (2018). http://dx.doi.org/10.1038/s41598-018-33138-y
9. Sekhar, L.N., Moossy, J., Guthkelch, A.N.: Malfunctioning ventriculoperitoneal shunts: clinical and pathological features. J. Neurosurg. **56**(3), 411–416 (1982)
10. Shenoy, P., Miller, K.J., Crawford, B., Rao, R.P.: Online electromyographic control of a robotic prosthesis. IEEE Trans. Biomed. Eng. **55**(3), 1128–1135 (2008)
11. Sun, Q., Zheng, R.: The resistance analysis of AUV based on variable buoyancy system. In: 2016 IEEE International Conference on Robotics and Biomimetics (ROBIO), pp. 819–822. IEEE (2016)
12. Suyambulingam, G.R.T., Jeyasubramanian, K., Mariappan, V.K., Veluswamy, P., Ikeda, H., Krishnamoorthy, K.: Excellent floating and load bearing properties of superhydrophobic ZnO/copper stearate nanocoating. Chem. Eng. J. **320**, 468–477 (2017)
13. Tan, H., et al.: Fluid flow forces and rhoA regulate fibrous development of the atrioventricular valves. Dev. Biol. **374**(2), 345–356 (2013)
14. Wissman, J.P., Sampath, K., Freeman, S.E., Rohde, C.A.: Capacitive bio-inspired flow sensing cupula. Sensors **19**(11), 2639 (2019)
15. Yue, C., Guo, S., Li, M., Li, Y., Hirata, H., Ishihara, H.: Mechatronic system and experiments of a spherical underwater robot: SUR-II. J. Intell. Robot. Syst. **80**(2), 325–340 (2015)
16. Yue, C., Guo, S., Shi, L.: Design and performance evaluation of a biomimetic microrobot for the father-son underwater intervention robotic system. Microsyst. Technol. **22**(4), 831–840 (2016)

Business Intelligence Analytics Tools

Teresa Guarda[1,2(✉)] (iD), Ana Carvaca[1], Ronald Gozabay[1], Mitzi Saquicela[1],
and Helen Tomalá[1]

[1] Universidad Estatal Penisula de Santa Elena, La Libertad, Ecuador
tguarda@gmail.com
[2] CIST – Centro de Investigación en Sistemas y Telecomunicaciones, La Libertad, Ecuador

Abstract. Information is one of the most important assets for organizations. In the current scenario of a stagnant economy and fierce competition, it is imperative for organizations to be proactive, and for this to be possible, it is necessary to have timely access to the necessary information, so that it supports the decision-making process, thus allowing anticipate business strategies to react in a timely manner. It is in this context that Business Intelligence (BI) and its tools arise. Through BI it is possible to have access to an integrated set of solutions that allow data analysis in order to capture the information and knowledge necessary to leverage the business. BI allows organizations to use tools to analyze, plan, predict, solve problems, understand, innovate and learn in order to increase organizational knowledge, allowing effective actions that help to establish and achieve concrete business objectives in order to increase its efficiency and competitiveness. There is a wide variety of BI tools available on the market, which facilitate the use of the right data and visualization in ways that allow you to understand what it means. It is pertinent that organizations know how to select the appropriate tools for their needs. In this sense, a comparative analysis will be carried out between the different BI tools. The characteristics, specifications, and attributes of each one of them will be detailed to know key aspects of the tools that help the different organizations, regardless of the service they offer, to achieve their processes in an effective and efficient way. This comparison will allow companies to have a new perspective when using BI tools and generating business strategies.

Keywords: Business intelligence · BI tools · Analytics tools · Competitive advantage

Technological progress and the great growth of data have been brought to the organizations to seek the way to use this information to excel before others, improve the flow of your company, have more customers, prevent sales or consumption, find market levels, and adjust your business strategy.

The organizations must have the relevance that they hold the data that are generated daily, so they must count on a correct management of information. This must be efficient so that they can be competitive, on the basis of which it is necessary to adopt BI tools for the analysis of this information and thus facilitate the understanding of their businesses for companies [1].

BI is the process through which users obtain accurate and consistent data from the storage of organizational data (internal and external). The data obtained from different

O. Gervasi et al. (Eds.): ICCSA 2022 Workshops, LNCS 13381, pp. 352–362, 2022.
https://doi.org/10.1007/978-3-031-10548-7_26

commercial contexts allow users to identify, analyze and detect trends, anomalies and make predictions.

In the competitive and dynamic environment where companies operate, it is necessary to use the data available in order to ensure the success of the organization. In general, organizations use BI systems to obtain useful information from the data obtained, in order to improve the decision-making process. An organization with BI solutions is capable of creating a high-quality data infrastructure, with greater usability and integration [2].

Within companies, decision-making is an action of great importance, since it marks their path and behavior in order to achieve the established objectives. For this reason, the use of BI plays a fundamental role, since it is possible to foresee the future, going from reactive to proactive, minimizing uncertainty, transforming information into knowledge and generating useful solutions to a given problem [3].

Business success is based on making decisions at the right time, however, it can be a bit complicated due to the large volumes of data that exist, so it is necessary to couple BI tools that allow you to include graphs and make reports with the needed information [4].

1   Business Intelligence

Business Intelligence is an abstract concept, in which techniques and tools that allow the organization and analysis of information that support decision-making are involved. The concept describes the capabilities of organizations to access data and explore information, analyze and develop perceptions and understandings about their businesses, which allows them to increase and make the necessary decision more guided by information [5, 6].

BI systems and tools play a key role in the strategic planning process of organizations. These systems allow the compilation, store, access and analysis of organizational data to support and facilitate decision making [6, 7].

BI can improve competitiveness, provide information necessary for the productive development of a company or organization, thus allowing better decision-making [8].

Another important point to refer to is about business modeling, this allows achieving certain objectives. Business modeling describes the relationships between the capture and representation of information within the enterprise. A model allows events to be specified, that is, to describe the behavior of each element or dependent on others based on conceptual criteria; measures and explains the influence of other elements; specify the results that analysts describe, in order to predict or modify. Therefore, it is intended to define what to measure and how it will be done, so it's possible analyze what happens, document, test and develop theories for the operation of the business [9].

BI allows organizations to reduce costs; the increase in income; improve the use of investment in ERP systems; and also improve internal communication [6]. The decrease in costs directly benefits an organization as it allows to eliminate delays in reports, allowing other activities to be carried out that conclude in a continuous improvement of the business, at the same time the decrease in costs based on BI allows to use opportunities that were previously wasted in the value chain, which produces new profits for the business [11].

BI facilitates the productivity of a company, since it allows the focus on information and its results, through the generation of reports or simply helps them make decisions.

Among the most popular benefits are best practices, decision-making support, process organization, since by including BI tools, a specific strategic, tactical and functional framework is provided for the analysis of business needs.

The benefits of BI are divided into cost savings; income increase; improve the use of the investment in ERP systems and finally improve internal communication [5,6]. The reduction of costs directly benefits an organization since it allows to eliminate delays in the reports, allowing other activities that conclude in a continuous improvement of the business, at the same time the reduction of costs based on BI allows to employ previously untapped opportunities in the value chain, producing new profits for the business [11].

Each of the benefits of adopting Business Intelligence is the total profit of the business, improve performance, improve analytical strategies, and satisfy the customer.

Despite having multiple benefits that Business Intelligence offers, it also has its drawbacks. Among them are making an investment where the economy must be considered and the training and time that the company has must also be taken into account [12].

2 Materials and Methods

This study uses a hybrid, descriptive and exploratory methodology, where the properties or characteristics of the Business Intelligence tools will be specified, subject to a comparative analysis [13].

The items used in this analysis are: tool name; developer; description; functions; features (license, GUI, plugins, compatible S.O, updates); advantages; and disadvantages.

Once the individual analysis of each tool has been carried out, a global assessment will be made in which what the tool enables will be considered: ETL Processes (ETL), OLAP Processes (OLAP), Report Generation (RG), Dashboard (DB), Support Technical (TS), Additional Components (AC), Tool Dependency (TD), Graphical Interface (GUI), Export Data (EXD), and whether or not it is licensed (LIC)) [14].

If a tool complies with the process or characteristic, it will receive a rating of 1, and if it does not comply, it will receive a rating of 0. In the end, all these values will be averaged and transformed in such a way that the final rating will be 5 points, with the ranges being 0 to 1.99 with a low score, from 2 to 3.49 with a medium score, and from 3.50 to 5 with a high score.

3 Analysis of BI Tools

Business Intelligence supports organizations to make appropriate and fast decisions that contribute to better performance and therefore makes them more competitive in the market. These types of tools are designed in an interactive and user-friendly way using graphics to make the information more accessible to the end user, which in this case is usually middle management or administrative [15].

Next we will go on to analyze the 19 selected BI tools: Open: OLAP DVP; Mondrian; Jedox OLAP; InstantOLAP; phpMyOLAP; RapidAnalytics; InetSoft; JasperReports; Eclipse BIRT; SpagoBI; Microsoft Dynamics NAV; Oracle BI; IBM Cognos Analytics;

SAP Business Objects; QlikSense; Power BI; Tableau; Microstrategy; and Domo BI (see Fig. 1).

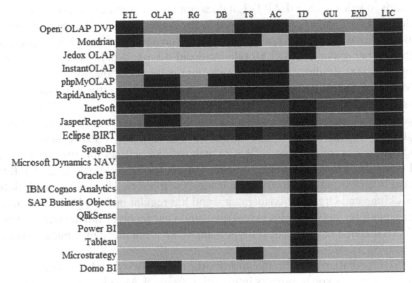

Fig. 1. Business intelligence tools scores (■ = 0, other colors = 1).

Open OLAP Data Visualization Plugin It is a complementary plugin created as an interface for Pentaho BI Server and Mondrian, it allows generating reports, creating dashboards, and viewing or querying data from an OLAP cube or relational databases through its interface graph. It has a GNU General Public License and maintenance service, it is compatible with all operating systems, it supports the Mondrian server, XMLA data, Microsoft SQL Server Analysis Services DB [16]. By receiving constant updates, it can be easily adapted to Mondrian and Pentaho, in addition to having an intuitive interface. It has commercial support and services that allow it to be implemented successfully. Its installation is tedious and the XMLA data source works exclusively for data belonging to the Mondrian tool.

Mondrian is a server to create and manage OLAP servers online, it supports XML files, allows you to manage OLAP servers and perform multidimensional queries. Its owner is Pentaho Corporation and it has an EPL (Eclipse Public License) type license, it does not contain a graphical interface, however, it is multiplatform.

Its complementary tools are JPivot, Saiku, Pentaho Analyzer, Pivot, EasyBi and it has updates made by the Pentaho community. It has four layers to display information, Presentation Layer is the top layer that determines the information displayed by the user and Queries are performed. Dimensional Layer which is the layer that executes the multidimensional queries towards the DB or OLAP cubes. Star Layer entrusts the program cache. Storage Layer adds data to the various dimensions of a relational database [17]. It enables the management of frontend tools, providing support for resolving incidents such as JIRA, the release times of Mondrian and Pentaho versions coincide. As it does not have a graphical interface, its use is intuitive, requiring programming knowledge. You also need complementary tools to be able to interpret data by the end user.

Jedox OLAP is a tool to manage and create OLAP servers and dashboards, produce Scorecards, queries to the OLAP DB, it does not have a graphical interface, however it provides an Excel plugin which is related to the Jedox OLAP DB synchronizing with each other. It has an LGPL type license and its owner is Jedox AG, it is compatible with the operating systems IOS Mobile, Android, Linux, Windows, and is in constant development [18]. It allows you to modify data in real time thanks to the integration with Microsoft Excel. It does not have technical support, and it is necessary to have a Microsoft Excel license.

Instant OLAP allows to query ROLAP and MOLAP databases, manage dimensions using Drillthrough and Drilldown expressions in real time. It also generates reports, dashboards, scorecards, manages OLAP databases, and allows information to be consulted from a web browser and exported in XML/A format to Microsoft Excel. It has a graphical interface and is multiplatform. It was developed by Thomas Behrends Softwareentwicklung und Organisationsberatung, and has regular updates [19]. It can be used from any platform, make queries in real time, and view reports from the web, it supports XML/A. It does not have technical support and there is not much information about this tool.

phpMyOLAP is an OLAP application for the use of MySQL, it has a simple graphical interface that allows you to process information from OLAP cubes in an analytical way for the generation of reports, it also allows you to manage data warehouse and import data. It is only compatible with Windows, it was developed by AlterVista and it has updates [20]. It is a simple reporting tool, however it is only used to generate unofficial reports.

RapidAnalytics allows to generate reports based on data processed and transformed by DataMining and RapidMiner for ad-hoc end users. It also generates Dashboards and has a graphical interface. It was developed by RapidMiner and has the AGPLv3 license, it is compatible with Windows, Linux and Mac [21]. Dashboards can be fully edited and its graphical interface is easy to use. It depends on the RapidMiner tool.

InetSoft allows to manage and create Dashboards and Scorecards. It also allows generating reports and querying relational databases and OLAP cubes in real time, it has a graphical interface. Its owner is InetSoft Technology Corp which has technical support [22]. It allows the use of suites that facilitate the use of the application and present the data in different ways in the Dashboards. It is only intended for the creation and management of Dashboards and Scorecards. On top of that, their reports are simple.

JasperReports is a tool to generate Dashboards, Scorecards and sophisticated reports capable of being exported in various formats and can be included in web applications, it also allows ETL processes. It has a graphical interface, its owner is TIBCO Software, Inc., which has a maintenance service and periodic updates, it is compatible with Windows, MacOS and Linux, it has an LGPL, Eclipse and AGPL license. Its plugins are Jasper products such as: Jaspersoft ETL, Ja-perReports Server, JasperReports Studio, JasperReports Library, and iReport Designer. You can export large volumes of output formats. It is necessary to have all the components installed.

Eclipse BIRT is a software project that allows you to access a wide variety of data warehouses, it also allows you to create data visualizations, reports, Dashboards and Scorecards. It contains a graphics engine that can be integrated with other applications, the designs that are generated in this tool are in XML format. It is in constant development by The Eclipse Foundation in collaboration with IBM, which is in charge of continuous development and updates, its license is EPL type. It has several add-ons and plugins and is multi-platform [22]. Capable of covering all types of Business Intelligence solutions, its integration is easy with other tools. It is necessary to have solid knowledge in programming.

SpagoBI is a BI suite capable of covering Business Intelligence project analysis areas. It allows creating Dashboards, Scoreboards, analysis models based on KPIs, and integrating ETL tools, Talend Open Studio Products and Datamining, as well as performing multidimensional database analysis, generating reports and exporting them in various formats. It was developed by Engineering Ingegnería Informatica S.p.A and has an Open Source license. Mozilla Public License v. 2.0 with constant maintenance and updates, its plugins are Meta, SpagoBI SDK, SpagoBI Studio, SpagoBI Server, SpagoBI and SpagoBI Applications [24]. BI solution that is required can be carried out. Allows to modify the views of the OLAP cubes. You need to know the tool to be able to use it.

Microsoft Dynamics Nav, is a solution (ERP) developed by Microsoft that adapts to small and medium-sized companies, developed by Microsoft which allows to create automated and integrated financial processes, manage data, processes, applications and systems connected to each other and be able to perform predictive analysis [24]. This BI tool allows users to access the system from anywhere and on any device. The integration of Microsoft Dynamics 365 Finance allows you to create a more productive and collaborative work environment. One of the downsides is that it is currently catching up with other CRMs on certain features which does not allow adjustments to the server code.

Oracle BI is one of the most complete tools on the market because it has real-time interactive panels which help take key actions and provide predictive responses by displaying statistical graphs [26]. This sophisticated tool offers us cloud-based services and data visualization, making individual interactive reports, allowing us to have integration with Office with ease of migration and updating of components. Oracle BI does not have a free version and does not offer a free trial.

IBM Cognos Analytics is an advanced business analytics solution that provides insights, data governance, and reporting. Which allows you to create data visualizations, infographics, dashboards, control panels and reports in a matter of minutes, and has compatibility with Cloud, SaaS, Web, Mac, windows, Linux, Android, iPhone [27]. One of the advantages of this tool is the fact that it allows users to have direct, productive and controlled access to data. Managed reports are created by professional report authors for other users or consumers. The only drawback is that a license is required to use all the tools.

SAP Business Objects provides comprehensive Business Intelligence functionality that enables users to make critical and effective decisions based on robust data and analysis [27]. This tool offers a very broad and complete solution for business management, it is designed taking into account the needs of small and medium-sized companies to facilitate their performance. One of the disadvantages of its use is the high cost of implementation for the first time due to the need for an adequate infrastructure and also the training of use is very expensive.

QlikSense is an advanced data visualization application, ideal for the analytical needs of groups, departments or an entire organization, allowing the management of high volumes of data and collaboration on any device, creating reports and dynamic tables [32]. It is a scalable product since it is compatible with a large number of data sources, it is capable of modeling data and performing complex calculations. One of the advantages of using this tool is that it allows to connect with multiple data sources to obtain an analysis in a complete visual way to communicate and collaborate more effectively with the work team. In addition, it is multiplatform, that is, it adapts automatically with a desktop and mobile version. One of its disadvantages is predictive analytics, as it is only possible through API connections with third-party software.

Power BI is a business intelligence solution in the cloud, which allows the use of different data sources, in order to process, analyze and present a report, allows access from any device to be shared by different users of the same company or organization; in such a way that all staff, administrative, financial, marketing, etc. can have business information in real time [30].

One of the advantages of the tool is the fact that it offers impressive interactive and customizable reports in any internal or external application, as well as fully secured data. It has an intuitive interface that is easy to use and its appearance is striking, which is why its user experience score is very high. It also has a large community of partner users and distributors that provide new functionalities and valuable informative content for new users. Unfortunately, the Power BI Free service is limited and you need to purchase a license, in addition, the business versions have a high price, but compared to other paid tools, this one is more affordable.

Tableau is a complete Business Intelligence solution, leader in the market and that allows decision makers to have all the necessary information in real time. Tableau allows the generation of advanced analyzes in record time, generating interactive visualizations and impressive demonstrations without the need for complex development with a very flexible configuration, since it can run under a server, locally on the user's computer or in the cloud, making it an easy-to-manipulate tool [31]. It offers the possibility of integration with cloud services in a simple way, it helps us to detect data correlations in a short time. In addition, it detects trends and erroneous behavior in the information. It has a community that contributes informative content and its manufacturer provides training available on the web. Its biggest disadvantage is that it is focused only on reporting tasks, without ETL and data transformation capabilities.

Microstrategy is a world leader in enterprise mobility and analytics software. A pioneer in the business intelligence and analytics space, MicroStrategy delivers innovative software that empowers people to make better decisions, available on Cloud, SaaS, Web, Mac (desktop), Windows (desktop), Linux (desk-top), Windows (local), Linux (local), Android (mobile) [32]. One of the advantages is that it has a high degree of personalization and real-time data analytics. Microstrategy has an SDK for data mining and predictive analytics. Its disadvantage is the need for highly trained human personnel to develop reports.

Domo BI is a subscription cloud platform that provides a business management solution that users can access from anywhere to perform analysis and generate reports from anywhere. It is compatible with all operating systems such as Windows, Mac and iOS. Domo offers a powerful and reliable cloud-based business intelligence (BI) system with the ability to display real-time data in a single dashboard [32]. This tool provides visibility and analysis through dashboards with data from various areas and performance metrics in real time, it has powerful data connection capabilities, which facilitates the integration of systems inside and outside the organization. Its disadvantage is that a license is needed to use all the tools.

4   Analysis and Results

Although both licensed and unlicensed BI tools were reviewed, only the free JedoxOLAP tool was able to obtain as good a rating as the ratings for the licensed tools. While only the Mondrian tool obtained a low evaluation since it only allows to manage and generate OLAP server online.

SpagoBI and Jedox OLAP were the ones that obtained the highest score compared to the other BI tools analyzed, obtaining a score of 4.94/5, followed by JasperReports and Eclipse BIRT, which obtained a score of 4.32/5 since they did not have OLAP processes, technical support or dependencies respectively. Open OLAP, InstantOLAP and Qlik Sense received 3.70/5, none of these three allowed to carry out ETL processes. phpMyOLAP, RapidAnalytics and InetSotf obtained a rating of 3.09/5 while Mondrian was the one with the lowest rating of 1.85/6 as it only allows OLAP processes and data export (see Fig. 2).

Among the BI tools analyzed, it is notable that among the licensing options they tend to be more complete to generate reports and make decisions within a company, in which QlickSense stands out. Power BI, Tableau, SAP Business Objects. However, these high scores should not be a straitjacket, since the choice of the best tool for a business depends on its needs and requirements based on functionality, architecture and cost.

Mondrain was the only solution with a low score. With a medium 3 tools (phpMy-OLAP, RapidAnalytics, and InetSoft), and all the rest had a high score (see Fig. 3).

To choose a tool it is necessary to know what characteristics the users of our organization have, these users may have profiles of information producers or information consumers" and a formal or informal selection process can be followed [8].

The informal process is one of the least recommended for choosing a BI tool since it can trigger unexpected results, resorting to forced changes after a few years, which would be reflected as a loss of both economic and time resources. These types of informal selection processes generally win the company that best sells its BI solution to the contracting company.

The formal process provides a greater probability of choosing the right tool for the type of business of the contracting company, and the selection of this must follow a formal process and be treated as a project, in addition, a selection committee must be created with few members made up of stakeholders from the different departments of the organization for the choice of the BI tool.

Once the committee is selected, it must determine the scenarios and users of use, since different types of users require different types of reports. Once the requirements

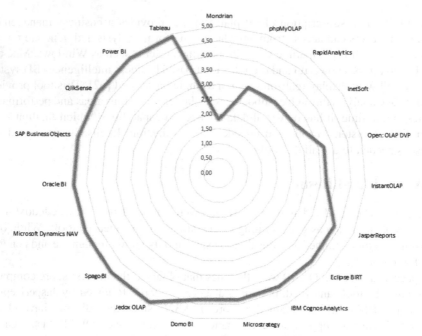

Fig. 2. Business intelligence tools scores.

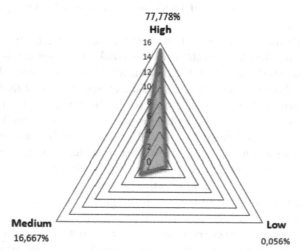

Fig. 3. Business intelligence tools scores ([0.00–1.99] low, [2.00–3.49] medium, [3.50–5.00] high).

have been defined, the different solutions provided by the different BI tools must be analyzed to achieve each requirement, and the selection committee must understand these differences and choose the one that comes closest to solving the requested requirements. Based on the requirements and solutions provided by each tool, the selection committee must also choose the one that best fits the organization in the short and long term.

5 Conclusions

In the competitive field in which companies find themselves, it is necessary for them to be able to get the most out of their data, and to stand out from the rest; due that, the incorporation of Business Intelligence in companies is of great importance. Although it means an investment on the part of the owners of the company, they will have more benefits in the end than disadvantages.

There are many Business Intelligence tools, in this case it is up to the company to make the correct selection of them, it is possible that the majority will go for unlicensed tools, but other companies will want to use and have more options so they choose licensed tools.

In this comparative study, all the theoretical content was first analyzed, to give a final approach to the tools that were going to be mentioned, some of these can be useful for large companies, while others are perfectly suited to small or medium-sized SMEs.

References

1. Yonatan, M.: Business Intelligence: herramientas para la toma de decisiones en procesos de negocio," Perú (2018)
2. Dodson, G., Arnott, D.: The use of business intelligence systems in Australia. In: ACIS 2008 Proceedings, vol. 74 (2008)
3. Alberto, R.: Impacto de la Business Intelligence en el Proceso de Toma de Decisiones. UPIICSA, México (2008)
4. MAYKROSYS: Inteligencia de Negocios. MAKROSYS (2016). http://www.makrosys.com/index.php/servicios-corporativos/bi-y-reporteria
5. Guarda, T., Santos, M., Pinto, F., Augusto, M., Silva, C.: Business intelligence as a competitive advantage for SMEs. Int. J. Trade Econ. Financ. 4(4), 187–190 (2013)
6. Guarda, T., Leon, M.A., Barrionuevo, M.F.O., Pesantes, M., Pomboza, E., Alvarez, J.: Business intelligence pervasive systems: BIPS model. In: 12th Iberian Conference on Information Systems and Technologies (CISTI) (2017)
7. Aaker, D.A., Kumar, V., Day, G.S., Leone, R.: Marketing Research, 10th edn., Wiley.com (2009)
8. Cano, J.L.: Business Intelligence. Banesto, Madrid (2015)
9. A. Rozenfarb, "Toma de Decisiones y Business Intelligence," Centro de Altos Estudios en Tecnología Informática - CAETI, Buenos Aires
10. Navarrete Carrasco, R.C.: Análisis de impacto del Business Intelligence: Expectativas y Realidades. Monterrey (2002)
11. Cipolla, A.I.: Business Intelligence. Que es y Beneficios? Open Webinars. https://openwebinars.net/blog/que-es-business-intelligence-y-cuales-son-sus-beneficios/

12. Guevara Alban, G.P., Verdesoto Arguello, A.E., Castro Molina, N.E.: Metodologías de investigación educativa (descriptivas, experimentales, participativas, y de investigación-acción). RECIMUNDO, pp. 163–173 (2020)
13. Vera García, A.C.: Análisis de herramientas BI en el mercado actual (2015)
14. Calzada Cantú, L.M., Abreu, J.L.: El impacto de las herramientas de inteligencia de negocios en la toma de decisiones de los ejecutivos. Int. J. Good Consci. **2**(4), 16–52 (2009)
15. Pentaho: HITACHI INSPIRE THE NEXT. https://forums.pentaho.com/threads/93595-OpenI-available-as-a-Pentaho-Plug-in-for-OLAP-Reporting/
16. Pentaho: Pentaho a Hitachi Group Compabby. https://mondrian.pentaho.com/documentation/installation.php
17. JEDOX: Jedox Knowledge Base. https://knowledgebase.jedox.com/jedox/how-jedox-works.htm
18. InstantOLAP: InstantOLAP. https://www.instantolap.com/
19. Apmuthu: Github. https://github.com/apmuthu/phpMyOLAP
20. RapidMiner: RapidMiner Community. https://community.rapidminer.com/discussion/53577/where-can-i-download-rapidanalytics
21. InetSoft: InetSoft Open Standars Innovation. https://www.inetsoft.com/solutions/dashboards/
22. ECLIPSE: Birt Home. ECLIPSE (2022). https://eclipse.github.io/birt-website/
23. SPAGOBI: Sopago BI. https://www.spagobi.org/
24. Microsoft: Dynamics NAV. Microsoft. https://dynamics.microsoft.com/es-es/nav-overview/. Accessed 5 Enero 2001
25. Oracle: Oracle Business Intelligence. https://www.oracle.com/es/business-analytics/business-intelligence/technologies/bi.html. Accessed 1 May 2022
26. IBM: IBM Cognos Analytics con Watson. https://www.ibm.com/products/cognos-analytics. Accessed 6 Enero 2022
27. SAP: ¿Qué es SAP BusinessObjects Business Intelligence? SAP. https://www.sap.com/latinamerica/products/bi-platform.html. Accessed 1 June 2022
28. Qlik: Qlik Sense® | Analítica en la nube moderna. https://www.qlik.com/es-es/products/qlik-sense. Accessed 1 June 2022
29. Microsoft: Power BI. https://powerbi.microsoft.com/es-es/what-is-power-bi/. Accessed 6 Enero 2022
30. tableau: Tableau Software. https://www.tableau.com/. Accessed 7 Enero 2022
31. MicroStrategy: Descubra MicroStrategy. Micro Strategy. https://www.microstrategy.com/es. Accessed 7 Jan 2022
32. Domo: Domo BI moderno para todos. Domo. https://www.domo.com/. Accessed 7 Jan 2022
33. Jaco, M.: Que es Business Intelligence Reporting - Una vision general completa Los in-formes de. 25 Julio 2020. https://zipreporting.com/es/business-intelli-gence-reporting.html
34. Jacovkis, D.: El software libre: producción colectiva de conocimiento. IDP. Revista de Internet, Derecho y Política **8**, 4--13 (2009)
35. Microsoft: Servicio Power BI para usuarios empresariales. 29 Septiembre 2021. https://docs.microsoft.com/es-es/power-bi/consumer/end-user-export#consider-ations-and-troubleshooting. Accessed 19 Jan 2022

Empirical Analysis of Data Sampling-Based Ensemble Methods in Software Defect Prediction

Abdullateef O. Balogun[1,2]([✉]), Babajide J. Odejide[1], Amos O. Bajeh[1],
Zubair O. Alanamu[3], Fatima E. Usman-Hamza[1], Hammid O. Adeleke[1],
Modinat A. Mabayoje[1], and Shakirat R. Yusuff[4]

[1] Department of Computer Science, University of Ilorin, Ilorin PMB 1515, Nigeria
{balogun.ao1,bajehamos,usman-hamzah.fe,
mabayoje.ma}@unilorin.edu.ng
[2] Department of Computer and Information Sciences, Universiti Teknologi PETRONAS,
Bandar Seri Iskandar, 32610 Perak, Malaysia
abdullateef_16005851@utp.edu.my
[3] Computer Services and Information Technology (COMSIT), University of
Ilorin, Ilorin PMB 1515, Nigeria
alanamu.zo@unilorin.edu.ng
[4] Department of Computer Science, Kwara State University, Malesse, Kwara State, Nigeria

Abstract. This research work investigates the deployment of data sampling and ensemble techniques in alleviating the class imbalance problem in software defect prediction (SDP). Specifically, the effect of data sampling techniques on the performance of ensemble methods is investigated. The experiments were conducted using software defect datasets from the NASA software archives. Five data sampling methods (over-sampling techniques (SMOTE, ADASYN, and ROS), and undersampling techniques (RUS and NearMiss) were combined with bagging and boosting ensemble methods based on Naïve Bayes (NB) and Decision Tree (DT) classifier. Predictive performances of developed models were assessed based on the area under the curve (AUC), and Matthew's correlation coefficient (MCC) values. From the experimental findings, it was observed that the implementation of data sampling methods further enhanced the predictive performances of the experimented ensemble methods. Specifically, BoostedDT on the ROS-balanced datasets recorded the highest average AUC (0.995), and MCC (0.918) values respectively. Aside NearMiss method, which worked best with the Bagging ensemble method, other studied data sampling methods worked well with the Boosting ensemble technique. Also, some of the developed models particularly BoostedDT showed better prediction performance over existing SDP models. As a result, combining data sampling techniques with ensemble methods may not only improve SDP model prediction performance but also provide a plausible solution to the latent class imbalance issue in SDP processes.

Keywords: Data sampling · Ensemble methods · Class imbalance · Software defect prediction

O. Gervasi et al. (Eds.): ICCSA 2022 Workshops, LNCS 13381, pp. 363–379, 2022.
https://doi.org/10.1007/978-3-031-10548-7_27

1 Introduction

The idea behind software defect prediction (SDP) is to deploy machine learning (ML) methods to predict software defects based on historical information such as bug reports and source code edit logs generated from the software development process [1]. SDP can help development teams use available resources more wisely in the software development process by concentrating on flawed or defect-prone modules or components before software product release [1, 2]. To anticipate defective modules in software systems, Data from software features which include source code complexity (Line of Code (LOC), McCabe, and Halstead), software development history, software cohesion, and coupling are used to build SDP models [3–5]. These software features are quantitatively measured to assess the degree of reliability and dependability of software systems [3].

SDP models can be developed using either supervised or unsupervised ML approaches [6–9]. The objective is to develop an SDP model that predicts defects in software systems with perfect certainty and accuracy. Nonetheless, the effectiveness of SDP models is reliant on the characteristics of the software datasets deployed. Particularly, the software attributes utilized to develop SDP models impact their efficacy [1, 2, 10]. By default, software attributes are muddled and skewed, which can be regarded as a class imbalance problem.

A class imbalance occurs in SDP if there is a disproportionality of class labels, having the non-defective and defective cases as majority and minority labels respectively. In addition, the class imbalance is a dormant issue that happens spontaneously in software attributes and impairs the prediction performance of deployed prediction algorithms. Addressing class imbalance as a data quality problem has piqued the interest of experts, as several kinds of research and techniques have been presented to handle the imbalance issue [7, 11, 12]. Based on previous research, SDP models developed using imbalanced datasets provide unreliable findings because the resulting SDP models produce poor performance. In other words, SDP models developed on imbalanced datasets preferentially identify the majority instances over the minority. However, it is crucial to re-affirm that correctly predicting the minority instances (in this case defective labels) is imperative, since neglecting the defective labels may be deleterious. Consequently, in the context of SDP, several researchers have adopted methodologies such as data sampling, cost-sensitive learning, and ensemble methods to address the problem of class imbalance [7, 11, 13]. Independently, these strategies have a positive influence on deployed prediction algorithms in SDP processes; nonetheless, the development of novel approaches to addressing the class imbalance in SDP is still ongoing research. The data sampling approach that increases and decreases the proportion of minority instances (over-sampling) and majority instances (under-sampling) respectively has been reported to overcome the class imbalance problem [14, 15]. Furthermore, the class imbalance has been shown to have negligible or no effect on ensemble techniques [7, 16]. In response to the foregoing reports, this research work proposes a hybrid of data sampling and ensemble approaches to overcome the class imbalance problem in SDP.

Data sampling approaches, especially data oversampling, have been proven in studies to have a positive influence on ML algorithms [17, 18]. However, as demonstrated in [19], they still suffer from excessive volatility and instability. To alleviate the large variance and instability of data sampling methods, ensemble methods such as boosting and bagging may be used [20]. The objective of this study is to conduct an empirical evaluation of the prediction performance data sampling-based ensemble methods. Specifically, models based on ensembled (Bagging and Boosting) Naïve Bayes (NB) and Decision Tree (DT) classifiers are deployed on newly generated datasets based on Random Over-Sampling (ROS), Synthetic Minority Over-Sampling Technique (SMOTE), Adaptive Synthetic (ADASYN), Random Under-Sampling (RUS), and Near Miss data sampling methods. Software defect datasets from the NASA repository are deployed in this study.

Summarily, the contribution of this study is as follows:

i.   Validate the effectiveness of ensemble methods over the conventional ML classifiers on data-sampled datasets in SDP.
ii. Compare the effectiveness of experimented data sampling methods on studied ensemble (bagging and boosting) methods.

The remainder of this research is structured as follows: Sect. 2 outlines the associated works that have been completed in this respect. Section 3 discusses the notion of imbalanced learning, and Sect. 4 presents the experimental data and analyses. Section 5 concludes this research work.

2   Related Works

This section investigates and analyses relevant developed SDP models based on ML methods and current solutions to the class imbalanced problem.

SDP is a method for detecting defects in software systems early on. It determines the characteristics of single code components to detect whether parts of it are prone to defects [7] or to forecast the number of defects in each component or module [2]. Experts have used a variety of ways to create SDP models based on static code metrics. NB [21], DT [14], artificial neural networks (ANNs) [22], support vector machines (SVM) [23], k-nearest neighbour (KNN) [24], and logistic regression (LR) [21] are just a few of the classical classifiers that have been used directly to develop SDP models. Nonetheless, these classifiers ignore the skewness and other inherent data quality problems in software defect datasets that could affect the effectiveness of SDP models [10]. For instance, SVM and KNN tend to overlook the minority class labels as they seek to maximise the accuracy values [25]. [26] reported that software defect datasets are very susceptible to the class imbalance problem, which is an example of the data quality problem.

Class imbalance is a latent anomaly of software defect data that consists of a small number of defective instances and a big number of non-defective instances [27]. NASA dataset PC1 exemplifies this, with just 6.59% of cases belonging to the defective class label. Since most classifiers aim to build classifiers that maximize overall prediction accuracy, this feature has a significant influence on both model training and predictive performance. Therefore, such models often neglect the valued minority (defective) class.

A considerable amount of study has been recommended to address the issue of class imbalance. [28] presented an overview of approaches for decreasing the detrimental impact of imbalance on prediction performance. [29] investigated whether various classifiers detect the same problems. To do this, they used NASA datasets to conduct a sensitivity analysis and evaluate the outcomes of RF, NB, RPart, and SVM. They concluded that certain flaws are more consistent in defect prediction than others and that each classifier identifies a distinct set of defects.

[30] addressed two procedures, undersampling and oversampling and then asserted that both data sampling approaches were successful. Furthermore, it was discovered that the adoption of advanced sampling procedures did not give any discernible improvement in addressing the class imbalance issue. Similarly, [31] observed that the RUS approach typically outperforms more complicated undersampling algorithms. In addition to undersampling procedures, oversampling methods are prominently deployed to solve the class imbalance issue. Aside from ROS with replacement, numerous more sophisticated data sampling techniques have been created. [15] proposed a unique oversampling approach termed the SMOTE, in which new minority samples are generated based on feature space similarities between existing minority cases. [32] used the borderline-SMOTE to oversample minority class samples close to the borderline. Both [18] and [13] found that oversampling outperforms undersampling. It can be noted that the aforementioned research on data sampling techniques is not conducted on software defect issues, and there is limited literature on evaluating data sampling methods for SDP. In [33], Tomek-Link, an undersampling technique was combined with Random Undersampling (RUS) and Synthetic Minority Oversampling SMOTE). It was reported that this combination showed an improvement in performance than other experimented methods.

Cost-Sensitive Learning is another technique that has been investigated by researchers. [34] evaluated data sampling techniques and MetaCost learning and there concluded that the sampling methods with replacement are effective for imbalanced learning. However, this method is still vague and needs to be more thoroughly investigated because assigning a cost penalty is not generic, it rather is dependent on some factors such as the dataset used, and the level of misclassification [35].

More recently, ensemble methods have been explored by researchers [7, 11, 16]. [36] suggested an ensemble technique for SDP based on object-oriented (OO) modules and compared the proposed method to some existing ML methods. They reported that the proposed method performed better than the studied ML methods. Furthermore, ensemble techniques have been also combined with resampling methods, which is known as the hybrid approach. [11] proposed a hybrid-SMOTE ensemble technique in what they simply referred to as <SMOTE + classifier>. In their experiment, they first resampled the dataset using SMOTE, and then the process of the ensemble was done using RF, AdaBoost, and Bagging. They observed that the suggested approach could effectively enhance the prediction accuracy of studied SDP models. [19] also researched this area, although their work was not in the domain of SDP, they demonstrated the effectiveness of ensembling resampled data over a single base classifier. They conducted their experiments using both simulated and real-world datasets.

3 Methodology

This section outlines and describes the data sampling techniques, prediction algorithms, ensemble methods, defect datasets examined, performance measures, and experimental strategy employed in this research work.

3.1 Data Sampling Method

In this study, five (5) data sampling approaches (SMOTE, ADASYN, ROS, RUS, and NearMiss) are studied. Data sampling techniques are broadly classified into two types: oversampling methods and undersampling methods [15]. The oversampling method's fundamental idea is to balance the dataset by raising or increasing the amount or frequency of minority class instances to an equal number of classes as majority class instances. In contrast, in undersampling approaches, the majority class instances are downsampled or lowered to the same number or frequency as the minority class occurrences. ROS, SMOTE, and ADASYN are instances of oversampling methods, while RUS and NearMiss are examples of undersampling methods. The samples to replicate in ROS are selected at random. This duplication of minority class instances often leads to overfitting and a poor prediction model. In SMOTE, however, the samples are selected using a (K-Nearest Neighbour) k-NN. The Euclidean distance between a feature vector and its nearest neighbour is used to generate a new vector [15]. ADASYN is an oversampling strategy based on k-NN that produces data adaptively based on density distribution [18]. RUS is an undersampling approach that removes examples of the majority class at random until both sets of instances are equal. Although some information may be lost in this process, it increases computation speed and power. NearMiss is another undersampling technique, but instead of randomly selecting samples to eliminate, it uses the k-NN approach [13].

3.2 Prediction Algorithms

In this study, NB and DT algorithms are used as prediction algorithms. NB is a probability-based classifier that is predicated on the Bayes theorem and the presumption that every pair of features is independent of one another [37]. DT is a type of non-parametric classifier whose goal is to create a model that predicts the value of a pre-determined instance using simple decision rules derived from data variables. The classifiers were chosen to bring heterogeneity into the prediction models and are based on their relative use and performance in previous SDP research. Table 1 gives a summary of the chosen models and their parameter values as employed in this research work.

Table 1. Selected prediction algorithms with parameter settings

Prediction algorithms	Parameter settings
DT	ConfidenceFactor = 0.25; MinObj = 2
NB	NumDecimalPlaces = 2; UseKernelEstimator = True

3.3 Ensemble Methods

This study investigated boosting and bootstrap aggregating (Bagging) ensemble methods. Ensemble methods generally combine multiple weak classifiers into a single strong and robust model to improve the effectiveness and stability of the model [26]. To learn the re-weighted training data, the boosting ensemble method utilizes a weak classifier in sequence. Finally, it uses a majority vote mechanism for its final judgement, including all weak hypotheses created by the weak classifiers into the final hypothesis [14]. In other words, boosting use weighted averages to transform weak classifiers into stronger classifiers, with each model choosing which qualities the next iteration focuses on. In the case of the Bagging ensemble, a bagging ensemble's baseline classifiers learn from a given dataset by extracting multiple samples from the original dataset. The classifiers' output is collected at prediction time. Consequently, the aggregation technique ensures that each classifier's variance is minimized while its bias is not raised. In layman's words, the bagging approach randomly resamples the original datasets, trains several base classifiers using the resampled subsets, and then creates a prediction based on the predictions of the many base learners [36]. Summarily, Table 2 depicts the investigated ensemble techniques and their parameters as they were used throughout the experimental phase of this research work.

Table 2. Experimented Ensemble Methods with parameter settings

Ensemble methods	Parameter settings
Bagging	Classifier = {NB, DT}, bagSizePercent = 100; numIteration = 10; seed = 1; calcOutOfBag = False; batchSize = 100
Boosting	Classifier = {NB, DT}, weightThreshold = 100; numIteration = 10; seed = 1; useResampling = True; batchSize = 100

3.4 Software Defect Datasets

The software defect datasets utilized in this research work were gathered from the NASA repository. In this research work, the [4] version of the NASA corpus was employed. The NASA datasets contain software features obtained from static code analysis centred on source code size and complexity [38–40]. Table 3 contains details of the datasets analysed as well as their corresponding imbalance ratios.

Table 3. Description of studied defect datasets

Datasets	Number of instances	Number of defective instances	Number of defective instances	Imbalance ratio (IR)
KC3	194	36	158	4
PC1	679	55	624	11
MW1	250	25	225	9

3.5 Evaluation Measures

According to available research, choosing performance evaluation criteria is crucial in SDP [41, 42]. This is because the datasets used to train and test the SDP models are unbalanced. Relying just on prediction accuracy values may not be sufficient. For example, in [1], an experiment was conducted to test the biasness of measurements such as Accuracy, F-Measure, and Area Under a ROC Curve (AUC). They concluded that Matthews Correlation Coefficient (MCC) is a more trustworthy statistic since it includes all confusion measures, as opposed to others that exclude the True Negative (TN). In this study, the prediction performances of the developed SDP models were evaluated using AUC, and MCC values. These chosen assessment measures have been used often and are reliable [1, 16, 21].

$$AUC = \frac{1 + TPR - FPR}{2} \tag{1}$$

$$MCC = \frac{TP * TN - FP * FN}{\sqrt{(TP + FP) * (TP + FN) * (TN + FP) * (TN + FN)}} \tag{2}$$

3.6 Experimental Procedure

This section discusses the experimental procedure employed in this research work as shown in Fig. 1.

The procedure is designed to experimentally investigate and evaluate the efficacy of the data sampling-based ensemble methods in SDP. Particularly, the original defect datasets and the newly generated datasets based on studied data sampling methods (ROS, SMOTE, ADASYN, RUS, and NearMiss) are deployed on ensembled NB and DT classifiers. That is, each of the studied data sampling methods is used to resolve the inherent class imbalance present in the defect datasets by balancing the number of the majority and minority class variables respectively, hence new datasets. The balancing of the original datasets is based on conclusions presented in previous research [21, 43]. The SDP models are created and tested using the K-fold (k = 10) Cross-Validation (CV) technique. The preference for the k-fold technique is based on its ability to develop prediction models while minimizing the influence of the class imbalance problem [27, 44]. Furthermore, the K-fold technique enables every variable to be deployed iteratively for the training and testing process. The investigated classifiers (NB and DT) and ensemble techniques (Boosting and Bagging) were chosen based on their application and performance in previous research [11, 36]. Table 1 (Sect. 3.3) and Table 2 (Sect. 3.4) indicate the parameter values for the classifiers and ensemble methods investigated in this research work. Following that, the prediction performances of the resulting models are evaluated using the chosen evaluation measures (AUC and MCC values). In addition, the prediction performances of the created model are compared to each other to determine the influence of data sampling techniques on the prediction models (NB and DT) and the effectiveness of the examined data sampling methods. Conclusively, the effectiveness of the created models is correlated with existing SDP models. The essence of the comparison is to validate the effectiveness of data sampling-based ensemble approaches in SDP procedures. The Python-Scikit ML library was utilized to develop the data sampling techniques, while the WEKA ML platform was used to construct the prediction models. These two ML resources are often employed in SDP and ML activities.

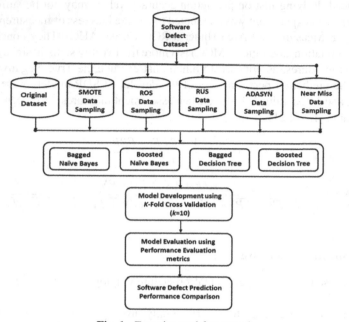

Fig. 1. Experimental framework

4 Results and Discussion

This section displays and analyses the results of evaluating the various constructed SDP models. It is crucial to show how the data sampling approach affects the effectiveness of SDP models. Furthermore, the performance of the studied data sampling-based ensemble models is one of the most important aspects of this study. As a result, the findings for investigated data sampling approaches, ensemble methods, and software defect datasets will be provided to reflect these impacts.

Table 4 and Table 5 display the AUC values of experimented prediction models using original and balanced NASA defect datasets.

From Table 4, NB and DT models developed using the balanced NASA datasets had better AUC values than when original NASA datasets are used. Models based on the studied datasets recorded significant increments in their respective AUC values except in the case of the RUS-balanced KC3 dataset. NB and DT models trained with SMOTE (NB: +9.52%; DT: +24.65%), ADASYN (NB: +8.16%; DT: +29.71%), ROS (NB: +4.23%; DT: +36.75%) and NearMiss (NB: +22.21%; DT: +39.36%)-balanced KC3 datasets had increments in AUC values when compared with the NB and DT models developed with the original KC3 dataset. On PC1 dataset, NB and DT models developed

Table 4. AUC values of NB and DT models on original and balanced datasets

		NB	DT
KC3	SMOTE	0.725	0.814
	ADASYN	0.716	0.847
	ROS	0.690	0.893
	RUS	0.584	0.595
	NearMiss	0.809	0.910
	No Sampling	0.662	0.653
PC1	SMOTE	0.831	0.919
	ADASYN	0.829	0.929
	ROS	0.818	0.964
	RUS	0.826	0.653
	NearMiss	0.858	0.840
	No Sampling	0.790	0.598
MW1	SMOTE	0.803	0.888
	ADASYN	0.812	0.875
	ROS	0.767	0.942
	RUS	0.734	0.588
	NearMiss	0.862	0.803
	No Sampling	0.314	0.503

with SMOTE (NB: +5.19%;DT: +53.68%), ADASYN (NB: +4.94%; DT: + 55.35%), ROS (NB: +3.54%; DT: +61.20%), RUS (NB: +4.56; DT: + 9.20%) and NearMiss (NB: +8.61%; DT: +40.47%)-balanced PC1 datasets had enhanced AUC values when compared with the NB and DT models. Also, a similar occurrence was observed in the MWI dataset. NB and DT models trained with the balanced MW1 dataset had superior AUC values than when the original MW1 dataset is deployed in most cases. NB models developed with SMOTE, ADASYN, ROS, NM, and RUS-balanced MW1 datasets had more than a +100% increment in AUC values while DT models developed with SMOTE (+76.54%), ADASYN (+73.96%), ROS (+87.28%), NearMiss (+59.64%), and RUS (+16.89%) had a significant increment in AUC values. These results proved that the experimented data sampling methods can enhance the performance of NB and DT in the presence of class imbalance.

Based on this observation, the performance of ensembled NB and DT models trained with balanced and original NASA datasets are further analyzed. Table 6 presents the AUC values of Ensemble NB and DT models on original and balanced NASA datasets. Specifically, ensembled NB models developed with SMOTE (BaggedNB: +5.93%; BoostedNB: +27.08%), ADASYN (BaggedNB: +7.42%; BoostedNB: +23.38%), ROS (BaggedNB: +5.64%; BoostedNB: +16.46%) and NearMiss (BaggedNB: +

24.04%; BoostedNB: +16.92%)-balanced KC3 datasets had increments in AUC values when compared with the ensemble NB model developed with the original KC3 dataset. A similar occurrence was observed with ensemble DT models developed with SMOTE (BaggedDT: +16.62%; BoostedDT: +30.06%), ADASYN (BaggedDT: +19.87%; BoostedDT: +33.15%), ROS (BaggedDT: +25.71%; BoostedDT: +39.88%) and NearMiss (BaggedDT: +14.68%; BoostedDT: +22.19%)-balanced KC3 datasets and original KC3 dataset. In the case of the RUS-balanced KC3 dataset, ensembled NB and DT models had poor AUC values that are lower than other experimented models.

Table 5. AUC values of ensemble NB and DT models on original and balanced datasets

		BaggedNB	BaggedDT	BoostedNB	BoostedDT
KC3	SMOTE	0.714	0.898	0.826	0.926
	ADASYN	0.724	0.923	0.802	0.948
	ROS	0.712	0.968	0.757	0.996
	RUS	0.591	0.546	0.545	0.584
	NearMiss	0.836	0.883	0.760	0.870
	No sampling	0.674	0.77	0.650	0.712
PC1	SMOTE	0.826	0.981	0.852	0.985
	ADASYN	0.829	0.988	0.821	0.991
	ROS	0.817	0.998	0.884	0.999
	RUS	0.812	0.785	0.882	0.756
	NearMiss	0.883	0.916	0.855	0.912
	No sampling	0.785	0.834	0.817	0.780
MW1	SMOTE	0.805	0.956	0.863	0.955
	ADASYN	0.813	0.971	0.897	0.980
	ROS	0.767	0.997	0.857	0.999
	RUS	0.722	0.666	0.690	0.533
	NearMiss	0.811	0.863	0.844	0.949
	No sampling	0.772	0.749	0.774	0.715

For the PC1 dataset, ensemble NB and DT models trained with the balanced PC1 dataset had superior AUC values than when the original PC1 dataset is utilized. Ensemble NB models developed with SMOTE (BaggedNB: +5.22%; BoostedNB: +4.28%), ADASYN (BaggedNB: +5.61%; BoostedNB: +0.49%), ROS (BaggedNB: +4.08%; BoostedNB: +8.20%), NM (BaggedNB: +12.48%; BoostedNB: +4.65%) and RUS (BaggedNB: +3.44%; BoostedNB: +7.96%)-balanced PC1 datasets had improved AUC values. Also, the ensemble DT model with a balanced PC1 dataset had better AUC values than when the original PC1 dataset is used.

In addition, on the MWI dataset, ensemble NB and DT models trained with the balanced-MW1 dataset had better AUC values than when the original MW1 dataset is deployed except in the case of the RUS-balanced MW1 dataset. Ensembled NB models developed with SMOTE (BaggedNB: +4.27%; BoostedNB: +11.49%), ADASYN (BaggedNB: +5.31%; BoostedNB: +15.89%), and NearMiss (BaggedNB: + 5.05%; BoostedNB: +9.04%)-balanced MW1 datasets had increments in AUC values when compared with the ensemble NB model developed with the original MW1 dataset. A similar occurrence was observed with ensemble DT models developed with SMOTE (BaggedDT: +29.63%; BoostedDT: +33.56%), ADASYN (BaggedDT: +29.64%; BoostedDT: +37.06%), ROS (BaggedDT: +33.11%; BoostedDT: +39.72%) and NearMiss (BaggedDT: +15.22%; BoostedDT: +32.73%)-balanced MW1 datasets and original KC3 dataset.

Furthermore, as recommended by [1], the performance of the developed models was analyzed using the MCC value. Table 6 and Table 7 present the MCC values of the developed models using both balanced and original NASA datasets. According to Table 6, NB and DT models created utilizing balanced datasets showed higher MCC values than original NASA datasets. NB and DT models based on the balanced datasets showed a considerable increase in their respective MCC values. This observation further supports the notion that data sampling methods can improve the prediction performance of SDP models in the presence of class imbalance.

Table 6. MCC values of NB and DT models on original and balanced datasets

		NB	DT
KC3	SMOTE	0.312	0.626
	ADASYN	0.308	0.694
	ROS	0.317	0.753
	RUS	0.321	0.396
	NearMiss	0.589	0.727
	No sampling	0.278	0.257
PC1	SMOTE	0.396	0.808
	ADASYN	0.386	0.839
	ROS	0.402	0.930
	RUS	0.417	0.273
	NearMiss	0.644	0.600
	No sampling	0.314	0.271

(*continued*)

Table 6. (*continued*)

		NB	DT
MW1	SMOTE	0.479	0.760
	ADASYN	0.469	0.743
	ROS	0.435	0.890
	RUS	0.500	0.280
	NearMiss	0.750	0.600
	No sampling	0.328	0.142

Table 7. MCC values of ensemble NB and DT models on original and balanced datasets

		BaggedNB	BaggedDT	BoostedNB	BoostedDT
KC3	SMOTE	0.328	0.708	0.504	0.728
	ADASYN	0.314	0.701	0.459	0.771
	ROS	0.338	0.817	0.407	0.875
	RUS	0.268	0.000	0.060	0.167
	NearMiss	0.626	0.701	0.589	0.556
	No sampling	0.233	0.137	0.298	0.223
PC1	SMOTE	0.396	0.861	0.541	0.909
	ADASYN	0.384	0.878	0.477	0.905
	ROS	0.406	0.944	0.402	0.972
	RUS	0.400	0.511	0.401	0.456
	NearMiss	0.644	0.711	0.644	0.691
	No sampling	0.287	0.194	0.300	0.315
MW1	SMOTE	0.466	0.810	0.609	0.840
	ADASYN	0.046	0.852	0.650	0.848
	ROS	0.431	0.898	0.536	0.923
	RUS	0.446	0.281	0.360	0.000
	NearMiss	0.718	0.725	0.750	0.600
	No sampling	0.333	0.267	0.279	0.332

Table 7 presents the MCC values of ensemble NB and DT models on both original and balanced datasets. Except in the case of the RUS-balanced dataset, the MCC values of ensemble NB and DT models developed using balanced KC3 datasets showed more than a +40% increase in MCC values. A similar phenomenon was observed with the ensemble NB and DT models using balanced-PC1 and balanced-MW1 datasets. Specifically, ensemble DT models on balanced-PC1 and balanced-MW1 datasets had a $+100\%$ increment in their MCC values in most cases.

Consequently, these findings indicate that the deployment of balanced datasets further enhances the prediction performances of the experimented ensemble NB and DT models. Table 8 shows the performance comparison of some of the developed models (ROS-BoostedDT, ADASYN-BoostedDT and SMOTE-BoostedDT) with existing methods on PC1. Specifically, the experimental results from El-Shorbagy, El-Gammal and Abdelmoez [16], Li, Zhou, Zhang, Liu, Huang and Sun [45], and Alsaeedi and Khan [7] are compared with ROS-BoostedDT, ADASYN-BoostedDT and SMOTE-BoostedDT. The developed methods had superior AUC and MCC values to existing SDP models.

Table 8. Comparison of some developed models with existing SDP results

Methods		AUC	MCC
PC1	Stacking (NB, MLP, J48) [16]	0.876	0.443
	Adaboost[45]	0.861	-
	AdaboostSVM[7]	0.760	-
	BaggedLR[7]	0.770	-
	*ROS-BoostedDT	0.999	0.972
	*ADASYN-BoostedDT	0.991	0.905
	*SMOTE-BoostedDT	0.985	0.909

*Indicates models from this study.

In summary, the analyses of the experimental results show that the investigated data sampling methods can ameliorate the class imbalance problem in SDP datasets while also improving the prediction performances of the SDP models. Furthermore, it was discovered that the analyzed data oversampling techniques (SMOTE, ADASYN, and ROS) outperformed the data undersampling approaches (NearMiss and RUS). There are considerable disparities in performance amongst the explored oversampling strategies since this changes throughout the explored datasets and chosen prediction models. However, it is worth mentioning that the RUS technique had the least influence on the prediction models and, in some instances, performed worse than when the original datasets were used. This finding may be ascribed to the random elimination of key data that might be critical for the SDP process. Although the NearMiss technique is likewise a data undersampling method, it eliminates instances based on their closest neighbour characteristics.

5   Conclusion and Future Works

Addressing SDP concepts and the class imbalance problem as described in research work is critical for successful SDP model development. Data sampling methods are utilized on software defect datasets in this study to alleviate the latent class imbalance problem by levelling the number of minority and majority class instances observed, resulting in new defect datasets with no class imbalance problem. Particularly, three data oversampling methods (SMOTE, ADASYN, and ROS) and two data undersampling methods (RUS and NM) are deployed on defect datasets from the NASA repository, while ensembled (Bagging and Boosting) NB and DT classifiers are employed on the original and newly developed software defect datasets.

Overall, the experimental findings showed that the data sampling methods investigated can address the class imbalance problem in SDP datasets. Furthermore, in most of the experimental scenarios, the studied data sampling method improved the prediction performances of the deployed ensembled NB and DT models. However, it should be noted that when combining ensemble models with data sampling methods, the choice of the data sampling method, as well as the base classifier, is critical if any significant result is to be achieved. In terms of the effectiveness of the data sampling methods, the oversampling approaches (ROS, SMOTE, ADASYN) had a greater (positive) impact on the prediction models than their undersampling counterparts (RUS and NearMiss).

As a result, it is recommended that data sampling operations, particularly oversampling approaches, be carried out during SDP activities. Implementing data sampling procedures may help to ease the underlying class imbalance issue and ensure the effectiveness of SDP models.

Following this, further study on the hybrid technique should be carried out utilizing other ensemble methods to investigate the data sampling method that best suits them as well as the classification algorithm that works well with those ensemble methods.

References

1. Song, Q., Guo, Y., Shepperd, M.: A comprehensive investigation of the role of imbalanced learning for software defect prediction. IIEEE Trans. Software Eng. **45**, 1253–1269 (2019)
2. Laradji, I.H., Alshayeb, M., Ghouti, L.: Software defect prediction using ensemble learning on selected features. Inf. Softw. Technol. **58**, 388–402 (2015)
3. El-Sharkawy, S., Yamagishi-Eichler, N., Schmid, K.: Metrics for analyzing variability and its implementation in software product lines: a systematic literature review. Inf. Softw. Technol. **106**, 1–30 (2019)
4. Shepperd, M., Song, Q., Sun, Z., Mair, C.: Data quality: some comments on the NASA software defect datasets. IIEEE Trans. Softw. Eng. **39**, 1208–1215 (2013)
5. Tiwari, S., Rathore, S.S.: Coupling and cohesion metrics for object-oriented software: a systematic mapping study. In: Proceedings of the 11th Innovations in Software Engineering Conference, pp. 1–11 (2018)
6. Balogun, A., Oladele, R., Mojeed, H., Amin-Balogun, B., Adeyemo, V.E., Aro, T.O.: Performance analysis of selected clustering techniques for software defects prediction. Afr. J. Comp. ICT **12**, 30–42 (2019)
7. Alsaeedi, A., Khan, M.Z.: Software defect prediction using supervised machine learning and ensemble techniques: a comparative study. JSEA **12**, 85–100 (2019)
8. Kumar, L., Dastidar, T.G., Goyal, A., Murthy, L.B., Misra, S., Kocher, V., Padmanabhuni, S.: Predicting software defect severity level using deep-learning approach with various hidden layers. In: Mantoro, T., Lee, M., Ayu, M.A., Wong, K.W., Hidayanto, A.N. (eds.) ICONIP 2021. CCIS, vol. 1517, pp. 744–751. Springer, Cham (2021). https://doi.org/10.1007/978-3-030-92310-5_86

9. Kumar, L., et al.: Deep-learning approach with Deepxplore for software defect severity level prediction. In: Gervasi, O., et al. (eds.) ICCSA 2021. LNCS, vol. 12955, pp. 398–410. Springer, Cham (2021). https://doi.org/10.1007/978-3-030-87007-2_28

10. Balogun, A., Bajeh, A., Mojeed, H., Akintola, A.: Software defect prediction: a multi-criteria decision-making approach. Niger. J. Technol. Res. **15**, 35–42 (2020)

11. Alsawalqah, H., Faris, H., Aljarah, I., Alnemer, L., Alhindawi, N.: Hybrid SMOTE-ensemble approach for software defect prediction. In: Silhavy, R., Silhavy, P., Prokopova, Z., Senkerik, R., Kominkova Oplatkova, Z. (eds.) CSOC 2017. AISC, vol. 575, pp. 355–366. Springer, Cham (2017). https://doi.org/10.1007/978-3-319-57141-6_39

12. Malhotra, R., Jain, J.: handling imbalanced data using ensemble learning in software defect prediction. In: 2020 10th International Conference on Cloud Computing, Data Science & Engineering (Confluence), pp. 300–304. IEEE (2020)

13. Batista, G.E., Prati, R.C., Monard, M.C.: A study of the behavior of several methods for balancing machine learning training data. ACM SIGKDD Expl. Newsl. **6**, 20–29 (2004)

14. Balogun, A.O., et al.: Data sampling-based feature selection framework for software defect prediction. In: The International Conference on Emerging Applications and Technologies for Industry 4.0, pp. 39–52. Springer, Cham (2020). https://doi.org/10.1007/978-3-030-80216-5

15. Chawla, N.V., Bowyer, K.W., Hall, L.O., Kegelmeyer, W.P.: SMOTE: synthetic minority over-sampling technique. J. Artif. Intell. Res. **16**, 321–357 (2002)

16. El-Shorbagy, S.A., El-Gammal, W.M., Abdelmoez, W.M.: Using SMOTE and heterogeneous stacking in ensemble learning for software defect prediction. In: The 7th International Conference, pp. 44–47. ACM Press (2018)

17. Tantithamthavorn, C., Hassan, A.E., Matsumoto, K.: The impact of class rebalancing techniques on the performance and interpretation of defect prediction models. IIEEE Trans. Softw. Eng. **46**, 1200–1219 (2020)

18. Xie, Z., Jiang, L., Ye, T., Li, X.: A synthetic minority oversampling method based on local densities in low-dimensional space for imbalanced learning. In: International Conference on Database Systems for Advanced Applications, pp. 3–18. Springer, Cham (2015). https://doi.org/10.1007/978-3-030-73200-4

19. Kamalov, F., Elnagar, A., Leung, H.H.: Ensemble learning with resampling for imbalanced data. In: Huang, D.-S., Jo, K.-H., Li, J., Gribova, V., Hussain, A. (eds.) ICIC 2021. LNCS, vol. 12837, pp. 564–578. Springer, Cham (2021). https://doi.org/10.1007/978-3-030-84529-2_48

20. Cai, X., et al.: An under-sampled software defect prediction method based on hybrid multi-objective cuckoo search. Concurr. Comput. Pract. Exp. **32**, e5478 (2020)

21. Balogun, A.O., Basri, S., Abdulkadir, S.J., Adeyemo, V.E., Imam, A.A., Bajeh, A.O.: Software defect prediction: analysis of class imbalance and performance Stability. J. Eng. Sci. Technol. **14**, 15 (2019)

22. Goyal, S.: Handling class-imbalance with KNN (Neighbourhood) under-sampling for software defect prediction. Artif. Intell. Rev. **55**, 1–42 (2021)

23. Cao, Y., Ding, Z., Xue, F., Rong, X.: An improved twin support vector machine based on multi-objective cuckoo search for software defect prediction. Int. J. Bio-Insp. Comput. **11**, 282–291 (2018)

24. Mabayoje, M.A., Balogun, A.O., Jibril, H.A., Atoyebi, J.O., Mojeed, H.A., Adeyemo, V.E.: Parameter tuning in KNN for software defect prediction: an empirical analysis. Jurnal Teknologi dan Sistem Komputer **7**, 121–126 (2019)

25. Yu, Q., Jiang, S., Zhang, Y.: The performance stability of defect prediction models with class imbalance: an empirical study. IEICE Trans Info Sys. **100**, 265–272 (2017)

26. Menzies, T., Greenwald, J., Frank, A.: Data mining static code attributes to learn defect predictors. IIEEE Trans. Softw. Eng. **33**, 2–13 (2007)

27. Balogun, A.O., et al.: SMOTE-based homogeneous ensemble methods for software defect prediction. In: Gervasi, O., et al. (eds.) ICCSA 2020. LNCS, vol. 12254, pp. 615–631. Springer, Cham (2020). https://doi.org/10.1007/978-3-030-58817-5_45

28. Mockus, A., Weiss, D.M.: Predicting risk of software changes. Bell Labs Tech. J. **5**, 169–180 (2000)

29. Bowes, D., Hall, T., Petrić, J.: Software defect prediction: do different classifiers find the same defects? Softw. Qual. J. **26**(2), 525–552 (2017). https://doi.org/10.1007/s11219-016-9353-3

30. Japkowicz, N.: The class imbalance problem: Significance and strategies. In: Proceedings of the International Conference on Artificial Intelligence, vol. 56, pp. 111–117. Citeseer (2000)

31. Peng, M., et al.: Trainable undersampling for class-imbalance learning. In: Proceedings of the AAAI Conference on Artificial Intelligence, vol. 33, pp. 4707–4714 (2019)

32. Han, H., Wang, W.Y., Mao, B.H.: Borderline-SMOTE: a new over-sampling method in imbalanced data sets learning. In: Huang, D.-S., Zhang, X.-P., Huang, G.-B. (eds.) ICIC 2005. LNCS, vol. 3644, pp. 878–887. Springer, Heidelberg (2005). https://doi.org/10.1007/115380 59_91

33. Elhassan, T., Aljurf, M.: Classification of imbalance data using tomek link (t-link) combined with random under-sampling (rus) as a data reduction method. Global J. Technol. Optim. S **1** (2016)

34. Malhotra, R., Kamal, S.: An empirical study to investigate oversampling methods for improving software defect prediction using imbalanced data. Neurocomputing **343**, 120–140 (2019)

35. Rodriguez, D., Herraiz, I., Harrison, R., Dolado, J., Riquelme, J.C.: Preliminary comparison of techniques for dealing with imbalance in software defect prediction. In: The 18th International Conference, pp. 1–10. ACM Press (2014)

36. Suresh Kumar, P., Behera, H.S., Nayak, J., Naik, B.: Bootstrap aggregation ensemble learning-based reliable approach for software defect prediction by using characterized code feature. Innov. Syst. Softw. Eng. **17**(4), 355–379 (2021). https://doi.org/10.1007/s11334-021-00399-2

37. Berrar, D.: Bayes' theorem and naive Bayes classifier. Encyclop. Bioinform. Comput. Biol. ABC Bioinform. **403** (2018)

38. Balogun, A.O., et al.: Empirical analysis of rank aggregation-based multi-filter feature selection methods in software defect prediction. Electronics **10**, 179 (2021)

39. Ghotra, B., McIntosh, S., Hassan, A.E.: A large-scale study of the impact of feature selection techniques on defect classification models. In: 2017 IEEE/ACM 14th International Conference on Mining Software Repositories (MSR), pp. 146–157. IEEE (2017)

40. Xu, Z., Liu, J., Yang, Z., An, G., Jia, X.: The impact of feature selection on defect prediction performance: an empirical comparison. In: 2016 IEEE 27th International Symposium on Software Reliability Engineering (ISSRE), pp. 309–320. IEEE (2016)

41. Tantithamthavorn, C., McIntosh, S., Hassan, A.E., Matsumoto, K.: An empirical comparison of model validation techniques for defect prediction models. IIEEE Trans. Softw. Eng. **43**, 1–18 (2016)

42. Tantithamthavorn, C., McIntosh, S., Hassan, A.E., Matsumoto, K.: Comments on "researcher bias: the use of machine learning in software defect prediction." IIEEE Trans. Softw. Eng. **42**, 1092–1094 (2016)

43. Yu, Q., Jiang, S., Zhang, Y.: The performance stability of defect prediction models with class imbalance: an empirical study. IEICE Trans **E100.D**. Inf. Syst., 265–272 (2017)

44. Balogun, A.O., Akande, N.O., Usman-Hamza, F.E., Adeyemo, V.E., Mabayoje, M.A., Ameen, A.O.: Rotation forest-based logistic model tree for website phishing detection. In: Gervasi, O., et al. (eds.) ICCSA 2021. LNCS, vol. 12957, pp. 154–169. Springer, Cham (2021). https://doi.org/10.1007/978-3-030-87013-3_12
45. Li, R., Zhou, L., Zhang, S., Liu, H., Huang, X., Sun, Z.: Software defect prediction based on ensemble learning. In: DSIT 2019: 2019 2nd International Conference on Data Science and Information Technology, pp. 1–6. ACM (2019)

MySQL Collaboration by Approving and Tracking Updates with Dependencies: A Versioning Approach

Dharavath Ramesh[1]([✉]) [iD] and Munesh Chandra Trivedi[2] [iD]

[1] Department of Computer Science and Engineering, Indian Institute of Technology (Indian School of Mines), Dhanbad 826004, India
drramesh@iitism.ac.in
[2] National Institute of Technology, Agartala, Tripura 799046, India
drmunesh.cse@nita.ac.in

Abstract. In recent times, data science has seen a rapid increase in the need for individuals and teams to analyze and manipulate data at scale for various scientific and commercial purposes. Groups often collaboratively analyze datasets, thereby leading to a proliferation of dataset versions at each stage of iterative exploration and analysis. Thus, an efficient collaborative system compatible with handling various versions is needed rather than the current most often used ad-hoc versioning mechanism. In a collaborative database, all the collaborators working together on a project need to interact together to perform extensive curation activities. In a typical scenario, when an update is made by one of the collaborators, it should become visible to the whole team for possible comments and modifications, which in turn aid the data custodian in making a better decision. Relational databases provide efficient data management and querying. However, it lacks various features to support efficient collaboration. In these databases, the approval and authorization of updates are based completely on the identity of the user, e.g., via SQL GRANT and REVOKE commands. In this paper, we present a framework well suited for collaboration and implemented on top of relational databases that will enable the team to manage as well as query the dataset versions efficiently.

Keywords: Collaborative databases · Versioning · Data cell · Database management

1 Introduction

Collaborative databases provide an efficient environment for team members working on a common dataset to work in a structured manner. It provides a mechanism allowing the collaboration members working on the same data to provide their inputs by interacting with each other. Each member is aware of all the updates made in the data by other collaborators and the current work carried out on the data. All the collaborators can discuss and comment on the data before it is finally approved and updated in the primary database after being thoroughly analyzed by an expert. With the advancement of data

O. Gervasi et al. (Eds.): ICCSA 2022 Workshops, LNCS 13381, pp. 380–395, 2022.
https://doi.org/10.1007/978-3-031-10548-7_28

science, there is an increase in the need for a collaborative database that will allow the collaborators to work in a collaborative environment, such as scientific databases, to develop and curate data from experimental and analytical processes [1, 2]. A collaborative bioinformatics database provides a typical scenario [5]. Bioinformatics databases require storing, retrieving, and analyzing large amounts of biological information. It requires different types of specialists to produce biological datasets (e.g., gene annotation database), share them among collaborators, share the updates among themselves for commenting, and keep updating the data until they converge and agree on the final content [3]. The data should be visible to all collaborators for discussion and resolution.

Moreover, all the updates need to be evaluated and approved by an expert, typically a data curator, data custodian, or the principal project investigators (PIs), to avoid any ambiguity or conflict in the derived update. Once the PI accepts the update, it is reflected in the primary database for further experimentation and analysis. Current database technologies, such as relational databases, provide an efficient mechanism to store, update, and read data [4, 6]. Data in a relational database is organized into tables in the form of rows and columns. A relational database such as MySQL provides various functionalities to carry out operations like create, read, update, and delete. MySQL includes functions that maintain the security, integrity, accuracy, and consistency of the data [10, 11, 33, 34]. It allows for easy updates and maintenance of the data. However, it lacks any support for Collaboration as any update needs to be approved first by the administrator before it is reflected in the database and is visible to the other collaborators. In this paper, we provide a framework to allow Collaboration in relational databases, namely MySQL.

Data Scientists need to work with databases daily. Data analysts and engineers need to be proficient in SQL and Database Management. Using a Relational Database Management System such as MySQL as a collaboration framework helps them access, communicate, and work on data more efficiently and robustly. The relational Database Management System is the core for storing and updating data for most projects. Thus using RDBMS as a collaboration framework makes the framework faster and more efficient than other collaboration frameworks such as git. This highlights the importance of this paper for building a collaborative framework using RDBMS.

Currently, MySQL does not provide any support for Collaboration. If a user updates a data item, it is not reflected in the database until and unless it is accepted by an update-issuer (PI). Only after being accepted the data is reflected in the database and is visible to the other collaborators. This limits the use of MySQL from being used in collaborative environments as PI becomes the bottleneck in the update process.

To better understand the need for our approach, we first illustrate how conventional update approval fails to support an efficient collaborative environment. Later we present our approach to overcoming these shortcomings. Assume that users A and B collaborate with PI in some tasks (as shown in Fig. 1). Suppose User A updates a data item X at time T1 and changes its value from x to y. At time T2, the PI is notified about the update made by User A on the data item X. Now, the updated value of X is visible to both A and PI. Still, B can see only the old value of X. Thus, PI becomes the bottleneck as every update needs to be approved by him before it is reflected in the database. Moreover, B cannot comment or discuss the update made by User A on the data item X before it is approved by the PI and committed into the database.

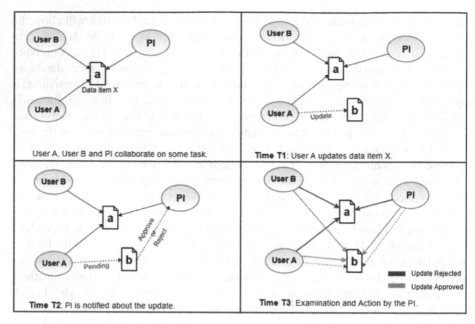

Fig. 1. An example of conventional update approval

This causes hindrance in the collaboration of work between Users A, B, and PI. Another drawback is that if B's work depends on the value of X, then knowing the updated value of X ahead of the time before it is committed will allow B to make necessary changes that need to be done in case the PI approves the update of X by A. Moreover, having prior knowledge of the new value of X will allow B to carry out his work with this new updated value and provide his feedback to the PI on the outcome of his experiment in case the update of X gets approved. From the figure, if the PI approves the new value of X at time T3, then B will be able to view the updated value of X after a time delay of T1 + T2 + T3. However, if at T3 PI rejects the update, then B will continue viewing the old value of X and will not learn from this experience. Also, as B is unaware of the change made on X by A, he may submit a similar change to X, which will be a waste of time both for B and PI.

To overcome the problem faced by the conventional update approval method in a collaborative environment, we propose a framework that will work on top of a relational database, namely MySQL, to handle the needs of a collaborative environment efficiently. As shown in Fig. 2, at a time, T1 collaborator A updates the value of data item X. Instead of directly committing the updated value in the database, it is marked pending approval. It is waiting for the PI to approve or reject the update. At the time, T2's PI is notified about the update. In the meantime, until the approval or rejection of the update takes place, any collaborator, say B, can see and comment on the update. Now the updated value is visible to B from time T2. Thus, PI is no longer a bottleneck as now all the collaborators can view and comment on the update even before it is committed in the database. Also, now PI can view the feedback of other collaborators on the update and accordingly decide whether to accept or reject the update. At time T3, the PI examines the update and approves or rejects it.

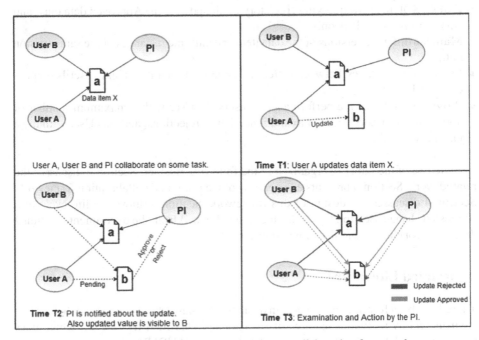

Fig. 2. Depiction of how things work in our collaboration framework

If the update gets accepted, then the new value of X is visible to B, and the status of the version of X with value b is changed to being "approved" (as shown in Fig. 2). Otherwise, if PI rejects the update, then the update status is marked as "rejected." After the value of the update is approved, it is finally reflected in the actual table and is removed from the pending table. We will discuss the role of the actual table and the pending table later in the paper. It is now compared with the conventional update model in Fig. 1. The delay for collaborator B to view the update is improved from T1 + T2 + T3 to 0. Such a model will provide efficiency in Collaboration as each user will give his feedback on the work being done by others before it is accepted and committed to the database.

1.1 Our Conributions

In this paper, we present an efficient system that realizes collaboration inside a relational database, namely MySQL. While MySQL allows easy updates and querying of data, it does not support different features needed in a collaborative scenario, namely update approval/rejection, commenting, versioning, history of updates, and dependency between different versions of data derived from each other. Hence, we extend MySQL with the following functionalities in the following manner.

- Perform Insert, Update, and Delete operations on the data item.
- Maintain the history of all the updates for a given data item or cell.
- Mark each update as either Approved, Rejected, or Pending Approval.
- Extend SQL to allow querying (i) history of all updates, (ii) Approved data only, and (iii) Most recent values only.
- Maintain different versions of the data item and multiple instances of the same version data.
- Establish dependency between different versions of data items and describe dependency rules.
- Provide metrics for the performance of users: (i) User with a maximum number of approvals, (ii) Users with a maximum number of rejections, and (iii) User with most numbers of updates.

The rest of the paper is organized in the following manner. Section 2 discusses the related work. Section 3 presents an overview of the presented collaboration framework. Section 4 discusses the design of this framework. Section 5 draws the life cycle of a suggested change. Section 6 presents the result obtained from the experiment. Section 7 draws the conclusion and lists down future work.

2   Related Literature

There have been few attempts to design databases frameworks to support a collaborative environment by including features like versioning. One such framework, which goes by the name AUDIT, has been proposed in the paper 'AUDIT: approving and tracking updates with dependencies in collaborative databases', and a query interface for this framework has been explained in the paper 'COACT: a query interface language for collaborative databases [14, 15]. The AUDIT framework has been implemented on top of Apache HBase [30–32]. HBase already supports version and history tracking of updates. However, nothing like this is facilitated by the commonly used relational databases like SQL. A drawback in the AUDIT framework is that it can consider only one instance of data at a particular version, i.e., if there is more than one instance of the data item at a particular version in the Pending table and one of them gets approved then all other instances will be automatically rejected. The framework presented in this paper considers all the instances of the data item at a particular version.

Orpheus database is another attempt at facilitating versioning capabilities on huge datasets [17, 18]. It is implemented on top of standard relational databases, and thus it supports most of the features supported by relational databases [16]. The OrpheusDB makes use of three models to represent different versions of the dataset:

- The combined table model supports versioning by including an attribute that stores a set of versions for each row.
- The second model uses a separate table that stores the versioning information by mapping versions to row IDs.
- The third model is used to store the mapping row IDs to versions.

OrpheusDB executes the operation 'checkout', which creates a new version of the table using the older versions. The other important operation is 'commit,' creating a new checkout version. However, the operations in the Orpheus database are performed on the complete dataset. In contrast, the framework suggested in this paper operates on a single data cell (a particular column of a particular row). Most of the frameworks proposed to date facilitate versioning only at the dataset level, contrary to the framework we are proposing, which supports versioning at the data cell level [7–9, 19]. Apart from these two models, there are other related works like temporal databases, collaborative databases, checkout and check-in systems, and active databases [26–29]. Temporal databases [12, 13], or multi-version databases [20–22] can track the histories of data with each update. However, these databases present zero support for mandatory features like pending approval or rejecting approvals by the PI. Thus these databases are not exactly used in collaborative environments.

An active database management system (ADBMS) [24, 24] is an event-driven system in which schema or data changes generate events monitored by active rules. Active database management systems are invoked by synchronous events generated by user or application programs and external asynchronous data change events such as changes in sensor value or time. Using various rules [23], active databases can handle pending approval and reject the pending approvals if they are invalid. However, such a system would be highly inefficient. However, there are a lot of shortcomings in using git. Git requires technical excellence and is much slower. It has poor GUI and usability.

3   System Overview

To explain how collaboration is carried out in a database, we need to understand various terminologies and processes that are carried out in a collaborative environment.

3.1   Update

The update refers to any changes made to the database by any collaborators. A collaborator updates the data item or cell in the actual table. This update can be of three types:

a) Insert - Insert a new row of data in the actual table.
b) Modify- Modify or change previous data already present in the cell of the actual table.
c) Delete - Delete an entire row from the actual table.

Any update made by the collaboration needs to be approved by the PI before it is finally reflected in the actual table. Each update creates a new version of the data on which the update was made. The version number of the updated data item is decided by the version number of the data item on which the update was made. We will elaborate on the versioning of data in the subsequent topic.

3.2 Approval/Reject of Updates

In a collaborative environment, every update made by a collaborator needs to be reviewed and examined before committing it to the actual database. This is done to maintain the authenticity and consistency of the database. It is the role of the Principal Investigator (PI) to ensure that the database does not contain any ambiguity by examining each update carefully. Once the PI has examined the update made by a collaborator, he decides whether to approve the update or reject it. If the PI approves the update, then the changes are reflected in the actual database else; if the update is rejected, no changes are made in the actual database. The record of this is maintained in history.

3.3 Pending Approval

When a collaborator makes an update in a data item, the update is set up as a request awaiting PI approval to be accepted and reflected in the original database. The update request is moved to a Pending table (explained later), where the PI can examine the updates made by the collaborators and take necessary actions (approval or rejection) on the pending updates. All such updates pending approval of the PI are termed as Pending Approval updated in this paper. On the other hand, all the updates in the pending table can further be updated by a collaborator resulting in a new update request, which will then be stored in the pending table awaiting approval of the PI.

3.4 Version

Each update of the data item results in the creation of a new version of that data item. Version no. of the updated data item is determined from the previous version of the data item from which the update has been derived. For example, if a collaborator updates a data item at version 1, then the newly updated data item will have version no. 2 (shown in Fig. 3a). In our collaboration framework, we are considering multiple instances of a version to exist simultaneously. This allowed introduction efficiency in the collaborative environment as multiple users could work on the same version of a data item. This will result in multiple instances having the same version no, all of which need to be considered. For example, assume a data item X having version 1 is updated by different collaborators. User A updates the data item X and creates version 2 of this data item (say version 2.1). Now, if another update is made by User B on data item X having version 1, then this will also result in the new version of data item X having version number 2 (say version 2.2). Thus, both instances of version 2 of data item X need to be considered to account for the work done by both the users on the same version of the data (Fig. 3b). Now to provide consistency among different instances of the same version, we assume the role of the Merger. We further explain the merging and role of a merger in the next topic.

3.5 Merging

Different users can create different instances of the same version derived from the previous data item. This can lead to inconsistencies and incompleteness in the version of data, as selecting a particular instance of the version of the data item will not show the entire changes made in that version. For example, assume two versions of X, version 2.1 and version 2.2, both derived from version 1 of X. Now version 2.1 may not contain the changes made in version 2.2 of the data item X and vice versa. Thus if a user views version 2.1 of X, he will not be getting complete knowledge about the changes made in the data-item X in version 2. This will result in inconsistency in the data among different versions. To overcome this issue, we introduce the concept of merging different instances of the same version to keep the data at a particular version consistent and complete. Thus all the different instances of a version, contributed by different collaborators, are combined, and only one instance of each version is maintained (shown in Fig. 4).

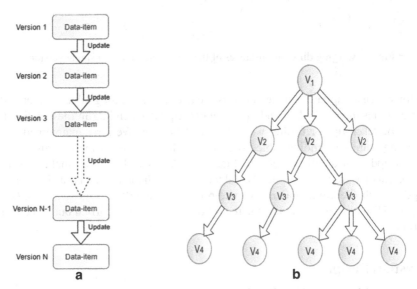

Fig. 3. **a** Numbering of different version of a data item, **b** Different instances of the same version of the data-item after update

3.6 Working of Collaborations in Databases

We have implemented our collaboration framework in a relational database. Data is stored in a relational database in the form of tables. Collaborators work on a common database that is accessible to all. In our collaboration framework, any changes made to a data item are not directly updated to the original table until and unless the PI approves it. We have assumed that the update is carried out in an Actual table that contains the data on which all the collaborators are working. We have implemented the framework for each cell of the Actual table. Thus, they allow the collaborators to change a particular column of a row from the table. Initially, the Actual table is empty, and when the data is inserted into the table, it is treated as the 1st version of the data. When a user updates a data item (or cell) in the Actual table, it is set as pending approval. This request is maintained in a separate table called the Pending table. So for each cell in the Actual

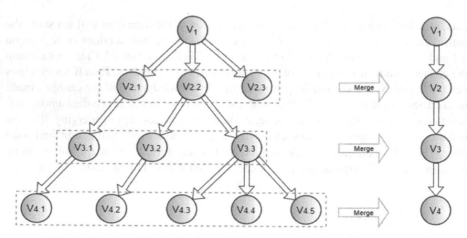

Fig. 4. Merging different instances of the same version into a single version

table for which an update is done, a row is created in the Pending table for that update, which contains the cell's data and other details. Updates pending in the Pending table can also be taken up for further work by a collaborator. We have maintained a Final table along with the Pending table. The Final table contains all the records regarding the latest update of a cell in the Actual table. Each row of both the Final and Pending table corresponds to the cell of the Actual table on which the update is carried out. Once the update in the Pending table is accepted/rejected by the PI, it is moved to the History table. The History table maintains the record of all the updates carried out in a data item over time.

4 System Design

This section describes the various tables used in designing the required framework. It discusses the schemas of the tables and their utility in making the framework sturdy and definitive. Apart from the Actual table (which stores the Actual data in its cells), we have used the following six tables:

Final Table: This table stores as a tuple, particularly the latest data approved by the PI corresponding to one of the Actual table cells. We identify a cell of the Actual table using the tuple <row number, column name>. Each tuple in this table has values corresponding to the following columns:

- Row no: It keeps the cell's row number in the Actual table to which this tuple belongs.
- Column name: It stores the name of the column of the cell in the Actual table to which this tuple belongs.
- Approved timestamp: It has the timestamp at which the PI approved this data.
- Data: This column has the md5 hash of the latest approved data.
- Latest contributor: It saves the id of the contributor who made the most recent change.
- Version no: It has the current version number of the data.

History Table: This table keeps the details of the changes which were either approved or rejected for all the cells in the Actual table. Each tuple in this table has values corresponding to the following columns:

- HS no (History Serial Number): This is an auto-increment column for identifying a row uniquely in this table.
- Row no: It keeps the cell's row number in the Actual table to which this tuple belongs.
- Column name: It stores the name of the column of the cell in the Actual table to which this tuple belongs.
- Data: This column has the md5 hash of the data.
- Version no: The current version number of the data.
- Operation: The operation is intended by the contributor to the cell's data, and it can take values from {'Insert,' 'Update,' 'Delete'}.
- Operation timestamp: The timestamp at which the change was implemented depends on whether it was approved or rejected by the PI.
- Status: The status of the change suggested, i.e., whether it was approved or rejected.
- Version seq no: The current sequence number of the data in a particular version (Assuming that there can be more than one data having the same version).
- Contributor:The Id of the contributor who suggested this change.

Pending Table: This table stores the changes submitted by the collaborators as a tuple, and these changes are yet to be approved or rejected by the PI. Each tuple in this table has values corresponding to the following columns:

- PS no (Pending Serial number): This is an auto-increment column for identifying a row uniquely in this table.
- Row no: It keeps the cell's row number in the Actual table to which this tuple belongs.
- Column name: It stores the name of the column of the cell in the Actual table to which this tuple belongs.
- Data: This column has the md5 hash of the data.
- Version no: It has the current version number of the data.
- Operation: The contributor intends the operation to the cell's data, and it can take values from {'Insert,' 'Update,' 'Delete'}.
- Submission timestamp: The timestamp at which the change was submitted.
- Version seq no: The current sequence number of the data in a particular version (Assuming that there can be more than one data having the same version).
- Contributor: The Id of the contributor who suggested this change.

Merge Table: Since we allow more than one data to have the same version, efficient merging of all the data having the same version number to get a single data is needed, and this Merge table just facilitates that. Each tuple in this table has values corresponding to the following columns:

- MS no (Merge Serial number): This is an auto-increment column for identifying a row uniquely in this table.
- Row no: It keeps the cell's row number in the Actual table to which this tuple belongs.

- Column name: It stores the name of the column of the cell in the Actual table to which this tuple belongs.
- Version no: It has the current version number of the data.
- Sequence count: It stores the number of data having the same version number, which has been merged for each cell corresponding to tuple <row number, column name>.
- Merged timestamp: It has the latest timestamp at which a new data having that particular version number was merged with already existing data at that version no.

Comment Table: This table keeps the details of all the comments made by collaborators on data waiting for approval in the Pending table. Each tuple in this table has values corresponding to the following columns:

- CS no (Comment Serial number): This is an auto-increment column for identifying a row uniquely in this table.
- PS no (Pending Serial number): It keeps the serial number of that row in the Pending table on which the comment was made.
- Comment: It has the comment made by one of the collaborators.
- Commenter: It stores the Id of the collaborator who commented.
- Timestamp: It keeps the timestamp at which this comment was made.

5 Life Cycle of the Proposed Framework

We assume that the Actual table is that table that has the original data, and a cell in this table is identified by the tuple <Row number, Column name> where Row number is an auto-increment column in the Actual table, as shown in Fig. 5.

Since this framework supports updates at a cellular level, so a collaborator might want to change the data in any of the cells and submit the changed data. The changed data of a cell, along with other details, is stored as a tuple (row) in the Pending table waiting for verification by the PI. In Fig. 5, the cell corresponding to the tuple <7, Col 2> has data equal to 'value 10'. A collaborator wants to update the cell data to 'value 12', hence corresponding to that cell, a row is inserted in the Pending table. The 'Data' column of the newly inserted row has data equal to 'value 12'. The change can be either rejected or approved by the PI depending on the authenticity of the new data suggested by the contributor and the feedback from other collaborators on this new data. Either way, this changed data, along with other details, is moved to the History table with 'Approved' or 'Rejected' status. If the PI approves the new data, then the version count is updated in the Merge table, and the new data is merged with other data of the same version so that a single unified data exists for a given version. As shown in Fig. 5, the change is approved by the PI, and hence 'value 12' and other columns are moved to the History table with status = 'Approved.' The data is updated in the Final table, which has < row no, column name > corresponding to the cell whose data is being changed and so corresponding to the tuple <7, col2 > in the Final table, we now have 'Data' equal to 'value 12'.

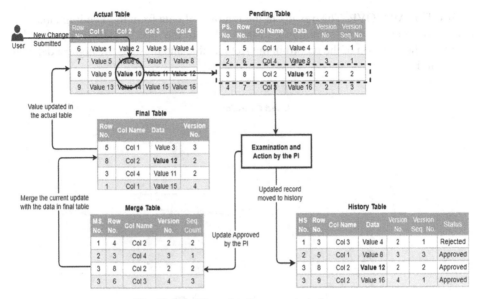

Fig. 5. The life cycle of a suggested change

6 Results and Discussions

In this section, we evaluate the performance of different framework Algorithms in the following manner. We evaluate the time taken by different functionalities under insert, update, and delete for the different numbers of records in the table. The corresponding output of the experiment is shown in Fig. 6, Fig. 7, and Fig. 8, which shows the total query delay for each operation.

Insert Operation: Issuing an INSERT algorithm by a collaborator involves inserting new rows in the Pending table having data corresponding to the row's cells, which are to be inserted. Issuing the APPROVE algorithm for the Insert operation will move the corresponding rows from the Pending table to the History table and insert the row in the Actual table. Invoking the REJECT algorithm instead of APPROVE will simply move the rows in the History table without affecting the Actual table. Figure 6 shows that the INSERT has the least delay, which is expected because it inserts data to the Pending table only. In contrast, REJECT inserts data to the History table and removes data from the Pending table.

Update Operation: Issuing an UPDATE algorithm by a collaborator involves inserting a new row in the Pending table having data corresponding to the cell of the Actual table, which is to be updated. Issuing the APPROVE algorithm for the Update operation will move the corresponding rows from the Pending table to the History table and updation of the row in the Actual table. Invoking the REJECTION algorithm instead of APPROVE will simply move the rows from Pending to the History table without affecting the Actual table. Figure 7 shows that the UPDATE operation on the Actual table results in the least delay. This is expected because it inserts a single row in the Pending table compared to

REJECT or APPROVE. This results in the removal of data from the Pending table and the insertion of a row corresponding to the update in the History table. Approve also results in the updation of the record in the Actual table and thus has the highest delay as visible in Fig. 7.

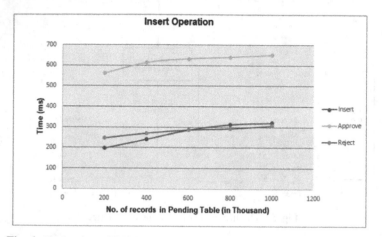

Fig. 6. Evaluation of INSERT, APPROVE and REJECT for insert operation

Delete Operation: Issuing a DELETE algorithm by a collaborator involves inserting a new row in the Pending table having data corresponding to the row of the Actual table, which is to be deleted. Issuing the APPROVE algorithm for the Delete operation will move the corresponding rows from the Pending table to the History table and updation the row in the Actual table. Invoking the REJECTION algorithm instead of APPROVE will simply move the rows from Pending to the History table without affecting the Actual table. Figure 8 shows that the Delete operation has similar behavior to the Update delay. Delete operation involves inserting a single row in the Pending table corresponding to the row to be deleted in the Actual table. APPROVE and REJECT both result in adding data in the History table and removing data from the Pending table with APPROVE, resulting in the deletion of the row from the Actual table. This is the same as the case discussed in the Update operation, resulting in the same trend in the graph. However, the delay of the Delete operation is less than that of the Update operation. This is because an update involves writing operations on the database, which increases the delay as no such operation occurs in the Delete operation.

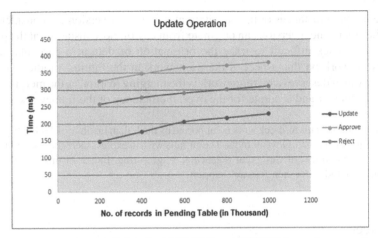

Fig. 7. Evaluation of UPDATE, APPROVE and REJECT for update operation

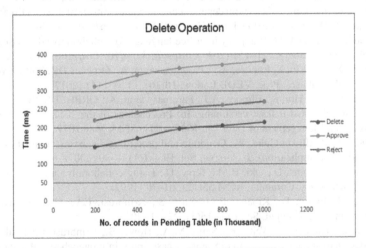

Fig. 8. Evaluation of DELETE, APPROVE and REJECT for delete operation

7 Conclusion and Future Scope

The framework suggested in this manuscript is implemented on top of standard relational databases like SQL, and unlike most other frameworks, it supports versioning at the data cell level. One more significant advantage of this framework is that it considers all the instances created by different collaborators for a data item at a particular version instead of just considering one of the instances and rejecting all others. The framework even includes certain contribution metrics that enable the PI to get an idea of the performance of different collaborators. A well maintainable interface can be easily concluded for the framework. We have described the algorithms and the prototypes for all the functionalities, making this framework easier to implement in a real-time collaboration scenario.

Since multiple instances of the data item at a particular version are considered, and the data item at the next version can originate from any of those instances at the previous version, it becomes difficult to trace the origination of data at a particular version. We intend to work on this aspect of the framework in the future. Another part of the framework which deserves a bit more work is the merging feature, as the merging feature needs to be efficient and accurate for the overall efficiency of the framework.

Acknowledgments. This research work is supported by the Indian Institute of Technology (Indian School of Mines), Dhanbad, Govt. of India. The authors wish to express their gratitude and heartiest thanks to the Department of Computer Science & Engineering, Indian Institute of Technology (ISM), Dhanbad, India, for their research support.

References

1. Mershad, K., Malluhi, Q.M., Ouzzani, M., Tang, M., Gribskov, M., Aref, W.G.: AUDIT: approving and tracking updates with dependencies in collaborative databases. Distrib. Parallel Databases **36**(1), 81–119 (2017). https://doi.org/10.1007/s10619-017-7208-y
2. Mershad, K., et al.: COACT: a query interface language for collaborative databases. Distrib. Parallel Databases **36**(1), 121–151 (2017). https://doi.org/10.1007/s10619-017-7213-1
3. Huang, S., Xu, L., Liu, J., Elmore, A.J., Parameswaran, A.: Orpheus DB: bolt-on versioning for relational databases. Proc. VLDB Endow. **10**(10), 1130–1141 (2017)
4. Xu, L., Huang, S., Hui, S., Elmore, A.J., Parameswaran, A.: ORPHEUSDB: a lightweight approach to relational dataset versioning. In: Proceedings of the 2017 ACM International Conference on Management of Data, pp. 1655–1658. ACM, May 2017
5. Navathe, S.B., Patil, U., Guan, W.: Genomic and proteomic databases: foundations, current status and future applications. J. Comput. Sci. Eng. **1**(1), 1–30 (2007)
6. Goldberg, D., Nichols, D., Oki, B.M., Terry, D.: Using collaborative filtering to weave an information tapestry. Commun. ACM **35**(12), 61–70 (1992)
7. Howe, B., Halperin, D., Ribalet, F., Chitnis, S., Armbrust, E.V.: Collaborative science workflows in SQL. Comput. Sci. Eng. **15**(3), 22–31 (2013)
8. Halperin, D., Ribalet, F., Weitz, K., Saito, M.A., Howe, B., Armbrust, E.: Real-time collaborative analysis with (almost) pure SQL: a case study in biogeochemical oceanography. In: Proceedings of the 25th International Conference on Scientific and Statistical Database Management, p. 28. ACM, July 2013
9. Eirinaki, M., Abraham, S., Polyzotis, N., Shaikh, N.: QueRIE: collaborative database exploration. IEEE Trans. Knowl. Data Eng. **26**(7), 1778–1790 (2014)
10. Harrington, J.L.: Relational Database Design and Implementation. Morgan Kaufmann (2016)
11. Coronel, C., Morris, S.: Database Systems: Design, Implementation, & Management. Cengage Learning (2016)
12. Nascimento, M.A., Sellis, T., Cheng, R.: Special issue on spatial and temporal database management. GeoInformatica **19**(2), 297–298 (2015). https://doi.org/10.1007/s10707-015-0224-z
13. Radhakrishna, V., Kumar, P.V., Janaki, V.: An efficient approach to find similar temporal association patterns performing only single database scan. Revista Tecnica De La Facultad De Ingenieria Universidad Del Zulia **39**(1), 241–255 (2016)
14. Collaborate your way to better SQL queries and data visualizations: https://blog.modeanaly tics.com/collaborate-your-way-to-better-sql-queries/

15. SqlDBM's Latest And Greatest: Team Project Collaboration: http://blog.sqldbm.com/team-collaboration/
16. Painless Data Versioning for Collaborative Data Science: https://medium.com/data-people/painless-data-versioning-for-collaborative-data-science-90cf3a2e279d
17. Bioinformatics Databases: https://www.ebi.ac.uk/training/online/course/bioinformatics-terrified-2018/what-bioinformatics
18. MySQL Database - very good thesis: http://www.engpaper.com/mysql-database-very-good-thesis.html
19. Relational Database Management System: https://searchdatamanagement.techtarget.com/definition/RDBMS-relational-database-management-system
20. Nambiar, U.B., Deshpande, P.M., Halasipuram, R.S., Iyer, B.R.: U.S. Patent No. 9,262,491. U.S. Patent and Trademark Office, Washington, DC (2016)
21. Alromema, N.A., Rahim, M.S.M., Albidewi, I.: Temporal database models validation and verification using mapping methodology. VFAST Trans. Softw. Eng. **11**(2), 15–26 (2016)
22. Alromema, N., Rahim, M.S.M., Albidewi, I.: An Efficient approach for modeling temporal database with interval-based timestamping in conventional database management systems. J. Comput. Theor. Nanosci. **14**(9), 4569–4575 (2017)
23. Kalanat, N., Kangavari, M.R.: Data mining methods for rule designing and rule triggering in active database systems. Int. J. Datab. Theory Appl. **8**(1), 39–44 (2015)
24. Berndtsson, M., Mellin, J.: Active database knowledge model. In: Liu, L., Özsu, M.T. (eds.) Encyclopedia of Database Systems. Springer, Boston (2009). https://doi.org/10.1007/978-0-387-39940-9_508
25. Veldhuizen, T.L.: U.S. Patent No. 9,424,304. Patent and Trademark Office, Washington, DC (2016)
26. Meagher, M.: U.S. Patent No. 8,822,848. U.S. Patent and Trademark Office, Washington, DC (2014)
27. Vance, J. R., et al.: U.S. Patent No. 9,277,833. Patent and Trademark Office. Washington, DC (2016)
28. Collins Jr., D.A., Amada, J.: U.S. Patent No. 8,925,811. U.S. Patent and Trademark Office. Washington, DC (2015)
29. Active Databases: http://web.cs.ucla.edu/classes/winter04/cs240A/notes/node1.html
30. Apache HBase Reference Guide: https://hbase.apache.org/book.html
31. The Architecture of Apache HBase: https://intellipaat.com/blog/what-is-apache-hbase/
32. Gómez, A., Benelallam, A., Tisi, M.: Decentralized model persistence for distributed computing. In: 3rd BigMDE Workshop, July 2015
33. Ramesh, D., Kumar, C.: An incremental protocol approach for secure collaboration between Byzantine processes in heterogeneous distributed processing systems. Glob. J. Technol. **3** (2013)
34. Ramesh, D., Khosla, E., Bhukya, S.N.: Inclusion of e-commerce workflow with NoSQL DBMS: MongoDB document store. In: 2016 IEEE International Conference on Computational Intelligence and Computing Research (ICCIC), pp. 1–5. IEEE, December 2016

Software Sentiment Analysis Using Machine Learning with Different Word-Embedding

Venkata Krishna Chandra Mula[1], Sanidhya Vijayvargiya[2(✉)], Lov Kumar[2], Surender Singh Samant[3], and Lalita Bhanu Murthy[2]

[1] Andhra University College of Engineering, Visakhapatnam, India
[2] BITS-Pilani Hyderabad, Hyderabad, India
{f20202056,lovkumar,bhanu}@hyderabad.bits-pilani.ac.in
[3] Graphic Era, Dehradun, India

Abstract. Software sentiment analysis has applications in numerous software engineering tasks ranging from code suggestions to evaluating app reviews which help to save the development team valuable time and increase productivity. In recent years, sentiment analysis has been used to study the emotional state of developers through sources like commit messages. State-of-the-art sentiment analysis techniques have been employed to accomplish these tasks with varying results. The goal of this paper is to provide a comparison between the performance of various models for possible applications of sentiment analysis in software engineering. We have used three different datasets to account for the possible applications: JIRA, AppReviews, and StackOverflow. In this work, six word embedding techniques have been applied on above datasets to represent the text as n-dimensional vectors. To handle the skewed distribution of classes present in the data, we have employed two class balancing techniques in the form of SMOTE and Borderline-SMOTE. The resulting data is subjected to six feature selection techniques, and finally, the sentiment of the text is classified using 14 different classifiers. The experimental results suggest that some models are very successful in accurately classifying the sentiment of the text, whereas choosing the wrong combination of ML techniques can lead to disappointing performance.

Keywords: Sentiment analysis · Word embedding · SMOTE

1 Introduction

Sentiment Analysis Tools and Techniques have witnessed an increase of usage in the Software Engineering World. Usually, Sentiment Analysis is used to identify the mood and feelings behind textual data and reviews, by leveraging Machine Learning Algorithms and Natural Language techniques. It is usually used by corporates to identify the sentiment behind user reviews, to garner feedback, be it positive, negative, or neutral, and to improve their products. In the area of

O. Gervasi et al. (Eds.): ICCSA 2022 Workshops, LNCS 13381, pp. 396–410, 2022.
https://doi.org/10.1007/978-3-031-10548-7_29

Software Engineering and its tasks, Sentiment Analysis can be used in various ways, such as to determine the polarity of user App Reviews, to evaluate the mood and mindset of software developers through their commit messages. Sentiment Analysis for Software Engineering Tasks aims to develop models which can accurately and efficiently predict the mood and feelings behind Software Engineering Tasks. The first thing to do to develop the predictive model is to perform word embedding techniques on the datasets, to convert textual data into vectorized data that is easier to analyze and process.

The experimental datasets were sourced from user's App Reviews, Stack Overflow comments and messages, JIRA issues tracked. All unnecessary spaces, symbols and stopwords were cleaned and Word embedding techniques were used on these datasets to express textual data as vectors. Six word embedding techniques have been applied in total to vectorize the data and preserve their semantic integrity. The application of the word embedding techniques now result in an abundance of features, of which not all are entirely useful to build predictive models. As a matter of fact, too many features can cause the accuracy of predictive models to plummet. We make use of six different Feature Selection Techniques to extract the most important and relevant features to improve the performance of the predictive model. The predictive ability of these techniques applied needs to be evaluated to make an informed decision on which word embedding technique is to be used to obtain the maximum performance and efficiency. The performance is evaluated by means of fourteen different classifiers. The application of classifiers on data that has been plagued with the Class Imbalance Problem will result in incorrect and unusable results. To rectify this, the classifiers are applied on the resulting datasets which have been rid of the Class Imbalance Problem, by the application of Synthetic Minority Oversampling Technique and Borderline Synthetic Minority Oversampling Technique. The challenges faced during the development of the model were:

- Word Embeddings: The dataset of user App Reviews, messages and comments on StackOverflow were represented as numerical features retaining their semantics in an n-dimensional space using six different word embedding techniques. The techniques used were Term Frequency and Inverse Document Frequency (TF-IDF), Continuous Bag of Words (CBOW), Skip-Gram (SKG), Global Vectors for Word Representation (GLOVE), Google news Word to Vector (GW2V), fasttext (FST).
- High Volume of Features: The application of the word embedding techniques have resulted in a very high volume of features data. Using all of the features data could affect the performance of the model adversely. So important features must be optimized. In this study, we have used six different Feature Selection Techniques to extract the relevant features to optimize the development of the model.
- Imbalanced Data: The data used to build the model is found to be imbalanced, which affects the performance of the model. A balanced dataset is one in which each class should have the same number of samples. Synthetic Minority Oversampling Technique (SMOTE) and Borderline Synthetic Minority

Oversampling Technique (Borderline-SMOTE) have been applied to resolve the class imbalance problem of the datasets.

This study aims to evaluate the performance of models developed using different Word Embedding and Feature Selection Techniques with the help of fourteen different classifiers, so that the model can accurately and effectively predict the sentiment behind Software Engineering Tasks.

2   Related Work

Different methods have been used to extract relevant features from textual content in the past. Rajni Jindal et al. have used the Term Frequency and Inverse Document Frequency (TF-IDF) to extract features from defect descriptions [3]. The classification of the defect reports has been done by the Radial Basis function of the Neural Network. The results have concluded that the model has performed very well in predicting high severity defects. Sari and Siahaan have also used Term Frequency and Inverse Document Frequency (TF-IDF) to tokenize the defect description. They have applied InfoGain Technique to extract the relevant features from the tokenized data. They have used a Support Vector Machine to develop Severities Prediction Models to predict the severity levels of defects [7].

Lov Kumar et al. have worked on applying word embedding techniques to predict software defect severity level [5]. They have also used seven different word embedding techniques to tokenize defect descriptions. Three Feature Selection Techniques have been used to extract the relevant features. The effectiveness of the word embeddings are evaluated by eleven different Classification Techniques with Synthetic Minority Oversampling Technique (SMOTE) to overcome the class imbalance problem. The results conclude that the word embedding, feature selection techniques and SMOTE can predict the severity level of a defect in a software.

Software sentiment analysis is a tool that has various applications but cannot yet produce satisfactory accuracy. Lin et al. attempted to solve this problem by retraining a state-of-the-art sentiment analysis tool exploiting deep learning on a set of 40k manually labelled sentences from StackOverflow [6]. They assigned a sentiment score to the 40k sentences, yet their effort yielded negative results with low accuracy levels. They conducted a comparison between Stanford CoreNLP SO and Stanford CoreNLP. They concluded that Stanford CoreNLP SO has a positive impact on the performance of sentiment analysis tools over Stanford CoreNLP. Another conclusion reached by the authors in their research was that the accuracy of sentiment analysis tools is, in general, poor on SE datasets.

Biswas et al. took a different approach by attempting to improve performance using software domain-specific word embeddings learned from StackOverflow [1]. They compared the impact on the performance of sentiment analysis tools using the domain-specific word embeddings with those that used generic word embeddings learned from Google News. Their results showed that the generic word embeddings performed at par or better than the domain-specific word embeddings. The domain-specific word embeddings led to a 10–20% decrease in precision compared to the generic word embeddings. Biswas et al. also studied the impact of oversampling and undersampling techniques for handling small SE datasets with a skewed distribution. They arrived at the conclusion that is oversampling alone, or a combination of undersampling and oversampling together, in the training of sentiment analysis tools resulted in improved performance. They achieved recall values of 56% for negative sentences and 46% for positive sentences, a major improvement on the work done by Lin et al.

Islam et al. proposed a tool for sentiment analysis, SentiStrength-SE, which achieved 73.85% precision and 85% recall [2]. In their work, they highlight some of the difficulties faced by sentiment analysis tools which include:

- Domain-specific meaning of words
- Context-sensitive variations in meanings of words
- Sentimental words in copy-pasted content (e.g., code)
- Difficulties in dealing with negation
- Wrong detection of proper nouns
- Difficulty in dealing with irony and sarcasm

These difficulties are faced by most state-of-the-art tools and highlight why achieving high accuracies in software sentiment analysis is still a challenging task.

3 Study Design

3.1 Experimental Dataset

In this experiment, three different datasets have been used, which are AppReviews, JIRA and StackOverflow. These datasets are collections of reviews, comments, etc. relating to Software Engineering and its tasks. Each dataset contains 'Sentence's' and their corresponding 'Oracles', by which the sentiment can be determined.

3.2 Word Embeddings

The textual data of the dataset is to be expressed as vectors in relation with each other. Six different word embedding techniques including Term Frequency and Inverse Document Frequency (TF-IDF), Continuous Bag of Words (CBOW), Skip-Gram (SKG), Global Vectors for Word Representation (GLOVE), Google news Word to Vector (GW2V), fasttext (FST) have been applied on the dataset. These techniques were used to represent the textual data as a vector in an n-dimensional space. We have also removed any and all stopwords, bad symbols and spaces before applying the word embedding techniques. These will now be used to develop models to determine the sentiment of Software Engineering Tasks.

3.3   Feature Selection Techniques

As we use the vectors as inputs to develop the model, the performance depends upon the optimization of the important features. To extract the important features from the existing set of vectors. We use six different Feature Selection Techniques, i.e. Principal Components Analysis, Analysis of Variance (ANOVA), GainRatioAttributeEval, InfoGainAttributeEval, ClassifierAttributeEval, OneRAttributeEval to remove irrelevant features and provide us with the set of relevant and important features.

3.4   Overcoming the Class Imbalance Problem

After analysis of the data, it becomes quite evident that the data is suffering from a class imbalance problem i.e., the number of samples in each class is not the same. So, the balancing of data is required, to improve the predictive ability of the developed Sentiment Analysis Models. We have performed Synthetic Minority Oversampling Technique (SMOTE) and Borderline Synthetic Minority Oversampling Technique (Borderline-SMOTE) on each dataset to balance the data.

3.5   Classification Techniques

The predictive ability of the different techniques used are evaluated using fourteen different classifiers such as Multinomial Naive Bayes (MNB), Bernoulli's Naive Bayes (BNB), Gaussian Naive Bayes (GNB), Complement Naïve Bayes (CNB), Decision Tree Classifier, KNeighbours Classifier, SVM with Linear Kernel (SVML), SVM with Polynomial Kernel (SVMP), SVM with RBF Kernel (SVMR), MinmaxScaler, BaggingClassifier, RandomForestClassifier, ExtraTreesClassifier, AdaBoostClassifier, GradientBoostingClassifier.

4   Research Methodology

In this work, we have applied five different word embedding methods to extract features from the software requirements in natural language, balanced the classes using SMOTE, selected features from both the balanced and imbalanced datasets, and used them as input to develop models for classification. These models are trained with eight different classifiers, with one of them being a soft voting ensemble classifier. The proposed methodology entails extracting features from text data using word embedding techniques, class balancing, deleting irrelevant and redundant features, and lastly, creating prediction models utilizing eight distinct classifiers. In this experiment, we employed the Rank-Sum test to identify features that may distinguish between functional and non-functional needs, as well as Principal component analysis to reduce the variance of the numerical features produced. Finally, eight distinct classifiers, including an ensemble classifier, are used to create the required classifications, which are then confirmed using 10-fold cross-validation. The accuracy, F-measure, and AUC of the developed requirement categorization models are extracted and compared using the Box-plot and Friedman test.

5 Empirical Results and Analysis

In this work, we have applied six different word embedding techniques, two class balancing techniques, six feature selection techniques, and fourteen different classification techniques to analyze the sentiment of the software engineering databases. Therefore, a total of 5292 [3 datasets * 6 word-embedding techniques * (2 sets of class-balancing techniques +1 set of original data) * 7 sets of features * 14 classifiers] distinct prediction models are built in this study. The predictive ability of these trained models is evaluated with Area Under Curve (AUC) and accuracy values, as seen in Tables 1 and 2 respectively. The first observation of note is that the range of accuracy from 13.73% to 98.68% shows that certain models perform exceedingly well but choosing the wrong combination of ML techniques can lead to very negative results. A second noteworthy observation is that the performance of the same ML model varies significantly between JIRA, AppReviews, and StackOverflow datasets. The performance metrics are lower for StackOverflow dataset than the other two datasets, which shows that sentiment prediction is a more challenging task for StackOverflow. This is corroborated by the fact that there was disagreement in 18.6% of the classifications, even when done by humans.

5.1 Comparative Analysis

The various models created utilizing word embedding techniques, class balancing methods, feature selection techniques, and different classifiers are compared in this section. The comparison is based on statistics like area under the ROC curve (AUC) and accuracy, with box plots serving as a visual depiction of the comparative performance. The Friedman test was used in this research to verify the findings. The Friedman test is used to accept or reject the following hypothesis.

- *Null Hypothesis-* The prediction ability of models constructed for sentiment analysis utilizing various combinations of word embedding, class balancing, feature selection, and classification methods is not significantly different.
- *Alternate Hypothesis-* The prediction ability of models constructed for sentiment analysis utilizing various combinations of word embedding, class balancing, feature selection, and classification methods is significantly different.

The Friedman test was carried out with a significance threshold of $\alpha = 0.05$ with degrees of freedom as 5 for word embedding, 2 for class balancing, 6 for feature selection, and 13 for different classifier comparisons.

Table 1. AUC: all features

		MNB	BNB	GNB	CNB	DT	KNN	SVC-LIN	SVC-Poly	SVC-RBF	BAG	RF	EXTR	AdaB	GRaB
ORGDATA															
TFIDF	AppReviews	0.90	0.90	0.82	0.91	0.81	0.82	0.88	0.85	0.89	0.87	0.89	0.90	0.83	0.83
TFIDF	JIRA	0.96	0.97	0.86	0.96	0.91	0.90	0.95	0.93	0.93	0.93	0.95	0.95	0.92	0.90
TFIDF	StackOverflow	0.73	0.73	0.56	0.74	0.58	0.66	0.66	0.65	0.69	0.70	0.67	0.65	0.66	0.59
CBOW	AppReviews	0.48	0.40	0.56	0.74	0.63	0.76	0.83	0.82	0.83	0.77	0.77	0.79	0.77	0.77
CBOW	JIRA	0.54	0.47	0.50	0.82	0.78	0.94	0.89	0.90	0.89	0.95	0.93	0.91	0.89	0.87
CBOW	StackOverflow	0.46	0.45	0.51	0.53	0.52	0.63	0.47	0.46	0.47	0.65	0.59	0.58	0.59	0.61
SKG	AppReviews	0.64	0.39	0.70	0.65	0.66	0.72	0.85	0.82	0.84	0.73	0.75	0.76	0.81	0.82
SKG	JIRA	0.79	0.50	0.75	0.80	0.82	0.94	0.93	0.95	0.91	0.95	0.93	0.95	0.91	0.91
SKG	StackOverflow	0.47	0.45	0.54	0.54	0.52	0.61	0.55	0.55	0.51	0.62	0.61	0.60	0.62	0.63
GLOVE	AppReviews	0.89	0.42	0.86	0.89	0.71	0.83	0.89	0.86	0.91	0.86	0.83	0.81	0.84	0.84
GLOVE	JIRA	0.96	0.50	0.96	0.96	0.82	0.96	0.97	0.96	0.97	0.96	0.94	0.94	0.94	0.94
GLOVE	StackOverflow	0.74	0.48	0.71	0.74	0.56	0.67	0.75	0.73	0.76	0.73	0.67	0.65	0.69	0.67
GW2V	AppReviews	0.91	0.44	0.86	0.91	0.72	0.86	0.92	0.91	0.93	0.88	0.85	0.83	0.83	0.82
GW2V	JIRA	0.97	0.50	0.92	0.97	0.83	0.97	0.98	0.98	0.99	0.98	0.95	0.97	0.93	0.93
GW2V	StackOverflow	0.79	0.46	0.78	0.80	0.52	0.71	0.77	0.77	0.83	0.77	0.62	0.67	0.67	0.63
FASTXT	AppReviews	0.63	0.37	0.70	0.64	0.58	0.68	0.69	0.71	0.77	0.67	0.65	0.67	0.75	0.70
FASTXT	JIRA	0.83	0.53	0.78	0.83	0.77	0.87	0.88	0.91	0.91	0.88	0.87	0.87	0.84	0.84
FASTXT	StackOverflow	0.59	0.45	0.60	0.59	0.51	0.62	0.50	0.59	0.58	0.60	0.56	0.57	0.59	0.60
SMOTE															
TFIDF	AppReviews	0.86	0.87	0.80	0.87	0.83	0.87	0.90	0.92	0.93	0.89	0.93	0.95	0.85	0.80
TFIDF	JIRA	0.96	0.97	0.87	0.96	0.94	0.95	0.97	0.96	0.95	0.96	0.97	0.97	0.94	0.93
TFIDF	StackOverflow	0.84	0.85	0.66	0.84	0.88	0.91	0.83	0.87	0.92	0.89	0.94	0.95	0.72	0.70
CBOW	AppReviews	0.52	0.46	0.56	0.75	0.76	0.86	0.84	0.84	0.86	0.87	0.89	0.92	0.78	0.79
CBOW	JIRA	0.64	0.49	0.52	0.87	0.84	0.97	0.89	0.94	0.86	0.97	0.97	0.97	0.91	0.92
CBOW	StackOverflow	0.51	0.48	0.52	0.56	0.82	0.97	0.76	0.78	0.76	0.98	0.98	0.98	0.74	0.75
SKG	AppReviews	0.61	0.44	0.64	0.62	0.78	0.86	0.86	0.89	0.87	0.84	0.90	0.91	0.82	0.81
SKG	JIRA	0.79	0.48	0.77	0.79	0.90	0.96	0.95	0.96	0.93	0.97	0.98	0.99	0.94	0.94
SKG	StackOverflow	0.50	0.48	0.54	0.60	0.85	0.96	0.80	0.81	0.80	0.96	0.98	0.99	0.78	0.79
GLOVE	AppReviews	0.86	0.45	0.87	0.87	0.78	0.91	0.93	0.94	0.97	0.92	0.93	0.93	0.86	0.85
GLOVE	JIRA	0.97	0.47	0.97	0.97	0.88	0.97	0.99	0.98	0.99	0.98	0.98	0.99	0.96	0.96
GLOVE	StackOverflow	0.76	0.47	0.76	0.76	0.85	0.96	0.89	0.99	0.99	0.98	0.98	0.99	0.81	0.80
GW2V	AppReviews	0.88	0.47	0.86	0.88	0.78	0.92	0.98	0.98	0.99	0.91	0.93	0.94	0.84	0.86
GW2V	JIRA	0.97	0.52	0.93	0.97	0.86	0.97	1.00	1.00	1.00	0.99	0.98	0.98	0.95	0.94
GW2V	StackOverflow	0.85	0.46	0.85	0.85	0.87	0.95	0.97	0.99	1.00	0.97	0.98	0.99	0.82	0.82
FASTXT	AppReviews	0.63	0.45	0.62	0.64	0.69	0.78	0.70	0.79	0.75	0.75	0.84	0.88	0.78	0.76
FASTXT	JIRA	0.84	0.56	0.77	0.84	0.82	0.93	0.90	0.95	0.94	0.93	0.96	0.97	0.88	0.88
FASTXT	StackOverflow	0.65	0.48	0.62	0.66	0.85	0.97	0.53	0.91	0.88	0.97	0.97	0.99	0.77	0.76
BLSMOTE															
TFIDF	AppReviews	0.87	0.88	0.77	0.87	0.83	0.87	0.90	0.89	0.93	0.89	0.93	0.93	0.85	0.81
TFIDF	JIRA	0.96	0.98	0.87	0.96	0.94	0.92	0.97	0.96	0.96	0.96	0.98	0.97	0.92	0.92
TFIDF	StackOverflow	0.87	0.89	0.70	0.87	0.91	0.94	0.87	0.91	0.95	0.93	0.96	0.97	0.75	0.74
CBOW	AppReviews	0.52	0.46	0.55	0.74	0.72	0.86	0.83	0.84	0.85	0.86	0.89	0.91	0.74	0.77
CBOW	JIRA	0.54	0.47	0.52	0.62	0.86	0.95	0.88	0.92	0.76	0.96	0.97	0.98	0.88	0.88
CBOW	StackOverflow	0.53	0.48	0.53	0.68	0.84	0.97	0.77	0.78	0.78	0.98	0.98	0.98	0.77	0.76
SKG	AppReviews	0.61	0.47	0.59	0.61	0.75	0.85	0.85	0.89	0.87	0.82	0.90	0.91	0.82	0.87
SKG	JIRA	0.66	0.49	0.61	0.66	0.88	0.94	0.91	0.94	0.89	0.96	0.99	0.99	0.90	0.91
SKG	StackOverflow	0.53	0.49	0.55	0.55	0.89	0.95	0.82	0.82	0.82	0.96	0.98	0.99	0.80	0.80
GLOVE	AppReviews	0.84	0.45	0.87	0.85	0.81	0.90	0.94	0.92	0.97	0.91	0.93	0.94	0.87	0.88
GLOVE	JIRA	0.92	0.50	0.93	0.93	0.86	0.94	0.97	0.98	0.99	0.97	0.98	0.98	0.93	0.93
GLOVE	StackOverflow	0.76	0.48	0.76	0.76	0.87	0.96	0.89	0.98	0.99	0.98	0.98	0.99	0.82	0.82
GW2V	AppReviews	0.88	0.45	0.90	0.89	0.78	0.89	0.96	0.98	0.98	0.89	0.93	0.94	0.84	0.84
GW2V	JIRA	0.97	0.49	0.98	0.97	0.89	0.92	0.99	1.00	1.00	0.98	0.99	0.99	0.95	0.95
GW2V	StackOverflow	0.85	0.45	0.85	0.85	0.86	0.95	0.97	0.98	1.00	0.97	0.98	0.99	0.84	0.84
FASTXT	AppReviews	0.60	0.44	0.60	0.61	0.69	0.80	0.66	0.79	0.75	0.77	0.87	0.90	0.78	0.79
FASTXT	JIRA	0.78	0.56	0.70	0.79	0.81	0.91	0.85	0.94	0.92	0.91	0.96	0.97	0.86	0.85
FASTXT	StackOverflow	0.65	0.48	0.62	0.65	0.86	0.96	0.56	0.92	0.89	0.96	0.98	0.99	0.76	0.78

Table 2. Accuracy: all features

AF

		MNB	BNB	GNB	CNB	DT	KNN	SVC-LIN	SVC-Poly	SVC-RBF	BAG	RF	EXTR	AdaB	GRaB
ORGDATA															
TFIDF	AppReviews	82.40	83.87	72.14	80.65	81.82	79.47	79.77	72.73	81.52	78.59	83.28	81.23	82.70	83.87
TFIDF	JIRA	90.39	92.33	81.64	91.25	90.71	82.07	90.93	84.56	91.25	87.69	91.68	91.79	92.01	91.47
TFIDF	StackOverflow	88.20	88.20	36.27	62.93	83.13	87.87	88.07	87.67	87.73	88.00	85.40	83.80	88.13	88.53
CBOW	AppReviews	61.88	58.36	47.51	51.32	65.69	74.78	61.58	76.83	61.88	75.66	72.43	73.02	72.14	73.61
CBOW	JIRA	68.68	68.57	67.82	68.03	80.56	90.06	68.79	87.91	68.68	90.28	87.47	87.91	84.56	83.59
CBOW	StackOverflow	88.13	87.33	19.20	76.93	76.53	87.87	88.13	88.13	88.13	88.13	85.80	87.33	87.20	87.33
SKG	AppReviews	61.88	57.48	59.82	58.94	68.04	68.33	77.71	79.47	76.83	68.33	68.62	70.97	74.49	75.95
SKG	JIRA	76.89	69.44	80.45	77.21	84.13	91.68	87.58	91.47	86.72	91.58	90.50	90.50	87.69	88.55
SKG	StackOverflow	88.13	87.67	21.87	50.20	78.27	86.60	88.13	88.13	88.13	87.80	86.87	86.87	87.87	87.33
GLOVE	AppReviews	72.14	57.77	76.83	80.65	71.85	78.01	81.82	78.01	84.46	76.54	75.07	75.37	76.54	78.01
GLOVE	JIRA	80.67	69.44	89.63	91.14	84.34	93.63	93.63	91.36	94.28	92.44	90.82	89.96	89.63	88.98
GLOVE	StackOverflow	88.13	87.53	73.93	68.93	79.60	86.93	88.00	84.40	88.13	87.93	86.53	87.60	86.60	86.80
GW2V	AppReviews	82.70	56.31	80.94	81.52	73.31	81.23	84.16	85.63	84.75	80.94	77.42	76.25	75.66	76.25
GW2V	JIRA	87.47	66.74	92.01	90.17	85.42	95.14	93.84	94.17	95.25	94.71	90.39	90.60	87.91	88.88
GW2V	StackOverflow	88.13	86.13	79.87	75.13	79.73	87.73	86.47	85.20	88.20	88.53	87.33	87.20	87.40	87.07
FASTXT	AppReviews	62.17	50.73	64.22	58.06	59.24	62.46	65.10	66.28	72.43	62.17	63.93	64.52	68.04	63.93
FASTXT	JIRA	82.59	68.11	69.95	78.70	79.78	84.00	84.86	85.19	86.16	83.78	83.68	84.11	80.65	80.54
FASTXT	StackOverflow	88.09	85.81	48.80	61.45	75.64	87.01	88.09	85.68	88.09	87.95	86.01	87.01	87.62	86.95
SMOTE															
TFIDF	AppReviews	81.90	81.36	66.49	75.99	83.87	81.54	84.23	80.82	89.07	80.20	85.66	80.96	83.33	84.59
TFIDF	JIRA	87.74	90.02	86.71	88.99	90.72	85.69	89.23	85.38	90.17	88.05	91.27	91.75	88.99	88.29
TFIDF	StackOverflow	74.95	79.85	55.56	72.07	87.91	84.83	78.25	79.46	86.12	82.26	88.41	90.23	74.78	76.49
CBOW	AppReviews	66.67	64.70	43.37	55.38	77.78	81.00	65.95	79.21	66.67	80.82	82.08	86.20	76.88	75.45
CBOW	JIRA	48.90	48.66	50.24	65.02	83.57	88.76	75.47	87.34	48.82	87.74	91.12	92.61	83.18	85.38
CBOW	StackOverflow	66.67	66.33	37.25	35.94	83.24	89.87	66.72	66.67	66.75	91.30	92.86	94.51	72.60	73.92
SKG	AppReviews	66.67	64.70	53.76	51.97	79.93	81.00	78.14	87.10	76.88	78.32	82.62	85.30	78.67	79.75
SKG	JIRA	72.64	49.61	75.08	72.56	89.70	88.60	86.95	91.35	83.33	89.62	92.61	94.50	86.16	87.50
SKG	StackOverflow	66.67	66.47	39.71	47.33	85.61	87.97	66.75	66.61	66.67	87.01	93.62	94.82	72.77	75.23
GLOVE	AppReviews	66.85	64.16	80.82	81.54	81.72	85.13	87.10	89.96	90.14	81.18	86.02	86.74	82.97	79.93
GLOVE	JIRA	89.70	47.64	90.57	89.39	87.66	88.13	94.26	95.13	95.60	90.33	93.40	94.03	87.66	88.36
GLOVE	StackOverflow	66.67	66.41	65.02	67.87	86.01	89.00	84.19	96.42	95.24	88.13	94.01	95.66	75.15	75.04
GW2V	AppReviews	82.26	63.26	77.06	78.67	80.29	84.05	92.83	93.91	91.94	80.11	85.66	88.17	79.39	79.21
GW2V	JIRA	86.48	52.99	88.60	86.40	86.01	86.64	96.31	96.70	97.80	87.58	93.40	94.10	86.48	86.32
GW2V	StackOverflow	69.07	65.91	76.91	75.45	87.41	87.29	93.59	96.78	98.18	86.23	94.29	95.52	76.60	77.53
FASTXT	AppReviews	67.92	61.47	54.84	63.98	72.94	73.84	71.86	77.24	73.30	70.43	78.32	82.97	76.88	72.76
FASTXT	JIRA	76.65	55.90	72.64	76.81	82.08	83.18	82.08	88.92	88.05	82.55	90.33	90.72	79.09	79.01
FASTXT	StackOverflow	66.64	65.99	53.50	61.91	85.32	88.86	66.67	87.48	79.58	88.19	91.84	94.85	73.64	74.51
							BLSMOTE								
TFIDF	AppReviews	80.11	81.36	59.68	73.84	83.69	80.65	84.95	79.21	87.99	79.39	88.53	89.61	84.59	83.69
TFIDF	JIRA	90.72	92.61	86.24	91.67	92.06	87.97	89.78	87.11	91.51	88.76	93.08	93.32	85.46	86.87
TFIDF	StackOverflow	76.07	81.50	59.78	77.02	90.79	87.99	78.65	80.24	88.19	85.50	91.13	92.33	76.85	77.16
CBOW	AppReviews	66.67	64.87	41.94	56.81	75.45	80.65	66.31	77.60	66.67	78.32	80.82	81.90	73.48	75.81
CBOW	JIRA	50.31	48.27	52.12	53.07	86.01	85.06	57.00	85.30	50.31	80.58	91.51	92.53	79.32	80.97
CBOW	StackOverflow	66.67	66.33	38.32	37.14	84.80	89.98	66.67	67.03	66.67	92.02	93.00	94.37	73.22	72.82
SKG	AppReviews	66.67	64.70	51.43	46.77	77.96	79.57	75.99	86.74	75.99	76.52	84.59	82.97	80.29	82.44
SKG	JIRA	57.55	50.55	60.53	58.57	88.05	85.38	80.66	88.29	74.61	82.70	95.05	94.10	81.21	84.98
SKG	StackOverflow	66.67	66.47	40.78	52.50	89.08	87.74	66.64	67.23	66.67	88.02	94.07	94.32	75.17	75.54
GLOVE	AppReviews	67.03	64.16	79.93	78.32	83.87	84.23	86.02	89.78	90.32	82.62	87.10	86.74	80.65	83.51
GLOVE	JIRA	84.36	49.61	83.81	84.75	86.32	82.86	92.53	94.73	95.83	80.50	93.40	94.18	84.75	84.83
GLOVE	StackOverflow	66.67	66.41	64.82	68.71	87.32	87.57	83.82	96.42	95.13	88.11	93.51	95.33	75.65	76.49
GW2V	AppReviews	78.49	63.26	81.90	78.14	80.65	80.65	91.40	92.11	94.44	77.06	87.46	87.10	79.21	79.75
GW2V	JIRA	89.47	52.83	93.47	89.23	88.68	79.32	96.78	97.25	98.66	76.34	93.47	95.99	88.29	88.76
GW2V	StackOverflow	68.88	65.91	76.66	77.05	86.93	86.65	94.29	96.25	98.07	85.73	95.02	96.08	77.92	78.90
FASTXT	AppReviews	66.49	62.37	53.76	56.45	72.40	72.76	67.74	74.01	69.89	70.43	79.93	81.54	73.12	74.91
FASTXT	JIRA	68.79	56.37	67.30	68.87	81.45	79.95	75.79	88.60	83.10	77.28	88.60	90.64	76.97	77.12
FASTXT	StackOverflow	66.61	65.94	52.97	63.04	86.02	88.72	66.67	87.51	81.49	87.51	93.45	95.11	73.84	74.68

5.2   Word-Embedding

The numerical vector of the three software engineering datasets was computed using six different word embedding techniques, such as Term Frequency and Inverse Document Frequency (TF-IDF), Continuous Bag of Words (CBOW), Skip-Gram (SKG), Global Vectors for Word Representation (GLOVE), Google news Word to Vector (GW2V), and fasttext (FST). The AUC statistic has been used to compare the prediction ability of models created using various word embedding approaches.

Box-Plot: Word-Embedding. Figure 1 graphically depicts the performance value of various word embedding algorithms. Models developed with the word vectors computed by GLOVE and GW2V are more predictive than other models, as shown in Fig. 1. The models created with CBOW have a low predictive performance when compared to other approaches. The average AUC of GW2V-created models is 0.84, with a maximum AUC of 1.00 and a Q3 AUC of 0.95, implying that 25% of GW2V-created models have an AUC greater than 0.95. The accuracy data of these models supports these conclusions, revealing that sentiment prediction models based on GW2V and GLOVE outperform models based on alternative word-embedding approaches.

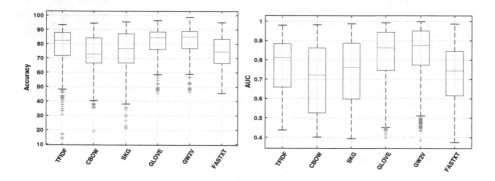

Fig. 1. Box-plot: word-embedding

Friedman Test: Word-Embedding. In this work, the Friedman Test is also utilized to examine the predictive ability of the models created using different word embedding techniques. The goal of the test is to see if the null hypothesis is correct or not. The null hypothesis asserts that "the various word embedding techniques have no discernible impact on the performance of the sentiment analysis models." Table 3 shows the mean ranks for the various word embedding algorithms. The lower the mean rank, the better the models' performance. GW2V has the lowest mean rank of 1.715, while CBoW has the highest mean rank of 4.906. GW2V outperforms GLOVE by a small margin, with a mean rank of 2.204. This performance supports the findings of Biswas et al. where word embedding with generic pre-trained vectors had a similar or better performance than other word embedding techniques, even software domain-specific word embeddings [1].

5.3   Feature Selection

In the proposed research, we use six different types of feature selection techniques- Principal Components Analysis, Analysis of Variance (ANOVA), GainRatioAttributeEval, InfoGainAttributeEval, ClassifierAttributeEval, OneRAttributeEval and in the seventh set of models, we use all of the original features for training predictive models for sentiment prediction.

Table 3. Friedman test: word-embedding

	TFIDF	CBOW	SKG	GLOVE	GW2V	FASTXT	Rank
TFIDF	1.00	0.00	0.00	0.00	0.00	0.00	3.51
CBOW	0.00	1.00	0.00	0.00	0.00	0.00	4.91
SKG	0.00	0.00	1.00	0.00	0.00	0.05	4.15
GLOVE	0.00	0.00	0.00	1.00	0.02	0.00	2.20
GW2V	0.00	0.00	0.00	0.02	1.00	0.00	1.72
FASTXT	0.00	0.00	0.05	0.00	0.00	1.00	4.52

Box-Plot: Feature Selection. Figure 2 suggests that all feature selection techniques resulted in high performance, with the original set of features having the highest mean of AUC. AF and Anova have a very close mean AUC of 0.81 for all features (AF), 0.80 for Anova test features, and 0.75 for PCA, 0.75 for GainRatioAttributeEval, 0.77 for InfoGainAttributeEval, 0.74 for OneRAttributeEval, and 0.76 for ClassifierAttributeEval. AF has a min of 0.37 AUC, max of 1.00 AUC, Q1 of 0.73 AUC, and Q3 of 0.94 AUC. AF and Anova seem to give

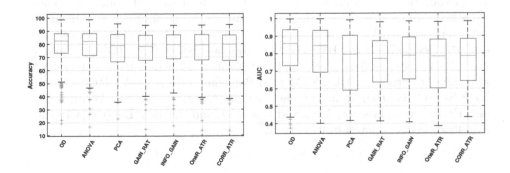

Fig. 2. Box-plot: feature selection techniques

similar results as per the box plot, with the original set of features marginally outperforming the Anova set of features.

Friedman Test: Feature Selection. To assess the different feature selection strategies based on their predictive ability, we used the Friedman test on the AUC values of the models, which were generated using seven distinct sets of features. "The sentiment prediction models created using different sets of features do not have a substantial difference in their predictive ability," is the null hypothesis, which must be accepted or rejected based on the Friedman test. The Friedman test was performed with degrees of freedom of 6 and a significance threshold of $\alpha = 0.05$. The mean ranks of the seven sets of features are shown in Table 4. The Friedman test's mean rankings can be used to compare the performance of various techniques under investigation. Lower mean ranks correspond to better performance in comparison to others. The models trained using the set of original features have the lowest mean rank of 2.42, followed by ANOVA with 2.56, and the worst-performing was OneRAttributeEval with 5.06. The mean ranks show that the models perform better when all features are included, and the use of feature selection techniques only regresses the performance of the models.

Table 4. Friedman test: feature selection techniques

	OD	ANOVA	PCA	GAIN_RAT	INFO_GAIN	OneR_ATR	CORR_ATR	Rank
OD	1.00	0.15	0.00	0.00	0.00	0.00	0.00	2.42
ANOVA	0.15	1.00	0.00	0.00	0.00	0.00	0.00	2.56
PCA	0.00	0.00	1.00	0.56	0.22	0.28	0.78	4.53
GAIN_RAT	0.00	0.00	0.56	1.00	0.03	0.54	0.34	4.92
INFO_GAIN	0.00	0.00	0.22	0.03	1.00	0.01	0.23	3.92
OneR_ATR	0.00	0.00	0.28	0.54	0.01	1.00	0.12	5.06
CORR_ATR	0.00	0.00	0.78	0.34	0.23	0.12	1.00	4.59

5.4   Classification Techniques

To predict the sentiment, the study used fourteen distinct classifiers. These classifiers are used with a variety of word-embedding approaches and on the three datasets, JIRA, AppReviews, and StackOverflow. Multinomial Naive Bayes (MNB), Bernoulli's Naive Bayes (BNB), Gaussian Naive Bayes (GNB), Complement Naive Bayes (CNB), Decision Tree Classifier, k-Neighbours Classifier, SVM with Linear Kernel (SVML), SVM with Polynomial Kernel (SVMP), SVM with RBF Kernel (SVMR), MinmaxScaler, Bagging Classifier, Random Forest Classifier, Extra Trees Classifier, AdaBoost Classifier, and Gradient Boosting Classifier classifiers were employed in this study.

Box-Plot: Classification Techniques. Figure 3 depicts the performance of the fourteen classifiers in visual form. With a mean AUC of 0.87, the models that were trained using the Extra Trees classifier achieved the greatest overall performance. The Multinomial Naive Bayes and Bernoulli's Naive Bayes classifiers performed the worst in contrast to other classifiers, with mean AUCs of 0.68 and 0.51, respectively. The Extra Trees classifier produces models with a maximum AUC of 0.99, a minimum AUC of 0.48, a Q1 AUC of 0.84, and a Q3 AUC of 0.97. The Bagging and Random Forest classifiers fared slightly worse than the Extra Trees classifier but far better than the others.

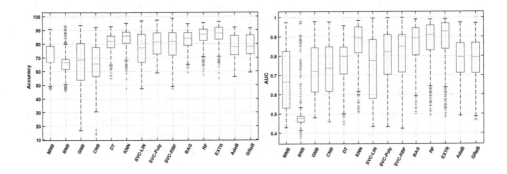

Fig. 3. Box-plot: machine learning

Friedman Test: Classification Techniques. In order to statistically compare the performance of the models, the Friedman test is also applied to the performance metrics of the various classifiers. The goal of the test is to see if the null hypothesis is correct or not. The null hypothesis for this test is that "the sentiment analysis models developed utilizing the different classifiers do not have a significant variation in their prediction abilities." The Friedman test was performed with degrees of freedom as 13 and a significance threshold of $=$ 0.05. After applying the Friedman test, the mean rank of several classifiers is shown in Table 5. We can see that the Extra Trees classifier has the lowest mean rank of all the classifiers, at 3.352. Bernoulli's Naive Bayes classifier has the highest mean rank of 12.847 and thus symbolizes that the classifier is the worst out of the fourteen. The Bagging classifier and the Random Forest classifier also perform well with mean ranks of 4.357 and 4.106, respectively.

Table 5. Friedman test: machine learning

	MNB	BNB	GNB	CNB	DT	KNN	SVC-LIN	SVC-Poly	SVC-RBF	BAG	RF	EXTR	AdaB	GRaB	Rank
MNB	1.00	0.00	0.00	0.00	0.00	0.00	0.00	0.00	0.00	0.00	0.00	0.00	0.00	0.00	10.95
BNB	0.00	1.00	0.00	0.00	0.00	0.00	0.00	0.00	0.00	0.00	0.00	0.00	0.00	0.00	12.85
GNB	0.00	0.00	1.00	0.32	0.00	0.00	0.09	0.00	0.00	0.00	0.00	0.00	0.00	0.00	9.05
CNB	0.00	0.00	0.32	1.00	0.00	0.00	0.38	0.00	0.00	0.00	0.00	0.00	0.00	0.00	8.64
DT	0.00	0.00	0.00	0.00	1.00	0.00	0.58	0.00	0.00	0.00	0.00	0.00	0.05	0.11	9.77
KNN	0.00	0.00	0.00	0.00	0.00	1.00	0.00	0.00	0.00	0.75	0.03	0.00	0.00	0.00	4.94
SVC-LIN	0.00	0.00	0.09	0.38	0.58	0.00	1.00	0.00	0.00	0.00	0.00	0.00	0.01	0.02	8.52
SVC-Poly	0.00	0.00	0.00	0.00	0.00	0.00	0.00	1.00	0.28	0.00	0.00	0.00	0.06	0.03	6.91
SVC-RBF	0.00	0.00	0.00	0.00	0.00	0.00	0.00	0.28	1.00	0.00	0.00	0.00	0.00	0.00	6.12
BAG	0.00	0.00	0.00	0.00	0.00	0.75	0.00	0.00	0.00	1.00	0.02	0.00	0.00	0.00	4.36
RF	0.00	0.00	0.00	0.00	0.00	0.03	0.00	0.00	0.00	0.02	1.00	0.01	0.00	0.00	4.11
EXTR	0.00	0.00	0.00	0.00	0.00	0.00	0.00	0.00	0.00	0.00	0.01	1.00	0.00	0.00	3.35
AdaB	0.00	0.00	0.00	0.00	0.05	0.00	0.01	0.06	0.00	0.00	0.00	0.00	1.00	0.81	7.63
GRaB	0.00	0.00	0.00	0.00	0.11	0.00	0.02	0.03	0.00	0.00	0.00	0.00	0.81	1.00	7.81

5.5   SMOTE

In this paper, there are three different types of models based on the data used for training the models. The first set is class-balanced using SMOTE, the second set is class-balanced using borderline-SMOTE, and the other set contains the original imbalanced classes.

Box-Plot: SMOTE. Figure 4 shows the visual depiction of the predictive ability of the models trained on the two balanced datasets compared to that of the models trained on the imbalanced dataset. The models trained using SMOTE outperformed the models trained on the original dataset in most box plot metrics while marginally outperforming borderline-SMOTE. The models trained with SMOTE had a mean AUC of 0.79, maximum AUC of 1.00, minimum AUC of 0.41, and 0.93 Q3 AUC.

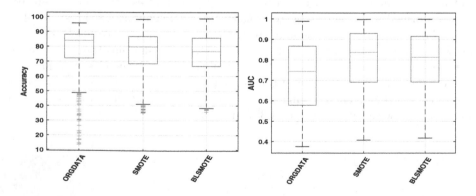

Fig. 4. Box-plot: ORIGINAL DATA and SMOTE

Friedman Test: SMOTE. The Friedman test is applied to the performance metrics of the models trained on the two class-balanced datasets and the imbalanced dataset to help compare the performance of the three sets of models. The purpose of this test is to accept or reject the null hypothesis, which is, "whether the models trained with balanced or imbalanced classes, there is no significant impact on their performance and the ML technique used to balance classes is also of no significance to the performance." The Friedman test was carried out with a significance level of $\alpha = 0.05$ with degrees of freedom as 2. The models trained on the SMOTE balanced dataset have the lowest mean rank of 1.67, whereas the models trained on the borderline-SMOTE balanced dataset have a mean rank of 1.86. The models trained on the original dataset with imbalanced classes have a mean rank of 2.47 (Table 6).

Table 6. Friedman test: ORIGINAL DATA and SMOTE

	ORGDATA	SMOTE	BLSMOTE	Rank
ORGDATA	1.00	0.00	0.00	2.47
SMOTE	0.00	1.00	0.01	1.67
BLSMOTE	0.00	0.01	1.00	1.86

6   Conclusion

Software sentiment analysis is a field with huge potential with applications ranging from evaluating project progress [4] to evaluating app reviews. Automated sentiment analysis can help save a lot of human labor and time. Various word embedding approaches, class balancing techniques, feature selection techniques, and numerous classifiers were used in this research. The goal of this paper is to improve the accuracy of sentiment analysis and help future researchers select the right combination of ML techniques for sentiment analysis. The results of this research can be compared with the results of software sentiment analysis using different classification techniques and help understand the merits and demerits of each technique. The key conclusions presented in this paper are:

- Models trained using GW2V and GLOVE outperformed models trained with other word-embedding techniques.
- The models with the Extra Trees classifier were markedly better than other classifiers at sentiment classification.
- The use of feature selection techniques resulted in a regression in performance, with the original set of features being the best choice.
- Class balancing helped improve the sentiment analysis models, with SMOTE achieving better results than BL-SMOTE.

Acknowledgements. This research is funded by TestAIng Solutions Pvt. Ltd.

References

1. Biswas, E., Vijay-Shanker, K., Pollock, L.: Exploring word embedding techniques to improve sentiment analysis of software engineering texts. In: 2019 IEEE/ACM 16th International Conference on Mining Software Repositories (MSR), pp. 68–78 (2019)
2. Islam, M.R., Zibran, M.F.: Leveraging automated sentiment analysis in software engineering. In: 2017 IEEE/ACM 14th International Conference on Mining Software Repositories (MSR), pp. 203–214 (2017)
3. Jindal, R., Malhotra, R., Jain, A.: Software defect prediction using neural networks. In: Proceedings of 3rd International Conference on Reliability, Infocom Technologies and Optimization, pp. 1–6. IEEE (2014)
4. Jurado, F., Rodriguez, P.: Sentiment analysis in monitoring software development processes: an exploratory case study on github's project issues. J. Syst. Softw. **104**, 82–89 (2015)
5. Kumar, L., Kumar, M., Murthy, L.B., Misra, S., Kocher, V., Padmanabhuni, S.: An empirical study on application of word embedding techniques for prediction of software defect severity level. In: 2021 16th Conference on Computer Science and Intelligence Systems (FedCSIS), pp. 477–484. IEEE (2021)
6. Lin, B., Zampetti, F., Bavota, G., Di Penta, M., Lanza, M., Oliveto, R.: Sentiment analysis for software engineering: how far can we go? In: Proceedings of the 40th International Conference on Software Engineering, pp. 94–104. ICSE 2018, Association for Computing Machinery, New York, NY, USA (2018)
7. Sari, G.I.P., Siahaan, D.O.: An attribute selection for severity level determination according to the support vector machine classification result. In: Proceedings of the 1st International Conference on Information Systems for Business Competitiveness (ICISBC) (2011)

Development of a Web-Based Knowledge Management Framework for Public-Private Partnership Projects in Nigeria

Akinbo Tomisin Faith[(✉)], Fagbenle Olabosipo, and Amusan Lekan

Department of Building Technology, Covenant University, Ota, Nigeria
tomisin.akinbo@covenantuniversity.edu.ng

Abstract. Public-private partnership (PPP) is a system implemented to improve the economic value of infrastructure outputs for the citizen of a country. Knowledge management (KM) has been seen as a way to develop successful and sustainable PPPs through constant learning and continuously improving the implementation of PPP processes. However, the presence of KM can hardly be seen on PPP project websites operated in Nigeria. The study developed a web-based knowledge management framework for PPP projects in Nigeria. The study examined existing PPP websites in Nigeria and noted that they do not have knowledge management frameworks. The system design was achieved using a use case diagram, system block diagram, and activity diagram. The web-based system is designed for the general public to access PPP project details and documents to aid accountability and transparency and help plan future PPP projects in Nigeria. The ICRC Admin, contractor's firm, and consultants on PPP projects are to populate the PPP data on the web-based knowledge management platform. The web-based knowledge management platform has six (6) primary interfaces. The essential interface is the knowledge management interface that archives the PPP project documents and is made available to users of the platform.

Keywords: Construction industry · Document control · Knowledge management · Public-private partnership (PPP) · Web-based systems

1 Introduction

Nigeria has a population of over 200 million people. This population size continues to put pressure on the provision of necessary infrastructure. Coupled with the lack of maintenance, the infrastructure gap continues to increase. Previous research works have shown evidence of infrastructural gap as witnessed in the housing deficit [1, 2], bad road rural road network [3], poor healthcare facilities [4], and so on. Currently, Nigeria needs an average of 100 billion dollars (One hundred billion dollars) annually to plug the infrastructural deficit in the country. This assertion was made by the President of the African Development Bank (AfDB). To achieve this mandate of delivering the required infrastructure to the Nigerian citizen, the government has embarked on numerous Public-private partnership (PPP) projects.

© The Author(s), under exclusive license to Springer Nature Switzerland AG 2022
O. Gervasi et al. (Eds.): ICCSA 2022 Workshops, LNCS 13381, pp. 411–421, 2022.
https://doi.org/10.1007/978-3-031-10548-7_30

There are many completed, ongoing, and proposed Public-private partnership (PPP) projects in Nigeria [5, 6]. One complex trait that cuts across these PPP projects is that it is difficult to access information on the cost, project documents, contractors, consultants, time of completion, or other contract details. These pieces of information are crucial to determining the accountability and transparency of PPP projects to the general public. The world in recent times is known as a global village characterized by the transfer of fast information via the internet across large geographic areas. At the same time, this PPP project information should be made accessible online, which could be helpful for citizen engagement, transparency, potential investors, and valuable for evaluating future Public-private partnership (PPP) projects.

Public-private partnership (PPP) is a system implemented to improve the economic value of infrastructure outputs, and it includes a large scale of public sector facilities broadly. Previous researchers have examined the utilization of PPP to enhance the effectiveness of infrastructure project delivery [7, 8]. PPP is used worldwide to deliver successfully various infrastructural projects. According to Li *et al.* [7], the PPP approach economically grows the value of infrastructure outputs. It enables the general development of facilities and infrastructure, including transportation facilities, sports infrastructure, airports, seaports, and so on. Despite the importance of this procurement system, there is still a lack of depth in the meaning of the concept of the public-private partnership (PPP) system [9].

Since the PPP system is a viable solution for providing the necessary infrastructure needed by the citizens of a country, there is a need to curate each project's knowledge. In PPP projects, Wojewnik-Filipkowska and Wegrzyn [10] and Ojelabi *et al.* [11] opined that vast amounts of information are generated from the public and private sector stakeholders within the project itself. Therefore, it is essential to manage this information appropriately to ensure the preservation, storage, and replication for project management in future PPP projects. This is the place knowledge management on PPP projects can help fill. According to Robinson *et al.* [12] and Boyer [13], knowledge management is critical to developing successful and sustainable PPPs through constant learning and continuously improving the implementation of PPP processes. Therefore, to enhance the performance of PPP projects in Nigeria, there is the need to integrate efficient knowledge management.

The study by Robinson *et al.* [12] supported the notion that knowledge management is crucial in PPP projects in countries such as Nigeria, where there are constraints in the public sector budgets and the necessity to increase public service delivery. Essentially, the knowledge created in any of the project phases during a PPP project will take a different shape due to the technical development of the project work from one stage to another. Moreover, when the project is not tracked during its construction process development, it will lose its context and intensely decrease the usefulness of the knowledge generated during the project [12]. There is a need to develop a framework for knowledge transfer on PPP projects tailored to the peculiar Nigerian building and construction industry. When this knowledge is available to PPP project stakeholders to use and reuse in subsequent public-private partnership projects, it can help address some challenges faced in some failed public-private partnership projects. The stakeholder can learn from the attributes of successful PPP projects. In this light, this study intends to develop a web-based knowledge management framework for public-private partnership projects in Nigeria. This study is motivated by the little or no information regarding plans, bill of quantities, pictures, and schedule of works of major PPP projects in Nigeria. The layout of this article presents the review of related literature, system design, system implementation, and the conclusion.

2 Review of Related Literature

According to Tupenaite *et al.* [14], different knowledge management (KM) models have been developed. The models usually revolve around four main components in the KM activity process [15, 16]. Tupenaite *et al.* [14] noted that most of these KM models are activity-oriented and are mostly not adapted for the construction industry. Nonoka and Takeuchi [15] and Davenport and Prusak [16] identified the four components: knowledge creation, diffusion, knowledge transfer, and knowledge inventory. This study evaluated past knowledge management models that have been created and used for knowledge creation and transfer. The survey by Maqsood et al. [17] developed a system that integrated knowledge management, organizational learning, and innovation. The system developed explained how an organization transforms over time through organizational learning. The study showed three phases in the organization's transformation: the pre-transformation stage, the transformation stage, and the ideal transformed stage. The system developed by Maqsood *et al.* [17] measured the knowledge that existed within the organization in the pre-transformation stage, then measured the organization's knowledge after being exposed to a particular learning-transformation stage. Finally, the knowledge in the organization was measured after exposure to more learning. These stages are a continuous process.

The study by Korsvold and Russak [18] developed a generic model that identified three main themes - collective knowing, relational knowledge, and knowing how. When applied, the interaction of these three main themes creates organizational innovation within the firm. The study showed the internal and external processes between tacit and encultured knowledge. Teerajetgul and Charoenngam [19] developed a model applied to the construction industry in Thailand. Their study examined the relationship between knowledge factors and the process of creating knowledge. The knowledge creation process comprises socialization, externalization, combination, and internalization. A framework was developed to test the relationship between these concepts, as identified in Teerajetgul and Charoenngam [19]. The framework in Teerajetgul and Charoenngam [19] showed that knowledge factors such as information technology (IT), incentives, and individual competency could influence creating knowledge. The success of the study in Teerajetgul and Charoenngam [19] emphasized the importance of IT in the knowledge management of construction projects.

Information technology (IT) has long been recognized as a critical success factor for knowledge management. Information technology is possibly a legacy of knowledge-based systems (KBS) growth in the eighties and early nineties. It has led to too much of the early work on knowledge management, focusing on delivering technological solutions [20]. While it is now recognized that good knowledge management does not result from the implementation of information systems alone [21], the role of IT as a critical enabler remains undiminished [20, 22]. The study by Tupenaite *et al.* [14] is an excellent example of an IT system developed for knowledge management. Their study developed a computerized knowledge-based decision support system for Construction Projects (DSS-CP). The automated system comprises the database management system, model-base, model-base management system, and a user interface. The user in the DSS-CP is allowed to input information on the building process' functional state; the building envelope's physical shape; the volume of work to be done; rationalize the energy consumption of the building; propose the required measures to increase the quality of air and indoor environment and analyze the construction processes scenarios by taking into account the system of criteria. According to Tupenaite *et al.* [14], a module base allows the DSS-CP's user to select the most suitable construction alternatives by comparing the measures that promote the most significant value to all interested bodies and organizations.

3 System Design

Existing websites capture project details of ongoing and completed PPP projects in Nigeria. Three (3) organizations mainly manage this: Infrastructure Concession Regulatory Commission (ICRC), the World Bank, and the Lagos State PPP Office. For instance, Fig. 1 shows ICRC's web page, which led project details of some PPP projects. It showed the project name, sector, state, project stage, sponsoring agency, and project value. It did not capture the knowledge generated on the projects in terms of project documents such as architectural, structural drawings, M&E drawings, the scope of work, bills of quantities, site meeting reports, progress reports, progress pictures, or other details that could be useful for future projects or potential investors to replicate the success of such PPP projects. Figure 2 shows the World Bank website, replicating the ICRC website and providing more minor details such as project name, sector, financial closure year, and the PPP project's investment cost. As this study posits, there is the need to implement knowledge management models on these web pages, whereby project documents regarding PPP projects can be accessed.

The system design explained the use case diagram, system block diagram, and system architecture of the proposed web-based knowledge management platform for PPP projects in Nigeria. Previous studies that have used this approach can be found in Afolabi et al. [23] and Afolabi et al. [24]. The use case diagram is designed mainly for the general public to access the contract information and project documents. However, the ICRC administrator and the contracting parties, such as the contractor and consultants, need to input the project documents and details on the website. Figure 3 shows the use case diagram of the web-based knowledge management platform for PPP projects in Nigeria.

Figure 4 shows the system block diagram for the web-based knowledge management platform for PPP projects in Nigeria. The Infrastructure Concession Regulatory Commission (ICRC) is in charge of collating PPP project information, as shown in Fig. 1. The ICRC was established to regulate the Public-Private Partnership (PPP) endeavors of the Federal government to address Nigeria's physical infrastructure deficit, hampers economic development. However, Fig. 4 proposes the integration of the contractor's firm and the different consultants' firms to input project documents in the web-based knowledge management system database.

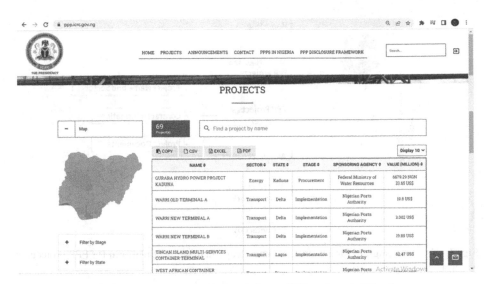

Fig. 1. Screenshot of ICRC website on PPP projects in Nigeria

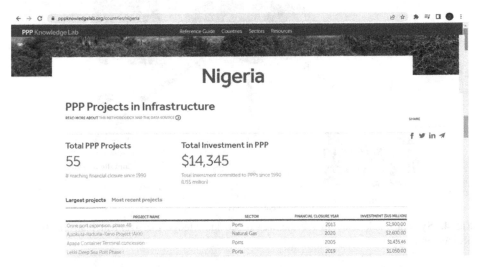

Fig. 2. Screenshot of World Bank website on PPP projects in Nigeria

Figure 5 shows the system architecture of the web-based knowledge management platform for PPP projects in Nigeria. In Fig. 5, the users can access the web-based system through the online URL through a browser. The database must be up-to-date by the ICRC Admin, Contractor's firm, and the PPP project Consultants. The general public can access the home page about Nigeria's PPP projects, PPP projects in Nigeria, Announcements from ICRC, a gallery, and a Contact Us interface. The primary interface is the PPP projects in Nigeria which shows states in Nigeria where PPP projects are situated. The user can view completed, ongoing, proposed, and future PPP projects by clicking on

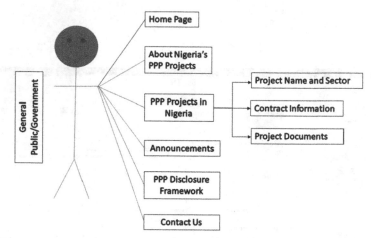

Fig. 3. Use case diagram for a web-based knowledge management platform for PPP projects in Nigeria.

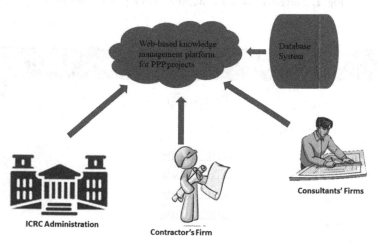

Fig. 4. System block diagram for the web-based knowledge management platform for PPP projects in Nigeria.

each state. This study's knowledge management aspect entails the user accessing the list of stakeholders and PPP documents. The list of stakeholders should show the public agencies involved in the project and the list of private participants, including contractors, financiers, consultants, and concessionaires. The PPP project documents that the users can view should include the contract description, drawings, working bills of quantities, a program of work, site reports, progress reports, pictures, and so on.

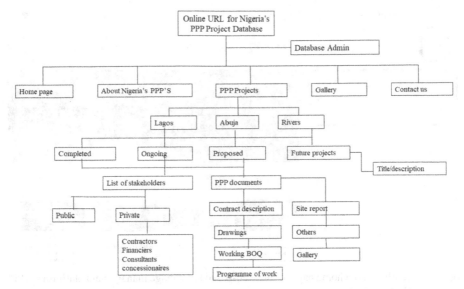

Fig. 5. System architecture of the web-based knowledge management platform for PPP projects in Nigeria

4 System Implementation

The web-based knowledge management platform for PPP projects in Nigeria was designed using Hyper Text Mark-up Language (HTML) to develop the web interfaces. In contrast, Cascading Style Sheet (CSS) was used to style the HTML tags. Most importantly, the knowledge management system required a database system designed using MySQL (Structured Query Language). PPP project documents can be stored on the database system in the web-based system. The study used C-Sharp (#) programming language. C# programming language can maximize possible performance and enable direct access to the underlying computer system parts. The system implementation for the web-based knowledge management platform for PPP projects in Nigeria is presented via a screenshot of some interfaces, as shown in Figs. 6, 7, 8 and 9. Once the user logs into the URL of the web-based knowledge management platform for PPP projects in Nigeria, the user enters the home page, as shown in Fig. 6. There is no requirement for providing login details such as username and password. This encourages the general public to access the PPP knowledge management documents.

Figure 7 shows the PPP project interface, which presents an interactive map of Nigeria with the states. Each location shows how many PPP projects are within the state. The page also showed the total number of PPP projects in Nigeria and a breakdown of the sectors. A click on each state takes the user to a new interface that lists the PPP projects within the state, as shown in Fig. 8. The user can click on any PPP project within the state. For example, the screenshot in Fig. 8 shows a list of some PPP projects in Lagos State. A click on any of the projects takes the user to the knowledge management section of the web-based system, as shown in Fig. 9. Figure 9 shows the screenshot of the knowledge management interface in the web-based knowledge management platform for

Fig. 6. Screenshot of the home page for the web-based knowledge management platform for PPP projects in Nigeria

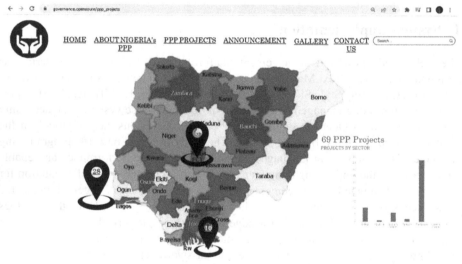

Fig. 7. Screenshot of the PPP project's page for the web-based knowledge management platform for PPP projects in Nigeria

PPP projects in Nigeria. The knowledge management details shown on the interface in Fig. 9 are the project description, type of PPP model, PPP parties, the value of the project, and the PPP project documents. Project documents such as the contract description, drawings (Architectural, Structural, M&E), bill of quantities, a program of work, site reports, and progress pictures (in gallery) are shown in Fig. 9. The significant difference between the ICRC and World Bank PPP websites is shown in Figs. 1 and 2. This study posits the need to integrate knowledge management into existing PPP project websites to curate and transfer project information for future projects and access to the general public.

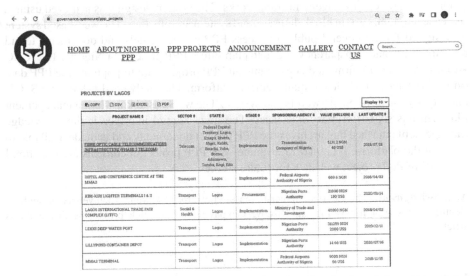

Fig. 8. Screenshot of the list of PPP projects in Lagos State interface for the web-based knowledge management platform for PPP projects in Nigeria

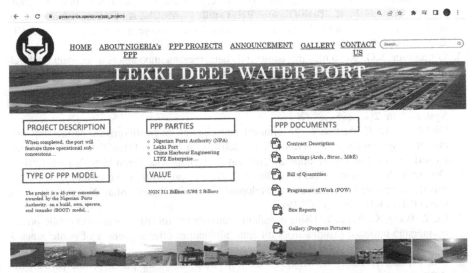

Fig. 9. Screenshot of knowledge management interface in the web-based knowledge management platform for PPP projects in Nigeria

5   Conclusion

The study developed a web-based knowledge management framework for PPP projects in Nigeria. The study examined existing PPP websites in Nigeria and noted that they do not have knowledge management frameworks. The system design was achieved using a use case diagram, system block diagram, and system architecture. The web-based system is designed for the general public to access PPP project details and documents to aid accountability and transparency and help plan future PPP projects in Nigeria. The ICRC Admin, contractor's firm, and consultants on PPP projects are to populate the PPP data on the web-based knowledge management platform. The study used HTML, CSS, C#, and MySQL to develop the web-based system. The web-based knowledge management platform has six (6) primary interfaces. The most crucial interface is the knowledge management interface that archives the PPP project documents and is made available to users of the platform. It is vital to examine why PPP project documents are not stored on existing PPP project websites for future studies.

Acknowledgment. The authors appreciate the kind efforts of Covenant University through its Centre for Research, Innovation, and Discovery in paying for the article processing charge of this article.

References

1. Ademiluyi, I.A., Raji, B.A.: Public and private developers as agents in urban housing delivery in Sub-Saharan Africa: the situation in Lagos State. Humanit. Soc. Sci. J. **3**(2), 143–150 (2008)
2. Afolabi, A., Ojelabi, R., Tunji-Olayeni, P.F., Omuh, I., Afolabi, A.: Quantitative analysis of socio-economic drivers of housing and urban development projects in megacities. Int. J. Civ. Eng. Technol. **9**(6), 1096–1106 (2018)
3. Olorunfemi, S.O.: Rural road infrastructural challenges: an impediment to agricultural development in Idanre local government area of Ondo State Nigeria. Ghana J. Geogr. **12**(2), 108–124 (2020)
4. Olusoji, A.: Health system in Nigeria: from underperformance to measured optimism. Health Syst. Reform **2**(4), 285–289 (2016)
5. Ojelabi, R.A.: Evaluation of government participation in public-private partnership procurement system for construction project delivery in Nigeria. Unpublished Ph.D. Thesis, Department of Building Technology Covenant University, Ota, Ogun State, Nigeria (2019)
6. Omoregie, M.J., Olanrewaju, O.I., Okorie, V.N.: Factors contributing to failure of public-private partnership in infrastructural development in Benin City, Edo State. Nigeria. J. Environ. Des. (JED) **14**(1), 126–133 (2019)
7. Li, Y., Wang, X., Wang, Y.: Using bargaining game theory for risk allocation of public-private partnership projects: Insights from different alternating offer sequences of participants. J. Constr. Eng. Manage. **143**(3), 04016102 (2016)
8. Cui, C., Liu, Y., Hope, A., Wang, J.: Review of studies on the public-private partnerships (PPP) for infrastructure projects. Int. J. Proj. Manage. **36**(5), 773–794 (2018)
9. Khanom, N.A.: Conceptual issues in defining public-private partnerships (PPPs). Int. Rev. Bus. Res. **6**, 150–163 (2010)
10. Wojewnik-Filipkowska, A., Wegrzyn, J.: Understanding of public-private partnership stakeholders as a condition of sustainable development. Sustainability **11**(1194), 1–16 (2019)

11. Ojelabi, R., Oyeyipo, O., Afolabi, A., Omuh, I.: Evaluating barriers inhibiting investors participation in public-private partnership project bidding process using structural equation model. Int. J. Constr. Manage. 1–10 (2020)
12. Boyer, E.J.: Identifying a knowledge management approach for public-private partnerships. Public Perform. Manage. Rev. **40**(1), 158–180 (2016)
13. Tupenaite, L., Kanapeckiene, L., Naimaviciene, J.: Knowledge management model for construction projects. Comput. Model. New Technol. **12**(3), 38–46 (2008)
14. Nonaka, I., Toyama, R.: The theory of the knowledge-creating firm: subjectivity, objectivity, and synthesis. Ind. Corp. Change **14**(3), 419–436 (2005)
15. Davenport, T., Prusak, L.: Working Knowledge: How Organizations Manage What They Know. Harvard Business School Press, Boston (1998)
16. Maqsood, T., Finegan, A., Walker, D.: Applying project histories and project learning through knowledge management in an Australian construction company. Learn. Organ. **13**(1), 80–95 (2006)
17. Korsvold, T., Ramstad, L.S.: A generic model for creating organizational change and innovation in the building process. Facilities **22**(11/12), 303–310 (2004)
18. Teerajetgul, W., Charoenngam, C.: Factors inducing knowledge creation: empirical evidence from Thai construction projects. Eng. Constr. Archit. Manage. **13**(6), 584–599 (2006)
19. Isaac, D., Amaka, I., Ogwueleka, C.: Assessing the use of ICT systems and their impact on construction project performance in the Nigerian construction industry. J. Eng. Des. Technol. **14**(2), 252–265 (2016)
20. Carrillo, P.M., Anumba, C.J., Kamara, J.M.: Knowledge management strategy for construction: key IT and contextual issues. In: Proceedings of CIT 2000, pp. 155–165, January 2000
21. Egbu, C.O.: The role of IT in strategic knowledge management and its potential in the construction industry. In: Proceedings of the UK National Conference on Objects and Integration for Architecture, Engineering, and Construction, vol. 13, issue number 14, pp. 106–114 (2000)
22. Afolabi, A., Afolabi, I., Akinbo, F., Misra, S., Ahuja, R.: Post-occupancy evaluation of building facilities in a university community using an electronic platform. In: Chillarige, R.R., Distefano, S., Rawat, S.S. (eds.) ICACII 2019. LNNS, vol. 119, pp. 351–361. Springer, Singapore (2020). https://doi.org/10.1007/978-981-15-3338-9_40
23. Afolabi, A., Afolabi, I., Eshofonie, E., Akinbo, F.: e-maintenance framework for strategic asset management in tertiary institutions. In: Misra, S., et al. (eds.) ICCSA 2019. LNCS, vol. 11623, pp. 266–277. Springer, Cham (2019). https://doi.org/10.1007/978-3-030-24308-1_22

Security Evaluation Criteria of Open-Source Libraries

Vivian Mills and Sergey Butakov[✉]

Concordia University of Edmonton, Ada Boulevard, Edmonton, AB 7128, Canada
{1vivian.mills,sergey.butakov}@concordia.ab.ca

Abstract. The use of freely available, open-source code to reduce the time needed to create new software or add functionality to existing software is a common practice. With analysis of recent high-profile cases of open-source software packages being corrupted by the original developer, or the introduction of remote backdoor functionality by malicious actors, it has been shown that there is much that can be done to help with simplifying the decision-making process of using any open-source code. This paper provides the basis for a simple-to-use checklist that can be used to quickly analyze open-source libraries for its suitability within an individual's or organization's code base. Fourteen projects were selected at random from a popular code hosting site that made use of specific biometric security libraries. The conclusions derived from the use of the checklist and the analysis of the selected projects will help with simplifying the decision-making process of using open-source code for software projects.

Keywords: Software security · Risk management · Supply chain attacks · Modern code review · Vulnerability management

1 Introduction

The number of public announcements regarding the corruption of popular open-source source code (OSSC) projects [1], or the discovery of back-doors [2] in popular packages has become more of a worry for developers and organizations [3, 4] that rely on OSSC to do their business. For example, in [1], the developer appears to have intentionally introduced issues to the libraries with the reasons not being clear as to why and having theories ranging from monetary compensation to a hacker protest. Shortly after that incident that particular project repository was forked and the development was taken over by a team of maintainers [5]. For [2], it is a case of a commercial company, that develops themes for a popular content management system (CMS), whose own systems were compromised at some point. From there their themes and plugins for that CMS were corrupted with code to allow attackers with backdoor access to the sites that use these source code objects. It could be argued that a theme or plugin should not be a high-security concern but any time you place code into a system it should be reviewed. While WordPress (WP) has had a number of security issues in the past, it was suggested that the main reason that these themes were able to do what they did, could be due to

O. Gervasi et al. (Eds.): ICCSA 2022 Workshops, LNCS 13381, pp. 422–435, 2022.
https://doi.org/10.1007/978-3-031-10548-7_31

any number of reasons like the use of older plugins, the misconfiguration of the instance permissions on the server, or not having a method of monitoring the instance files and configuration for changes [2]. These, along with regular audits of any third-party plugins have been recommended to help secure WP instances [6, 7].

Many users of free source code packages are not large companies that have dedicated software development teams, nor do they generally have the capability to scan the code for security issues. Scanning source code for security issues is a specialized skillset that requires vast amounts of time, or money for the specialized software to automate those tasks, or both. It was for these reasons that a different approach was developed to assist in reducing the amount of effort needed to begin the evaluation process of OSSC projects. The target audience of the proposed checklist is intended to be developers who may not be trained in security analysis of code or quality assurance teams that need to develop a code review tool tailored to the specific needs of the company. The research focused on reviewing OSSC library projects, found on GitHub, for the iOS local authentication Application Programming Interface (API). Specifically, it is focused on the Touch ID and Face ID, biometric authentication features of the Operating System (OS) and devices that support associated biometrics hardware.

The scope of the research was specifically chosen to match what could be reasonably expected of a developer to focus on when looking for a library to use. Specifically, for this project, the Local Authentication API for iOS was selected. There were a number of criteria that this particular feature set met, those included Biometric security, mobile devices, and it had to be an OSSC project found on GitHub. These requirements were chosen to help limit the number of project repositories that could be found on GitHub, but also to bring a level of real-world similarity to what an organization, or single developer, would be doing when starting to look for library projects that met their needs for a given task. The list that was eventually selected for this paper was not exhaustive, nor completely free of issues. For example, during the selection process it was discovered that a number of project repositories were forks of another project already in the list, with minor changes from the original project repository. Given the relatively small scale of this research project, its scope was limited to a small number of repositories that were found on GitHub that claimed the use of the iOS API criteria outlined earlier. From that starting point, using the software developed to help speed up the evaluation process, the repositories were analyzed using the criteria outlined in the following sections of this document.

The rest of the paper is organized into the following sections, Sect. 2 further reviews the previous work on analyzing OSSC Biometric API support. In Sect. 3, the non-code analysis part of the checklist is further defined and with justification provided. The results of the gathered research data are shown, where it is analyzed and broken down to show the patterns of what the checklist can expose when given evaluation criteria. In Sect. 4 we conclude the paper and suggestions for future research directions.

2 Related Works

The amount of work done in the field of code security and secure development methodologies is significant. With numerous organizations and researchers writing whitepapers or frameworks that can be used to help provide direction with security analysis or supporting the decision-making process with respect to Risk Management in software development.

The National Institute of Standards and Technology (NIST) has developed documents such as Recommendations for Mitigating the Risk of Software Vulnerabilities (NIST SP 800-218) [8], detailing the Secure Software Development Framework (SSDF), or the Security and Privacy Controls for Information Systems and Organizations (NIST SP 800-53) [9].

Primarily, the SSDF framework is intended to help with the risk management factors of business risk mitigation. Both NIST standards can be used by independent developers but generally takes a lot of effort to make the best use of them given the size and scope of the frameworks. The SSDF does have a guideline that details a "subset of what an organization may need to do" [8]. The items in the guideline provide reference referrals to other documents like NIST SP 800-53 (SA-1, SA-8, SA-15, and SR-3). That these items lack are specific directions that can be modified or adjusted to specific needs. For example, in Table 1 of the SSDF, the first task is "Identify and document all security requirements for the organizations software development infrastructures and processes and maintain the requirements over time." Further on in the Practices column is the item "Reuse Existing, Well-Secured Software When Feasible Instead of Duplicating Functionality" where it essentially recommends that the user "Acquire and maintain well-secured software components … from commercial, open-source, and other third-party developers for use by the organization's software" [8]. Most smaller development departments do not maintain their third-party code themselves as they do not typically have the resources or ability to do so, except by continuing to acquire newer updated copies of the code on a regular basis.

By design, the NIST frameworks and the task items found in them are developed to be very generic in the guidance and direction for any organization that has the ability to look at and understand those frameworks. The SSDF is an exhaustive framework and implementing it would require a set of dedicated resources that most single developers, or even small development shops, would not have access to. It makes recommendations and provides reasoning for what it is suggesting with defined examples for every task, but because of the number of tasks and references to other frameworks or documents it makes it very challenging for someone to implement and follow on a regular basis.

There has been other research done using similar criteria as those defined in the evaluation criteria proposed in part 1 of the methodology. In [10], Thompson and Wagner, also used GitHub to review OSSC projects but from the perspective of the second part of the checklist, code reviews, where they attempted to create better policies for conducting code reviews for the code itself. As such the focus of Thompson and Wagner was more on the security aspect of using OSSC as a practical concept of the code review process [10]. While they focused on the actual code, their use of the GitHub APIs to look for correlations between the different statistics of a project like the numbers of stars, pull requests, contributors, and issues to try and identify what they could mean when compared to the quality and security of the code. Specifically, they focused on the relationship between code review coverage with the number of issues and issues that are security bugs. In [15] the focus was on the analysis of the literature available that discussed ways to evaluate the OSSC and models for measuring the quality of the code. This is different than the approach taken by this paper in that the outcome of this paper should be a customizable and measurable way to analyze OSSC projects to cover quality, security, and usability of the code. For [16] the approach on the surface appears to be similar to the developed checklist for this paper, but their outcome was to help with the selection of existing evaluation frameworks to select open-source applications not libraries. This once again differs from this paper since the focus of this paper is to produce a workable checklist that can be used to analyze OSSC libraries for inclusion in a software project, rather than the selection of an application.

The goal of the research being presented in this paper is to provide a practical method that helps bridge a gap for individuals or small organizations who may not have the same resources yet still leave the thresholds for usability up to the team using it.

3   Proposed Approach

3.1   Methodology

The evaluation process methodology developed in this paper consists of 2 main parts with multiple items in each section. The first part is based on the evaluation of code repositories from a management and risk assessment point of view for characteristics such as freshness, number of contributors, and responsiveness of the developer(s). The research, data gathering, and evaluation consists of a number of smaller steps.

1. GitHub REST API – Researching what API calls were available and what data was publicly available from those calls.
2. Criteria evaluation rules – The rules used to determine the pass/fail values that the software tool would use to evaluate the selected repositories.
3. Software tool – Creation of a software tool that used the API calls and the evaluation criteria to gather the data for evaluation and comparison.
4. Build a list of target repositories – The repositories were filtered and selected based on the criteria of iOS, Touch ID/Face ID, and a library for other developers to use.
5. Gather the data on the repositories – The use of the developed software was key in gathering the data on the selected repositories.
6. Dataset evaluation – The task of evaluating the data and determination of the overall pass/fail of a given repository, to be completed by the user of the tool.

The second part of the evaluation process, the actual code review, was left for the reason that it had already been covered in other research, like that found in [10, 11] and further enhancements were out of scope for this project. Given that the initial intent to develop a checklist was more focused on the iOS Touch ID and Face ID API calls and how they were being used, the research could be expanded to any OS security API call, but for the sake of brevity the Touch ID and Face ID API calls were chosen. While the original method was designed to have a good balance between the steps, it was discovered that there was an imbalance in the original weightings of Step 1 and Step 2. One of the repositories reviewed was found to have an issue where it was no longer working on a later version of the iOS software, that the bug was more than a year old, and that it was still open. The original weightings did not allow for the repository to be immediately disqualified for use.

The underlying basis for the checklist is to provide a measure of confidence for the evaluation of OSSC projects that are under consideration for inclusion in application software being developed by an individual or organization. Given the criteria that is found in NIST SP 800-218 the checklist is a useful companion methodology for initial evaluation of risk management.

The SSDF tasks listed in Table 1, is not a complete list of items found within the SSDF that the checklist covers. However, it does highlight why the checklist, when used, can help to provide a non-technical evaluator to a decision that can be aligned within a Risk Management framework if needed.

Table 1. Mapping of Secure Software Development Framework (SSDF) items to the CHECK-LIST STEPs.

SSDF task	Checklist	Details
PO.1.1 PO.1.2	Evaluation criteria for the checklist	Review all security requirements at least annually. With every OSSC project update, security needs to be reviewed
PS.1.3	Step 1e, Step 1g	When defining the evaluation criteria that is acceptable for evaluating OSSC projects, the end-user is setting boundaries for attributes like documentation requirements and vulnerability disclosures
PO.3.1	Step 1i	Use of automated security tools and review of results
PO.3.3	Results of using the checklist	Use existing tools to create an audit trail of secure development-related actions. By keeping track of the results of the checklist an audit trail can be kept between updates of the OSSC projects
PO.4.1	Evaluation criteria for the checklist	By defining the evaluation criteria, the risk appetite is defined. When the checklist is used with the evaluation criteria it is a step in managing that risk
PS.1.1	Step 1b, Step 1d	Overtime, the continued use of the checklist to monitor the contributors and code releases of the OSSC project, and with thorough auditing of the results to possibly identify patterns where a project might be in trouble or not adequate to the risk management requirements
PW.1.1	Step 1g	Reviewing the open issues of the OSSC project can highlight issues that may be of concern to using the code
PW.4.1	Step 1c, Step 1e, Step 1h	Evaluating a OSSC project, attributes like provenance needs to be considered. Other characteristics like is it a forked project, has it been archived and superseded, and is it up to date and compatible for what it's intended use is (iOS 12 vs iOS 15)

3.2 Evaluation Criteria

This is the first part of the non-code analysis checklist and should be considered the initial sniff test of a library project. Any project that cannot standup to the initial scrutiny of the following items should not be considered for use in a project that is being built for production use. The following items are not in any predetermined order of importance. This part of the analysis process should be considered more of a holistic view of what should be considered for further analysis if it passes the preliminary test. There may also be the possibility for this section to be automated using a REST API through the GitHub website, further research will be required.

Items **a** to **i** of Step 1 in checklist:

a. **Age of the Project** – The age of the project repository will be a good indicating factor of longevity and stability. The more mature the code base the greater the complexity of the code conversely, less maturity will mean it is easier to understand the code as there is less cruft [12].
b. **Code Releases** – This means that active development is occurring, and the likelihood of bugs being fixed is higher than a stale project. This should be considered a critical section when being considered with the results of the Project Freshness. The speed of releases and time between releases can also be significant [13].
c. **Project Freshness** – The freshness of a project repository can be gauged by the support for the latest versions of the OS or APIs that is supported. A stale project will be a couple of versions behind the current production version or programming language version. This should be considered a critical section when combined with Code Releases. If the Code Releases and the Project Freshness is too far out of date or the targeted OS version is more than a major release version apart this should be a failure for the entire analysis section. It might be mitigated by the Code Analysis section if the API calls being wrapped by the library has not changed between major release versions. Currently there is not a good, automated way of determining this with any accuracy with an automated tool. This should be completed by the user of the checklist.
d. **Contributor Strength** – If the library project is supported by multiple developers, then the project is likely to survive loss of team members. If the project is supported by only a single developer, then the likelihood of it becoming abandoned is greater. This does have a negative side in that the more contributors there are the more likely that something could be slipped into the code as well [13].
e. **Documentation** – Documentation does not have to be written pages but may include code examples on how to use the library. Similarly, to Item C, there is currently no good, automated way of determining this with any accuracy with an automated tool. This should be completed by the user of the checklist.
f. **Popularity** – While popularity is not something that should be used by itself, when combined with the other analysis items of this section, it can be useful measurement of the project whereby the more popular the library is, the less likely it is to have glaring errors [10]. At least ones that have not already been discovered and listed in the issues of the project's repository
g. **Open Issues** – The number of open issues registered on the project may be an indicator of the state of the project. Any decently sized project may have open

issues, but the age of the open issues and the responsiveness of the developer on those issues will need to be considered when evaluating the library. This should be considered a critical section depending on the age and severity of the issues. Failing this section should be a failure for the entire analysis [14].

h. **Repository State** – If the repository is marked as archived then it should be an immediate failure for any use in future projects.

i. **Automated Code Analysis** – One of the new features introduced by GitHub is the ability for any public repository to look for known code issues like those found on the Common Weakness Enumerations website (https://cwe.mitre.org). If this is available for a given repository it should be considered a critical part of the analysis that should being considered. If the repository doesn't have this turned on, then it should be considered a failure.

The above checklist items are comparatively similar to items proposed in the research of Thompson and Wagner [10] for filtering their initial dataset. In their paper they examine the code reviews for OSSC on the GitHub platform and the filtering criteria they considered regarding the repositories that they were including as a part of their review process included items like the creation date when combined with the last push date to determine if they had an actively developed project or a just a place holder. Others included a minimum number of issues (>5), contributor strength (>4), and other items such as the project age and the repository language details [10]. While some of these items are not strictly related to programming, Thomson and Wagner showed that their repository filtering rules for applicability to their paper were similar to how the use of the items in the checklist can be used. When used to filter repositories for evaluation that are being considered for inclusion into a software project. Since their paper has to do with code reviews and software security their work and the work provided by this checklist could benefit each other when used together.

3.3 Analysis

Table 2 details the specific evaluation criteria used in determining the pass/fail rate of each checklist item for the library projects under review. While the factors listed here are what was used during the testing process for this paper, it should be noted that everything on the checklist should be adjusted to suit the needs of the organization or individual using it, ultimately basing it on their risk appetite and other factors that would be unique to them. By allowing the flexibility of defining the evaluation criteria based on risk appetite it allows the user to change the way that the criteria can be considered. For example, if the OS that is being targeted by the code has not had a major change in more than a year, the number of updates to the repository may not meet the criteria as it was defined, for example, in this paper. By changing the focus of that step to having a longer time frame, it decreases the weighting on that step which then increases it on other steps.

Table 2. Specific evaluation criteria used in the checklist analysis.

Checklist item	Additional testing criteria	Explanation
Step 1a	Within the last 5 years	Limit the project repositories that were no older than 5 years. Ozment and Schechter found that the number of foundational vulnerabilities decreased with age, and that new vulnerabilities were reported and code was added. "The average age of foundational vulnerabilities have a median lifetime of 2.6 years." [12]
Step 1b	Within the last 12 months	Limit to actively developed/updated repositories. The more active a project is with code churn, the more likely it is to have issues occur [13]
Step 1c	Not assessed (Not automated)	This item left to the end user of the checklist to determine
Step 1d	More than 1	The more developers that actively work on a project the more likely it is to survive a developer leaving it. For single developer projects the likelihood that the project would become abandon-ware is significantly higher. It also can increase the number and quality of the code reviews and architectural decisions [10]
Step 1e	Not assessed (Not automated)	This item left to the end user of the checklist to determine
Step 1f	More than 15 stars	The higher the number of stars a project has the more likely it is to continue to be actively developed. It also means the more people who would report issues [10]
Step 1g	Open issue count/project age is less than 100	The number of issues is not a clean target but the number of issues when combined with the age of the oldest and newest issues and the volume of issues brings a clearer picture of projects that work to maintain and control issues
Step 1h	(Pass/Fail)	Any archived project should be considered an automatic failure
Step 1i	Automated testing in use	Since GitHub.com has several fully automated tests that can scan a repository for common vulnerabilities each repo should consider turning that feature on. Currently, the major issue with this feature is that Github.com does support more than a half dozen specific languages for such scanning and none of the repos that were chosen for evaluation used one of the supported languages

While it may seem that injecting additional testing requirements to the checklist items should not be necessary, it must be noted that any risk analysis that an organization undertakes for any system that they use, will always be unique to that organization. Thus, it makes sense that defining of testing criteria for the first part of the checklist should also have those same steps taken when considering the use of OSSC for inclusion on internal projects. It may not be common for a single developer to do a risk analysis, based on NIST 800-218, of someone else's code prior to using it. Evaluation software having user definable levels of acceptance criteria would help to highlight the possible need for individuals to make use of it.

Appendix B provides a summary output of the application that produces Part 1 of the non-code analysis portion of the checklist that was generated when the analysis was run on the fourteen repositories selected for evaluation.

All fourteen repositories were evaluated using the application developed. The method of selecting the projects that were used came from finding public projects that made use of the Face ID and Touch ID security API features offered by iOS devices. The application was then used to evaluate all the repositories which then generated the raw data found in Appendix B.

For example, a single project repository, *suxinde2009/touchidkit,* it passed five of the seven test cases. When manually reviewing the two test cases that were not automated, it passed an additional item to bring its total up to six of nine. Based on the outcome of the checklist and the evaluation criteria used during the research for this paper, this project repository is a nearly successful candidate for moving on to the second part, or code review, of the checklist.

By reviewing the results of each checklist item for this project we can see the overall details of the *touchidkit* project:

Step 1a – The project creation date was February 26, 2020, this is within the past five years. (Passed)
Step 1b – The project had a check-in on May 30, 2021, this fell within the 12-month timeframe that was set. (Passed)
Step 1c – The project does not list what version of the programming language or OS version it is intended for in the repository details. (Failed, manually examined)
Step 1d – It appears as though there has not been another contributor to this project beyond the initial creation and check-in. (Failed)
Step 1e – The developer provided both documentation and some sample code. (Passed, manually examined)
Step 1f – Twenty stars compared to the required fifteen stars. (Passed)
Step 1g – There were no open issues, with 1 closed. (Passed)
Step 1h – The project repository is marked as Active. (Passed)
Step 1i – There is no apparent automated testing setup on GitHub. Simply due to the fact that Swift is not currently a supported programming language. (Failed)

One mark against this project that is not as well highlighted is the fact that there has not been a code update for over two years. This is where the flexibility in the design of the checklist comes into play. Not having a code check-in for so long should have affected its Code Release (Step 1b) score but it did not. The reason for this is due to the fact that the readme.md file for the repository was updated and counts as a check-in. However, since there are no outstanding issues and the popularity is high enough to meet the evaluation criteria for the project, it should be considered for the code review process. That failure to identify a non-code check-in could be corrected in a future version of the software developed for this research.

3.4 Discussion

In their paper, Thompson and Wagner talk about the Modern code review as being the heavyweight process of formal code inspection [10], and it is essential that the code review is done on any OSSC that is to be brought into a project even if that code is worked on directly by the individual or team that is looking to use it. To get to that point they setup and used several evaluation criteria similar to the checklist which they used to generate a base list of 48,612 candidate repositories, from that list they randomly selected 5000. They then used a second set of evaluation criteria to further refine their dataset down to 3,126 repositories. All of the filtering they used can be matched onto similar items of the checklist. What stands out from their list of filtering criteria, that differs from the checklist, are the attributes of the repositories like popularity (Stars), or that a project may have been Archived. While that may not have mattered to them for the purposes of their research it points to a type of blind spot that should not be overlooked. The checklist explicitly uses these items to try and raise the awareness that using a project that has been Archived by the maintainer may be problematic in the future. Similarly, a project that does not have any interest from the rest of the development community may not have the same forward momentum to continue to be developed by the maintainer. Either item could highlight a possible issue for use of the OSSC in the future. By using several of the same criteria, in a similar fashion to the steps being proposed in the methodology of this paper, it demonstrates that there can be useful datapoints extracted that can help to winnow out OSSC projects that should be avoided without starting with the code review first.

The summarized values in Table 3 does not paint a great picture of the fourteen OSSC projects that were selected for evaluation. In two of the nine checklist items we can see that the number of repositories that passed the evaluation criteria was one or less and that in most of the checklist items less than half of the repositories were considered to have passed the testing. The summarized numbers, while they look significant, are meaningless without a greater understanding of what the checklist items evaluation criteria were, and that they need to be further broken down to gain a full understanding of what the numbers mean.

For Step 1a, thirteen of fourteen projects passed, but to determine if the chosen criteria was valid would depend on what the requirements are for the end-user. Choose a cutoff date that is too short and the results will only show very young projects. Does that mean that there could be an inherent bias against mature projects or vice versa? There is no simple answer to that question since it will differ between projects, as well as organizations, using the checklist. When looking at the results for Step 1b, where only four of the fourteen projects passed, it could be inferred that the majority of the projects may have been abandoned since the last check-in was outside of the established criteria. This inferred result can also be misleading in multiple ways. For example, the project that was reviewed in Sect. 3.2 also did not have a code check-in within the criteria period, yet it was marked as having passed. This is an established issue within the developed software used but could be corrected by looking for code changes vs any other type of changed document. It leads to the question of what would be considered a valid code check-in. Should the evaluation criteria also look for specific source code file changes and then the number of lines modified to match a minimum requirement? What if the only lines that have changed are comments? It could be viewed that any modifications show that the code is still being maintained and thus could meet some evaluation criteria of the organization.

The rest of results in Table 3 can also be viewed in the same manor, but what can be extrapolated from those results is that the evaluation criteria are critical to the use of the checklist and that the amount of effort spent in defining those criteria is going to pay off when used appropriately. Further to the effort of properly defining the evaluation criteria is the weighting of every item in the checklist to each other item. If a project passes six of nine items, but fails on what is considered a critical item does that failure negate the six passed items? What each user, or organization, who uses the checklist must understand is the weighting of each item and balance that with their risk appetite and risk mitigation strategies. If the team is willing to accept that risk then there is no reason that a single failed, heavily weighted, item should immediately negate a project evaluation.

Table 3. Checklist item evaluation rate as defined by the evaluation criteria.

Checklist items	Pass rate
Step 1a	13/14 (92.9%)
Step 1b	4/14 (28.6%)
Step 1c	Not assessed
Step 1d	1/14 (7.1%)
Step 1e	Not assessed
Step 1f	5/14 (35.7%)
Step 1g	9/14 (64.3%)
Step 1h	14/14 (100%)
Step 1i	0/14 (0%)

4   Conclusion

In view of the general availability of open-source source code library projects, the use of such code becomes more likely in the projects of a single developer or a small team of developers. The issues that arise from relying on such code are numerous. With corruption of the source by the developer or from a malicious third-party actor to a lack of on-going maintenance it becomes important to have a methodology that can be used to evaluate every third-party open-source library. The proposed checklist should be looked at as a tool that needs to be adjusted and refined by the user of the tool to reflect the risk appetite, and development practices that are acceptable to the development team. The target audience is not strictly intended to be the developers themselves, but anyone who needs to evaluate source code for inclusion into any project.

The checklist, as it is proposed, should be considered as a part of a larger risk management process. In both the NIST SP 800-53 and SP 800-218 frameworks, there are multiple steps of risk management from the analysis and appetite determination to the mitigation processes. The creation of the checklist was originally intended for software development, but the general use for such a system is not limited to the examination of software. It could be universally extended and developed for any kind of system where an evaluation by an individual not trained or experienced in doing such an analysis could be developed and implemented.

When the checklist is used in conjunction with a proper modern code review process for software development, the overall number of OSSC project repositories to consider should be reduced. This should have an overall positive effect on the time to evaluate OSSC repositories and risk level of using them. It is important that the determination of the categories and fundamental testing criteria are predetermined to match the needs of the implementors of the checklist to get the most benefit. There are at least two possible future research paths to improve the checklist, one would be to further refine it for the use in software development such that it could be applied to commercial software source code. The second would be to look at creating a generalized checklist for use in other industries that utilize open source approach to the development.

Appendix A: List of Repositories Used in Analysis

See Table A.1.

Table A.1. List of repositories used in analysis.

Framework	Description
https://github.com/g212gs/LocalAuthentica tion	iOS API example
https://github.com/roninprogrammer/Biomet ricAuthentication	iOS API example
https://github.com/gabrieltodaro/Biometric Examples	iOS code example. Additional code for storing user id/password in local keychain system
https://github.com/AppliedRecognition/Face-Template-Utility-Apple	This application template uses the following project library. It also demonstrates how to use the library
https://github.com/AppliedRecognition/Ver-ID-UI-iOS	Advanced middleware security library. Providing more features that the base API

(continued)

Table A.1. (*continued*)

Framework	Description
https://github.com/expo/expo	Entire framework that can build apps on either iOS or Android using React
https://github.com/rushisangani/Biometric Authentication	Security middleware library
https://github.com/vasilenkoigor/Biometric Auth	Security middleware library
https://github.com/tejas-ardeshna/TJBioAuth entication	Security middleware library
https://github.com/yankodimitrov/SwiftPass codeLock	Security middleware library
https://github.com/Meniny/BioAuthenticator	Security middleware library
https://github.com/BabyShung/Splash Window	Security middleware library
https://github.com/suxinde2009/TouchIDKit	Security middleware library
https://danielsogl.github.io/capacitor-face-id/	Security middleware library

Appendix B: Summary Results of Repository Analysis

Table B.1. Summary results of repository analysis.

Repository	Step 1a	Step 1b	Step 1c	Step 1d	Step 1e	Step 1f	Step 1g	Step 1h	Step 1i
g212gs/localAuthentication	Pass	Fail	n/a	Fail	n/a	Fail	Pass	Pass	Fail
roninprogrammer/biometricAuthentication	Pass	Fail	n/a	Fail	n/a	Fail	Pass	Pass	Fail
gabrieltodaro/biometricExamples	Pass	Fail	n/a	Fail	n/a	Fail	Pass	Pass	Fail
appliedRecognition/face-Template-Utility-Apple	Pass	Fail	n/a	Fail	n/a	Fail	Pass	Pass	Fail
appliedRecognition/Ver-ID-UI-iOS	Pass	Pass	n/a	Fail	n/a	Fail	Pass	Pass	Fail
expo/expo	Pass	Pass	n/a	Pass	n/a	Pass	Fail	Pass	Fail
rushisangani/biometricAuthentication	Pass	Pass	n/a	Fail	n/a	Pass	Fail	Pass	Fail
vasilenkoigor/biometricAuth	Pass	Fail	n/a	Fail	n/a	Fail	Pass	Pass	Fail
tejas-ardeshna/TJBioAuthentication	Pass	Fail	n/a	Fail	n/a	Fail	Fail	Pass	Fail
Yankodimitrov/SwiftPasscodeLock	Fail	Fail	n/a	Fail	n/a	Pass	Fail	Pass	Fail
Meniny/BioAuthenticator	Pass	Fail	n/a	Fail	n/a	Fail	Pass	Pass	Fail
BabyShung/SplashWindow	Pass	Fail	n/a	Fail	n/a	Fail	Fail	Pass	Fail
suxinde2009/TouchIDKit	Pass	Pass	n/a	Fail	n/a	Pass	Pass	Pass	Fail
danielsogl.github.io/capacitor-face-id	Pass	Pass	n/a	Fail	n/a	Pass	Pass	Pass	Fail

References

1. Roth, E.: Open source developer corrupts widely-used libraries, affecting tons of projects - The Verge, The Verge, 9 January 2022. https://www.theverge.com/2022/1/9/22874949/developer-corrupts-open-source-libraries-projects-affected. Accessed 18 Jan 2022
2. Martin, B.: AccessPress Themes Hit with Targeted Supply Chain Attack, Sucuri, 20 January 2022. https://blog.sucuri.net/2022/01/accesspress-themes-hit-with-targeted-supply-chain-attack.html. Accessed 9 Feb 2022
3. Microsoft: Third-party notices|Microsoft Legal, Microsoft (2022). https://www.microsoft.com/en-us/legal/third-party-notices. Accessed 18 Jan 2022
4. Microsoft: "Open Source|Microsoft Legal," Microsoft (2022). https://www.microsoft.com/en-us/legal/intellectualproperty/open-source. Accessed 18 Jan 2022
5. An update from the Faker team, 14 January 2022. https://fakerjs.dev/update.html. Accessed 8 Mar 2022
6. Eckert, J.: The Ultimate WordPress Security Guide for 2022, Parachute Design, 14 January 2022. Accessed April 2022
7. Koskinen, T., Ihantola, P., Karavirta, P.: Quality of WordPress Plug-Ins: an overview of security and user ratings. In: 2012 International Conference on Privacy, Security, Risk and Trust and 2012 International Conference on Social Computing (2012)
8. Souppaya, M., Scarfone, K., Dodson, D.: SP 800-218, Secure Software Development Framework (SSDF) Version 1.1: Recommendations for Mitigating the Risk of Software Vulnerabilities, February 2022. https://nvlpubs.nist.gov/nistpubs/SpecialPublications/NIST.SP.800-218.pdf. Accessed 22 Feb 2022
9. NIST Joint Task Force: SP 800-53, Security and Privacy Controls for Information Systems and Organizations, September 2020. https://nvlpubs.nist.gov/nistpubs/SpecialPublications/NIST.SP.800-53r5.pdf. Accessed 22 Feb 2022
10. Thompson, C., Wager, D.: A large-scale study of modern code review and security in open source projects. In: 13th International Conference on Predictive Models and Data Analytics in Software Engineering (PROMISE), New York (2017)
11. Davila, N., Nunes, I.: A systematic literature review and taxonomy of modern code review. J. Syst. Softw. 177(0164–1212), 110951 (2021)
12. Ozment, A., Schechter, S.E.: Milk or wine: does software security improve with age? In: 15th USENIX Security Symposium (USENIX Security 06), Vancouver (2006)
13. Nagappan, N., Ball, T.: Use of relative code churn measures to predict system defect density. In: 2005 Proceedings. 27th International Conference on Software Engineering, ICSE 2005 (2005)
14. Aljedaani, W., Javed, Y., Alenezi, M.: Open source systems bug reports: meta-analysis. In: Proceedings of the 2020 the 3rd International Conference on Big Data and Education (ICBDE 2020), New York (2020)
15. Adewumi, A., Misra, S., Omoregbe, N., Crawford, B., Soto, R.: A systematic literature review of open source software quality assessment models. Springerplus 5(1), 1–13 (2016). https://doi.org/10.1186/s40064-016-3612-4
16. Adewumi, A., Misra, S., Omoregbe, N., Sanz, L.F.: FOSSES: framework for open-source software evaluation and selection. Softw. Pract. Experience 49(5), 780–812 (2019)

Lean Robotics: A Multivocal Literature Review

Adis Jasarevic and Ricardo Colomo-Palacios[✉]

Østfold University College, BRA veien. 4, 1757 Halden, Norway
{adisj,ricardo.colomo-palacios}@hiof.no

Abstract. Lean, as a business approach, has gained popularity in several functional areas. One of these applications is Lean Robotics that focus on the utilization of Lean aspects to improve robotic deployment. This study aims to be the first to conduct a Multivocal review on what Lean Robotics is, its main components, its benefits, and challenges and how it evolved. It was found that Lean Robotics is defined differently by some sources, and that its components can be understood both theoretically and practically. The benefits of Lean Robotics are found to resonate from the prioritization of human and machine collaboration, and the use of various Lean tools via continuous improvement. However, some challenges of Lean Robotics like cost and fear might arise if organizations are uneducated in what Lean Robotics offers regarding its knowledge.

Keywords: Multivocal literature review · Lean robotics · Robot · Machine · Performance · Applications

1 Introduction

The Lean concept was coined by the Japanese automotive company Toyota after the second world war. This concept has been gaining considerable interest from various organizations worldwide [1]. Businesses in areas like manufacturing, service and other sectoral domains have been trying to assimilate and operationalize the Lean concept in order to gain success [2]. However, adopting said concept has not consistently been a steady or straightforward journey, because of various barriers known to arise during the implementation stages of Lean. [3] Most of these barriers are mainly linked to human and organizational errors, such as the improper transmittal of knowledge, attitude or behavior when implementing Lean. [4] Tackling said errors has therefore put stress on the necessity to reconsider the way Lean is actually understood in terms of its practical and theoretical aspects. For instance, Pettersen [5] asserts that organizations that missionize to fully understand Lean, requires to first acknowledge it dimensionally at two levels, such as 1) understanding it practically as a set of operational tools that support users with discrete improvement efforts, and 2) understanding it strategically as a set of philosophical principles of continuous improvement efforts. Both levels are suggested to be hard to formulate into a single definition that classifies one clear understanding of Lean [5]. Nevertheless, the main focus of Lean is still centralized around the improvement efforts from both levels of understanding. These efforts are understood as the systematic identification and elimination of all sources of waste, variabilities and inflexibilities that

O. Gervasi et al. (Eds.): ICCSA 2022 Workshops, LNCS 13381, pp. 436–446, 2022.
https://doi.org/10.1007/978-3-031-10548-7_32

might jeopardize the cost, quality and delivery of an organization [6]. Because of the two-folded understanding of Lean, a plethora many specific definitions have arisen and entered the management lexicon over the years [7]. Whilst these definitions might be interpreted to contain aspects that tilt towards one understanding of Lean or the other, the distinction between them might reside with their applications or industries [7]. Some examples of this distinction may include extensions, such as *"Lean IT"*, *"Lean star-tup"*, or *"Lean UX"*[8–10]. These said extensions are some of the evidence that suggest that Lean has expanded over a long period of time from what was primely confined to automotive industries decades ago. Most of these extensions mentioned have been researched and evaluated for their benefits and challenges within their confined application. However, there still exists other extensions that have not shared enough research. This is reflected by the low number of academic papers available. One such extension is the application of Lean Robotics.

Lean Robotics is a novel term that has arisen, but its concept seems still in its infancy. This concept employs the knowledge of Lean and tries to align it with the field of robotics in order to improve the deployment of robots [11]. Robotics by itself is an engineering discipline [12], a science that involves the utilization of robots for automating different tasks within various settings. Such robots can be industrial robots that can be programmed with functions *to move* objects in the physical world to perform tasks [12]. Traditionally, robotics was viewed *as the utilization of machines performing a mechanized task or series of tasks automatically to multiply the impact of human effort* [13]. However, as advancements in science progressed, this view of robotics began to be surrounded by ethical rules that protect and prioritizes humans. This is reflected by the laws that arose over the years after the term robot came into existence. Whilst these laws originated because of the potential fear of robots harming humans, it is important to note that this harm might both be physically and psychologically caused [13]. Introducing robots into work environments by increasing automation can have detrimental effects on the workers [14]. In lean, the best degree of automation is deployed in a manner where both humans and robots can collaborate. This is emphasized by the Lean pillar known as *Jidoka*, which means *automation with a human touch* [15]. Considering this pillar, Lean and robotics might complement each other if robotics considers human efforts before robotics.

In this paper, an extensive deep dive of the topic Lean Robotics, its definition, main components, evolution, and its benefits and challenges will be studied in order to get a better understanding of said topic. To the best of our knowledge there is not a previous literature review carried out on Lean Robotics. The remaining sections of this paper are as follows: Second, the literature review process will be described. Third, the findings of the literature review will be discussed. Last and foremost, the literature review will be concluded.

2 Methodology

2.1 Multivocal Literature Review

For obtaining relevant knowledge regarding the topic of Lean Robotics, this paper will carry out a Multivocal Literature Review (MLR) approach. This approach was chosen, due to its extendibility of reaching publications that are within and outside of academia. For instance, in [16] authors show that this approach can be extended upon the respected systematic literature review approach (SLR) to include both grey and formal literature. Grey literature can be classified in blog posts, videos, and whitepapers, whilst formal literature can be classified in journals and conference papers. This is perfect for topics that lacks necessary formal evidences [16].

2.2 Research Questions

Because of the novelty of Lean Robotics, the objective is to understand what Lean Robotics is (its meaning and definition), its main components, its benefits, and challenges, and how it evolved. In doing so, four research questions were formulated to guide the search process. See Table 1.

Table 1. Research questions

RQ1	How is Lean robotics defined?
RQ2	What are the main components of Lean Robotics?
RQ3	What are the benefits/challenges of Lean Robotics?
RQ4	How did Lean Robotics evolve?

2.3 Review Protocol

The review protocol can be viewed as a strategic process on how a review of the literature can be executed [16]. In this paper, a model was constructed in order to plan out and descript the review process. This model includes the quantity of publications fetched and extracted from the chosen databases, the main search string employed to conduct the search, and the selection criteria for identifying the correct data. The parameters chosen within the model is justified in the following sections. See Table 2 for a view of the model.

2.4 Data Source

To find publications about Lean Robotics, the databases Google and Google scholar were selected as the main sources of data for formal and grey literature. Both Google and Google scholar are excellent and well-known data sources, due to their vast library of various publications on topics across the board. This is perfect for novel topics that require an exhaustive literature review because these databases fetch data that are included within other databases. Another reason for the choice is that Google utilizes a world-class algorithm that automatically filter out data that are not relevant during the search. For info about how Google works and how it performs in regard to other search engines, please refer to its documentation and the benchmarking study tested [17, 18].

Table 2. Review process

Databases	Publications	Extractions
Google	270	17
Google Scholar	63	15
Search string (search strategy)		
("Lean robotics" OR "Lean robotization") AND (definition OR benefits OR barriers OR challenges) AND (robot OR machine)		
Selection criteria		
Publications that specifically mention or discuss the utilization of Lean Robotics	Publications that are inaccessible	
Publications that discuss the effects of Lean Robotics	Publications that use other languages	
	Publications that are similar (Duplicates)	

2.5 Search Strategy

As seen below, most of the terms used within the search string is based on the research questions found in Table 1.

- ("Lean robotics" OR "Lean robotization") AND (definition OR benefits OR barriers OR challenges) AND (robot OR machine)

In making sure that relevant publications are reached, the term *"Lean Robotization"* was included within the search string. This is because *"robotization"* by itself means *automation of a system or process* using *robotic devices* [19]. However, separating the term *"Lean"* from *"robotics"* or robotization will give irrelevant results. This is because Lean by itself means many things depending on its context. For instance, Lean can mean fit or to cast weight to a position [20]. Other terms that are included within the search string are *"machine"* and *"robot"*. This is to make sure that the search reaches publications that utilizes the term *"machine"* and not necessarily *"robot"* within a Lean context, and wise versa. *"Machine"* is a broad term and can be applied to "robot" [21]. Nevertheless, adding both terms together with the operator "OR" in between will help reach publications that talk about robotics in Lean contexts without including *"Lean robotics"*. The other terms, such as *"barriers"* and *"challenges"* can have the same meaning. However, *"barriers"* was utilized as an extra, due to it often being mentioned in Lean studies [22].

2.6 Search Results

The process conducted for finding relevant publications was operationalized in three steps. The first step was reading the abstracts and keywords for relevancy in accordance with the selection criteria. The second step was extracting the relevant publications. The third step was analyzing the publications and placing them into their classification corpus. See Table 3 in the third section for a view of the corpus.

2.7 Selection Criteria

As Table 3 below displays, the selection criteria inclusion and exclusion were applied to filter out irrelevant publications that could clutter up the search results. The term *"inclusion"* [23] means basically the action of including something in, whereas the term *"exclusion"* means the opposite of said action. In this paper, it was opted to include anything related to automation in the context of Lean Robotics. Any other form of automation in Lean that is not Lean Robotics is therefore excluded. This exclusion is also applied with publications that are inaccessible, are similar in nature (e.g., duplicates), or are written in languages other than English.

Table 3. Review process

Selection criteria	
Inclusion	Exclusion
• Publications that specifically mention or discuss the utilization of Lean Robotics • Publications that discuss the effects of Lean Robotics	• Publications that are inaccessible • Publications that use other languages • Publications that are similar (Duplicates)

3 Findings

As Table 2 from **23** displayed, 333 publications were fetched in totality from both databases. Google had 207 publications more than Google scholar using the same search string. Nevertheless, after filtration was applied in accordance with the selection criteria, the total amount of results got reduced to 32 publications respectively. These results were later on categorized and placed into a classification corpus. See Table 4 for a view of the corpus.

Table 4. Classification corpus

Discusses Lean Robotics	Mentions Lean Robotics
23	10

As Table 4 displays, 23 publications discuss the topic of Lean Robotics, whereas 10 publications mention the topic of Lean Robotics. In the following subsections, the findings will be discussed in accordance with the posed research questions.

3.1 How is Lean Robotics Defined?

Defining Lean Robotics can be a complex task to conduct, due to Lean not having a clear definition itself. Nevertheless, this does not mean that some publications have not opted to define it. For instance, most of the publications extracted from the databases exhibits indications that Lean Robotics is either defined as a *"methodology"* for efficiently incorporating robots in factory environments, [24–30] a *"project"* that investigates robotics with Lean, [31–33] a *"framework"* that help efficiently integrate robots [34, 35], or as *"automation"* that help on-going problem-solving [36]. Most of these definitions signify that Lean Robotics is defined differently by some of the extracted publications. However, this does not mean that some definitions do not share a similar understanding of Lean Robotics. For instance, the most significant definition utilized was *methodology*. This definition shares a common source of knowledge as the ones that defined it as a *framework*. According to [11], Lean Robotics *is a method for efficiently deploying robotic cells in factories.* This said source also utilizes the terms method, methodology, guide, way, and framework throughout its publication interchangeable, despite them having different meanings in theory. The other publications that define Lean Robotics as a *project* or as *automation* do not share a common source of knowledge. The ones that define Lean Robotics as a *project* are of an investigative nature, in which the authors specifically refer Lean Robotics as the name of the research endeavor. This means that a conceptual definition of Lean Robotics was not necessarily implied here, but rather the naming of the research project itself that was partaken by the researchers. The one publication that defines Lean Robotics as *automation*, implies a more general definition of understanding. In this definition, the author suggests that Lean Robotics is *automation which supports an ongoing and distributed problem-solving activity with strong emphasis on the knowledge and competence of the company's human resources.* The *automation* definition stresses the challenge of continuously improving robotic automation at a holistic level in order to maintain the innovative capacity of the workforce. This said definition also falls more in line with the Lean concept itself, in which the main focus is to centralize and propel the continuous improvement efforts conducted by each of the individuals in an organization. The only difference here is that the *automation* definition of Lean Robotics specifically refers to the continuous improvement efforts as being activities operationalized for robotic automation. However, looking back at the *methodology* definition, it seems to suggest a more limited understanding of Lean Robotics as opposed to the suggested *automation* definition. This is because the *methodology* definition only applies to the deployment of robots in factory domains. The *automation definition* does not mention any specific type of application domain, but rather provides an indication that Lean Robotics can be interpreted at different levels in terms of continuous improvement, innovation, and robotic automation. Nevertheless, this does not mean that the *methodology* definition applied to Lean Robotics is wrong in contrast to the *automation* definition. Perhaps, the vital question to ask here is what the consensus conforms about the main components of Lean Robotics and if these components contain any knowledge that compliment or contradict Lean as a concept.

3.2 What are the Main Components of Lean Robotics?

The main components of Lean Robotics are discussed by some of the extracted publications, some more detailly than others. For instance, most of these publications [27–29] explain the main components as being principles, such as 1) putting people before robots, 2) focusing on the robotic cell output, 3) eliminating waste, and 4) leveraging the skills.

Each of these publications refers to a common source [11] when explaining said principles. The source stresses that the first principle exhibits that the robotic cells must be safe and usable for all humans. This said principle touches on aspects of risk avoidance, continuous improvement, and the centrality of humans. The second principle is stressed as the importance of serving the internal customer so that value is generated. With this principle, the internal customer can be any robotic station that comes after the first station deployed. By serving the internal customer (the robotic station) with the proper resources at the right time will help create flow in the production. The third principle is stressed as minimizing any form of waste during the production flow. With this principle, the waste might be anything that bottlenecks the whole robotic cell station to adequately carry out the operation. Typically, in Lean, there are seven forms of waste, but the one that is often left out by Lean studies is the *"Underutilization of human potential"*. In Lean Robotics, this waste is prioritized as one of the most important ones [11]. The final principle is stressed as leveraging the skills from the early robotic deployments and taking small steps towards perfection. This principle guides the robotic users to improve upon previous skills continuously through learning. This principle is similar to the last principle exhibited in Lean, which is about continuously improving, (e.g., kaizen in Lean) so that a certain state of perfection might be obtained [37]. The difference between Lean and Lean Robotics here, is that the latter orients its improvement efforts solely on robotics. Operationalizing said principles in practice is stressed to be carried out via three steps. The first step is to design the robotic cell by planning out the potential requirements and resources. The second step is to integrate the robotic cell into action by assemble and installation. This step also includes the necessary preparation of the robotic cell and training of the deployment staff. The third step is the operation of the robotic cell by monitoring and improving its performance. In this step, the Lean aspect *"Gemba"* might come into play, in which means *"the real workplace"* where value is created. This aspect encourages the user to continuously monitor the workplace to identify problems and improvements [37]. Looking at these components of Lean Robotics, they can be understood both theoretically and practically. For instance, at a theoretical level, some might understand these components only as mere principles of Lean Robotics, whereas at a practical level, these components might be understood only as mere activities in operationalizing the principles. Just like the barriers companies face with Lean [3] during the implementation stages, Lean Robotics might encounter the same barriers if the transfer of knowledge is not sufficiently communicated. This stresses the importance of formally evaluating Lean Robotics as a full concept and exploring its potential in organizations that utilize Robotics.

3.3   What are the Benefits and Challenges of Lean Robotics?

Some benefits of Lean Robotics have been discussed by some of the extracted publications. For instance, [24] mentions that Lean Robotics prioritizes the utilization of collaborative robots or cobots more than traditional robotics. Cobots are robots that directly work alongside human workers by sharing their workplace. These robots have exhibited great results as strategies within Lean settings that are prone to variable and hazardous contexts. For instance, this [38] publication exhibits that these robots integrated with Lean can reduce the production time, improve ergonomic conditions and the wellbeing of the workers. Other publications explains that cobots are enablers of prosperous automation in Lean [39] and that Lean as a concept in the digital age best can be sustained through human and machine mutual learning [15]. Other benefits of Lean Robotics identified is that it borrows most of the core philosophical aspects found in Lean. For instance, it borrows the aspects of putting humans at the centrum, continuous improvement and the continuous removal of any form of waste in the production setting [11]. All of these aspects of Lean have been evaluated and proven by the Japanese company Toyota and other studies to increase performance if implemented properly by an organization [40]. For instance, the first aspect of putting humans at the center has been configured in Lean Robotics as the first principle to mean *putting humans before robots*. The takeaway with this principle is that in no matter which circumstances, robotic cells must be safe and usable for all humans. This principle also touches upon the laws of robotics by Asimov, in which signify that humans should not be harmed by robots, whether the harm is physiologically or psychologically caused [11]. Another vital benefit of Lean Robotics is that it provides robotic deployers with the knowledge on how to operationalize the three steps of deployment via the lens of a variety of Lean tools. For instance, [11] provides a dynamic framework that guides and encourages the robotic deployers in what Lean tools to utilize in each of the steps of deployment. One example of this can be utilizing the Lean tool value-stream mapping in order break down processes and identify value-adding activities during the design of deployment. Another example can be utilizing the Lean tools called 5S and Poke Yoke for order and error-proofing. Most of the Lean tools has been well established to be versatile procedures that help organizations in creating standards that can be executed in workplace environments and maintained for continuous improvement efforts [40]. Some challenges of Lean Robotics might manifest from the perceptions and understanding people have of the concept. Since Lean Robotics contains terms like robotics, robots and automation, people might worry or fear that its main purpose is to take over or steal jobs. For instance, in [14] authors exhibit that fear of robots at work can partly be understood to reside from variables of self-interest and cultural differences. Managers in higher position in an organization might like and interest the idea of robotics, but the workforce downstream with cultural differences might fear and reject it. The publication further stresses that the level of education is amongst the strongest predictors of fear of robots at work. Another challenge of Lean Robotics is that some might perceive it as being costly to deploy. In [41], authors emphasize the need to deal with the cost associated with robotics, instead of fearing it. The publication exhibits that there are cost-effective solutions to robotics and that organizations require to move forward in how they think about automation in order to survive in the future. Both of these challenges are highly linked to the lack of knowledge on how people might perceive and understand the term robotics. It is therefore suggested that Lean Robotics as a concept is properly communicated in order to overcome said challenges.

3.4   How has Lean Robotics Evolved?

As Table 5 below displays, the idea of integrating Lean with Robotics was not mentioned before the year of 1994. During this time, the idea was termed as *"Lean Robotization"* [42]. Afterwards, the term *"Lean Robotics"* entered the lexicon in year 2007 as a research project for Lean and Robotics [31]. However, it was not until the year 2017 that Lean Robotics was hyped as a method of efficiently deploying Robotics [11].

Table 5. Publication timeline

Year	Publications
1994–1997	3
2007–2011	5
2017–2019	8
2020–2022	12
Unknown	5

4 Conclusion

This paper describes a multivocal literature review operationalized on the topic of Lean Robotics. The paper also discusses the findings of said topic regarding its definition, main components, benefits/challenges, and evolution. The findings suggests that Lean Robotics is defined with different terms, but that the most prominent one utilized was that of a methodology. The components of Lean Robotics exhibit a two-leveled understanding in terms of theoretical principles and activities utilizing Lean tools. The benefit of Lean Robotics exhibit that it borrows proven aspects of Lean, such as continuous improvement (kaizen), waste removal and the centralization of humans. The challenges of Lean Robotics indicate that it might be perceived negatively, due to the terms robot or robotics. These terms have been discussed to affect people who are culturally different and afraid of the unknown. Other challenges of Lean Robotics might also be that people perceive it as highly costly to apply in an organization.

Future work will be concentrated on the inclusion of security and safety aspects in Lean Robotics.

Acknowledgements. This research was partially funded by "User-centered Security Framework for Social Robots in Public Space", project code 321324, funded by Norwegian Research Council.

References

1. Chiarini, A.: Lean Organization: from the Tools of the Toyota Production System to Lean Office: From the Tools of the Toyota Production System to Lean Office, vol. 3, p. 180. Springer, Milano (2012). https://doi.org/10.1007/978-88-470-2510-3
2. Lawal, O.R., Elegunde, A.F.: Lean management: a review of literature. EAI. **26**, 25–33 (2020). https://doi.org/10.35219/eai15840409102
3. Jadhav, J.R., Mantha, S.S., Rane, S.B.: Exploring barriers in lean implementation. Int. J. Lean Six Sigma **5**, 122–148 (2014). https://doi.org/10.1108/IJLSS-12-2012-0014

4. Čiarnienė, R., Vienažindienė, M.: Lean manufacturing implementation: the main challenges and barriers. Manage. Theory Stud. Rural Bus. Infrastruct. Dev. **35**, 43–49 (2013)

5. Pettersen, J.: Defining lean production: some conceptual and practical issues. TQM J. **21**, 127–142 (2009). https://doi.org/10.1108/17542730910938137

6. Drew, J., McCallum, B., Roggenhofer, S.: Journey to Lean: Making Operational Change Stick. Palgrave Macmillan, New York (2004)

7. Bhamu, J., Singh Sangwan, K.: Lean Manufacturing: literature review and research issues. Int. J. Oper. Prod. Manag. **34**, 876–940 (2014). https://doi.org/10.1108/IJOPM-08-2012-0315

8. Bell, S., Orzen, M.A.: Lean IT: Enabling and Sustaining Your Lean Transformation, 1st edn. Productivity Press, New York (2010)

9. Bortolini, R.F., Nogueira Cortimiglia, M., Danilevicz, A. de M.F., Ghezzi, A.: Lean Startup: a comprehensive historical review. MD **59**, 1765–1783 (2021). https://doi.org/10.1108/MD-07-2017-0663

10. Liikkanen, L.A., Kilpiö, H., Svan, L., Hiltunen, M.: Lean UX: the next generation of user-centered agile development? In: Proceedings of the 8th Nordic Conference on Human-Computer Interaction: Fun, Fast, Foundational, pp. 1095–1100. ACM, Helsinki (2014). https://doi.org/10.1145/2639189.2670285

11. Bouchard, S.: Lean Robotics: A Guide to Making Robots Work in Your Factory. Samuel Bouchard (2017)

12. Xie, M.: Fundamentals of robotics: linking perception to action. World Scientific Publishing, River Edge (2003)

13. Carroll, K.: Robotics: considerations for practice. Nurs. Sci. Q. **34**, 253–255 (2021). https://doi.org/10.1177/08943184211010451

14. OUP accepted manuscript: Soc. Econ. Rev. (2017). https://doi.org/10.1093/ser/mwx005

15. Romero, D., Gaiardelli, P., Powell, D., Wuest, T., Thürer, M.: Rethinking Jidoka systems under automation and learning perspectives in the digital lean manufacturing world. IFAC-PapersOnLine. **52**, 899–903 (2019). https://doi.org/10.1016/j.ifacol.2019.11.309

16. Garousi, V., Felderer, M., Mäntylä, M.V.: Guidelines for including grey literature and conducting multivocal literature reviews in software engineering. Inf. Softw. Technol. **106**, 101–121 (2019). https://doi.org/10.1016/j.infsof.2018.09.006

17. Google Search - Discover How Google Search Works. https://www.google.com/search/how searchworks/. Accessed 19 Apr 2022

18. Lewandowski, D.: The retrieval effectiveness of web search engines: considering results descriptions. J. Documentation. **64**, 915–937 (2008). https://doi.org/10.1108/002204108109 12451

19. Definitions.net: Robotization. https://www.definitions.net/definition/Robotization. Accessed 19 Apr 2022

20. Definitions.net: Lean. https://www.definitions.net/definition/lean. Accessed 19 Apr 2022

21. Definitions.net: Machine. https://www.definitions.net/definition/machine. Accessed 19 Apr 2022

22. Almeida Marodin, G., Saurin, T.A.: Managing barriers to lean production implementation: context matters. Int. J. Prod. Res. **53**, 3947–3962 (2015). https://doi.org/10.1080/00207543. 2014.980454

23. Definitions.net: Inclusion. https://www.definitions.net/definition/inclusion. Accessed 19 Apr 2022

24. Will Automation Help Improve Lean Manufacturing. https://lean-manufacturing-junction. com/2019/11/will-automation-help-improve-lean-manufacturing/. Accessed 17 Apr 2022

25. Get Started With Your Collaborative Robot Project - The Right Way! https://olympus-controls. com/2021/08/19/get-started-with-your-collaborative-robot-project-the-right-way/. Accessed 17 Apr 2022

26. How Can Manufacturers Benefit From Lean Robotics? https://lean-manufacturing-junction. com/2021/11/how-can-manufacturers-benefit-from-lean-robotics/. Accessed 17 Apr 2022
27. RBR Staff: Cobots, Lean Robotics Will Help Automation Ease of Use, Says Robotiq CEO. https://www.roboticsbusinessreview.com/manufacturing/cobots-lean-robotics-help-with-ease-of-use-says-robotiq-ceo/. Accessed 17 Apr 2022
28. Medium.com: A Lean Robotics Approach To Maximizing Automation Output. https://aug mentus.tech/a-lean-robotics-approach-to-maximizing-automation-output/ Accessed 17 Apr 2022
29. What Can 80 Engineers Do with 40 Robots in 24 Hours? https://www.engineering.com/story/ what-can-80-engineers-do-with-40-robots-in-24-hours. Accessed 17 Apr 2022
30. "Lean Robotics" Method Empowers Manufacturers To Deploy Robots Faster Than Ever. https://www.manufacturing.net/operations/press-release/13195377/lean-robotics-met hod-empowers-manufacturers-to-deploy-robots-faster-than-ever. Accessed 17 Apr 2022
31. Hedelind, M., Hellström, E.: Programming of reconfigurable robotic working cells programming. IFAC Proc. Vol. **40**, 277–282 (2007). https://doi.org/10.3182/20070927-4-RO-3905. 00047
32. Hedelind, M., Jackson, M.: Industrial robotics in the lean enterprise - a case study. In: The 6th International Conference on Manufacturing Research. Brunel University, UK (2008)
33. Mikael, H., Erik, H., Mats, J.: Robotics for SME's – investigating a mobile, flexible, and reconfigurable robot solution (6). In: Proceedings of the 39th ISR (International Symposium on Robotics), pp. 15–17, October 2008
34. How to Decide If You Should Bother With Lean Robotics. https://robotswetrust.com/how-to-decide-if-you-should-bother-with-lean-robotics/. Accessed 17 Apr 2022
35. Louw, L., Deacon, Q.: Teaching Industrie 4.0 technologies in a learning factory through problem-based learning: case study of a semi-automated robotic cell design. Procedia Manuf. **45**, 265–270 (2020). https://doi.org/10.1016/j.promfg.2020.04.105
36. Segelod, E.: Studies in Industrial Renewal: Coping with Changing Contexts. Malardalen University, Vasterås (2011)
37. Wittenberg, G.: Kaizen—the many ways of getting better. Assem. Autom. **14**, 12–17 (1994). https://doi.org/10.1108/EUM0000000004213
38. Colim, A., et al.: Lean manufacturing and ergonomics integration: defining productivity and wellbeing indicators in a human-robot workstation. Sustainability. **13**, 1931 (2021). https:// doi.org/10.3390/su13041931
39. Malik, A.A., Bilberg, A.: Framework to implement collaborative robots in manual assembly: a lean automation approach. In: Katalinic, B. (ed.) DAAAM Proceedings. DAAAM International Vienna, pp. 1151–1160 (2017). https://doi.org/10.2507/28th.daaam.proceedin gs.160
40. Gupta, S., Jain, S.K.: A literature review of lean manufacturing. Int. J. Manage. Sci. Eng. Manage. **8**, 241–249 (2013). https://doi.org/10.1080/17509653.2013.825074
41. Fiaidhi, J., Mohammed, S., Mohammed, S., Fiaidhi, J.: The robotization of extreme automation: the balance between fear and courage. IT Prof. **20**, 87–93 (2018). https://doi.org/10. 1109/MITP.2018.2876979
42. Hollingum, J.: ABB focus on "lean robotization." Ind. Robot Int. J. **21**, 15–16 (1994). https:// doi.org/10.1108/01439919410068140

Multiperspective Web Testing Supported by a Generation Hyper-Heuristic

Juliana Marino Balera(✉) and Valdivino Alexandre de Santiago Júnior

Instituto Nacional de Pesquisas Espaciais (INPE),
Av. dos Astronautas 1758, São José dos Campos, SP, Brazil
{juliana.balera,valdivino.santiago}@inpe.br

Abstract. Web interface testing is a sort of system testing level and it is laborious if accomplished manually, since it is necessary to map each of the elements that make up the interface with its respective code. Furthermore, this mapping makes test scripts very sensitive to any changes to the interface's source code. Approaches for automated web testing have been proposed but the use of hyper-heuristics, higher-level search techniques aiming to address the generalization issues of metaheuristics, for web testing are scarce in the literature. In this article we present a multi-objective web testing method, MWTest, which automates the generation of test cases based only on the URL of the web application and a new proposed generation hyper-heuristic, called GECOMBI. The GECOMBI hyper-heuristic takes into account combinatorial designs to generate low-level heuristics to support our goal. Moreover, the implementation of the MWTest method creates a Selenium test script quickly and without human interaction, exclusively based on the URL in order to support the automated execution of test cases too. In our evaluation, we compared GECOMBI to another generation hyper-heuristic, GEMOITO, and four metaheuristics (NSGA-II, IBEA, MOMBI, NSGA-III). Results show superior performance of GECOMBI compared to the other approaches.

Keywords: Web testing · Hyper-heuristics · Combinatorial designs · System testing

1 Introduction

Interface testing is an important part of the testing cycle of a web application. The goal is to identify failures from the externally visible behavior of the application [13]. However, this type of test depends on the mapping of each of the components of the interface to the source code and this is a cumbersome task if performed manually. Moreover, this mapping makes test scripts very sensitive to any changes to the interface's source code. Due to the rapid evolution of software nowadays, including web applications, following practices such as continuous integration (CI), effective test cases/data generation must resort to

© The Author(s), under exclusive license to Springer Nature Switzerland AG 2022
O. Gervasi et al. (Eds.): ICCSA 2022 Workshops, LNCS 13381, pp. 447–462, 2022.
https://doi.org/10.1007/978-3-031-10548-7_33

automated approaches to ensure that high quality web systems are produced. Therefore, manually generating and executing web test cases is not feasible in this context.

Testing of web applications has naturally been addressed by researchers where the most common types of testing are functional, security, usability, performance, compatibility, and structural testing [4]. However, one interesting direction is trying to address different perspectives, e.g., functional and non-functional, altogether to generate test cases. Hence, several different characteristics are considered together to generate the test suites (sequences of test cases)

Search-based software testing (SBST) is a subfield of search-based software engineering (SBSE) which is formed by the combination of software testing and optimization [6, 18, 25]. SBST is precisely suitable to deal with the previous multi-perspective test case generation approach. In SBST, testing a software system is formulated as an optimization problem and the main reasoning is that test objectives can be considered as objective functions, and hence optimization algorithms can be used to help in this regard.

As for SBST, metaheuristics such as evolutionary algorithms (EAs) (genetic algorithm (GA) [23,24]), particle swarm optimization (PSO) [21,30], simulated annealing (SA) [16] have been employed, indeed dominating the subfield [6]. However, researchers claim that metaheurisitics suffer from the lack of generalization. With the goal of tackling the generalization issue, hyper-heuristics [14,26] emerged as general-purpose high-level optimization methods controlling or building (components of) low-level (meta)heuristics (LLHs), and they have been preferred less than the metaheuristics for SBST [6].

Moreover, to the best of our knowledge, no previous work has used hyper-heuristics for test case generation for web interface systems following the multi-perspective point of view we have just mentioned above.

Currently, the most used technology for automating web interface testing is the Selenium framework. With Selenium, it is possible to automate the execution of test flows in several programming languages such as Java, Javascript, Ruby and Python.

In this article we present a Multi-objective Web Testing method, MWTest, which automates the generation of test cases based only on the URL of the web application and a new proposed generation hyper-heuristic, called GEneration hyper-heuristic via COMBInatorial designs (GECOMBI)(the code can be access in [1]). As its name implies, GECOMBI takes into account combinatorial designs [5] to generate LLHs to support our goal. Within our method, we used as LLHs four metaheuristics: Indicator-Based Evolutionary Algorithm (IBEA) [32], Metaheuristic for Many-objective Optimization based on the R2 Indicator (MOMBI) [17], Nondominated Sorting Genetic Algorithm-II (NSGA-II) [12] and III (NSGA-III) [11]. Moreover, the implementation of the MWTest method creates a Selenium test script quickly and without human interaction, exclusively based on the URL in order to support the automated execution of test cases too.

In our experiment, we then compared GECOMBI to these four meta-heuristics and one other generation hyper-heuristic: Grammatical Evolution hyper-heuristic for the Multi-objective Integration and Test Order problem (GEMOITO) [22]. Moreover, case studies come from five different web applications developed by the *Instituto Nacional de Pesquisas Espaciais* (INPE).

This article is organized as follows. Section 2 presents some relevant related studies. The MWTest method and GECOMBI hyper-heuristic are presented in Sect. 3. Experimental evaluation and results are in Sect. 4. Conclusions and future directions are in Sect. 5.

2 Related Work

Several approaches have been proposed for web applications testing [4,13]. We mention here some relevant studies related to ours.

2.1 Web Testing

The study proposed by [29] proposes the A POGEN tool. Using the Page Object pattern, the tool is able to automatically produce transformed Java page objects for Selenium WebDriver through a combination of clustering and static analysis. However, an approach possibly requires intervention, in addition, only the human elements that have an id are automatically identified.

The work proposed in [28] proposes a tool capable of creating a test specification at different levels of abstraction. To implement it, it is necessary to use the TTCN-3 language, which allows more robust test cases. The approach however, is dependent on human interaction and considerable knowledge of software testing techniques to be able to apply it.

The approach proposed in [9] allows non-functional requirements such as security to be explored in web test cases. However, the tool does not offer the generation of an automatic test script, and like the approaches mentioned above, it requires knowledge in software testing for your application.

The approach proposed in [20], like the previous approach, focuses on test cases based on non-functional requirements, specifically vulnerability. However, the approach does not support automated test case generation.

All the approaches mentioned above are very promising approaches for this aspect of software engineering. However, in general, it can be said that they do not offer full support to the developer who will use them, since it requires knowledge in software testing, or does not support the generation of automated test case scripts. Furthermore, some of the approaches did not unite the exploration of functional and non-functional requirements. The approach proposed in this work, unites all these differential in a single tool: automatic generation and without interaction of a test script and exploration of functional and non-functional requirements simultaneously.

2.2 Hyper-Heuristics

Hyper-heuristics are high-level optimization methods where the search is performed in the space of heuristics (or heuristics components) instead of being performed directly in the decision variable space (space of solutions) [14,26]. One domain to classify hyper-heuristics is in accordance with the nature of the heuristic search space which defines the characteristics of the search space. In the space of LLHs, there can be **selection hyper-heuristics**, which are methodologies designed to select an already existing set of LLHs, and **generation hyper-heuristics**, which are methodologies that generate new LLHs from other preexisting ones.

As recently reported, within SBST, more selection hyper-heuristics have been used compared to the generation ones [6], even if some authors argue that generation hyper-heuristics possess more features for greater level of generalization compared to the selection counterparts [10]. Hence, in this study we also aimed to realize the performance of a new proposed generation hyper-heuristics for web testing. However, we present below some studies relying on generation hyper-heuristics.

The GEMOITO geneation hyper-heuristic was proposed in [22]. GEMOITO was designed for the solution of the integration and test problems. The approach makes use of the grammatical evolution (GE) technique, explained in Sect. 3, and consequently, defines a specific grammar that contemplates several parameter values common to evolutionary algorithms (EAs).

In [15], authors presented an adaptation of the GEMOITO [22] hyper-heuristic, as we have just mentioned originally designed for the solution of integration and test order problems, to solve software production line (SPL) problems. This adaptation consisted in the change of the values of four parameters (mutation probability, crossover probability, mutation operator type, and crossover operator type) to values more appropriate to the class of target problems.

The differences between our research and all the previous ones are basically two. Firstly, no previous work has used a generation hyper-heuristic for test case generation for web interface systems. Since the claims of higher generalization capabilities of hyper-heuristics, we felt motivated to follow this direction. Secondly, the multi-perspective point of view, combining cost, functional, and non-functional properties (in this case, vulnerability of web applications) together is another interesting feature of our approach.

3   The MWTest Method

In this section we present our method, MWTest, whose main component is the GECOMBI generation hyper-heuristic. However, some important definitions are necessary before going on as shown in the sequence.

Definition 1. *Abstract test case: An abstract test case is one whose representation does not allow it to be effectively executed against the SUT. Such an abstract test case serves as a guide for generating the truly executable test case. Particular, in our case, an abstract test case is a sequence of vertices of the Event Flow Graph (EFG).*

Definition 2. *Solution as a test suite with variable size: A solution of a population created by an optimization algorithm is indeed a test suite, i.e. a sequence of abstract test cases. The number of abstract test cases a solution may have depends on the number of terminal vertices of the EFG, and which are present in the solution.*

Definition 3. *Decision variable as test step: A decision variable is one element of a solution. The value of the decision variable of a solution identifies a vertex of the EFG. It is therefore considered a test step of an abstract test case.*

From this point onward, unless otherwise noted, we will denote an **abstract test case** simply as a **test case** for simplicity. Basically, our method starts by handling a web site url which is its input. Hence, the method proposes the automated generation of an EFG [8] based only on the source code of the web application. Considering a set of objective functions (functional and non-functional properties) and this EFG, GECOMBI generates LLHs which are responsible for the creation of (abstract) test suites. Finally, the method proposes that one or more test suites are randomly selected to stimulate the web application.

In order to better explain our method, Fig. 1 shows one instance of the MWTest method. In other words, this is an actual implementation of our method, with a set of tools that we developed or adapted. We used this implementation to accomplish the experiment presented in Sect. 4.

Basically, our method (instance) starts by downloading a website's source code from its URL, using a crawler written in Python. This crawler relies on the BeautifulSoup [3] library. It takes as input the URL of the website being tested, downloads the source code, and stores it in a text file. This source code is just the client code, that is, the code downloaded by the browser when the user accesses the site.

The next step is the generation of the EFG model. For this, there is also a specialized module that receives as input the text file that contains the code downloaded in the previous step. From this text, the elements that correspond to the implementation of some component of the web interface are identified, such as a text box. After identifying all these components, the EFG model will be generated, which consists of a directed graph where each of its nodes correspond to elements of the web interface and the edges are the possible interactions between them. Nodes that do not have edges that depart from it are terminal nodes, corresponding to buttons to close or cancel something.

The main module of our approach, the GECOMBI hyper-heuristic. See detailed explanation of our hyper-heuristic in Sect. 3.1).

The set of LLHs that compose the GECOMBI hyper-heuristic will be executed and the product will be a test suite, where each position corresponds to an interaction with the target web interface. After that, an executable script will be generated using the Selenium framework. This script can be generated in different programming languages, depending on the tester's needs. This script is generated by the Selenium Generator module. When executing the generated script, it will simulate a user flow (defined by the test suite sequence) in a "fake" browser, Webdriver.

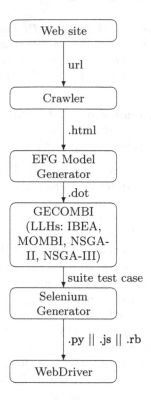

Fig. 1. An instance of the MWTest method

3.1   The Gecombi Hyper-Heuristic

In the context of generation hyper-heuristics applied to software testing, grammatical evolution (GE) [15] stands as the main option. GE is a type of genetic programming technique capable of generating new heuristics by means of a grammar, which defines the rules of adjustment of values for the configuration parameters of a generic EA, such as crossover probability, mutation probability.

However, the use of a grammar will eventually make a search limited since, regardless of the problem class, the parameters values will always be the same, which will require an adaptation of the grammar for each type of problem. In addition, GE allows all possibilities of parameters combinations to be explored but it does not define a systematic form of searching, which leads to the problem of the blast of combinations.

The basic idea of the GECOMBI generation hyper-heuristic is that the parameters of an EA do not act independently of each other, since they operate in the same population, i.e. the interaction of the effects of each configuration parameter tends to influence the quality of the solution as a whole. For example, it is not interesting to have both a very high crossover and mutation probabilities, since this can cause the population change to be so large that each offspring population will be totally different from the previous population, and hence the algorithm never converges.

Hence, one possible strategy for parameter tuning of an EA would be to try all interactions of values for these parameters, not considering parameter interactions that do not make sense. However, this is not achievable with an exhaustive approach (all combinations) because the number of combinations is generally very high.

On the other hand, combinatorial designs with constraints allows the evaluation of interactions between the different values of the metaheuristics configuration parameters, since the aim of the technique is to try to "group" all these interactions into a smaller set, not considering combinations that do not make sense (e.g. mutation and crossover probabilities simultaneously high). Within software testing, combinatorial designs are known as combinatorial interaction testing (CIT), a well-studied strategy to generate test cases/data [5].

The GECOMBI generation hyper-heuristic is split into two parts: generating LLHs and creating test suites. The generating LLHs phase is described in Algorithm 1. GECOMBI receives, among other inputs, the EFG related to the simple/smallest web application and a set of objective functions (Obj in Algorithm 1). Hence, we relied on the T-tuple Reallocation (TTR) [5] CIT algorithm to generate the t-tuples where each t-tuple is formed by a single value of each parameter. Here, a t-tuple is also known as a **configuration** (C_i in Algorithm 1) of an LLH. VP in Algorithm 1 means sets of sets of parameter values. Let us consider the following elements (sets) of VP: crossover_prob_val = {0.01, 0.9}, mutation_prob_val = {0.01, 0.9}, population_size_val = {100, 1000, 10000}.

Moreover, let the strength (t in Algorithm 1) for TTR be equal to two (pairwise interaction). All pairwise interactions are shown in Table 1. Note that lines 1 and 4 (gray) will not be considered (constraints), since they are combinations of values that are mostly inadequate in the context of EAs. This is done in line 4 ($removeConfigs$) in Algorithm 1.

The final set of configurations after line 4 is shown in Table 2. Thus, we have this set of configurations indicated as $\langle C_1, \cdots, C_m \rangle$ in Algorithm 1.

The set of LLHs (LLH; $n = |LLH|$) is also an input to the GECOMBI's generating LLHs phase. From lines 6 to 13 we define how to select the definite LLHs that will compose GECOMBI. Thus, we execute all LLHs considering all configurations, C_i, as defined for each LLH, and get the populations Pop_i, where $0 \leq i < n$. Since TTR's output can be really large, even if a lower strength is defined, the parameter β indicates a percentage of the best generated LLHs to be considered as the ones GECOMBI definitely indicate to create the test suites. To select the LLHs which will be indeed considered as the final ones, we use quality indicators (e.g. hypervolume [33] and IGD+ [19]). Hence, the LLHs with the best values in accordance with these quality indicator are the generated (i.e. selected) ones. The output of Algorithm 1 is precisely the LLHs generated by GECOMBI (set L) illustrated in Table 2.

The second phase is to create the test suites as shown in Algorithm 2. The set L of generated LLHs are input to this procedure as well as the EFG, Obj, and the population size ($pSize$). Note that the EFGs now are from any web application

Algorithm 1. GECOMBI: Generating LLHs

input: $EFG, Obj, VP, t, LLH, \beta$
output: L

1: $Prob \leftarrow adaptProblem(EFG, Obj)$
2: $M \leftarrow TTR(VP, t)$
3: $< C1, C2, ..., C_k > \leftarrow splitRows(M)$
4: $< C1, C2, ..., C_m > \leftarrow removeConfigs(< C1, C2, ..., Cn >)$
5: $Pop_h \leftarrow \emptyset$
6: $i \leftarrow 0$
7: **while** $i < n$ **do** // $n =$ the number of LLHs.
8:    **for** $j \in Ci$ **do** // all configurations for an LLH[i]
9:       $Pop_i \leftarrow Pop_i \cup runLLH(LLH[i], j, Prob)$
10:    **end for**
11:    $i \leftarrow i + 1$
12: **end while**
13: $L \leftarrow generateLLHs(< Pop_1, Pop_2, \cdots, Pop_n >, \beta)$
14: **return** L

Table 1. Matrix with all pairwise interactions of parameters

i	crossover_prob_val	mutation_prob_val	population_size_val
1	0.01	0.01	
2	0.01	0.9	
3	0.9	0.01	
4	0.9	0.9	
5		0.01	100
6		0.01	1000
7		0.01	10000
8		0.9	100
9		0.9	1000
10		0.9	10000
11	0.01		100
12	0.01		1000
13	0.01		10000
14	0.9		100
15	0.9		1000
16	0.9		10000

and not only the smallest one. The set of test suites (TSs in Algorithm 2) is indeed the final population due to GECOMBI obtained by generating the nondominated solutions (procedure $generateND$), and by the adjustment of the population size in accordance with $pSize$ (procedure $adjustPop$).

Table 2. Final set of configurations

Config	crossover_prob_val	mutation_prob_val	population_size_val
CONF_1	0.01	0.01	100
CONF_2	0.01	0.9	1000
CONF_3	0.01	0.01	10000
CONF_4	0.9	0.9	100
CONF_5	0.9	0.01	1000
CONF_6	0.9	0.9	10000

Algorithm 2. GECOMBI: Creating Test Suites

---

input: $EFG, Obj, L, pSize$
output: TSs

1: $Prob \leftarrow adaptProblem(EFG, \ Obj)$
2: $TSs \leftarrow \emptyset$
3: **for** $l \in L$ **do**
4:     $TSs \leftarrow TSs \cup runLLH(l, Prob)$
5: **end for**
6: $TSs \leftarrow generateND(TSs)$
7: $TSs \leftarrow adjustPop(TSs, pSize)$
8: **return** TSs

---

4   Experimental Design and Evaluation

In this section, we present the design and characteristics of the experiment we conducted to evaluate our method.

4.1   Objective, Algorithms and Quality Indicators

The objective of this evaluation is to identify which out of six optimisation algorithms is the best regarding test case generation for web applications. We considered our new proposed generation hyper-heuristic, GECOMBI, the GEMOITO hyper-heuristic, and the metaheuristics IBEA, MOMBI, NSGA-II, and NSGA-III. Note that these metaheuristics are used as LLHs of GECOMBI.

Note that each metaheuristic was configured as follows: SBX crossover with probability 0.0001, Polynomial mutation with probability 0.00125, population and archive size equal to 20. On the hand, the GEMOITO hyper-heuristic and GECOMBI had the same sets of values. As for GECOMBI, the parameter settings are shown later in Sect. 4.5.

As quality indicators to evaluate the performance of the algorithms, we used the hypervolume and IGD+. In our case, we took into the front-normalized values of these indicators. Note that as higher the (front-normalized) hypervolume value the better the algorithm, and as lower the (front-normalized) IGD+ value, the better the approach.

4.2   Research Question and Variables

We want to answer the following research question:

- **RQ_1** - Which of the six algorithms is the best regarding each quality indicator?

   The independent variables are the optimisation algorithms. The dependent variables are the values of the quality indicators: hypervolume and IGD+.

4.3   Objective Functions

The objective functions we considered are described below:

- **test case consistency:** we defined no constraints to the problem instances. Hence, the algorithms have total flexibility to generate the test cases. But, it is usually necessary that the sequence of values of the decision variables within a (abstract) test case is consistent with the sequence of vertices (edges) of the graph, otherwise an inconsistent test case will be generated. Thus, we want to maximize the test case consistency. Note that by generating consistent test cases we are traversing correctly the EFG, and hence this can be seen as a function related to functional properties;
- **length of the test suite:** this objective function has as purpose to control the amount and the position in which the terminal vertices of the EFG appear in a solution. This is a cost measure where we want to minimize the amount of test cases in the test suite;
- **vulnerability:** this objective function is related to the vulnerability of web interface applications. One of the most well-known attacks is SQL Injection. In this attack, the text fields present in the interface are exploited, and SQL commands are inserted into them that can cause some damage to the website's database. We want to maximise the number of vulnerabilities in order to create more suitable test cases. This is a function related to non-functional properties (vulnerability).

4.4   Case Studies

Case studies are 18 case web interfaces whose source code is based on Javascript extracted from the web sites from the Instituto Nacional de Pesquisas Espaciais (INPE).

4.5   Generating LLHS

As for the GENERATING LLHs phase (see Sect. 3.1, Algorithm 1), we considered the smallest (less number of vertices in the corresponding EFG) web interface among all the 18 web interfaces. Parameters are described in Table 3. Altogether, 162 LLHs were generated by GECOMBI, and we set $\beta = 0.06$. Note that since this is a real problem, we created the True Known Pareto Front according to the execution of the LLHs. Hence, GECOMBI suggests the top 10 LLHs/configurations in accordance with the highest hypervolume values.

After identifying the top 10 LLHs, we moved on to the next step where we were able to compare GECOMBI to the other algorithms. It is very important to emphasize that the final population due to GECOMBI is adjusted to fit the size of the population of the metaheuristics run in isolation (see procedure *adjustPop* in Algorithm 2). Hence, the final population of GECOMBI is 20.

Table 3. Parameter settings for GECOMBI

Parameters	Values
Population size	20, 50
Crossover probability	0.0001, 0.009, 0.005
Mutation probability	0.0001, 0.009, 0.005
Crossover operator	*TwoPoint, SinglePoint, SBX*
Mutation operator	*Polynomial, Random, CDG*
Archive	(2,3)*population_size

4.6   Results

After the training of GECOMBI and the generation of LLHs in conjunction with the Pareto Frontier of the problem, the execution phase was started. For each of the web interface under test an EFG model was generated, and each of these models was submitted to GECOMBI so that the comparison of the results obtained was compared with the results of the Pareto Frontier obtained during the training phase. This goal was achieved by calculating hypervolume and IGD+ comparators.

After obtaining the data referring to the approach proposed in this work, the data for the comparison were obtained by submitting the same problem to the GEMOITO, NSGA-II, NSGA-III, IBEA and MOMBI were also run, configured according to the literature. The configuration of the native algorithms, we considered the parameter values for the solution of the *Traveling Salesman* problem, also implemented in the jMetal tool. The Traveling Salesman problem is of the same nature as the problem of generating test cases for web interface, so it was selected. In these applications, the city concept represents the test case, and the distance concept represents the cost of the test case.

Tables 4 and 5 bring the results of all 18 GUIs submitted. In all cases, the first column corresponds to the ID of each case study. The other column is the value obtained by the algorithm corresponding to the indicator referring to the table (i.e. hypervolume or IGD). The results obtained by the GEMOITO, NSGA-II, NSGA-III, IBEA, MOMBI and GECOMBI, although are very similar, in most of cases the GECOMBI algorithm obtained slightly better results. This is further evidence of the applicability of GECOMBI to real problems.

Table 4. Hypervolume values

Case study	NSGA-II	IBEA	MOMBI	NSGA-III	GEMOITO	GECOMBI
1	0.268782	0.120026	0.131513	0.257367	0.431783	**0.516108**
2	0.333638	0.180318	0.196101	0.459991	0.441912	**0.527794**
3	0.347497	0.193399	0.160884	0.515277	**0.521259**	0.508557
4	0.341984	0.256996	0.233039	**0.593170**	0.460526	0.543643
5	0.347971	0.220834	0.221348	0.512301	0.485573	**0.528132**
6	0.339228	0.203439	0.100345	0.434617	**0.468291**	0.383098
7	0.194871	0.109718	0.088416	0.297875	0.391903	**0.420904**
8	0.212474	0.196170	0.088853	0.529682	0.529376	**0.530784**
9	0.401964	0.193806	0.126963	0.563866	0.456579	**0.605975**
10	0.241677	0.209873	0.134434	0.523692	0.528122	**0.634823**
11	0.154823	0.079160	0.070553	0.214052	**0.440771**	0.358798
12	0.243821	0.158441	0.093224	0.478388	**0.517422**	0.324694
13	0.308754	0.248139	0.096751	**0.532646**	0.518316	0.432973
14	0.348418	0.192111	0.135408	**0.510069**	0.412745	0.428427
15	0.298458	0.173096	0.197651	**0.562706**	0.498127	0.459960
16	0.256699	0.188478	0.103281	0.437255	**0.453236**	0.386052
17	0.304820	0.115310	0.143298	0.241853	0.363048	**0.488897**
18	0.429585	0.264860	0.231269	0.454193	0.461678	**0.462882**

However, it is important to apply a statistical evaluation to verify if there is a significant difference between the results obtained by GECOMBI and the other algorithms compared. For this, we follow the experiment proposed in [7], for a statistical evaluation to provide greater confidence in results.

For the statistical verification, the values of the hypervolumes and IGD+ indices obtained by each algorithm were analyzed for each case study. Just as in [7], the first step is to verify the normality of the data. For this purpose, we apply the Shapiro-Wilk test [27] with significance level $\alpha = 0.05$. This test shows that the data is not normally distributed. In this way, the nonparametric Wilcoxon test (Signed Rank) [2] was applied, with significance level $\alpha = 0.05$. The results are presented in Table 6.

According to these results, some p-values are below 0.05, there is difference between the GECOMBI and other algorithms compered, with the advantage for the GECOMBI. In other cases, there is no difference between the GECOMBI and other algorithms compered, which leads to the conclusion that GECOMBI has the potential to be used as a solution as well as algorithms already established in the literature.

Just as the studie [31] that propose new hyper-heuristics aimed at solving problems in the context of Software Testing, use hypervolume as one of the evaluation metrics. In all cases, the relational experiments include the comparison of

Table 5. IGD+ values

Case study	NSGA-II	IBEA	MOMBI	NSGA-III	GEMOITO	GECOMBI
1	0.190867	0.264044	0.254507	0.196629	0.335454	**0.116704**
2	0.178105	0.226365	0.223408	0.132267	0.309283	**0.108458**
3	0.140721	0.194362	0.211330	**0.097364**	0.265463	0.099995
4	0.193979	0.209409	0.221629	**0.091531**	0.293613	0.109736
5	0.192311	0.229109	0.235112	0.137427	0.290119	**0.116768**
6	0.173407	0.242507	0.315417	**0.130213**	0.291789	0.184460
7	0.267496	0.323623	0.343992	0.277611	0.290227	**0.156939**
8	0.235092	0.249626	0.321397	**0.082650**	0.239363	0.120851
9	0.167383	0.236273	0.305631	0.106392	0.307430	**0.086991**
10	0.211442	0.237703	0.277094	0.088141	0.247280	**0.079455**
11	0.289887	0.368626	0.386215	0.254050	0.295715	**0.173608**
12	0.219030	0.272827	0.328390	**0.104665**	0.248476	0.176153
13	0.179412	0.202748	0.294480	**0.096213**	0.236766	0.143670
14	0.163677	0.236982	0.269477	0.107956	0.335256	**0.141035**
15	0.201289	0.245688	0.235549	**0.096922**	0.255825	0.143700
16	0.192261	0.215661	0.266578	**0.112177**	0.323162	0.135705
17	0.189252	0.297050	0.256142	0.203925	0.346667	**0.114139**
18	0.142135	0.186448	0.200636	0.137599	0.287251	**0.119112**

Table 6. *Wilcoxon* test

Comparison	*p-value* (Hypervolume)	*p-value* (IGD+)
GECOMBI ↔ GEMOITO	0.4951	7.629e–06
GECOMBI ↔ NSGAIII	0.5798	0.8317
GECOMBI ↔ MOMBI	7.629e–06	7.629e–06
GECOMBI ↔ IBEA	7.629e–06	7.629e–06
GECOMBI ↔ NSGAII	7.629e–06	1.526e–05

the proposed hyper-heuristic with other algorithms in the literature. In the same way that the experiment for evaluating GECOMBI showed very close results with the values of the algorithms compared, with the studies cited the same situation also occurred. This is further evidence that GECOMBI is a scalable solution for solving real problems.

5   Conclusions

This work proposed a multi-objective web testing method, MWTest, which automates the generation of test cases based only on the URL of the web application and a new proposed generation hyper-heuristic, called GECOMBI. The GECOMBI hyper-heuristic takes into account combinatorial designs to generate low-level heuristics to support our goal. Preliminary results were obtained with the preliminary version of GECOMBI based on the execution of 18 GUIs derived from the real case studys.

Experiments were performed for comparated the NSGA-II, NSGA-III, IBEA, MOMBI and GEMOITO algorithms, configured based on values obtained in the literature. The results sought to evaluate the potential to produce good GECOMBI solutions, as well as other approaches proposed in the literature. These preliminary results show that the application of GECOMBI to the 18 case studies were slightly better than the results found in the literature.

In addition, to verify that there is a statistically significant difference between the results obtained by the compared algorithms, a statistical evaluation was performed. This test showed in some cases, that there is a statistical difference between the results obtained by GECOMBI and the other algorithms compared.

Based on the results obtained, it is possible to conclude that GECOMBI has as much potential for solving problems as well as established approaches in the literature, since the experiments related to the 18 case studies had positive results. These results obtained are encouraging for GECOMBI to continue to be exploited. Future work includes the application of GECOMBI to generate test cases that explore non-functional aspects through the modeling of new objective functions, e.g. the ones that address usability and security. In addition, we intend to carry out rigorous experiments involving GECOMBI, comparing it with other hyper-heuristics, meta-heuristics, and even for many-objective problems.

References

1. Gecombi repository. https://github.com/BaleraJuliana/GECOMBI_code. Accessed 13 July 2019
2. The Wilcoxon signed-rank test. http://www.r-tutor.com/elementary-statistics/non-parametric-methods/wilcoxon-signed-rank-test. Accessed 13 July 2019
3. (2022). https://www.crummy.com/software/BeautifulSoup/bs4/doc/
4. Al-Ahmad, B., Al-Debei, K.: Survey of testing methods for web applications. Eur. Int. J. Sci. Technol. 9(12), 1–22 (2020)
5. Balera, J.M., Santiago Júnior, V.A.: An algorithm for combinatorial interaction testing: definitions and rigorous evaluations. J. Softw. Eng. Res. Dev. 5(1), 10 (2017). https://doi.org/10.1186/s40411-017-0043-z
6. Balera, J.M., Santiago Júnior, V.A.: A systematic mapping addressing hyper-heuristics within search-based software testing. Inf. Softw. Technol. 114, 176–189 (2019). https://doi.org/10.1016/j.infsof.2019.06.012, http://www.sciencedirect.com/science/article/pii/S0950584919301430
7. Balera, J.M., Santiago Júnior, V.A.d.: An algorithm for combinatorial interaction testing: definitions and rigorous evaluations. J. Softw. Eng. Res. Dev. 5(1), 10 (2017). https://doi.org/10.1186/s40411-017-0043-z
8. Banerjee, I., Nguyen, B., Garousi, V., Memon, A.: Graphical user interface (GUI) testing: systematic mapping and repository. Inf. Softw. Technol. 55(10), 1679–1694 (2013). https://doi.org/10.1016/j.infsof.2013.03.004, http://www.sciencedirect.com/science/article/pii/S0950584913000669

9. Bozic, J., Wotawa, F.: Planning-based security testing of web applications with attack grammars. Softw. Qual. J. **28**(1), 307–334 (2020). https://doi.org/10.1007/s11219-019-09469-y

10. Burke, E.K., et al.: Hyper-heuristics: a survey of the state of the art. J. Oper. Res. Soc. **64**(12), 1695–1724 (2013). https://doi.org/10.1057/jors.2013.71

11. Deb, K., Jain, H.: An evolutionary many-objective optimization algorithm using reference-point-based nondominated sorting approach, part i: Solving problems with box constraints. IEEE Trans. Evol. Comput. **18**(4), 577–601 (2014). https://doi.org/10.1109/TEVC.2013.2281535

12. Deb, K., Pratap, A., Agarwal, S., Meyarivan, T.: A fast and elitist multiobjective genetic algorithm: NSGA-II. IEEE Trans. Evol. Comput. **6**(2), 182–197 (2002). https://doi.org/10.1109/4235.996017

13. Di Lucca, G.A., Fasolino, A.R.: Testing web-based applications: the state of the art and future trends. Inf. Softw. Technol. **48**(12), 1172–1186 (2006). https://doi.org/10.1016/j.infsof.2006.06.006, https://www.sciencedirect.com/science/article/pii/S0950584906000851

14. Drake, J.H., Kheiri, A., Özcan, E., Burke, E.K.: Recent advances in selection hyper-heuristics. Eur. J. Oper. Res. **285**(2), 405–428 (2020). https://doi.org/10.1016/j.ejor.2019.07.073, https://www.sciencedirect.com/science/article/pii/S0377221719306526

15. Filho, H.L.J., Lima, J.A.P., Vergilio, S.R.: Automatic generation of search-based algorithms applied to the feature testing of software product lines. In: Proceedings of the 31st Brazilian Symposium on Software Engineering, SBES 2017, pp. 114–123. ACM, New York, NY, USA (2017). https://doi.org/10.1145/3131151.3131152

16. Garvin, B.J., Cohen, M.B., Dwyer, M.B.: Evaluating improvements to a meta-heuristic search for constrained interaction testing. Empir. Softw. Eng. **16**(1), 61–102 (2011). https://doi.org/10.1007/s10664-010-9135-7

17. Gómez, R.H., Coello, C.A.C.: MOMBI: a new metaheuristic for many-objective optimization based on the R2 indicator. In: 2013 IEEE Congress on Evolutionary Computation, pp. 2488–2495 (2013). https://doi.org/10.1109/CEC.2013.6557868

18. Harman, M., Jia, Y., Zhang, Y.: Achievements, open problems and challenges for search based software testing. In: 2015 IEEE 8th International Conference on Software Testing, Verification and Validation (ICST), pp. 1–12, April 2015. https://doi.org/10.1109/ICST.2015.7102580

19. Ishibuchi, H., Masuda, H., Nojima, Y.: A study on performance evaluation ability of a modified inverted generational distance indicator. In: Proceedings of the 2015 Annual Conference on Genetic and Evolutionary Computation, pp. 695–702. GECCO 2015, ACM, New York, NY, USA (2015). https://doi.org/10.1145/2739480.2754792, http://doi.acm.org/10.1145/2739480.2754792

20. Jan, S., Panichella, A., Arcuri, A., Briand, L.: Search-based multi-vulnerability testing of xml injections in web applications. Empir. Softw. Eng. **24**, 3696–3729 (2019). https://doi.org/10.1007/s10664-019-09707-8

21. Mahmoud, T., Ahmed, B.S.: An efficient strategy for covering array construction with fuzzy logic-based adaptive swarm optimization for software testing use. Expert Syst. App. **42**(22), 8753–8765 (2015). https://doi.org/10.1016/j.eswa.2015.07.029, http://www.sciencedirect.com/science/article/pii/S0957417415004893

22. Mariani, T., Guizzo, G., Vergilio, S.R., Pozo, A.T.R.: Grammatical evolution for the multi-objective integration and test order problem. In: Proceedings of the Genetic and Evolutionary Computation Conference 2016, pp. 1069–1076. GECCO 2016, Association for Computing Machinery, New York, NY, USA (2016). https://doi.org/10.1145/2908812.2908816

23. McCaffrey, J.D.: An empirical study of pairwise test set generation using a genetic algorithm. In: 2010 Seventh International Conference on Information Technology: New Generations, pp. 992–997, April 2010. https://doi.org/10.1109/ITNG.2010.93

24. Petke, J., Cohen, M.B., Harman, M., Yoo, S.: Practical combinatorial interaction testing: empirical findings on efficiency and early fault detection. IEEE Trans. Softw. Eng. **41**(9), 901–924 (2015). https://doi.org/10.1109/TSE.2015.2421279

25. Saeed, A., Ab Hamid, S.H., Mustafa, M.B.: The experimental applications of search-based techniques for model-based testing: taxonomy and systematic literature review. Appl. Soft Comput. **49**, 1094–1117 (2016). https://doi.org/10.1016/j.asoc.2016.08.030, https://www.sciencedirect.com/science/article/pii/S1568494616304240

26. Santiago Júnior, V.A., Özcan, E., Carvalho, V.R.: Hyper-heuristics based on reinforcement learning, balanced heuristic selection and group decision acceptance. Appl. Soft Comput. **97**, 106760 (2020). https://doi.org/10.1016/j.asoc.2020.106760, https://www.sciencedirect.com/science/article/pii/S1568494620306980

27. Shapiro, S.S., Wilk, M.B.: An analysis of variance test for normality (complete samples). Biometrika **52**(3–4), 591–611 (1965)

28. Stepien, B., Peyton, L., Xiong, P.: Framework testing of web applications using TTCN-3. STTT **10**, 371–381 (2008). https://doi.org/10.1007/s10009-008-0082-1

29. Stocco, A., Leotta, M., Ricca, F., Tonella, P.: APOGEN: automatic page object generator for web testing. Softw. Qual. J. **25**(3), 1007–1039 (2016). https://doi.org/10.1007/s11219-016-9331-9

30. Wu, H., Nie, C., Kuo, F.C., Leung, H., Colbourn, C.J.: A discrete particle swarm optimization for covering array generation. IEEE Trans. Evol. Comput. **19**(4), 575–591 (2015). https://doi.org/10.1109/TEVC.2014.2362532

31. Zamli, K.Z., Din, F., Kendall, G., Ahmed, B.S.: An experimental study of hyper-heuristic selection and acceptance mechanism for combinatorial t-way test suite generation. Inf. Sci. **399**, 121–153 (2017). https://doi.org/10.1016/j.ins.2017.03.007, http://www.sciencedirect.com/science/article/pii/S0020025517305820

32. Zitzler, E., Künzli, S.: Indicator-based selection in multiobjective search. In: Yao, X., et al. (eds.) Parallel Problem Solving from Nature - PPSN VIII, pp. 832–842. Springer, Heidelberg (2004). https://doi.org/10.1007/978-3-540-30217-9_84

33. Zitzler, E., Thiele, L.: Multiobjective evolutionary algorithms: a comparative case study and the strength pareto approach. IEEE Trans. Evol. Comput. **3**(4), 257–271 (1999). https://doi.org/10.1109/4235.797969

On the Machine Learning Based Business Workflows Extracting Knowledge from Large Scale Graph Data

Mert Musaoğlu[1]([✉]), Merve Bekler[1], Hüseyin Budak[1], Celal Akçelik[1], and Mehmet S. Aktas[2]

[1] R&D Department GTech, Istanbul, Turkey
{mert.musaoglu,merve.bekler,huseyin.budak,celal.akcelik}@gtech.com.tr
[2] Computer Engineering Department, Yildiz Technical University, Istanbul, Turkey
aktas@yildiz.edu.tr

Abstract. The data created by web users while navigating on a website constitutes graph data. Large-scale graph data is generated on websites many users visit with high frequency. Analyzing large-scale graph data using artificial intelligence techniques and predicting user behavior by creating models is an actively studied research topic. Within the scope of this research, a machine learning business process is proposed that will allow the interpretation of graph data obtained from web user navigation data. A prototype application was developed to demonstrate the usability of the proposed business process. The developed prototype application was run on graph data obtained from websites with intense user-system interaction. A comprehensive evaluation study was carried out on the prototype application. The results obtained from the empirical evaluation are promising and show that the proposed business process is used.

Keywords: Machine learning · Sequential pattern mining · Customer journey · Funnel analysis · Encoding

1 Introduction

A series of conversions, sales, and registrations are performed on websites that receive visitors daily. Funnel analysis is used to understand the traffic in this set of transactions. Funnel analysis is a method of understanding the steps required to reach a result within the website and how many users pass through these steps [1]. In other words, this analysis allows us to analyze the splits in the conversion path, understand which path has the splits, and interfere with these splits to impact the overall conversion rate. It is clear that improving conversion rates is essential, but funnel analysis is not just tracking conversion rates. Funnel analysis also allows us to understand how the conversion rate changes based on user characteristics or

TUBITAK supported this study under project ID# 3200698.

behavior. Thus, it is understood which users are more likely to convert, the reasons for leaving, and what users who leave are doing. This feature improves the funnel performance and finds potential flaws in critical funnels and user flows. Depending on the complexity of a product or the question it is trying to answer, the funnel can be incredibly simple or overly complex. Therefore, it is crucial to correctly define a funnel to gain accurate insights from the analysis. Funnels, also called conversion funnels or sales funnels, are widely used in various marketing functions. They help identify the barriers that cause users to leave before reaching a conversion point. The navigation click flow data subject to the funnel analysis reveals evidence that will inform about the usability and functionality of the web application. The web crawl graph data in Fig.1(a-1) consists of navigation URLs served by corners and links. Each link between two vertices corresponding to navigation URLs refers to a single user's action, such as a visited URL [2]. These tours within site are evaluated at various stages of funnel analysis. As in the image in Fig.1(a-2) here, funnel analysis consists of various stages, including awareness, interest, interaction, action, and advocacy. One of the most effective points of funnel analysis as a marketing activity is that it gives information about which stage has the most room for improvement. This study argues that clickstream data contains an essential signal for predicting future user action. We argue that the conversion rate can be increased by estimating people who could not reach the "action" stage in funnel analysis for any reason but are likely to access it. We formulate the problem of simultaneously predicting future user actions given a user's clickstream history. To solve this new problem, we treat user click data on web pages as a classification problem by preparing it for modeling with preprocessing and embedding methods. We perform experiments on a real dataset and predict the person's next step using supervised learning-deep learning algorithms.

The structure of this work is as follows. Section 2 gives an overview of the fundamental concept, followed by literature. Section 3 describes the problem description. Our proposed methodology is explained in Sect. 4. Section 5 describes the prototype and experimental design, while Sect. 6 provides our experiments. Section 7 covers the critical conclusion related to the research summary and future research directions.

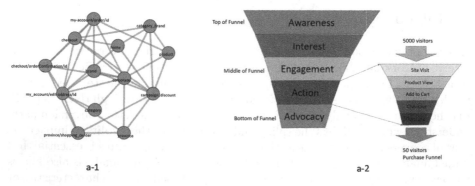

a-1   a-2

Fig. 1. a-1) Visualization of an example user browsing graph data, a-2) Conversion funnel

2   Fundamental Concept and Literature Review

2.1   Fundamental Concept

In this study, we propose an end-to-end business process that aims to predict the subsequent movements of users in the conversion path in the stages of the funnel analysis. Navigation sequence data generated from user navigations are first subjected to different data transformation applications and data pre-processing. Embedding methods are the focus of these data pre-processing processes. Although many embedding methods are used in the literature, various versions of Word2Vec, CountVectorizer, and TF-IDF with the help of N-Gram are frequently used, especially in studies on clickstream data. This study uses five different data transformations, including these three methods and their variants. After the data pre-processing process, the data is labeled according to the user movement to be predicted and made suitable for the relevant machine learning and deep learning algorithms. While training the mentioned algorithms, models are trying to predict users' subsequent movements in the conversion path. Many models are trained using different embedding methods and different estimation algorithms, and the most successful one is selected according to the relevant metric.

Embedding Methods: The textual clickstream data input to machine learning models is called word embedding. These methods provide the extraction of semantic information between words. Methods are gathered under two different representations as frequency-based and estimation-based.

TF-IDF (Term Frequency-Inverse Document Frequency) method, which is one of the frequency-based word embedding methods, is one of the frequently used embedding methods [3]. A statistical approach determines how much each word represents the document it contains. For each word, a score is calculated, indicating the value of the word in the relevant document and word dictionary (corpus) [4].

– Number of occurrences of the relevant word in the document, term frequency (TF).
– Reverse document frequency (IDF) of related word.

This score is calculated with the help of two basic metrics. Ramos observed that TF-IDF works much more successfully in documents containing information on similar topics in his study [5].

Term Frequency (TF) value is the frequency of each word in the document. It is a metric that is directly related to the length of the document. Since there is no relationship between the lengths of the documents and their order of importance, normalization is applied over the frequency value. As Yang and Korfhage [6] pointed out, the longer the documentation lengths, the better the performance of word conversions. In the next step, the documents are converted into vectors.

The vectorization process is applied over the whole word dictionary for documents. In this way, the change due to the difference between the document lengths is prevented [7] TF value takes a value between 0 and 1 according to the importance of the word in the document. If a word does not appear in the document at all, it takes the value 0, and if all the words in the document are the same word, the word's TF score will be the value 1.

TF(t,d) = number of occurrences of word t in document/number of words in document

Reverse Document Frequency (IDF) is the inverse of document density (DF); it is calculated by taking the logarithm of document density. Document frequency is calculated by dividing the number of documents by the number of documents containing the relevant word.

$$DF(t) = \text{occurrence of t word in n documents}$$

When calculating the IDF, if there are frequently repeated words such as stop words in the document, this value will receive a low score. While calculating the IDF value, one is added to the denominator to eliminate possible ambiguity, taking into account the possibility that the word will never occur in the document.

$$IDF(t) = log(N/(DF + 1))$$

Thus, the TF-IDF value can now be produced by combining the formulas from both sides.

$$TF - IDF(t, d) = TF(t, d) * log(N/(DF + 1))$$

The TF-IDF score can be used with N-Gram sequences to better measure associations. N-Gram series are defined as pieces of text that come together N times that are used together in texts or documents. The variable N here can be a character, word, or sentence [8].

CountVectorizer, another frequency-based embedding method, creates a new column in the matrix for each different word in the documents and represents the words with the help of columns. The matrix also includes other documents in its rows, each cell represents the number of times the relevant word occurs in the relevant document [9].

Word2Vec, one of the prediction-based embedding methods, is an unsupervised learning model that can detect the contexts and semantic dependencies between words, unlike other methods. As Church [10] stated in his study, Word2Vec was accepted by large groups in a short time due to its ease of use and accessibility and was used in most studies. The Word2Vec model detects the relationships between words and creates word vectors depending on them. An embedding matrix is made from these extracted vectors and given to deep learning models as an embedding layer. Looking at the working logic, in the first step, as in the CountVectorizer, using the tokenizer creates a column in the matrix for each different word. In each document, 1 or 0 is assigned depending on whether the relevant word is included or not. One of the ways Word2Vec differs from other methods is the window size parameter. With the Window size parameter, information on how many words can be left and right of the relevant word as a bundle is given to the model [11].

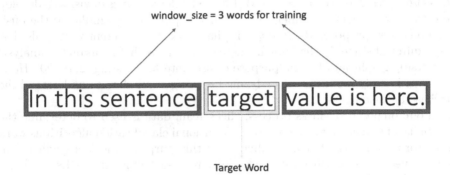

Fig. 2. Example of window size parameter

When we look at the preliminary stages of Word2Vec, Word2Vec models are divided into two structures. In models with CBOW and Skip-Gram. CBOW structure, the word in the center is selected as the target variable, and the other words in the window size are used as input. In Skip-Gram models, the related word predicts other words in window size. Words used as inputs are transferred to the modeling stage of Word2Vec as vectors. The model, which is in the artificial neural network structure, contains N neurons in the hidden layer, and the output module generates a vector of V length. The Word2Vec model does not include an activation function between the input and hidden layers. The softmax function is located between the hidden layer and the output layer. Related processes are applied to each document, and then the model is made ready by using a mapping.

2.2 Literature Review

Customers proceed on a purchasing journey to meet their needs [12]. The classic AIDA (Attention, Interest, Desire, and Action) model depicts the consumer journey as a buying funnel (Strong 1925; Howard and Sheth 1969) [13]. The journey in this funnel; includes stages such as awareness, interest, desire, and action. It also consists of a buying process in which customers' implicit purchasing tendencies can be influenced by their goals or situational factors in the shopping environment. Considering all aspects, it is critical not to lose the customer who comes to the final stage of purchasing funnel. In this respect, we recommend a business process that supports the completion of the conversion path by finding people who are most likely to make the transition to the purchase stage. Within the proposed business process, studies were carried out using the leading websites of companies in the automotive and retail sectors. When we look at the literature, although no study performs this funnel analysis and directly deals with websites in the automotive and retail industries, some studies make sense of customer behavior through search data in many channels such as search engines, video screens, redirect engines. Moe ve Fader (2004) [14] used different types of visits to develop a model that predicts consumers' probability of purchasing, similar to the business process we propose. Moe (2003) [15] has worked on different visit goals that reflect different stages in the funnel. There exist studies that focus on the analysis of browsing graph-data for the purpose of user interface testing [2,16–20]. However, in this study, we focus on analyzing browsing graph data to understand the purchase behaviour.

In our proposed business process, clickstream data is used to determine the possibility of purchasing the next step. Traditional classification algorithms work on vectors consisting of real numbers. For this purpose, the focus will be on creating vectors that will most successfully represent dynamic URLs. Defining dynamic URLs is a current research topic in the literature. We see that Yuan et al. use the word2vec method to represent dynamic URLs as vectors (Yuan et al. 2018) [21]. In another study, Li et al. generate representation vectors by applying the word2vec method after further segmenting URLs into non-numeric characters (Li et al. 2019) [22]. These transformations are made with the general name of embedding methods. In the literature, many studies use machine learning methods to a group and make sense of user browsing behaviors involving similar clickdata flows (Su 2015), (Ting 2005), (Wang 2013) (Sadagopan 2008). When the methods used to predict online shopping behavior are examined, it is seen that supervised machine learning methods and mainly deep learning are used. Kohn, Dennis Lessmann, Stefan Schaal, Markus (2020) [23] emphasizes that supervised machine learning is conceptually unsuitable due to the sequential nature of click data but that the iterative neural networks (RNNs) framework can unlock the full potential of clickstream data. In his studies, Logistic Regression, Gradient Boosting Machine, etc., from supervised learning algorithms. Furthermore, RNN comparisons were made with GRU, LSTM, which are deep learning algorithms. In the proposed business process, we use both supervised learning algorithms and deep learning algorithms compared to different embedding methods. In this way, we aim to collect the strengths of other studies in the literature. We observe studies that analyzes the graph data to extract information on the data lineage [24–27]. Different from these studies, we focus on analyzing browsing graph-data.

3   Problem Definition

The business process we recommend is intended to predict users' future actions and consider their clickstream history. For this process, customer navigation data is divided into customer sessions needed. Various pre-processing and embedding methods have been applied to the navigation data. The new data became the input for machine learning and deep learning algorithms. As a result of the process, users who are most likely to enter the conversion path you want to go in the funnel are estimated from the users who continue to browse the site. For a better understanding, the following questions are asked.

1. What should a business process look like by modeling click-stream and showing the purchase target?
2. How can tagged sequence data be created and automatically tagged in the business process that models customer behavior?
3. What are the most appropriate embedding methods to model customer behavior?
4. Which machine learning–deep learning models give the best results for predicting sequences?

4   Proposed Methodology

The proposed business process is modularly designed. The end-to-end module-based flow from the data collection stage to the estimation results is illustrated in Fig. 3. At the same time, Fig. 3 image is the first of the research questions, "What should a business process look like by modeling click-stream and showing the purchase target?" answers the question.

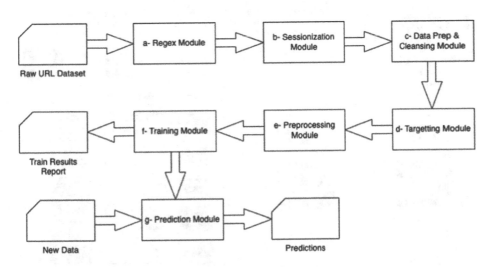

Fig. 3. Proposed supervised machine learning based business work flow

Modules a, b, c, d, e in the flow cover the data flow process to get the data ready for modelling. Other modules e and f include modeling and estimation studies.

The collected data set is passed to the first module, **a-regex module**, in order to mark predefined topics. Each page URL is grouped and tagged according to which topic-specific navigation it contains using the relevant regex. After the tagged URLs, they move to **b-sessionization module** and are grouped here as SessionID, Page URL, Time. At the same time, observations with missing data were excluded from the analysis. In **c-data prep & cleansing module**, the number of crawls in the same session is limited. The goal here is to get people's real browsing. In this restriction, if there is a long wait at the relevant URL, the session is divided into two. Afterward, the number of navigation steps is limited to 10. The reason behind this action is to avoid data loss. The last ten tours of the sessions with more than ten crawls are included in the analysis. Single trips in the same session were removed from the analysis. As a result of these sequential modules, a cleansed sequence dataset was obtained. In order to predict the next step, the last movements of the cleaned session-based data obtained are reserved as the target variable. With this study, we have answered the second of the research questions. In this study, which is included in **d-targetting module**, as seen in Fig. 4, label encoding is made for the selected target, and a 0-1 assignment is made. After the assignment, the variable set that will enter the training is inserted into the embedding methods to make the text data mathematical in the **e-preprocessing module** in order to make it suitable for modeling.

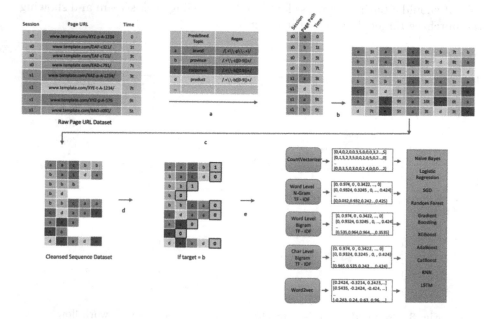

Fig. 4. Data flow

In this module, datasets are created using five (CountVectorizer, Word Level N-Gram TF-IDF, Word Level Bi-Gram TF-IDF, Char Level Bi-Gram TF-IDF, Word2Vec) embedding methods. As a result of this process, the data sets are ready for modeling. In **f-training module**, then different algorithms are trained. Eight algorithms are machine learning algorithms (Naive Bayes, Logistic Regression, Stochastic Gradient Descent, Random Forest, Gradient Boosting, XGBoost, AdaBoost, CatBoost), and two algorithms are deep learning algorithms (RNN, LSTM). Analyzes were carried out using different algorithms. In the proposed end-to-end process, different embedding methods and algorithms were compared. A design was made by finding the embedding method and estimation algorithm that gave the best results according to the metrics selected for the problem. These comparisons are recorded in reports based on success metrics and working times. The estimation of the new incoming user behavior flow is performed in **g-prediction module** with the algorithm and embedding method that gives the best results based on metrics.

5   Prototype and Experimental Study

5.1   Prototype

The modules described in the methodology section are implemented using various Python-3.9 libraries. While collecting navigation data on the website, javascript scripts were used. In the modeling and preprocessing part, libraries such as sklearn (1.0.2), TensorFlow (2.7.0), Keras (2.7.0), gensim (4.1.2), catboost (1.0.3), xgboost (1.5.1) were used. MongoDB was used for saving datasets.

5.2   Experimental Design

Within the scope of this study, a raw data e-commerce site data set of approximately 6 million lines have been studied. On this raw data, the pre-processes in modules a, b, c, d, and e in the modular business process described in the methodology section were completed, and approximately 160 thousand rows of data entered the modeling. It has been tried to find the probability that the next step of the people browsing the e-commerce site will be "sales." 70% of the dataset is reserved for training during the modeling phase, while 30% is reserved for testing. The training set, approximately 70 thousand, was divided into 5 folds by k-fold cross-validation. The success rate of the embedding methods and algorithms according to the error metrics and working times followed in the study is recorded as a table. The error metrics used in the study are as follows, respectively:

– Accuracy
– Precision
– Recall
– F1 Score
– Roc-Auc.

In the study, the embedding method, algorithm, target, and the desired fold number in the k-fold cross-validation are written dynamically, allowing the user to change it.

6   Experiments

As a result of the proposed work process, success scores were obtained based on the metrics explained in the experimental design section. As seen in Fig. 5, when looking at the F1 score values, it is seen that the TF-IDF embedding method is better at the character level, while XGBoost is in the first place as an algorithm, followed by CatBoost. Naive Bayes algorithm and CountVectorizer embedding method gave the lowest results. These results will vary depending on the target variable and selected data set. In addition, 3 and 4 of the research questions were answered together with Fig. 5.

Fig. 5. F1-score results

When we look at the accuracy results in Fig. 6, it is seen that the TF-IDF embedding method is better at the character level in parallel with the F1 score, and tree-based models have higher success as an algorithm.

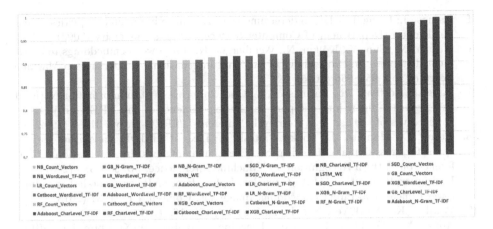

Fig. 6. Accuracy results

7   Conclusions and Future Research Directions

With the proposed business process, the website navigation data have been used to find which topic will be the next move in people's navigation. Different embedding methods and machine learning/deep learning algorithms represent textual data with mathematical expressions. As a result of the study, different success metrics and methods were compared. As a result, it has been seen that the character-level TF-IDF method is more successful in this data set, and tree-based algorithms are much better.

We carried out our studies on the data set we obtained from an e-commerce site in this study. We aim to expand the use of this study in other e-commerce sites. We focused on a study aiming at purchasing within the scope of the business process, and we will implement this study for different purposes in other studies. In addition, it is another aim of ours to increase the embedding methods we use in future studies.

References

1. Daugherty, T., Djuric, V., Li, H., Leckenby, J.: Establishing a paradigm: a systematic analysis of interactive advertising research. J. Interact. Adv. **17**(1), 65–78 (2017)
2. Olmezogullari, E., Aktas, M.: Representation of click-stream DataSequences for learning user navigational behavior by using embeddings. In: 2020 IEEE International Conference on Big Data (Big Data), pp. 3173–3179 (2020). https://doi.org/10.1109/BigData50022.2020.9378437
3. Aizawa, A.: An information-theoretic perspective of TF-IDF measures. Inf. Process. Manag. **39**(1), 45–65 (2003)
4. Zhang, W., Yoshida, T., Tang, X.: A comparative study of TF-IDF, LSI and multi-words for text classification. Exp. Syst. Appl. **38**(3), 2758–2765 (2011)

5. Ramos, J.: Using TF-IDF to determine word relevance in document queries, Technical report, Department of Computer Science, Rutgers University (2003)
6. Kusner, M., Sun, Y., Kolkin, N., Weinberger, K.: From word embeddings to document distances. In: Proceedings of the 32nd International Conference on Machine Learning, pp. 957–966 (2015)
7. Yang, J., Korfhage, R., Rasmussen, E.: Query improvement in information retrieval using genetic algorithms-a report on the experiments of the TREC project. In: Proceedings of the 1st Text Retrieval Conference (TREC-1), pp. 31–58 (1992)
8. Atanu, D., Mamata, J., Thakkar Jitesh, J.: Lexical TF-IDF: an n-gram feature space for cross-domain classification of sentiment reviews. In: International Conference on Pattern Recognition and Machine Intelligence, pp. 380–386 (2007)
9. Rodríguez, P., Bautista, M.A., Gonzàlez, J., Escalera, S.: Beyond one-hot encoding: lower dimensional target embedding. Image Vis. Comput $\mathbf{75}$, 21–31 (2018)
10. Ward, C.K.: Word2Vec. Nat. Lang. Eng. $\mathbf{23}$, 155–162 (2017)
11. Rong, X.: Word2vec Parameter Learning Explained, arXiv preprint (2014). arXiv:1411.2738
12. Li, A. Ma, L.: Charting the path to purchase using topic models. J. Mark. Res. $\mathbf{57}$(6), 1019–1036 (2020)
13. Howard, J.A., Sheth, J.N.: The Theory of Buyer Behavior, pp. 83–114. John Wiley Sons, New York (1969)
14. Moe, W., Fader, P.: Dynamic conversion behavior at E-commerce sites. Manag. Sci. $\mathbf{50}$, 326–335 (2004). https://doi.org/10.1287/mnsc.1040.0153
15. Moe, W.W.: Buying, searching, or browsing: differentiating between online shoppers using in-store navigational clickstream. J. Cons. Psychol.. $\mathbf{13}$(1–2), 29–39 (2003)
16. Erdem, I., Oguz, R.F., Olmezogullari, E., Aktas, M.S.: Test script generation based on hidden Markov models learning from user browsing behaviors. In: 2021 IEEE International Conference on Big Data (Big Data), pp. 2998–3005. IEEE (2021)
17. Oz, M., Kaya, C., Olmezogullari, E., Aktas, M.S.: On the use of generative deep learning approaches for generating hidden test scripts. Int. J. Softw. Eng. Knowl. Eng. $\mathbf{31}$(10), 1447–1468 (2021)
18. Oguz, R.F., Oz, M., Olmezogullari, E., Aktas, M.S.: Extracting information from large scale graph data: case study on automated UI testing. In: Euro-Par 2021: Parallel Processing Workshops. Euro-Par 2021, LNCS, vol. 13098. Springer, Cham (2021). https://doi.org/10.1007/978-3-031-06156-1_29
19. Olmezogullari, E., Aktas, M.S.: Pattern2Vec: representation of clickstream data sequences for learning user navigational behavior. Concurr. Comput. Pract. Exp. $\mathbf{34}$(9) (2022)
20. Uygun, Y., Oguz, R.F., Olmezogullari, E., Aktas, M.S.: On the large-scale graph data processing for user interface testing in big data science projects. In: 2020 IEEE International Conference on Big Data (Big Data), pp. 2049–2056 (2020)
21. Yuan, H., Yang, Z., Chen, X., Li, Y., Liu, W.: URL2Vec: URL modeling with character embeddings for fast and accurate phishing website detection. In: 2018 IEEE International Conference on Parallel & Distributed Processing with Applications, Ubiquitous Computing & Communications, Big Data & Cloud Computing, Social Computing & Networking, Sustainable Computing & Communications (ISPA/IUCC/BDCloud/SocialCom/SustainCom) (2018)
22. Li, B., Yuan, G., Shen, L., Zhang, R., Yao, Y.: Incorporating URL embedding into ensemble clustering to detect web anomalies. Fut. Gener. Comput. Syst. $\mathbf{96}$, 176–184 (2019)

23. Köhn, D.L., Stefan Schaal, M.: Predicting online shopping behaviour from clickstream data using deep learning. Exp. Syst. Appl. **150**, 113342 (2020). https://doi.org/10.1016/j.eswa.2020.113342
24. Tufek, A., Gurbuz, A., Ekuklu, O.F., Aktas, M.S.: Provenance collection platform for the weather research and forecasting model. In: 2018 14th International Conference on Semantics, Knowledge and Grids (SKG 2018) (2018)
25. Baeth, M.J., Aktas, M.S.: Detecting misinformation in social networks using provenance data. In: 2017 13th International Conference on Semantics, Knowledge and Grids (SKG 2017) (2017)
26. Yazici, I.M., Karabulut, E., Aktas, M.S.: A data provenance visualization approach. In: 2018 14th International Conference on Semantics, Knowledge and Grids (SKG 2018) (2018)
27. Riveni, M., Baeth, M, Aktas, M.S., Dustdar, S.: Provenance in social computing: a case study. In: 2017 13th International Conference on Semantics, Knowledge and Grids (SKG 2017) (2017)

Augmented Intelligence Multilingual Conversational Service for Smart Enterprise Management Software

Abidemi Emmanuel Adeniyi[1,4] , Mukaila Olagunju[2],
Joseph Bamidele Awotunde[3(✉)] , Moses Kazeem Abiodun[1] ,
Jinmisayo Awokola[4] , and Morolake Oladayo Lawrence[5]

[1] Department of Computer Science, Landmark University, Omu-Aran, Nigeria
{adeniyi.emmanuel,moses.abiodun}@lmu.edu.ng
[2] Department of Computer Science, Federal University, Oye-Ekiti, Nigeria
mukaila.olagunju@fuoye.edu.ng
[3] Department of Computer Science, University of Ilorin, Ilorin, Nigeria
awotunde.jb@unilorin.edu.ng
[4] Department of Computer Science, Precious Cornerstone University, Ibadan, Nigeria
jinmi.awokola@pcu.edu.ng
[5] Department of Computer Science, Baze University, Abuja, Nigeria
morolake.lawrence@bazeuniversity.edu.ng

Abstract. Conversational agents are gaining popularity in the corporate world as a way to increase customer experience and economic competitiveness. Additionally, developments in augmented intelligence systems employ natural language processing to provide the industry with natural and clear interaction experiences. Multilingual conversational bot or Chabot is important in every area of life, especially in a multicultural community recognized for its numerous accents and slang among many social groupings Moreover, most present Chabot systems only handle one language at a time, and the training session is cumbersome since it needs various dialects for different purposes. This research presents a multilingual chatbot that allows clients to converse in many languages as if they were conversing with a real person to achieve a smart enterprise management software. The proposed system was implemented using React.JS and python programming language on a Pentium III processor speed of 600 MHz minimum. The proposed multilingual service will deal with the limitation of the existing system by developing a system that will allow multiple languages on chatbot agents. The system will allow the users to converse in their languages, which will make communication easy between the system and the users. The proposed system will include a user-friendly interface that will assist in guiding each user on how to utilize it effectively without any specialized training.

Keywords: Augmented Intelligence · Chatbot · Conversational agent · Rule base · Software development

---

A. E. Adeniyi—Landmark University SDG 4 (Quality Education) and Landmark University SDG 11 (Sustainable Cities and Communities)
M. K. Abiodun—Landmark University SDG 4 (Quality Education) and Landmark University SDG 16 (Peace and Justice, Strong Institution)

O. Gervasi et al. (Eds.): ICCSA 2022 Workshops, LNCS 13381, pp. 476–488, 2022.
https://doi.org/10.1007/978-3-031-10548-7_35

1 Introduction

An Augmented intelligence entails humans and robots collaborating to maximize company value by appealing to their respective strengths. This is an alternate paradigm of artificial intelligence that emphasizes AI's assisting role in developing human skills, reflecting AI's continual effect on enhancing human creativity. Artificial intelligence is being used in a wide range of everyday tasks [1, 2]. Among the most commonly used applications include navigation, which can forecast road congestion; real-time language transcription using cameras; online platforms, which help individuals explore different information of personal value or involvement; movie proposals; email spam and ransomware filtering; online customer assistance; Chabot, among others.

Multilingual Conversations or Chatbots are software applications that use natural language to connect with individuals. This technology began almost six decades ago to see if chatbot software might deceive consumers into thinking they were actual humans [3]. Chatbot systems, on the other hand, are not just designed to replicate human communication; they are also beneficial in a variety of industries like education, knowledge discovery, industry, and e-commerce. Chatbot apps improve customer experience by streamlining communication between humans and enterprises [4]. Chatbots have become increasingly important in a variety of businesses [5]. Chatbots such as Apple's Siri, Microsoft's Cortana and XiaoIce, Google Assistant, Facebook Messenger bots, IBM's Watson Assistant, and Amazon's Alexa have all received significant interest [6]. Nevertheless, developing bots with simulated cognitive capacities is still in the works. Studying complicated user behavior under numerous settings and circumstances can be essential to improving a system's user experience [7]. Chatbots ought to be able to do more than only comprehend things offered in message queries to better replicate human emotional skills, such as reading the mood of text/voice and assessing facial gestures [8]. This is where augmented intelligence of Things comes into implementing an intelligence chatbot for a smart enterprise management system.

The physical world is transformed into being digitized and makes everything connected [9]. The development of mobile and network devices, along with modernization, has changed the way people interact with each other and engage with organizations [10]. The proliferation of wireless networks and mobile devices has resulted in the expansion of electronic business [11, 12]. Which presents several benefits for entrepreneurs by facilitating the growth of commercial activity and enabling operations that were previously impossible [13]. As a result, various firms, including airlines, fashion labels, and insurance organizations, have begun to provide services to their clients using chat applications. Airlines now allow passengers to check-in, make suggestions, and receive the latest information via Facebook messaging. Fashion firms provide clients with stylistic tips based on prior purchasing or personal tastes, and insurance companies manage claims using chat applications. Customers and businesses may engage via text messaging, a generally known form of communication, and a basic interface when using mobile messenger software [14]. Customers may quickly reach out to firms by messaging, rather than phoning, e-mailing, or launching an app, at a time that is convenient for them.

Augmented intelligent multilingual conversational services can be used to facilitate interactions between a business and its customers to enable a smart enterprise management system [15]. The conversation service achieves this by creating natural language as output [16]. The use of chatbots by corporations is not a new concept. Chatbots have been around for quite a long period in electronic web-based applications and are often employed to ease customer care. Chatbots, on the other hand, are now migrating to the mobile messaging platform. The use of mobile messenger chatbots for business reasons is at the start of a trend known as 'conversational commerce.' Chatbots can answer via the messengers interface with comments, suggestions, changes, links, or call-to-action buttons, and users can browse for items by scrolling through a product carousel [17, 18]. A chatbot can identify the buyer's purpose and adjust products depending on the buyer's preferences and tastes. It can then help with the purchase, ordering, and delivery processes [19].

The focus of this study is to enhance the chatbot agent with the augmented intelligence of things for multiple language interactions among the users with rule base approach to achieve a smart enterprise management software. This study switched between English and French during the conversation with the client. This will cause the conversational agents to find it enticing since it can consolidate and reduce the steps of the purchasing process to become a "one-stop shopping" platform.

The remaining part of this research is structured into various sections: Sect. 2 describes the review of related works, and Sect. 3 described the material and methods. Section 4 presented the result and discussion while Sect. 5 presented the concluding part of the research.

2   Related Works

Ralston *et al.* [2] investigated the chatbot-related API packages provided by Google, Amazon, and IBM, and suggests a chatbot system for student support. The study used Watson Tone Analyzer to analyze the student mood and Watson Language Translator API to provide the standard chatbot base. The study's comparative analysis indicated that IBM Watson provided the most effective alternatives for assessing textual tone information in terms of attitude. However, the question-answer bank for all possible questions needs to be inputted manually and Assign them to intentions in the chatbot's expertise specification to respond correctly to user interaction requests.

Kasinathan, Mustapha, and Bin [20] the study presented a multilingual chatbot system that will enable businesses and organizations to build and launch their customized multilingual chatbot solution with enhanced capabilities The research implemented Type-Script for frontend web application development and Go for backend development while Dart was used for the mobile application. The constructed prototypes are then tested using a research instrument, with the results indicating that the suggested scheme might help local firms and enterprises establish their chatbot system as a substitute for conventional customer support. However, the limitation to the study was that of adding support for more languages and improving language models for better matching accuracy.

Vanjani, Aiken, and Park [21] the study surveyed chatbots for multilingual conversations. The study established that chatbots may be used to deliver multilingual supportive services to customers Conversely, while several chatbots have been built in other languages, the majority now talk solely in English, with only a handful able to interact in many languages. Multilingual chatbots, when properly constructed, can provide an online communications alternative that crosses language borders. A team of undergraduates assessed the English translations of the chatbot's responses in this investigation. The results suggest that German and Spanish comments were clear and natural, whereas Korean ones were less so. The study indicates encouraging findings in the future usage of multilingual chatbots to enable global communication, with business potential in the employment of such chatbots to provide customer support and online live connection with clients worldwide.

Zheng et al. [22] surveyed hybrid-augmented intelligence, collaboration, and, cognition. The study outlines a basic framework for human-computer cooperative hybrid-augmented knowledge, as well as the fundamental features of cognitive-based hybrid-augmented intellectual capacity. Common implementations of hybrid-augmented intellectual ability are explored, including controlling manufacturing intricacies and threats, participatory decision-making in organizations, online smart learning, medical and universal health care, public safety and security, human-computer interactive driving, and cloud robotics. The study encourages both business and academics to research and improve hybrid-augmented intelligence, both theoretically and practically.

Li et al. [23] The IBM Watson Language Translator API was used to establish an efficient billing transaction processing for a global corporation that provides safe language translation across many dialects. The system also contains a review method that enables users to rate how well their lexical items are converted on a routine basis, which helps to improve the learning algorithm.

Marbouti et al. [24] IBM Tone Analyzer was used to scan online tweets to uncover pertinent information that may be useful in an emergency case. The Tone Analyzer was included in this application to assess the emotional resonance of a given tweet. Using this information, as well as an assessment may be done to classify and categorize twitter posts in process of extracting vital information in the event of an emergency based on information about the operator and the receiver(s) of the message. This is an appropriate use case that suggests combining IBM Tone Analyzer with our proposed chatbot.

Mlakar et al. [25] work on an execute-related investigation that links artificial intelligence (expressed speech methods, conversational intellect) and natural sciences (encapsulated interactive bots) to create a system that permits symmetrical computer-mediated communication. Its task is to gather client data and integrate it into medical workflows as electronic health materials (the Fast Healthcare Interoperability Resources). The research utilizes the system's core elements, including the mHealth software, the Open Health Connect framework, and techniques to provide voice voice-enabled conversational agents to cancer survivors in five distinct languages. The system suggested a way to incorporate potential advantages and distribute them to people.

Nuruzzaman and Hussain [26] the article give an overview of contemporary chatbots and the methods used to construct them. It examines and evaluates the connections, variances, and limitations of existing chatbots. The research looked at the functionality and technological attributes of the top 11 chatbot technology platforms. According to studies, around 75% of customers have experienced poor customer service, and delivering relevant, comprehensive, and insightful responses remains a challenging task. Earlier, methods for developing chatbots relied on hand-written guidelines and patterns. When deep learning become prominent, end-to-end neural networks quickly surpassed them. Deep Neural Networks, in particular, is a powerful generative-based methodology for overcoming conversational response generating challenges. This paper conducted an in-depth review of recent literature by examining over 70 articles relevant to chatbots published in the last 5 years. This study examined selected studies depending on the approach adopted, based on a review of the literature. This study also examined why previous chatbot models fail to consider when creating responses and how this affects dialogue effectiveness.

Hussain, Ameri, and Ababneh [27] focus on chatbot categorization and chatbot creation strategies, in which the authors investigated chatbot categories of task-oriented and non-task-oriented chatbots. These categories were discussed during a discussion on how chatbots utilize conversational context. The authors investigated a variety of machine learning methodologies, including Recurrent Neural Networks, Sequence to Sequence neural concepts, and Long Short-Term Memory networks.

Bavaresco *et al.* [28] the paper provide a thorough review of the literature on the usage of conversational agents in commercial domains. The study addressed three basics, three specific, and two statistical research issues using a selected literature corpus. The corpus was created by scanning information sources for publications, using inclusion and exclusion criteria, and then filtering them. The study questions addressed the business areas studied, as well as the fundamental aims and future difficulties. This review's contributions demonstrate that the study area of conversational agents in business lacks this method of enriching the agents. The findings and outcomes of this review may influence future research possibilities in conversational agents in business domains.

Kaghyan *et al.* [29] outline the reasons for the increased utility of chatbots and their future in the corporate context. They also advocated a dialogue on platform development by comparing skills, strengths, and constraints. Meyer et al. [30] carried out the investigation that most closely resembles this work. The authors organized a literature analysis of chatbots in digital workplaces, analyzing employee support in their regular job. They propose a system of searching and filtering using scientific databases as a source of papers in the study. The primary goals of the research were to categorize the chatbot application fields and to assess the potential and objectives of the articles In addition to business uses.

From the list of works of literature, it can be concluded that chatbot is an important aspect of enterprise management software development and many other related fields. In recent times, corporations have discovered uses for chatbots that go beyond service delivery. Chatbots are playing important roles in advertising and promotion. They're quickly gaining popularity among firms trying to automate customer care, marketing, or sales. People are eager to interact with chatbots, and some even prefer this mode of contact to human representatives. Therefore, this study contributes to the body of knowledge by engaging the use of augmented intelligence to develop a multi-language conversation software for various organizations to achieve smart enterprise management software.

3 Material and Methods

This section presents the methodology used to conduct the study. The system is designed using a rule-based method that makes it entitled Conversation Training Data. The training is categorized into three major subsystems which are; Facts, insights, and guidelines from NLU Utilizing top tier keys, the training sample parser identifies the training data type. The area utilizes the same YAML structure as the learning algorithm and can be divided into numerous files or concatenated into a single file. The domain covers reaction and form specifications. Each of the subsystems described above serves a unique purpose for the platform.

A. Stories

Stories are made up of:

Narrative: The title of the story. The name is generic and is not utilized in coaching; nevertheless, it can be used as a human-readable description for the tale.

Metadata: random and unnecessary; not used in training; can be used to hold necessary details about the tale, such as the author's name.

A step-by-step guide: The tale is made up of respondents and activities.

Each of the subsequent steps can be taken:

- A user statement comprised of purpose and entities.
- An Or Expression that contains two or more user messages.
- A bot operation.
- A form.
- A time slot was assigned to the event.
- A checkpoint that links one tale to another (Figs. 1 and 2).

```
stories:
- story: story with a form
  steps:
  - intent: find_restaurant
  - action: restaurant_form
  - active_loop: restaurant_form    # Activate the form
  - active_loop: null               # This form is current
  - action: utter_restaurant_found  # Form complete, no form
```

Fig. 1. Structure of a form. A form is a type of customized activity that provides the logic to cycle over a list of needed slots and ask the user for this knowledge.

B. Checkpoints

Checkpoints are indicated using the guard post: key, either at the start or conclusion of a tale. Checkpoints are used to link storylines. They might be the first or last stage in a tale (Fig. 3).

```
stories:
- story: story with a slot
  steps:
  - intent: celebrate_bot
  - slot_was_set:
    - feedback_value: positive
  - action: utter_yay
```

Fig. 2. Structure of a slot. A slot activity is defined by the key slot was set: with the space title and, possibly, the space values.

```
stories:
- story: story_with_a_checkpoint_1
  steps:
  - intent: greet
  - action: utter_greet
  - checkpoint: greet_checkpoint

- story: story_with_a_checkpoint_2
  steps:
  - checkpoint: greet_checkpoint
  - intent: book_flight
  - action: action_book_flight
```

Fig. 3. Structure of a checkpoint. Checkpoints can assist to clarify training sets and eliminate duplication, but they should not be used excessively.

C. Rules

The guidelines are given under the principles area and resemble tales. A rule also includes a steps key, which holds the same set of steps that tales do. Rules might also include the discussion beginning and criteria keys. These are used to define the parameters under which the policy must be applied.

Regulation with a prerequisite that appears just like (Fig. 4):

```
rules:
- rule: Only say `hey` when the user provided a name
  condition:
  - slot_was_set:
    - user_provided_name: true
  steps:
  - intent: greet
  - action: utter_greet
```

Fig. 4. Structure of a rule

D.   Test Stories.

Test tales determine if a statement is appropriately categorized as well as the response forecasts.

Test scenarios have the same syntax as narratives, with the exception that user communication steps might include a user defining the user message's actual content and object descriptions. Here's an illustration of a test narrative (Figs. 5, 6, 7 and 8):

```
stories:
- story: A basic end-to-end test
  steps:
  - user: |
    hey
    intent: greet
    action: utter_ask_howcanhelp
  - user: |
    show me [chinese]{"entity": "cuisine"} restaurants
    intent: inform
    action: utter_ask_location
  - user: |
    in [Paris]{"entity": "location"}
    intent: inform
    action: utter_ask_price
```

Fig. 5. Structure of aest stories.

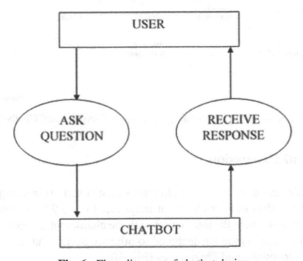

Fig. 6. Flow diagram of chatbot design

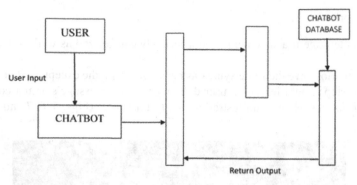

Fig. 7. Sequence diagram representing design of the proposed chatbot.

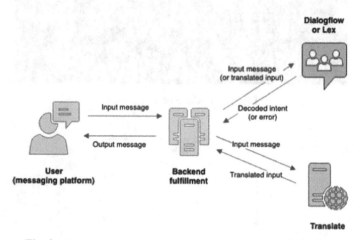

Fig. 8. Diagram representing the proposed multilingual Chatbot.

4 Results and Discussion

This program is designed to enable users to interact with chatbots in multiple Languages, as well as get the replies in their choice of language. Figure 9 Shows the NLU simple chatbot system, this is where the interaction with the chatbot takes place. As it is using a rule-based approach, the system is designed to offer support for adverse drug reactions, Blood Pressure, Hospitals, and Pharmacies (Fig. 10).

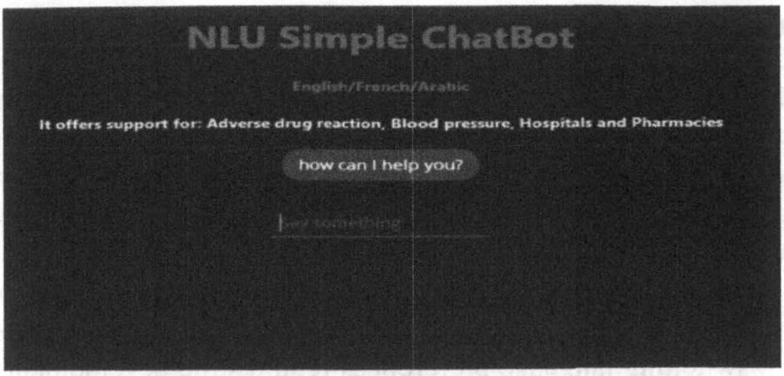

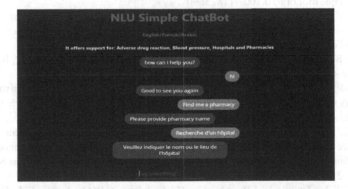

Fig. 9. NLU Multilingual chatbot interface.

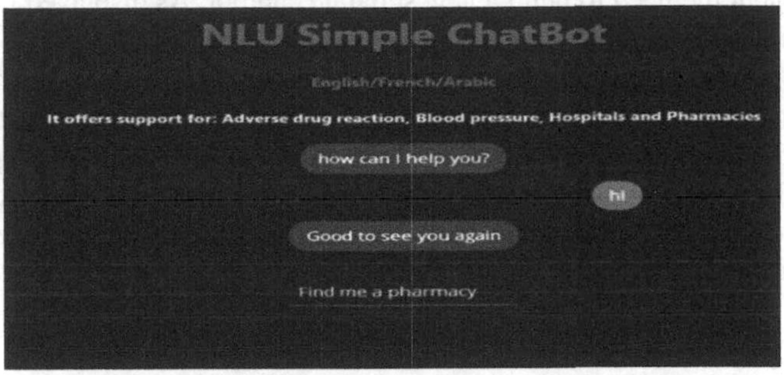

Fig. 10. Interaction with the chatbot in English.

Fig. 11. Interaction with the chatbot in both English and French.

Figure 10 Shows the interaction with the system in English, the User starts the conversation with greetings like "Hi there", "How are you", "Is anyone there?", "Hey", "Hola", "Hello", "Good day". Figure 11 Shows the interaction with the Chatbot in French language, User start the conversation with greetings like "Bonjour", "Comment allez-vous", "Quelqu'un est-il là?", "Hé", "Hola", "Bonjour", "Bonjour" Or it can also start by asking questions related to the support the chatbot offers like asking "Recherche d'un hôpital". And the system replies to the conversation with the same language French.

5   Conclusion and Recommendation

Augmented Intelligence Multilingual Conversational service is a way to increase organizational functional efficiency and minimize expenses while offering clients comfort and significant operations. They enable firms to respond swiftly to a wide range of consumer inquiries and concerns while reducing the need for human intervention. This research developed a multilingual conversational bot software development to converse with clients speaking languages enhancing engagement and conversations. Modern chatbots were designed with the incapacity to communicate in many languages at the same time; however, switching language preferences requires the development of a distinct chatbot, which adds time complexity and costs [31]. Our proposed system is flexible in terms of time complexity as a single chatbot converses both in English and French language without the need to build a new separate chatbot. As displayed in Fig. 11, our proposed system can converse in multiple languages simultaneously.

Chatbots are a smarter method to ensure that clients get the fast response they need without having to wait in line. Conversational multilingual bots are constantly accessible to engage clients and provide them with rapid responses to frequently requested questions. Therefore this proposed system will help to engage customers which is perhaps the most effective approach to reduce bounce rates and, as a result, increase conversions in multilingual mode simultaneously.

References

1. Cai, Y., Abascal, J.: Ambient Intelligence in Everyday Life. LNCS. Springer, Heidelberg (2006). https://doi.org/10.1007/11825890
2. Ralston, K., Chen, Y., Isah, H., Zulkernine, F.: A voice interactive multilingual student support system using IBM Watson. In: 2019 18th IEEE International Conference on Machine Learning and Applications (ICMLA), pp. 1924–1929. IEEE, December 2019
3. Shawar, B.A., Atwell, E.: Chatbots: are they useful? In: LDV Forum, vol. 22, issue number 1, pp. 29–49 (2007)
4. Awotunde, J.B., Chakraborty, C., Adeniyi, A.E.: Intrusion detection in industrial internet of things network-based on deep learning model with rule-based feature selection. Wirel. Commun. Mob. Comput. **2021**(2021), 7154587 (2021)
5. Vaira, L., Bochicchio, M.A., Conte, M., Casaluci, F.M., Melpignano, A.: MamaBot: a system based on ML and NLP for supporting women and families during pregnancy. In: 2018 Proceedings of the 22nd International Database Engineering and Applications Symposium, pp. 273–277. ACM (2018)
6. Adeniyi, E.A., Awotunde, J.B., Abiodun, K.M., Adeboye, W.O., Ajamu, G.J.: Development of secured smart display for art industry. In: Misra, S., Oluranti, J., Damaševičius, R., Maskeliunas, R. (eds.) ICIIA 2021. CCIS, vol. 1547, pp. 256–267. Springer, Cham (2022). https://doi.org/10.1007/978-3-030-95630-1_18
7. Mostafa, M., Crick, T., Calderon, A.C., Oatley, G.: Incorporating emotion and personality-based analysis in user-centered modelling. In: Bramer, M., Petridis, M. (eds.) Research and Development in Intelligent Systems XXXIII, pp. 383–389. Springer, Cham (2016). https://doi.org/10.1007/978-3-319-47175-4_29
8. Justo, A.C., dos Reis, J.C., Calado, I., Bonacin, R., Jensen, F.R.: Exploring ontologies to improve the empathy of interactive bots. In: 2018 IEEE International Conference on Enabling Technologies: Infrastructure for Collaborative Enterprises (WETICE), pp. 261–266 (2018)

9. Awotunde, J.B., Abiodun, K.M., Adeniyi, E.A., Folorunso, S.O., Jimoh, R.G.: A deep learning-based intrusion detection technique for a secured IoMT system. In: Misra, S., Oluranti, J., Damaševičius, R., Maskeliunas, R. (eds.) ICIIA 2021. CCIS, vol. 1547, pp. 50–62. Springer, Cham (2022). https://doi.org/10.1007/978-3-030-95630-1_4

10. Eeuwen, M.V.: Mobile conversational commerce: messenger chatbots as the next interface between businesses and consumers. Master's thesis, University of Twente (2017)

11. Pavlou, P.A., Lie, T., Dimoka, A.: An integrative model of mobile commerce adoption. In: Proceedings of the Conference on Information Systems and Technology (CIST/INFORMS), Seattle, WA, November 2007

12. Mustapha, A.M., Arogundade, O.T., Misra, S., Damasevicius, R., Maskeliunas, R.: A systematic literature review on compliance requirements management of business processes. Int. J. Syst. Assur. Eng. Manage. 11(3), 561–576 (2020). https://doi.org/10.1007/s13198-020-009 85-w

13. Ogundokun, R.O., Arowolo, M.O., Misra, S., Awotunde, J.B.: Machine learning, IoT, and blockchain integration for improving process management application security. In: Misra, S., Kumar Tyagi, A. (eds.) Blockchain Applications in the Smart Era. EAI/Springer Innovations in Communication and Computing. Springer, Cham (2022). https://doi.org/10.1007/978-3-030-89546-4_12

14. Oluwamayowa, A., Adedeji, A., Sanjay, M., Faith, A.: Empirical framework for tackling recurring project management challenges using knowledge management mechanisms. In: Gervasi, O., et al. (eds.) ICCSA 2020. LNCS, vol. 12254, pp. 954–967. Springer, Cham (2020). https://doi.org/10.1007/978-3-030-58817-5_67

15. Griol, D., Carbó, J., Molina, J.M.: An automatic dialog simulation technique to develop and evaluate interactive conversational agents. Appl. Artif. Intell. 27(9), 759–780 (2013). https://doi.org/10.1080/08839514.2013.835230

16. Constine, J.: Facebook launches messenger platform with chatbots|TechCrunch, 12 April 2016. https://techcrunch.com/2016/04/12/agents-on-messenger

17. Abioye, T.E., Arogundade, O.T., Misra, S., Adesemowo, K., Damaševičius, R.: Cloud-based business process security risk management: a systematic review, taxonomy, and future directions. Computers 10(12), 160 (2021)

18. Shopify: Conversational Commerce Definition – What is Conversational Commerce (2016). https://www.shopify.com/encyclopedia/conversational-commerce

19. Adeniyi, E.A., Ogundokun, R.O., Misra, S., Awotunde, J.B., Abiodun, K.M.: Enhanced security and privacy issue in multi-tenant environment of green computing using blockchain technology. In: Misra, S., Kumar Tyagi, A. (eds.) Blockchain Applications in the Smart Era. EAI/Springer Innovations in Communication and Computing. Springer, Cham (2022). https://doi.org/10.1007/978-3-030-89546-4_4

20. Kasinathan, V., Mustapha, A., Bin, C.K.: A Customizable multilingual chatbot system for customer support. Ann. Emerg. Technol. Comput. (AETiC) 5(5), 51–59 (2021)

21. Vanjani, M., Aiken, M., Park, M.: Chatbots for multilingual conversations. J. Manage. Sci. Bus. Intell. 4(1), 19–24 (2019)

22. Zheng, N.N., et al.: Hybrid-augmented intelligence: collaboration and cognition. Front. Inf. Technol. Electron. Eng. 18(2), 153–179 (2017). https://doi.org/10.1631/FITEE.1700053

23. Li, Y., Muthiah, M., Routh, A., Dorai, C.: Cognitive computing in action to enhance invoice processing with customized language translation. In: 2017 IEEE International Conference on Cognitive Computing (ICCC), pp. 136–139. IEEE, June 2017

24. Marbouti, M., Mayor, I., Yim, D., Maurer, F.: Social media analyst responding tool: a visual analytics prototype to identify relevant tweets in emergency events. In: ISCRAM (2017)

25. Mlakar, I., et al.: Multilingual conversational systems to drive the collection of patient-reported outcomes and integration into clinical workflows. Symmetry 13(7), 1187 (2021). https://doi.org/10.3390/sym13071187

26. Nuruzzaman, M., Hussain, O.K.: A survey on chatbot implementation in customer service industry through deep neural networks. In: 2018 IEEE 15th International Conference on e-Business Engineering (ICEBE), pp. 54–61. IEEE, October 2018

27. Hussain, S., Ameri Sianaki, O., Ababneh, N.: A survey on conversational agents/chatbots classification and design techniques. In: Barolli, L., Takizawa, M., Xhafa, F., Enokido, T. (eds.) WAINA 2019. AISC, vol. 927, pp. 946–956. Springer, Cham (2019). https://doi.org/10.1007/978-3-030-15035-8_93

28. Bavaresco, R., et al.: Conversational agents in business: a systematic literature review and future research directions. Comput. Sci. Rev. **36**, 100239 (2020)

29. Kaghyan, S., Sarpal, S., Zorilescu, A., Akopian, D.: Review of interactive communication systems for business-to-business (B2B) services. Electron. Imaging **2018** (6) (2018) 1–11 (2018)

30. Meyer von Wolff, Hobert, S., Schumann, M.: How may i help you? State of the art and open research questions for chatbots at the digital workplace. In: 2019 Proceedings of the 52nd Hawaii International Conference on System Sciences, vol. 6, pp. 95–104 (2019). https://doi.org/10.24251/HICSS.2019.013

31. Ranade, N., Catá, A.: Intelligent algorithms: evaluating the design of chatbots and search. Tech. Commun. **68**(2), 22–40 (2021)

Recommendation of Microservices Patterns Through Automatic Information Retrieval Using Problems Specified in Natural Language

Álex dos Santos Moura(iD), Mário Alan de Oliveira Lima(iD),
Fabio Gomes Rocha(iD), and Michel S. Soares(✉)(iD)

Federal University of Sergipe, São Cristòvão, Brazil
michel@dcomp.ufs.br

Abstract. Microservices are becoming increasingly popular for the development of distributed systems. However, in order to adopt microservices in practice, one has to deal especially with decomposition, communication and deployment of services. These issues can be solved by applying design patterns to microservices. Although it seems simple, developers may present difficulties when selecting the correct pattern to solve a given problem. This situation happens both to beginners and experienced professionals, as there are a considerable number of patterns to master. This study proposes an information retrieval-based approach to recommend patterns applied to microservices considering problems expressed by developers in natural language. To evaluate the proposed approach, we created two corpus, the first one containing 10 patterns, and the second 10 problems. When performing the experiments, we were able to achieve a precision rate of 60%. From this study, it is possible to support developers in selecting patterns applied to microservices, which facilitates their adoption and the development of higher quality systems, also benefiting organizations, as well as assisting researchers in future studies, presenting a possible way to recommend these patterns.

Keywords: Automatic recommendation · Design patterns · Microservices · Information retrieval · Machine learning

1 Introduction

The Microservice architecture, a variant of the Service-Oriented Architecture (SOA) [1–3], has been recently proposed with the objective of designing software systems as a collection of loosely-coupled services. Microservices are defined as independent, small, and limited context services, and together they constitute a software system [4].

Microservices have been increasingly adopted in large organisations such as Netflix, SoundCloud, and Amazon. Organisations are adopting microservices as

O. Gervasi et al. (Eds.): ICCSA 2022 Workshops, LNCS 13381, pp. 489–501, 2022.
https://doi.org/10.1007/978-3-031-10548-7_36

a solution for software architecture as they allow the development of systems that are easier to scale, deploy and maintain [5]. However, despite these advantages, processes and methods for adopting microservices are not simple, since it is necessary to deal with complex problems, including the decomposition of the system in microservices, how they will communicate, and, finally, the definition of the implementation plan for each microservice [6]. Even though microservices are often discussed, there is little guidance on refactoring processes of legacy applications [7]. Regarding guidance on adopting design patterns in microservices, there is a shortage number of works.

For many years, developers, according to their experiences, have produced proven solutions to common design problems in software projects [8]. These solutions are known as software design patterns. Usually, a design pattern is part of a collection, such as the popular collection presented by Gamma et al., in the book "Design Patterns: Elements of Reusable Object-Oriented Software" [9], which deals with problems related to object-oriented design and development. These patterns are also known in Software Engineering as the Gang of Four (GoF) Patterns, containing 23 patterns that are classified into 3 categories: creational, structural and behavioural.

Design patterns are also proposed for microservices. To solve the aforementioned problems and others present when adopting microservices, developers can apply the patterns pointed out by Richardson in his book named "Microservices Patterns: With Examples in Java" [10], where 42 patterns are presented and classified into 14 groups, such as decomposition, communication style, and deployment.

Although it seems simple, beginners and even experienced developers may present difficulties when choosing the appropriate pattern to solve a given problem. One important reason for these difficulties is the substantial amount of patterns to be mastered [11]. Therefore, it may be difficult to choose the most suitable design pattern for a given problem.

As a matter of fact, to help developers overcome this difficulty, and facilitate the adoption of microservices, this study proposes a recommendation approach that is based on information retrieval, where the developer can express a given problem in natural language and then receive the appropriate pattern to solve it. With this work, it is also possible to assist researchers in the development of future studies, since it presents an open approach to receiving improvements, thus, this study serves as a basis.

This paper contains four additional sections. Section 2, where related works are presented. Section 3 exposes the methodology, that is, the proposed approach, Sect. 4, where experiments and results are shown, and finally Sect. 5, which presents the conclusion and proposal for future work.

2   Related Works

Sanyawong and Nantajeewarawat [11] seek to improve the approach of recommending GoF (Gang of Four) patterns [9] that they developed in a previous work

[12]. Their approach is based on a pattern usage hierarchy, where the developer can identify the pattern to solve a given problem. After subjective evaluation, the authors concluded that it would be necessary to automate the levels of hierarchy to facilitate the selection of a specific pattern. Thus, they presented a way to automate the first level of the hierarchy, through textual classification, since this level associates the problem with a category of patterns. Therefore, they used algorithms such as Naive Bayes, J48, K-NN, and SVM. Also, they used 26 real problems to test the classifiers, and metrics like precision, recall, and F-measure to evaluate them. From the results, the authors concluded that it is possible to apply in practice this approach in projects in the software industry.

Hussain et al. [8], Duyne's HCI [13], Douglass [14] and Security [15] propose a recommended approach for GoF patterns, through information retrieval and the use of "Learning to Rank" to order the patterns according to their relevance for a given problem. The authors used three algorithms, Coordinate Ascent, AdaRank, and LambdaMART. The authors considered 47 real problems to test the approach, and two metrics to evaluate it, MAP (Mean Average Precision), and NDCG (Normalized Discounted Cumulative Gain). The results indicate that in terms of NDCG and MAP, LambdaMART outperforms the other algorithms. Thus, the authors concluded that the proposed approach is promising.

Silva-Rodriguez et al. [16] present a way of recommending interaction patterns to obtain satisfactory user interfaces aligned with user requirements. The authors use text classification, where a pattern is recommended according to a given requirement. Four algorithms were used, they are Logistic Regression, Multinomial Naive Bayes, Linear SVM, and Random Forest. Linear SVM proved to be superior to other algorithms in terms of Accuracy, Precision, Recall, and F1-Score.

Celikkan and Bozoklar [17] present a recommended approach for GoF design patterns that is based on the combination of 3 existing techniques in the information retrieval domain, they are text-based recommendation, case-based recommendation, and question-based recommendation. To evaluate the approach, the authors relied on 120 problems, where the text-based and case-based recommendation phases placed the appropriate pattern in first place for 56 problems, second place for 16, and third place for 8. This means that for 65% of the problems, the correct pattern was ranked among the top three, for 76% the correct pattern was among the top five, and for 86% the correct pattern was placed in the top 7. In the question-based recommendation phase, the answers of the most experienced developers caused a significant improvement in recommending the appropriate pattern.

Rahmati et al. [18] present a new method to select the GoF design patterns using information retrieval methods and cosine similarity. They proposed a more accurate method for automatically selecting GoF design patterns. The proposed method specifies the similarity between user-defined requirements and patterns definition text. This method is implemented based on the extended version of the vector space model (VSM), but the explicit semantic analysis (ESA) was considered a candidate to determine a similarity between the two texts.

The authors used Wikipedia as a broad external knowledge base. Two scenarios are considered to implement the ESA method: scenario 1, determining the semantic similarity between the user input text and the available texts in the repository of patterns; and scenario 2, determining the semantic similarity between the user input text and a set of keywords extracted from each available text in the repository of patterns. For evaluation, the proposed method used 23 design patterns, 29 object-oriented related design problems, and 9 real-world problems. The results of the first scenario were better than the second scenario, and between ESA method and the extended version of VSM, VSM has better performance. In addition, the authors found respectively 8.5%, 1.2%, and 5.2% improvement in terms of precision, recall, and accuracy of the proposed method compared to other methods.

Hamdy and Elsayed [19] proposed a novel approach for the automatic selection of the fit design pattern. Their approach is based on using the Latent Dirichlet Allocation (LDA) topic model. LDA was trained and used to analyze the corpus of pattern descriptions and extract the topics, then transferring each design pattern description and each problem scenario to a VSM of features, building a VSM of unigrams, the VSM is concatenated such that each pattern will be represented by a vector of features for each target design problem scenario, then discover the similarity between the target problem scenario, and the collection of patterns using Improved Sqrt-Cosine similarity measure (ISCS). The selected pattern is the closest to the problem scenario. The proposed approach was evaluated using a design patterns repository and a design problem repository. In the first, there is the textual description of the Gof design patterns and, in the second, there are 29 real design problem scenarios collected from various sources. The authors labelled each design problem manually, and the pre-processing was performed using the natural language toolkit NLTK. The best precision obtained during experiments is about 72% with 10 topics. The results showed that the proposed approach outperforms approaches based on the VSM.

Different from the works previously presented, this study deals with the recommendation of patterns applied to microservices. Thus, we use information retrieval, since the effectiveness of classification-based systems depends on a large and representative dataset [20], which is not easy, as we would have to elaborate this on the dataset, since we did not find any, in addition to having to use several classifiers to obtain good results, according to the works described before.

3   Methodology

In this section, the suggested approach is presented as an answer to the following research question: How to Recommend Microservices Patterns through Automatic Information Retrieval using Problems Specified in Natural Language?

It is worth mentioning that the patterns used were collected from Richardson's popular book called "Microservices Patterns: With Examples in Java" [10] and the design problems were created by the authors, as we could not find databases with similar problems in real systems based on microservices. In Sect. 4, the data used are commented in detail.

The proposed approach is organized into 3 steps: textual pre-processing, the weighting of terms, and similarity calculation. These steps are depicted in Fig. 1 and are described in the first three subsections as follows.

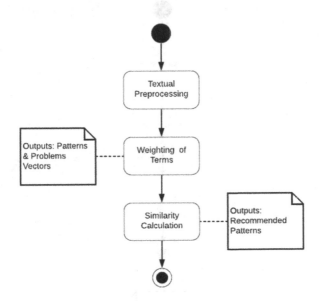

Fig. 1. Steps of the proposed approach

3.1 Textual Pre-processing

This step intends' is to prepare data for use. The three main tasks performed in it are depicted in Fig. 2 and are explained below.

In this work, a token is a word. Tokenization consists of extracting tokens from a text. Stop-word Removal corresponds to the elimination of words that are not relevant, such as articles and pronouns. Finally, stemming is the reduction of an inflected word in its stem. In this task, we apply the algorithm presented by Porter [21].

3.2 Weighting of Terms

In this step, pre-processed patterns and problems are represented by vectors of words in a vector space model. The dimensions of these vectors correspond to different words or terms. To use vector operations, we assign a weight to each term to compare patterns with problems.

$$TF * IDF(t, d, D) = TF(t, d) \cdot IDF(t, D) \tag{1}$$

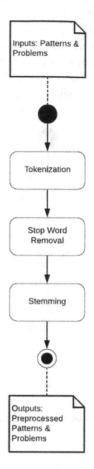

Fig. 2. Main tasks of text pre-processing

We calculate this weight through Eq. 1, which consists of the product of two statistics, named TF (Term Frequency) and IDF (Inverse Document Frequency), where TF(t,d) is the number of times a term (t) appears in a document (d), and IDF(t,D), calculated through Eq. 2, is equivalent to the inverse of DF(t,D), which stands for Document Frequency and indicates the number of documents that have a term (t) in a corpus (D).

$$IDF(t, D) = \frac{1}{DF(t, D)} \tag{2}$$

Thus, the resulting value of Eq. 1 is known as TF*IDF (Term Frequency-Inverse Document Frequency), its purpose is to indicate how important a term is for a document in a corpus. In this work, a document can be a pattern or a problem.

3.3   Similarity Calculation

This is the last step of the presented approach, where we apply a similarity measure that expresses the distance between two vectors. Thus, the appropriate pattern to solve a given problem is the one that has its vector closest to the problem vector.

Because of this, we employ the cosine similarity measure, given that it is popular in the field of information retrieval and is given by Eq. 3, as follows:

$$CS(V, W) = \frac{\sum_{i=1}^{n} V_i W_i}{\sqrt{\sum_{i=1}^{n} V_i^2} \sqrt{\sum_{i=1}^{n} W_i^2}} \tag{3}$$

V is the pattern vector, W is the problem vector, and n is the size of the vectors.

3.4   Evaluation Metric

To evaluate the suggested approach, we use a metric called Precision. It indicates the rate of recommendations that were performed correctly. This metric is obtained from Eq. 4, where TP and FP represent, respectively, the total number of recommendations made correctly and incorrectly.

$$Precision = \frac{TP}{TP + FP} \tag{4}$$

4   Implementation and Results

In this section, the implementation of the proposed approach is presented throughout the following Subsect. 4.1, 4.2 and 4.3. Also, in this section, the results of the recommendations made are reported, in Subsect. 4.4, where, in addition, in this same subsection, some ways to improve our approach are described.

4.1   Data About Design Patterns

The design patterns used in this study are aimed at software developed using the microservices architecture, because as seen in Sect. 1, this work intends is to facilitate the selection of these patterns so that developers can apply them properly, which makes these professionals more productive, in addition to favouring the quality of this software.

Thus, we have selected 10 of these patterns from Richardson's popular book called "Microservices Patterns: With examples in Java" [10]. From there, we look for pertinent information about each one of these patterns, this information added together makes up what we call a "description", in this way, we form the description of each pattern taken from the book.

Table 1 presents the information used to create the description of a pattern. In total, there are 11 pieces of information. After elaborating the descriptions

Table 1. Information used to create the description of a pattern

Information	Definition
Name	Term by which the pattern is called
Group	Group in which the pattern is a part
Subgroup	Subgroup in which the pattern is a part
Layer	Layer where the pattern is applied
Context	Context in which the pattern is applied
Problem	Problem the pattern solves
Forces	Issues that must be addressed when solving a problem in a given context
Solution	Way in which the pattern solves the problem
Resulting context	Benefits, drawbacks and issues, arising from the application of the pattern
Issues	Issues that must be addressed to use the pattern
Related patterns	Patterns that have some relationship with the pattern

of the patterns, we generate a corpus with them. This corpus is retrieved when a pattern needs to be recommended to solve a design problem. A detail worth mentioning is that some information that constitutes the description of a pattern was extracted from Richardson's website [22].

4.2   Data About Design Problems

In this work, design problems are difficult scenarios that can occur during the development or maintenance of a system based on the microservices architecture. They are important for the evaluation of our approach, which is given by the metric called "precision", that has already been presented in Subsect. 3.4. In short, the more problems that have adequate recommendations, the greater the precision of our approach. This means something positive, as it indicates how effective the approach is.

Because of this, we created 10 design problems that are part of a corpus, each of these problems is labelled with the correct pattern to solve it. We did this to calculate the precision later, here are 5 of these 10 problems as examples:

Problem #1: A company that develops software systems received a new demand, where it is necessary to develop a clinical management system. Because of this, requirements analysts performed the requirements elicitation, and from the given set of requirements, software architects concluded that the microservices architecture would be the most suitable for the system. Then, systems analysts created a top-level domain model, identified command and query operations, and finally mapped business capabilities with the help of requirements analysts. Now systems analysts want to define system services. These services must be independent, small, and contextually limited.

Problem #2: OnShop is a monolithic software system that will be migrated to microservices. Professionals participating in this migration want to use Domain-Driven Design (DDD) concepts to decompose the system into services, as they are familiar with DDD.

Problem #3: The fictional company XGO is designing a microservices architecture for its main system and it needs to make the microservices communicate. This communication must be request/response based and synchronous.

Problem #4: After making the services communicate through REST, it was observed that when the mobile app makes multiple requests to the order service, through an API gateway, and the order service is down or responding to the requests extremely slowly, the API gateway is unable to serve new requests.

Problem #5: Instances of ordering, payment and other services need to make their network address available in some way, as customers need this information to make requests.

Table 2. Example of problems and the correct pattern to solve each one

Problem #	Correct pattern
1	Decompose by business capability
2	Decompose by subdomain
3	Remote procedure invocation
4	Circuit breaker
5	Self registration

In Table 2, the correct pattern to solve each exemplified problem is presented. An issue worth mentioning is that we did not find in the literature any set of design problems that are aimed at software based on the microservices architecture, for this reason, we had to create a corpus with these problems.

4.3   Tools Used to Develop the Approach

To implement the proposed approach of recommending design patterns used in software based on the microservices architecture, we use Python [23], NLTK (Natural Language Toolkit) [24], Scikit-Learn [25] and Collaboratory.

The Python programming language was chosen for being simple, prioritising code readability with its syntax that is clear and concise, having powerful native resources, libraries and frameworks and, finally, it is familiar to the researchers.

Thus, we implemented our approach in the Collaboratory, which is a free cloud service offered by Google. Collaboratory makes it possible to work with Python in a collaborative environment, in this way, the researchers were able to work together.

NLTK is a leading platform for developing Python programs that need to handle human language data. Given this, we use NLTK in the description of each pattern and in the design problems, where we extract the tokens, remove the stop words and reduce each inflected word to its stem. These processes have already been detailed in Subsect. 3.1.

To weight the words and calculate how similar each design problem is to each design pattern, we made use of the Scikit-Learn library, as it is easy to use, efficient, and quite popular when it comes to machine learning. It is worth noting that the weighting of words and the calculation of similarity between design problems and design patterns have already been addressed, respectively, in Subsect. 3.2 and 3.3.

4.4   Recommended Patterns for Design Problems

With the corpus ready and our approach implemented, we put it into action and obtained several recommended patterns for each problem, where these patterns were ordered in descending order by the similarity rate given by Eq.3. Thus, we considered only the first 3 recommended patterns for each problem, Table 3 sets out the first 3 recommended patterns for design problem #1.

Table 3. The first 3 recommended patterns for design problem #1

Placing	Recommended pattern	Similarity rate
1st	Decompose by business capability	0.28283
2nd	Decompose by subdomain	0.24633
3rd	Server-side discovery	0.11662

Table 4. Recommended patterns for each problem given as an example in Subsect. 4.2

Problem #	1st recommended pattern	2nd recommended pattern	3rd recommended pattern
1	Decompose by business capability	Decompose by subdomain	Server-side discovery
2	Decompose by subdomain	Decompose by business capability	Remote procedure invocation
3	Remote procedure invocation	Messaging	Decompose by subdomain
4	Remote procedure invocation	Client-side discovery	Server-side discovery
5	Server-side discovery	Remote procedure invocation	Client-side discovery

In view of this, Table 4 shows the recommended patterns for each problem given as an example in Subsect. 4.2. The first recommended pattern is considered the most suitable candidate to solve the problem. In this way, it is possible to confirm this information by checking if it is equal to the correct pattern to solve the problem. Table 2, previously presented, shows the correct pattern to solve each of the 5 problems presented as examples in Subsect. 4.2.

Thus, out of 10 problems, 4 had the correct pattern recommended in first place, 2 in second, and the other 4 below the third. This means that the precision of the proposed approach is equivalent to 40% and that 20% of the problems had the correct pattern recommended in second place, which indicates that the correct pattern for 60% of the problems happens in first and second place.

In search of the reasons that contributed to 4 of 10 problems having their correct pattern recommended below third place, we reviewed these problems. With that, we found that they are problems related to microservices communication, and that the first 3 patterns recommended for each one are patterns that solve problems related to microservices communication, that is, this happened because these patterns share similar terms, and because the problems did not have more specific terms for each pattern, ended up impacting the recommendation.

5   Conclusion and Future Work

This study proposes an approach for recommending design patterns used in microservices-based systems to solve common problems that occur in systems of this type. It is based on information retrieval, where a developer can report a problem in text and then get a pattern that could solve it. To evaluate the proposed approach, we created two corpora, the first one containing 10 patterns, and the second 10 problems. Its precision is equal to 60%.

When developing using the microservices architecture, the adoption of standards is facilitated, providing a higher quality of source code development. Developers who make migrations and new implementations of microservices-based systems can benefit from recommendations that will help them solve problems that may occur during the process of developing these systems. Organizations can also benefit in two ways, by reducing problems in adopting patterns, and by improving the software process. Finally, this work may contribute to future research, presenting a possible way to recommend these patterns.

For future work, the intention is to evolve the two corpora generated in this study, that is, to enrich them with more data, and look for ways to improve the approach, such as replacing the current similarity measure with ISCS (Improved Sqrt-Cosine Similarity) [26], which seems to be better when dealing with smaller documents.

References

1. França, J.M.S., Soares, M.S.: SOAQM: quality model for SOA applications based on ISO 25010. In: Proceedings of the 17th International Conference on Enterprise Information, pp. 60–70 (2015)

2. Soares, M.S., França, J.M.S.: Characterization of the application of service-oriented design principles in practice: a systematic literature review. J. Softw. **11**(4), 403–417 (2016)
3. Niknejad, N., Che Hussin, A.R., Prasetyo, Y.A., Ghani, I., Fajrillah, A.A.N.: Service oriented architecture adoption: a systematic review. Int. J. Integr. Eng. **10**(6) (2018)
4. Dragoni, N., et al.: Microservices: yesterday, today, and tomorrow. In: Present and Ulterior Software Engineering, pp. 195–216. Springer, Cham (2017). https://doi.org/10.1007/978-3-319-67425-4_12
5. Chen, R., Li, S., Li, Z.: From monolith to microservices: a dataflow-driven approach. In: 2017 24th Asia-Pacific Software Engineering Conference (APSEC), pp. 466–475 (2017)
6. Balalaie, A., Heydarnoori, A., Jamshidi, P.: Migrating to cloud-native architectures using microservices: an experience report. In: Celesti, A., Leitner, P. (eds.) ESOCC Workshops 2015. CCIS, vol. 567, pp. 201–215. Springer, Cham (2016). https://doi.org/10.1007/978-3-319-33313-7_15
7. Bogner, J., Fritzsch, J., Wagner, S., Zimmermann, A.: Industry practices and challenges for the evolvability assurance of microservices. Empir. Softw. Eng. **26**(5), 104 (2021)
8. Hussain, S., et al.: A methodology to rank the design patterns on the base of text relevancy. Soft. Comput. **23**(24), 13433–13448 (2019)
9. Gamma, E., Helm, R., Johnson, R., Johnson, R.E., Vlissides, J.: Design Pattern: Elements of Reusable Object-Oriented Software. Addison-Wesley, NewYork (1995)
10. Richardson, C.: Microservices Patterns: With Examples in Java. Simon and Schuster (2018)
11. Sanyawong, N., Nantajeewarawat, E.: Design Pattern Recommendation: A Text Classification Approach (2015)
12. Sanyawong, N., Nantajeewarawat, E.: Classifying design-level requirements using machine learning for a recommender of interaction design patterns. In: IEEE, pp. 134–139 (2014)
13. Landay, J.A., Hong, J.I.: The Design of Sites: Patterns, Principles, and Processes for Crafting a Customer-Centered Web Experience. Addison-Wesley Professional, Reading (2003)
14. Douglass, B.P.: Real-Time Design Patterns: Robust Scalable Architecture for Real-Time Systems. Addison-Wesley Professional, Reading (2003)
15. Schumacher, M., Fernandez-Buglioni, E., Hybertson, D., Buschmann, F., Sommerlad, P.: Security Patterns: Integrating Security and Systems Engineering. John Wiley & Sons, Hoboken (2013)
16. Silva-Rodríguez, V., Nava-Muñoz, S.E., Castro, L.A., Martínez-Pérez, F.E., Pérez-González, H.G., Torres-Reyes, F.: Classifying design-level requirements using machine learning for a recommender of interaction design patterns. IET Softw. **14**(5), 544–552 (2020)
17. Celikkan, U.; Bozoklar, D.: A consolidated approach for design pattern recommendation. In: 2019 4th International Conference on Computer Science and Engineering (UBMK). IEEE, pp. 1–6 (2019)
18. Rahmati, R., Rasoolzadegan, A., Dehkordy, D.T.: An automated method for selecting GoF design patterns. In: 9th International Conference on Computer and Knowledge Engineering (ICCKE 2019), 24–25 October 2019, Ferdowsi University of Mashhad (2019)
19. Hamdy, A., Elsayed, M.: Topic modelling for automatic selection of software design patterns. In: ICGDA 2018, 20–22 April 018, Prague, Czech Republic (2018)

20. Uysal, A.K.: An improved global feature selection scheme for text classification. Expert Syst. Appl. **43**, 82–92 (2016)
21. Jones, K.S., Willett, S. (eds.): Readings in Information Retrieval. Morgan Kaufmann, San Francisco (1997)
22. Microservices Homepage, https://microservices.io. Aaccessed 16 Mar 2022
23. Python Homepage, https://www.python.org. Accessed 16 Mar 2022
24. NLTK Homepage, https://www.nltk.org. Accessed 16 Mar 2022
25. Scikit-Learn Homepage, https://scikit-learn.org. Accessed 16 Mar 2022
26. Sohangir, S., Wang, D.: Improved sqrt-cosine similarity measurement. J. Big Data **4**(1), 1–13 (2017). https://doi.org/10.1186/s40537-017-0083-6

Crime Detection and Analysis from Social Media Messages Using Machine Learning and Natural Language Processing Technique

Xolani Lombo, Olaide N. Oyelade(✉), and Absalom E. Ezugwu(✉) (iD)

School of Mathematics, Statistics, and Computer Science, University of KwaZulu-Natal,
King Edward Road, Pietermaritzburg 3201, KwaZulu-Natal, South Africa
218014246@stu.ukzn.ac.za, {oyeladeo,Ezugwua}@ukzn.ac.za

Abstract. Social media has dramatically influenced and changed the rate and the nature of crime in our society. The perpetrators cut across different age groups, social standing, and beliefs. The ability to be anonymous on social media and the lack of adequate resources to fight cybercrime are catalysts for the rise in criminal activities, especially in South Africa. We proposed a system that will analyse and detect crime in social media posts or messages. The new system can detect attacks and drug-related crime messages, hate speech, and offensive messages. Natural language processing algorithms were used for text tokenisation, stemming, and lemmatisation. Machine learning models such as support vector machines and random forest classifiers were used to classify texts. Using the support vector machine to detect crime in texts, we achieved 86% accuracy and using the random forest for crime analysis, 72% accuracy was achieved.

Keywords: Crime detection · Social media · Natural language processing · Support vector machine · Random forest

1 Introduction

Crime detection in social media messages identifies the presence of crime in social media posts or messages. Crime analysis is the study of crime and law enforcement data with other information to apprehend criminals and prevent crime [1]. According to South African Police Service (SAPS), social media crime is fast-growing because more criminals or ordinary people exploit anonymity and lack adequate resources to detect the crime. The crime that we focus on is attack and drug-related crimes, hate speech, and offensive messages.

Many people use social media, especially Twitter and Facebook, which is why it is a target for criminal activities. There are numerous reports of cyberbullying, fraud, online threats, and people getting scammed online. Law enforcement agencies are slow and sometimes handicapped to respond to cybercrime due to limited resources [2]. This study was proposed as a base for other researchers to use in real-time to monitor and detect crime in social media posts or messages, which is better than facing the consequences of the crime.

© The Author(s), under exclusive license to Springer Nature Switzerland AG 2022
O. Gervasi et al. (Eds.): ICCSA 2022 Workshops, LNCS 13381, pp. 502–517, 2022.
https://doi.org/10.1007/978-3-031-10548-7_37

Natural Language Processing (NLP) is a branch of artificial intelligence that helps computers understand, manipulate, and interpret natural language (human language). The Term Document Inverse Document Frequency (TF-IDF) is used to prepare and represent the output data after processing the data. This gets ready the data to be passed to Machine Learning (ML) models. On the other hand, ML is a branch of artificial intelligence based on the idea that systems can learn from data, identify patterns, and make decisions with the minimal human intervention [3] The NLP was used for text pre-processing (for cleaning and formatting operations) and have also been successfully applied in email filtering [4], recommendation system [5–7], medicine [8–11] r, several ML models have been used for text classification in different crime categories [12–15] Therefore, this study employs the use of ML over deep learning considering the performance track records of ML algorithms in solving the peculiarity associated with the problem considered in the study [16].

An enhanced computational framework with increased accuracy in detecting crime in social media criminal activities is essential to apprehending criminals. A comparative study of classification algorithms known for high accuracy was first carried out in this paper to investigate the high accuracy model. The ML models, support vector machine (SVM), K-nearest neighbor (KNN), and Naïve bayesian were studied for crime detection within the binary classification paradigm. For crime analysis and multi-class classification of texts, random forest (RF) and SVM were used, respectively. As the data for crime analysis was imbalanced, we applied the RF, which is widely reported to demonstrate good performance in cases of imbalanced data. Similarly, we also used an SVM classifier to address such peculiarities for cost sensitivity in imbalanced data.

The paper aims to successfully use NLP for data pre-processing and comparatively study the classification algorithms used for text classification. The specific objectives of the study include:

- To model a framework for accurate detection and analysis of social media messages.
- To accurately detect and analyse crime from social media messages using NLP and ML algorithms, namely SVM and RF.
- To investigate the performance of similar classification algorithms, namely, K-Nearest Neighbor and Naïve Bayes, to detect and analyse crime in social media messages accurately.

The rest of the paper is organised as follows: Sect. 2 consists of a literature review that justifies the importance of the research by reviewing related research. The research methods and techniques of how the problem was addressed are discussed in Sect. 3. In Sect. 4, results and discussion describing the findings and results of the study are presented. Conclusion and future research direction are presented in Sect. 5.

2 Literature Review

Many researchers have addressed text classification problems using NLP algorithms and ML models. This section will discuss techniques that have been used in literature for classifying text, for example, spam detection in messages, as many of the related research are based.

Ashok [17] looked at data mining and sentiment analysis on the online network to help detect crime patterns. Data was collected from Twitter using -related tweets that include the following keywords "gun," 'crime,' "kill," and so forth. Then data was cleaned and processed using a natural language algorithm. The research was a success as it was concluded that tweets with "very negative" sentiment were identified as contributing to crime intensity. Although this research did not strictly follow the traditional NLP methods, it was a success. Following the approach of using all standard NLP algorithms would have resulted in a more accurate study.

Sharma et al.'s [18] research focused on data pre-processing using traditional NLP algorithms in classifying emails as spam or non-spam. The steps for this study were data pre-processing, representation of data, and classification. The following steps were followed during data pre-processing: removing words lesser in length, removing alphanumeric words (words that contain both characters and numbers), removing stop words, and stemming. This research shows that pre-processing plays a crucial role in classifying texts. Another NLP algorithm, lemmatisation after stemming, could be useful. Removing words with lesser length may affect finding the pattern of spam; for example, a word like "sex" are essential in identifying spam.

Shirani-Mehr [19] used five ML models, namely SVM, RF, KNN, Multinomial NB, and Adaboost, as classifiers of SMS spam datasets for SMS Spam Detection. Their work aimed to investigate different ML algorithms for the classification of SMS spam. The only NLP algorithm that was used for data pre-processing was for tokenisation. The research was a great success because he could catch 90.62% of the Spam SMS with an accuracy of 98.57% using RF, the best in the five algorithms being investigated. The researcher caught 92.99% of Spam SMS using SVM with an accuracy of 98.86%. The problem faced by the researcher is that there are fewer datasets for SMS spam compared to email spam. Due to text messages having a small length, the number of features used for their classification is smaller than the corresponding number of emails.

Andrews et al. [20] describe an approach for detecting the presence of organised crime signals on social media. Formal concept analysis is used to group information sources according to crime type and location. NLP algorithms are used to identify, extract, and corroborate information from open web sources, identifying the early onset of organised crime. They used this to establish the idea of 'weak signals' as keywords and phrases that point to criminality.

McCord and Chuah [21] investigated spam detection using the traditional classifiers, SVM, KNN, RF, and Naïve Bayesian. They evaluate the usefulness of the features suggested by Twitter spam policies and observe spammers' behaviours in spammer detection using the mentioned traditional classifiers using the Twitter dataset they collected. Then use these features to help identify spammers. They found that the RF classifier gave the best performance, which achieved 95.7% precision. The second-best performance was the SVM model with an accuracy of 93.5%, and KNN was the third-best got an accuracy of 92.8%, which is also good. This approach of training the data was effective in detecting crime in messages.

Malmasi and Zampieri [19] examine social media methods to detect hate speech. They achieved 78% accuracy in identifying posts across three classes: hate, offensive, and no offensive. For data pre-processing, they convert all texts to lowercase, tokenise and remove URLs and emojis. The approach they used for data pre-processing was very poor. If they had used all traditional NLP methods, the accuracy might have increased. The model that these researchers used is a Support Vector Machine (SVM) classifier to perform multi-class classification in their experiment.

Using ML techniques, the theoretical study for classification by Ikonomakism et al. [22] investigated the text classification process. They mentioned that text classification includes reading the document, tokenising text, stemming, vector representation of text, deleting stop-words, feature selection, feature transformation, and learning algorithms. Lim proposed a method that improves K-Nearest Neighbor-based text classification performance by using well-estimated parameters [23].

Johnson et al. [24] use the rule simplification method that converts the decision tree into a logically equivalent and the sparsity of text data taken by a decision tree algorithm. Kim, Rim, and Yook [25] deduced that Naïve Bayes is often used in text classification applications and experiments because of its simplicity and effectiveness. Shanahan and Roma [26] mention that the SVM applied to text classification provides excellent precision but poor recall. The research's similarity is that they cover major theoretical issues to guide researchers to exciting research directions. One of the disadvantages of these kinds of research is that they are theory information that was not tested, so they might not work in other types of data or applications.

Machine learning methods have been well harnessed to solve the challenge of crime detection. Studies in [16] applied the combination of ML and computer vision algorithms to improve the accuracy and detailing of crime prediction. The approach depends on data sourced from cameras and microphones in public spaces so that algorithmic solutions based on their hybrid model are then applied to detect crime using a social security number database. Similarly, neural networks have also been applied to crime detection using geo-spatiality to support the detection process [27]. A study in [28] combined the big data technique with an optimised ML algorithm to extract key features suggesting the occurrence of crime, the location, and potential hotspots. Other related works are those in [29] and [30].

Based on the literature reviewed, all traditional NLP algorithms were used to process the data in this research. The SVM and RF classifier were used for crime detection and analysis.

3   Research Methodology

Based on the ideas and approach of the previous research in text classification using NLP algorithms. In this paper, the techniques used for accurate crime detection include pre-processing with traditional NLP algorithms, comparing different ML models, and using the most suitable models that produce accurate results. This section explains in detail the methodology and techniques used to implement the proposed crime detection concepts. More so, Fig. 1 shows the summary of the steps we took.

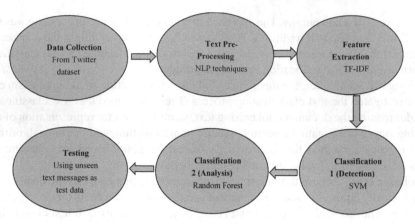

Fig. 1. Summary of the approach

3.1 Dataset

Twitter Spam dataset was used for crime detection. Twitter spam is unwanted content manifesting in many ways, including profanity, insults, hate speech, malicious, link and fraudulent reviews. By closely inspecting the data/tweets in this dataset, we saw that this data is crime-related. Twitter hate speech dataset was used for crime analysis. This data was used to create two more other classes for Attack and Drug- "crime," "gun," and more were used to group attack-related tweets. Keywords such as "drug," "cocaine," "overdose" were used to group drug-related crime messages. Table 1 and Table 2 show the distribution of the texts across different classes. The analysis dataset indicates the imbalance between the classes, but the ML algorithm works well with imbalanced data due to the classifiers applied in this study. Table 3 and Table 4 show the example of the records of the dataset. Moreover, several studies have demonstrated outstanding performances with Twitter datasets when used with ML algorithms [31, 32].

Table 1. Crime twitter dataset (detection dataset)

Class	Texts
Crime	5804
Quality	5983
Total	11787

3.2 Text Pre-processing

Natural Language Learning techniques were used for text cleaning. Text message data contains much noise and no text data like emoji and numbers. The process of data cleaning will include converting emojis to text, converting all characters to lower cases, converting numbers to words, removing punctuations, mentions, white spaces, stop words,

Table 2. Twitter hate speech dataset (analysis dataset)

Class	Texts
Hate speech	5097
Offensive	3245
Attack	2456
Drug	348
Normal	6979
Total	20122

Table 3. Sample of detection dataset

Tweet	Type
'Gun for hire': how Jeff Sessions used his prosecuting power to target Democrats	Crime
I posted a new photo to Facebook http://fb.me/2Be7LiyuJ	Quality

Table 4. Sample of analysis dataset

Tweet	Label
I don't think I'm getting my baby them white 9 he has two white j and Nikes not even touched	Normal
@Libre, I am a bit confused coz Chinese ppl cannot access Twitter than how this Ching Chong using it. I think he Pakistani 😄😄😄	Hate speech
All my exes were cute, but they were hoes I guess I only attract fly looking thots 😒	Offensive
Overthink can kill yourself too <happy>	Attack
common blacked on get em high	Drug

and replacing URLs with the word "URL". The NLP techniques such as tokenisation, stemming, and word lemmatisation are used to reduce words to their most basic form. Figure 2 shows the summary of data pre-processing.

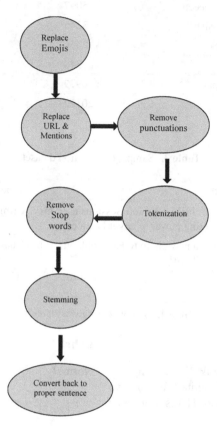

Fig. 2. Data pre-processing steps

3.2.1 Replacing Emojis with Text

We decided not to remove the emojis but to replace them with text because they have meaning and will support detecting the crime.

Example 1: Input: "Take some 💊 they will make you high"
Output: "Take some pill they will make you high."
Example 2: Input: "Did you 🔫 him?"
Output: "Did you fire him?"

If emojis were removed, sentences one and two would lose meaning, resulting in the training model losing the crime pattern in them. This will result in models yielding negative reports.

3.2.2 Replacing URL and User Mentions

Every URL is replaced with the word "URL", that is because we want to keep track of the text that contains a URL in it so that if a model detects a crime and it's not hate speech, offensive, attack, and drug-related, we can know that that text contains a malicious link. Every mention such as (@XolaniLombo are not removed but replaced with the word "USER" so that the training model can find the pattern that describes certain words said or posted by certain users. This step also includes converting all numbers to word form as they can be used to detect the crime pattern when we know the quantity.

Example 1: Input: "Go to http://MaliciousWebsite.com for"
Output: "Go to URL"
Example 2: Input: "I hate @JamesCordan you should die"
Output: "I hate USER you should die."
Example 3: Input: "We need to be 4 to successfully steal the money"
Output: "We need to be four to successfully steal the money."

Examples 1 and 2 may lose the crime pattern if the URL and the user mention are removed. Although the numbers are not very important in identifying the crime pattern, knowing the quantity (number) associated with certain words can help detect the crime, especially in attack and drug-related texts.

3.2.3 Removing Punctuations

Our focus is only on the texts (words), so punctuations (including hashtags) are unnecessary. That is why we removed all the punctuations in the texts in this step.

Example 1: Input: "How many grams do you want???"
Output: "How many grams do you want"
Example 2: Input: "Can you deliver weed, crack and cocaine, please?"
Output: "Can you deliver weed crack and cocaine please"

This step ensures the characters are shown clearly for the next step, such as tokenisation for easy splitting of the words.

3.2.4 Tokenisation

Tokenisation is the essential basic step of NLP, where you identify words that constitute a string of characters. This is important because the meaning of the text could be interpreted by analysing the terms present in the text. This step includes converting all the words to lower cases.

Example 1: Input: "This is fun"
Output: ['this', 'is', 'fun']
Example 2: Input: "Drugs are bad for your health"
Output: ['Drugs', 'are', 'bad', 'for;', 'your', 'health']

This makes it easy for the following steps to perform their function as words are separated nicely.

3.2.5 Removing Stop Words

One of the essential steps in NLP is to filter out useless data. In NLP, useless words (data) are referred to as stop words. Figure 3 shows an example of stop words. This list can be modified by adding words of your choice in English.

{'ourselves', 'hers', 'between', 'yourself', 'but', 'again', 'there', 'about', 'once', 'during', 'out', 'very', 'having', 'with', 'they', 'own', 'an', 'be', 'some', 'for', 'do', 'its', 'yours', 'such', 'into', 'of', 'most', 'itself', 'other', 'off', 'is', 's', 'am', 'or', 'who', 'as', 'from', 'him', 'each', 'the', 'themselves', 'until', 'below', 'are', 'we', 'these', 'your', 'his', 'through', 'don', 'nor', 'me', 'were', 'her', 'more', 'himself', 'this', 'down', 'should', 'our', 'their', 'while', 'above', 'both', 'up', 'to', 'ours', 'had', 'she', 'all', 'no', 'when', 'at', 'any', 'before', 'them', 'same', 'and', 'been', 'have', 'in', 'will', 'on', 'does', 'yourselves', 'then', 'that', 'because', 'what', 'over', 'why', 'so', 'can', 'did', 'not', 'now', 'under', 'he', 'you', 'herself', 'has', 'just', 'where', 'too', 'only', 'myself', 'which', 'those', 'i', 'after', 'few', 'whom', 't', 'being', 'if', 'theirs', 'my', 'against', 'a', 'by', 'doing', 'it', 'how', 'further', 'was', 'here', 'than'}

Fig. 3. Example of stop words

Example 1: Input: ['this', should', 'stay', 'between', 'us']
Output: ['stay', 'us']
Example 2: Input: ['he', 'killed', 'her', 'not', 'me']
Output: ['killed']

Removing stop words helps remove all the unwanted words because they mostly include pronouns, prepositions, and conjunctions that are unimportant in this scope.

3.2.6 Stemming

Stemming removes the suffix from a word and reduces it to its root word. For example, "Killing" is a word and its suffix "ing", if "ing" is removed from "Killing", then we get the root word or base word which is "Kill". This step helps, so the word like "Killed" and "Killing" be considered as one-word "Kill" to narrow the unique words our model will process. Porter Stemmer algorithm was used for stemming because it is fast, most common, and is a gentle stemmer (Tables 5 and 6).

Example 1: Input: ['bombing', 'execution', terrorist]
Output: ['bomb', 'execut', 'terrorist']
Porter's algorithm consists of five phases of word reductions, applied sequentially.

Table 5. Rules of porter stemmer

Rule	Example
SSSES -> SS	Caresses -> Caress
IES -> I	Bullies -> Bulli
SS -> SS	Caress -> Caress
SS ->	Pills -> Pill

Table 6. Few examples of words with their stem

Words	Stem
Killing	Kill
Ponies	Poni
Caress	Caress
Feed	Fe
Sing	Sing
Liked	Like
Laundering	Launder
Troubling	Troubl

3.2.7 Lemmatisation

Lemmatisation is not that different from stemming. In both lemmatisation and stemming, we try to reduce the word to its root. The root in the stemming process is called a stem, and in the lemmatisation process is called a lemma. The difference is that in stemming, a part of the word at the tail end is removed to arrive at the stem of the word, with no understanding of the meaning. In lemmatisation, the algorithm has this knowledge. It is like the algorithm referring to a dictionary to understand the word's meaning before reducing it to its root word (lemma). The lemmatisation algorithm knows that the word better is derived from the word good, and hence the lemma of better is good. We decided to use both algorithms for better results, first applying the stemming operation followed by lemmatization (Table 7).

Table 7. Few examples of words with their lemma

Words	Lemma
Has	Have
Helped	Help
Better	Good
Am	Be
Relatives	Relative
Study	Study
Studying	Study
Studies	Study

3.2.8 Converting Word List to Sentence

This is the final step of data pre-processing, where the output of the above steps is converted to a proper sentence to prepare for the next step.

Example: Input: ['student', 'study, 'smart']
Output: "student study smart"

3.3 Feature Extraction

Machine learning models deal with numbers while we are dealing with text. So, we need to transform and represent the text to numbers, known as text vectorisation, for the classification model to learn. The commonly used algorithm TF-IDF (Term Frequency-Inverse Document Frequency) is used for this study. This statistical measure evaluates how relevant a word is to a document in a collection of documents. The highest-scoring word of a document is most relevant to that document (considered keywords for that document). This is done by multiplying two metrics: how many times a word appears in a document and the inverse document frequency of words across a set of documents. Figure 4 shows the crime word cloud (Table 8).

TF-IDF of a term word in a text:

tf-idf (word, text) = tf (word, text)*idf (word)
tf (word, text) = (frequency of term word in text/number of words in the text)
idf (word) = log [(n+1)/(df(word)+1)] + 1
(n = total number of texts, df(word) = number of texts where the word occurs)

For an example of TF-IDF calculations, suppose you have:

Text A: "killing humans is fun to psychopaths."
Text B: "killing other humans is bad."

Results features for the above examples would be:

Fig. 4. Crime word cloud

Table 8. Example of TF-IDF calculations

Word	tf		idf	tf * idf	
	A	B		A	B
Killing	1/6	1/5	Log (3/3) + 1	0.167	0.200
Humans	1/6	1/5	Log (3/3) + 1	0.167	0.200
Is	1/6	1/5	Log (3/3) + 1	0.167	0.200
Fun	1/6	0/5	Log (3/2) + 1	0.196	0
To	1/6	0/5	Log (3/2) + 1	0.196	0
Psychopaths	1/6	0/5	Log (3/2) + 1	0.196	0
Other	0/6	1/5	Log (3/2) + 1	0	0.235
Bad	0/6	1/5	Log (3/2) + 1	0	0.235

[[0.167, 0.167, 0.167, 0.196, 0.196, 0.196, 0.000, 0.000]
[0.200, 0.200, 0.200, 0.000, 0.000, 0.000, 0.235, 0.235]]

4   Results and Discussion

The next step after TF-IDF was to train the models for crime detection to achieve binary classification and crime analysis using multi-class classification. If the accuracy of a model falls within the range of 0%–69%, then such model is considered as bad, 70%–79% good, 80% to 89% excellent and 90%–100% overfitting. For crime detection in text SVM, Naïve Bayesian and KNN classification algorithms were used. Notably, 70% (8251 texts) of data was used to train the models and 30% (3536 texts) for testing. Table 9 shows the classification results obtained.

Table 9. Classification results for crime detection in texts

Model	Accuracy	Precision	Recall
SVM	85.69%	85.85%	85.46%
Naïve Bayesian	60.02%	56.59%	85.92%
KNN	50.21%	73.33%	06.00%

The results show that SVM achieved higher accuracy than other models, which yielded 85.69% accuracy. This is regarded as an excellent accuracy as it shows that the model is not overfitting. Therefore, this model will be used to detect crime in texts. As the dataset for crime analysis in the text was imbalanced, two ML algorithms that are good with imbalance datasets were investigated, RF and Cost-Sensitive SVM for imbalanced data. So, both models ensure all the classes get equal chances of getting to a training model. In this case, 70% (14085 texts) of training data was used to train the models and 30% (6037 texts) for testing. Table 10 shows the classification results obtained.

Table 10. Classification results for crime analysis in texts

Model	Accuracy	Precision	Recall
RF	72.16%	72.16%	72.16%
Cost-Sensitive SVM	69.33%	69.33%	69.33%

The results show that RF achieved higher accuracy than Cost-Sensitive SVM, achieving 72.16%, which is regarded as good accuracy. Therefore, this model was used to analyse texts for the crime. The main challenge encountered in this study is that there is no social media (Twitter) dataset that has its texts classified as a crime. We analysed the data and noticed that data labels as spam are all crime-related to circumvent this. However, this approach can lead to other messages not being detected as a crime. To prevent this, we ensured that the models missed no message.

As the Attack and Drug classes were self-generated based on keywords, not all the texts that are labelled as Attack or Drug may have anything to do with these classes. Other drug or attack-related texts cannot be labelled as drug or attack because the keywords used did not pick them. The same thing in the detection dataset, as the owner regards the label as spam, not crime. Due to a thorough analysis of the dataset, we noted that the labels classified as spam are crime-related. It can happen that other texts that are labelled as spam are not strictly crime-related. The implemented system ensures that it checks for crime-related keywords if they are missed by the models (classified as normal while there is a crime) to detect and analyse crime in text messages accurately.

The implemented system ensures that it checks for crime-related keywords if they are missed by the models (classified as normal while there is a crime) to detect and analyse crime in text messages accurately.

5   Conclusion and Future Work

This paper applied NLP techniques to detect and analyse crime in social media messages. The crime that this paper focused on is hate speech, offensive (lite crime), attack, and drug-related crimes. We used two datasets to detect crime in texts (binary classification) and analyse crime (multi-class classification). We investigated three ML models for crime detection in the text: SVM, Naïve Bayesian, and KNN. It was found that the SVM is the most accurate achieving 85.69% accuracy. In addition, we investigated two good models with imbalanced data for crime analysis in text, RF and Cost-Sensitive SVM classifier. More so, it was also discovered that the RF achieved an accuracy of 72.16%.

This research focused more on normal English text messages. However, if non-English or slang words are absent in a text message, this may negatively impact the learning algorithm. In future work, we would like to investigate the use of NLP in non-English languages and internet slang. An error analysis could also help better understand the challenges of this task, and this could be used to provide insights into the work of NLP algorithms.

References

1. Boba, R.: Introductory guide to crime analysis and mapping. Community Oriented Policing Services, USA (2001)
2. Dlamini, S., Mbambo, C.: Understanding policing of cybe-rcrime in South Africa: the phenomena, challenges and effective responses. Cogent Soc. Sci. 5(1), 1675404 (2019)
3. SAS: SAS: Machine Learning: What it is and why it matters. https://www.sas.com/en_us/insights/analytics/machine-learning.html. Accessed 27 Apr 2021
4. Salloum, S., Gaber, T., Vadera, S., Shaalan, K.: Phishing email detection using natural language processing techniques: a literature survey. Procedia Comput. Sci. 189, 19–28 (2021)
5. Guo, W., et al.: Deep natural language processing for search and recommender systems. In: Conference: the 25th ACM SIGKDD International Conference (2019)
6. Chavare, S.R., Awati, C.J., Shirgave, S.K.: Smart recommender system using deep learning. In: 2021 6th International Conference on Inventive Computation Technologies (ICICT) (2021)
7. Chakraoui, M., Elkalay, A., Mouhni, N.: Recommender system for information retrieval using natural language querying interface based in bibliographic research for Naïve users. Int. J. Intell. Sci. 12(1), 9–20 (2022)
8. Olaide, O., Kana, A.D.: OWL formalization of cases: an improved case-based reasoning in diagnosing and treatment of breast cancer. Int. J. Inf. Secur. Priv. Digit. Forensics (IJIS) 3(2), 92–105 (2019)
9. Oyelade, O.N., Ezugwu, A.E.: COVID19: a natural language processing and ontology oriented temporal case-based framework for early detection and diagnosis of novel coronavirus. Preprints (2020)

10. Oyelade, A.O.S.J.S.A.O.N.: Patient symptoms elicitation process for breast cancer medical expert systems: a semantic web and natural language parsing approach. Future Comput. Inform. J. **3**(1), 72–81 (2018)
11. Oyelade, O.N., Ezugwu, A.E.: A case-based reasoning framework for early detection and diagnosis of novel coronavirus. Inform. Med. Unlocked **20**, 100395 (2020)
12. Osorio, J., Beltran, A.: Enhancing the detection of criminal organisations in mexico using ML and NLP. In: 2020 International Joint Conference on Neural Networks (IJCNN) (2020)
13. Meira, J., Carneiro, J., Bolón-Canedo, V., Alonso-Betanzos, A., Novais, P., Marreiros, G.: Anomaly detection on natural language processing to improve predictions on tourist preferences. Electronics **11**(5), 779 (2022)
14. Zhang, T., Schoene, A.M., Ji, S., Ananiadou, S.: Natural language processing applied to mental illness detection: a narrative review. NPJ Digital Med. **5**(46) (2022)
15. Wang, M., Xu, L., Guo, L.: Anomaly detection of system logs based on natural language processing and deep learning. In: 2018 4th International Conference on Frontiers of Signal Processing (ICFSP) (2018)
16. Shah, N., Bhagat, N., Shah, M.: Crime forecasting: a machine learning and computer vision approach to crime prediction and prevention. Vis. Comput. Ind. Biomed. Art **4**(1), 1–14 (2021)
17. Bolla, R.A.: Crime Pattern Detection Using Online Social Media. Missouri University of Science and Technology (2014)
18. Sharma, A., Jain, R.: Data pre-processing in spam detection. IJSTE Int. J. Sci. Technol. Eng. **1**(11) (2015)
19. Shirani-Mehr, H.: SMS spam detection using machine learning approach, Stanford University (2013)
20. Malmasi, S., Zampieri, M.: Detecting hate speech in social media, arXiv preprint arXiv:1712.06427 (2017)
21. Andrews, S., Brewster, B., Day, T.: Organised crime and social media: a system for detecting, corroborating and visualising weak signals of organised crime online. Secur. Inform. **7**(1), 1–21 (2018)
22. Ikonomakis, E., Kotsiantis, S., Tampakas, V.: Text classification using machine learning techniques. WSEAS Trans. Comput. **4**(8), 966–974 (2005)
23. Lim, H.S.: Improving KNN based text classification with well estimated parameters. In: Pal, N.R., Kasabov, N., Mudi, R.K., Pal, S., Parui, S.K. (eds.) ICONIP 2004. LNCS, vol. 3316, pp. 516–523. Springer, Heidelberg (2004). https://doi.org/10.1007/978-3-540-30499-9_79
24. Johnson, D.E., Oles, F.J., Zhang, T., Goetz, T.: A decision-tree-based symbolic rule induction system for text categorization. IBM Syst. J. **41**(3), 428–437 (2002)
25. Kim, S.-B., Rim, H.-C., Yook, D., Lim, H.-S.: Effective methods for improving naive bayes text classifiers. In: Ishizuka, M., Sattar, A. (eds.) PRICAI 2002. LNCS (LNAI), vol. 2417, pp. 414–423. Springer, Heidelberg (2002). https://doi.org/10.1007/3-540-45683-X_45
26. Shanahan, J.G., Roma, N.: Improving SVM text classification performance through threshold adjustment. In: Lavrač, N., Gamberger, D., Blockeel, H., Todorovski, L. (eds.) ECML 2003. LNCS (LNAI), vol. 2837, pp. 361–372. Springer, Heidelberg (2003). https://doi.org/10.1007/978-3-540-39857-8_33
27. Walczak, S.: Predicting crime and other uses of neural networks in police decision making. Front. Psychol. **12** (2021)
28. Palanivinayagam, A., Gopal, S.S., Bhattacharya, S., Anumbe, N., Ibeke, E., Biamba, C.: An optimised machine learning and big data approach to crime detection. Wirel. Commun. Mob. Comput. **2021** (2021)
29. Bharati, A., Sarvanaguru, R.A.K.: Crime prediction and analysis using machine learning. Int. Res. J. Eng. Technol. (2018)

30. Navalgund, U.V., Priyadharshini, K.: Crime intention detection system using deep learning. In: 2018 International Conference on Circuits and Systems in Digital Enterprise Technology (ICCSDET) (2018)

31. Rodrigues, A.P., Fernandes, R., Shetty, A., Lakshmanna, K., Shafi, R.M.: Real-time twitter spam detection and sentiment analysis using machine learning and deep learning techniques. Comput. Intell. Neurosci. (2022)

32. Yadav, N., Kudale, O., Gupta, S., Rao, A., Shitole, A.: Twitter sentiment analysis using supervised machine learning. In: Hemanth, J., Bestak, R., Chen, J.I.Z. (eds.) Intelligent Data Communication Technologies and Internet of Things. Springer, Singapore (2020). https://doi.org/10.1007/978-981-15-9509-7_51

Residential Water Consumption Monitoring System Using IoT and MQTT Communication

Jacqueline del Pilar Villacís-Guerrero[1] (iD), Daniela Yessenia Cunalata-Paredes[2],
José Roberto Bonilla-Villacís[3], Angel Soria[4] (iD), and Fátima Avilés-Castillo[5]([⊠]) (iD)

[1] Carrera de Ingeniería Industrial, Facultad de Ingeniería y Tecnologías de la Información y la
Comunicación, Universidad Tecnológica Indoamérica, Quito 170103, Ecuador
jacquelinevillacis@uti.edu.ec

[2] Facultad de Ingeniería en Sistemas, Electrónica e Industrial, Universidad Técnica de Ambato,
Ambato 180206, Ecuador
dcunalata8286@uta.edu.ec

[3] Carrera Ingeniería Industrial, Colegio de Ciencias e Ingenierías, Universidad San Francisco de
Quito, Cumbayá 170901, Ecuador
jbonillav@estud.usfq.edu.ec

[4] Electrical and Computer Engineering, Purdue University, Lafayette 47907, USA
asoriach@purdue.edu

[5] Escuela de Posgrados, Pontificia Universidad Católica del Ecuador, Quito 170525, Ecuador
faaviles@puce.edu.ec

Abstract. Water shortage across the globe causes changes in the life of the human being, not to mention that water is a resource that must be preserved for future generations. The companies that distribute and charge fees for residential water services have problems performing the periodical manual readings. Thus, showcasing inaccuracy in the costumer statements at the end of every month. The following paper describes the development process of a low-cost intelligent control and monitoring system of residential water consumption. The system design uses a flow sensor that measures the influx of liquid as it passes through the pipes. Based on the value that the conventional meter marks at the beginning of the day, it is possible to determine the daily consumption. The processing of acquired data is performed with a low-cost controller (SBC). Also, the respective control actions were transmitted towards a solenoid valve, which controls the passage of water to the house. Next, an access and communication point is established applying bidirectional MQTT (Message Queue Telemetry Transport) protocol to send and receive data wirelessly through Internet of Things (IoT). Data was stored and managed on a local server. The prototype displays information through an LCD screen and in a web page. To achieve this, the server sends information such as date-time, username, meter number, etc. The results showcase that the measurements were performed as expected. Thus, validating the possibility of using it in a larger sample.

Keywords: Flow sensor · IoT · MQTT · Water measurement

O. Gervasi et al. (Eds.): ICCSA 2022 Workshops, LNCS 13381, pp. 518–533, 2022.
https://doi.org/10.1007/978-3-031-10548-7_38

1   Introduction

Water as a resource represents a crucial role in sustaining and enabling life on planet earth (above oxygen or other nutrients) [1]. Water can be found in its natural state, or it might have undergone a modification process [2]. Despite, the attempts to raise awareness in the population about its decrease due to climate change and incorrect use that ultimately led to excessive waste, these objective to this date has not been possible to meet. According to the reports presented by the United Nations Organization (UN) in the last decade, approximately one fifth of the world's inhabitants experience water shortages [3]. Predictions state that by the year 2030 hundreds of millions of people will be displaced in search of water resources due to its widespread shortage [4].

Even though, Latin America has approximately 31% of the global water sources, this region could be heavily affected in a possible future crisis [5]. The country with the highest consumption of drinking water (237 L per inhabitant/day) is Ecuador, surpassing the average for the region by 40% (169 L inhabitant/day) [6]. A large part of the population ignores this problem and does not consume water consciously. Contributing to the current environmental deterioration. Leaks produced from defective water pipes, leaving open faucets produces excessive water consumption [7]. The monthly consumption bills issued by the residential water management institutions showcase these problems. These companies collect data readings from residential water meters manually, a difficult task to perform due to urban and rural demographic growth. Based on the mentioned problems, the need to implement interconnected technological tools to facilitate the management of residential water consumption, both for the user and for the private company is generated [8].

In each residence there is an analog meter that is installed by the local water service provider, on a mandatory basis. The process consists of the mobilization of personnel to the user's home, the identification of the meter and the reading of the current value of consumption. This is repeated periodically with an interval of 30 days, on exceptional or improbable cases this would not be performed. According to the data collected from the manual readings, the accounting department performs the manual calculation, and issue the customer invoice afterwards. This invoice is uploaded to the company's web portal and in this way the client can download it and decide to pay it. However, poor readings and human errors cause a mismatch of the real consumption values, causing inconveniences for the client and the supplier. Therefore, this scenario shows the need to automate this process since human errors are difficult to eliminate and can only be reduced [9].

The continuous progress of society requires the optimization of daily processes [10]. In order to, mitigate the effects of climate change. Based on a bibliographic review, several research works related to residential water monitoring systems have been found. Despite, efforts to standardize these devices, as mentioned in [4] the various components used, and the constantly evolving technologies do not allow this. In [8] a prototype that goes in series with a conventional meter that is part of a complex SCADA system was presented. The study by Li et al. [11] implements a self-powered meter that works based on a turbine design and Bluetooth. While Fuentes and Mauricio [12] make a smart residential water meter using IoT, showing good results in reading water consumption and detecting water leaks. Wang [13] implements ultrasound sensors to make a water consumption meter. However, the research paper lacks the results data that validates the designed equipment. The study presented in [14] allows the monitoring of water consumption through M2M-LoRa of rural villages in India, with this waste can be avoided. However, there is no evidence of the operation of this system either. Finally, Kumar Jha et al. [15] developed a smart meter using Arduino, Raspberry Pi and an interface for data presentation. This system evaluates the quality of the water by measuring the levels of pH, temperature, turbidity, dissolved oxygen, and conductivity.

The waste of water represents a greater expenditure for the user, while leaks and other failures in the system represent a problem for the residential water distribution service company. Current meters and the actual manual consumption measurement methods require a process of innovation. Furthermore, the proposed research work describes a device that performs the numerical estimation of residential water consumption in an urban residential unit using bidirectional communication under the MQTT protocol. The primary objective is to provide accurate data on a daily, weekly, or monthly basis and to send notifications to the user when excessive consumption occurs. Researchers and the open-source software, hardware development communities will benefit indirectly. Furthermore, the application of secure protocols in this prototype enables the replication and improvement in future research studies. All electronic components and integrated circuits (ICs) were adapted to the Latin American regional standards of availability and application, for easy acquisition. Thus, the content of this research paper will show the feasibility of the proposed implementation, from a technological and economic standpoint.

This document has four sections, including the introduction in Sect. 1. The materials and methods used in the development of the prototype are described in Sect. 2. The results are presented in Sect. 3 and the conclusions in Sect. 4.

2 Materials and Methods

Documented bibliographical research was performed, to collect information about the theoretical concepts involved in the design of the data acquisition and monitoring stages of the system [16]. This academic paper focuses on the domain of applied research type, since its purpose is the generation of knowledge with direct application to the problems of society and various industries. In addition, a systematic study was carried out during field research activities to determine the characteristics of the system to be designed. Data acquisition and validation of proper operation was executed in a university laboratory. Several performance tests were required to validate each of the design stages, and the final prototype. The results were documented in this experimental research proposal. Figure 1 shows the block diagram of the system which is divided into three stages. In the first stage, data acquisition and preprocessing were performed at regular intervals. This was achieved using a water flow sensor that sends electrical signals to the controller system. In the second stage, calculations quantify the amount of residential water consumption and display the values on the system LCD screen. Through wireless communication the system connects to the local server applying MQTT protocol that uses minimal bandwidth to avoid the loss of data. Enabling the operation of the database that acquires information in real time. In addition, it has alarms (notifications) that notify the user when a pre-defined limit of residential water consumption in the residential unit is exceeded.

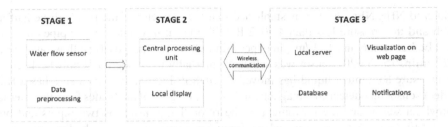

Fig. 1. General diagram of the proposed system.

2.1 Hardware

The elements that are part of the wireless system have been selected according to the design provided in Fig. 2. A technical analysis of each of the components and/or devices involved in each of the design phases was performed. The overall system is composed of six modules that are power supply, sensing, control and data processing, communication, visualization and monitoring.

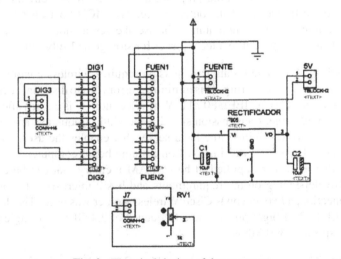

Fig. 2. Electrical design of the prototype.

Power Supply. The system requires a Direct Current (DC) voltage of 5 V for all electronic components. The prototype will be placed in a residential unit that provides direct access to an Alternate Current (120 VAC) power outlet that is close to residential water meter equipment, therefore the power supply must be regulated. A L7805 voltage regulator and two electrolytic capacitors were used to generate a stable DC 5 V power supply output.

Sensing. The use of a water flow sensor makes it possible to quantify the amount of water that passes through the pipe in domestic residential units. According to the Ecuadorian standard NHE NEC-2011, it is stablished that the diameter of the pipe will be half an inch and the pressure less than 4.9032 Bar. The usual flow rate for this pipe diameter will be between 6 and 12 L/m (liters per minute), for this proposal the flow rate was at 12 L/min. The YF201 sensor was selected. Internally it's made up of pinwheel sensor to measure how much liquid has moved through it. Externally, the camera has a Hall Effect sensor that detects the magnetic field of the magnet of the blades from the internal pinwheel sensor and the movement of the rotor. The sensor has two inputs and one output that sends a square wave whose frequency is proportional to the flow rate. Both its conversion factor from frequency (Hz) to flow rate (L/min) and the diameter of its liquid inlet are suitable for this study. In addition, a half-inch solenoid valve was used to control the flow of water to the sensors by switching between open and closed states. The activation of this solenoid valve will be triggered when the user has unpaid values. A water solenoid was selected because it has an operating voltage of 12 V and was designed specifically for residential water flow.

Control and Data Processing. The controller of this system is the Node Micro Controller Unit (MCU) ESP8266 card, due to its features and low cost. Sensor readings and measurements were analyzed. For this proposed design the flow that circulates is directly proportional to the frequency of the output wave. The MCU board has built-in Wi-Fi wireless communication, without requiring the use of external modules. After this stage, the processed data will be sent to a local server for storage and subsequent monitoring.

Communication. The system data transmission requires wireless communication, in order to minimize the use of wiring. This minimizes errors due to disconnection and facilitates its installation at home. IEEE 802.11 (Wi-Fi) technology is chosen after analyzing parameters such as range, transmission speed, bandwidth, frequency, and modulation. The information was transmitted to a local server that enables the user to observe the data in real time. The server was installed on a single board computer, for this design a Raspberry Pi B4+ will be applied. It has a RAM memory that can be expanded to 2 GB or 4 GB depending on the requirements and has 2 micro-HDMI ports. For the wireless connection, a two antennas Cisco Wireless Router was used. The device works under the IEEE 802.11 b/g/n protocol at a frequency of 2.4 GHz in a single band and a transmission speed of 300 Mbps.

Visualization. The selected component is a 16×2 liquid crystal LCD screen that is connected to the Node MCU card through an I2C serial communication adapter.

2.2 Software

Data acquisition begins with the initialization of variables and parameters for the quantification of the value of water consumption. Figure 3 shows the aforementioned.

The flow sensor provides information in the form of a square wave, which corresponds to a Hall effect pulse output whose frequency in Hz is proportional to the flow rate Q (l/min) as shown in Eq. (2), starting from (1). The K factor depends on the build-in parameters of the sensor and in the case of the YFS201 flow sensor it is 7.5 with a precision margin of 10% and the Q variable corresponds to the flow value obtained. To

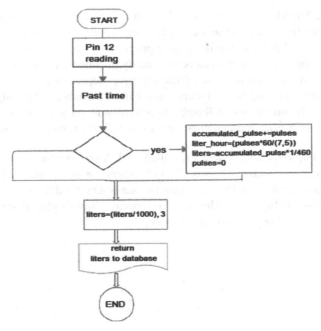

Fig. 3. Process flowchart for sensor data acquisition.

configure and program the board, the frequency of the square wave from the sensor is required. The measurement was calculated by implementing a periodic check that counts pulses in certain time intervals and then divide this value by the length of this interval in seconds. The source code for the board is found in Appendix 4 in the Arduino IDE interface.

$$f(Hz) = K * Q \tag{1}$$

$$Q = \frac{f(Hz)}{K} \tag{2}$$

Communication Protocol. IoT protocols are sets of M2M (machine to machine) communication standards established so that the devices that are part of the network can communicate efficiently, are scalable, and have interoperability. The MQTT protocol is ideal for IoT as it represents a lightweight method for messaging via a publish/subscribe model with low power devices, uses low bandwidth and requires minimal system requirements. MQTT provides three specific levels of quality of service (QoS). Based on the level of difficulty, the broket guarantees the reception of a message from the client side. Therefore, as the QoS level increases the necessary bandwidth increases too. Security is a key factor to consider in any communication system. The MQTT protocol has different security measures that can be applied to shield these communication link. This includes SSL/TLS transport, authentication by username and password, or by certificate. However, the design must consider that many of the IoT devices have limited memory space, so SLL/TLS can be a significant process to load.

Local Server. The Mosquitto server was developed with the MQTT protocol. The server works from level 0 of quality of service and can be developed with C programming language. Broker installation instructions were programmed in the Raspberry board. For this, Raspbian operating system must be previously installed. The operation of the local server is centered on a LAMP server, these acronyms represent the acronym for a system that uses the following free software tools: Linux, Apache, and MySQL/MariaDB. Therefore, after the installation of Raspbian each software packages were installed from the console, since it is an operating system based on Debian of GNU/Linux.

Database. In PhpMyAdmin, a database called AQUA was created, and it contains different tables such as: “meters”, “history” and “owners”, which contain all the variables necessary to identify the user, the water flow measurement, the date, and the current system state, as shown in Fig. 4. In addition, the information was displayed on the developed website in a clear and organized user interface.

Result Grid | Filter Rows: | Edit: | Export/Import: | Wrap Cell Content:

id	cedula	nombre	apellido	direccion	telefono	celular	email	estado	created
1	1804388286	Daniela	Cunalata	Ambato	032548976	0998755638	danielacunalata@gmail.com	1	2020-04-28 07:41:15
2	1804493565	Juan	Morales	Pelileo	038867649	0984403580	juank_jc@gmail.com	1	2020-05-15 21:48:27
NULL	NULL	NULL	NULL	NULL	NULL	NULL	NULL	NULL	NULL

Result Grid | Filter Rows: | Edit: | Export/Import: | Wrap Cell Content:

id	numero	medicion	fecha	medidore_id	estado	created
60	333444	0.00000	2020-05-11	1	1	2020-05-11 04:38:11
61	333444	1.47200	2020-05-13	1	1	2020-05-13 04:38:28
62	333444	2.95500	2020-05-15	1	1	2020-05-15 04:36:56
65	333444	4.18500	2020-05-17	1	1	2020-05-17 04:38:45
66	333444	6.73600	2020-05-19	1	1	2020-05-19 04:39:00
67	333444	8.40100	2020-05-21	1	1	2020-05-21 04:39:12
68	333444	9.82000	2020-05-23	1	1	2020-05-23 04:39:25
69	333444	12.41100	2020-05-25	1	1	2020-05-25 04:39:41
70	333444	13.67200	2020-05-27	1	1	2020-05-27 04:39:57

Fig. 4. Database table

Monitoring. The last stage is related to the display of information through an HMI interface on a web page. Both PHP and HTML programming languages were used to display the information contained in the database in a friendly user interface experience. The web page implements security levels for access. The available roles are user and administrator, to access into the web page the user need to enter with a registered email account. The administrator interface contains a home tab that allows you to view the data of all system users with the following information: identity card, names, surnames and address. The administrator role can manage the information and edit it if necessary. The list of owners can be completely managed as shown in Fig. 5. Also, as system security configuration the access passwords for the administrator and each of the users can be modified at any time.

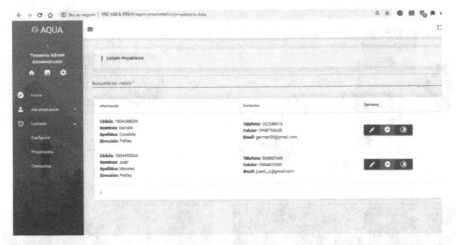

Fig. 5. Owners list.

Email Notification. Consumption control is extremely important, so the administrator can set a maximum value previously agreed with the user. As soon as, the flow rate measurement present data closer to the maximum value, an alarm gets triggered, and the user receives email notifications. Similarly, under prior agreement with the user, the system emits a signal to close the solenoid valve and stop the normal flow of residential water into the residential unit. To carry out the email notification system, the Google SMTP server was used, the same one that is used for the transfer of emails between various devices and has become more relevant with the growth of IoT platforms. The creation of an exclusive Gmail account for the system was require. This account serves as a source that sends email notifications to the users. It is essential to enable access to less secure applications, Gmail identifies an account as a vulnerable due to the static address configuration. If consumption is classified as above the stablished high threshold, the discussed countermeasures can be applied.

2.3 Implementation

Figure 6 shows the design of the electronic circuit boards of the system. A circuit case was designed, so that all the elements have protection and the display of water consumption on the LCD screen is as clear and legible as possible.

The prototype got installed in a user's residential unit with the build in characteristics that were specified specially for the solenoid valve and the flow sensor in the initial pipe and agreed by the user and the design team. Additional pipes and pipeline connectors were require to complete the installation and to have the system operating properly, as shown in Fig. 7.

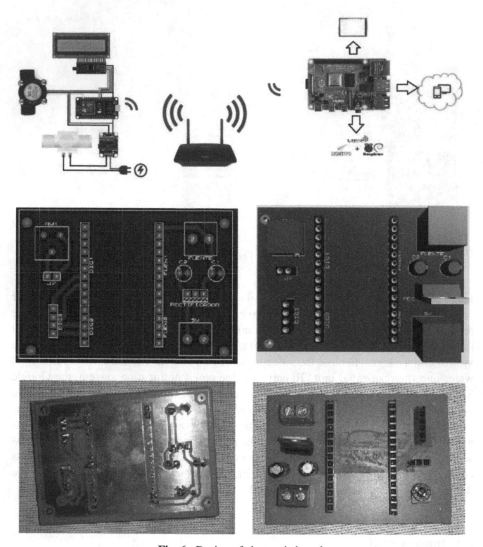

Fig. 6. Design of electronic boards

Fig. 7. Prototype installation in the user's residential unit.

3   Results

The system was successfully implemented, and the prototype performance was demonstrated by applying it in a residential unit. The system monitors water consumption, possible leaks, and enables the service company to cut off the residential water supply for cases of non-payment. In addition, performance was evaluated in conjunction with the conventional meter provided by the residential water service provider.

Figure 8 shows the user interface, with the administrator access that provides ease of learning and use. The main window is shown in Fig. 9, in this visual dashboard the water consumption readings are measured in cubic meters and are updated in real time including the user's data. Thus, enabling a quick and efficient response to any fortuitous event, since the user's location is known exactly.

Fig. 8. User interface presented on the web.

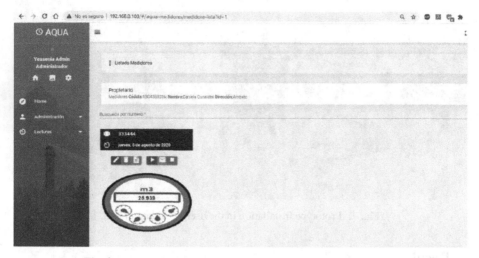

Fig. 9. Monitoring of residential water consumption in real time.

Table 1 shows the residential water consumption in the residential unit used for this proposal in a 30-day period. Measurements were taken with the conventional meter and with the prototype system. The range of error obtained between the measured values by both devices fluctuates in a 0,5% range as evidenced in Fig. 10. Moreover, it was observed that with the used the proposal prototype, exact and precise values of residential water consumption were obtained. Therefore, increasing the reliability of the system collecting the required data. In addition, the users will benefit from these insights by paying fair and precise measured values for their monthly consumption bills. On the other hand, the residential water service provider can analyze the collected data to optimize the management of the residential water supply network and reduce leaks.

For the purposes of this investigation, the needs of the user and the provider were satisfied. Table 2 shows a detailed budget for the electronic residential water monitoring system including design and implementation costs of the entire system. For this design, accessible components in the national markets and qualified labor were used.

3.1 Discussion

The designed equipment demonstrated a satisfactory performance. However, it cannot be compared with all the available proposals. Manoharan in [14] used more robust sensors and Lora technology, said technology amplifies the scope of implementation for a residential water monitoring system in a village. The previously mentioned research proposal does not provide results that can be compared and analyzed against our results. On the other hand, the economic aspect of this academic paper was preserved due to the similarity of this proposal aimed to be used in places with scarce resources. Likewise, the study by Alvisi [8] presents a SCADA system with a higher complexity and difficulty that makes it unfeasible to be developed under a limited budget. Li et al. [11] shows an interesting approach that includes a self-powered turbine. Although, this design has a remarkable limitation because it uses Bluetooth and limits the device to operate in

Table 1. Summary of measurements made with a conventional meter and the prototype.

Day	Daily consumption	Accumulated consumption	Reading number	Accumulated reading
1	0,000	0,000	2969	0
2	1,472	1,472	2970	1
3	1,483	2,955	2972	1
4	1,230	4,185	2973	1
5	2,551	6,736	2976	3
6	1,665	8,401	2977	1
7	1,419	9,829	2979	2
8	2,591	12,411	2981	2
9	1,261	13,672	2983	2
10	1,652	15,324	2984	1
11	1,284	16,608	2986	2
12	2,545	19,153	2988	2
13	1,487	20,640	2990	2
14	1,365	22,005	2991	1
15	2,546	24,552	2994	3
16	1,387	25,939	2995	2

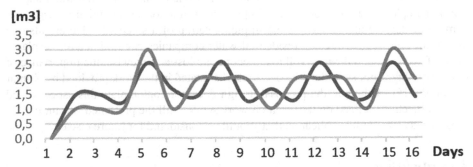

Fig. 10. Graphic representation of the variations between a commercial device and the prototype.

shorter ranges. Moreover, the designed equipment described in this research work was developed for a higher scale infrastructure. As a result, it is not able to detect water flows lower than 200 L/h. Over and above that, the Bluetooth module has a short range of operation. The presented proposal discussed in this academic paper showcases a higher accuracy and a wider range due to the communication through MQTT protocols.

On the other hand, Wang [13] uses ultrasonic sensors. However, tests were not performed to validate their use in practical scenarios. Whereas, in this research proposal

Table 2. Prototype cost summary.

Item	Description	Amount	Unir value	Total value
1	Raspberry Pi 4+	1	89,00	89,00
2	LCD displayCs	1	10,00	10,00
3	Case	1	18,00	18,00
4	Buzzer module	1	1,00	1,00
5	ESP8266 NodeMCU	1	9,00	9,00
6	Solenoid valve	1	12.0	12,0
7	L7805CV	1	0,80	0,80
8	Terminal board	5	0,50	2,50
9	Resistors	12	0,03	0,36
10	Printing	1	12,00	12,00
11	YF201 sensor	1	12,00	12,00
12	USB cable	1	1,50	1,50
13	Tin	1	0,50	0,50
14	Female sprats	2	0,50	1,00
Total				170,66

flow rate sensors have shown positive results. Fuentes and Mauricio [12] likewise use flow sensors. However, a valve that can shut off or enable the residential water supply was not implemented. Although, it is important to monitor consumption in real time, complementary solutions such as the implementation of a solenoid valve are also an important offering. As a result, residential water companies can mitigate the displacement of workers, and the user will avoid economic losses. Likewise, the importance of having quality water should not be overlooked as stated in the work provided by Kumar Jha et al. [15]. Although, the proposal design does not contemplate this aspect based on the objectives defined on the research work scope. Still the presented variant in [15] proposes an interesting application that should be considered for future research papers.

4 Conclusions

Currently, residential water metering is performed manually, and it is infrastructure relies on the use of residential water flow meters. Consumption bills of a home or property are traditionally calculated using the difference in volume in m^3 of a previous value and a current value over a 30-day period. Therefore, the customer does not know his daily or weekly consumption or the presence of faults or breaks in their pipeline infrastructure that would let them apply the necessary corrective measures. The development of IoT technologies focused on water flow measurement and wireless communication represent an ideal alternative to solve this problematic. Wi-Fi technology provides a wide range of operation, as well as a good operating frequency, cost, and availability of equipment.

It uses communication protocols for IoT devices that enables the implemented network to have scalability, security, efficiency, and interoperability between devices connected to the same network. Thus, offering greater functionality.

A thorough analysis was required upfront to understand the size of the network. This previous analysis led to the proper selection of the best IoT communication protocol, so that the advantages offered by each one were maximized. In such manner, traditional methods of measurement and billing of residential water consumption could be replaced with lower-cost proposals that provide clear and reliable measurements. Remote access for both users and administrators enable the streamlining of procedures. Thereby, reducing work time, expenditure of resources, and reducing human or systematic errors in the metering process. The proposal prototype was developed following the same guidelines as the proposals developed in the works of [3–7]. Being low cost one of the key aspects as well as the use of IoT. Therefore, it is demonstrated that efficient devices can be developed in the Latin American context.

To have a stable input voltage in the electronic circuit design a parallel circuit between two electrolytic capacitors is recommended as well as placing a voltage rectifier at the beginning of the circuit design. Device components such as the flow sensor, the solenoid valve, and the Node MCU board will not produce variations to the measured signal. All the outputs of the circuit must be connected to ground to avoid current fluctuations that alter the proper functioning of the electronic components. An aspect that stands out for this system is that it must be implemented in a place where it does not represent an obstacle for the inhabitants of the house and is protected from rain, wind, dust, or other environmental factors that may alter the performance of the internal circuits.

One of the limitations that were faced in this research work relates to the accuracy of the chosen sensor, in referenced bibliography the application of ultrasound sensors will be consider as an optimization upgrade that can be applied in the future research work. Despite this, the implemented sensors have an acceptable performance, and lie in the low-cost thresholds applicable for the system design budget. In addition, it should be noted that this process does not require such a high accuracy standard, so these sensors could be considered acceptable.

This proposal is aligned with the initiatives of smart cities management that aims to provide technology and efficiency to households. Although, the economic factor is a limiting factor in many countries. The availability of research projects like this aims for the improvement of the quality of life of the inhabitants. Reducing the environmental impact of wasted water resources and promoting a more efficient and conscious use of natural resources. As for future work, it is proposed to carry out tests in more residential units and perform analysis of the gathered data. As a result, the provision of continuous flow of information can be achieved. Resulting in increased agility and efficiency coupled with the benefits of cloud technologies. Similarly, a data analytics platform could be implemented with the use of Big Data. Further expanding the analysis and to adhere to other approaches found in the researched literature. Some extra implementations and optimizations could be considered such as the use of other sensors, communication protocols and the analysis of the quality of the residential water consumed on a daily basis by the users.

Acknowledgments. Thanks to the Universidad Tecnológica Indoamérica for funding this research work.

References

1. Subrahmanya, T.M., et al.: A review of recent progress in polymeric electrospun nanofiber membranes in addressing safe water global issues. RSC Adv. **11**, 9638–9663 (2021). https://doi.org/10.1039/d1ra00060h
2. Yánez-Naranjo, J., Hidalgo-Almeida, L.E.: Carved leather for a leather goods using mixed organic and inorganic tanning. Publicare **1**, 13–21 (2021)
3. Ray, I., Smith, K.R.: Towards safe drinking water and clean cooking for all. Lancet Glob. Heal. **9**, e361–e365 (2021). https://doi.org/10.1016/S2214-109X(20)30476-9
4. Li, J., Yang, X., Sitzenfrei, R.: Rethinking the framework of smart water system: a review. Water **12**, 412 (2020). https://doi.org/10.3390/w12020412
5. Kumar, R., et al.: Emerging technologies for arsenic removal from drinking water in rural and peri-urban areas: methods, experience from, and options for Latin America. Sci. Total Environ. **694**, 133427 (2019). https://doi.org/10.1016/j.scitotenv.2019.07.233
6. Balarezo, J.C., Buele, J., Naranjo-Avalos, H., Castillo, F., Vargas, W.G., Salazar, F.W.: Monitoring system for physical water quality parameters and automatic control for chlorine dosing in a aerator treatment plant. J. Phys. Conf. Ser. **1878**, 012065 (2021). https://doi.org/10.1088/1742-6596/1878/1/012065
7. Buele, J., et al.: Interactive system to improve the skills of children with dyslexia: a preliminary study. In: Rocha, Á., Pereira, R.P. (eds.) Developments and Advances in Defense and Security. SIST, vol. 152, pp. 439–449. Springer, Singapore (2020). https://doi.org/10.1007/978-981-13-9155-2_35
8. Alvisi, S., et al.: Wireless middleware solutions for smart water metering. Sensors **19**, 1853 (2019). https://doi.org/10.3390/s19081853
9. Venkataramanan, V., Geere, J.A.L., Thomae, B., Stoler, J., Hunter, P.R., Young, S.L.: In pursuit of â safe' water: the burden of personal injury from water fetching in 21 low-income and middle-income countries. BMJ Glob. Heal. **5**, e003328 (2020). https://doi.org/10.1136/bmjgh-2020-003328
10. Pilatásig, M., et al.: Interactive system for hands and wrist rehabilitation. In: Rocha, Á., Guarda, T. (eds.) ICITS 2018. AISC, vol. 721, pp. 593–601. Springer, Cham (2018). https://doi.org/10.1007/978-3-319-73450-7_56
11. Li, X.J., Chong, P.H.J.: Design and implementation of a self-powered smart water meter. Sensors **19**, 4177 (2019). https://doi.org/10.3390/s19194177
12. Fuentes, H., Mauricio, D.: Smart water consumption measurement system for houses using IoT and cloud computing. Environ. Monit. Assess. **192**(9), 1–16 (2020). https://doi.org/10.1007/s10661-020-08535-4
13. Wang, J.X., et al.: Smart water Lora IoT system. ACM Int. Conf. Proceeding Ser. 48–51 (2018). https://doi.org/10.1145/3194244.3194260
14. Manoharan, A.M., Rathinasabapathy, V.: Smart water quality monitoring and metering using Lora for smart villages. In: 2nd International Conference on Smart Grid Smart Cities, ICSGSC 2018, pp. 57–61 (2018). https://doi.org/10.1109/ICSGSC.2018.8541336

15. Jha, M.K., Sah, R.K., Rashmitha, M.S., Sinha, R., Sujatha, B., Suma, A.: Smart water monitoring system for real-time water quality and usage monitoring. In: Proceedings of International Conference on Inventive Research in Computing Applications, ICIRCA 2018, pp. 617–621 (2018). https://doi.org/10.1109/ICIRCA.2018.8597179
16. Buele, J., Franklin Salazar, L., Altamirano, S., Abigail Aldás, R., Urrutia-Urrutia, P.: Platform and mobile application to provide information on public transport using a low-cost embedded device. RISTI - Rev. Iber. Sist. e Tecnol. Inf. 476–489 (2019)

CALint: A Tool for Enforcing the Clean Architecture's Dependency Rule in Python

Clevio Orlando de Oliveira Junior[1], Jonathan Carvalho[1],
Fábio Fagundes Silveira[1(✉)], Tiago Silva da Silva[1],
and Eduardo Martins Guerra[2]

[1] Federal University of São Paulo – UNIFESP,
São José dos Campos, São Paulo, Brazil
{fsilveira,silvadasilva}@unifesp.br
[2] Free University of Bolzen-Bolzano – UNIBZ, Bozen-Bolzano, Italy

Abstract. Clean Architecture (CA) aims to address the need for more loosely coupled components and better cohesion. CA focuses on preparing software engineers to write more stable, durable, and flexible applications capable of distinguishing between details (e.g., what framework it uses) and the business logic requirements. A literature review shows that considerable effort has been devoted to cataloging and solving code smells related to code, often called code smells. However, the same does not apply to architecture smells – its software architecture counterpart. Similar research regarding other programming languages such as Java, PHP, or C# represents noteworthy works in the area, but they do not address Python applications directly. This work directs efforts towards redesigning and adapting existing Python programs to the CA principles by detecting the code smells that break the CA constraints through the developed CALint tool. Moreover, this approach proposes two extended refactoring techniques to solve these smells efficiently by grouping and comparing static code analysis and reuse them to enforce Clean Architecture's Dependency Rule programmatically. To demonstrate the feasibility of the two refactoring techniques described in this work and the CALint tool, we applied them to three different case studies. The major findings of this work include two extended refactoring techniques and the development of a tool to verify non-conformities related to the Clean Architecture dependency rule. The results show common cases where the dependency rule was violated and highlighted by the CALint tool, which are fixed with the support of refactoring steps.

Keywords: Software engineering · Clean architecture · Code smells · Refactoring

© The Author(s), under exclusive license to Springer Nature Switzerland AG 2022
O. Gervasi et al. (Eds.): ICCSA 2022 Workshops, LNCS 13381, pp. 534–549, 2022.
https://doi.org/10.1007/978-3-031-10548-7_39

1   Introduction

Refactoring techniques are constantly needed in the software development process. In fact, in multidisciplinary software projects, it is expected that due to tight deadlines software developers choose shortcuts, which result in trade-offs that allow the customer's expectations to be met in the short term, accumulating technical debts that inflate the long-term maintenance cost of an application [11].

For a long time, refactoring meant hiding the parts of the code that dealt with input and output through subroutines. Nowadays, one can see that refactoring means something different. This time closer to exposing the I/O operations and hiding the operations that deal with the business logic [20]. Among the methods that allow such detection, is it possible to cite the analysis of the program dependency graph [5]. This directed graph represents a dependency between elements of a program and can be used, for example, to detect duplicate codes [13], which configures a code smell proposed by [8].

Currently, the maintenance benefits that architectural styles such as the Clean Architecture or the Hexagonal Architecture [4] provide are widely discussed. However, there is a lack of discussions about adapting existing programs to a specific architecture or even detecting violations of their fundamental constraints.

This article proposes two code refactoring techniques to adapt existing Python codes to the Clean Architecture constraints. Furthermore, it shows a tool named *CAList*, developed to automate this process, responsible for creating a set of rules, based on existing static code analysis tools, capable of identifying and warning about smells that violate the dependency rule Clean Architecture principle in Python applications. Although our proposed tool and refactoring techniques are an ongoing research project, preliminary results show that they are feasible when applied to a few selected case studies from the Python developer community.

The remaining of this paper is structured as follows: Sect. 2 presents an overview of current work involving architecture smells detecting and refactoring techniques for the Clean Architecture. Section 3 describes the tool structure and Sect. 4 presents two extended refactoring techniques proposed in this work. Section 5 presents the application of the tool in three different case studies, aiming to demonstrate the feasibility of our approach. Finally, Sect. 6 concludes the paper and points out future works.

2   Related Works

Garcia et al. [9] describe what architecture smells are and compare them with other code smells. They list and define new architectures smells, citing examples in industrial systems and showing these smells with diagrams, possible causes, and tradeoffs. This paper also makes efforts to catalog architecture smells. However, differently from the work proposed by Garcia et al. [9], we focus only in the architecture smells related to the Clean Architecture. Further, we propose explanations and solutions for refactoring them with a programmatic approach.

Bui [2] proposes refactoring techniques for Clean Architecture but in a different context. First, the author explains various design patterns and architectural models, as well as mentions principles like the dependency rule, but does not have a focus on code smells and refactoring techniques. Also, several good practices are mentioned as well as their reasons within the context of Android and reactive programming applications.

The work of Velasco-Elizondo et al. [22] has the goal of proposing smells and refactoring techniques for a specific architectural pattern. However, as the Clean Architecture has more layers and rules than the MVC one, the techniques for finding and solving smells need to be adapted.

A refactoring method for architecture smells, more specifically, the *Cyclic Dependency Smell* is proposed by Rizzi et al. [21]. They also extend functions of an existing application based on graphs (*Arcan* [6]), and perform an experiment in a large base of programs. However, the work does not focus on Python language neither the CA's specific rules.

Beltrão et al. [1] present a project called *"Project Case"*. The aim is to reduce technical debt (TD), a metaphor in which developers take shortcuts during software development and negatively impact quality, completeness, or safety. The work implements technical debt detection rules through a plugin developed to the *SonarQube*[1], a continuous code quality inspection tool based on static analysis.

Even though there are important related works in the literature, neither of them focuses on analyzing and justifying these code smells nor focuses on the Python programming language.

3   The CALint Tool

3.1   General View

CALint is a tool developed to check if a given Python project complies with the Clean Architecture dependency rules and, if not, to point out the places where the non-conformities were detected. The objectives of this tool are:

- Use the own proposed tool as an object of study, pointing out during development the times when the dependency rule was violated, in a process analogous to *bootstrapping*;
- Facilitate the configuration of other existing tools on the market to efficiently establish rules shaped for the Clean Architecture. Besides, to accelerate the process of development and refactoring of existing programs to the constraints of the Clean Architecture, more specifically, the dependency rule one;
- Start a development project where checking for dependency rules becomes continuous and simplified through the whole software life cycle, integrating it with tools used in the market;
- Create an approach that follows and/or checks the Clean Architecture constraints differently from those commonly found, which primarily focus on data reading and storing operations.

---

[1] https://www.sonarqube.org.

3.2 Architecture and Development

As pointed out by Martin [15], the folder structure should reveal the features of the program and not be strictly framework-oriented or driven to *I/O* mechanisms. This project adheres to this premise regarding its organization. Figure 1 depicts the folders and location of its architectural layers.

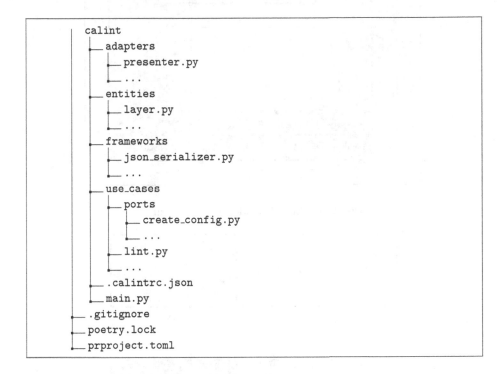

Fig. 1. CALint folder structure

CALint has five architectural layers: main, frameworks, adapters, use_cases, and entities (Fig. 2). There is an extra layer, named Main. It is the gateway to the application. The function that calls the use cases in order, sending parameters and injecting dependencies on each one is in the Main. First, it calls the use case responsible for configuring the entities create_config, then the use case that creates the results (lint).

The following frameworks are used in the CALinst:

– Click (click_printer.py): responsible for formating and coloring the output from the command-line interface.
– Import Linter (importlinter_linter.py): the main framework in the project, it analyzes the dependencies between layers of the application based on the rules specified by the user.
– json (json_serializer.py), despite being a standard library provided by Python, it is crucial that the programmer has the freedom to change it and choose

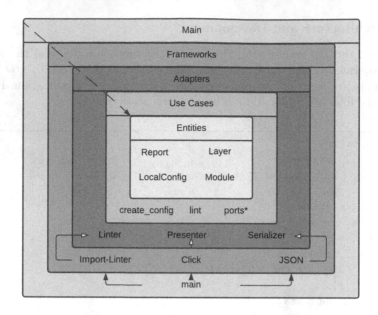

Fig. 2. CALint dependency architecture

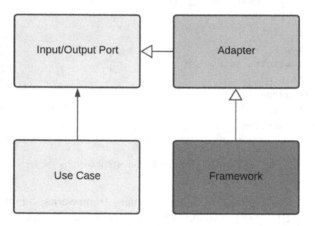

Fig. 3. Flow of dependencies from the use case to frameworks

alternatives of data serializers in the project. After all, serializing is an I/O process. This way, if there is a requirement to use another serializer framework (e.g. a serializer for toml, an alternative library of json), it can be changed easily, due to dependency injection [19].

The adapters are the project's adapters, both input, and output. An adapter can have ports for one or more input or output use cases. In this case, they make the connections between the libraries and the use cases through the implementation of the use case ports (Fig. 3). The CALint adapters are:

- LinterAdapter: it implements LintPort. This adapter implements the linter output method, calling an abstract method, later implemented by one of the classes that use the frameworks, called lint. It receives a configuration of type LocalConfig and returns a Report.
- PresenterAdapter, it implements the PrinterPort. This adapter implements the call to present passing the contents of the Report so that the responsible framework presents the contents of the Report.
- SerializerAdapter, it implements CreateConfigPort, calling the deserialize. In addition, SerializerAdapter also provides the signature of serialize, which, unlike deserialize, takes a dictionary and returns a string.

Use cases coordinate the application's business logic and populate and regulate entity data required by the application. They do not know about adapters, as they define the input and output ports (abstract classes). In this way, adapters that implement the same ports can be inserted or removed as needed without knowledge of the use cases. There are three ports (Fig. 4):

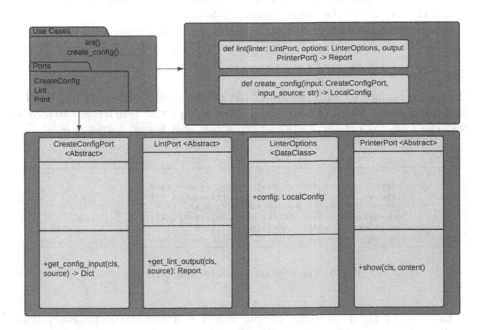

Fig. 4. CALint use cases and ports

- LintPort: responsible for defining the signature of the output after executing the linter. Defines that the configuration must be of type LocalConfig and the return must be an entity, Report.
- PrinterPort: responsible for defining the signature of the method that displays the return contents, regardless of the program's output interface. Requires that it must have a name with only one dynamic typed argument and must return nothing.
- CreateConfigPort: responsible for defining the architecture of an abstract method and receiving an arbitrary source, returning a dictionary (Dict).

Entities describe the enterprise business or the business objects of an application. They also represent objects and instructions and how to handle them. This part of the system must be unaware of which technologies implementation are accessing them. The main entities of CALint are:

- Layer: represents an architectural layer. Stores the priority data, the physical path of the import, and the virtual name of the Layer.
- LocalConfig: represents the local configuration, that is, the layers and the root of the project to be analyzed.
- Module: represents a module, contains the physical path and Layer to which this module belongs.
- BrokenRule: represents a broken rule. Contains the start and the end modules and the line where the nonconformity is found.
- Report: represents a report, that is, the listing of the broken rules.

3.3 Setting up the CALint

The tool is configured with the JSON file .calintrc.json, which must be placed in the project's root folder. Within this configuration file, it is necessary to have at least the following entries: roots and the subsequent layers' names (Fig. 5).

```
1    {
2        "roots": ["root_folder_one", "root_folder_two"],
3        "frameworks": ["root_folder_two.frameworks", 0],
4        "adapters": ["root_folder_two.adapters", 1],
5        "use-cases": ["root_folder_one.use_cases", 2],
6        "entities": ["root_folder_one.entities", 3]
7    }
```

Fig. 5. The CALint JSON configuration file

Here, every key is a string (as per JSON requirements), and every value consists of an array. The array will always contain one string and one integer (works like a tuple), except when the key is the root one. Roots must be an array of strings where every string is a root directory, and this is especially useful when there is no "main" folder and folders are scattered around the root folder.

For every other possible key-value pair, the key represents the virtual name of an architectural layer (e.g., "use cases"). The value will contain the layer's module path (e.g., `root_folder_one.use_cases`) and an integer value, representing how external that architectural layer is. The numbering sequence must start at "0" (the outermost layer), while the innermost layer should have the highest number (e.g., "3").

4   Proposed Refactoring Techniques

This section describes two proposed refactoring techniques applied to pave the way for existing Python code to adhere to the CA dependency rule.

4.1   Extract Port – Adapting the Existing Source Code

In order to refactor the non-conformities found to adhere to the CA's dependency rules, it is necessary to know where a module should be located in the application and which modules it is allowed to import.

During the case studies, we noticed that developers commonly forget that adapters should not be called directly from the use cases or entity layer. By doing that, use cases and adapters get tightly coupled to each other. In order to solve this issue, it is necessary to refactor the code so that the adapters become use case-dependent.

Consider the architecture smell represented in Fig. 6. The solution applied to this case consists of the following steps:

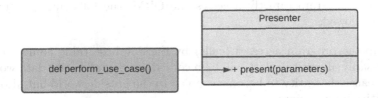

Fig. 6. Violating the dependency rule – a scenario where a use case is dependent on an adapter

1. Check what exactly the use case output needs to be and what is available to pass as a parameter;
2. Verify if such a situation is an input or output operation;
3. Create a use case centric function signature, specifying the parameters as well as the returning values;

4. Extract this information as an interface or as an abstract class (*Extract Interface* [8]), making the adapter dependent on or inheriting from this new class;
5. Replace adapter function calls with use cases;
6. Inject dependencies.

In the Sect. 5.1 we describe an application of this refactoring technique to handle non-conformities reported by CALint.

4.2   Extract Repository – Refactoring Code that Accesses Storage

As stated by Cockburn [4], there are primarily two types of adapters: primary and secondary. This nomenclature exemplifies that some adapters tend to be more responsible for the input of a program, whereas others are more for the output. According to the author, there are three technical solutions (which depend on the programming language): i) define interfaces and inject dependencies; ii) inject anonymous functions (also known as lambda expressions), and iii) inject objects that have common signatures (*duck typing* and dynamic typing [17]).

A program that manages repositories or data storage services, option "i" [4] can commonly be used to perform refactoring of programs that depend directly on an ORM. The ORM or *Object Relational Mapping* refers to a type of framework that tries to abstract and encapsulate the database code, mapping the data present in the database to objects of a programming language [3]. However, ORMs are nothing more than frameworks. In order to keep them flexible and allow replacement, keeping the decoupling between the application and the database, *Repository Patterns* [16,18] is commonly used, as shown in the Python Clean Architecture example (Sect. 5).

When a program directly accesses the ORM, the following best practices must be followed:

1. Group the program accesses (calls) by the database table name. Since not necessarily all entity's data will be recorded, storing all entity data would not only cause the entity to become coupled to the outside world but also expose sensitive information;
2. Create an interface using the *Repository Pattern* for every database table. Group typical operations within the generic repository, such as searching, creating, deleting, updating, and sorting;
3. Make the generic repository logic implemented concretely within each framework. In the composition root, frameworks are then injected. So, the repository works as a gateway to one or more use cases.

Figure 7 illustrates this situation and shows a possible solution by using this refactoring technique. It is quite common to call frameworks in the use case layer, especially when the use case itself deals with CRUD operations. Nevertheless, that violates the CA dependency rule, as shown in the source code example

(Fig. 7, line 7), since there is a calling to the *SQLAlchemy* directly from the use case. Although a repository can be seen as a use case port, the database contents or wherever that repository host is not part of the use case. They are implementation details.

```
1     from config import session
2     from models import User
3
4     def list_users():
5         # CODE SMELL! Use Case calling the
6         # SQLAlchemy ORM framework directly...
7         return session.query(User).all()
```

```
8     # Snippet code #1
9     # on usecases/ports
10    class UserRepository(ABC):
11        @staticmethod
12        @abstractmethod
13        def all():
14            pass
15
16    # Snippet code #2
17    # on frameworks/DB
18    # stuff directly related to the db
19    from sqlalchemy import create_engine
20
21    from .config import session
22    from .models import User
23
24    class DBUserRepository(UserRepository):
25        @staticmethod
26        def all():
27            return session.query(User).all()
28
29    # Snippet code #3
30    # on usecases
31    def list_users(repository: UserRepository):
32        return repository.all()
33
34    # now when calling list_users, somewhere else
35    list_users(DBUserRepository())  # here we inject the repository as a
                                                                 dependency
```

Fig. 7. Extract repository refactoring technique example

To solve this code smell, one can create a repository (e.g., UserRepository) to host the function signatures as an abstract class (line 10). Then, a concrete class (e.g., DBUserRepository) provides the details to the repository in the framework layer (lines 24–27). From now on, the use case only knows about UserRepository (line 31).

5   Case Studies and Result Analysis

To demonstrate the feasibility of the CALint tool and the two refactoring techniques described in this work, we applied them to three different case studies.

5.1   Bootstraping the CALint Itself

One practice in computer science is the *bootstrapping* [14]. Bootstrapping is the technique used by a newly created compiler to compile itself. In other words, the idea is to produce a self-compiling compiler.

Thus, we applied this technique to guide and verify whether the dependency rule is achieved or not during the development of the own CALint tool. The configuration JSON file of dependencies is depicted in Fig. 8.

```
1  {
2      "roots": ["calint"],
3      "main": ["calint.main", 0],
4      "frameworks": ["calint.frameworks", 1],
5      "adapters": ["calint.adapters", 2],
6      "use_cases": ["calint.use_cases", 3],
7      "entities": ["calint.entities", 4]
8  }
```

Fig. 8. The CALint JSON dependency file configuration for the CALint verification

With this structure, the next subsections describe times when there were non-conformities.

In one of the tool's first versions, as depicted in Fig. 9, it was possible to run the program and figure out that the use cases did not create a port, but rather the adapter was driving the development of business logic, a visible violation of the dependency rule and therefore a code smell according to the Clean Architecture constraints.

A new port was created in the use cases as an abstract class to refactor this code. The adapter had to inherit to be called by the use case after injecting dependencies, thus causing the adapter to depend on the instructions provided by the use case, not the other way around.

An example of such a situation can be seen in the snippet code of Fig. 10, where a use case imports an adapter. In the lint method, the first parameter is the adapter itself, not a port. Thus, to make it compliant with the clean architecture dependency rules and address this smell, we need to extract the port and use it as the first parameter of the lint use case method.

A similar problem was detected in one of the latest versions of the CALint tool. At this time, a use case layer was directly importing a presenter from the adapter layer (Fig. 11). Again, this situation was fixed by using the same refactoring technique. Due to the lack of space, reduced reports from CALint are depicted from now on.

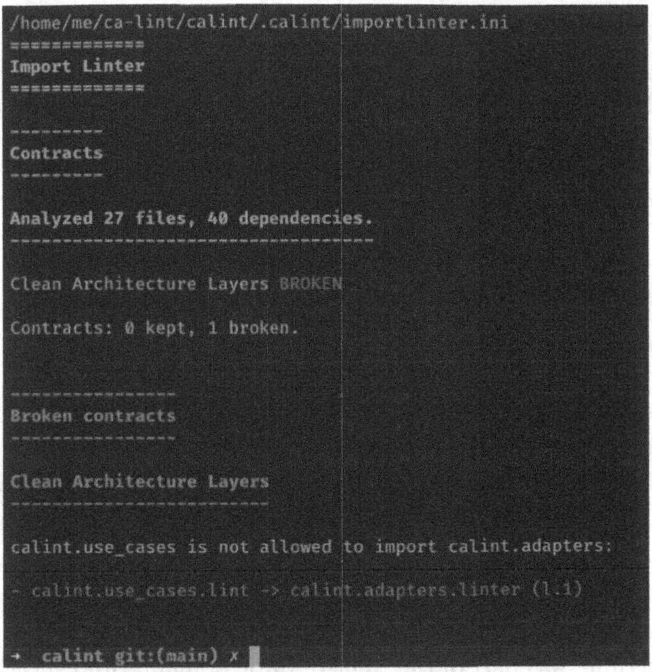

Fig. 9. Example of a dependency rule-breaking problem identified by CALint

```
1    from calint.adapters.linter import LinterAdapter
2    from calint.use_cases.ports import LinterOptions
3
4    def lint(linter: LinterAdapter, options: LinterOptions):
5        return linter.lint(options.config)
```

```
1
2    from calint.use_cases.ports import LinterOptions, LintPort
3
4    def lint(linter: LintPort, options: LinterOptions):
5        return linter.lint(options.config)
```

Fig. 10. Extract port refactoring technique example

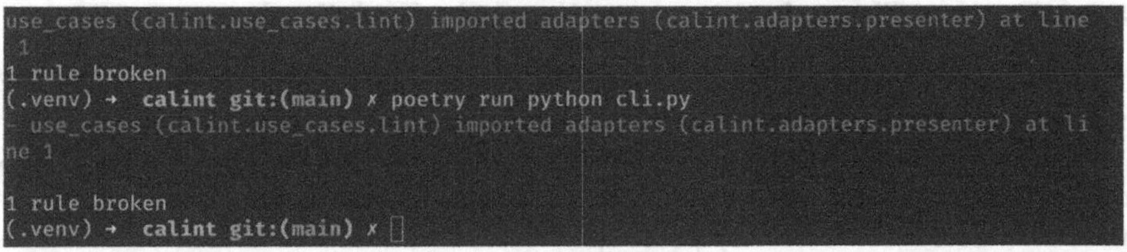

Fig. 11. CALint detecting a non-conformity in the CALint architecture design: the use case layer importing a presenter from the adapter layer

5.2 *Rent-o-Matic* Project Case Study

Rent-o-Matic is a demo project[2], comprising a companion repository to [10]. As the physical files tend to differ from project to project, first, we need to conduct a pre-processing step to create the files __init__.py, need by the Python language to solve the modules problem import issue [7]. Shortly, it was necessary to restructure some folders of the application as well as create the JSON dependency rule file (Fig. 12).

```
1  {
2      "roots": ["rentomatic"],
3      "main": ["rentomatic.app", 0],
4      "frameworks": ["rentomatic.rest", 1],
5      "adapters": ["rentomatic.repository", 2],
6      "use-cases": ["rentomatic.use_cases", 3],
7      "entities": ["rentomatic.domain", 4]
8  }
```

Fig. 12. Rent-o-Matic CALint JSON configuration file

An empty abstract class was also detected, where its only purpose was to check if something was part of the Rent-o-Matic domain. However, this class was in the use cases folder, and CALint detected it correctly, as shown in Fig. 13. To fix this nonconformity caused by the relocation of the folders, the tool just moves it to the entities folder.

```
→  rentomatic git:(master) ✗ calint
-  entities (rentomatic.domain.storageroom) imported use-cases (rentomatic.use_cases.sha
red.domain_model) at line 1

1 rule broken
```

Fig. 13. CALint detecting a non-conformity in the *Rent-O-Matic* design: the domain layer importing a class from the use case layer

5.3 Python Clean Architecture Example Case Study

The *Python Clean Architecture Example* [12][3] is an open source project on *GitHub* with the aim of illustrating the Clean Architecture in a *Flask* application.

Considering the study case architecture diagram (Fig. 14), we set the JSON dependency rules file (Fig. 15), creating the folder called frameworks with the modules main and in_memory_post_repository. In addition to that, the interfaces folder moved into the use cases folder because this folder represents the ports. Since CALint did not detect any problem, no code changes were required.

---

[2] https://github.com/lgiordani/rentomatic.
[3] https://github.com/heumsi/python-clean-architecture-example.

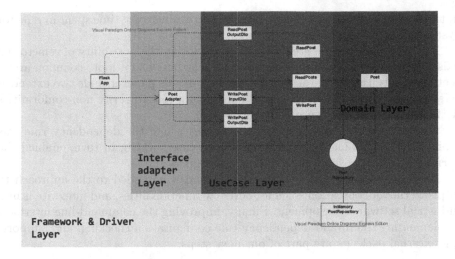

Fig. 14. Python CA example architecture diagram [12].

```
1  {
2      "roots": ["frameworks", "domain", "adapter"],
3      "frameworks": ["frameworks", 0],
4      "adapter": ["adapter", 1],
5      "use_cases": ["domain.use_case", 2],
6      "entities": ["domain.entity", 3]
7  }
```

Fig. 15. The Python Clean Architecture example JSON dependency configuration file

As shown by Fig. 16, CALint reports no nonconformities regarding the CA dependency rule in this case study.

```
→  python-clean-architecture-example git:(master) ✗ calint
No rules broken.
```

Fig. 16. CALint not highlighting any nonconformities

6   Conclusion and Future Work

Clean Architecture defines rigid communication layers by centering the program on its domain rather than its composing frameworks. As a result, it is possible to make the program completely configurable, as the details become flexible enough to be rewritten and plugged in on demand.

However, it is possible to refactor and adapt existing programs to the Clean Architecture since most refactorings involve principles well established in the literature, such as dependency inversion and dependency injection. Experiments in the industry are still necessary to verify and evaluate the time spent in refactor systems with large code bases.

The work herein presented focuses on exploring the possibility of refactoring existing programs to generate step-by-step instructions for more common architecture smells. Hence, the significant findings of this paper include two extended refactoring techniques and the development of a tool to verify non-conformities with the Clean Architecture dependency rule.

Our approach results show common cases where the dependency rule was violated. The CALint tool highlighted these cases, which, in turn, enabled the correction with the support of the refactoring steps.

Regarding future works, some extensions can be added to the approach to improve the tool operation, such as, add new functionalities, and integrate it into industrial software development. Finally, improving the command-line interface, implementing the invalid dependency rule configuration checking, and supporting external packages are part of our next steps.

Acknowledgments. The authors would like to thank the São Paulo Research Foundation (FAPESP) grant 2018/22064-4 – for financial support.

References

1. Beltrão, A., Farzat, F., Travassos, G.: Technical debt: a clean architecture implementation. In: Anais Estendidos do XI Congresso Brasileiro de Software: Teoria e Prática. SBC, Porto Alegre, RS, Brasil, pp. 131–134 (2020). https://doi.org/10.5753/cbsoft_estendido.2020.14620. https://sol.sbc.org.br/index.php/cbsoft_estendido/article/view/14620
2. Bui, D.: Reactive programming and clean architecture in Android development. Metropolia Ammattikorkeakoulu (2017)
3. Chen, T.H., et al.: An empirical study on the practice of maintaining object-relational mapping code in Java systems. In: 2016 IEEE/ACM 13th Working Conference on Mining Software Repositories (MSR), pp. 165–176. IEEE (2016)
4. Cockburn, A.: Hexagonal architecture (2005). https://alistair.cockburn.us/hexagonal-architecture/
5. Ferrante, J., Ottenstein, K.J., Warren, J.D.: The program dependence graph and its use in optimization. ACM Trans. Program. Lang. Syst. (TOPLAS) **9**(3), 319–349 (1987)
6. Fontana, F.A., Pigazzini, I., Roveda, R., Tamburri, D., Zanoni, M., Di Nitto, E.: Arcan: a tool for architectural smells detection. In: 2017 IEEE International Conference on Software Architecture Workshops (ICSAW), pp. 282–285. IEEE (2017)
7. Python Software Foundation: Python language reference, modules (2022). https://docs.python.org/3/tutorial/modules.html
8. Fowler, M.: Refactoring: Improving the Design of Existing Code. Addison-Wesley, Reading (1999)
9. Garcia, J., Popescu, D., Edwards, G., Medvidovic, N.: Toward a catalogue of architectural bad smells. In: Mirandola, R., Gorton, I., Hofmeister, C. (eds.) QoSA 2009. LNCS, vol. 5581, pp. 146–162. Springer, Heidelberg (2009). https://doi.org/10.1007/978-3-642-02351-4_10

10. Giordani, L.: Clean Architectures in Python, 2nd edn. Leanpub (2018). https:// leanpub.com/clean-architectures-in-python
11. Guo, Y., et al.: Tracking technical debt - an exploratory case study. In: ICSM 2011: Proceedings of the 2011 27th IEEE International Conference on Software Maintenance, pp. 528–531, September 2011. https://doi.org/10.1109/ICSM.2011. 6080824
12. Heumsi: Python clean architecture example (2020). https://github.com/heumsi/ python-clean-architecture-example
13. Hotta, K., Higo, Y., Kusumoto, S.: Identifying, tailoring, and suggesting form template method refactoring opportunities with program dependence graph. In: 2012 16th European Conference on Software Maintenance and Reengineering, pp. 53–62. IEEE (2012)
14. Louden, K.C.: Compiler Construction. Cengage Learning, Boston (1997)
15. Martin, R.C.: Clean Architecture: A Craftsman's Guide to Software Structure and Design. Robert C. Martin Series. Prentice Hall, Boston (2017). https://www. safaribooksonline.com/library/view/clean-architecture-a/9780134494272/
16. Microsoft:net microservices - architecture e-book (2021). https://docs.microsoft. com/en-us/dotnet/architecture/microservices/microservice-ddd-cqrs-patterns/ infrastructure-persistence-layer-design
17. Milojkovic, N., Ghafari, M., Nierstrasz, O.: It's duck (typing) season! In: 2017 IEEE/ACM 25th International Conference on Program Comprehension (ICPC), pp. 312–315. IEEE (2017)
18. Prajapati, M., et al.: ASP.NET MVC-generic repository pattern and unit of work. Int. J. All Res. Writ. 1(1), 23–30 (2019)
19. Razina, E., Janzen, D.S.: Effects of dependency injection on maintainability. In: Proceedings of the 11th IASTED International Conference on Software Engineering and Applications, Cambridge, MA, p. 7 (2007)
20. Rhodes, B.: The clean architecture in Python (2014). https://archive.org/details/ pyvideo_2840__The_Clean_Architecture_in_Python
21. Rizzi, L., Fontana, F.A., Roveda, R.: Support for architectural smell refactoring. In: Proceedings of the 2nd International Workshop on Refactoring, pp. 7–10 (2018)
22. Velasco-Elizondo, P., Castañeda-Calvillo, L., García-Fernandez, A., Vazquez-Reyes, S.: Towards detecting MVC architectural smells. In: Mejia, J., Muñoz, M., Rocha, Á., Quiñonez, Y., Calvo-Manzano, J. (eds.) CIMPS 2017. AISC, vol. 688, pp. 251–260. Springer, Cham (2018). https://doi.org/10.1007/978-3-319-69341-5_23

Genetic Data Analysis and Business Process Management Platform for Personalized Nutrition Service

Jitao Yang[(✉)]

School of Information Science, Beijing Language and Culture University,
Beijing 100083, China
yangjitao@blcu.edu.cn

Abstract. Vitamins and minerals are essential micro-nutrients required by our bodies to optimize health and maintain well-being. Currently, our nutrient recommendations are one-size-fits-all or one solution for a large group of persons, however, due to the difference of each individual's genetic background, lifestyle, and health condition, individual's nutrition requirement is different from each other, therefore, we should compute and provide personalized nutrition supplementation solution for each person. At the beginning of this paper, we describe the importance of personalized nutrition for keeping healthy; then we give a description of our personalized nutrition intelligent service platform by analyzing genetic data, lifestyle data and physical examination data together to generate genetic interpretation report and personalized nutrition report, and further place order to produce customized nutrition packs for each customer. To promote management efficiency and reduce errors in business processes, we developed multiple business process management systems such as laboratory information management system (LIMS), bioinformatic pipelines, genetic interpretation system, customer relationship management (CRM) system and etc. All the systems were integrated together to have the ability of processing tens of thousands of samples in parallel.

Keywords: Genetic testing · Nutrigenetics · Personalized nutrition platform · Business process management

1 Introduction

The traditional nutrient recommendations: Dietary Reference Intakes (DRIs) [1] are estimated average daily nutrient intake levels to meet the requirements of a group of population.

However, the difference of genetic background will affect the digestion, absorption, transport, metabolism and storage of food and nutrients, and the steady-state regulation of internal environment to varying degrees, reflecting the differences of different individual's response to nutrition and susceptibility to disease.

O. Gervasi et al. (Eds.): ICCSA 2022 Workshops, LNCS 13381, pp. 550–559, 2022.
https://doi.org/10.1007/978-3-031-10548-7_40

Nutrigenetics can study how individual's genetic composition affects diet response and susceptibility to diet related diseases through retrospective analysis of the interaction between individual's genetic variations and diet as well as diseases.

As a new interdisciplinary subject born from the benefit of the human genome project, nutrigenetics has produced many scientific research achievements, such as individual's dietary behaviors, vitamin and other nutritional needs, as well as metabolic factor regulation, are all significantly different due to the composition of individual's genetic background. Genetic defects may cause the body to be unable to obtain nutrition from food, then health will be damaged, therefore, it is necessary to evaluate nutrient requirements according to genetic composition, so as to make more accurate nutritional supplementation.

Vitamin D, is a fat soluble vitamin, and it's a necessary nutrient to maintain the life of human. Its main forms are vitamins D_3 and D_2, which form active vitamin D through hydroxylation in liver and kidney, and then exert its biological activity. Vitamin D is hydroxylated to 25-hydroxy vitamin D at position 25 and is further hydroxylated to 1,25-dihydroxy vitamin D [1,25 (OH) 2D] by 1α-Hydroxylase (encoded by the gene CYP27B1) in the kidney; vitamin D binding protein (DBP) binds to vitamin D for transport, 1,25 (OH) 2D is released into the blood circulation of the intestine, and then through the mechanism mediated by vitamin D receptor (encoded by the gene VDR), passively reabsorbed in the kidney [2].

Nutrigenetics research shows that the genetic polymorphisms of multiple genes involved in vitamin D metabolic pathway affect the activation, transport and absorption of vitamin D. For example, the serum concentration of 1,25(OH)2D3 in hepatitis C virus (HCV) patients with CYP27B1-1260 AA genotype is higher than that in HCV patients with CYP27B1-1260 AC or CC genotype, and the sustained virological response rate (SVR) of the HCV patients with CYP27B1-1260_AA homozygous genotype was significantly increased [3].

The GC gene's mutation can encode different GC protein mutants, the Gc2-2 protein mutant encoded by 436KK mutation has the lowest concentration of vitamin D binding protein in individual's plasma [4].

As a ligand, active vitamin D binds to vitamin receptor (VDR) and enters into the cell, and forms a complex with retinoid X receptor (RXR) in the nucleus. RXR-VDR binds to vitamin D response element (VDRE) and affects gene expression regulation as a transcription factor [5].

The Cdx2 gene's polymorphisms are located in the promoter region of VDR gene, allele A can improve the transcriptional activity of VDR gene. The FokI gene's restriction enzyme cutting site is located in the coding region of VDR gene, which has an impact on the activity of receptor. The BsmI, ApaI and TaqI genes' restriction enzyme cutting sites are located at the 3' end of VDR gene. The VDR gene's polymorphisms can limit the process of vitamin D entering cells [6].

With the development and application of functional genomics and next-generation sequencing technology, the time and cost of whole genome sequencing

(WGS) are greatly shortened. The establishment of genomics database based on population cohort research, the coding and interpretation of basic genome information by bioinformatics analysis technology, and the use of polygenic risk scoring (PRS) model, make the application of individual genome information possible, which can provide effective technical support for the accurate evaluation of individual's health status and the formulation of intervention strategies.

In recent years, bioinformatics has become more and more mature, and the application of single nucleotide polymorphism (SNP) based genetic risk score (GRS), PRS and other genetic risk assessment models have gradually expanded, more and more studies have focused on the field of nutrigenetics, such as the GRS based vitamin D insufficiency genetic risk assessment model [7], the risk allele frequency based vitamin D deficiency genetic risk assessment model [8], the intervention effect evaluation [9], and the evaluation model of vitamin E supplement response based on partial least squares (PLS) regression model [10].

2   Genetic Data Analysis

To analyze a customer's genetic data, we provide an non-invasive and self-administered DNA collection solution that, we send customer a DNA collection kit, which includes a saliva collecting tube, in the tube is the stabilization chemistry reagent used to keep the stabilization of saliva and DNA. After spiting saliva to the saliva collection tube, the customer should post the DNA collection kit to our molecular genetic testing laboratory. The laboratory will extract DNA from the saliva, and after a series of complex experimental processes, the DNA samples will be sequenced by different genome sequencing equipment such as iScan [11], Novaseq [12] and etc. The sequencer will generate millions of reads data, and the gene sequencing data will be stored in cloud storage disks. Multiple bioinformatic pipelines will analyze the reads data and give the genetic risk scores. Based on the genetic risk scores, the genetic interpretation system will generate genetic interpretation report using the gene-disease associations databases such as the databases of AutDB [13], DisGeNET [14,15], OMIM [16,17], and other published clinical scientific literature.

Figure 1 left is the user interface of precision nutrition genetic testing report, which lists the nutrition related genetic testing items, such as Vitamin A (VA), Calcium, Vitamin C (VC), Iron, Vitamin D (VD), Zinc, Vitamin E (VE), Selenium, Vitamin K (VK), Magnesium, Vitamin B_2 (VB$_2$), Phosphorus, Folic acid, Vitamin B_3 (VB$_3$), Lactose Tolerance, Vitamin B_{12} (VB$_{12}$), Alcohol Metabolism, Vitamin B_6 (VB$_6$), Caffeine Metabolism, Omega-3 Intake, Sweetness Sensitivity, Bitter Sensitivity, and etc. Under the genetic testing item name, the color bar represents the customer's nutrition requirement levels (*i.e.*, high, higher, medium, low). Click the name of each genetic testing item in the report, more detail information will be displayed to: 1) explain the genetic testing result, 2) give life style suggestions, 3) recommend personalized nutrition solutions, 4) list loci's genotypes, and 5) provide scientific evidences.

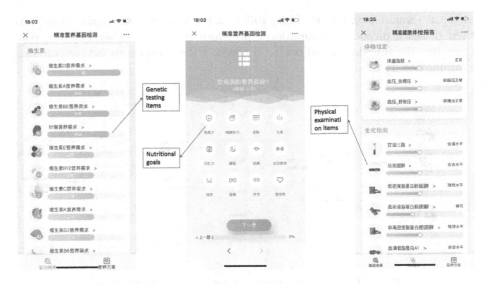

Fig. 1. The user interfaces of personalized nutrition service reports.

The genetic interpretation reports are embedded in WeChat app using the APIs [18] of WeChat. By embedding the genetic interpretation reports in WeChat, we can reach and communicate with customers conveniently, rather than persuade customers to download a new app or open a web page to access the genetic report. Since WeChat is the most popular chatting software in China, and more than 1 billion people in China use WeChat for communication everyday, therefore, customers can find and read the genetic interpretation reports easily, and we can also send notifications to customers through WeChat for notifying the status of samples.

3   Personalized Nutrition Service

To get customers' lifestyle data, we provide online food frequency questionnaires (FFQs) [19–21] to collect customers' diet, sports, sleep, and other health related data, including the questions related to health status/physical conditions, dietary habits, and medical histories. Figure 1 middle is the user interface of online food frequency questionnaires. The questions in the online FFQs are dynamic that, at the beginning, the questionnaire will list multiple nutritional goals, based on different nutritional goals selected by customers, the system will generate different questions, and the answer of the current question can decide the content of next question.

Additionally, we provide an interface for customers to upload their physical examination report to our platform, including the physical examination data of: heart rate, complete blood count, throat, urinalysis, ears, blood pressure, respiration rate, thyroid, nose, eyes, and etc. Figure 1 right is the user interface of physical examination report. Since different physical examination centers have their different physical examination report formats in PDF, therefore, our platform has the function to adjust to different PDF formats to extract physical examination data.

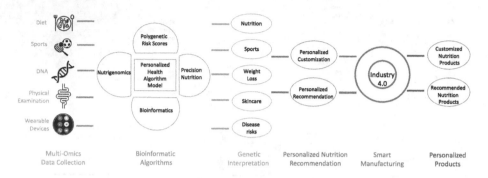

Fig. 2. Personalized nutrition intelligent service platform.

Figure 2 demonstrates the personalized nutrition intelligent service (PNIS) platform. Combing the genetic testing data, lifestyle data, physical examination data, PNIS platform will analyze the data together using bioinformatic algorithms, genetic interpretation algorithms, and nutrition requirement evaluation algorithms, to generate genetic interpretation reports, and further generate personalized nutrition report. Based on the personalized nutrition report, PNIS platform can order smart manufacturing machine in nutrition factory directly to produce unique customized nutrition product for each customer.

Genome sequencing has multiple platforms, different sequencing platform requires different laboratory experimental methods and process, and generate the sequence data in different formats. PNIS platform can start different bioinformatic pipelines to execute quality control and analyze the genomic sequencing data from different genome sequencing equipment.

PNIS platform can analyze tens of thousands of genetic testing samples in parallel, the bioinformatic analysis pipelines were implemented in cloud environment and scheduled by Kubernetes [22]. Each bioinformatic analysis software was en-capsuled in a docker engine, and multiple bioinformatic analysis software dockers can be chained together to form pipelines. When there are large amount of samples need to be analyzed, the platform will start more computing nodes elastically.

PNIS can generate multiple genetic interpretation reports, including precision nutrition, precision sports, weight loss, precision skincare, disease risks, mother care, men's health care, strengthen immune system, and anti-fatigue.

Based on the nutrigenetics, dietary guidelines, population nutrition big data, and customer's personal data, PNIS will compute and give a personalized nutrition report for each person. The personalized nutrition report includes two solutions: personalized customization, and personalized recommendation.

The personalized customization solution will order the smart manufacturing nutrition factory to produce personalized and customized daily nutritional supplement packs for each customer. Figure 3 left is the user interface that lists the recommended daily nutritional supplements; Fig. 3 middle shows the nutrition packs that going to be produced by factory, every user's name will be printed on the nutrition pack and our system allows each customer to define his/her name on the pack, the name of the tablets and capsules inside the nutrition pack will also be printed on the pack so that to let customer know the ingredients of the nutrition pack.

The personalized nutrition packs will be produced and then posted to user's home or office directly from the nutrition factory. The personalized recommendation solution lists the suggested foods that can help customer to supplement the nutrients that customer's body required, as described in Fig. 3 right.

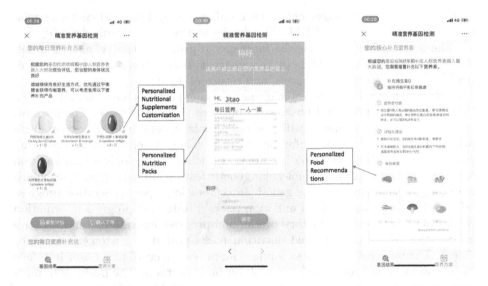

Fig. 3. The user interfaces of personalized customization and personalized recommendation reports.

4   Personalized Nutrition Service Business Process Management

To support the processing of large amount of samples in parallel and the collaboration with multiple business partners, we developed several systems including laboratory information management system (LIMS), bioinformatic pipelines scheduling system, genetic interpretation system, personalized nutrition report

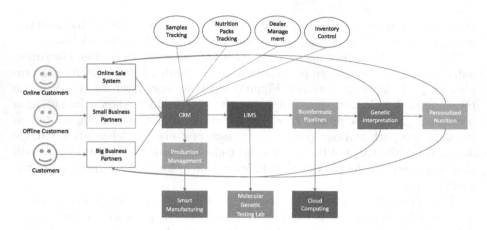

Fig. 4. Business process management systems for personalized nutrition service.

system, production management system, online sale system, and customer relation management system (CRM). Our business process is described in Fig. 4.

The online sale system has the functions of products display, placing order, shopping cart, multiple addresses management, order status tracking, logistics tracking, online payment, coupons, and return of goods.

The customer relationship management system provides both business to customer (B to C) service and business to business (B to B) service. The business to customer service connects with the online sale system, managing customer's personal information, order information, after sale service, as well as providing genetic testing sample tracking information (including the logistics information of sample mailed back to the molecular genetic testing laboratory, sample experiment progress information, and genetic interpretation report generation progress information) and personalized nutrition packs' production progress information (including manufacturing factory production progress information and logistics information of the personalized nutrition packs posted to customer's home or office). The business to business service can provide a customized user interface (using business partner's logo) for small business partners. The business to business service also provides APIs to communicate with big business partner's sale system to 1) provide sample tracking information, genetic interpretation reports, and personalized nutrition packs production information, as well as 2) exchange other information with big partner's system.

The LIMS manages all the sample experimental procedures such as sample reception, DNA extraction, library construction, polymerase chain reaction (PCR) [29] amplification, pooling, sequencing, sample tracking, and etc.

The bioinformatic pipelines scheduling system manages and schedules multiple bioinformatic pipelines to analyze large amount of genetic testing samples in parallel.

The genetic interpretation system interprets the analyzed genomic data, and generates different genetic interpretation reports such as precision nutrition genetic interpretation report, weight loss genetic interpretation report, precision skincare genetic interpretation report, and so on based on customer's order.

The personalized nutrition report system can generate tailored nutrition report for each person combing customer's genetic data, lifestyle data, and physical examination data.

The production management system will receive personalized nutrition packs production order from CRM system and then place the order (including customer's name, tablet and capsule information, customer's address information) to smart manufacturing nutrition factory to produce daily personalized nutrition packs. After production, the daily personalized nutrition packs will be mailed to user's home or office directly.

As decribed in Fig. 4, the systems are integrated together and can exchange data conveniently between each other. Each system was developed using Spring Boot [23], MyBatis [24], BootStrap [26], Html5, CSS [27], and javascript, and implemented as micro services in Spring Cloud [28]. All the systems have backup and standby systems to stabilize the service for personalized nutrition solution.

5 Conclusions

Currently, most of the nutrition products are one-size-fits-all, and the traditional nutrient recommendations are estimated to meet the requirements of a large group of population.

However, studies found that genetic background will affect the digestion, absorption, transport, metabolism and storage of food and nutrients; additionally, individual's lifestyles and health conditions also have impact on individual's nutrition requirement. Therefore, different individuals should supplement different kinds and different amounts of foods and nutrients.

In this paper, based on nutrigenetics and nutriology, we developed a personalized nutrition intelligent service (PNIS) platform. PNIS collects individual's genetic data through genetic testing and bioinformatic analysis, harvests lifestyle data through food frequency questionnaires, and retrieves individual's physical examination data through individual's uploading of physical examination report. Through bioinformatic analysis and genetic interpretation, PNIS generates genetic interpretation reports for each person, and further combines lifestyle data and physical examination data to analyze and generate personalized nutrition reports. Based on personalized nutrition report, the smart manufacturing nutrition factory will produce daily customized nutrition packs for each consumer. To verify the effectiveness of our personalized nutrition solution, we have collaborated with a physical examination center to conduct a population cohort study, after personalized nutrition supplementation, the result showed that our personalized nutrition solution could effectively supplement the nutritional needs of consumers.

We also developed multiple information systems such as online sale system, CRM system, LIMS and so on to support the business process management of large amount of samples. The systems have been delivered online and can provide service for tens of thousands of customers in parallel in one day.

We will continue to optimize our personalized nutrition solution by analyzing more individual's personal data such as the sensor data of sports, sleep, and etc.

Acknowledgment. This research project is supported by Science Foundation of Beijing Language and Culture University (supported by "the Fundamental Research Funds for the Central Universities") (Approval number: 22YJ080008)

References

1. Dietary Reference Intakes (DRIs). https://www.nal.usda.gov/fnic/dietary-reference-intakes. Accessed 2 May 2022
2. Wu, X., Cheng, J., Yang, K.: Vitamin D-related gene polymorphisms, plasma 25-Hydroxy-Vitamin D, cigarette smoke and non-small cell lung cancer (NSCLC) risk. Int. J. Mol. Sci. **17**(10), 1597 (2016)
3. Lange, C.M., Bojunga, J., Ramos-Lopez, E., et al.: Vitamin D deficiency and a CYP27B1-1260 promoter polymorphism are associated with chronic hepatitis C and poor response to interferon-alfa based therapy. J. Hepatol. **54**(5), 887–893 (2011)
4. Malik, S., Fu, L., Juras, D.J., et al.: Common variants of the vitamin D binding protein gene and adverse health outcomes. Crit. Rev. Clin. Lab. Sci. **50**(1), 1–22 (2013)
5. Irimie, A.I., Braicu, C., Pasca, S., et al.: Role of key micronutrients from nutrigenetic and nutrigenomic perspectives in cancer prevention. Medicina (Kaunas) **55**(6), 283 (2019)
6. Wjst, M.: Variants in the vitamin D receptor gene and asthma. BMC Genet. **6**(2) (2005)
7. Wang, T.J., Zhang, F., Richards, J.B., et al.: Common genetic determinants of vitamin D insufficiency: a genome-wide association study. Lancet **376**(9736), 180–188 (2010)
8. Yoon, B.W., Shin, H.T., Seo, J.: Risk allele frequency analysis of single-nucleotide polymorphisms for Vitamin D concentrations in different ethnic group. Genes **12**(10), 1530 (2021)
9. Sallinen, R.J., Dethlefsen, O., Ruotsalainen, S., et al.: Genetic risk score for serum 25-Hydroxyvitamin D concentration helps to guide personalized Vitamin D supplementation in healthy Finnish adults. J. Nutr. **151**(2), 281–292 (2021)
10. Borel, P., Desmarchelier, C., Nowicki, M., Bott, R., Tourniaire, F.: Can genetic variability in α-tocopherol bioavailability explain the heterogeneous response to α-tocopherol supplements? Antioxid. Redox Signal. **22**(8), 669–678 (2015)
11. iScan System. https://www.illumina.com/systems/array-scanners/iscan.html. Accessed 2 May 2022
12. Novaseq. https://www.illumina.com/systems/sequencing-platforms/novaseq.html. Accessed 2 May 2022
13. AutDB: a Genetic Database for Autism Spectrum Disorders. http://www.mindspec.org/products/autdb/. Accessed 8 May 2022
14. DisGeNET - a database of gene-disease associations. https://www.disgenet.org/dbinfo. Accessed 8 May 2022
15. Pinero, J., Bravo, A., Queralt-Rosinach, N., Gutierrez-Sacristan, A., et al.: DisGeNET: a comprehensive platform integrating information on human disease-associated genes and variants. Nucleic Acids Res. **45**(D1), D833–D839 (2017)

16. OMIM-Online Mendelian Inheritance in Man. https://www.omim.org/. Accessed 8 May 2022
17. Amberger J. S., Hamosh A.: Searching online Mendelian inheritance in man (OMIM): A knowledgebase of human genes and genetic phenotypes. Curr. Protoc. Bioinform. **58**, 1.2.1–1.2.12 (2017)
18. WeChat open platform. https://open.weixin.qq.com/. Accessed 8 May 2022
19. Johns, R., Kusuma, J., Lie, A., Shiao, S.P.K.: Validation of macro- and micronutrients including methyl donors in social ethnic diets using food frequency questionnaire and nutrition data system for research (USDA computerized program). SDRP J. Food Sci. Technol. **3**(4), 417–430 (2018)
20. Affret, A., Fatouhi, D.E., Dow, C., Correia, E., Boutron-Ruault, M.C., Fagherazzi, G.: Relative validity and reproducibility of a new 44-Item diet and food frequency questionnaire among adults: online assessment. J. Med. Internet Res. **20**(7), e227 (2018)
21. Thompson, F.E., Subar A.F.: Chapter 1 - Dietary Assessment Methodology. Nutrition in the Prevention and Treatment of Disease, 4th edn. Academic Press, ISBN: 9780128029282 (2017)
22. Kubernetes. https://kubernetes.io/. Accessed 8 May 2022
23. Spring Boot. https://spring.io/projects/spring-boot Accessed 10 May 2022
24. MyBatis. https://mybatis.org/mybatis-3/. Accessed 10 May 2022
25. HTML Living Standard. https://html.spec.whatwg.org/. Accessed 10 May 2022
26. What is Bootstrap? https://www.w3schools.com/whatis/whatis_bootstrap.asp. Accessed 10 May 2022
27. Starting with HTML + CSS. https://www.w3.org/Style/Examples/011/firstcss.en.html. Accessed 10 May 2022
28. Spring Cloud. https://spring.io/projects/spring-cloud. Accessed 10 May 2022
29. Lorenz T.C.: Polymerase chain reaction: basic protocol plus troubleshooting and optimization strategies. J. Vis. Exp. (63), e3998 (2012)

Electric Monitoring System for Residential Customers Using Wireless Technology

Jorge Buele[1,3] (ID), Juan Carlos Morales-Sánchez[2], José Varela-Aldás[1,3] (ID), Guillermo Palacios-Navarro[3] (ID), and Manuel Ayala-Chauvin[1,4](✉) (ID)

[1] SISAu Research Group, Facultad de Ingeniería y Tecnologías de la Información y la Comunicación, Universidad Tecnológica Indoamérica, Ambato 180103, Ecuador
{jorgebuele,josevarela,mayala}@uti.edu.ec
[2] Universidad Técnica de Ambato, Ambato 180206, Ecuador
jmorales3565@uta.edu.ec
[3] Department of Electronic Engineering and Communications, University of Zaragoza, 44003 Teruel, Spain
guillermo.palacios@unizar.es
[4] Centro de Investigaciones de Ciencias Humanas y de la Educación, Universidad Tecnológica Indoamérica, Ambato 180103, Ecuador

Abstract. Power grids continue to develop and it is increasingly difficult to guarantee the quality of service offered to the user. In several developing countries, consumption is calculated on the basis of visual inspection, which is prone to errors. Consequently, this document outlines the construction of electrical consumption telemetering equipment. This is designed to reduce human error through manual measures and have a web backup that can be accessed from anywhere. To develop the prototype voltage and current sensors are used, and the signal is conditioned for the control stage. The processing unit is the Arduino Mega embedded board, which incorporates a GPRS Shield (General Packet Radio Services) that handles communication with a LAMP server (Linux, Apache, MySQL, PHP) connected to the Internet. It also incorporates a block of connection and disconnection of the electrical service that would leave the whole house without service. Two functionalities are used to present the data, one is local on the LCD display of the equipment installed in the home (user) and the second is remote access to a website (server). The results show that in comparison with a standard voltage device it presents an error of 0.28% and 4.12% in current. In this way, the use of this prototype for real-time monitoring of electricity consumption is validated, since it works similarly to a conventional one.

Keywords: Electrical networks · Telemetry · LAMP

1 Introduction

The rapid growth of electrical networks has made it difficult to monitor their quality That has been replaced by the development of smart grids (SG) [1]. Their purpose is to support today's complex electrical systems, providing greater reliability and safety [2].

O. Gervasi et al. (Eds.): ICCSA 2022 Workshops, LNCS 13381, pp. 560–575, 2022.
https://doi.org/10.1007/978-3-031-10548-7_41

With information channels, you can learn about supplier and customer requirements for improved system efficiency and value for money. Implementation of the technology in existing networks could reduce existing emissions by 5% or more according to research described in [1]. The main issues are sudden power outages affecting industrial activities worldwide. It has a direct impact on the economy that needs electricity to develop its activities [3]. Consequently, investigations have been conducted when smart grids (SG) are used to prevent power outages, as in [4].

In conventional networks is not precisely known as customer load consumption and trends. Other factors include system congestion, obsolete infrastructure, lack of maintenance, increased demand, and lack of investment. Monitoring allows to define the places where the demand is highest, as well as the schedules and their frequency, and to manage accordingly an adequate decision. Conventional active energy meters register information on an energy meter that is read monthly by company personnel. Thus, a form is generated by the department, where this information is available to the user after the end of the month. It is very common for the supplier not to obtain the actual reading numbers and to make an approximate estimate of consumption whereas the user only knows the consumption produced at home at the end of each month. It is difficult to define whether there are defects in the home network or heavy consumption in the devices to damage them [5].

Nowadays, efforts have been made to improve the performance of this equipment by combining advances in information and communication technologies (ICT). In addition, the problems mentioned above have promoted the development of several investigations where innovative technological proposals are made. The use of smart meters has gained notoriety among consumers as exposed in [6]. In [7], the acceptance of this equipment in Malaysia is described, demonstrating the interest of users in energy-saving and their remarkable environmental awareness. Similarly, [8] shows that smart meters are widely used in the European Union, as a tool to reduce costs. The surveys were carried out to reveal the desire of households to acquire these devices and the need to incorporate more tools to take care of the environment. Not only do users require service improvements, but providers constantly lose resources to non-technical losses (NTL). Therefore, in [9] they have implemented a control algorithm based on hybrid deep neural networks that allow the detection of operating problems and anomalies in smart meters. This proposal does not require data pre-processing, which simplifies the system that shows good results.

In many Latin American countries, the measurement of monthly electricity consumption is manual and prone to human error. This is adhered the failures described above do not allow evidence of reality and service providers make an inefficient estimate of monthly consumption. Nor is there a mechanism that allows the automatic disconnection or connection of the electrical service for customers who have not paid their bills on time. For this reason, the need to implement smart devices for telemetering consumption in real-time, which emit alarms in the event of problems, has become evident. Current commercial equipment is expensive and its integration with the current system would mean a significant investment. This results in technological stagnation for nations with limited resources and higher charges for consumers. That is why, in this research, it is proposed to develop a meter for residential electricity. Thus, daily consumption can be evidenced and reported when there are signs of damage to the system or the internal connections of the home. As a hypothesis, it is expected that the built device will have a good performance, with an error of less than 5% compared to a commercial device.

This document consists of four sections, including the introduction in Sect. 1. Section 2 describes the materials and methods used and Sect. 3 the results. Finally, conclusions are presented in Sect. 4.

2 Methods and Materials

The electrical energy telemetry equipment is made up of three main blocks: measurement equipment, communication, and the server. This is indicated in Fig. 1 which shows the general diagram for electrical telemetry.

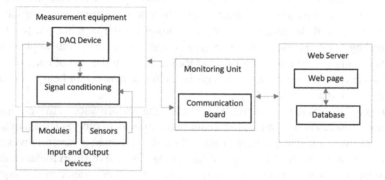

Fig. 1. Block diagram telemetering equipment.

2.1 Measurement Equipment

The measurement equipment is a set of electronic elements, designed to be installed independently in the home. Its purpose is to collect information on current and voltage sensors to send them to the server through the communication board.

Data Acquisition. For this, there is a sensing stage, hardware data acquisition, and software information processing. The voltage sensor is responsible for providing a signal that can be read by the microcontroller and used to calculate power consumption. The voltage transformer was selected since it measures AC voltage directly from the electrical network, which works at a nominal 120 V. For total current measurement, the SCT013-000 alternating current sensor is used, which detects variations in magnitude and generates a proportional signal that can be voltage, analog current or a digital signal. This hall effect type sensor has a clamp-like structure that facilitates its installation on the phase or neutral line and can measure up to 100 A.

Signal Conditioning. This stage performs a signal preparation that is used as a current limiting and coupling circuit, in addition to standardizing the data from the sensors. The current sensor has an output of 500 mA for a current of 100 A, so its conditioning is done through a shunt resistor (RL) where the voltage drop is measured. Two 470 KΩ resistors are used and the voltage is measured at RL, which is linked to one microcontroller port. A controller with a 10-bit ADC converter is used, that is, at the time of quantization of the analog signal, it is represented in values from 0 to 1023. A similar circuit is used for conditioning the voltage signal, considering that the transformer output is 12 VAC when there is 120 VAC at its input. To reduce this voltage, a voltage divider is used between resistors, while the remaining resistors generate a DC component of 2.5 V, which is the midpoint of the microcontroller's analog pin input signal.

2.2 Monitoring Unit

The microcontroller is the specialized hardware that is responsible for processing the data delivered by the conditioning stage after sensing. It executes all kinds of calculations, processes, and required instructions. The Arduino Mega 2560 was selected as it has 54/54 digital I/O pins and 16 analog input pins, I2C, EMI, SPI and USART interfaces. Also, an analog converter with a resolution of 10 bits, as indicated above. Using the DS1307 module, it is possible to obtain date and time data in real-time, using I2C communication with the processor unit. This information is kept up-to-date as it has a built-in battery that maintains power when the main power is off. Using the Arduino compatible SIM900 SIMCOM module provides wireless communication via the GSM/GPRS cellular network. This is because no data transport network of its own connects the meter to the webserver. In addition, its coverage range is practically global since it communicates through the existing mobile network. To register on the mobile network, it is necessary to use a sim from any local operator that is compatible with the module.

This information obtained is registered using the Micro SD module that uses the SPI communication protocol compatible with Arduino. The time, date, voltage, current, and consumption data are stored here. Finally, a two-channel contact relay module is incorporated, with an output of 10 A for a 250 VAC input. In the prototype, it is used as a control to perform a disconnection/connection of the electrical service in the terminal block of the energy meter. This is when the user is in default due to non-payment of their service bill on time, prior authorization from the electricity distribution company. The display screen is used to present the electrical energy data that is accumulated in the controller. Therefore, a 16×2 LCD with I2C communication has been chosen, which facilitates the exchange of information with Arduino.

2.3 Software

Data Processing. A program was developed in the Arduino development environment (IDE). The microcontroller inputs and outputs are configured, and the ports for serial communication with the modules and communication with the webserver connection manager module are initialized. The calculation of current, voltage, and power consumption is performed in a script. Furthermore, communication is established with the real-time module to request the time and date. The data is saved in a micro SD memory as a backup and has two display methods. They can be viewed locally on a liquid crystal display and also through a web server from any browser.

Server. For the management of information, a concept called client-server architecture is used. From a communications standpoint, a server process listens on a TCP communications port (by default, 80), and waits for connection requests from Web clients. Once the connection is established, the TCP/IP protocol is responsible for maintaining the communication and guaranteeing an error-free data exchange; to access the server you need an internet domain, without this, it is not possible to access the information that is stored in a database, to be able to communicate the client uses HTTP. This model attempts to provide usability, flexibility, interoperability, and scalability in communications.

The LAMP server functions are programmed on one machine and the other operates as a client. The server is Apache, which operates under the HTTP hypertext transfer protocol, keeping the information available 24 hours a day, with a secure connection that prevents possible failures or errors in the services. Once the Apache package is installed, the static IP of the computer is configured, this address will be the one used to access the server. To check that the Apache installation was successful, you can enter the server address from a web browser and the configured message will be displayed. All data on power, consumption, voltage, date, and time, reach the server via the Internet.

Client. A web browser must be used which must be installed in the application layer on the client-side, HTTP is based on simple request/response operations. The client establishes a connection to the server and sends a message with request data, while the server replies with a similar message, containing the status of the operation and its possible result. All operations can attach an object or resource on which they act; each web object (HTML document, media file, or CGI application) is known by its URL. The web browser that is used can be any, but it will depend on the platform or device that is used to request the server. This guarantees that regardless of the operating system, the generated information will be displayed transparently. The client manages all the functions related to data handling and display, so they are developed on platforms that allow the construction of graphical user interfaces, as well as access to services distributed anywhere in the network.

Database. The database management system used is MariaDB, which fulfills the same functions as MySQL, including important improvements such as compatibility with multiple storage managers, faster queries and subqueries, open-source code, and fewer errors. Once installed, the system will ask you to provide a password for the root user and when the service is restarted it is already operational.

2.4 Implementation

For the implementation, a connection diagram is made that is detailed in Fig. 2. In the diagram, you can see the location of each element used in the development of the prototype. The embedded Arduino mega 2560 card is in charge of executing all the mathematical operations and the program that controls the inputs and outputs. There is also a SIMCOM 900 wireless communication module that establishes communication via GPRS with the webserver. Additional two STC 013-100 current sensors and two 120 VAC-12 VAC voltage sensors are responsible for sending electrical signals to the data acquisition card. The DS1307 real-time module provides the time and date, an 8 GB micro SD module for recording electrical parameters, a relay module responsible for connecting and disconnecting the user, and an LCD screen to display electrical consumption.

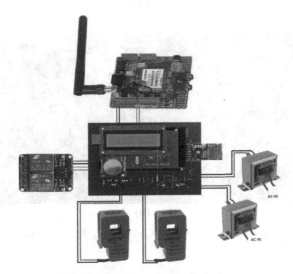

Fig. 2. Prototype electronic design.

Continuing with the implementation process, begins with the conditioning of the sensors, for this, a PCB is made, as shown in Fig. 3(a) The PCB is mounted on top of the Arduino Mega 2560 development board; With this, compact and functional equipment is obtained. In conditioning, a direct connection is made pins A0, A1, A4 and A5 are taken. The current and voltage sensors are installed at the terminal board of the conventional electric energy meter as indicated in Fig. 3(b).

Data Transmission. For data transmission, the prototype was programmed to send the information to the server at intervals of 1 min. It should be noted that the data sending time can be configured according to the system requirements. Once the connection with the webserver database is established, a table assigned for registration is entered and the entered data is saved. Figure 4 shows the table assigned to this record, which contains 7 fields. In order, they are user ID (integer), phase 1 and phase 2 utility voltage values

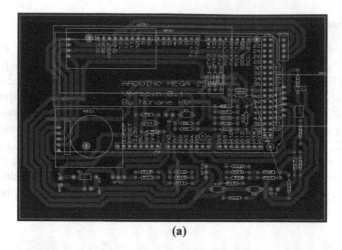

(a)

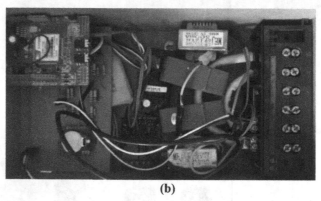

(b)

Fig. 3. Prototype electronic design. Arduino Conditioning-DAQ Shield: (a) PCB design. (b) Actual implementation.

assigned as Vrms1 and Vrms2 respectively (units are in V). The fourth column records the power (Watts) and the fifth the accumulated electrical consumption (kWh). The sixth column indicates the address where the meter is installed (location) and the last column records the date and time when all this information was taken.

3   Results

3.1   Voltage Measurement

For the execution of the tests, the measurement equipment was installed in a house and the values of voltage, current, and power were analyzed. These measurements were taken at the input terminal blocks of the prototype, previously connected to the electrical network that supplies a home. For the voltage sensor, the data displayed on the screen of the remote measurement equipment is compared with the values measured with a Fluke

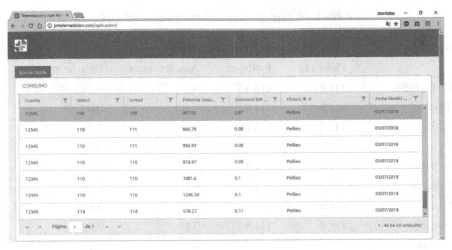

Fig. 4. Consumption information on the website.

111 multimeter (pattern). Table 1 shows the average voltage values of 10 measurements for each of the 12 items evaluated and the absolute and relative errors calculated for each sample using (1) and (2). The similarity in the measurements can be appreciated in a better way in Fig. 5. Voltage values remain similar when connecting different types of loads, with semi-industrial equipment generating a slight voltage drop. The measurements made with the prototype show a relative error of less than 0.3%, which allows inferring that there is a good accuracy. It should be clarified that the Fluke device is only used as a reference to analyze the measurements obtained, but it does not function by itself as a measurement device similar to the one proposed.

$$\text{Absoluteerror} = |V_{\text{PROTOTYPE}} - V_{\text{COMMERCIALMETER}}| \tag{1}$$

$$\text{Relativeerror} = (\text{Absoluteerror}/V_{\text{COMMERCIALMETER}}) * 100\% \tag{2}$$

3.2 Current Measurement

Similarly, a comparison of the measurements of the prototype and a commercial equipment is made. A Fluke 322 clamp meter was used, which has an AC measurement range of 400A with an accuracy of 2% ±5 digits, in frequency from 45 to 65 Hz and 2,5% from 65 to 400 Hz. Table 2 shows the respective values and errors, while Fig. 6 shows their graphic representation. The current values obtained by the prototype tend to approach the values of the measuring instrument. However, when using a Hall Effect current sensor, the measured value can vary due to poor handling or impurities (garbage in the ferrite) found in its core, causing measurement errors when the current values are small. This percentage error decreases when the connected load is greater, reaching a

Table 1. Voltage measurement multimeter/prototype.

Appliance	Voltage measurement		Voltage error	
	Fluke 111	Prototype	Absolute error	Relative error [%]
DVD reader	115,6	115,3	0,3	0,26
Talking	115,0	114,9	0,1	0,09
Saving focus	115,0	115,1	0,1	0,09
TV	114,1	114,4	0,3	0,26
Soldering iron	114,9	114,7	0,2	0,17
Refrigerator	113,4	113,2	0,2	0,18
Blender	114,5	114,4	0,1	0,09
Washer	114,6	114,5	0,1	0,09
Sewing machine	114,1	113,9	0,2	0,18
Cloth cutter	114,4	114,1	0,3	0,26
Heater	111,0	110,9	0,1	0,09
Industrial iron	109,9	109,6	0,3	0,27
Motor	105,4	105,7	0,3	0,28

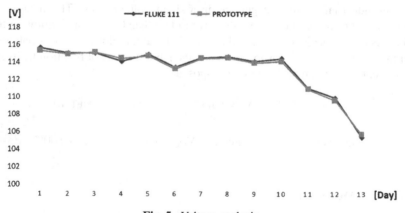

Fig. 5. Voltage analysis.

relative error of 0,14%, *i.e.,* behavior is close to optimal. With respect to Table 1 it can be seen that now the current values do vary considerably according to the connected load. When small equipment is connected, the current consumption is low, while when larger equipment such as a washing machine is operating, the current is higher.

3.3 Power Calculated

In the area of electrical consumption, it is usual to know the power consumed by a device, because the energy consumption will be based on this. The power of an electrical device

Table 2. Current measurement multimeter/prototype.

Appliance	Voltage measurement		Voltage error	
	Fluke 322	Prototype	Absolute error	Relative error [%]
DVD reader	0,12	0,12	0,00	0,00
Talking	0,11	0,13	0,02	18,18
Saving focus	0,17	0,19	0,02	11,76
TV	0,31	0,34	0,01	9,68
Soldering iron	0,32	0,35	0,03	9,37
Refrigerator	1,82	1,92	0,1	5,49
Blender	1,94	2,02	0,08	4,12
Washer	2,23	2,27	0,04	1,79
Sewing machine	2,75	2,78	0,03	1,09
Cloth cutter	4,55	4,59	0,04	0,88
Heater	6,87	6,83	0,04	0,58
Industrial iron	8,36	8,42	0,06	0,72
Motor	14,61	14,59	0,02	0,14

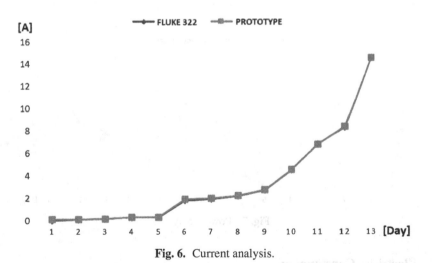

Fig. 6. Current analysis.

is the product of the voltage (V) to which it is connected and the intensity of the current (I) passing through it, as shown in the equation in (3). For the power comparison, the average voltage and current values from the previous tables were used. The data is presented in Table 3 and graphically in Fig. 7.

$$P = V * I \tag{3}$$

Table 3. Power calculated.

Appliance	Voltage measurement		Voltage error	
	Calculated	Prototype	Absolute error	Relative error [%]
DVD reader	13,872	12,683	1,18	0,00
Talking	12,65	14,937	2,28	1,99
Saving focus	19,55	21,869	2,31	2,02
TV	35,371	38,896	3,52	3,09
Soldering iron	36,768	40,145	3,37	2,94
Refrigerator	206,388	217,344	10,95	9,66
Blender	222,13	231,088	8,95	7,82
Washer	255,558	259,915	4,35	3,80
Sewing machine	313,775	316,642	2,86	2,51
Cloth cutter	520,52	523,719	3,19	2,80
Heater	762,57	757,447	5,12	4,62
Industrial iron	918,764	922,832	4,06	3,70
Tape recorder	1539,894	1542,163	2,26	2,15
Average				3,62

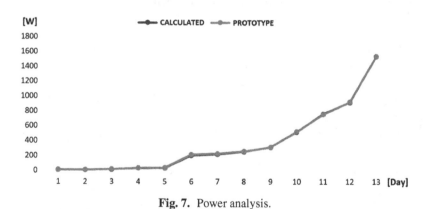

Fig. 7. Power analysis.

3.4 Electricity Consumption

Subsequently, to compare the measurement of electricity consumption, standard equipment from the local service provider was used (electronic two-phase measurement of electrical energy). The data from six days were evaluated, obtaining the data shown in Table 4. The equipment taken as a pattern only displays whole figures, while the prototype has decimal figures, presenting an average error of 3.42%.

Figure 8 shows voltage variations suffered by the electrical network during certain time intervals, a phenomenon known as voltage profile. The evaluation interval is from

Table 4. Comparison of consumption measurements.

Day	Commercial meter	Prototype	Absolute error	Relative error [%]
1	0	0,0	0,0	0,00
2	1	0,9	0,1	4,30
3	3	3,1	0,1	5,00
4	7	7,1	0,1	2,50
5	10	9,9	0,1	3,30
6	15	15,1	0,1	2,00
Average				3,42

17:27 to 17:38. Changes in the network voltage reading are observed and then its return to the initial state during another time interval. Similarly, in Fig. 9 an overview of the power profile corresponding to the load connected in the prototype is presented. As in the previous figure, jumps are observed that are generated by the change in the load of the dwelling.

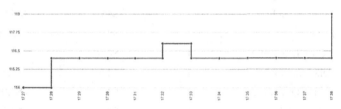

Fig. 8. Voltage profile.

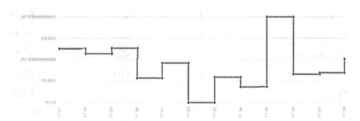

Fig. 9. Load power profile.

Within Fig. 10 there is an orange box that shows the accumulated consumption of electrical energy [kWh], which is stored in the database and changes as energy is consumed in the home.

3.5 Cost Analysis

Based on the budget indicated in Table 5, it has been established that the approximate cost of the implemented prototype is $167, a value that justifies all the characteristics

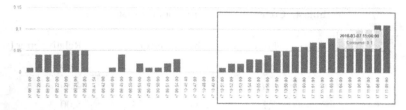

Fig. 10. Accumulated consumption.

presented. This provides a more accessible alternative through the use of free hardware and software.

Table 5. Summary of costs of materials used.

Item	Description	Amount	Unit value	Total value
1	Voltage sensor	2	$10	$20,00
2	Current sensor	2	$15	$30,00
3	Arduino Mega 2560	1	$12,5	$12,50
4	GPRS module	1	$45	$45,00
5	LCD	1	$8	$8,00
6	I2C LCD module	1	$3,5	$3,50
7	Relay module	1	$4,5	$4,50
8	MicroSD module	1	$4	$4,00
9	RTC module	1	$4,5	$4,50
10	Battery	1	$7,5	$7,50
11	Resistor	32	$0,1	$3,20
12	Capacitor	4	$0,1	$0,40
13	Male sprat	1	$2,5	$2,50
14	Case	1	$10	$10,00
	PCB	1	$3	$3,00
Total				$167,00

Given that the average useful life of this type of equipment is established at 10 years, the time required to recover the investment is analyzed. The internal rate of return expressed in Table 6 refers to the current value of the measurement equipment, in each year until its useful life is fulfilled, at the end of the 10 years it will have a residual value of $42,70.

Table 6. Internal rate of return.

Year	Operational flows	t	1+r	(1+r)t	1/(1+r)t	BN*(1/(1+r))t
0	−$167,00	1	1,08	1,00	1,00	−$167,00
1	$30,1	2	1,08	1,08	0,93	$27,9
2	$30,1	2	1,08	1,17	0,86	$25,8
3	$30,1	3	1,08	1,26	0,79	$23,9
4	$30,1	4	1,08	1,36	0,74	$22,1
5	$30,1	5	1,08	1,47	0,68	$20,5
6	$30,1	6	1,08	1,59	0,63	$19,0
7	$30,1	7	1,08	1,71	0,58	$17,6
8	$30,1	8	1,08	1,85	0,54	$16,3
9	$30,1	9	1,08	2,00	0,50	$15,1
10	$30,1	10	1,08	2,16	0,46	$21,7
Residual value						$42,70

3.6 Discussion

One point that should be highlighted is how the technology is reaching all households, institutions and industries around the world. Smart meters are already a reality of common use in Europe as shown in [6, 8]. Similarly, in Asia they are having a good acceptance due to the benefits they have presented for a better monitoring of existing networks [7]. It should be noted the importance that smart devices have nowadays in the industry and in the home. Smart meters have greater interconnectivity with other elements of the house, which translates into greater convenience for the person. There is greater security, because the readings are now reliable, which translates into energy efficiency and therefore economic savings.

Temneanu & Ardeleanu [10] developed a smart meter for measuring the consumption of various electrical appliances, but they did not compare it with a commercial one, so we cannot compare it with ours either. Zainab et al. [11] developed a meter that incorporates distributed computing, however they focused on communication data and also do not allow a proper comparison. The equipment developed by Koutroumpina et al. [12] allows to identify when the appliance is off, this is due to the use of sensors with higher resolution. The results show an accuracy of 97%, however, they have not been compared with a standard equipment and because of its high cost it cannot be incorporated in the region of this study. Although it has not been possible to adequately compare this study with other similar studies, it is clear that there are different approaches and that the economic aspect must be considered in this case. However, there is much to be expanded in the future as technology advances.

4 Conclusions

Current distribution networks require renewal and the implementation of proposals that merge the conventional with technology. The theoretical foundation made it possible to demonstrate the need to change conventional electric meters, providing them with intelligence to enhance their performance. This document has described the process of designing and building a prototype for remote measurement that has been tested in a residence but can also be used in industrial environments. Through the measurement tests and when comparing it with a standard FLUKE 111 instrument, a difference of 0,3 V on average is observed, with an error of ±0.28% (in a range of 110 V a 130 V). The current tests with loads from 0 to 20 A presented an error of ±4,12% concerning the standard Fluke 321 equipment. The current measurement presents a greater error than the voltage measurement, this is attributed to the fact that the current sensor has a range of measurement of 0 a 100 A and it is less accurate to measure relatively low currents (less than 5 A).

The prototype calculates the instantaneous power using the measured current and voltage values. When performing the tests, the calculated error is 3,16%, this error for a measurement range between 0 and 1550 W. While when carrying out the consumption analysis, an error of 3,42% was generated, since the conventional meter only presents the information in whole figures, and the prototype if it has decimal figures. Despite this, it has been verified that this error does not affect the reading. It is recommended that this equipment be installed in a visible and easily accessible place with the transmission antenna since obstacles interfere with the cellular network signal.

For the use of the equipment, it must be considered that the design was made for the Latin American environment where it operates at a maximum of 220 V in residential meters, i.e., two phases and one neutral. In the case of replicating, it in Europe or other parts of the world, the necessary changes in the design must be considered. Also, to prevent injuries, the personnel making these connections must have electrical knowledge to couple the voltage sensors to the electrical network. Likewise, it is advisable to review the installation of the current sensors so that they do not present erroneous measurements and therefore an adequate calculation of the instantaneous power. Another advantage it has over commercial devices is the ease of its integration with other platforms because it is developed with free software. Greater security can also be added to the network, which is difficult on a standard device that is mass-produced. In case the DC and AC sources are different, the prototype should be adjusted according to the working conditions. If there are many variations in the network, a conditioning stage should be included to regulate the input to a reference value so that the rest of the system is not altered and can be coupled to the AC source.

The main limitation of this study is that the current sensor does not present ideal linearity at the output. Also, they cannot detect small voltage and current variations, so if there were small loads, they would be automatically disregarded. To carry out the measurements and reduce their error, other devices with a lower relative error could be evaluated, but which will increase the cost proportionally.

Acknowledgments. To the Universidad Tecnológica Indoamérica for its support and financing under the project "Big data analysis and its impact on society, education and industry".

References

1. Hledik, R.: How green is the smart grid? Electr. J. **22**, 29–41 (2009). https://doi.org/10.1016/j.tej.2009.03.001
2. Ayala, M., Huaraca, D., Varela-Aldás, J., Ordóñez, A., Riba, G.: Anthropization and growth of the electricity grid as variables for the analysis of urban infrastructure. Sustain. (2020). https://doi.org/10.3390/su12041486
3. Ayala-Chauvin, M., Kavrakov, B.S., Buele, J., Varela-Aldás, J.: Static reactive power compensator design, based on three-phase voltage converter. Energies **14**, 2198 (2021). https://doi.org/10.3390/EN14082198
4. Rahimi, S., Chan, A.D.C., Goubran, R.A.: Usage monitoring of electrical devices in a smart home. In: Proceedings of the Annual International Conference of the IEEE Engineering in Medicine and Biology Society EMBS, pp. 5307–5310 (2011). https://doi.org/10.1109/IEMBS.2011.6091313
5. Chaudhari, A., Mulay, P.: A bibliometric survey on incremental clustering algorithm for electricity smart meter data analysis. Iran J. Comput. Sci. **2**(4), 197–206 (2019). https://doi.org/10.1007/s42044-019-00043-0
6. Belton, C.A., Lunn, P.D.: Smart choices? An experimental study of smart meters and time-of-use tariffs in Ireland. Energy Policy **140**, 111243 (2020). https://doi.org/10.1016/j.enpol.2020.111243
7. Alkawsi, G.A., Ali, N., Baashar, Y.: An empirical study of the acceptance of IoT-based smart meter in Malaysia: the effect of electricity-saving knowledge and environmental awareness. IEEE Access. **8**, 42794–42804 (2020). https://doi.org/10.1109/ACCESS.2020.2977060
8. Rausser, G., Strielkowski, W., Štreimikienė, D.: Smart meters and household electricity consumption: a case study in Ireland. Energy Environ. **29**, 131–146 (2018). https://doi.org/10.1177/0958305X17741385
9. Buzau, M.M., Tejedor-Aguilera, J., Cruz-Romero, P., Gómez-Expósito, A.: Hybrid deep neural networks for detection of non-technical losses in electricity smart meters. IEEE Trans. Power Syst. **35**, 1254–1263 (2020). https://doi.org/10.1109/TPWRS.2019.2943115
10. Temneanu, M., Ardeleanu, A.S.: Hardware and software architecture of a smart meter based on electrical signature analysis. In: 2013 – 8th International Symposium On Advanced Topics In Electrical Engineering. ATEE 2013 (2013). https://doi.org/10.1109/ATEE.2013.6563499
11. Zainab, A., Refaat, S.S., Abu-Rub, H., Bouhali, O.: Distributed computing for smart meter data management for electrical utility applications. In: Proceedings of the 30th International Conference Cybernetics and Informatics, K I 2020 (2020). https://doi.org/10.1109/KI48306.2020.9039899
12. Koutroumpina, C., Sioutas, S., Koutroubinas, S., Tsichlas, K.: Evaluation of features generated by a high-end low-cost electrical smart meter. Algorithms. **14**, 311 (2021). https://doi.org/10.3390/a14110311

Computer-Aided Forensic Authorship Identification in Criminology

András Kicsi[1,2(✉)] , Péter Sánta[2], Dániel Horváth[2], Norbert Kőhegyi[2],
Viktor Szvoreny[2], Veronika Vincze[1] , Eszter Főző[3], and László Vidács[1,2]

[1] MTA-SZTE Research Group on Artificial Intelligence,
Tisza Lajos krt. 103, Szeged 6720, Hungary
{akicsi,vinczev,lac}@inf.u-szeged.hu
[2] Department of Software Engineering, University of Szeged,
Dugonics tér 13, Szeged 6720, Hungary
{speter,hoda,knorbert,szvoreny}@inf.u-szeged.hu
[3] Special Service for National Security, Törökvész út 32-34,
Bégu, Budapest 1022, Hungary
fozo.eszter@nbsz.gov.hu

Abstract. The increasingly anonymous methods people use to communicate in the modern world allow for more freedom of speech. The safety of anonymity, however, can enable criminals to cause harm to others through various means, such as blackmail, verbal abuse, threat letters and numerous other ways. These culprits, often hiding behind computer screens, can be extremely difficult to identify and especially difficult to find definitive proof of their wrongdoings. They are not completely untraceable, however, as they are bound to leave clues in the text, linking it to them. The way they phrase sentences, the words they use, how often they use them and other parts of their idiolect can be used to identify them and even connect them to other texts. Through analyzing the text, it becomes possible to catch these individuals. This analysis is neither simple nor cheap, the aid of linguistic experts is critical, and even they are likely to encounter difficulties. This article explores the way in which the work of such experts can be assisted through computer analysis based on machine learning techniques and the role Artificial Intelligence plays in bringing these criminals to justice. Our current paper investigates how linguistic features can be automatically extracted to be used in the field. Through a total of 61 real text artefacts written in the Hungarian language by four different individuals, we extract various syntactic and semantic linguistic features which reflect the author's idiolect and aid the expert's work. We demonstrate how the technique can aid author identification in criminology.

Keywords: Author identification · Stylometry · Criminalistics · Nlp

O. Gervasi et al. (Eds.): ICCSA 2022 Workshops, LNCS 13381, pp. 576–592, 2022.
https://doi.org/10.1007/978-3-031-10548-7_42

1   Introduction

When people talk on the Internet, they generally don't worry too much about the consequences of their comments, they feel safe since they are anonymous. On the one hand, this allows people to talk freely, be honest, to not worry about what others might think of them. On the other hand, this same safety can be exploited in dangerous ways. In the modern world, people are sending text messages anonymously all the time, be it through a forum, a chat room, or even through e-mail with a fake address. This is generally harmless, however, sometimes, things can go very wrong: what people can do with the anonymity they have ranges from lighter wrongdoings such as verbal abuse and deception to very severe crimes such as blackmail, stalking messages or even death threats. The thought of some person one doesn't even know stalking, or perhaps even threatening to harm an individual, can be quite frightening. Perhaps the better question to ask here, however, is not the "is it possible", but rather "how it is possible" to identify the authors of such a malicious message. In criminology, there are linguistic experts who are tasked with solving this problem. Their job is rather difficult and expensive, but it is very important, aiding them could be a worthwhile effort.

There are many features one can use to describe a text. For example, one can analyze how many words there are in a text, how many sentences, or perhaps the average length of these sentences. One can also investigate a text's semantics. For example, the text might be using overwhelmingly negative or positive words, or maybe it contains a lot of racist or aggressive remarks. These features, among others, are all parts of an author's idiolect, and many of them can be used to potentially get a hint about the writer's identity. While some of these are obvious indicators of an author's identity -such as the number of aggressive words they use-, some give more subtle clues about the writer: for example, somebody who uses complex sentences could be said to prefer writing in a live speech style [20].

These features -although very useful- can prove to take a lot of time and effort to extract from the text, and for this reason, automation of this process is crucial. This is where modern technology, equipped with artificial intelligence, can play a significant part. Using technology based on machine learning, we can not only speed up the process of said feature extraction, but we can also take a lot of burden off of the experts so that they can focus more on actually utilizing said features. Of course, it is critical for said systems to be as accurate as they can possibly be, in order for them to be reliable, as precision is of especially high importance in criminology.

Research surrounding the application of linguistic features has been done in several languages, including, for instance, German [9], where the author looked into the usefulness of certain features when it comes to identifying authors. They relied on likelihood ratios (or LR for short) for this purpose. However, in some languages -particularly Hungarian - less research has been done. In Hungarian, feature extraction has mainly been done by hand, and there are tools out there for linguistic analysis, for example, Laurence Anthony's software [2]. Considering how morphologically rich and complex this language is, the possibilities for automated linguistic feature extraction for forensic applications are vast, and research in this field is both highly motivated and necessary. In this article, we will detail our approach for this task aided by the Hungarian linguistic processing tool called magyarlanc, which was developed using machine learning [22], and inspect our system that allows experts to analyze texts through a graphical user interface. We will also be discussing the implications of our research and potential future directions.

2   Background

The basis of criminalistic or forensic linguistics is the unique use of a language (idiolect). An idiolect is a way a person uses a language, their relationship to it or even how they came to learn it. People master a language (in our case, the Hungarian language) to some degree through socializing. The tools it gives us are then varied, filtered and combined in our heads. The way we go about this can depend on our close environment, our social status, our education, what we read, how well we grasped the language, our age, our gender and other factors as well [19]. Some aspects of how we use a language depend on the topic or the text's genre, or maybe even the target audience, but other aspects can be subconscious decisions, such as repeating words, connectives and function words used, the complexity of the sentences, how often we use multiword expressions and phrasemes and the way we use them, etc. Experts compare the suspect's texts with the incriminating text using these features, then decide how likely it is that the authors match. Features influenced by subconscious decisions can be especially reliable for this goal, as they are much more difficult to fake. Comparisons in our case are primarily made on the morphological, syntactical, semantical and pragmatic levels, both quantitatively and qualitatively. The expert can also compare features of the suspect's text with features of a generalized corpus, then looks for any abnormalities, features that differ from the norm greatly.

Criminals acting in an online environment can, in most cases, be traced, and this approach is usually both faster and cheaper than analyzing texts with linguistic experts. However, this method of identifying criminals does not always work, especially with modern tools that mask the author's identity, such as virtual private networks (VPN) and browsers that enable anonymous communication; for example, The Onion Router [3]. In such cases, one may have to rely on analyzing the text itself. This does not come without its own difficulties, however, as texts of this nature are often very differently written than texts from the real world, such as ones people would send in a mail. When online, people usually write very casually, not paying much attention to punctuation or correct spelling. Slang is often used alongside emojis. Abbreviations are very common, affixes are somewhat ignored, words are often repeated, and sometimes even the language used is mixed: seeing IM (Instant Messaging) texts that are written in half English and half Hungarian is increasingly common. Even in these cases, identifying the author behind the anonymous messages can be of critical importance.

In many countries forensic linguistics is an active field of research [4,11,13, 15,17], and much work has been done regarding computer analysis for forensic purposes as well, with a wide range of bibliography [5,8,14,16,18,21], even examining cross-language methods [7,10]. In Hungary, however, the area is a lot less covered, with only six linguistic experts even being registered in The Ministry of Justice, and the only forensic institute working with linguistic experts is the Institute for Expert Services within the Special Service for National Security. It is no coincidence that research involving authorship analysis using computers is also done within the organization. Experiences of foreign partners and international research also help direct their own research in order to deliver to clients as efficiently as possible.

The organization's modernization in this field is moving in the following directions:

1. Computer text analysis: The first stage is to develop text analysis using computers on as many linguistic levels as possible. For texts that can be processed either manually or with existing software, this should be automated. Depending on the experiences, this could be followed by an attempt to implement feature extraction with computers from shorter or incomplete sentences as well.
2. Computer text comparison: Automatic one-to-one text comparisons could be implemented with an expert's control, utilizing computer analysis that reliably and effectively processes text on multiple linguistic levels. The expert could prioritize certain linguistic features by determining their value in distinguishing authors. The goal is to automate this as well, after some testing and fine-tuning.
3. Computer text comparison on an existing database: Point number two could serve as a basis for one-to-many text comparisons, which can then be used to compare newly written anonymous texts with texts from previous cases in order to find patterns and schemes (for example, one could infer some general traits of threat letters). It could also be used for serial offenders (the same person threatening/blackmailing/slandering other people, at different times, in different places) to identify reoccurring motifs. The goal is for a computer to make rankings of texts based on how similar they are (according to some kind of score).
4. LR-based ranking: Likelihood Ratio based identification using a population database (referential corpus). The computer compares the text in question both with a sample text and with the database, then outputs an LR value indicating how much more likely it is that the text is authored by the suspect instead of anyone else. This method is largely independent of the human expert. The computer determines whether the suspect is guilty or innocent. The introduction of this method to the field of expert linguistics is not underway yet; the composition of the populational database and the effectiveness and reliability of feature extraction are critical for this process.

The first stage of our current research involves developing computer analysis and comparisons, alongside making feature extraction require less and less

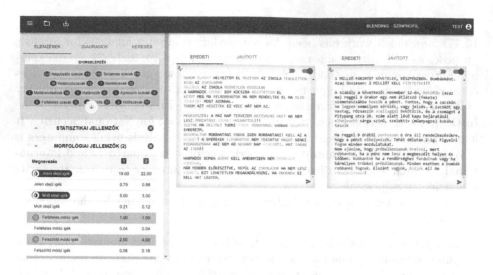

Fig. 1. A preview of the system in use.

human input. The extracted data should be statistically comparable in order to enable the computer to make a judgment about the likelihood of texts being written by the same authors, relying solely on statistical data.

3   Methods

In this section, we will be inspecting how our system operates and the possibilities it opens up to linguistic experts. We will demonstrate the system using example texts about bomb threats in Hungarian. We also present data on a real corpus on which experiences are to be conducted in the next section.

3.1   Automatized Extraction

As seen in Fig. 1, our system accepts one or two texts and then extracts their numerous linguistic features automatically. The features are categorized into nine different categories: statistical, morphological, part-of-speech, semantic (for example, aggressive words), semantic uncertainty (for example, peacock words), semantic emotions (for example, words used to express anger), syntactic and indices for textual structure, pragmatic, and finally spelling associated features. Next to each category's name, one can see how many features are currently selected, and one can deselect all of them at once with the X button.

The user can see the quantity associated with each feature for both texts side-by-side, making it simple to compare them. Where it is reasonable to show both a ratio and a quantity for a feature, both are shown as two separate features with the same name. However, the quantity features are easily distinguishable by their darker grey background. Clicking on features with a darker background

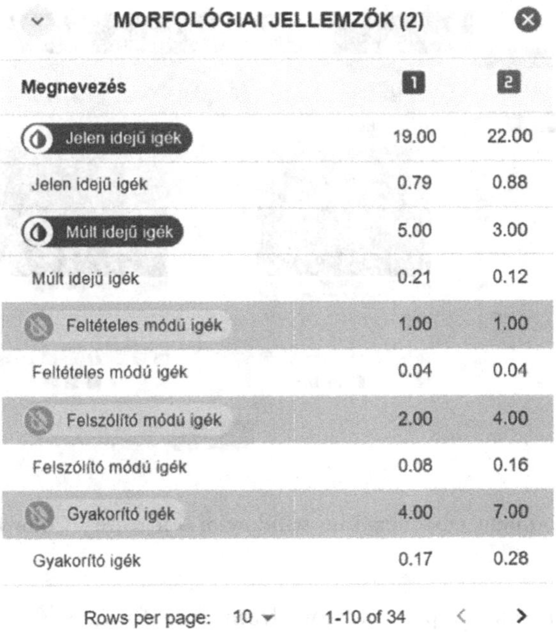

MORFOLÓGIAI JELLEMZŐK (2)		
Megnevezés	**1**	**2**
Jelen idejű igék	19.00	22.00
Jelen idejű igék	0.79	0.88
Múlt idejű igék	5.00	3.00
Múlt idejű igék	0.21	0.12
Feltételes módú igék	1.00	1.00
Feltételes módú igék	0.04	0.04
Felszólító módú igék	2.00	4.00
Felszólító módú igék	0.08	0.16
Gyakorító igék	4.00	7.00
Gyakorító igék	0.17	0.28

Rows per page: 10 ▾   1-10 of 34   <   >

Fig. 2. A closeup of features in a category, with two of them highlighted.

highlights the related tokens in the text: for example, by clicking on the past tense verbs feature, one can highlight all the past tense verbs in both texts. The system is made for Hungarian texts (to be used by the Hungarian Special Service for National Security), so the feature names are also Hungarian. Figure 2 demonstrates a possible setting. "Jelen idejű igék" means present tense verbs, while "Múlt idejű igék" means past tense verbs, and these are among the highlighted words. Negative words and misspelled words are also highlighted, the former with purple and the latter with green. The color which the user wants to highlight words can be freely adjusted, and they can also be highlighted by making them bold, italic or underlined. The configuration window can be seen in Fig. 3 If a word is highlighted multiple times (for example, if the word is a verb and also negative, and both verbs and negative words are highlighted), the colors are combined by default, but this behavior can also be configured.

Most of these features are calculated using magyarlanc [22], a Hungarian text analysis tool developed through machine learning. More simple features, such as dates (for example, the name of a month, or 2022-04-21) or racist words, are detected simply by using regular expressions or customizable word lists. The system can also detect location names, names of people or names of organizations with the aid of a Named-entity recognition (NER), using the huBERT [12] model. huBERT is a machine learning model based on the groundbreaking BERT

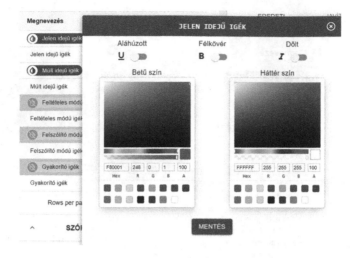

Fig. 3. The highlight customization window of a feature. (Color figure online)

(Bidirectional Encoder Representations from Transformers [6]). Unlike the regular BERT model, huBERT was trained specifically for the Hungarian language, on Hungarian corpora, using the structure and mechanics of BERT.

For texts that have very long sentences, text analysis with magyarlanc can occasionally take a long time, so there is an option to use fast-analysis on the text (this can be toggled in the upper-right corner of the text box with the left-side button). The fast analysis automatically puts punctuation marks after a certain number of tokens in the sentence if it is too long. This process is repeated until the sentence is deemed short enough for a fast analysis. Normally, the text is analyzed upon changing the contents of the text box and waiting for a few seconds, but this behavior can be disabled in favor of manually starting the analysis by using the right-side toggle in the upper-right corner of the text box.

For detecting misspelled words, we used HunSpell, a popular free spell checker and morphological analyzer library [1] with some rule-based distinctions. An example of detecting misspelled words can be seen in Fig. 4. The figure shows multiple misspelled words, "hétőfőn" is supposed to be "hétfőn", "szallaggal" is spelled with only one l ("szalaggal"), "elhejezett" is written with the wrong j/ly character (correctly, it is "elhelyezett"). In the Hungarian language, the letter "j" is sometimes written with the letter "ly" instead: it depends on the word which letter should be used. This can lead to spelling errors very often, so there is even a separate feature for this in our system, called "j-ly hibák" (j-ly errors). If the linguistic expert analyzing the text wishes to see the text written in the correct form, they can ask the computer to make a corrected version of the text, by pressing the button in the top left corner of the text box. Afterwards, the correct version of the text will appear in the separate "Javított" (corrected) tab.

Fig. 4. A closeup of an analyzed (left) and corrected (right) text. Misspelled words are highlighted with green. All the previously misspelled words are now spelled correctly. (Color figure online)

The corrected text is also made using Hunspell. It is important to have the option to correct texts automatically because some features will be more accurately evaluated in this form of the text. For example, misspelled verbs will not be recognized as verbs (as most of the time, the misspelled word is not even a proper, existing word in the language). For this reason, text analysis (except for spell checking, naturally) is automatically done on the corrected form of the text instead of the original form. The expert may also wish to see the corrected form of the text, so it is important to let them see that as well. This can be especially important for texts that have a great number of misspelled words. They might also want to correct the text (or some parts of the text) manually, instead of letting the computer handle it, so text in the corrected tab can be manually edited as well, and the automatic correction only shows in the text box after pressing the corresponding button.

In order to make the expert's work faster and smoother, there are several helper functions available in the system. The most significant differences are displayed in a quick preview as seen on the left side of Fig. 5. While using the system, the expert is also logged in with a profile that they can use to save highlight and word list configurations.

On the diagrams tab, visualized analysis of the data is also available, this is visible on the right side of Fig. 5.

Users can also search in the text in the search tab. While searching, they can use filters that examine whether certain words or lemmas of a specific POS type are within a given range. For example, if the text contains "three bombs, two bombs", and one searches for the "bomb" lemma, normally, they would find both occurrences. By using a filter such as "the word three must also appear before the word within a range of 1 token", only the first occurrence will be counted. An example is displayed in Fig. 6.

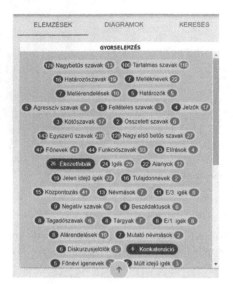 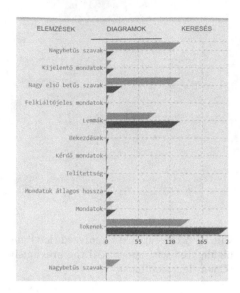

Fig. 5. Left: A quick overview of the analysis as seen in the system. Right: Diagrams of the system. Diagrams alternate between feature values and ratios (first diagram is for values, second is for ratios). Green bars are for the text in the left box, while blue bars are for the text on the right. Exact values can be seen by hovering the cursor over the bars. (Color figure online)

3.2   Experimental Corpus

During our experiments, we will examine how various linguistic features can help determine whether two corpora were authored by the same person and also how they can give hints about the author's identity. The texts themselves are written in the Hungarian language, but we provide a brief summary of their contents in English:

Corpus A has texts from postcards and letters written by a woman with a high school diploma as her highest form of education. She is jealous of her former partner's current relationship and strives to ruin it by sending anonymous messages regarding an affair to the man and his current partner. **Corpus B** contains mails sent by a hunter with a university degree. The man falsely accuses his hunting mates of illegally obtaining highly expensive deer horns. **Corpus C** contains letters and e-mails sent by a man. In these texts, he is blackmailing a bank's CEO, attempting to extort money, and threatening to expose their supposed tax fraud and misappropriation of public funds. His highest form of education is a university degree in economics. The last corpus, **corpus D**, contains postcards, letters and e-mails written by a woman with a university degree in liberal arts. She is jealous like author A and is in a similar situation. She, however, goes even further, going as far as sending defamatory texts to the new girlfriend's workplace and even sending bomb threats. She also uses many aliases, using both fictional and real (other people's) identities. She also sent anonymous letters and used a great number of different signatures, such as "a father", "a benefactor" or "a grandmother". The ages of all four authors are between 33 and 55 (middle-aged), and they all contain both handwritten and digital letters, except for corpus C, which doesn't contain handwritten texts. Further information about the corpus can be found in Table 1.

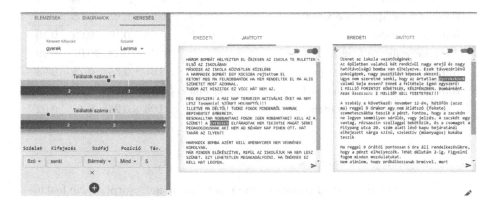

Fig. 6. An example of the advanced search. The lemma "gyerek" (child) is searched, and the word "senki" (nobody) has to appear in a range of 5 words in either direction. In this case, the POS type of the "senki" word is not considered. At the blue and red bars, the dot visualizes the location of the word in the text.

Table 1. Parameters of the corpus used in the experiments

Author	Number of tokens	Number of sentences	Number of documents
A	7 101	528	10
B	2 932	97	6
C	5 940	296	13
D	15 254	812	32
Total	31 227	1 733	61

4 Results

This section displays the most important results of the comparative analysis made between the texts of the four authors detailed above. Only the ratios of the features will be considered, as the available text between authors varies greatly, and the quantities of the linguistic features would reflect this greatly.

4.1 Statistical Features

Table 2 shows the quantified results of the most important statistical features. Note that the words length rate is calculated as follows: (total length of tokens, except for punctuations)/(total number of tokens − total number of punctuations)

Table 2. The most important statistical features.

Feature	A	B	C	D
Rate of lemmas	0.17	0.22	0.18	0.12
Saturation	1.06	2.45	1.58	0.84
Words length rate	5.39	7.02	6.38	5.77
Rate of fully uppercase words	0.04	0.03	0.05	0.06
Rate of capitalized words	0.08	0.10	0.09	0.10
Average sentence length	13.45	30.23	20.07	18.79
Rate of declarative sentences	0.61	0.55	0.75	0.93
Rate of sentences ending with an exclamation mark	0.33	0.20	0.12	0.05
Rate of interrogative sentences	0.06	0.26	0.14	0.02

4.2   Morphologic Features

Table 3 shows the quantified results of the most important morphologic features.

Table 3. The most important morphologic features. Sg-singular, Pl-plural.

Feature	A	B	C	D
Rate of present tense verbs	0.67	0.50	0.53	0.63
Rate of past tense verbs	0.34	0.49	0.48	0.38
Rate of conditional verbs	0.08	0.06	0.03	0.07
Rate of imperative verbs	0.07	0.05	0.08	0.09
Rate of frequentative verbs	0.13	0.11	0.17	0.17
Rate of causative verbs	0.00	0.02	0.01	0.01
Rate of modal verbs	0.02	0.02	0.07	0.03
Rate of 1Sg verbs	0.35	0.30	0.18	0.31
Rate of 2Sg verbs	0.10	0.00	0.01	0.09
Rate of 3Sg verbs	0.46	0.48	0.57	0.49
Rate of 1Pl verbs	0.04	0.00	0.07	0.03
Rate of 2Pl verbs	0.00	0.00	0.00	0.00
Rate of 3Pl verbs	0.05	0.22	0.17	0.09
Rate of superlatives	0.02	0.02	0.02	0.00
Rate of comparatives	0.05	0.02	0.03	0.04
Rate of plural nouns	0.08	0.08	0.12	0.14

4.3   Part-of-Speech Features

Table 4 shows the quantified results of the most important part-of-speech features.

Table 4. The most important part-of-speech features.

Feature	A	B	C	D
Rate of verbs	0.14	0.07	0.09	0.13
Rate of nouns	0.20	0.30	0.26	0.19
Rate of adjectives	0.06	0.07	0.07	0.06
Rate of numerals	0.01	0.01	0.01	0.01
Rate of adverbs	0.12	0.05	0.08	0.12
Rate of conjunctions	0.08	0.05	0.05	0.08
Rate of pronouns	0.08	0.05	0.04	0.11
Rate of proper nouns	0.00	0.04	0.02	0.00

4.4   Syntactic Features

Table 5 shows the quantified results of the most important syntactic features.

Note: the rate of clauses is calculated as follows: total number of clauses/total number of sentences

Table 5. The most important syntactic features.

Feature	A	B	C	D
Rate of subjects	0.05	0.03	0.06	0.06
Rate of objects	0.05	0.04	0.04	0.04
Rate of adverbials	0.04	0.02	0.02	0.04
Rate of attributives	0.05	0.08	0.07	0.05
Rate of coordinations	0.05	0.08	0.08	0.06
Rate of subordinations	0.05	0.03	0.03	0.05
Rate of clauses	2.12	2.67	2.31	2.64
Rate of simplex sentences	0.39	0.29	0.34	0.32
Rate of complex sentences	0.61	0.71	0.66	0.68
Rate of clauses in complex sentences	2.84	3.35	2.99	3.40
Rate of complex sentences with two clauses	0.30	0.25	0.30	0.23
Rate of complex sentences with three clauses	0.20	0.22	0.19	0.20
Rate of complex sentences with four clauses	0.05	0.14	0.10	0.14

4.5   Semantic Features

Table 6 shows the quantified results of the most important semantic features.

Table 6. The most important semantic features.

Feature	A	B	C	D
Rate of positive words	0.02	0.02	0.03	0.02
Rate of negative words	0.02	0.02	0.03	0.02
Rate of simplex words	1.00	0.98	0.99	0.99
Rate of compound words	0.02	0.04	0.03	0.02
Rate of content words	0.54	0.57	0.53	0.54
Rate of function words	0.46	0.43	0.47	0.46
Dividedness of sentence units	1.53	2.95	2.33	1.79
Saturation rate for sentence units	3.40	6.44	4.62	3.82
Contentness	7.22	17.20	10.69	10.08

4.6   Pragmatic Features

Table 7 shows the quantified results of the most important pragmatic features.

Table 7. The most important pragmatic features.

Feature	A	B	C	D
Rate of private verbs	0.16	0.08	0.13	0.16
Rate of public verbs	0.07	0.06	0.07	0.06
Rate of speech acts	0.20	0.15	0.14	0.19
Rate of punctuation	0.19	0.23	0.25	0.18

5   Discussion

Overall, between authors A, B, C and D, intuitively, authors B and C should be somewhat close as both their gender and education match, and the nature of their letters are also somewhat similar. Authors A and D are also very similar, as both are women and both are in a very similar situation: however, their degree of education differs, and their methods differ greatly as well. Generally, A and D -although similar- are not as close to each other as B and C, and looking at it as a whole, author A seems to be an odd one out in general, being the only one with only a high school diploma. We will now investigate how the results reflect this.

There are a number of interesting distinctions one can make between the four corpora by analyzing the results. Author B, for instance, seems to prefer writing long and complex sentences, which are also quite saturated. Not only are his sentences lengthy, but they also contain many meaningful words. This is all contrary to author A, who uses the shortest sentences amongst the four, and said sentences are also one of the least saturated: though D's sentences are a little less saturated even. The average length of the words used is also highest in the case of B and lowest in the case of A. The same goes for the rate of sentences with four clauses, which can be considered very complex. On the other hand, author A writes a lot of sentences with two clauses, she's only matched in this regard by author C, so one can't say that A avoids sentences with multiple clauses altogether, but she does seem to feel comfortable with less than four clauses. The rate of clauses shows that altogether, author A avoids complex sentences the most, and author B prefers them the most, although he's very closely matched with D. This may point to author D having a degree in liberal arts, which can also indicate a humanistic sense.

One should also note the different types of sentences the authors use. D appears to use declarative sentences the most. In fact, the vast majority of her sentences are declarative. One can also infer that B uses a lot of interrogative sentences, so it appears they tend to ask a lot of questions. As for exclamatory (and imperative and conditional) sentences, it appears that A prefers using them the most. It's an interesting contrast between her and D, as both are in a similar situation, yet D avoids them the most. Perhaps D attempts to mask her emotions more than A. She also uses a lot of aliases. It is apparent that she does try to cover her tracks.

One can also detect differences between the four by the way they use verb tenses. A and D both talk a lot more about the present than both B and C. The past tense appears to be preferred by B and C, compared to A and D. This is arguably somewhat of a surprise, as A and D would intuitively have a lot to reflect on, as they are both trying to revive a past relationship. However, neither seems to behave accordingly and instead, they appear to focus on the now in their texts. As for B and C, the most probable reason they both prefer the past tense is that they are both accusing another party of having done something, so they talk a lot about what another person has done in the past. Looking at it this way, it makes sense that A and D focus on the present, as in order to break up their ex's current relationship, they would probably prefer to point out flaws in their new relationship rather than the old one, and flaws in the people they are in the present. The usual verb tenses of one's text can indicate an underlying personal preference, but as it is visible, it is more likely to be influenced by the subject and goals of the text than stylistic choices.

Another point of interest is the person each author focuses on in their texts. A, B and D all seem to be focusing a lot on themselves, but C sticks out in this regard: he focuses on himself a lot less, only barely using first-person conjugated verbs compared to the other three. The rate of third-person verbs appears to indicate that all four focus on a third party a lot, especially C, but it's worth noting that in the Hungarian language, in formal writing, the second-person verb form is often discarded in favor of the third-person form. C actually does write in this manner, which is the true reason his rate of third-person verbs is this high. A B and D, however, all talk about a third person in their messages. Taking all this into consideration, it's evident that one must be very careful with interpreting features, as their meaning can change very significantly from language to language.

We can also use the system's search function in order to uncover some very interesting findings: A has the tendency to misuse the Hungarian connective "is" by incorrectly concatenating it to the preceding word. In Hungarian, the "is" connective should always be written separately from the preceding word. The other three authors do not make this same mistake. Only B uses the "összefüggésben" (in Hungarian) structure. We say something is in "összefüggésben" with something else if something is related to that something else, but there are other ways of expressing this too. D has some unique traits as well, she is the only one who ends words with the "képpen" affix, and she uses it four times, showing a clear tendency. In Hungarian, the "képpen" affix is easily replaceable, so D did not necessarily have to use it in any of the instances. She also often uses the word "kép" (picture in English) in her structures, for example, "out of the picture". This structure is common in both the Hungarian and English languages. This, too, can easily be phrased differently, and the other three authors do not use it as often. There is also an example of a word that two authors, B and D, both use, but even though they use it to express the same thing, they use it in different ways: In Hungarian, the word "továbbá" (in English, this translates to "furthermore", or "in addition") can be used both at the start of a sentence or somewhere in the middle. B consistently uses it mid-sentence, while D consistently uses it at the beginning of the sentence.

6   Conclusions

The goal of this research was to show that through the aid of machine learning, helping linguistic experts in identifying authors even behind short, digitally written texts is possible. We implemented a highly customizable system that combines machine learning technologies and simpler technologies to allow automated feature extraction from Hungarian texts. The system allows the expert to smoothly analyze and visualize the data with numerous tools, such as highlighting certain features, correcting texts and advanced searching in texts. We discussed how the experts can use the data and these tools to get hints about the author and ultimately identify them by pairing their texts with texts from known authors. In the future, our goal is to also automate the process of determining whether two bodies of text (or a query text and a corpus) were authored by the same person based on the data extracted and could even contribute to comparison to a population database to inspect traits of criminals writing malicious texts.

Acknowledgements. The research (conducted by the Special Service for National Security and the University of Szeged) was supported by the Ministry of Innovation and Technology NRDI Office within the framework of the Artificial Intelligence National Laboratory Program (RRF-2.3.1-21-2022-00004).

References

1. Hunspell. http://hunspell.github.io/. Accessed 21 Mar 2022
2. Laurence Anthony's linguistic analysis software. https://www.laurenceanthony. net/software.html. Accessed 21 Mar 2022
3. Tor project. https://www.torproject.org/. Accessed 21 Mar 2022
4. Coulthard, M., Johnson, A.: The Routledge Handbook of Forensic Linguistics (2010)
5. Crespo, M., Frías, A.: Stylistic authorship comparison and attribution of Spanish news forum messages based on the TreeTagger POS tagger. Procedia. Soc. Behav. Sci. **212**, 198–204 (2015)
6. Devlin, J., Chang, M.W., Lee, K., Toutanova, K.: BERT: pre-training of deep bidirectional transformers for language understanding. In: NAACL HLT 2019–2019 Conference of the North American Chapter of the Association for Computational Linguistics: Human Language Technologies - Proceedings of the Conference, pp. 4171–4186. Association for Computational Linguistics (ACL), October 2019
7. Faqeeh, M., Abdulla, N., Al-Ayyoub, M., Jararweh, Y., Quwaider, M.: Cross-lingual short-text document classification for Facebook comments. In: International Conference on Future Internet of Things and Cloud, pp. 67–98 (2014)
8. Ishihara, S.: E-mail authorship verification for forensic investigation. In: Proceedings of the 2010 ACM Symposium on Applied Computing (SAC), Sierre, Switzerland, vol. 24 (2010)
9. Ishihara, S.: Strength of forensic text comparison evidence from stylometric features: a multivariate likelihood ratio-based analysis. Int. J. Speech Lang. Law **24**, 67–98 (2017)
10. Llorens, M., Delany, S.: Deep level lexical features for cross-lingual authorship attribution. In: Proceedings of the First Workshop on Modeling, Learning and Mining for Cross/Multilinguality (MultiLingMine 2016), Padova, Italy (2016)
11. McMenamin, G.: Advances is Forensic Stylistics. CRC Press, Boca Raton (2002)
12. Nemeskey, D.M.: Natural language processing methods for language modeling. Ph.D. thesis, Eötvös Loránd University (2020)
13. Nini, A.: Authorship profiling in a forensic context. Ph.D. thesis (2014)
14. Nirkhi, S., Dharaskar, R., Thakare, V.: Authorship verification of online messages for forensic investigation. Procedia Comput. Sci. **78**, 640–645 (2016)
15. Olsson, J.: Forensic Linguistics: An Introduction to Language, Crime, and the Law. Bloomsbury Publishing, New York (2004)
16. Rexha, A., Kröll, M., Ziak, H., Kern, R.: Authorship identification of documents with high content similarity. Scientometrics **115**(1), 223–237 (2018). https://doi. org/10.1007/s11192-018-2661-6
17. Shuy, R.: Linguistics in the Courtroom: A Practical Guide. Oxford University Press, New York (2006)
18. Sousa-Silva, R.: Computational forensic linguistics: an overview of computational applications in forensic contexts. Lang. Law **5**, 118–143 (2018)
19. Szilák, J.: Az írásszokások néhány formai jegyének hátteréről. Belügyi Szemle **16**, 67–68 (1980)

20. Veronika, V., András, K., Eszter, F., László, V.: A gépi elemzők kriminalisztikai szempontú felhasználásának lehetőségei. XVII. Magyar Számítógépes Nyelvészeti Konferencia, pp. 275–288 (2021)
21. Zhang, C., Wu, X., Niu, Z., Ding, W.: Authorship identification from unstructured texts. Knowl.-Based Syst. **66**, 99–111 (2014)
22. Zsibrita, J., Vincze, V., Farkas, R.: magyarlanc: a toolkit for morphological and dependency parsing of Hungarian. In: Proceedings of RANLP, pp. 763–771 (2013)

Improved CNN Based on Batch Normalization and Adam Optimizer

Roseline Oluwaseun Ogundokun[1,2,3]([✉]) [iD], Rytis Maskeliunas[1], Sanjay Misra[4], and Robertas Damaševičius[5]

[1] Department of Multimedia Engineering, Kaunas University of Technology, 44249 Kaunas, Lithuania
rosogu@ktu.lt
[2] Department of Computer Science, Landmark University, Omu Aran, Nigeria
[3] Landmark University SDG 11 (Sustainable Cities and Communities Research Group), Omu Aran, Nigeria
[4] Department of Computer Science and Communication, Østfold University College, 1757 Halden, Norway
[5] Department of Applied Informatics, Vytautas Magnus University, 44404 Kaunas, Lithuania

Abstract. After evaluating the difficulty of CNNs in extracting convolution features, this paper suggested an improved convolutional neural network (CNN) method (ICNN-BNDOA), which is based on Batch Normalization (BN), Dropout (DO), and Adaptive Moment Estimation (Adam) optimizer. To circumvent the gradient challenge and quicken convergence, the ICNN-BNDOA uses a sequential CNN structure with the Leaky rectified linear unit (LeakyReLU) as the activation function (AF). The approach employs an Adam optimizer to handle the overfitting problem, which is done by introducing BN and DO layers to the entire connected CNN layers and the output layers, respectively, to decrease cross-entropy. Through a small regularization impact, BN was utilized to substantially speed up the training process of a neural network, as well as to increase the model's performance. The performance of the proposed system with conventional CNN (CCNN) was studied using the CIFAR-10 datasets as the benchmark data, and it was discovered that the suggested method demonstrated high recognition performance with the addition of BN and DO layers. CCNN and ICNN-BNDOA performance were compared. The statistical results showed that the proposed ICNN-BNDOA outperformed the CCNN with a training and testing accuracy of 0.6904 and 0.6861 respectively. It also outperformed with training and testing loss of 0.8910 and 0.9136 respectively.

Keywords: Convolutional Neural Network · Batch normalization · Dropout · Adam optimizer · CIFAR-10

1 Introduction

Classification of images, acquisition of knowledge, and semantic segmentation of images using the convolutional neural network (CNN) have gotten a lot of consideration because

O. Gervasi et al. (Eds.): ICCSA 2022 Workshops, LNCS 13381, pp. 593–604, 2022.
https://doi.org/10.1007/978-3-031-10548-7_43

of its success in object recognition [1, 19]. As a result, enhancing its performance is a popular topic in a study by Vieira, Pinaya and Mechelli [1]. The central processing unit (CPU) manages the whole procedure including data preparation of the CNN when solving the image or object detection, while the graphics processing unit (GPU) advances the convolution computation in the neural network (NN) unit and the execution speed of the full-joint layer-integration cell [2].

Even though the neural network's learning speed has been improved recent, the time cost of data preprocessing and preparation for the CPU and the GPU has increased, and a feeble GPU platform is susceptible to execution disruption. The involvement of BN in deep learning (DL) [1] has improved the efficiency of deep CNN and simplified the training procedure. Due to different issues faced during training, training them gets more difficult as the network grows deeper.

The output of the convolutional layers is regularized with extra scaling and ever-changing processes after the convolutional layers (CL) and before the activation layers (AL) [20]. These are introduced after forwarding the output to the AL and then to the next CL [1]. Just by adding this layer, the network improves test data accuracy and trains quicker than a comparable model without BN. BN lowers the internal covariate shift, resulting in improved outcomes. The impact of BN on several of the most lately postulated existing networks, including the Residual Network [4], Dense Network [4], VGG Network [5], and the Inception (v3) Network [6], are investigated. The architecture's inclusion of Batch Normalization layers has not been acknowledged explicitly.

The authors presented that adding BN layers to shallow networks improves performance when compared to a network without BN. They also showed that BN is required to train a deep network in the first place. We go one step more and demonstrated that when BN is employed, Exponential Linear Units [7–9] for Residual Networks perform better than Rectified Linear Units for all other networks.

With operator theory as the AF, reference [10] integrated multi-variable all-out product and interpolation operator theory into the CNN framework, focusing on CNN convergence speed. Their research provides a comprehensive mathematical formula derivation but no findings from the experimental testing. By incorporating companion objective functions (COF) at the entire hidden layers with an inclusive objective function at the output layer, Lee et al. [11] presented deeply-supervised nets. Companion goal functions are frequently used to provide another constraint or regularization to the learning process. As a result, the effectiveness of this strategy is dependent on the creation of a COF, which is not straightforward to achieve. The CNN technique introduces a novel way of extracting image features.

After evaluating the difficulties of CNNs in extracting convolution features, this paper suggested an improved convolutional neural network (ICNN) algorithm (ICNN-BNDA), which is based on batch normalization, dropout layer, and Adaptive Moment Estimation (Adam) optimizer. The ICNN-BNDA uses a seven-layered CNN structure with the LeakyReLU unit as the activation function to circumvent the gradient problem and accelerate convergence. The approach employs an Adam optimizer to handle the overfitting problem, which is done by introducing a BN layer into the overall connected and output layers to reduce cross-entropy.

The core contributions made in this study are as follows:

1. Batch normalization is used to minimize overfitting, increase generalization, and help the model converge rapidly, reducing training time. a greater learning rate was utilized to optimize the model's training duration, and a batch size of 32 was selected since small batch sizes perform better with batch normalization and help provide the needed regularization in the proposed system.
2. Dropout (0.2) was introduced to assist prevent overfitting by randomly setting an input unit with a frequency rate of each step during the training period.
3. The Adam optimization technique is used to make the model more computationally efficient, as well as to optimize the model with big data and parameters.

The rest of this article is prearranged as follows: Sect. 2 discussed a few correlated kinds of literature that have been conducted on CNN. Section 3 presented the rudiments of our proposed model and its details. Section 4 discussed the experimental results, analysis, and interpretations. Section 5 finally concludes the article and a few further study directions were also suggested and presented.

2 Literature Review

Drop-Activation is a regularization approach suggested by Liang et al. [12], which introduces randomization into the activation function. Drop-Activation employs a deterministic network with modified nonlinearities for prediction and drops nonlinear activations in the network at random during training. The proposed technique has two distinct advantages. First, as the numerical tests show, Drop-Activation is a simple yet efficient approach for regularization.

Yamada et al. [13] presented ShakeDrop, an innovative stochastic regularization approach that can be effectively used with ResNet and its enhancements as long as the residual blocks are normalized in batches. Experimentations on the CIFAR-10 and CIFAR-100 datasets confirmed their usefulness. ShakeDrop outperformed the competition in both datasets used for the implementation.

Zhang et al. [14] introduced an innovative Residual network (RN) of Residual network architecture (RoR), which was shown to achieve a new image classification performance on CIFAR-10 and CIFAR-100. Their approach not only improved image classification performance through empirical research, but also has the potential to be a successful supplement to the RN family in the upcoming.

The exponential linear units (ELUs) were suggested by Clevert et al. [9] for quicker and further precise learning in deep NN. The network can drive the mean activations closer to zero by using ELUs with negative values. As a result, ELUs reduce the distance between the normal and unit natural gradients, speeding up learning. In its negative regime, ELUs have a distinct saturation plateau, permitting them to absorb an extra robust and durable system. On various visual datasets, experimental results reveal that ELUs greatly outperform numerous activation functions.

Furthermore, ELU networks outperform ReLU networks that have been trained with BN. Without the necessity for multi-view test, assessment, or model averaging, ELU networks obtained one of the highest ten superlative conveyed outcomes on CIFAR-10 and established an innovative state-of-the-art in CIFAR-100. Furthermore, ELU networks on the ImageNet delivered competitive results in many fewer epochs than an equivalent ReLU network.

For (static) object recognition, Liang and Hu [15] suggested a recurrent convolutional neural network (RCNN). The primary concept was to include recurrent connections in each of the feedforward CNN's convolutional layers. This structure allowed units in the same layer to modulate the units, improving CNN's capacity to grasp statistical regularities in the context of the object. By weight sharing between layers, the recurrent connections enhanced the depth of the innovative CNN while keeping the number of parameters the same. The advantages of RCNN over CNN for object identification were proved in experiments. RCNN beat the existing models on four benchmark datasets with fewer parameters. Enlarging the number of variables resulted in even improved results.

Although many researchers have sought to enhance the performance of deep learning algorithms [16], the issues encountered when utilizing DL models for picture categorization are as follows.

a. DL normally requires a huge amount of dataset for training and this is lacked
b. Imbalanced dataset
c. Interpretability of dataset
d. Uncertainty scaling
e. Catastrophic forgetting
f. Model compression
g. Overfitting
h. Vanishing gradient problem
i. Exploding gradient problem
j. Underspecification

To overcome these issues, this work developed an enhanced activation function that includes dropout layers and batch normalization layers between the fully connected and output layers of CNN to raise the convergence rate. This overcomes the problem of overfitting caused by increasing the number of repetitions by adding the Adaptive Moment Estimation (Adam) optimizer to the gradient descent technique, which reduces the cumulative error and increases training speed. Internal covariate shift is also addressed by batch normalization. It is possible to employ a faster learning rate, which has a regularizing impact. As a result, an improved CNN algorithm (ICNN-BNDA) is suggested, which is based on dropout, batch normalization, and the Adam optimizer.

3 Materials and Methods

3.1 Dataset

Alex Krizhevsky, Vinod Nair, and Geoffrey Hinton got the CIFAR-10. There are 60,000 32×32 color photos in the collection. It is divided into ten classes, each having 6000 photos. The number of training photos is 50,000, whereas the number of testing images is 10,000. The dataset is split into five training batches, each of which contains precisely 1000 photos from each class. The remaining photos are arranged in a random order in the training batches. The test and validation datasets are encompassed in Table 1, and the suggested approach employed in this study is depicted in Fig. 1.

Table 1. Training and test datasets for CIFAR-10

Size of training data	Size of test data	Number of image category
50, 000	10, 000	10

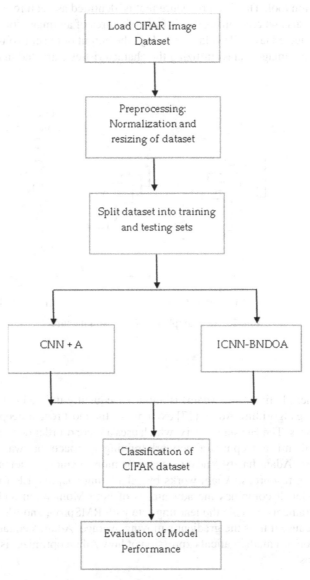

Fig. 1. Schematic illustration for the proposed system

3.2   CNN

Convolutional layers (CL), pooling layers (PL), and fully-connected (FC) layers are the 3 main layers made up by the CNN algorithm. In the algorithm, architecture will be constructed when the layers are layered. The DO layer and the AF are 2 extra key factors in addition to these 3 layers. The architecture is further diverged into 2 components, as shown in Fig. 2.

a.   A convolution tool: This is a procedure that is identified as Feature Extraction (FE), which discerns and recognizes the different features of an image for analysis.
b.   A fully connected layer: This layer employs the output of the convolution execution to forecast the image's class utilizing the characteristics extracted in earlier stages.

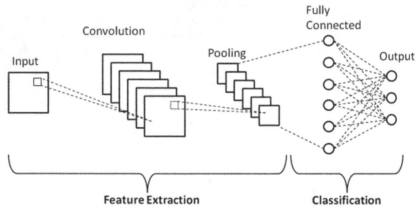

Fig. 2. An example of a CNN Architecture

3.3   Adam

Adaptive Moment Estimation (Adam) is another frequently utilized optimization app-roach or learning algorithm. Adam [17] exemplifies the most recent deep learning opti-mization advances. The Hessian matrix, which uses a second-order derivative, is used to express this. Adam is a deep neural network training approach that was created exclu-sively for Adam. Adam has two advantages: it is more memory efficient and requires fewer processing resources. Adam works by calculating adaptive LR for each param-eter in the model. It combines the advantages of both Momentum and RMSprop. It uses squared gradients to scale the learning rate with RMSprop, and it's comparable to momentum because it uses the gradient's moving average. Adam's equation is given in E1. The equation is a mathematical expression of how Adam optimizer is used in image classification task.

$$w_{ij^t} = w_{ij^{t-1}} - \frac{\eta}{\sqrt{E[\delta^2]^t} + \epsilon} * \widehat{E[\delta^2]}^t \tag{1}$$

where w is the model weights, eta (look like the letter n) and is the step size which can depend on iteration.

3.4 Activation Function Based on LeakyReLU

The following are the characteristics of the ReLU function $f(x) = \max(0, x)$ $(x(0, +)$: (1) Gradient that is unsaturated: $Ix > 0$ is the formula for the gradient. As a result, the reverse propagation process' gradient dispersion problem is solved, and the parameters in the first layer of the neural network may be updated quickly. (2) Simplicity of computation: The thresholds are determined by the ReLU function: if x 0, then $f(x) = 0$; if $x > 0$, then $f(x) = x$. Regrettably, ReLU units might be brittle and "die" during training [17]. The value generated by a "dead" ReLU is always the same. The "dead" problem of ReLU was solved with the Leaky ReLUs AF [18], which has a modest positive gradient for negative inputs. The Leaky ReLU AF has the formula $f = \max(0.01x, x)$, which offers all of the benefits of the ReLU AF but without the "dead" issue. Due to LeakyReLU advantages in solving the gradient saturation problem and improving convergence speed, this AF in this study.

3.5 The Proposed Approach

This research created a seven-layer CNN model that includes an input layer with BN and DO layers, two hidden layers with BN and DO layers composed of convolution and pool layers, a flatten layer with DO layer (0.3), a fully connect-ed layer, two dense layers with BN and DO layers, and an output layer with sigmoid activation. The layers' activation functions are all rectified linear unit (LeakyReLU) functions, with the exception of the output. Conv2D is a function that performs 2D convolution operations. The ICNN founded on Batch normalization, Dropout and the Adam Optimizer (ICNN-BNDOA) is created on the foundation of the CNN architecture, the LeakyReLU AF, and the overfitting avoidance approach that is based on batch normalization and the Adam. A 3x3 matrix is used in the pooling procedure to guarantee that the image input and output after FE are of the same size. In each stage, the LeakyReLU activation function is employed to activate the neuron.

4   Implementation and Evaluation

4.1 Proposed Execution Environment

The seven-layers CNN learning method is developed using the python programming language on a 64-bit Windows 10 system. To evaluate the performance of the established model, Tensorflow is deployed. The performance of the CNN algorithm based on batch normalization and Adam optimizer is tested, assessed, and compared to that of the traditional CNN method at various Adam learning rates. This research compares CNN with and without BN and DO between layers.

4.2 Implementation Evaluation Results

BN and DO layers were supplied to evaluate the performance of the proposed model and determine the effects of the various added layers, according to the implementation setup stated in the preceding section. With the addition of BN and DO to the CIFAR-10 dataset, the model's identification rate rises. The following are the specifics of the two algorithms utilized in the implementation:

1. Conventional CNN is the first algorithm. This approach achieves input signal processing by using a SoftMax function as the activation function and a convolution and pooling layer.
2. Improved CNN algorithm. A convolutional neural network with batch normalization and a dropout of 0 is used in this approach. 2. The sigmoid function was utilized in the last dense layer as the AF. The addition of BN and DO layers, as well as an Adam optimizer with a learning rate of 0.0001 to maximize the cross entropy, enhances model performance.

4.3 Comparative Analysis of the Two Algorithms

The proposed algorithms run using 50 epochs. The two algorithms are compared using metrics like training loss, validation loss, testing loss, training accuracy, testing accuracy, and validation accuracy. Figures 3, 4, 5 and 6 show the model accuracies and losses for the two algorithms.

Figure 3 shows the ICNN-BNDOA training and testing accuracy of 0.6904 and 0.6861 respectively. Figure 4 shows the ICNN-BNDOA training and testing loss of 0.8910 and 0.9136 respectively. Figure 5 show the CNN-A training and testing accuracy of 0.4954 and 0.6739 respectively with their training and testing loss of 1.4170 and 0.9636 respectively as shown in Fig. 6.

Table 2 shows the parameters set and used for the execution (training, validation, and testing) of the proposed model. Table 3 shows the comparative analysis results for the two algorithms implemented and it was deduced that the introduction of BN and DO in the CNN layers produced an improved training and test accuracies with lower value for their losses.

Table 2. Parameter set for the model execution

Parameters	Values
Epochs	50
Batch size	32
Validation split	20
Training split	80
Optimizer learning rate	0.0001
Loss	Categorical cross-entropy

Table 3. Comparative analysis of the two algorithms

Algorithm	Training loss	Training accuracy	Validation loss	Validation accuracy	Test loss	Test accuracy
Proposed ICNN-BNDA	0.8910	0.6904	0.9137	0.6861	0.9136	0.6861
CNN-A	1.4170	0.4954	1.3374	0.5337	0.9636	0.6739

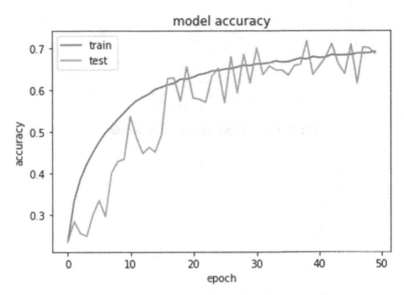

Fig. 3. ICNN-BNDOA training and testing accuracies

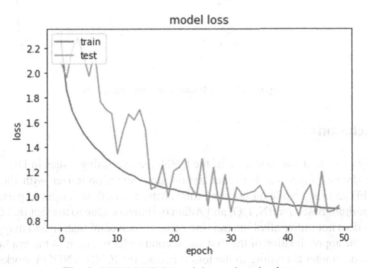

Fig. 4. ICNN-BNDOA training and testing losses

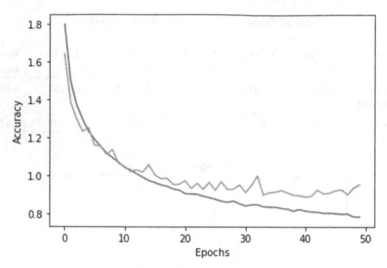

Fig. 5. CNN-A training and testing accuracies

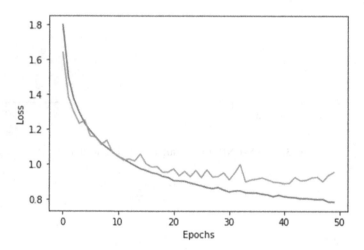

Fig. 6. CNN-A training and testing losses

5   Conclusion

This study looks at the architecture of the CNN, the overfitting issues in DL, and combines the dropout layer, batch normalization, and Adam optimizer with the CNN to increase FE accuracy while minimizing time costs. Tensorflow is used to parallelize an ICNN algorithm based on BN, DO, and Adam optimizers. Due to the fact that the Adam optimizer does not utilize all of the training cases in each combination and may energetically alter the approximation of the first and second-order matrices of the gradient of the individual parameter according to the loss function, the ICNN-BNDOA works quicker.

Additionally, by enhancing the AF, the technique evades the problem of the neuron node output being 0, enhances recognition accuracy, and shortens the processing time.

Since the current test data is small, future research will necessitate employing more test datasets to increase the algorithm's classification accuracy performance. Furthermore, limiting the number of neurons in the CNN can reduce calculations during the training, validation, and testing stages; nevertheless, the dropout layer technique employed during the learning stage upsurges processing time. At the start of the study, we concentrated on enhancing detection accuracy. The amount of time each stage takes necessitates additional examination.

References

1. Vieira, S., Pinaya, W.H., Mechelli, A.: Using deep learning to investigate the neuroimaging correlates of psychiatric and neurological disorders: methods and applications. Neurosci. Biobehav. Rev. **74**, 58–75 (2017)
2. Li, S., Dou, Y., Niu, X., Lv, Q., Wang, Q.: A fast and memory saved GPU acceleration algorithm of convolutional neural networks for target detection. Neurocomputing **230**, 48–59 (2017)
3. Ioffe, S., Szegedy, C.: Batch normalization: accelerating deep network training by reducing internal covariate shift. In: International Conference on Machine Learning, pp. 448–456. PMLR, June 2015
4. Simonyan, K., Zisserman, A.: Very deep convolutional networks for large-scale image recognition (2014). arXiv preprint arXiv:1409.1556
5. Szegedy, C., Vanhoucke, V., Ioffe, S., Shlens, J., Wojna, Z.: Rethinking the inception architecture for computer vision. In: Proceedings of the IEEE Conference on Computer Vision and Pattern Recognition, pp. 2818–2826 (2016)
6. He, K., Zhang, X., Ren, S., Sun, J.: Deep residual learning for image recognition. In: Proceedings of the IEEE Conference on Computer Vision and Pattern Recognition, pp. 770–778 (2016)
7. Huang, G., Liu, Z., Van Der Maaten, L., Weinberger, K.Q.: Densely connected convolutional networks. In Proceedings of the IEEE Conference on Computer Vision and Pattern Recognition, pp. 4700–4708 (2017)
8. Clevert, D. A., Unterthiner, T., & Hochreiter, S. (2015). Fast and accurate deep network learning by exponential linear units (elus). arXiv preprint arXiv:1511.07289
9. Costarelli, D., Vinti, G.: Pointwise and uniform approximation by multivariate neural network operators of the max-product type. Neural Netw. **81**, 81–90 (2016)
10. Lee, C.Y., Xie, S., Gallagher, P., Zhang, Z., Tu, Z.: Deeply-supervised nets. In Artificial Intelligence and Statistics, pp. 562–570. PMLR, February 2015
11. Liang, S., Khoo, Y., Yang, H.: Drop-activation: implicit parameter reduction and harmonious regularization. Commun. Appl. Math. Comput. **3**(2), 293–311 (2021)
12. Yamada, Y., Iwamura, M., Kise, K.: Shakedrop regularization (2018)
13. Zhang, K., Sun, M., Han, T.X., Yuan, X., Guo, L., Liu, T.: Residual networks of residual networks: multilevel residual networks. IEEE Trans. Circuits Syst. Video Technol. **28**(6), 1303–1314 (2017)
14. Liang, M., Hu, X.: Recurrent convolutional neural network for object recognition. In Proceedings of the IEEE Conference on Computer Vision and Pattern Recognition, pp. 3367–3375 (2015)
15. LeCun, Y., Bottou, L., Bengio, Y., Haffner, P.: Gradient-based learning applied to document recognition. Proc. IEEE **86**(11), 2278–2324 (1998)

16. Zhang, Z.: Improved Adam optimizer for deep neural networks. In 2018 IEEE/ACM 26th International Symposium on Quality of Service (IWQoS), pp. 1–2. IEEE, June 2018
17. Jin, X., Xu, C., Feng, J., Wei, Y., Xiong, J., Yan, S.: Deep learning with s-shaped rectified linear activation units. In: Proceedings of the AAAI Conference on Artificial Intelligence, vol. 30, No. 1, February 2016
18. Awotunde, J.B., Ogundokun, R.O., Ayo, F.E., Matiluko, O.E.: Speech segregation in background noise based on deep learning. IEEE Access **8**, 169568–169575 (2020). 3024077
19. Odusami, M., Maskeliunas, R., Damaševičius, R., Misra, S.: Comparable study of pre-trained model on Alzheimer disease classification. In: Gervasi, O., et al. (eds.) Computational Science and Its Applications – ICCSA 2021. LNCS, vol. 12953, pp. 63–74. Springer, Cham (2021). https://doi.org/10.1007/978-3-030-86976-2_5

The Application of SISO LSTM Networks to Forecast Selected Items in Financial Quarterly Reports – Case Study

Adam Galuszka[1](✉) , Eryka Probierz[1] , Adrian Olczyk[1], Jerzy Kocerka[1],
Katarzyna Klimczak[2] , and Tomasz Wisniewski[3]

[1] Institute of Automatic Control, Silesian University of Technology, Akademicka 16,
44-100 Gliwice, Poland
{adam.galuszka,eryka.probierz,adrian.olczyk,
jerzy.kocerka}@polsl.pl
[2] SGH Warsaw School of Economics, Niepodleglosci 162, 02-554 Warsaw, Poland
katarzyna.klimczak@sgh.pl
[3] The Warsaw Stock Exchange, Ksiazeca 4, 00-498 Warsaw, Poland
tomasz.wisniewski@gpw.pl

Abstract. Automatic analysis of financial data is the subject of many ongoing research. The aim of this study was to explore deep learning methods to predict and forecast the value of selected financial data included in financial quarterly reports based on historical data in a given future horizon, assuming incomplete data. The study considered the quarterly financial reports of selected companies listed on the Warsaw Stock Exchange (WSE), in the period from September 2010 to December 2021, where each report consists of about 250 indices. Basing on the principles of financial analysis and the interdependencies between financial indicators, a selection of interdependent indicators has been established to forecast future indices values based on historical data. The reinforced learning technique was used to see if it improves forecast results relative to the classic deep learning technique. Results indicate good prediction of the financial statement values up to one-year horizon, i.e., up to four future quarterly reports, considering both complete and incomplete financial data. Also, it is shown how observation update (reinforced learning) influences the forecast result. Forecast results are supporting tool for financial analysis for WSE.

Keywords: Automated reasoning · Time series analysis · Forecasting ·
Ai-supported simulation · Financial indices · Financial report analysis · LSTM
network

1 Introduction

Financial forecasting is an increasingly used tool in corporate finance management. Since forecasting allows for rational and scientific forecasting of future events, it allows making decisions (e.g. investment decisions) with the possibility of relatively precise

O. Gervasi et al. (Eds.): ICCSA 2022 Workshops, LNCS 13381, pp. 605–616, 2022.
https://doi.org/10.1007/978-3-031-10548-7_44

estimation of their impact on the financial situation of the enterprise. This is essential in the economic realities where economy practitioners more and more often use data from financial statements and financial analysis to make decisions based on them. Preparation of a financial forecast is associated with the need to accept the uncertainty it carries with it. However, even though making an accurate forecast (due to the presence of random factors that cannot be taken into account at the stage of forecast preparation) is extremely difficult, it allows for a detailed analysis of the company's future financial situation and taking into account elements that are not taken into account during the standard analysis financial (Franc-Dąbrowska and Zbrowska 2008). Thus, it enables a more detailed identification of opportunities and threats in the financial sphere of the company's operation. Therefore, it seems that financial forecasting will be increasingly used in economic practice, especially in entities operating on international or global markets, as a supplement to traditional methods of financial analysis. The basic methods of financial analysis require supplementation. Summarising, there is a need to develop practical methods that allow for a relatively simple forecast of the company's financial situation in the perspective of at least several financial reports ahead, which is not easy due to the complexity of forecasting methods and the occurrence of random factors, impossible to predict when building the forecast.

Along with the development of data collection tools, there are solutions that allow for their analysis, i.e. digital platforms that provide automated financial planning services, based on algorithms and hardly supervised by man. This type of platform obtains information about the financial situation and future goals from the client point of view. Then, it uses such data to provide consulting services (using, among others, data from reports) and automatically investing client funds. Artificial intelligence (AI)and especially deep learning is increasingly being used in data analysis, and 70% of companies are already declaring in their research that they intend to introduce AI-based solutions in nearest future. The newest research (e.g. Hedayati et al. 2016; Burba 2019) indicates that AI techniques based on deep learning are useful in analysis of stock market indicators, successfully extending classical approaches based on technical analysis.

Many existing implementations of deep learning in financial area are focused on forecasting on a given financial series (Korczak and Hemes 2017; Sezer et al.2020; Mateńczuk et al. 2021). The main focus is on predicting the next movement of the asset – including stock price forecasting, index prediction, forex price prediction, commodity price prediction, bond price forecasting, volatility forecasting, cryptocurrency price forecasting. Relatively little attention is paid to the analysis of financial data contained in periodic reports, ie annual and quarterly.

One of the most frequently applied deep learning method in financial time series forecasting is LSTM (e.g. Chen 2015; Zhao et al. 2017; Roondiwala et al. 2017; Qiu et al. 2020; Fischer and Krauss 2018; Galuszka et al. 2020a, b). However, some initial decisions when applying AI in stock index analysis need to be made. They are connected e.g. with time window of analysed data, since improper choice of it may lead to unsatisfactory results and similar difficulties are met in any time-series domains (Kyoung-jae 2003; Shumway and Stoffer 2017).

The paper is organized as follow: in next section aim, methods and scope of the research is formulated, in Sect. 2 methodology is presented, in Sect. 3 forecasts results are shown. All is concluded in Sect. 4.

1.1 Aim, Methods and Scope of the Research

In the paper we are focused on financial quarterly reports. The aim of the work is to prepare and evaluate the forecast of a set of selected basic financial statement items included in financial quarterly reports:

- revenues from sales
- operating profit/loss
- net profit/loss attributable to equity holders of the parent
- total comprehensive income attributable to equity holders
- depreciation
- assets
- non-current assets
- equity shareholders of the parent

for a selected group of companies representing enterprises of various types with different behaviors, listed on WSE. Results of the work are expected to be a supporting tool in analysis of financial reports on WSE.

A set of five companies (limited due to data delivered for tests) with a division into companies dealing with industry, finance and services was used in the study, representing industry, finance and services. The training period covered the years 2010–2020 and the forecast were done for 2021. Intentionally the research does not cover pandemic period since its influence for financial statements was unpredictable.

In the analysis Matlab's DeepLearnig Toolbox (www.mathworks.com) to forecast time series using deep learning has been used. In particular, time series data forecasts using long-short-term memory (LSTM) networks with single input and single prediction (thus SISO structure) has been applied.

2 Methodology

2.1 LSTM Networks

The LSTM network is being developed in order to forecast future index values based on historical data. LSTM networks are a type of recursive neural network (RNN) designed to avoid the problem of long-term relationships, in which each neuron contains a memory cell capable of storing prior information used by RNN or forgetting it when needed (Hochreiter and Schmidhuber 1997). They are now widely used successfully in time series prediction problems (e.g. Elsaraiti and Merabet 2021). The LSTM-RNN is designed with a memory cell that stores long-term dependencies. In addition to the memory cell, the LSTM cell includes an input gate, an output gate, and a forget gate. Each gate in the cell receives the current input, the hidden state in the previous time, and the state information of the cell's internal memory in order to perform various operations and determine whether to activate using activation function. To predict the values of future time steps of a sequence, it is assumed that the answers are training sequences with values shifted by one time step. This means that at each stage of the input sequence, the LSTM network learns to predict the value of the next time step. To forecast the value of multiple time steps in the future, the PredestAndUpdateState function from the toolbox was used to predict time steps one by one and the network status was updated with each forecast. The training parameters of the network are given in the Table 1.

Table 1. The training parameters of the network

No. of hidden units	200
Solver	Adam
Max epochs	250
Gradient threshold	1
Initial learn rate	0.005
Learn rate drop period	125
Learn rate drop factor	0.2

Input data for the analysis is excel report file, containing 277 financial items published each quarter over 11 years, i.e. size of the data vector for each item is 44 with some missing values. Piece of data is shown in Table 2.

Table 2. Piece of quarterly financial data.

Accounting period	07.01-09.01	10.01-12.01	01.02-03.02	04.02-06.02	07.02-09.02	10.02-12.02
Basic information						
End of period	2001-09-30	2001-12-31	2002-03-31	2002-06-30	2002-09-30	2002-12-31
Start of period	2001-07-01	2001-10-01	2002-01-01	2002-04-01	2002-07-01	2002-10-01
Revenues from sales	233 788	257 077	225 646	215 734	279 438	271 347
Operating profit/loss	21 215	8 235	12 729	5 610	18 500	4 492
Net profit/loss attributable to equity holder	3 331	7 375	2 628	-2 249	5 851	-3 479
Total comprehensive income attributable to equity holders						
Depreciation	16 392	16 058	15 148	15 112	15 308	15 635
Cash flow from operating activities	21 203	20 721	4 442	23 370	18 755	16 179
Cash flow from investing activities	-19 341	-41 770	-4 595	-23 868	-13 619	29 509
Cash flow from financing activities	-743	19 105	13 674	-3 606	-8 574	-50 526
Aktywa	685 879	644 951	695 951	702 836	764 332	727 941
Non-current assets	431 400	413 970	419 617	414 335	404 343	403 693
Current assets	254 479	230 981	276 334	288 501	359 989	324 248
Equity shareholders of the parent	193 066	198 375	188 822	183 735	188 723	220 012
Non-current liabilities	202 526	214 508	216 924	188 476	191 349	176 924
Current liabilities	290 287	232 068	286 635	326 541	380 143	327 786

The output data for our analysis are:

– Statement forecast up to four (4) quarterly periods (up to 1 year),
– Normalized error,
– Statement forecast with observation updates,
– Normalized error of forecast with updates,
– LSTM training progress data.

2.2 Data Preparation

The data in quarterly reports very often were incomplete. There are different methods of replacing missed data with numbers and most often used are: linear interpolation of neighboring, nonmissing values; specified constant value; previous nonmissing value; next nonmissing value; moving median with specified window size or moving mean with specified window size (see e.g. mathworks.com). Without further justification in the research missing data are filled with moving median method with fixed window size. The method returns an array of local k-point median values, where each median is calculated over a sliding window of length k across neighboring elements of A. When k is odd, the window is centered about the element in the current position. When k is even, the window is centered about the current and previous elements. The window size is automatically truncated at the endpoints when there are not enough elements to fill the window (Matlab 2021).

2.3 Error Normalization

The comparison of the forecasts efficiency has been done using the root-mean-square error (RMSE) calculated from the standardized data, i.e.:

$$RMSE = \sqrt{\frac{\sum_{i=1}^{n}(X_{test,i} - X_{pred,i})^2}{n}}, \tag{1}$$

where X_{test} are test values and X_{pred} are predicted values at time i. To be able to compare the forecasts quality RMSE has been normalized in two ways:

1) using the difference between maximum and minimum of the test data:

$$NRMSE1 = RMSE/(X_{test\,max} - X_{test\,min}), \tag{2}$$

2) using the mean (average) of the test data:

$$NRMSE2 = RMSE/(X_{test\,mean}). \tag{3}$$

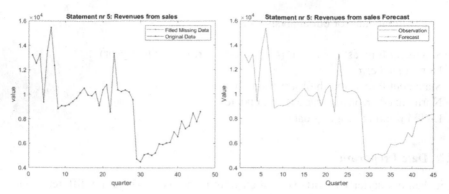

Fig. 1. Revenues from sales data (left) and data with forecast (right)

3 Forecasts

3.1 Example of Forecasts for Industry Companies for Complete Data

The example data file contains a single time series, with time steps corresponding to quarter and values corresponding to financial statement items, here revenues from sales. The output is an array of cells in which each element is a single time step. In the Fig. 1. revenues from sales data and data with forecast are presented.

The Fig. 2 (left) shows the forecasts for the values actually observed along with the prediction error. If actual index values of forecasts is known, one can update the network status with the observed values instead of the predicted ones, thus confronting the learning results with the actual values (the so-called reinforced learning technique). The results are shown in the Fig. 2 (right). In this case, the observation update significantly (not in a statistical sense) improves the prediction result.

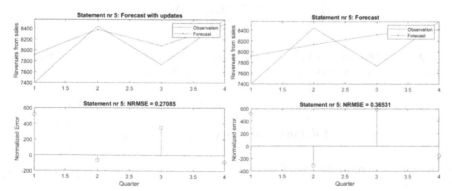

Fig. 2. Revenues from sales forecast with NRMSE (left) and forecast with updates with NRMSE (right)

3.2   Example of Forecasts for Finance Companies for Slightly Incomplete Data

The example data file contains a single time series, with time steps corresponding to quarter and values corresponding to financial statement items, here operating profit/loss. The output is an array of cells in which each element is a single time step. In the Fig. 3. operating profit/loss data and data with forecast are presented.

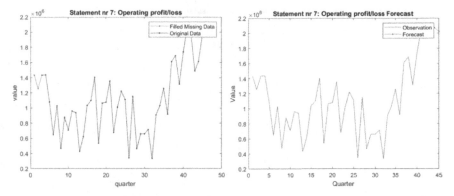

Fig. 3. Operating profit/loss data (left) and data with forecast (right)

The Fig. 4 (left) shows the forecasts for the values actually observed along with the prediction error. If actual index values of forecasts is known, one can update the network status with the observed values instead of the predicted ones, thus confronting the learning results with the actual values. The results are shown in the Fig. 4 (right). In this case, the observation update significantly (not in a statistical sense) worsens the prediction result.

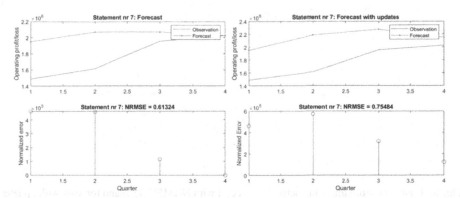

Fig. 4. Operating profit/loss forecast with NRMSE (left) and forecast with updates with NRMSE (right)

3.3 Example of Forecasts for Service Companies for More Incomplete Data

The example data file contains a single time series, with time steps corresponding to quarter and values corresponding to statement values, here cash flow from financing activities. The output is an array of cells in which each element is a single time step. In the Fig. 5 cash flow from financing activities data and data with forecast are presented.

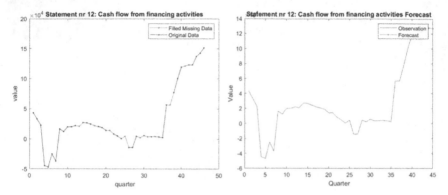

Fig. 5. Cash flow from financing activities data (left) and data with forecast (right)

The Fig. 6 (left) shows the forecasts for the values actually observed along with the prediction error. If actual index values of forecasts is known, one can update the network status with the observed values instead of the predicted ones, thus confronting the learning results with the actual values. The results are shown in the Fig. 6 (right). In this case, the observation update slightly improves the prediction result.

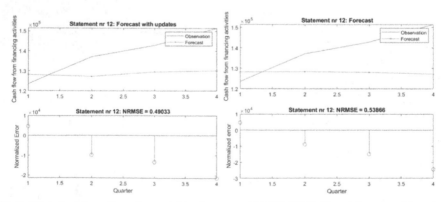

Fig. 6. Cash flow from financing activities forecast with NRMSE (left) and forecast with updates with NRMSE (right)

3.4 Accuracy of Financial Statements Forecast in One-Year Horizon

In Tables 3 and 4 NRSME1 (2) for each analyzed financial statement item and for each considered company are presented. In Tables 5 and 6 NRSME2 (3) for each analyzed financial statement item and for each considered company are presented. Minimal values in each column are marked bold. One should note that for M-LSTM in each case we received significantly lower values for minima of the NRSME, significantly higher values for maxima of the NRSME and similar or even worse NRSME values for averages. We do not include SD parameter due to too few analyzed companies.

Table 3. NRSME1 forecast for each analyzed financial statement item and for each considered company

Financial statement item	Forecast NRMSE1		
	Min	Max	Avg
-revenues from sales	0,3653	0,8165	0,52545
-operating profit/loss	**0,3105**	**0,5923**	**0,4915**
-net profit/loss attributable to equity holders of the parent	0,3457	1,5549	0,77953
-total comprehensive income attributable to equity holders	0,4914	0,8949	0,69375
-depreciation	0,3553	0,8631	0,60553
-assets	0,4824	2,2116	1,22135
-non-current assets	0,6237	2,3993	1,15548
-equity shareholders of the parent	0,4499	0,7359	0,5497

Table 4. NRSME1 forecast with updates for each analyzed financial statement item and for each considered company

Financial statement item	Forecast with updates NRMSE1		
	Min	Max	Avg
-revenues from sales	**0,2708**	**0,5744**	0,44515
-operating profit/loss	0,4205	0,781	0,5638
-net profit/loss attributable to equity holders of the parent	0,3274	10,3016	3,021875
-total comprehensive income attributable to equity holders	0,6024	1,055	0,7548
-depreciation	0,3572	0,8566	0,592867
-assets	0,5015	2,4117	1,2166
-non-current assets	0,5289	2,6683	1,22575
-equity shareholders of the parent	0,487	0,6984	**0,557667**

4   Conclusion and Future Works

The scheme resulting from the multi-criteria optimization for passenger communication analysis - the access point in the vehicle is shown in the Fig. 3.

The results obtained do not clearly indicate the quality of the forecasts and the size of the prediction horizon. The wide range of NRMSE1 and NRMS2 is caused by assumed normalization method, which returns high values of NRMSE in case of not varying test data. The problem is that future values of financial statement items depend not only on past values (except fully determined systems with known excitations and without undetermined disturbances) but also on other external signals that can occur occasionally taking the form of non-time series data (non-predicted market conditions).

Table 5. NRSME2 for each analyzed financial statement item and for each considered company

Financial statement item	Forecast NRMSE2		
	Min	Max	Avg
-revenues from sales	0,0713	1,2949	0,504733
-operating profit/loss	0,0287	1,9763	0,743533
-net profit/loss attributable to equity holders of the parent	0,4639	0,9564	0,7233
-total comprehensive income attributable to equity holders	0,223	48,7909	17,5413
-depreciation	0,0513	0,1394	0,09535
-assets	0,0368	0,2585	0,116767
-non-current assets	0,0334	0,3423	0,2285
-equity shareholders of the parent	**0,0002**	**0,0944**	**0,033**

The forecast result in financial report case should be treated rather as a supporting tool in automatically noting possible unusual changes in financial data reporting than an efficient forecasting tool.

Future works will be focused on:

1) Perform analysis for other simulation scenarios, considering cross-correlations of the data, changing:

   a.   methods of missed data management,
   b.   forecasting horizon size,
   c.   normalization methods.

2) On the basis of performed analysis, indicate the optimal sets of LSTM parameters.
3) The indications should be subject to expert opinions.

Table 6. NRSME2 forecast with updates for each analyzed financial statement item and for each considered company

Financial statement item	Forecast with updates NRMSE2		
	Min	Max	Avg
-revenues from sales	0,076	1,3071	0,511033
-operating profit/loss	0,0267	1,3675	0,537467
-net profit/loss attributable to equity holders of the parent	0,7013	4,3616	2,070567
-total comprehensive income attributable to equity holders	0,1584	36,9211	13,45953
-depreciation	0,0534	**0,1016**	0,0775
-assets	0,0403	0,2687	0,1249
-non-current assets	0,037	0,3008	0,200267
-equity shareholders of the parent	**0,0002**	0,1206	**0,041333**

Acknowledgements. The work of Adam Galuszka, Adrian Olczyk and Jerzy Kocerka was supported by the SUT Grant the subsidy for maintaining and developing the research potential, in 2022. The work of Eryka Probierz was supported in part by the European Union through the European Social Fund as a scholarship under Grant POWR.03.02.00-00-I029, and in part by the Silesian University of Technology (SUT) through a grant: the subsidy for maintaining and developing the research potential in 2022 for young researchers in data collection and analysis.

References

Burba, D.: An overview of time series forecasting models *towardsdatascience.com* (2019). Accessed 3 Oct 2019

Galuszka, A., Dzida, T., Klimczak, K., Jedrasiak, K., Wisniewski, T.: Short time series of share prices with financial results in day-ahead forecast –the Warsaw stock exchange main market example. In: Nketsa, A., Baron, C., Ostend, C.F. (eds.) The European Simulation and Modelling Conference 2020. ESM 2020, 21–23 October 2020, Toulouse, France, pp. 115–117. EUROSIS-ETI 2020 (2020a)

Galuszka, A., Dzida, T., Klimczak, K., Jedrasiak, K., Wisniewski, T.: LSTM network with reinforced learning in short and medium term Warsaw Stock Market index forecast. In: Nketsa, A., Baron, C., Ostend, C.F. (eds.) The European Simulation and Modelling Conference 2020. ESM 2020, 21–23 October 2020, Toulouse, France, pp. 118–122. EUROSIS-ETI 2020 (2020b)

Hedayati, M.A., Hedayati, M.M., Esfandyari, M.: Stock market index prediction using artificial neural network. J. Econ. Finan. Admin. Sci. **2**, 89–93 (2016)

Korczak, J., Hemes, M.: Deep learning for financial time series forecasting in A-Trader system. In: 2017 Federated Conference on Computer Science and Information Systems (FedCSIS), Prague, pp. 905–912 (2017)

Kim, K.J.: Financial time series forecasting using support vector machines. Neurocomputing **55**(1–2), 307–319 (2003)

Shumway, R.H., Stoffer, D.S.: Time Series Analysis and its Applications: With R Examples. 4th edn. Springer, Cham (2017). https://doi.org/10.1007/978-3-319-52452-8

Franc-Dąbrowska, J., Zbrowska, M.: Prognozowanie finansowe dla spółki X – spółka logistyczna. Zeszyty Naukowe SGGW w Warszawie. Ekonomika i Organizacja Gospodarki Żywnościowej **64**, 251–270 (2008). (in polish)

Elsaraiti, M., Merabet, A.: Application of long-short-term-memory recurrent neural networks to forecast wind speed. Appl. Sci. **11**, 2387 (2021)

Hochreiter, S., Schmidhuber, J.: Long short-term memory. Neural Comput. **9**(8), 1735–1780 (1997)

Chen, K., Zhou, Y., Dai, F.: A LSTM-based method for stock returns prediction: a case study of China stock market. IEEE Int. Conf. Big Data (Big Data) **2015**, 2823–2824 (2015)

Qiu, J., Wang, B., Zhou, C.: Forecasting stock prices with long-short term memory neural network based on attention mechanism. PLOS ONE **15**, 1 (2020)

Fischer, T., Krauss, C.: Deep learning with long short-term memory networks for financial market predictions. Eur. J. Oper. Res. **270**(2), 654–669 (2018)

Zhao, Z., Rao, R., Tu, S., Shi, J.: Time-weighted LSTM model with redefined labeling for stock trend prediction. In: 2017 IEEE 29th International Conference on Tools with Artificial Intelligence (ICTAI), pp 1210–1217 (2017)

Roondiwala, M., Patel, H., Varma, S.: Predicting stock prices using LSTM. Int. J. Sci. Res. (IJSR) **6**(4), 1754–1756 (2017)

Sezer, O.B., Gudelek, M.U., Ozbayoglu, A.M.: Financial time series forecasting with deep learning: a systematic literature review: 2005–2019. Appl. Soft Comput. J. **90**, 106181 (2020)

Mateńczuk, K., et al.: Financial time series forecasting: comparison of traditional and spiking neural networks. Proc. Comput. Sci. **192**, 5023–5029 (2021)

Design Assertions: Executable Assertions for Design Constraints

Yoonsik Cheon[✉]

The University of Texas at El Paso, El Paso, TX, USA
ycheon@utep.edu

Abstract. An assertion is a Boolean expression embedded in a program that must hold during the execution. Executable assertions are a simple but practical way to check assumptions and code logic at runtime. Assertions are written by referring to concrete program states. In this paper, we recognize a variety of assertions that we call *design assertions*. These are assertions written to ensure design constraints and properties, not detailed implementation decisions, and thus can detect major problems in the implementation such as design drift or corrosion. However, they are written by referring to concrete program states, thus causing readability and maintenance problems. To address these problems, we propose to write design constraints at a higher abstraction level by referring to abstract program states. We explain our approach using the Dart/Flutter platform, but it should work in other languages and platforms with similar assertion facilities.

Keywords: Assertion · Abstract model · Assertion-only method · Design constraint · Dart

1 Introduction

An assertion is a Boolean expression embedded at a specific place in a program that must hold during program execution. As evidenced by the presence of the *assert* statement and similar constructs in programming languages, assertions are recognized as a simple but practical programming tool. They provide a way to embed a programmer's assumptions and logic in source code in a form that can be checked at runtime. Assertions are written by referring to concrete program states, e.g., implementation-dependent data structures and algorithms. Therefore, when there are changes in implementation decisions, assertions have to be reformulated and rewritten. Furthermore, there are assertions to check design-level assumptions, constraints, or properties that should hold regardless of specific choices of implementation data structures and algorithms. In fact, assertions are said to be more effective when generated from design constraints and decisions. These assertions can detect a deviation or drift of implementation from its design, called *design corrosion* [14] or *decay* [11], one of the main problems associated with software maintenance.

In this paper, we study the use of assertions on the Flutter/Dart platform. Flutter is a cross-platform development framework for building apps that runs on multiple

O. Gervasi et al. (Eds.): ICCSA 2022 Workshops, LNCS 13381, pp. 617–631, 2022.
https://doi.org/10.1007/978-3-031-10548-7_45

platforms, e.g., Android and iOS [10]. Dart [4], the language of Flutter, provides an *assert* statement to write an executable assertion. In Flutter, a common pattern is to use assertions to perform preliminary checks on the constructor's arguments of a widget class. A Flutter widget is created and rendered automatically when its state changes. In Flutter, *assert* statements are enabled only in debug mode and are removed from production code in release mode. Flutter uses a dead code elimination technique called *tree shaking* to reduce compiled code size. This means that functions and classes used only in assertions are eliminated from the compiled code. Assertions, therefore, provide a simple yet effective way to check code logic in debug mode by stating the effects of a portion of code. We would like to promote the use of executable assertions for detecting bigger problems such as design drift or corrosion on the Dar/Flutter platform.

In this paper, we first show that there are two different kinds of executable assertions that we write in our code: *design assertions* and *code assertions*. Design assertions are assertions to check design constraints – design decisions, properties, and business rules – and must hold regardless of implementations. If expressed properly, they don't need to be reformulated or rewritten upon implementation changes such as data structures and algorithms. On the other hand, code assertions are for checking implementation-specific assumptions, properties, and decisions, e.g., choices of data structures and algorithms, and thus may need to be rewritten when there are changes in implementation decisions. We then propose an approach for writing design assertions abstractly in an implementation-independent way to make them more readable and maintainable. Two key elements of our approach are *assertion-only methods* and *abstract models*. Assertion-only methods are getters (special access methods in Dart) and observer methods whose sole purpose is to write assertions. We can also define a special assertion-only method called an *abstraction function* to map a concrete program state to an abstract model. The idea is to write assertions in terms of the abstract model rather than a concrete program representation. The assertion-only methods and the abstract models provide a vocabulary to write assertions at a higher level of abstraction without directly referring to concrete program states. Therefore, changes in implementation details have minimal or no impact on design assertions. Furthermore, this approach better supports some of the required properties of executable assertions such as transparency and plug-and-playability [6, 7].

An assertion-only method is similar to a specification-only method found in behavioral interface specification languages (BISL) such as JML [13]. It is a pure or side-effect-free method to be used only in assertions. An abstract model is similar to a model variable or a specification-only variable found in BISLs (e.g., [9]). It is a derived attribute or field to write assertions at a higher level of abstraction. Unlike in BISLs, we blend these specification concepts in the assertion facility of a programming language without extending the language or requiring special tool support. We enrich the vocabulary of Dart/Flutter assertions and make them more expressive. Our work was inspired by existing work on translating design constraints written in OCL [17] to runtime checks (e.g., [2]). The focus of our work, however, is the Dart/Flutter platform and its assertion facility. We think our approach is more practical and less holistic in that we suggest translating only key design constraints directly to executable assertions using the assert facility of the programming language. Thanks to the expressiveness of the language, most methods in well-written Dart/Flutter code are short and straightforward to the extent that they don't need assertions. Assertions, for example, are frequently redundant and longer than the code itself. In previous work, the translation is done indirectly with the use of BISL such as JML [1, 12] or an aspect-oriented programming language such as AspectJ [5, 8, 15]. There is also a BISL proposed for Dart [6], but it doesn't include specification-only methods or abstract models.

The rest of this paper is organized as follows. In Sect. 2 below, we identify two different kinds of assertions that we call design and code assertions. We explain them with examples taken from a Flutter app that will be used as a running example throughout this paper. In Sect. 3, we first describe the problems of the conventional way of writing design assertions and then propose our approach for writing them at a higher level of abstraction – assertion-only methods and abstract models. In Sect. 4, we show more examples along with some interesting observations, findings, and discussions on writing design assertions. In Sect. 5, we conclude this paper with a concluding remark.

2 Design and Code Assertions

In this section, we identify two different kinds of assertions that we write in our code. We explain them by showing example assertions picked from a small app for playing connect-four games that we will use as a running example in this paper. Connect Four is a classic two-player connection game in which the players take turns to drop their discs, or tokens, from the top into a seven-column, six-row vertically suspended grid (see Fig. 1). The discs fall straight down, occupying the next available space within the column. The objective is to be the first to connect four of one's discs next to each other vertically, horizontally, or diagonally.

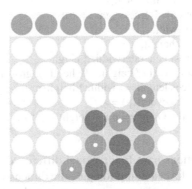

Fig. 1. Connect-four game

The class diagram in Fig. 2 shows one possible design for the model part of the connect-four app. A board representing the grid consists of a collection of places representing the spaces in the grid. Each place may be associated with one of the two players. The association indicates that a place is taken by a player and thus has a disc of the player. There are several different ways to realize the Board class in an implementation. We can use different data structures to store all the places of a board: a two-dimensional array-like structure (an array of columns or an array of rows), a one-dimensional array (stored in column/row/arbitrary order), a map from indexes to places, etc.

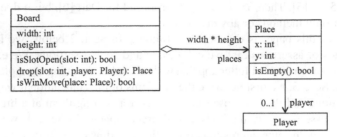

Fig. 2. Connect-four class diagram

The following code snippet of the Board constructor shows one possible implementation choice. All places are stored in a list (*_places*) in column-major order; in Dart, a name starting with an underscore (_) is private. The code also shows three *assert* statements, the Dart way of writing executable assertions. The first statement checks the parameters. The *assert* statement is very commonly used to check assumptions or the precondition of a method or constructor. For example, it is a common pattern for Flutter widget classes to perform preliminary checks on the constructor's parameters. The last two statements check code logic – postconditions or facts on the state that the code has to establish.

```
Board(int width, int height) {
  assert(width >= 7 && height >= 6);
  this.width = width;
  this.height = height;
  _places = List.generate(width * height,
        (i) => Place(i ~/ height, i % height), growable: false);
  assert(_places.length == width * height);
  assert(_places.every((p) =>
    _places.indexOf(p) == p.x * height + p.y));
}
```

The above three assertions have fundamental differences in their natures. The first assertion is about a design-level assumption, i.e., the dimension of a board or a connect-four grid. On the other hand, the other two are concerned with an implementation-level decision, i.e., a particular choice of data structure. A list is used to store all the places on a board, and thus its length is constrained. Similarly, the indexes of elements are constrained because the elements are stored in column-major order. The assertions may need to be reformulated and rewritten if the implementation decision changes. In this paper, we will use the terms *design assertions* and *code assertions* to refer to these two kinds of assertions. Design assertions are assertions to check design constraints – design decisions, properties, and business rules – and must hold regardless of implementations. If expressed properly, they don't need to be reformulated or rewritten when there are implementation changes such as data structures and algorithms. On the other hand, the purpose of code assertions is to check implementation-specific decisions, e.g., choices of data structures and algorithms, and thus may need to be rewritten upon changes in implementation decisions.

Below we show another code snippet with assertions. One key operation of the Board class is to place a player's disc in an empty place. The *drop()* method shown below implements this operation. Given a 0-based column index and a player, the method drops a disc of the player in the column. The *for* loop finds the last empty place in the column and associate it with the player.

```
Place drop(int slot, Player player) {
  assert(0 <= slot && slot < width);
  for (var i = (slot + 1)  * height -1; i >= slot * height; i--) {
    if (_places[i].isEmpty) {
      _places[i].player = player;
      assert(_places.getRange(slot * height, i)
        .every((p) => p.isEmpty));
      assert(_places.getRange(i, (slot + 1) * height)
        .every((p) => p.isFilled));
      return _places[i].;
    }
  }
  assert(_places.getRange(slot * height, (slot + 1) * height)
    .every((p) => p.isFilled));
  return null;
}
```

The code has three *assert* statements, and their usage pattern is very similar to the previous example. The first assertion is the precondition of the method and checks the validity of the parameters. The other three check the effect of the code in the post-state just before the control returns to the caller. The two nested *assert* statements together state that a player's disc is placed in the bottom-most empty place of a column. The last statement asserts that if a disc isn't placed, the column has no empty place. The way the three assertions are written gives the impression that they are code assertions. The assertions are formulated in terms of implementation-specific features such as the index of the _places list. Are they really code assertions? They assert (partial) behavior of the operation that should hold regardless of implementations; it is an operation postcondition expressed in terms of an implementation-specific data structure. In fact, it asserts partially a key invariant of the Board class: each column of a board is filled from the bottom to the top.

```
assert(Iterable.generate(width).every((slot) =>
  _places.getRange(slot * height, (slot + 1) * height )
    .every((p) => p.isEmpty ? true :
      _places.getRange(_places.indexOf(p) + 1,
      (slot + 1) * height)
      .every((q) => q.isFilled))));
```

3 Writing Design Assertions

3.1 The Problem

As shown in the previous section, assertions are written by referring to concrete program states – variables, fields, and methods. For code assertions, it may be acceptable because they have to be rewritten anyway if the program representation changes. It is often desirable to express the required relationships among elements of the program state, e.g., the x and y coordinates of a place and the position of the place in the containing list. For design constraints, however, there are several problems associated with expressing them in terms of the concrete program state. One problem is that when the representation, e.g., data structure, changes, assertions have to be reformulated and rewritten. As an example, consider changing the representation of the Board class. Instead of storing all the places in a one-dimensional list, we can organize them as a list of columns. This change requires us to review all occurrences of the _places field in the code including the assertions. For example, we need to rewrite the last three assert statements of the drop() methods as follows.

```
for (var i = height -1; i >= 0; i--) {
  if (_places[slot][i].isEmpty) {
    _places[slot][i].player = player;
    assert(_places[slot].getRange(0, i)
      .every((p) => p.isEmpty));
    assert(_places[slot].getRange(i, height)
      .every((p) => p.isFilled));
    return _places[slot][i].;
  }
}
assert(_places[slot].getRange(0, height)
  .every((p) => p.isFilled));
```

The required changes may be small or the rewritings may be done systematically. However, the concern is that all design assertions have to be rewritten manually, causing maintenance issues. Another problem is that when assertions are written by referring to concrete program states, it is not clear or easy to tell whether they are code assertions or design assertions. It is said that assertions are more effective when they are generated from design constraints and properties. These assertions called design assertions can detect major issues or problems compared with those of code assertions. They can detect when an implementation deviates from its design, often called *design corrosion* [14] or *design decay* [11], one of the main problems associated with software development and maintenance. We will need to pay more attention when design assertions are violated. Ideally, design assertions should be written in terms of the design vocabulary – design elements and concepts – not the implementation vocabulary. In the following two subsections, we propose two different ways to solve the above problems by writing design assertions abstractly.

3.2 Algebraic-Style Assertions

We can eliminate or minimize direct references to concrete program states by using get-ters or observer methods. In Dart, getters are special methods that provide read access to an object's properties or fields. For example, instead of accessing a place in a list directly, e.g., _places[slot * height + y], we can use an observer method, say _getPlace(int slot, int y). If there is no such method already defined, we can introduce one just for the purpose of writing assertions. The getters and observer methods allow us to access the concrete program states indirectly. Therefore, if we change the program representation, i.e., data structure, we need to make changes only to the getter and observer methods, thus minimizing the impact of the change to the assertions. The assertions also become more readable, as they are written in the vocabulary of a higher level of abstraction. In a sense, we enrich the vocabulary of the assertion language by providing model- or design-level operations. As an example, let us rewrite the drop() method of the Board class (see Sect. 2). The code snippet below shows the rewritten method. We introduce a new observer method _getColumn(int) that, given a slot index, returns a column of places. With this method, we can eliminate the use of the _places field from the two assertions in the middle. For the last one, we can also replace the whole assertion with a call to the isSlotFull() method that checks whether a given slot is filled completely.

```
Place drop(int slot, Player player) {
  assert(0 <= slot && slot < width);
  for (var i = (slot + 1) * height - 1; i >= slot * height; i--) {
    if (_places[i].isEmpty) {
      _places[i].player = player;
      assert(_getColumn(slot).getRange(0, i - slot * height)
        .every((p) => p.isEmpty));
      assert(_getColumn(slot).getRange(i - slot * height, height)
        .every((p) => p.isFilled));
      return _places[i];
    }
  }
  assert(isSlotFull(slot));
  return null;
}

@assert_only
List<Place> _getColumn(int slot) =>
  _places.getRange(slot * height, (slot + 1) * height);
```

When introducing getters and observer methods only for assertions, it would be a good idea to indicate it. We can define an annotation for this, say @assert_only, as shown above. The annotation also means that the annotated method should have no observable side-effect. An assertion expression may have side effects for the purpose of assertion checking, but the side-effect shouldn't be observable by the implementation code [7]. An assertion-only method should not be used in the implementation code. On the Flutter platform, assertions are enabled only in debug mode and are completely ignored in release mode in that they are not evaluated. Flutter also uses a dead code elimination technique called *tree shaking* to reduce code size. Functions and classes that are never used are removed from the compiled code. Therefore, assertion-only methods are not compiled in the production code in release mode.

As shown in the above example, we can write more abstract assertions by accessing the concrete program representation indirectly through getters and observer methods. If needed, we can also introduce assertion-only getters and observers, thus enriching the vocabulary for writing assertions. The set of getters and observers used in assertions defines implicitly an abstract view of a concrete program state. This style of writing assertions is in a sense algebraic. An operation is constrained by other operations – getters and observers. In other words, an assertion specifies a relationship or constraint among operations. Therefore, one fundamental question of this approach is: how do we write assertions for the getters and observer methods themselves? Ultimately, we will need to refer to the concrete program states. This algebraic style assertions may require a large number of assertion-only methods and may be less intuitive to a programmer because assertions are not constructive.

3.3   Abstract Model

The previous approach defines an abstract model of a program implicitly by the set of getters and observer methods used in assertions. We can define an abstract model explicitly and use it in assertions. An abstract model is an assertion's view on a concrete program state and provides the vocabulary to write assertions (see Fig. 3). Since an abstract model will be used only in assertions, it should be immutable or no mutation method should be allowed. By manipulating an abstract model in assertions, we may be able to write assertions in a constructive fashion, which may be more intuitive than an algebraic style to most programmers (see Sect. 4).

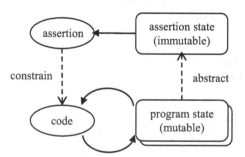

Fig. 3. Abstract model approach

In our implementation of the Board class, all places of a board are stored in a one-dimensional list in column-major order for performance reasons. Assertions, however, are enabled only in debug mode and stripped off from production code in release mode. And we are not or less concerned about performance of assertions, so, it would be advantageous to view all places as a list of columns. We can define explicitly a mapping, called an *abstraction function*, from a concrete program representation to an abstract representation or model. For example, we can define a private getter named *_model* as shown follows.

```
@assert_only
List<List<Place>> get _model => List.unmodifiable(
   Iterable.generate(width).map((slot) => List.unmodifiable(
      _places.getRange(slot * height, (slot + 1) * height))));
```

The getter returns an abstraction of the current program state, i.e., the *_places* field. It returns an immutable list to avoid side effects in assertions. If needed, we can also introduce assertion-only classes to express an abstract model just like we do with assertion-only methods (see Sect. 4). Once we define an abstraction function, we can write assertions to check various design constraints and properties in terms of the abstract model. For example, the following two assertions check class invariants saying that (a) a board has *width* * *height* number of places, and (b) the *x* and *y* indexes of each place are unique and are in the range of 0 and *width* - 1 and 0 and *height* - 1, respectively. They can be added to the constructors to ensure the establishment of the invariants and to the mutation methods to ensure the preservation [7].

```
assert(_model.length == width &&
   _model.every((column) => column.length = height));
assert(Iterable.generate(width).every((x) =>
   Iterable.generate(height).every((y) =>
      _model[x][y].x == x && _model[x][y].y ==y));
```

Of course, we can use the abstract model to rewrite assertions for methods and get rid of direct references to a concrete program state (see below).

```
Place drop(int slot, Player player) {
   assert(0 <= slot && slot < _model.length);
   for (var i = (slot + 1) * height -1; i >= slot * height; i--) {
     if (_places[i].isEmpty) {
      _places[i].player = player;
      assert(_model[slot].every((p) =>
         p.y < _places[i].y ? p.isEmpty : p.isFilled));
      return _places[i];
     }
   }
   assert(_model[slot].every((p) => p.isFilled));
   return null;
}
```

Two most common types of design constraints are class invariants and operation pre and postconditions. The ways these constraints are written are different. An invariant is a constraint on a single state and thus needs to refer to only a single abstract model.

It only needs to observe the values in a single state, not the changes of the values. On the other hand, a postcondition is frequently a constraint on two states, pre- and post-states, to specify the side effect of an operation, and documents state changes or transformations by referring to two abstract models. It needs to constrain the changes to the state, i.e., from the pre-state to the post-state. We can make the whole pre-state or some parts available to the post-state *assert* statements by introducing (assertion-only) local variables.

```
Place drop(int slot, Player player) {
  assert(0 <= slot && slot < _model.length);
  final y_ = _model[slot].lastIndexWhere((p) => p.isEmpty);
  for (var i = (slot + 1) * height -1; i >= slot * height; i--) {
    if (_places[i].isEmpty) {
      _places[i].player = player;
      assert(y_ >= 0);
      assert(_model[slot][y_].player == player);
      return _places[i]; // assert(places[i] == _model[slot][_y]);
    }
  }
  assert(y_ < 0);
  return null;
}
```

The local variable $y\_$ was introduced to store a pre-state value of an expression. It is initialized with the last row index of an empty place contained in the column under consideration. The three post-state assertions can be written in terms of this assertion-only local variable. The use of assertion-only local variables improves the expressiveness of assertions and thus lets us write more rich assertions. We can assert not only the side effects of a section of code but also when the side effects should happen. The above three assertions, for example, state that when there is an empty place in the given slot ($y\_ > = 0$), the place is filled; otherwise ($y\_ < 0$), no change in the state assuming an appropriate frame axiom such as "and nothing else changes" [3]. One downside of introducing a local variable for the sole purpose of writing assertions is that it may produce an "unused variable" warning in a release build because all *assert* statements are removed.

The abstract model approach can be thought of as a restricted form of the algebraic style approach where one assertion-only method defines an abstract model and the others, if any, are defined in terms of this abstract model. And design assertions are written in terms of this model without directly referring to the concrete program states. Therefore, one clear advantage is that when there are changes in the program representation, only a single assertion-only method, i.e., the abstraction function, needs to be reformulated and rewritten. By making the model immutable, we can also ensure the side-effect freeness of assertions. Another benefit is that we can tell easily which assertions are sort of more important design-level constraints and which are code-level constraints. However, one shortcoming is that an assertion violation is reported in terms of an abstract model, and thus we need to map it to a concrete program state to track and find the cause. In summary, the key idea of the abstract model approach is to define a model at a higher level of abstraction to write design assertions with the vocabulary of design concepts and elements.

4 More Examples, Observations, and Discussions

Another key operation of the Board class is to determine whether there is a winning sequence of discs, four discs of the same player next to each other vertically, horizontally, or diagonally. The *isWinMove()* method below implements this operation. Given a place (of the last drop), it checks whether there exists a winning sequence containing the place. If a winning sequence exists, the method also has the side effect of storing the sequence in a field named *winRow*.

```
bool isWinMove(Place place) {
assert(place.isFilled);
var result = false;
// ... omitted code to find a winning sequence
// assertion-only nested functions: isWin and seqs
isWin(seq) => seq.fold(0, (cnt, p) => cnt >= 4 ? cnt :
  (p.player == place.player ? cnt + 1 : 0)) >= 4;
seqs(places) => [
  places.where((p) => p.x == place.x),
  places.where((p) => p.y == place.y),
  places.where((p) => p.x - place.x == p.y - place.y),
  places.where((p) => p.x - place.x == -(p.y - place.y))];
assert(result == seqs(_model.expand((col) => col))
  .where((seq) => isWin(seq)).isNotEmpty);
assert(result ? winRow.length == 4 && isWin(winRow)
  : winRow == null);
return result;
}
```

The above code shows that we can also introduce assertion-only nested functions. The *isWin()* function tests if a given sequence of places contains a winning sequence, and the *seqs()* function finds the row, column, and two diagonals containing the place in question. The last two assertions constrain the return value and the side effect of the method, respectively.

As said previously, invariants are an important type of design constraint that can be checked with assertions. More interesting invariants are those that involve multiple objects and constrain relationships among them. Below we show several assertions for class invariants to show some interesting observations and findings. We have a class named ViewModel to manage the app state. It stores data that is shared by multiple widgets. When there is a change in the app state, all widgets are notified, rebuilt, and rendered again.

```
class ViewModel extends Model {
  final Board board;
  bool gameOver;
  final List<Player> _players;
  Player _currentPlayer;
  // ... other fields and methods
}
```

Below we have two invariants involving players. The first invariant states that there are two distinct players, and the current player, the player who has the turn, is one of the two players. The second invariant states that for every place on the board, its player should be one of the two players.

```
bool _inv1() => _players.contains(_currentPlayer)
  && _players.length == 2 && _players[0] != _players[1];

bool _inv2() => board.places.every((p) =>
  p.isEmpty || _players.contains(p.player));
```

The two invariants are similar in that we can write them by using the vocabulary of the implementation code, i.e., getters and observers. However, there is a big difference in their natures. The objects involved in the first invariant, the two players and the current player, are owned and managed by the ViewModel class, and the ViewModel class is responsible for ensuring the invariant. Therefore, we can call the invariant method in the *assert* statements embedded in the constructors and mutation methods such as *change-Turn()* of the ViewModel class. The invariant should be established by the constructors and preserved by the mutation methods of the ViewModel class. On the other hand, the places of the board referenced in the second invariant are not owned or managed by the ViewModel class; they are owned by the Board class. Therefore, the second invariant has to be checked by the Board class or its component class Place – i.e., when a place changes its state. The problem is the assertion can't be written inside the Board class because the two players are not available there and there is no reference from the Board class to the ViewModel class. One finding is that the right class in which to write a class invariant may not be the right class to check the invariant. It is future work to address this problem. A possible intrusive workaround would be to pass the assertion (or callback) to the Board class, e.g., through an assertion-only parameter or setter method.

There is also an invariant that is concerned with the *gameOver* field. The field can be thought of as a derived attribute in that its value can be calculated from other elements of the class. It is true when the board is full or contains a winning sequence. The following shows an incorrectly written assertion. The problem is that the *isWinMove()* method has a side effect and thus shouldn't be used in an assertion. And the Board class doesn't provide its client with a vocabulary suitable for writing the assertion.

```
bool _inv3() => gameOver == (board.isFull()
  || board.places.indexWhere((p) =>
    p.isFilled && board.isWinMove(p)) >= 0);
```

The real cause of the above problem is that when we write assertions outside a class, we have a limited vocabulary, i.e., public getters and observer methods of the class, as we can't access directly the hidden representation of the class. This vocabulary, a subset of the public API of the class, is for writing client code, and thus may not be suitable for writing client assertions. This raises an interesting discussion. Should a class provide assertion-only public features such as getters and observer methods for its clients? Would it be a good idea to have an assertion-only API for a class? For the above invariant, for example, we can introduce an assertion-only observer, say *hasWin*(), or make the abstract model public. Making the abstract model public seems to be the most general solution, and this is another strength of the abstract model approach.

We can write assertions in two different styles: *constrained* and *constructive styles*. In the constrained style, we constrain the value of a variable by specifying the properties that it has to satisfy without expressing it explicitly. In the constructive style, we specify the value explicitly by calculating it. We can use both styles to assert the return value of an operation or the state change that an operation has to establish. As an example, consider the *changeTurn*() method that alternates the two players' turns. We can assert its side-effect in the two different styles as follows.

```
bool changeTurn() {
  final oldCurrentPlayer_ = _currentPlayer;
  ...
  assert(_currentPlayer != oldCurrentPlayer_); // constrained
  assert(_currentPlayer ==                     // constructive
    _players.firstWhere((p) => p != oldCurrentPlayer_);
}
```

The first assertion written in the constrained style states that the new value of the *_currentPlayer* field should not be the same as its previous value. As there are only two players, the new value should be the other player. The second assertion is written in the constructive style in that it calculates the new value of the *_currentPlayer* field. It selects a player from the players list that is not the same as the pre-value of the *_currentPlayer* field. A constructive assertion is written in the form of $x == E$, where x is a variable and E is one specific value. Which style is preferred? It depends on the assertion, but our preference is the style that can express the intention of the assertion clearly and concisely. For the above assertion, we prefer the constrained style.

We found that with a suitable representation of a class, most methods are short and straightforward to the extent that they don't need assertions or assertions are redundant. In fact, oftentimes, assertions are longer than the code.

```
bool isFull() => _places.every((p) => p.isFilled);

bool isFull() { // rewritten to add an assertion
  var result = _places.every((p) => p.isFilled;
  assert(result ==
  _model.expand((col) => col).every((p) => p.isFilled));
  return result;
}
```

Most assertions shown in this paper are concerned with collections of values, e.g., a list of places and a list of two players. To write these assertions, we used higher-order methods defined on collections such as *every()*, *expand()*, *firstWhere()*, *fold()*, *indexWhere()*, and *where()*. These higher-order methods are indispensable for writing assertions involving a collection, but they are all read-only operations for accessing or observing the elements of a collection iteratively. In assertions, we can't use write operations that have side effects, e.g., adding new elements, removing existing elements, and performing an action on each element. However, to manipulate a collection of values in various ways, we need such operations but without side effects, e.g., an *add()* operation that returns a new collection. We, therefore, think that a mathematical toolkit or immutable collection library found in formal specification languages such as Z [16] and OCL [17] would be also useful for writing executable assertions. Such a library would be particularly helpful for defining abstract models as well as writing design assertions in a constructive style.

5   Conclusion

We presented our approach for writing executable assertions to check design constraints such as class invariants at runtime. The key idea of our approach is to write these assertions called *design assertions* at a higher level of abstraction without directly referring to the concrete program state. For this, we can introduce so-called *assertion-only* methods – getters and observer methods whose sole purpose is to write assertions. We can also define a getter called an *abstraction function* to map a concrete program state to an abstract model, and then we can write assertions in terms of the abstract model rather than a concrete program representation. The assertion-only methods and the abstract model provide a vocabulary to write assertions at a higher level of abstraction. Our approach allows programmers to embed runtime checks of important design decisions in code in a more readable and maintainable fashion. Changes in the implementation-level decisions such as data structures require no or minimal rewriting of design assertions; e.g., only the abstract function needs to be redefined. The two key contributions of our work include (a) recognition of an important class of assertions that we call design assertions, and (b) ways to write them at a higher level of abstraction. We also made several interesting observations, findings, and discussion topics, e.g., constrained- vs. constructive-style assertions, checking invariant assertions, and assertion-only APIs.

References

1. Avila, C., Flores, G., Cheon, Y.: A library-based approach to translating OCL constraints to JML assertions for runtime checking. In: International Conference on Software Engineering Research and Practice, Las Vegas, Nevada, 14–17 July, pp. 403–408 (2008)
2. Avila, C., Sarcar, A., Cheon, Y., Yeep, C.: Runtime constraint checking approaches for OCL, a critical comparison, In: International Conference on Software Engineering and Knowledge Engineering, 1–3 July, San Francisco, CA, pp. 393–398 (2010)
3. Borgida, A., Mylopoulos, J., Reiter, R.: '. . . and nothing else changes': the frame problem in procedure specifications. In: Proceedings of 1993 15th International Conference on Software Engineering, pp. 303–314. IEEE (1993)
4. Bracha, G.: The Dart Programming Language. Addison-Wesley, Boston (2016)
5. Briand, L., Dzidek, W., Labiche, Y.: Instrumenting contracts with aspect-oriented programming to increase observability and support debugging. In: International Conference on Software Maintenance, Budapest, Hungary, 25–30 September, pp. 687–690. IEEE (2005)
6. Chalin, P.: Ensuring that your dart will hit the mark: an introduction to dart contracts. In: International Conference on Information Reuse and Integration, Redwood City, CA, 13–15 August, pp. 369–377. IEEE (2014)
7. Cheon, Y.: Toward more effective use of assertions for mobile app development. In: International Conference on Progress in Informatics and Computing, Shanghai, China, 17–19 December, pp. 319–323. IEEE (2021)
8. Cheon, Y., Avila, C., Roach, S., Munoz, C.: Checking design constraints at run-time using OCL and AspectJ. Int. J. Softw. Eng. 2(3), 5–28 (2009)
9. Cheon, Y., Leavens, T., Sitaraman, M., Edwards, S.: Model variables: cleanly supporting abstraction in design by contract. Softw. Pract. Exp. 35(6), 583–599 (2005)
10. Flutter Homepage. https://flutter.dev/. Accessed 6 Nov 2021
11. Fowler, M.: Refactoring: Improving the Design of Existing Code. Addison-Wesley, Boston (1999)
12. Hamie, A.: Translating the object constraint language into the java modeling language. In: ACM Symposium on Applied Computing, Nicosia, Cyprus, 14–17 March, pp. 1531–1535. ACM (2004)
13. Leavens, G., Cheon, Y., Clifton, C., Ruby, C., Cok, D.: How the design of JML accommodates both runtime assertion checking and formal verification. Sci. Comput. Program. 55(1–3), 185–208 (2005)
14. Perry, D., Wolf, A.: Foundations for the study of software architecture. ACM SIGSOFT Softw. Eng. Notes 17(4), 40–52 (1992)
15. Richters, M., Gogolla, M.: Aspect-oriented monitoring of UML and OCL constraints. In: AOSD Modeling with UML Workshop, San Francisco, CA, 20 October 2003 (2003)
16. Spivey, S.: The Z Notation: A Reference Manual. Prentice Hall, Hoboken (1992)
17. Warmer, J., Kleppe, A.: The Object Constraint Language: Getting Your Models Ready for MDA, 2nd edn. Addison-Wesley, Hoboken (2003)

DC Health: Node-Level Online Anomaly Detection in Data Center Performance Data Monitoring

Walter Lopes Neto⬭ and Itamir de Morais Barroca Filho[(✉)]⬭

Metropole Digital Institute, Federal University of Grande do Norte Natal,
Natal, Brazil
walter.lopes@ifrn.edu.br, itamir.filho@imd.ufrn.br
http://www.imd.ufrn.br, http://www.ufrn.br

Abstract. Data centers are critical environments for the availability of technology-based services. Aiming at the high availability of these services, performance metrics of nodes such as Virtual Machines (VM) or VMs clusters are widely monitored. These metrics, such as CPU and memory utilization, can show anomalous patterns associated with failures and performance degradation, culminating in resource exhaustion and total node failure. Thus, early detection of anomalies can enable remediation measures, such as VM migration and resource reallocation, before losses occur. However, traditional monitoring tools often use fixed thresholds for detecting problems on nodes and lack automatic ways to detect anomalies at runtime. In this sense, machine learning techniques have been reported to detect anomalies in computer systems with online and offline approaches. Thus, this work aims to propose and evaluate the DC Health application, pursues to anticipate the detection of anomalies in data center nodes. For this, this research was conducted from i) Systematic Literature Review previously performed, ii) problem modeling from real VM data and iii) DCH evaluation using the prequential method in 6 real-world datasets. Preliminary results showed that DCH excelled in constant memory usage and detection accuracy above 75% in the worst of the 5 cases and accuracy of 90% at best when applied in the real node datasets and an accuracy of 85% on the shuttle dataset. As a continuation of this research, it is expected to develop a case study with data center operators and the evaluation of the tool in a large volume of nodes.

Keywords: Anomaly detection · Monitoring · Data center · Fault-detection · Machine learning · Half-Space-Trees · Data mining · Predictive analytics · VM-level anomalies · Node-level anomaly

1 Introduction

Network infrastructure monitoring systems for data centers are essential to maintain observability and high availability of operation in these critical environments. In this sense, existing and widely used systems for this purpose, such as

O. Gervasi et al. (Eds.): ICCSA 2022 Workshops, LNCS 13381, pp. 632–649, 2022.
https://doi.org/10.1007/978-3-031-10548-7_46

Zabbix [20], enable detailed monitoring of physical and virtual servers as well as applications. Among these collected data, the health and performance data of the nodes, such as logs and metrics, can present sets of anomalous patterns associated with failures as reported by Ibidunm et al. [14], Guan et al. [11] and [26]. The accumulation of anomalies of different natures can be a significant cause of incremental performance degradation, culminating in resource exhaustion or even the total failure of the host [26]. In this way, techniques that enable the analysis of these patterns aiming at the early detection of performance anomalies have become increasingly present in the literature and the industry as a report for Notaro et al. [25]. Early detection of anomalies in data center nodes, such as performance degradation, can make it possible to apply corrective measures before damage occurs. Examples of corrective measures are virtual machine migration and resource allocation adjustment [23]. The classic machine learning approach to this type of problem is to split the stored data into datasets, train the model on that data, i.e. it is required early access to the entire dataset, and then use it for prediction. Although this classic approach has been used to detect performance anomalies in works in the literature, as presented in Sects. 2 and 3, it faces challenges such as naturally suffering from the aging of the model as reported by Xiao et al. [37]. In this sense, the field of online machine learning has been established to address this problem. The online learning field seeks to carry out the learning process from potentially infinite data streams [29]. Thus, unlike classical methods, the model is exposed only once to each sample and must be ready to perform prediction at any time, in addition, to dynamically adapting to changes in streams, for example, due to concept drift. In this sense, the term concept drift refers to a common challenge in the machine learning area, which occurs when changes in the forecast target variable lead the model to lag, impairing the accuracy over time [36]. Online anomaly detection has been applied in several domains such as network intrusion detection, financial fraud detection, fault detection, and anomaly detection in the context of public health, among others [5]. Among the application domains, we highlight fault detection, which is a field that has attracted interest for more than 30 years and focuses on subareas such as fault tracking, and symptom monitoring, reporting of detected errors, and auditing undetected errors [29]. In this context, online failure prediction refers to identifying whether a failure will occur shortly (during runtime), based on an assessment of the current state of the monitored system [29]. Concerning critical environments such as data centers, online forecasting methods are especially interesting, since they focus on the aspect of short-term forecasts being useful to prevent potential disasters and limit the damage caused by computer system failures. By incorporating system performance metrics at runtime, the prediction of failure occurrence can be on the order of seconds or minutes [29]. However, because they have big data characteristics, dynamically dealing with failure data from monitoring systems in data centers is challenging. Sometimes these failures are unpredictable and it becomes complex and expensive to identify their root cause [26] or individually model the factors that potentially generate each type of failure, being in some cases unfeasible. Additionally, predicting failures in systems where there is no labeled data (in this case, where each instance used to train the model is previously classified as failure or normal) is a challenge. Real-world computer systems, especially newly deployed systems, do not always have fault-labeled data available or have such data reliably [12]. In this context, generally, the volume of data representing normal behavior is significantly greater than that of failure data so, in that case, it is possible to use unsupervised techniques to reveal hidden patterns in the data, and thus determine also conditions that deviate from the normal operating condition (anomalies). In this sense, the performance degradation of hosts and services can be an early indication of resource exhaustion, which causes failures. In this way, the unsupervised anomaly detection approach is better suited. Regarding node performance and fault identification and performance degradation, current infrastructure monitoring systems such as Zabbix and Cactie generally make use of fixed thresholds [35]. Examples of node performance items monitored with fixed thresholds are CPU or memory usage above a certain fixed value or free disk space below a certain fixed value. This detection format culminates in making monitoring systems overly dependent on manual adjustments by operators. This context becomes especially problematic when it comes to complex and dynamic systems such as data centers, and a greater extent in cloud data centers. In this sense, identifying thresholds related to an anomaly is more complex than using a single value, like 75% CPU usage, for example, as reported by Mendoza et al. [19]. Based on the exposed elements, the following research question will be addressed in this work: **How to early identify anomalies in datacenter nodes, such as virtual machines or virtual machine clusters, from performance measurements, such as CPU and memory utilization, at runtime?** Thus, the objective of this article is to propose and evaluate the DC Health application, which is a solution aimed at anticipating the detection of node anomalies in an online manner. The DC Health application, presented in this work, is a solution aimed at detecting anomalies in an online manner based on performance data from data center nodes, collected as a data stream. The tool is based on the framework skmultiflow [21] (A Python library focused on stream data) and the implementations of Half-Space-Trees, well known and state-of-the-art anomaly detection algorithm for data streams [34]. Introduced by Tan et al. [32] as a fast anomaly detector for evolving data stream.

2   Background

The anticipation of anomaly detection is potentially advantageous for the operation of data centers from the point of view of increasing the availability of nodes and services that depend on them. Anomaly detection can be performed in advance, by taking advantage of intrinsic characteristics of machine learning techniques when training a model and seeking to improve it over time. Thus, as new data is collected (with each new instance of the data stream), the model can be updated automatically.

Data Centers and Cloud Services Infrastructure. Data center (DC) refers to an information technology infrastructure aimed at housing information systems (IS) to minimize all types of interruptions. DCs main components are computers, servers, storage, cooling, and power systems according to Saha et al. [28]. In this sense, the prediction of the failure propensity of data center nodes can be performed based on the analysis of historical performance and failure data and can improve the availability of services in several ways, among them through the allocation of virtual machines in healthy nodes or even migration without disconnecting from the client (live migration) [17]. However, dealing with the volume of performance metrics data can be challenging. Monitoring tools such as Zabbix [20] often collect a large number of performance metrics from the data center and nodes. Among these metrics, we can highlight the level of CPU utilization (at the system or user level), CPU idle time, memory utilization level, and volume of I/O operations, among others [11]. Data centers are usually monitored through network infrastructure monitoring systems, which are essential to maintain the observability and high availability of these environments. Examples of specialized monitoring systems include Zabbix, Nagios, and proprietary systems. In general, these systems collect health and performance data from nodes (logs and metrics) that may present anomalous patterns associated with failures. Which, when accumulated, can cause performance degradation and lead to resource exhaustion and failures.

Anomaly Detection in Data Centers. Anomaly Detection (AD) refers to the problem of identifying patterns in the data that do not conform to the expected behavior according to Chandola et al. [5]. Among the several areas of research that address AD problems, we can highlight the area of machine learning, focusing on the application domain of fault detection from the perspective of performance data, the focus of this work. In this sense, regarding AD in data centers, we considered in this research the hypothesis that in environments designed for high availability such as data centers, anomaly data is significantly rarer when compared to the volume of data of normal operation. Thus, obtaining accurate data, where each instance is clearly labeled as normal or anomalous, and which is representative of all types of behavior, is generally prohibitively expensive [5]. Generally, data labeling to obtain the training dataset is done by human experts or based on the modeling of specific and not very generalizable cases, such as failures in HD's [3,13], and [40]. Additionally, anomalous behavior is dynamic in nature, so new types of uncharacterized anomalies often arise in the model training process. This factor is relevant in the context of reliability, since anomalous events, although very rare, can translate into catastrophic scenarios in certain cases [5]. In this way, the provision of mechanisms that enable the early detection of these events is relevant for the efficient operation of data centers.

Online Anomaly Detection. Online Anomaly Detection (DAO), similarly to online failure prediction, aims to predict the occurrence of failures in a system based on the current state of the system and during runtime [29]. Thus, DAO, especially applied to sequential data, is a relevant topic in fields such as intrusion and failure detection [6]. In this sense, online learning is superior to offline learning when it comes to applying sequential data, allowing online prediction with low memory usage [8]. In the context of anomaly detection, machine learning can be used to enable the statistical model of the normal behavior of the data to be learned, and so this model can predict future values and identify anomalies, as new data is received online, comparing the predicted with the actual values [19]. In this sense, works like [27,38], and [31] apply online anomaly detection, so that each of the test instances receives an anomaly score, as well as helping to update the model, which evolves incrementally. Approaches and methods aimed at online anomaly detection can be classified into statistical-based, cluster-based, nearest-neighbor-based, and isolation-based. Of these, we highlight the isolation-based methods, which differ from the others in that they do not compute the distance or density of the dataset. Isolation-based methods, like HS-Trees, prove to be scalable and suitable for datastream [33]. In this sense, the sliding window strategy has been used as a way to adapt offline methods for data in-stream format as in [7] and [22]. The application of the sliding window strategy allows online fault detection, for example, to adapt to variations in system behavior. This is because this technique assumes that recent data is more important than old data and thus discards the oldest samples from the window [41].

Unsupervised Anomaly Detection (UAD). Unsupervised Anomaly Detection (UAD) refers to the challenge of applying anomaly detection to data that has not been previously labeled. Unlike standard classification methods, UAD is generally applied to take into account only the internal structure of the data [10]. In this case, each instance can be associated with only one attribute (univariate) or with multiple attributes (multivariate) [5]. In scenarios such as production data centers, it is natural that system metrics change over time due to several factors, such as configuration changes, demand characteristics, software updates, among others. In these cases, models need to identify the new normal behavior in an unsupervised way in order to adapt [1]. Techniques that need pre-labeled data, such as supervised classification-based methods, are generally not suitable for anomaly detection and continuous learning [1]. Among the unsupervised techniques aimed at detecting anomalies in datastream, we can highlight Half-Space-Trees (HS-Trees), introduced by Tan et al. as a fast one-class anomaly detector for evolving data streams [32]. The method used works based on a Haflt-Space-Trees committee in which each HS-Trees is composed of a set of nodes that capture a given set of items. After executing HS-Trees, the identification of an instance as being or not being an anomaly can be done in two ways: **i)** Through the predict function, in which the sample is labeled with a specific value if it is considered anomalous, or **ii)** Based on the visual analysis of the output of the decision function, in which a threshold can be drawn.

Challenges Related to Early Identification of Anomalies in Data Center Nodes. Among the challenges related to the early identification of anomalies in data center nodes, we can mention: **i) Faults of different origins** Nodes of complex systems such as data centers can have their failures of very different origins (hardware, software, bugs, among others). Identifying the root cause or individually modeling each factor that potentially generates the failure can be very complex and costly [39] and **ii) Lack of labeled data in data centers** Predict failures in systems where there is no data previously labeled as failures. That's usually the case for data centers.

3   Related Works

The field of anomaly detection in data streams has been extensively researched and has applications in several domains such as detection of financial fraud, network attacks, in the field of individual and public health and fault detection. In regard of fault detections, several recent works have addressed techniques and tools aimed at detecting anomalies online. The development of DH Health was inspired as a result of some recent work with the approaches described as follows.

A supervised anomaly detection strategy was proposed by Liu et al. [18], applying Self Organizing Maps (SOM). They demonstrate that anomalies within VMs can be detected in certain regions of the infrastructure using unified modeling to detect the node performance. Differently, we propose the application of a different anomaly detector to each node, so each detector can learn from the behavior of an specific node monitored, without being affected by the others.

The work present by Sirbu et al. [30] is a study of cluster data from Google dataset, collected from a 12K-node cluster with the goal of building and evaluating predictive models for node failures. Although the work presents relevant contributions, the application is designed to be applied in a supervised manner. In contrast to the method proposed by the authors, our work proposes an unsupervised approach, due to the restriction of the data collected in our research. This occurs as a result of the data provided does not have clear markings indicating which samples refer to faulty nodes and which refer to normal behavior.

A method extending HS-Trees was proposed by Wetzing et al. [35] to detect anomalies on IoT-Gateway devices. The authors propose an unsupervised anomaly detection algorithm based on the concept of HS-Trees. The proposed method extends the HS-Trees through online adaptive thresholds for resourced constrain IoT-Gateway devices. In contrast to these, our work is based on the use of virtual machines in the data center, in a context where there is usually no severe restriction of resources.

The Streaming Half-Space-Trees (HS-Trees) was presented by Tan et al. [32] as an anomaly detector with a focus on detection speed for one-class anomalies applied to the data stream. The presented algorithm works in an unsupervised way, so it only needs normal data for training. In the evaluation, the method presented a favorable performance in terms of detection accuracy and runtime performance, when compared to state-of-the-art algorithms. Also applying online anomaly detection, the work by Togbe et al. [33] presents a quick survey of existing anomaly detection methods for the data stream and provides an implementation of iForestASD, an adaptation of iForest for data streams. Our work, in a similar manner to Tan et al. [32] and Tobe et al. [33], performs the evaluation of the HS-Trees method using the prequential method. However, our work differs in the sense of using real performance data from data center nodes.

4   DC Health

DC Health is proposed as a solution aimed at anticipating the detection, in an online manner, of anomalies in data center nodes.

4.1   DC Health Overview

DC Health (DCH) is a system whose objective is realize early detection of anomalies in data center nodes. For this, the tool consumes data streams composed of performance samples of data center nodes, such as usage level CPU, memory, and network. These samples are collected by the DCH, from network monitoring systems like Zabbix. It is noteworthy that currently, the DCH is in the prototype stage of development. The DCH uses the Half-Space Trees (HS-Trees) algorithm to perform anomaly detection. Thus, within the scope of DCH, anomaly detection is carried out in an unsupervised online manner, that is, without the need to train the system with pre-labeled data. In addition, due to the use of HS-Trees, the DCH has constant memory consumption requirements for each instance of the anomaly detection model. These constant memory requirements are achieved due to the working format of HS-Trees, which processes each sample only once, that is, testing and updating the model for each sample. DCH is designed to perform anomaly detection at a host level in order to be applied to physical servers, virtual machines or virtual machine clusters nodes. In this way, the DCH monitors certain nodes of interest and, by learning from their behavior considered normal, makes it possible to alert datacenter operators in advance if any abnormal events are detected. The application of these techniques makes it possible to learn the behavior considered normal for the data centers performance metrics, in an online manner, making it possible to alert anomalous behaviors in advance, since it makes the use of thresholds more flexible, making them more dynamic, as well as enabling alerts based on abnormal behavior.

The Fig. 1 presents the overview of DC Health. In this overview, it is possible to identify the multiple instances of online anomaly detectors that aim to detect anomalies in advance based on the metrics of each node of interest.

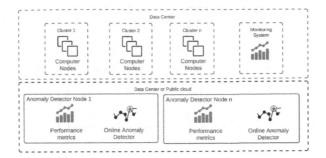

Fig. 1. DC Health overview.

4.2   DC Health Architecture

DC Health is composed of software components called modules. Each component implements a certain set of system functionality. The main modules currently implemented in the DCH prototype are the Stream Collection Module (MCS), the Online Anomaly Detection Module (MDAO) and the Messenger Module (MM). In general, anomaly detection occurs when the Anomaly Detection Module Online understands that there is an anomalous event in a certain node of the datacenter, which is being observed. In this sense, the observed node refers to a host (for example a cluster of virtual machines), which has been previously associated with a Detector. In this way, when using the system, the datacenter operator can create and remove Anomaly Detectors associated with the nodes. Thus, if an anomaly is detected, the operator is alerted via the Messenger Module. Finally, for the DCH to work, it must be hosted on a Linux operating system based on ×86 host. The collection of performance data from the nodes is carried out through the Stream Collection Module (MCS), which communicates with the datacenter monitoring server, such as Zabbix, and starts to receive samples of metrics from performance. Examples of performance metrics are the level of CPU, memory, and network utilization. The Fig. 2 presents the basic architecture of DC Health through an example of a working flow. Observe the data flow where the performance metrics of the nodes are collected and stored by the monitoring server (Number 1). In parallel, the anomaly detection module instantiated for a given node consumes the collected instances one by one from the monitoring server and performs anomaly detection (Number 2). Then, if an anomalous event is detected, the operator is alerted (Number 3). During this process, with each data sample consumed, the model is updated. The operator can perform basic query and configuration operations on the DCH through access using the command line interface (Number 5), as well as query report of anomalies detected by host.

4.3   DC Health Components

Online Anomaly Detector Module (MDO). MDO is the module that performs the main DC Health online anomaly detection function. MDO works online

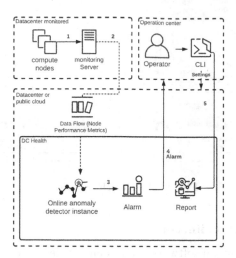

Fig. 2. Basic architecture of DC Health.

and is based on registered nodes. For each node of interest registered with DC Health, a new online anomaly detector is created and keeps track of the flow of performance data streams from this node. Several detectors can be created so that each detector is composed of an instance of HS-Trees that monitors the datastream. For each new data sample associated with a given node, an anomaly score is associated with the instance and a label of normal or anomalous. Additionally, the sample is used for an incremental update of the model. In case the sample is identified as anomalous, the MOD sends, via the Message Module, and identified anomaly alert to the operator, with the related context. The MOD also logs all activities on disk. The entire analysis is considered for a given sample window.

Stream Collection Module (MCS). The MCS communicates with Monitoring Systems through queries via API. After the query, the MCS performs data extraction and transformation and sends the samples in data stream format to the Anomaly Detection Module Online. In the current implementation, MCS supports the Zabbix monitoring system [20].

4.4   Methodology

As a proof of concept, we performed anomaly detection assessment on real data using the DC Health prototype. The phases of the methodology adopted in this research were briefly presented in Fig. 3. Initially, a Systematic Literature Review was conducted (phase 1) to help understand the current state and future trends of the application of machine learning techniques in data center monitoring, aimed at early detection of failures [24]. Based on the techniques and strategies identified in the SLR, such as unsupervised strategies aimed at detecting anomalies based on the degraded behavior of resource consumption in the [16] and [2] targeting data center, an iterative phase of data analysis and solution development was conducted. In the analysis, historical performance data of nodes from a real data center in production were used to model the problem as a Machine Learning problem. After modeling the problem, during the development of the application, activities such as data collection, exploration and preparation were carried out. In the third phase 3 of development, and evaluation of the detection performance was carried out. The proposed solution was evaluated (phase 3) based on the comparison of anomaly detection results obtained through DC Health against performance metrics of virtual machines from the real data center in production at Instituto Metropole Digital, a unit of the Federal University of Rio Grande do Norte, Brazil (IMD), as well as well-known datasets from the area of machine learning. The evaluation was based on the prequential method (interleaved test-then-train), an alternative to the traditional holdout, commonly adopted in the literature because it is specific to the datastream. The method consists of using each sample to make a prediction (i.e. testing the model), and then the same sample is used to train the model (partial fit). In this way, the model is always tested on samples not yet used in training. Each sample is evaluated in order of arrival and immediately becomes inaccessible (natural from a data stream), serving for testing and training.

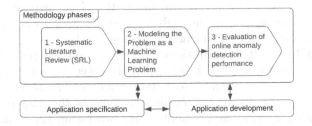

Fig. 3. Methodology phases.

Overview. We propose to approach the problem as an online anomaly detection problem, for that we use the HS-Trees that works in an unsupervised way and can deal with samples from the stream of unlabeled data. In this way, the model is built based on performance data at runtime, collected by the monitoring tool and representing the nodes in their normal behavior (without failures).

In this research we use the implementation of the algorithm HS-Trees presented by [32], as an ensemble of HS-Trees, a fast anomaly detector for data streams that requires only normal data for training. Also, HS-Tree and works well when (as presented in the context of this work), the anomalous data are rare [32]. The method based on HS-Tree was chosen because it is feasible with the use of unclassified data (in an unsupervised way) in addition to being able to use only normal data for training, to create the anomaly detection model.

This choice was made due to the problem of insufficient failure data for training due to natural limitations of the data center data collection process, identified earlier. There are two outputs of the anomaly detection algorithm: The label for each instance, identifying whether the instance is normal or anomalous, and the value of Anomaly Score, which indicates the degree of abnormality.

Methodology Steps. The methodology of this research was developed in 3 steps, as described below:

Step 1 - Systematic Literature Review (SRL). A systematic literature review was conducted following the method of [15]. The following research questions (RQ) were addressed: **RQ1:** What are the main characteristics of the machine learning algorithms and models being applied to monitoring data center infrastructure? **RQ2:** What types of data are being used in the proposed models? (eg sensor data, images, event logs). **RQ3:** What are the main challenges in applying machine learning to data center infrastructure monitoring? **RQ4:** What are the most common types of failures identified in data center infrastructure monitoring?

Step 2 - Modeling the problem as a Machine Learning problem. The approach chosen for the machine learning problem was to consider performance anomalies as potential failures and failure precursors and approach anomaly detection in an online and unsupervised way. With each new instance received, the model is updated and labels the given instance as normal or anomalous. The instances, once labeled, can be used as a source for fault detection through supervised classification methods.

Step 3 - DC Health evaluation. The evaluation was performed by comparing performance metrics during anomaly detection for different existing datasets and for data from a real data center environment. As described in [4], the key criteria for evaluating classifiers in the data stream context (depending on specific requirements) are: processing time, memory usage, adaptability, and prediction performance. In this work, we will use prediction performance. As described by Gama et al. [9], performance measurements on data streams can be performed using prequential evaluation. The evaluation method will be briefly described: **1)** Choice of datasets. As detailed earlier, a reference dataset was chosen along with 5 new experimental datasets. **2)** Choice of evaluation parameters. For the sliding windows, different sizes (32, 64, 128 and 256) were adopted. **3)** Choice of the detection algorithm execution discipline. With each new sample added to the window, the detection algorithm is executed using the contents of the window as a training set. **4)** Choice of main metric for comparison. The chosen metrics were accuracy. Unsupervised methods do not need labeled data, however, for performance evaluation, labeled data and well-known datasets are generally used [10].

5   Experimental Evaluation

In this section, the procedures used in the evaluation experiment, and the characteristics of the data from the experimental environment will be briefly described.

Datasets. The data used in the experiment came from two sources. The first was the Shuttle dataset, which was chosen because it is commonly used in the literature for the evaluation of anomaly detectors in streaming data. Among the works that applied this dataset, we can mention the work by Ding et al. [7], in a witch, the authors proposed the algorithm iForestASD and evaluate this dataset, and also Tan et al. [32], that authors applied the HS-Trees algorithm. Additionally, this dataset contains known anomalies, being used as a baseline for performance reference. The Shuttle dataset is an unbalanced dataset, which contains 80% of the data associated with one of the classes. Additionally, unlike the second data source, has the class attribute available and used during the evaluation. The second data source was the datasets created based on collecting data from hosts in a real data center during the execution of the experiment. For this, we chose to compute nodes that presented known problems related to performance and unavailability (Processor load is too high and Unreachable for more than 10 min). The data collection period was 1 year (01/01/2020 to 12/31/2021). Node 1 to 5 datasets were created containing the following attributes: CPU Load (Average 1 min), Ping (milliseconds), Ping (0 or 1), Memory, and Amount of free space in the file system. Additionally, the data were normalized. Regarding the data nature of the experimental datasets, multivariate data with continuous numerical attributes were considered. Regarding the relationship between the instances, sequential instances were considered.

The Table 1 briefly presents the characteristics of the datasets in terms of a number of instances and attributes. To facilitate the reproducibility of this research, the datasets node 1 to 5 was made available.[1]

Table 1. Summary of the characteristics of the datasets adopted for the experiment.

Summary of the characteristics of the adopted datasets		
Dataset	Number of instances	Number of attributes
Shuttle	49097	9
Node 1 to Node 5	1698	6

Description of the Experimental Environment. Aiming at evaluating the feasibility of the proposal, we defined a controlled environment for the experiment. The experimental environment configuration used to host DC Health was: One server with 2 CPUs: Intel(R) Xeon(R) CPU E5-4610 v4 @ 1.80 GHz, 4 GiB of memory, using de OS CentOS Linux release 7.9.2009 (Core), with a disk of 50 GB (SCSI) and Network interface as Gigabit Ethernet.

---

[1] https://github.com/walter-ln/datasets_dch.

Execution of the Experimental Evaluation. The experiments aimed at validating the DC Health anomaly detection model were performed as described in the following steps: **1. Experimental environment definition** - the experimental environment was defined as described in this section; **2. Data collection for the experiment** - data collection was performed from the Extraction Module (MET) and Treatment of the DC Health prototype, with the target being the monitoring system (Zabbix) of the data center of the Instituto Metrópole Digital (IMD/UFRN). The MET, according to its configuration, requested all available data for each of the pre-defined hosts. After collection, MET performed preprocessing and created a dataset file for each of the 5 hosts with known issues, as described. In-depth details on how the MET works can be described in Sect. 4.3; **3. Loading of experimental data and conversion into data stream** - the reading of the experimental datasets was performed by the Stream Collection Module (MCS) and this transferred the data in data stream format to the Detection Module of Anomalies Online (MDAO); **4. Model training and evaluation, for each set of parameters** - a total of 24 experiments were performed. For each of the 6 data sets, the model was run considering the sample window value varying between the values 32, 64, 128, and 256 samples. At each sample window value, the model was instantiated, trained over 1000 samples, and performed the prequential evaluation. The prequential method consists of using each sample to test the model and then the same sample is used to train the model, i.e. to perform the partial fit. In this way, the model is always tested on samples not yet used in training. Each sample is evaluated on a first-come, first-served basis and is immediately inaccessible for testing and training. After the evaluation of each model, the result metrics, in this case, in particular, the accuracy, were saved in auxiliary text files.

6   Results and Limitations

In this research, the DC Health system, aimed at detecting anomalies in data center nodes, was presented. Table 2 presents the results obtained for each combination of sample window sizes, with w varying between 32, 64, 128, and 256 samples. The results presented show that DC Health obtained an accuracy of 75% in the worst of the 5 cases and 90% accuracy in the best case. These accuracy values occurred when applied to datasets from real data center nodes (datasets from nodes 1 to 5). As shown in Table 2, the same system obtained an accuracy of 85% in the dataset Shuttle, with window size w = 64 samples. The preliminary experimental results indicate that the proposed solution achieved satisfactory performance, considering the detection accuracy above 75% for the detection of anomalies in real data, both in datasets from nodes 1 to 5, as well as with well-known data of literature. However, considering the natural trade-off between execution speed and accuracy, and in the context of applying early anomaly detection on datacenter nodes, we understand that a faster, even if less accurate, model is usually more desirable than a more accurate model, but slower in terms of detection. This hypothesis is based on the sense that, in critical

Table 2. Comparison of results from the application of the proposed system in different real-world data sets. For each dataset, window size combinations (32, 64, 128, and 256) were tested on 1000 samples.

Dataset node 1			
Window (w)	Accuracy	Memory (kB)	Execution time (s)
32	0.033033	755201	96
64	0.868869	755202	60
128	0.828829	755204	45
256	0.657658	755207	34
Best	**0.868869**	**755201**	**34**

Dataset node 2			
Window (w)	Accuracy	Memory (kB)	Execution time (s)
32	0.034034	755201	95
64	0.837838	755202	61
128	0.825826	755204	41
256	0.688689	755207	37
Best	**0.837838**	**755201**	**37**

Dataset node 3			
Window (w)	Accuracy	Memory (kB)	Execution time (s)
32	0.034034	755201	88
64	0.479479	755202	62
128	0.827828	755204	41
256	0.720721	755207	35
Best	**0.827828**	**755201**	**35**

Dataset node 4			
Window (w)	Accuracy	Memory (kB)	Execution time (s)
32	0.034034	755201	93
64	0.755756	755202	59
128	0.649650	755204	44
256	0.683684	755206	35
Best	**0.755756**	**755201**	**35**

Dataset node 5			
Window (w)	Accuracy	Memory (kB)	Execution time (s)'
32	0.032032	755201	89
64	0.906907	755202	59
128	0.858859	755204	41
256	0.720721	755206	35
Best	**0.906907**	**755201**	**35**

Dataset shuttle			
Window (w)	Accuracy	Memory (kB)	Execution time (s)'
32	0.7888	154677	1313
64	0.8509	116430	1507
128	0.8298	843094	1670
256	0.7197	580721	1572
Best	**0.8509**	**116430**	**1313**

environments, anomalous events, although very rare, can translate into catastrophic scenarios in certain cases [5]. In this way, the system obtained the best execution time of 34 s for the evaluation of 1000 instances. Finally, as shown in Table 2, the memory consumption requirements of the model remained constant for different sizes of windows w. **Limitations** This study has a number of limitations. The set of hyperparameters used to find the best configuration for the model was identified but was restricted so that other configurations can identify better results. Due to time limitations for the research, the prototype was evaluated only through the metrics of accuracy, processing time, and memory usage. Other comparison metrics were not explored, such as Area Under the Receiver Operating Characteristics (AUROC), Area Under The Curve (AUC), Receiver Operating Characteristics (ROC), F1 measure, Precision, and Recall. Due to the availability of data from the real data center, the evaluation was performed based on data from 5 real data center nodes, with known problems in a given time interval. An evaluation with a quantity with a large-scale volume of nodes could reveal different aspects to be considered.

7   Conclusions and Future Work

In this work, we propose and evaluate the early detection of anomalies through DC Health, which used the HS-Trees algorithm as a basis. This method was used to obtain a data anomaly score on each performance sample of nodes operating in a given data center and was chosen due to characteristics such as online and unsupervised detection. The main contributions of this work are listed as follows: **i)** development and availability of the DC Health solution prototype, aiming to facilitate the early detection of anomalies in datacenter nodes for data center infrastructure operators, **ii)** providing a dataset that compiles node performance data from a real industry data center and **iii)** evaluation of the anomaly detection method through *prequential* method in a real industry datacenter. The availability of a specialized tool for early detection of anomalies in data center hosts provides a set of possibilities with the potential to benefit data center operators, users of ICT services, and organizations that finance datacenters and costs relating to the unavailability of ICT services. Among these possibilities, we can highlight the early detection of failures, the possibility of developing advances such as the automation of diagnosis of the root cause of problems, the automation of remediation actions as well as the minimization and grouping of monitoring alerts. In addition, paths such as the possibility of developing specialized tools for early detection in certain fields of application, such as attack detection, and optimization of resource provisioning, among others. As a continuation of the studies carried out in this research, the following proposals for future work are suggested: **i)** conducting a case study involving the application of DC Health in a real data center and thereby collecting the experience and evaluation of data center operators, **ii)** development of new features in DC Health, which facilitate its use and adoption by datacenter operators. To facilitate adoption and use by data center operators, it is suggested to develop a version based on the web for the anomaly detection tool, **iii)** evaluation of the tool in a large volume of nodes with greater statistical relevance, as well as identifying the best adjustments of *hyperparameters* for the model, as one of the works futures to be developed, it is suggested the evaluation based on datasets representing more nodes of the data center, **iv)** it is also suggested to extend the functionality of the DC Health tool, aiming to evaluate the early detection of anomalies applied to cloud computing nodes, in hybrid datacenters and cloud data centers, **v)** development of automated mechanisms for diagnosis and remediation and **vi)** we also suggest the development of specialized anomaly detectors in certain fields of application, such as in-network attacks.

References

1. Ahmad, S., Lavin, A., Purdy, S., Agha, Z.: Unsupervised real-time anomaly detection for streaming data. Neurocomputing **262**, 134–147 (2017)
2. Ahmed, J., et al.: Automated diagnostic of virtualized service performance degradation. In: NOMS 2018–2018 IEEE/IFIP Network Operations and Management Symposium, pp. 1–9. IEEE (2018)
3. Alter, J., Xue, J., Dimnaku, A., Smirni, E.: SSD failures in the field: symptoms, causes, and prediction models. In: Proceedings of the International Conference for High Performance Computing, Networking, Storage and Analysis, pp. 1–14 (2019)
4. Brzezinski, D., Stefanowski, J.: Prequential AUC: properties of the area under the ROC curve for data streams with concept drift. Knowl. Inf. Syst. **52**(2), 531–562 (2017). https://doi.org/10.1007/s10115-017-1022-8
5. Chandola, V., Banerjee, A., Kumar, V.: Anomaly detection: a survey. ACM Comput. Surv. (CSUR) **41**(3), 1–58 (2009)
6. Chandola, V., Banerjee, A., Kumar, V.: Anomaly detection for discrete sequences: a survey. IEEE Trans. Knowl. Data Eng. **24**(5), 823–839 (2010)
7. Ding, Z., Fei, M.: An anomaly detection approach based on isolation forest algorithm for streaming data using sliding window. IFAC Proc. **46**(20), 12–17 (2013)
8. Fontenla-Romero, Ó., Guijarro-Berdiñas, B., Martinez-Rego, D., Pérez-Sánchez, B., Peteiro-Barral, D.: Online machine learning. In: Efficiency and Scalability Methods for Computational Intellect, pp. 27–54. IGI Global (2013)
9. Gama, J., Sebastião, R., Rodrigues, P.P.: On evaluating stream learning algorithms. Mach. Learn. **90**(3), 317–346 (2012). https://doi.org/10.1007/s10994-012-5320-9
10. Goldstein, M., Uchida, S.: A comparative evaluation of unsupervised anomaly detection algorithms for multivariate data. PLoS One **11**(4), e0152173 (2016)
11. Guan, Q., Zhang, Z., Fu, S.: Proactive failure management by integrated unsupervised and semi-supervised learning for dependable cloud systems. In: 2011 Sixth International Conference on Availability, Reliability and Security, pp. 83–90. IEEE (2011)
12. Guan, Q., Zhang, Z., Fu, S.: Ensemble of Bayesian predictors and decision trees for proactive failure management in cloud computing systems. J. Commun. **7**(1), 52–61 (2012)
13. Huang, S., Liang, S., Fu, S., Shi, W., Tiwari, D., Chen, H.B.: Characterizing disk health degradation and proactively protecting against disk failures for reliable storage systems. In: 2019 IEEE International Conference on Autonomic Computing (ICAC), pp. 157–166. IEEE (2019)

14. Ibidunmoye, O., Lakew, E.B., Elmroth, E.: A black-box approach for detecting systems anomalies in virtualized environments. In: 2017 International Conference on Cloud and Autonomic Computing (ICCAC), pp. 22–33. IEEE (2017)
15. Kitchenham, B., Brereton, P.: A systematic review of systematic review process research in software engineering. Inf. Softw. Technol. **55**(12), 2049–2075 (2013)
16. Lanciano, G., et al.: SOM-based behavioral analysis for virtualized network functions. In: Proceedings of the 35th Annual ACM Symposium on Applied Computing, pp. 1204–1206 (2020)
17. Lin, Q., et al.: Predicting node failure in cloud service systems. In: Proceedings of the 2018 26th ACM Joint Meeting on European Software Engineering Conference and Symposium on the Foundations of Software Engineering, pp. 480–490 (2018)
18. Liu, J., Chen, S., Zhou, Z., Wu, T.: An anomaly detection algorithm of cloud platform based on self-organizing maps. Math. Probl. Eng. **2016** (2016)
19. Mendoza, M.A., Amistadi, H.R.: Machine learning for anomaly detection on VM and host performance metrics. Technical report, MITRE Corp. Bedford, MA (2018)
20. Mescheryakov, S.V., Shchemelinin, D.A.: Analytical Overview of Zabbix International Conference 2013 (1(188)), pp. 91–98 (2014)
21. Montiel, J., Read, J., Bifet, A., Abdessalem, T.: Scikit-Multiflow: a multi-output streaming framework. J. Mach. Learn. Res. **19**(72), 1–5 (2018). http://jmlr.org/papers/v19/18-251.html
22. Mouratidis, K., Papadias, D.: Continuous nearest neighbor queries over sliding windows. IEEE Trans. Knowl. Data Eng. **19**(6), 789–803 (2007)
23. Nagarajan, A.B., Mueller, F., Engelmann, C., Scott, S.L.: Proactive fault tolerance for HPC with Xen virtualization. In: Proceedings of the 21st Annual International Conference on Supercomputing, pp. 23–32 (2007)
24. Neto, W.L., de Morais Barroca Filho, I.: Failures forecast in monitoring datacenter infrastructure through machine learning techniques: a systematic review. In: Gervasi, O., et al. (eds.) ICCSA 2021. LNCS, vol. 12957, pp. 27–42. Springer, Cham (2021). https://doi.org/10.1007/978-3-030-87013-3_3
25. Notaro, P., Cardoso, J., Gerndt, M.: A survey of AIOps methods for failure management. ACM Trans. Intell. Syst. Technol. (TIST) **12**(6), 1–45 (2021)
26. Pellegrini, A., Di Sanzo, P., Avresky, D.R.: A machine learning-based framework for building application failure prediction models. In: 2015 IEEE International Parallel and Distributed Processing Symposium Workshop, pp. 1072–1081. IEEE (2015)
27. Pokrajac, D., Lazarevic, A., Latecki, L.J.: Incremental local outlier detection for data streams. In: 2007 IEEE symposium on computational intelligence and data mining. pp. 504–515. IEEE (2007)
28. Saha, S., Sarkar, J., Dwivedi, A., Dwivedi, N., Narasimhamurthy, A.M., Roy, R.: A novel revenue optimization model to address the operation and maintenance cost of a data center. J. Cloud Comput. **5**(1), 1–23 (2015). https://doi.org/10.1186/s13677-015-0050-8
29. Salfner, F., Lenk, M., Malek, M.: A survey of online failure prediction methods. ACM Comput. Surv. (CSUR) **42**(3), 1–42 (2010)
30. Sîrbu, A., Babaoglu, O.: Towards operator-less data centers through data-driven, predictive, proactive autonomics. Clust. Comput. **19**(2), 865–878 (2016). https://doi.org/10.1007/s10586-016-0564-y
31. Snyder, D.: On-line intrusion detection using sequences of system calls (2001)
32. Tan, S.C., Ting, K.M., Liu, T.F.: Fast anomaly detection for streaming data. In: Twenty-Second International Joint Conference on Artificial Intelligence (2011)

33. Togbe, M.U., et al.: Anomaly detection for data streams based on isolation forest using scikit-multiflow. In: Gervasi, O., et al. (eds.) ICCSA 2020. LNCS, vol. 12252, pp. 15–30. Springer, Cham (2020). https://doi.org/10.1007/978-3-030-58811-3_2

34. Togbe, M.U., Chabchoub, Y., Boly, A., Barry, M., Chiky, R., Bahri, M.: Anomalies detection using isolation in concept-drifting data streams. Computers **10**(1), 13 (2021)

35. Wetzig, R., Gulenko, A., Schmidt, F.: Unsupervised anomaly alerting for IoT-gateway monitoring using adaptive thresholds and half-space trees. In: 2019 Sixth International Conference on Internet of Things: Systems, Management and Security (IOTSMS), pp. 161–168. IEEE (2019)

36. Widmer, G., Kubat, M.: Learning in the presence of concept drift and hidden contexts. Mach. Learn. **23**(1), 69–101 (1996). https://doi.org/10.1023/A:1018046501280

37. Xiao, J., Xiong, Z., Wu, S., Yi, Y., Jin, H., Hu, K.: Disk failure prediction in data centers via online learning. In: Proceedings of the 47th International Conference on Parallel Processing, pp. 1–10 (2018)

38. Yamanishi, K., Takeuchi, J.I., Williams, G., Milne, P.: On-line unsupervised outlier detection using finite mixtures with discounting learning algorithms. Data Min. Knowl. Discov. **8**(3), 275–300 (2004). https://doi.org/10.1023/B:DAMI.0000023676.72185.7c

39. Yang, Y., Dong, J., Fang, C., Xie, P., An, N.: FP-STE: a novel node failure prediction method based on spatio-temporal feature extraction in data centers. Comput. Model. Eng. Sci. **123**(3), 1015–1031 (2020)

40. Zeydan, E., Arslan, S.S.: Cloud2HDD: large-scale HDD data analysis on cloud for cloud datacenters. In: 2020 23rd Conference on Innovation in Clouds, Internet and Networks and Workshops (ICIN), pp. 243–249. IEEE (2020)

41. Zhang, L., Lin, J., Karim, R.: Sliding window-based fault detection from high-dimensional data streams. IEEE Trans. Syst. Man Cybern. Syst. **47**(2), 289–303 (2016)

An Antibot-Based Web Voting System for Higher Institutions

Jessen Japheth[1], John Wejin[2(✉)], Sanjay Misra[3], and Jonathan Oluranti[2]

[1] Taraba State University, Jalingo, Taraba, Nigeria
[2] Covenant University, Ota, Ogun, Nigeria
John.wejinpgs@stu.cu.edu.ng,
jonathan.oluranti@covenantuniversity.edu.ng
[3] Ostfold University College, Halden, Norway
Sanjay.misra@hiof.no

Abstract. The Internet has caused an evolution in how people socialize, work, and do business. The emergence and improvement in cloud computing and web technologies make interactions and remote processes possible. This advancement has presented an opportunity for the people and their representatives to meet during the voting process. Voting is making a choice or decision within a particular group. However, the conventional voting process that uses the paper-based approach faces the challenges of multiple voting, overvoting, cost, high voting fraud, and delay in declaring election results due to long counting times. Various methods have been proposed to overcome the multiple challenges prevalent in the traditional voting system. This paper proposes an antibot-based web voting platform that enables voters to vote within any location. It uses the hash technique and the antibot checking features to enforce security and voters' confidentiality. PHP and HTML languages were used to implement the front-end of the system. SQL database and the Apache server were used for the back-end. On implementation and testing, our system shows good security enhancement and a reduction in the time consumed for counting and declaring election results.

Keywords: Anti-bot · E-voting · Cloud computing

1 Introduction

The Internet, which started as an interconnection between four large computers (Mainframes) connecting a few universities and research institutes, has significantly evolved. The modern high-speed global interconnection known as the Internet is a vital commodity for both individuals and governments. In the 21st century, exploring emergent technologies to connect people is rising. This drive has been extended to the frontiers of democracy, as electronic involvement presents an opportunity for people and their representatives to meet during the voting process [1]. Voting is making a choice or decision regarding something within a specific group. Various voting systems have different standards and requirements for the entire process, but the goal remains unchanged, giving utmost consideration to voters' decisions regarding something.

O. Gervasi et al. (Eds.): ICCSA 2022 Workshops, LNCS 13381, pp. 650–661, 2022.
https://doi.org/10.1007/978-3-031-10548-7_47

Conventional voting systems have been identified as ineffective in terms of their requirements: ballot paper, voting in proxy, lack of transparency in counting of votes (a severe issue for Nigeria), and over-dependence of the voting process on a centralized committee [2]. In modern times, the digitization of the electioneering and voting process is becoming increasingly adopted by various countries and organizations. The most prominent example is digital voting for local authorities in countries like Estonia, the USA, Switzerland, Netherlands, India, Namibia, and Nigeria. Though this means of voting addresses the inefficiency in the conventional voting system, the electronic system still faces some challenges, especially in vulnerabilities regarding the central checking of all results, and recently the use of software-bot for anonymous voting [3].

This paper proposes an anti-robot voting system for voting in educational institutions. It prevents anonymous voting through a soft bot and securely protects the e-voting platform and process. The rest of the paper is structured as follows. An overview of the voting system and the hashing system are presented in Sects. 2 and 3. Related works are discussed in Sect. 4, and the proposed system is presented in Sect. 5. Results and discussions are presented in Sect. 6, while the conclusion and future works are presented in Sect. 7.

2   Types of Voting System

Voting has been identified as a duty and a fundamental right of citizens in a given country. It gives the people the privilege to decide who champions the affairs of their nation within a specified democratic dispensation or period. There are various means of voting processes or methods in the world. These methods are based on the agreement of the majority of the people via their various representatives. The well-known techniques commonly employed by various governments are as follows.

1. Paper-Based Voting System
   The paper type of voting was the earliest or most traditional voting system employed by various nations, especially in developing countries of the African continent. In this method, the voters vote using papers on which different political parties and their candidates are written. The eligible voters will select the party or candidate using the agreed marker (usually with the thumb or a stamp), then fold the ballot paper, and drop it in a ballot box positioned in a given location where individuals and party representatives can see it or monitor. The votes are then counted after the election at the polling station in the hearing and observation of party officials, collated, and signed by party representatives for onward transmission to the central collation center. The paper-based voting system comes with the advantage of voting ease. The voter only needs to make a mark beside his candidate of choice to vote [4]. However, many disadvantages come with this method of voting system. Theses are:

   • Time Demanding: The paper-based system allows voting one at a time. This is time tasking.

- Delay in Counting. The election results usually take a long time (sometimes days) before they are declared. This is because counting is done manually in every polling station.
- Ballot Fraud: The ballot papers can be easily copied and altered to conceal any change.
- Hoodlums can quickly snatch ballot papers.
- The cost of printing ballot papers adds to the cost of paper-based voting systems.

2. Electronic Voting Machine (EVM) Method

The electronic voting machine was proposed and implemented to overcome the drudgery prevalent in the paper-based voting method. The EMV consists of two essential parts: the control unit and the ballots unit. The ballot unit has buttons that enable candidates to vote. Unused buttons are usually covered within the control unit. It is capable of recording about 3840 votes. With EVM, only eligible voters can vote, which happens only once. Thus, over-voting and multiple voting challenges at different polling stations are eliminated. The demerits of such a voting system, as enumerated in [4], are:

- Transparency: Voters are critical of the EVM machine because they lack knowledge of the working principle of the voting procedure within the machine.
- The tendency for Fraud: Digital systems can be hacked by individuals who know the working principle of a particular system. Access to the EVM storage can alter votes within the system.
- Power: An electronic system depends on power to function. EVM voting system deployment becomes difficult or nearly impossible in areas where electric power supply is erratic.
- Cost: The cost of obtaining an EVM and its maintenance in the event of mechanical or software failure is highly expensive.

3 Common Security Approach for E-Voting Systems

3.1 Hashing

Hash functions are vital in most information systems. The hash function is a mathematical expression that converts streams of characters and maps them to a value of a particular length. This value is usually a smaller version of the original streams of characters. The hashing algorithm retrieves data at a shorter time from a database and is also commonly used for either encryption or decryption of signatures or keys [5]. Furthermore, hashing can be used for password storage to identify users that can have access to use a particular system. A logon scenario that explains hashing in our proposed system is shown in Fig. 1. The password is wrapped, making it have a table pair consisting of the user ID and the h(p) table. This makes it difficult for a hacker to access a system [6]. Various researches make use of hashing to enforce security. In [7], hashing was employed for constant checking of application vulnerability, an optimized hashing technique based on Convolutional Neural Network (CNN) was developed in [8], speech encryption [9], etc.

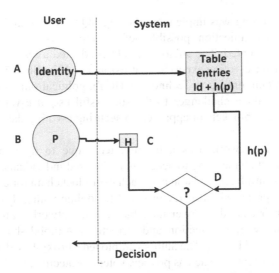

Fig. 1. Hashing operation in password application

3.2 Homomorphic Encryption

Homomorphic encryption techniques have become prominent cryptographic approach, especially for processes that are cloud-based. Unlike other cryptographic techniques that act on data at inertia or in transit, homomorphic encryption acts on data that is in use. It provides computation on data that has been encrypted, thus, enabling confidentiality in data as it is being processed or used. This security approach allows mostly two key algebraic operation on encrypted text namely, addition and multiplication. Other mathematical operations are resultants of the combination of these two operations [25]. Based on the function or number of mathematical operations on an encrypted data, homomorphic security technique can be grouped into the following:

- Additive homomorphic technique: Only addition operation is allowed on the encrypted data.
- Partial homomorphic technique: Allows for addition and limited number of multiplication operation.
- Fully homomorphic technique: Allows for both addition and multiplication operations in unlimited fashion.

Homomorphic encryption technique find application in e-voting during the ballot counting process. The e-counting process can use homomorphic encryption e.g. the addition operation to calculate votes without the choice of the voters being known or disclosed, thus, enabling confidentiality and privacy in the voting process.

4 Related Works

In [10], the authors reviewed the state of implementation of e-voting around the world, especially in Estonia and Switzerland. Based on their analysis of the Indian scenario, a design for internet voting was implemented using SQL. Testing and evaluation of the proposed system, SQL injection, possible defense mechanisms, and future directions for e-voting were presented. The authors in [11] conducted a review on e-voting. The authors focused on the e-voting experience of Estonia and Namibia. Their study reveals that Information Communication Technology (ICT), political dimensions, and voters' illiterate level are critical challenges to the successful use of e-voting, especially in developing nations. A blockchain approach to securing e-voting data was proposed in [12].

The proposed framework uses a hashing technique to dynamically adjust the blockchain, making it challenging to access unauthorized individuals. To optimize and ensure a secure decentralized decision approach over blockchain for e-voting purposes, the authors in [13] proposed a privacy protocol for online voting. It allows connected peers to choose their candidates over their blockchain network without using a third party, ensuring privacy, fraud detection, and corrections. A mobile-based approach to e-voting was implemented in [14]. The authors employed a proxy-based signature scheme that provides security features such as privacy, voters' protection, and message verification. Evaluation of the system reveals a reduction in computational cost and enhanced security. The concealment of voters' identities during an election is critical in the election process. This is usually known as secret suffrage. The authors in [15] investigated how the various proposals of e-voting adhere to the secrecy of voters during elections. The authors in [16] proposed a homomorphic encryption approach to ensure the online system of voting security. Voter confidentiality is ensured by enforcing security on ballots using encryptions. Evaluation reveals that the system has a good time submission verification rate and high voter confidentiality. Blockchain and machine learning are highly accepted in securing e-voting platforms and systems [17–24].

5   Proposed Approach

To actualize implementing the proposed antibot web-based voting system, we adopted the design in [2] and modified it to suit our designs and functionalities. The proposed design considered using antibot techniques and keys to enable security in the voting system. The proposed system has 5 phases: eligible voters' registration, vote casting, end of the day stage, collection stage, and final repository stage. These stages are briefly described below.

- Voters Registration Stage
  Unlike other systems that allow systems to register voters directly, our system first has, before the voters' registration via the web interface, a complete list of eligible voters is included in the database (in this case, the number of students). This enables the system to check the status of the voter (students or not students) before generating keys that will be used in the voting process.
- Vote Casting
  This is the phase where the voting takes place. The voter visits the voting site, where he will be prompted to enter his student ID and the key generated during the voter registration phase. On successful login, the various contesting positions with the names

of candidates are displayed for the voter to elect the candidate of their choice. After selecting their choices, the voter clicks on the vote button to submit his vote. A prompt is activated to help verify voters of their choice before submission. On submission, a hash key is generated for the candidate. The key enables the voter to log in to check the election results.

- Collation Stage
  To reduce fraud and ensure transparency, collation of results is done by a neutral party in the presence of candidates' representatives. However, this phase is conducted using an offline means.
- Voting close
  At this phase, the election process is ended after the set time for the election has ended. During this period, the voter can log in to vote. However, voters can check the election results using the hash key generated after voting. Data gathering and compilation are done automatically. System checks are carried out (verification of hashes against several voters and votes count). After the confirmation, the election committee and various representatives sign and ratify the election process.

5.1 Proposed System Flowchart

The voting process using the proposed system is shown in Fig. 2. The voters' eligibility is first checked using the record on the database. The user-generated user ID and password are used as login details for the voters, and an electronic ballot sheet for voting on successful login. Successful voting is saved on the database, the vote count is updated, and a confirmation message is displayed to assure the voter that his vote has been accepted.

5.2 The Antibot Security Process

The proposed system uses a two-way verification process namely, the voter/password authentication and the antibot security mechanism. During the registration of voters, an automated voter's ID based on Extended Binary Coded Decimal (EBCD) is generated for each voter. The voter then creates a unique password they can recall. These two security keys are first verified during the login process as shown in Fig. 3. On successful authentication, the system activates the antibot mechanism that checks for soft-bots. In modern days, it has become common for malicious programs (commonly referred to as soft-bots) that automates task to find presence over the internet. These bots can generate fraudulent accounts, ticket purchase, and even infiltrate a voting process by acting as legitimate voters. This motivates the integration of antibot mechanism in the proposed electronic voting system. In our proposed solution, we adopted the google authenticator and API security features to implement the antibot mechanism. We first created an account on google console and then used the checkbox antibot feature of the google authenticator. The google SDK shell was run on the server to enable offline authentication and verification.

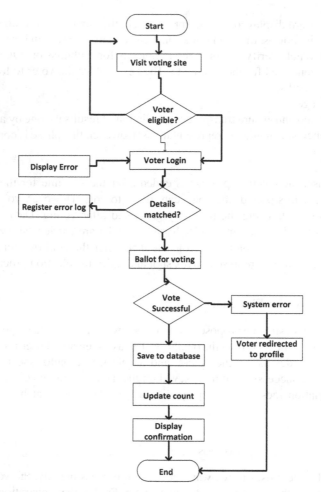

Fig. 2. Proposed voting system flowchart

6 Results and Discussion

SQL and Apache servers were employed to implement the proposed system for the back-end design and the server. PHP and HTML were used to implement the front-end. The hardware component consists of a Windows 10-based PC of 5G dual core intel processor with 250G. After the design and implementation, the antibot web-based system was deployed on the school's network and tested by running a departmental election. The results from the implementation are shown in this section.

Figure 3 shows the login page for the voters to sign in and vote. The users insert their login details as provided, and on verification and authentication, the voter is ready to begin voting. The antibot mechanism is integrated with the user login authentication process. At login, the voter is also verified to ascertain their soft-bot status by the system, as depicted in Fig. 3.

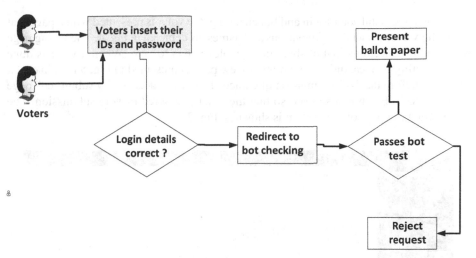

Fig. 3. The proposed security approach

Fig. 4. Voters' login page

Upon successful voter login and bot checking, the voter is presented with a page that holds the various candidates' positions and names, as depicted in Fig. 4. The voting page serves as the electronic ballot sheet that enables voters to vote. When a voter is done with selecting their candidates, a voting review page is presented in Fig. 5 to help check selection before the final submission of choice. The "vote successfully submitted" page as depicted in Fig. 6 is displayed so that the voter is assured of vote submission. The voting tracking page of the system is shown in Fig. 7.

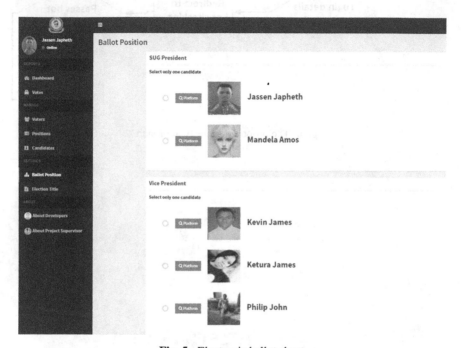

Fig. 5. Electronic ballot sheet

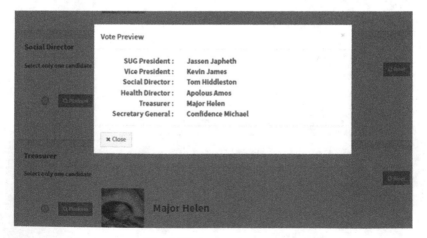

Fig. 6. Voting preview page

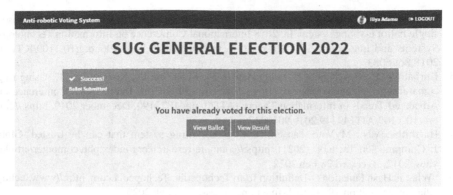

Fig. 7. Vote submission page

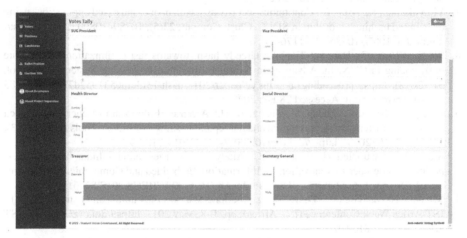

Fig. 8. Voting tracking page

7 Conclusion

This paper proposes an antibot-based web voting platform that enables voters to vote within their comfort zones. The proposed system uses the hash technique and the antibot checking features to enforce security and voters' confidentiality. This system eliminates the possibility of non-human voting that threatens the fidelity of the e-voting system. Furthermore, the eligibility of voters and their submissions are easily verified. Voters can track the result process by having a unique login that enables only registered, accredited, and voted individuals to track the progress. Using a machine learning approach that holds the potential for a more secure and efficient e-voting system is a good research direction.

References

1. Zissis, D., Lekkas, D.: Securing e-Government and e-Voting with an open cloud computing architecture. Gov. Inf. Q. **28**(2), 239–251 (2011). https://doi.org/10.1016/j.giq.2010.05.010

2. Rodiana, I.M., Rahardjo, B., Aciek Ida, W.: Design of a public key infrastructure-based single ballot e-voting system. In: 2018 International Conference on Information Technology Systems and Innovation (ICITSI), pp. 6–9, October 2018. https://doi.org/10.1109/ICITSI.2018.8696083

3. Kurbatov, O., Kravchenko, P., Poluyanenko, N., Shapoval, O., Kuznetsova, T.: Using ring signatures for an anonymous e-voting system. In: 2019 IEEE International Conference on Advanced Trends in Information Theory (ATIT), pp. 187–190, December 2019. https://doi.org/10.1109/ATIT49449.2019.9030447

4. Harshitha, V.N.: MyVote - an effective online voting system that can be trusted. Glob. J. Comput. Sci. Technol. (2021). https://computerresearch.org/index.php/computer/article/view/2012. Accessed 28 Feb 2022

5. "What is Hash Function? - Definition from Techopedia. Techopedia.com. http://www.techopedia.com/definition/19744/hash-function. Accessed 28 Feb 2022

6. Cryptography Hash Functions. https://www.tutorialspoint.com/cryptography/cryptography_hash_functions.htm. Accessed 28 Feb 2022

7. Vijayakumar, K., Arun, C.: Continuous security assessment of cloud based applications using distributed hashing algorithm in SDLC. Clust. Comput. **22**(5), 10789–10800 (2017). https://doi.org/10.1007/s10586-017-1176-x

8. Su, S., Zhang, C., Han, K., Tian, Y.: Greedy hash: towards fast optimization for accurate hash coding in CNN. In: Advances in Neural Information Processing Systems 2018, vol. 31 (2018). https://proceedings.neurips.cc/paper/2018/hash/13f3cf8c531952d72e5847c4183e6910-Abstract.html. Accessed 28 Feb 2022

9. Zhang, Q., Zhou, L., Zhang, T., Zhang, D.-H.: A retrieval algorithm of encrypted speech based on short-term cross-correlation and perceptual hashing. Multimed. Tools Appl. **78**(13), 17825–17846 (2019). https://doi.org/10.1007/s11042-019-7180-9

10. Singh, V.P., Pasupuleti, H., Babu, N.S.C.: Analysis of internet voting in India. In: 2017 International Conference on Innovations in Information, Embedded and Communication Systems (ICIIECS), pp. 1–6, March 2017. https://doi.org/10.1109/ICIIECS.2017.8276137

11. Mpekoa, N., van Greunen, D.: E-voting experiences: a case of Namibia and Estonia. In: 2017 IST-Africa Week Conference (IST-Africa), pp. 1–8, May 2017. https://doi.org/10.23919/ISTAFRICA.2017.8102303

12. Shahzad, B., Crowcroft, J.: Trustworthy electronic voting using adjusted blockchain technology. IEEE Access **7**, 24477–24488 (2019). https://doi.org/10.1109/ACCESS.2019.2895670

13. Zhang, W., et al.: A privacy-preserving voting protocol on blockchain. In: 2018 IEEE 11th International Conference on Cloud Computing (CLOUD), pp. 401–408, July 2018. https://doi.org/10.1109/CLOUD.2018.00057

14. Chiou, S.-Y., Wang, T.-J., Chen, J.-M.: Design and implementation of a mobile voting system using a novel oblivious and proxy signature. Secur. Commun. Netw. **2017**, e3075210 (2017). https://doi.org/10.1155/2017/3075210

15. Rodríguez-Pérez, A.: Secret suffrage in remote electronic voting systems. In: 2017 Fourth International Conference on eDemocracy eGovernment (ICEDEG), pp. 277–278, April 2017. https://doi.org/10.1109/ICEDEG.2017.7962550

16. Yang, X., Yi, X., Nepal, S., Kelarev, A., Han, F.: A secure verifiable ranked choice online voting system based on homomorphic encryption. IEEE Access **6**, 20506–20519 (2018). https://doi.org/10.1109/ACCESS.2018.2817518

17. Djanali, S., Nugraha, D.P., Studiawan, H., Pratomo, B.A.: Vote identification and integrity of ballot in paper-based e-voting system. Electron. Gov. **14**(3), 240–254 (2018). https://doi.org/10.1504/EG.2018.093416

18. Abou-Rizka, M., Shedeed, A.: Secure E-voting scheme through polling stations, vol. 1–3, pp. 250–256 (2009)

19. Roopak, T.M., Sumathi, R.: Electronic voting based on virtual ID of Aadhar using blockchain technology, pp. 71–75 (2020). https://doi.org/10.1109/ICIMIA48430.2020.9074942
20. Taş, R., Tanriöver, Ö.Ö.: A manipulation prevention model for blockchain-based E-voting systems. Secur. Commun. Netw. **2021** (2021). https://doi.org/10.1155/2021/6673691
21. Baudier, P., Kondrateva, G., Ammi, C., Seulliet, E.: Peace engineering: the contribution of blockchain systems to the e-voting process. Technol. Forecast. Soc. Change **162**, 120397 (2021). https://doi.org/10.1016/j.techfore.2020.120397
22. Anwar ul Hassan, Ch., et al.: A liquid democracy enabled blockchain-based electronic voting system. Sci. Program. **2022** (2022). https://doi.org/10.1155/2022/1383007
23. González, C.D., Mena, D.F., Muñoz, A.M., Rojas, O., Sosa-Gómez, G.: Electronic voting system using an enterprise blockchain. Appl. Sci. **12**(2), 531 (2022). https://doi.org/10.3390/app12020531
24. Xu, D., Shi, W., Zhai, W., Tian, Z.: Multi-candidate voting model based on blockchain. IEEE/CAA J. Autom. Sin. **8**(12), 1891–1900 (2021). https://doi.org/10.1109/JAS.2021.1004207
25. Challa, R.: Homomorphic encryption: review and applications. In: Borah, S., Balas, V.E., Polkowski, Z. (eds.) Advances in Data Science and Management. LNDECT, vol. 37, pp. 273–281. Springer, Singapore (2020). https://doi.org/10.1007/978-981-15-0978-0_27

Efficient GitHub Crawling Using the GraphQL API

Adrian Jobst$^{(\boxtimes)}$, Daniel Atzberger, Tim Cech, Willy Scheibel(ID),
Matthias Trapp(ID), and Jürgen Döllner

Hasso Plattner Institute, Digital Engineering Faculty,
University of Potsdam, Potsdam, Germany
{adrian.jobst,daniel.atzberger,tim.cech,willy.scheibel,
matthias.trapp,juergen.doellner}@hpi.uni-potsdam.de

Abstract. The number of publicly accessible software repositories on online platforms is growing rapidly. With more than 128 million public repositories (as of March 2020), GitHub is the world's largest platform for hosting and managing software projects. Where it used to be necessary to merge various data sources, it is now possible to access a wealth of data using the GitHub API alone. However, collecting and analyzing this data is not an easy endeavor. In this paper, we present Prometheus, a system for crawling and storing software repositories from GitHub. Compared to existing frameworks, Prometheus follows an event-driven microservice architecture. By separating functionality on the service level, there is no need to understand implementation details or use existing frameworks to extend or customize the system, only data. Prometheus consists of two components, one for fetching GitHub data and one for data storage which serves as a basis for future functionality. Unlike most existing crawling approaches, the Prometheus fetching service uses the GitHub GraphQL API. As a result, Prometheus can significantly outperform alternatives in terms of throughput in some scenarios.

Keywords: Mining software repositories · *GitHub* crawling · GraphQL API · Microservices · Event-driven

1 Introduction

Today's software development projects are characterized by a large number of stakeholders and a comprehensive technology stack. The activities of the stakeholders and their communication with each other are systematically stored

We want to thank the anonymous reviewers for their valuable feedback to improve this article. This work is part of the "Software-DNA" project, which is funded by the European Regional Development Fund (ERDF or EFRE in German) and the State of Brandenburg (ILB). This work is part of the KMU project "KnowhowAnalyzer" (Förderkennzeichen 01IS20088B), which is funded by the German Ministry for Education and Research (Bundesministerium für Bildung und Forschung).

O. Gervasi et al. (Eds.): ICCSA 2022 Workshops, LNCS 13381, pp. 662–677, 2022.
https://doi.org/10.1007/978-3-031-10548-7_48

in various software repositories, be they code repositories, source code control repositories, bug repositories, archived communications, or artifacts from builds, testing, or deployment. The Software Analytics domain generates interesting and actionable insights about the software development process by analyzing the extensive data available in software repositories [34]. For example, machine learning methods are used that require training data. This data is usually extracted from online software repositories as they contain large amounts of openly available data. Various systems have been developed to generate datasets from publicly available software repositories. There are already large collections of raw or enriched software data that can be used for studies [6,14,28]. In addition, end-to-end approaches have also been proposed to support scientists and engineers throughout the process, from data collection to analysis [7,31]. However, although existing datasets contain large amounts of data, they may be incomplete, the pre-processing steps may be unclear or obstructive, or the chosen format may be inappropriate.

In this work, we propose Prometheus, a system that is based on an event-driven microservice architecture. In a microservice architecture, functionality is separated into services. This separation reduces the need to understand implementation details of existing functionality, as new services communicate via REST-like API's, events, or a mixture of both. Being able to connect to event streams also facilitates the development of live analytic scenarios, which is especially interesting for industry use cases [26]. Prometheus consists of two components, a GitHub crawling service and a storage service that is important to overcome API throughput limitations. We chose the GitHub project management platform as it contains a large number of software artifacts, i.e., source code control information, software development information, and metadata like developer information and comments. The latter two are less represented in Mining Software Repositories (MSR) research [8]. Through the redesigned GitHub GraphQL API, Prometheus can access all information available on GitHub and retrieve it in less time than other systems that use the prior REST API.

The remainder of this work is structured as follows: In Sect. 2 we review existing work related to our approach. We provide an overview of our concept in section Sect. 3. In Sect. 4 we present a detailed description of our system and provide implementation details. The experimental setup and the results of our evaluation are presented and discussed in section Sect. 5. We conclude this paper in Sect. 6 and present directions for future work.

2   Related Work

Various systems have been proposed which acquire data from online repositories. Linstead et al. presented Sourcerer, an infrastructure for analyzing source code repositories [22]. The authors processed source code files from GitHub projects and analyzed them using Latent Dirichlet Allocation [2] and its variant, the Author-Topic Model [29]. The results may serve as a summary for program function, developer activities and more. A system developed to support scientists and practitioners in MSR research is Boa, presented by Dyer et al. [7]. The system provides the infrastructure and a domain-specific language for accessing large software repositories such as GitHub. Researchers can access the service and create datasets for their experiments through a web-based interface. Another system for generating large datasets of open source projects was presented by Ma et al. [23]. The authors created World of Code, a very large and frequently updated collection of version control data for open source software projects that is updated monthly. In their work, the authors explore several issues related to the structure of open source projects. Trautsch et al. presented the SmartSHARK ecosystem to support MSR research [32]. It consists of four parts, which are tools for crawling data from different hosting platforms, e.g., GitHub or Jira, a storage system, a web application that can be used for data collection and a web application that provides an overview of the collected data. While the aforementioned systems combine crawling and processing functions, other systems focus more on crawling to create datasets that can be used as a research base. Gousios and Spinellis presented the GHTorrent project [14]. Ultimately, GHTorrent aims to create an offline mirror of GitHub. To this end, it retrieves event data from the GitHub REST API, from which the original GitHub data schema has been reconstructed, and makes everything available in database dumps. In a follow-up study, Gousios presented a dataset created by GHTorrent [15], and in another follow-up study, Gousios et al. described a new feature to obtain customizable data dumps on demand [16]. Another mentionable project in this context is GH Archive (www.gharchive.org/), which is an open source project to record and archive the public GitHub timeline (event data). GH Archive data is often used as a data basis in MSR related research [1,12,17].

In general, a deeper understanding of data sources and potential use cases helps in the design and development of MSR systems. Kalliamvakou et al. analyzed the data quality of GitHub data in more detail [20]. The study showed that there are some dangers to be aware of when using GitHub data for research or analysis purposes. For example, 40% of all pull requests do not appear as merged, even though they were. Also, many projects are personal or inactive. This could be a potential threat for analysis purposes Munaiah et al. addressed the issue and developed a classifier to identify whether a repository is a developed software project or not [27]. Another study that analyzed GitHub metadata was conducted by Borges et al. In their work, they investigated what factors influence the popularity of GitHub repositories [3].

As previously described, systems often use REST API's of repository hoster to gather data. But in the case of GitHub, there is also a GraphQL based alternative. Due to the growing popularity and adoption of GraphQL in general, academia has also turned to the topic. Motivated by the lack of a formal definition, Hartig and Pérez formalized the semantics of GraphQL queries and then analyzed them [18]. This allowed them to prove certain things, such as that the GraphQL evaluation problem is NL-complete and that GraphQL answers can be prohibitively large for Internet scenarios. Wittern et al. studied 16 commercial GraphQL schemas and 8,399 GraphQL schemas to investigate GraphQL interfaces. They found that the majority of APIs are vulnerable to denial of service through complex queries, which also introduces security risks [33]. A direct comparison between the REST and GraphQL architectural models was made by Seabra et al. [30]. Three target applications were implemented in both models, from which performance metrics could be derived. Two-thirds of the applications tested saw performance improvements in terms of average number of requests per second and data transfer rate when using GraphQL. But in general, performance was also below that of its REST counterpart when the workload exceeded 3000 requests. Similarly, Brito et al. migrated seven REST-based systems to use GraphQL [4]. The migration reduced the size of JSON responses by up to 94% in the number of fields and 99% in the number of bytes (median results). In another study, Brit and Valente described a controlled experiment in which students had to implement similar queries, once in REST, once in GraphQL [5]. Their results showed that students were faster at implementing GraphQL queries, especially when the REST endpoints contained more complex queries. Surprisingly, the results held true for the more experienced groups of graduate students as well. As mentioned earlier, GraphQL queries can be unexpectedly large, not least because of their nested structure, making query cost estimation an important feature. Estimating costs based on a static worst-case analysis of queries has had limited success, leading Mavroudeas et al. to propose a machine learning-based approach. Testing their approach on publicly available commercial APIs, they found that their framework is able to predict query costs with high accuracy and consistently outperforms static analysis.

The presented systems come with limitations when used for data generation. Some systems have obstructive data transformations of raw data [22] or provide a fixed set of processing functionality [7] which excludes them as usable tools when a different transformation or format is needed. Systems which are able to provide raw data [14,32] do usually only leverage a subset of available data, e.g. issue tracking and version control history. Additionally most systems use the GitHub REST API, whose rate limit is rather conservative which introduces the need for multiple API tokens, otherwise crawling additional information takes long. By using the GraphQL API, a single API token can crawl significantly more information, which makes it more suitable for most users.

3   Concept

The Prometheus architecture follows an event-driven microservice architectural style. At first, the implemented system will consist of two components. A fetching component to crawl data from the GitHub GraphQL API, and a database component that stores the responses in a database management system. As there is no common formal definition of microservices and event-driven applications, we will start by outlining important aspects of these, before describing the fetching component in Sect. 3.2 and database component in Sect. 3.3.

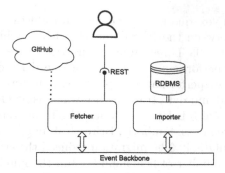

Fig. 1. General concept of the Prometheus system architecture.

3.1 Architecture Considerations

According to Fowler and Lewis, a microservice architectural style means that an application is developed as a suite of small services. These services usually communicate via lightweight mechanisms and are built around business capabilities. Furthermore, each service runs in its's own process, which means that they can be deployed independently [10]. Figure 1 shows the general concept of the Prometheus System, including two services, one for crawling and one for persisting crawled data. Fowler and Lewis also described the main characteristics of microservices derived from practice, since there is no formal definition. Some of them also apply to our system.

In software engineering, a component usually refers to a unit of software, that encapsulates a certain functionality, e.g., via a library. In monolithic applications, components are tightly coupled to the code that uses them, thus making a complete redeployment necessary when a component is changed. The microservice approach mitigates this problem by dividing the application into services, each of which can be deployed individually. So in the architecture seen in Fig. 1, a change related to the importing service would not affect the fetching service at all. In monolithic applications, components communicate via method invocation or function call which execute in-process. Microservices use a coarser-grained approach where the communication medium should be as simple as possible. Usually, an HTTP request-response or lightweight message bus is used for asynchronous communication with routing, which is also used in our system to control the crawling component. The right tool for the right job is a philosophy that microservice architectures follow. Unlike centralized governance, where standardization of certain technologies leads to restrictions on the choice of development tools, developers of microservice architectures choose the tools they need to create a particular service. When one wants to extend the Prometheus system, the only technology restriction will be the component that manages services. While a single data model seems reasonable, it is often not realistic, as different components may have slightly different views of the data. It may be useful for each service to use its own appropriate conceptual model, which has the advantage that each service can use a database system that is most suitable, also known as "polyglot persistence" [21]. In our system, the Importer service stores the raw data collected from GitHub, and new services, even if they build on this data, may use a new storage component. We believe this also has usability benefits, as single conceptual models are easier to understand than a complicated mixture.

Event-driven architectures are also not formally defined, most likely because there are many different notions of what an event is and what it is used for. An event contains at least the form or action of the event and a timestamp of when the event occurred. In summary, three purposes of events can be formulated [11]. In the simplest case, an event just serves as a mere notification that something happened. For instance, in our system, the fetching service publishes data from the crawling process as events. As mentioned earlier, two systems or services, even if they use conceptually different data models, can still have similar attributes. In this case, state changes from one service must be transmitted to others that have a similar view of the data which can be done in the form of an event. In our system, the importing service publishes state changes via events so that dependent or related components can react to them. For a small monolithic application with a single data model, the state of the application is usually mirrored in the database or can be derived from it in case of failure. In contrast, the state of a distributed system is mirrored in all data of all services together. However, because services can change state individually or event-driven state transfers can occur, accessing older state is not as easy as with a single database log. One way to maintain this capability in a distributed system is event sourcing, where all changes to the system are recorded as events [9]. In theory, the event log can be used to recover the system state at any point in time. This feature will not be used in the current version of Prometheus but may be relevant for future use-cases where it can be implemented without any architectural change.

3.2   GitHub Fetcher

The crawling component uses the GraphQL API from GitHub to fetch metadata. Mainly because the rate limit is more liberal than in the case of the REST API. But also because one GraphQL call can replace multiple REST calls and therefore returns more data. But using the GraphQL paradigm also imposes differences in crawling logic which can be seen in Fig. 2. For instance, when crawling metadata for a repository and its issues on GitHub, the entry point is the according /repos/ URL path as seen in Fig. 2a. The response of such a call then contains URLs to linked entities, e.g. repository issues. Paginated endpoints usually just include summary information of entities, so in order to get all information, subsequent calls for every single entity must be made. With GraphQL, all these entities can be included in a single call which is shown in Fig. 2b. Since we need a cursor to fetch more than 100 results, the crawling is more complex making it difficult to get a parallel connection. Furthermore, responses do not contain information about linked entities, so in the case of Fig. 2b, the system must infer how to formulate a query that fetches user information of issue authors.

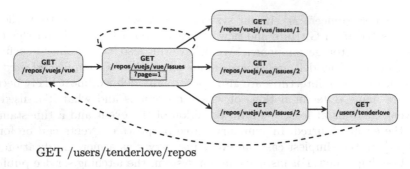

(a) REST API crawling. Pagination information is encoded in URL parameters.

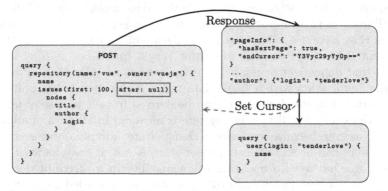

(b) GraphQL API crawling. A cursor from the response is needed to paginate.

Fig. 2. A comparison of how entities of the GitHub REST and GraphQL API's are crawled. Red parts specify pagination settings. (Color figure online)

Since it is good practice to combine services that change frequently and the GitHub data schema may change often [10], our service could also address data persistence. We argue that it is unlikely that there will be frequent changes to the GitHub data model as GitHub has a long history of how people use the API and has put a lot of thought into the GraphQL schema. So it is more likely that the data model just gets extended for new features, which will not break the existing ones. GraphQL also makes it easy to handle minor changes, for example, attributes that will soon be dropped can be marked as deprecated, and new changes can simply be added as nullable attributes.

Therefore, storage capabilities will be handled explicitly by a separated service as described in Sect. 3.3.

The interface of this service will only be used to control the crawling process which means sending crawling jobs and monitoring progress. In our system job descriptions will be defined as GraphQL queries. Using GraphQL for job descriptions makes sense since it is the same paradigm as the GitHub API, and because it seems easier for developers to form GraphQL queries instead of e.g. REST queries [5]. These queries will be the same as regular GitHub GraphQL API queries but allow for additional or different parameters. For instance, the query seen in Fig. 2b uses 100 as the first argument value, which is the allowed maximum in the GitHub API. In our system values beyond the allowed value, e.g. 10.000 are possible. By allowing additional or changed arguments, the system needs logic on how to handle them. For example, it needs to be able to paginate automatically when more than 100 elements are requested. An additional problem is when we nest connections and require more than 100 elements in the nested connection. Pagination requires a cursor of the previous page, which is specified as the after argument as seen in Fig. 2b. The response to a query with nested pagination returns multiple cursors for the nested entities since the cursor refers to the parent entities. But since there can only be supplied one cursor, there is no correct way to map these in a consecutive query. But in most cases, the nested pagination problem can be solved by resolving it in separate queries. This can be achieved by replacing a connection field with a field that queries just one entity. In the left query of Fig. 2b, *issues* can be replaced with *issue* which returns only a single issue. This would resolve nesting if any, but requires splitting the query into one that fetches all issues and a second one that paginates the nested connection.

3.3 Database Importer

The sole purpose of the database import service is to capture the data published by the GitHub fetching service and store it in a database. An important design decision is the choice of database, as it has a large impact on the schema, database interface, and transactional properties.

The GraphQL API provides a schema for GitHub's data model so it is normalized to some extent since the schema provides the relationships between structured entities. In some cases, it seems tempting to store this data in a denormalized form in a document store. For instance, if repository entities are stored, the corresponding topics can simply be stored in a nested list in a document store. Bulk loading this data could be faster since no join operations are required. However, this would result in the repetition of data, and the increased storage requirements that would result may not be feasible since GitHub provides huge amounts of data. Since, if a topic name changes, every occurrence in all objects must be changed, it is more challenging to keep the data consistent. Moreover, it is not possible to nest every type of entity in this way, as the size of the documents would become very large. Also, some relationships would still need to be modeled, such as the relationship between repositories and their forks. A mixture of relationships and nested properties would lead to a cluttered data model and complicated application logic and a performance decrease [25].

Finally, no caching strategy is implemented. This means that even if entities were already fetched and stored in the database, they will always be fetched again in new queries. Systems that rely on the REST API often use such a strategy, in the GraphQL context it makes less sense. This is because in the REST API ETags can be used. ETags are GitHub's REST APIs way to determine if a resource has changed. This makes it easy to check in advance if an entity stored

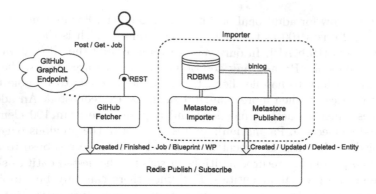

Fig. 3. Prometheus system architecture docker setup. Event subscriptions are excluded for clarity.

in the database needs an update. In GraphQL, one could check the `updatedAt` field, but unlike the REST API, this consumes rate limit, so one could also simply ask for all attributes and update the entity if needed.

4   Prometheus System

The individual services are developed and deployed as Docker containers. These coincide with the conceptual requirements for microservice architectures. In fact, it has been shown that Docker can be a good fit when implementing microservices [19]. Figure 3 shows the general Docker setup of Prometheus. The importer service consists of two containers, and one for importing fetched entities, one for publishing changes in the database. Separating service functionality in several containers is not uncommon. This way the system can spawn multiple containers of the desired functionality in case of a heavier workload. Both use the same relational database. The fetching functionality resides in one single container. The GitHub fetcher is using the GitHub GraphQL endpoint to query data. Querying jobs can be submitted via a REST API, as well as getting job progress summaries. The GitHub fetcher as well as the metastore publisher are publishing events via an event service when service state changes occur. Redis is chosen as the event system, whose basic publish/subscribe as well as a queuing mechanism is sufficient for a prototype implementation of the proposed architecture.

GitHub Fetcher. One of the most important functions of the crawling service is the processing of the job definitions. This includes splitting the query if there is nested pagination. In addition, pagination must continue until the parameters entered by the user are satisfied or there are no more objects. It must also pass parameters from responses to consecutive queries resulting from the splitting process if any. If a query has nested pagination, the way to resolve it is to first query the top paginated node, e.g. issues of a repository, and then for every

```
1   queries = [initial_query]
2   consecutive_info = []
3
4   current_query = initial_query
5
6   while True:
7     actual_query, info = remove_nested_pagination(current_query)
8
9     if actual_query != current_query:
10      remove_field_nodes(queries[-1], info.obsolete_nodes_left)
11      remove_field_nodes(actual_query, info.obsolete_nodes_right)
12
13      queries.append(actual_query)
14      consecutive_info.append(info.consecutive_info)
15    else:
16      break
17
18    current_query = actual_query
```

Listing 1: Nested pagination split algorithm

node in the response query the nested nodes, e.g. assignees of every single issue. This approach is not always applicable, more precisely it is only possible if the returned entities of the paginated top node can also be accessed directly.

Pseudocode on how to do that can be seen in code Listing 1. The algorithm starts with the query originally supplied, then `remove_nested_pagination` replaces connection nodes containing a nested connection with their direct-access counterpart (e.g. issue instead of issues). It is important that the top node is replaced and the rest of the branch remains untouched, even if it contains more nested connections. If a substitution has taken place, the nested pagination will be removed from the previous query (e.g. assignees of issues). Also, obsolete nodes are removed from the new query, i.e. all connection nodes that do not have a nested connection. These are already crawled by the previous query and are not needed in the new query. Finally, the new query and follow-up parameter information, e.g. an issue number, are added. The loop continues to replace nested connections until there are none left.

5 Evaluation

This section evaluates the performance of *Prometheus* fetching and import services. As a performance metric, we will measure throughput in fetched and stored entities per second. This is done for Prometheus and *Microsoft's ghcrawler*, a REST-based GitHub crawler, to see if the promised speed increase through the GraphQL API is true. Two experiments are performed, one simple and another with deeper relationships.

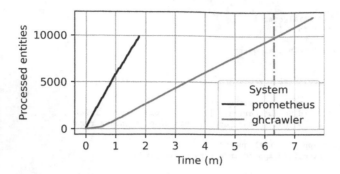

Fig. 4. Comparison of crawling performance between Prometheus and ghcrawler. In the GitHub REST API, every pull request is an issue, so the issues endpoint return issues and pull requests. The vertical line indicates at what point pure issues (without pull requests) would have been completed. Considering that, Prometheus is still 3.5 times faster.

5.1   Simple Fetching Scenario

In the simple fetching scenario, the *vuejs/vue* repository (github.com/vuejs/vue) and all the issues it contains are crawled. The repository contains 327 open issues and 9 370 closed issues. So, theoretically, 9 698 entities are being fetched (9 697 issues plus 1 repo). Currently, there is only one adjustable parameter for retrieval performance in Prometheus, which is the number of work packages that are combined in a query. Combining more work packages increases performance, but can also lead to timeouts. Currently, this parameter cannot be dynamically adjusted and is set to 100 for both experiments. This is quite aggressive and sometimes leads to API timeouts, but so far never to unresolvable timeouts. For ghcrawler, the required visitor maps are implemented in the source code. Four tokens and ten concurrent processing loops are used for both tasks.

Figure 4 shows the result of the simple job. The first thing to notice is that ghcrawler processes more entities than Prometheus. This is because the GitHub REST API considers each pull request as an issue, but not vice versa [13]. Thus, the REST API also returns all pull requests in the issues endpoint, and therefore ghcrawler processes them (2 169 additional entities). The GitHub GraphQL API explicitly separates pull requests and issues, so there is no such overhead in Prometheus job execution. A unique feature of this job in Prometheus is that the work packages are completely sequential. Getting the next page of Issues requires the last cursor, which means there is no advantage to combining work packages. In terms of overall job execution, Prometheus is 4.2 times faster, with an average throughput of 92 entities per second, while ghcrawler has a throughput of 26 entities per second. If we assume that ghcrawler does not retrieve the unwanted pull requests, Prometheus is still 3.5 times faster at retrieving all entities. On average, the processing loop of the Prometheus fetching service took 1.14 s with a standard deviation (SD) of 0.46 to process a work package. The majority of

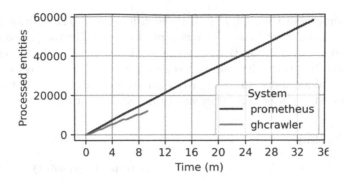

Fig. 5. Comparison of crawling performance between Prometheus and ghcrawler on a job with nested pagination. Prometheus takes 3.7 times longer because a large number of consecutive work packages are generated, which increases fetching and processing time. However, more entities are still fetched per unit time.

that time is used to make the actual API request, which took 1.09 s (SD = 0.46) on average.

5.2   Complex Fetching Scenario

In the complex fetching scenario, the repository with all issues is also fetched, but in addition, the assigned users of the issues are also captured. In this case, the number of additional entities cannot be estimated in advance.

Figure 5 shows the result of the complex scenario. This time Prometheus took significantly longer than in the previous example, 3.7 times longer than ghcrawler. The reason is that the current implementation of Prometheus strictly separates nested queries. So there is one query that retrieves a page with 100 issues, which results in 100 new individual queries for each issue that paginates the connection of the assignees. So in this example, Prometheus has 9 794 queries (97 + 9 697) to fetch. In the actual processing loop, up to 100 queries can now be combined per call. Therefore, only two more calls to the API are required for this job than for the previous job. However, since the queries are now more complex, one processing loop now takes 19.48 s (SD = 2.69) on average. The actual API calls take 6.12 s (SD = 0.48). Although most of the combined queries have about twice the number of nodes and the same number of points as the queries in the previous example, the API calls take about 5.6 times longer. The loop execution time is also longer due to the need to decompose the response, extract more cursors, and create more consecutive work packages.

Prometheus also has significant overhead in this situation. We still only crawl a single repository, but it is fetched in each of the 9 794 queries. In addition, we now fetch 222 entities related to accounts, 97 repository owners when fetching issue pages as in the last example, and 125 users assigned to issues. Of these 222 accounts, only 20 are unique. Since only 125 issues have a user assigned, 9 572 queries return only an empty connection to assignees, making them redundant.

Overall, Prometheus throughput in this scenario relates to 28 entities per second. Ghcrawler, on the other hand, behaves almost exactly like the previous example with a throughput of 21 entities per second. This is because the issues endpoint response already returns the summary representation of the assignees. Also, there are only 20 unique users, so previously queried users that exist in the database are not queried again because they are retrieved from storage.

5.3 Discussion

In the simple use case – fetching all issues from a repository – Prometheus clearly outperforms ghcrawler in both execution time and token consumption. Even if we exclude the discussed pull request overhead when retrieving issues, Prometheus is still 3.5 times faster when retrieving all issues. Looking at token consumption, the difference is drastic. While ghcrawler requires at least three tokens to fetch all requests from the REST API, Prometheus consumes only about two percent of the rate limit of one token. The result of the second experiment is different, Prometheus is slower in this case. This is because the current implementation incurs unnecessary overhead when fetching empty connections. Also, at the moment it is fully synchronous in terms of the actual API calls. Although Prometheus is 3.7 times slower, it still has higher throughput and lower token consumption. The token consumption has remained almost the same even though the queried nodes were much more, which is since queries could be combined in this query. This is a particularly interesting result, as another study suggests that GraphQL API responses are smaller than those of REST API's [4]. While this is true for an end-user application, crawling application developers must be careful to avoid this pitfall. Especially because GraphQL may perform worse on heavier loads than a REST counterpart [30], one does not want to flood GraphQL endpoints with unnecessary calls. Even if not present in this experiment, the opposite can also be the case, badly chosen calls can lead to unexpectedly complex queries which may either overload the server or even the client [24].

6 Conclusion

In this work, we presented Prometheus, a system for crawling software repositories from GitHub at scale. We demonstrated that an event-driven microservice architecture is applicable in the context of mining software repositories. Traditional systems used the REST API, but the new GraphQL API promises a significant throughput and token consumption advantage. To show whether these promises hold, we compared Prometheus, which uses the GraphQL API, to Microsoft's ghcrawler, which is based on the REST API. The throughput achieved by Prometheus is higher in all test scenarios, while token consumption is significantly lower. The job execution time is 3.5 times faster in a simple scenario but 3.7 times slower in a more complex scenario due to the currently synchronously implemented fetching loop.

Future Work. Originating from the performed experiments, we plan to make future upgrades to Prometheus. One is using more elaborate queries. Instead of the strict splitting, we can still query items from the nested connection. When querying paginated fields, one can also retrieve the total count of items available. If we do both, we can eliminate all the redundant queries that made the second experiment slow. We can also further optimize for throughput. For example, a consecutive query always fetches parents of the paginated node of interest, resulting in severe overhead that should be omitted. Furthermore, the processing loop should be asynchronous so that the high response times do not affect the execution time. Lastly, more use cases have to be implemented and tested to verify the system's effectiveness.

References

1. Bjertnes, L., Tørring, J.O., Elster, A.C.: LS-CAT: a large-scale CUDA AutoTuning dataset. In: 2021 International Conference on Applied Artificial Intelligence (ICA-PAI), pp. 1–6. IEEE (2021). https://doi.org/10.1109/ICAPAI49758.2021.9462050
2. Blei, D.M., Ng, A.Y., Jordan, M.I.: Latent dirichlet allocation. J. Mach. Learn. Res. **3**, 993–1022 (2003)
3. Borges, H., Hora, A., Valente, M.T.: Understanding the factors that impact the popularity of github repositories. In: 2016 IEEE International Conference on Software Maintenance and Evolution (ICSME), pp. 334–344 (2016). https://doi.org/10.1109/ICSME.2016.31
4. Brito, G., Mombach, T., Valente, M.T.: Migrating to GraphQL: a practical assessment. In: Proceedings of 26th International Conference on Software Analysis, Evolution and Reengineering, SANER 2019, pp. 140–150. IEEE (2019). https://doi.org/10.1109/SANER.2019.8667986
5. Brito, G., Valente, M.T.: REST vs GraphQL: a controlled experiment. In: Proceedings of International Conference on Software Architecture, ICSA 2020, pp. 81–91. IEEE (2020). https://doi.org/10.1109/ICSA47634.2020.00016
6. di Cosmo, R., Zacchiroli, S.: Software heritage: why and how to preserve software source code. In: iPRES 2017–14th International Conference on Digital Preservation, pp. 1–10 (2017)
7. Dyer, R., Nguyen, H.A., Rajan, H., Nguyen, T.N.: Boa: Ultra-large-scale software repository and source-code mining. ACM Trans. Softw. Eng. Methodol. **25**(1), 1–34 (2015). https://doi.org/10.1145/2803171
8. de F. Farias, M.A., Novais, R., Júnior, M.C., da Silva Carvalho, L.P., Mendonça, M., Spínola, R.O.: A systematic mapping study on mining software repositories. In: Proceedings of the 31st Annual ACM Symposium on Applied Computing, SAC 2016, pp. 1472–1479. ACM (2016). https://doi.org/10.1145/2851613.2851786
9. Fowler, M.: Event sourcing (2005). https://martinfowler.com/eaaDev/EventSourcing.html. Accessed 17 May 2022
10. Fowler, M., Lewis, J.: Microservices (2014). https://www.martinfowler.com/articles/microservices.html. Accessed 17 May 2022
11. Fowler, M.: What do you mean by "Event-Driven"? (2017). https://martinfowler.com/articles/201701-event-driven.html. Accessed 17 May 2022
12. Gasparini, M., Clarisó, R., Brambilla, M., Cabot, J.: Participation inequality and the 90-9-1 principle in open source. In: Proceedings of the 16th International Symposium on Open Collaboration, pp. 1–7. ACM (2020). https://doi.org/10.1145/3412569.3412582

13. Github: List repository issues. https://docs.github.com/en/rest/reference/issues# list-repository-issues. Accessed 17 May 2022
14. Gousios, G., Spinellis, D.: GHTorrent: Github's data from a firehose. In: Proceedings of 9th International Workshop on Mining Software Repositories, MSR 2012, pp. 12–21. IEEE/ACM (2012). https://doi.org/10.1109/MSR.2012.6224294
15. Gousios, G.: The GHTorrent dataset and tool suite. In: Proceedings of the 10th Working Conference on Mining Software Repositories, MSR 2013, pp. 233–236. IEEE (2013). https://doi.org/10.1109/MSR.2013.6624034
16. Gousios, G., Vasilescu, B., Serebrenik, A., Zaidman, A.: Lean GHTorrent: GitHub data on demand. In: Proceedings of the 11th Working Conference on Mining Software Repositories, MSR 2014, pp. 384–387. ACM (2014). https://doi.org/10.1145/2597073.2597126
17. Hagiwara, M., Mita, M.: Github typo corpus: a large-scale multilingual dataset of misspellings and grammatical errors. arXiv preprint arXiv:1911.12893 (2019)
18. Hartig, O., Pérez, J.: Semantics and complexity of GraphQL. In: Proceedings of World Wide Web Conference, WWW 2018, pp. 1155–1164. International World Wide Web Conferences Steering Committee (2018). https://doi.org/10.1145/3178876.3186014
19. Jaramillo, D., Nguyen, D.V., Smart, R.: Leveraging microservices architecture by using docker technology. In: SoutheastCon 2016, pp. 1–5 (2016). https://doi.org/10.1109/SECON.2016.7506647
20. Kalliamvakou, E., Gousios, G., Blincoe, K., Singer, L., German, D.M., Damian, D.: The promises and perils of mining github. In: Proceedings of the 11th Working Conference on Mining Software Repositories, MSR 2014, pp. 92–101. ACM (2014). https://doi.org/10.1145/2597073.2597074
21. Leberknight, S.: Polyglot persistence (2008). http://www.sleberknight.com/blog/sleberkn/entry/polyglot_persistence. Accessed 17 May 2022
22. Linstead, E., Bajracharya, S., Ngo, T., Rigor, P., Lopes, C., Baldi, P.: Sourcerer: mining and searching internet-scale software repositories. Data Min. Knowl. Disc. 18(2), 300–336 (2009). https://doi.org/10.1007/s10618-008-0118-x
23. Ma, Y., Bogart, C., Amreen, S., Zaretzki, R., Mockus, A.: World of code: an infrastructure for mining the universe of open source VCS data. In: Proceedings of 16th International Workshop on Mining Software Repositories, MSR 2019, pp. 143–154. IEEE/ACM (2019). https://doi.org/10.1109/MSR.2019.00031
24. Mavroudeas, G., et al.: Learning GraphQL query cost. In: Proceedings of 36th International Conference on Automated Software Engineering, ASE 2021, pp. 1146–1150. IEEE/ACM (2021). https://doi.org/10.1109/ASE51524.2021.9678513
25. Mei, S.: Why you should never use mongodb (2013). http://www.sarahmei.com/blog/2013/11/11/why-you-should-never-use-mongodb. Accessed 17 May 2022
26. Menzies, T., Zimmermann, T.: Software analytics: so what? IEEE Softw. 30, 31–37 (2013). https://doi.org/10.1109/MS.2013.86
27. Munaiah, N., Kroh, S., Cabrey, C., Nagappan, M.: Curating GitHub for engineered software projects. Empir. Softw. Eng. 22(6), 3219–3253 (2017). https://doi.org/10.1007/s10664-017-9512-6
28. Ortu, M., Destefanis, G., Adams, B., Murgia, A., Marchesi, M., Tonelli, R.: The JIRA repository dataset: understanding social aspects of software development. In: Proceedings of the 11th International Conference on Predictive Models and Data Analytics in Software Engineering, PROMISE 2015, pp. 1–4. ACM (2015). https://doi.org/10.1145/2810146.2810147

29. Rosen-Zvi, M., Griffiths, T., Steyvers, M., Smyth, P.: The author-topic model for authors and documents. In: Proceedings of 20th Conference on Uncertainty in Artificial Intelligence, UAI 2004, pp. 487–494. AUAI Press (2004)

30. Seabra, M., Nazário, M.F., Pinto, G.: REST or GraphQL? A performance comparative study. In: Proceedings of XIII Brazilian Symposium on Software Components, Architectures, and Reuse, SBCARS 2019, pp. 123–132. ACM (2019). https://doi.org/10.1145/3357141.3357149

31. Tiwari, N.M., Upadhyaya, G., Rajan, H.: Candoia: a platform and ecosystem for mining software repositories tools. In: 2016 IEEE/ACM 38th International Conference on Software Engineering Companion (ICSE-C), pp. 759–761 (2016)

32. Trautsch, A., Trautsch, F., Herbold, S., Ledel, B., Grabowski, J.: The SmartSHARK ecosystem for software repository mining. In: Proceedings of the ACM/IEEE 42nd International Conference on Software Engineering: Companion Proceedings, pp. 25–28. ACM (2020). https://doi.org/10.1145/3377812.3382139

33. Wittern, E., Cha, A., Davis, J.C., Baudart, G., Mandel, L.: An empirical study of GraphQL schemas. In: Yangui, S., Bouassida Rodriguez, I., Drira, K., Tari, Z. (eds.) ICSOC 2019. LNCS, vol. 11895, pp. 3–19. Springer, Cham (2019). https://doi.org/10.1007/978-3-030-33702-5_1

34. Zhang, D., Han, S., Dang, Y., Lou, J.G., Zhang, H., Xie, T.: Software analytics in practice. IEEE Softw. 30, 30–37 (2013). https://doi.org/10.1109/MS.2013.94

Software Functional Requirements Classification Using Ensemble Learning

Sanidhya Vijayvargiya[1(✉)], Lov Kumar[1], Aruna Malapati[1],
Lalita Bhanu Murthy[1], and Sanjay Misra[2]

[1] BITS-Pilani Hyderabad, Hyderabad, India
{f20202056,lovkumar,arunam,bhanu}@hyderabad.bits-pilani.ac.in
[2] Østfold University College, Halden, Norway
sanjay.misra@covenantuniversity.edu.ng

Abstract. Software requirement classification is crucial in segregating the user requirements into functional and quality requirements, based on their feedback or client demand. Doing so manually is time-consuming and not feasible. This can lead to delays in satisfying the requirements which in turn can lead to unhappier clients and users. Thus, machine learning techniques are used to optimize this task. In this work, five different word embedding techniques have been applied to the functional and non-functional (quality) software requirements. SMOTE is used to balance the numerical data obtained after word embedding. Dimensionality reduction and feature selection techniques are then employed to eliminate redundant and irrelevant features. Principal Component Analysis (PCA) is used for dimensionality reduction, and Rank-Sum test (RST) is used for feature selection. The resulting vectors are fed as inputs to eight different classifiers- Bagged k-Nearest Neighbors, Bagged Decision Tree, Bagged Naive-Bayes, Random Forest, Extra Tree, Adaptive Boost, Gradient Boosting, and a Majority Voting ensemble classifier, with Decision Tree, k-Nearest Neighbors, and Gaussian Naive Bayes. The experimental results suggest that the combination of word embedding and feature selection techniques with the various classifiers are successful in accurately classifying functional and quality software requirements.

Keywords: Functional requirements · Non-functional requirements · Ensemble learning

1 Introduction

Software requirements are the conditions that a system must meet in order to fulfill a contract or meet a standard. They can be classified into two types- functional and non-functional. Functional requirements are the demands that the end-user specifies as essential features that the system should provide. These are described as operation to be conducted, input to be delivered to the system, and expected output. Non-functional or quality requirements are the basic quality criteria that the system must meet, which include aspects such as portability, security, maintainability, reliability, etc. As the software requirements increase for larger projects, manual classification becomes a tedious task requiring domain experts. Using natural language processing to classify the requirements helps streamline this process. A critical challenge that needs to be addressed is the inconsistency between terminologies used by stakeholders and requirements engineers, which leads to misclassifications [1]. Our aim in this paper is to create highly accurate software requirements classification models while analyzing-

- The word embedding techniques that best suit the task of software requirements classification using Word2Vec (w2v), Term Frequency-Inverse Document Frequency (TF-IDF), Global vectors for word representation (GloVe), Skip-Gram (SKG), and Continuous bag of words (CBOW).
- The impact of class balancing technique, SMOTE, on the classification compared to models trained without SMOTE.
- How feature selection and dimensionality reduction techniques like Rank-Sum Test (RST) and Principal Component Analysis (PCA) respectively impact the accuracy of the classification models compared to the set of the original features.
- The performance of eight different classifiers: Bagged k-Nearest Neighbors (Bag-kNN), Bagged Decision Tree (Bag-DT), Bagged Naive-Bayes (Bag-NB), Random Forest (RF), Extra Tree (EXTR), Adaptive Boost (AdaB), Gradient Boosting (GraB), and Majority Voting ensemble classifier (MVE).

We perform the above analysis by comparing the performance of models using accuracy, F-measure, and Area under ROC curve (AUC). We use the Friedman test to evaluate if the ML techniques used have a significant effect. The PROMISE dataset, which contains 625 labeled requirements taken from a group of 15 projects, is used in this investigation.

The primary contribution of this paper is to provide a thorough comparison of various ML techniques and algorithms for each step of the software requirements classification pipeline, starting from the feature extraction step, to the classification step. These comparisons, which are performed using AUC, F-measure, and accuracy as the performance metrics, help analyze the impact of the most commonly used ML techniques on the performance and single out those that work best for software requirements. Statistical testing in the form of Friedman test is used to further validate the findings.

The rest of the paper is organized as follows: Literature Review on software requirements classification and various word embedding techniques is presented in Sect. 2. The experimental dataset collection, as well as the various ML techniques used, are described in Sect. 3. Section 4 details the research methodology through an architecture framework. The findings of the experiments, as well as their analysis, are reported in Sect. 5. The comparative study of models generated using various word-embedding techniques, sets of features, and machine learning models is described in Sect. 5. Finally, Sect. 6 wraps up the material presented and suggests research directions for future studies.

2   Related Work

Researchers have previously explored the effectiveness of different classifiers in segregating functional and non-functional requirements. The impact of various word embedding techniques has also been studied, and the key conclusions of the research are discussed in this section. Tiun et al. [8] proposed models based on classifiers like Logistic Regression, Support Vector Machine (SVM) and Convolutional Neural Network (CNN) to classify the software requirements into functional and non-functional, and explored the impact of word embedding techniques on the performance. They concluded that Doc2Vec was a worse choice than fastText for feature selection as it faced the issue of sparsity due to a small vocabulary. Word2Vec performed at par with fastText, giving a highest F1-score of 91.6%. TF-IDF with SVM gave the worst performance with an F1-score of 38.42% due to the same reasons for the poor performance as Doc2Vec.

Rahimi et al. [6] attempted to improve the accuracy of software requirement classification using ensemble learning techniques with SVM, SVC, and Logistic Regression as classifiers. TF-IDF and CountVectorizer were used for feature extraction. CountVectorizer outperformed TF-IDF in all aspects and was used for word embedding. SVM, Support Vector Classifier (SVC), and Logistic Regression produced accuracies of 99.0%, 97.0%, and 99.0%, respectively, and were used to monitor the accuracy of the ensemble approach. On the constructed dataset, the proposed strategy was compared to other existing ensemble approaches, and their technique had the highest accuracy, with 99.45%.

Improving on their previous work, Rahimi et al. [7] proposed three different ensemble techniques to enhance the accuracy: mean ensemble, accuracy per class as a weight ensemble, and accuracy as a weight ensemble, with a combination of four different Deep Learning models- LSTM, BiLSTM, GRU, and CNN. The DL models achieved accuracies of 93.22%, 94.49%, 92.37%, and 93.22%, respectively. Ensemble learning helped boost these results by achieving 95.7% accuracy per class as a weight and 94.9% accuracy as a weight. The accuracy per class weight ensemble approach was used to reach 0.96 for the other performance evaluation parameters.

Abad et al. [1] made a key contribution to software requirements classification by first classifying the requirements into functional and non-functional and then further classifying the non functional requirements into their sub-categories. They used three methods for the latter. Topic modeling with Latent Dirichlet Allocation (LDA) algorithm and Biterm Topic Model (BTM) method in which highly correlated words are grouped into topics was employed. BTM generated better models and topics but performed much worse than LDA as BTM does all of its modeling at the corpus level, and biterms are generated independently of topics. On evaluating the clusterings using Hopkins statistic on the non-functional requirements it was shown that the dataset under examination is unstructured, and sub-categories are not effectively segregated. Thus, unsupervised approaches are not ideal. On the other hand, a Binarized Naive-Bayes approach resulted in accuracy of 90%.

3   Study Design

This section contains information on the various design settings used in this study.

3.1   Experimental Dataset

The proposed software requirement solution is validated using the same datasets as Cleland-Huang and his team [2,6]. With the support of MS students from DePaul University, Cleland-Huang and his team retrieved the data and made it available for public research via the PROMISE repository. Figure 1 depicts the functional and quality characteristics of this dataset. The first point to note about Fig. 1 is that the PROMISE repository is unbalanced in terms of functional and non-functional requirements, with 382 out of 625 being quality requirements.

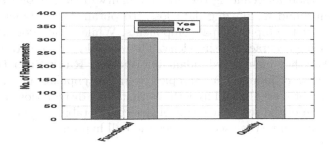

Fig. 1. Data-Sets

3.2   Data Normalization

Prior to feeding data into the model, data preprocessing is critical since it aids in data normalization [5]. To normalize the dataset, the following stages were followed in order:

– In the requirements specifications, all characters are transformed to lowercase letters.
– All alphanumeric and symbol characters are maintained, but others are removed.
– Stop-words are often used terms like 'a' and 'the,' and words with lengths less than two are deleted due to their insignificance.
– Finally, the corpus's phrases are tokenized into words.

3.3   Word Embedding

Vectorization techniques aid in efficient information retrieval and relevance ranking, which helps ML models perform better. In the classification phase, this research examines the performance of five word embedding techniques: Skip-Gram (SKG), Word2Vec, TF-IDF, Global Vectors for Word Representation (GloVe)[1], and Bag of Words (CBOW)[2]. After being normalized, each requirement is vectorized using the aforementioned vector space models, resulting in a two-dimensional array with dimensions.

3.4   Feature Selection and Dimensionality Reduction Techniques

After performing word embedding on the data, we select essential feature vectors that impact the performance of the models. Rank Sum Test (RST) and Principal Component Analysis (PCA) are used to get rid of redundant and irrelevant features that might negatively impact the performance of the models. The performance of models with these features is compared with the original features to see the difference. This step helps reduce overfitting and training time [3]. **PCA** is a method for reducing the dimensionality of such datasets, improving interpretability, and minimizing data loss. To obtain lower dimensional data, we merely select the top principal components. While some information is lost, we are sacrificing accuracy for simplicity. The variables are sometimes so highly connected that they include redundant information. **Rank Sum test** - When the data consists of independent samples from two populations, the rank-sum test can be used to test the null hypothesis that their distributions are identical. When the value of the test statistic is either considerably large or significantly small, the rank-sum test is used to reject the null hypothesis.

3.5   SMOTE

Many machine learning algorithms have the flaw of ignoring the minority class in imbalanced datasets, despite the fact that it is often the performance on those that matters. It is critical to use the SMOTE approach on the imbalanced data in our dataset in order to apply subsequent Machine Learning techniques. SMOTE (Synthetic Minority Oversampling Technique) is a data augmentation technique in which current minority class instances are duplicated, or new minority class examples are generated. Although it does not provide any new data to the dataset, it overcomes the imbalance problem, allowing us to use machine learning techniques later [4].

3.6   Classifiers

To prevent the bias produced by distinct features measured at different scales, Min-Max Scaling is conducted prior to training the Machine Learning model. Using K-Fold Cross-validation with a k value of 10, the dataset is separated

---

[1] https://nlp.stanford.edu/projects/glove/.
[2] https://towardsdatascience.com/word2vec-skip-gram-model-part-1-intuition-78614 e4d6e0b.

into training and testing subsets and categorized using eight machine learning classifiers: Bagged k-Nearest Neighbors, Bagged Decision Tree, Bagged Naive-Bayes, Random Forest, Extra Tree, Adaptive Boost, Gradient Boosting, and Majority Voting ensemble classifier [3].

4   Research Methodology

In this work, we apply five different word embedding methods to extract features from the software requirements in natural language, balanced the classes using SMOTE, selected features from both the balanced and imbalanced datasets, and use them as input to develop models for classification. These models are trained with eight different classifiers, with one of them being a soft voting ensemble classifier. The proposed methodology entails extracting features from text data using word embedding techniques, class balancing, deleting irrelevant and redundant features, and lastly, creating prediction models utilizing eight distinct classifiers. In this experiment, we employ the Rank-Sum test to identify features that may distinguish between functional and non-functional requirements, as well as PCA to reduce the variance of the numerical features produced. Finally, eight distinct classifiers, including an ensemble classifier, are used to create the required classifications, which are then confirmed using 10-fold cross-validation. The accuracy, F-measure, and AUC of the developed requirement categorization models are extracted and compared using the Box-plot and Friedman test.

5   Empirical Results and Analysis

In this work, we apply five different word embedding techniques, a class balancing technique, two feature selection techniques, and eight different classification techniques to categorize the software requirements into functional or non-functional. Therefore, a total of 480 [5 word-embedding techniques * 2 requirements datasets (1 functional requirements dataset + 1 quality requirements dataset) * (1 balanced dataset + 1 imbalanced dataset)* 3 sets of features * 8 classifiers] distinct prediction models are built in this study. The predictive ability of these trained models is evaluated with Area Under Curve (AUC), F-measure, and accuracy performance values, as shown in Table 1. The first noteworthy finding is that all of the models trained for software requirement classification have an AUC value larger than 0.7, indicating that the trained models can classify functional and non-functional requirements. The second noteworthy finding is that software requirement classification models trained on SMOTE balanced data perform better than their imbalanced counterparts in most cases.

Table 1. AUC: SMOTE and Original Data

	BAG-KNN	BAG-DT	BAG-NB	RF	EXTR	ADaB	GRaB	MVE	BAG-KNN	BAG-DT	BAG-NB	RF	EXTR	ADaB	GRaB	MVE
	OD								SMOTE							
TFIDF																
FUN																
AF	0.75	0.84	0.86	0.86	0.90	0.74	0.71	0.89	0.76	0.85	0.85	0.85	0.89	0.68	0.70	0.88
PCA	0.87	0.85	0.88	0.85	0.86	0.70	0.70	0.88	0.87	0.84	0.91	0.84	0.85	0.73	0.71	0.89
RST	0.78	0.77	0.73	0.76	0.71	0.76	0.79	0.80	0.79	0.77	0.72	0.75	0.70	0.79	0.82	0.81
QUA																
AF	0.85	0.87	0.91	0.90	0.91	0.73	0.73	0.92	0.91	0.91	0.92	0.95	0.95	0.80	0.78	0.95
PCA	0.92	0.91	0.93	0.91	0.91	0.76	0.70	0.94	0.93	0.93	0.93	0.94	0.94	0.77	0.77	0.96
RST	0.84	0.84	0.75	0.78	0.77	0.84	0.82	0.85	0.84	0.88	0.80	0.88	0.88	0.87	0.85	0.88
CBOW																
FUN																
AF	0.80	0.72	0.72	0.71	0.71	0.75	0.76	0.78	0.83	0.72	0.70	0.72	0.73	0.78	0.79	0.79
RST	0.86	0.76	0.80	0.78	0.76	0.79	0.79	0.83	0.85	0.75	0.80	0.78	0.76	0.79	0.78	0.82
PCA	0.69	0.70	0.66	0.68	0.66	0.73	0.71	0.72	0.72	0.72	0.67	0.72	0.71	0.70	0.70	0.76
CBOW																
QUA																
AF	0.87	0.79	0.70	0.76	0.78	0.77	0.79	0.81	0.91	0.85	0.71	0.83	0.86	0.80	0.80	0.86
RST	0.89	0.79	0.81	0.83	0.81	0.80	0.80	0.87	0.93	0.87	0.81	0.89	0.89	0.81	0.83	0.89
PCA	0.79	0.77	0.73	0.77	0.72	0.78	0.80	0.80	0.83	0.82	0.71	0.83	0.87	0.79	0.79	0.86
SKG																
FUN																
AF	0.81	0.73	0.73	0.78	0.79	0.73	0.75	0.79	0.82	0.77	0.73	0.77	0.76	0.75	0.73	0.79
RST	0.83	0.76	0.75	0.78	0.80	0.75	0.74	0.78	0.83	0.76	0.77	0.78	0.77	0.76	0.77	0.79
PCA	0.81	0.75	0.72	0.73	0.78	0.79	0.80	0.80	0.85	0.78	0.72	0.76	0.77	0.76	0.78	0.81
SKG																
QUA																
AF	0.87	0.84	0.80	0.81	0.83	0.82	0.81	0.85	0.91	0.89	0.82	0.90	0.91	0.87	0.86	0.89
RST	0.89	0.85	0.82	0.81	0.85	0.82	0.81	0.86	0.92	0.90	0.84	0.90	0.92	0.84	0.86	0.90
PCA	0.86	0.79	0.75	0.80	0.80	0.80	0.77	0.86	0.92	0.89	0.78	0.90	0.90	0.83	0.83	0.91
GLOVE																
FUN																
AF	0.86	0.79	0.81	0.77	0.77	0.73	0.73	0.85	0.86	0.75	0.80	0.78	0.80	0.76	0.75	0.84
RST	0.87	0.77	0.83	0.80	0.80	0.75	0.77	0.87	0.86	0.78	0.82	0.79	0.80	0.74	0.75	0.85
PCA	0.82	0.70	0.75	0.71	0.74	0.71	0.71	0.81	0.81	0.73	0.71	0.71	0.66	0.69	0.71	0.81
GLOVE																
QUA																
AF	0.90	0.79	0.84	0.81	0.84	0.82	0.80	0.88	0.93	0.89	0.86	0.91	0.94	0.82	0.83	0.93
RST	0.90	0.81	0.86	0.82	0.85	0.79	0.77	0.88	0.94	0.89	0.88	0.91	0.91	0.83	0.82	0.92
PCA	0.85	0.75	0.76	0.73	0.75	0.75	0.71	0.85	0.91	0.85	0.79	0.82	0.85	0.80	0.77	0.89
W2V																
FUN																
AF	0.88	0.80	0.82	0.79	0.79	0.77	0.76	0.86	0.88	0.82	0.83	0.77	0.81	0.79	0.80	0.88
RST	0.88	0.82	0.84	0.81	0.79	0.80	0.79	0.87	0.89	0.81	0.85	0.83	0.81	0.81	0.80	0.86
PCA	0.82	0.73	0.75	0.68	0.70	0.74	0.76	0.83	0.85	0.74	0.78	0.73	0.72	0.76	0.76	0.83
W2V																
QUA																
AF	0.90	0.85	0.86	0.83	0.83	0.81	0.82	0.89	0.95	0.89	0.89	0.90	0.91	0.85	0.85	0.93
RST	0.92	0.85	0.88	0.85	0.86	0.82	0.80	0.90	0.95	0.89	0.90	0.92	0.92	0.85	0.84	0.93
PCA	0.87	0.79	0.82	0.75	0.77	0.83	0.82	0.89	0.91	0.83	0.82	0.86	0.87	0.85	0.84	0.90

5.1 Comparative Analysis

In this section, the performance of different software requirement classification models trained using different ensemble learning on original data and balanced data with reduced sets of vectors of embedding techniques are compared using

Area under ROC curve (AUC), simulated F-measure, and accuracy. We have used box plots acting as a visual representation of the comparative performance and Friedman test has been employed in this paper to corroborate the results. The below is tested using Friedman test:

- *Null Hypothesis*- The predictive ability of software requirements classification models do not depends on different ML techniques, balancing techniques, embedding techniques, and feature selection techniques.
- *Alternate Hypothesis*- The predictive ability of software requirements classification models depends on different ML techniques, balancing techniques, embedding techniques, and feature selection techniques.

The above null hypothesis is accepted if calculated p-value of Friedman test is less than 0.05 with degrees of freedom as 4 for word embedding, 1 for class balancing, 2 for feature selection, and 7 for different classifier comparisons.

5.2   Word-Embedding

Initially, we have used five different embedding techniques to extract numerical value of software requirement text. The quality of finding best numerical vectors using these techniques are compared using AUC Accuracy, Recall, Precision, and F-measure.

Box-Plot: Word-Embedding. The performance value of various word embedding approaches is visually depicted in Fig. 2. The information present in Fig. 2 suggested that the models trained by taking numeric vectors computed by W2V and TF-IDF more better ability to classify requirements as compared to other techniques. Similarly, the models built with CBoW have a low predictive performance. W2V-created models have an average accuracy of 75.64%, a maximum accuracy of 86.26%, and a Q3 accuracy of 78.97%, which implies that 25% of W2V-created models have an accuracy of higher than 78.97%. These conclusions are supported by the AUC data and F-measure of these models, which reveal that classification models based on W2V and TF-IDF outperform classification models based on other word-embedding techniques.

Friedman Test: Word-Embedding. The Friedman Test is also used to compare the predictive ability of the models constructed using various word embedding techniques in this study. The test's purpose is to determine if the null hypothesis is true or false. "The various word embedding strategies have no meaningful impact on the performance of the classification models," asserts the null hypothesis. The mean ranks for the various word embedding approaches are

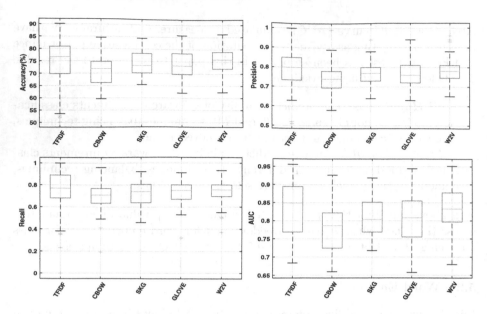

Fig. 2. Box-plot: word embedding approach

listed in Table 2. The better is the models' performance, the lower is the mean rank. The lowest mean rank is 2.07 for W2V, while the highest mean rank is 4.28 for CBoW. W2V slightly outperforms TF-IDF, which has a mean rank of 2.30. It's possible that TF-IDF's strong performance is related to the fact that requirements documents have many similar phrases and terms. TF-IDF can successfully prevent frequent terms used in articles from having an impact on the categorization better than other word-embedding algorithms because of its way of allocating weights to each term.

Table 2. Friedman test: word-embedding

	TFIDF	CBOW	SKG	GLOVE	W2V	Rank
TFIDF	1.00	0.00	0.03	0.02	0.71	2.30
CBOW	0.00	1.00	0.00	0.00	0.00	4.28
SKG	0.03	0.00	1.00	0.85	0.01	3.02
GLOVE	0.02	0.00	0.85	1.00	0.01	3.32
W2V	0.71	0.00	0.01	0.01	1.00	2.07

5.3   Feature Selection

We employ two different forms of feature selection strategies in the proposed research: Rank Sum test and PCA, and we use all of the original features for training predictive models for requirements classification in a third set of models. Both the functional and non-functional needs datasets are subjected to these feature selection strategies.

Box-Plot: Feature Selection. RST appears to produce a better set of features than any other feature selection technique as shown in Fig. 3. The average accuracy of RST is 76.52%, with a minimum of 63.36% and a maximum of 89.14%. With an average accuracy of 70.56%, the features generated using PCA had the weakest performance among the three sets of features.

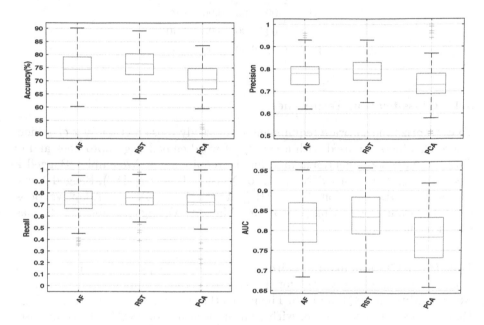

Fig. 3. Box-plot: feature selection

Friedman Test: Feature Selection. We also use the Friedman test to assess the different feature selection strategies based on their predictive ability on the performance metrics of the models, which are generated using three different sets of features. "The requirements classification models created using different sets of features do not have a substantial difference in their predictive ability" is the null hypothesis, which must be accepted or rejected based on the Friedman test. The Friedman test was performed with degrees of freedom of 2 and a significance threshold of $= 0.05$. The mean ranks of the three sets of features are shown in Table 3. The Friedman test's mean ranks can be used to compare the performance of various techniques under investigation. In comparison to others, lower mean ranks indicate higher performance. The models trained with the set of RST features had the lowest mean rank (1.40), followed by the original set of features (1.97), and lastly, PCA (2.63). The mean ranks show that when RST features are included, the models perform better, while using dimensionality reduction techniques like PCA only regresses the models' performance.

Table 3. Friedman test: feature selection

	AF	RST	PCA	Rank
AF	1.00	0.03	0.00	1.97
RST	0.03	1.00	0.00	1.40
PCA	0.00	0.00	1.00	2.63

5.4   Classification Techniques

To categorize the software requirements, the study uses eight distinct classifiers. These classifiers are used with a variety of word-embedding approaches and on datasets with both functional and quality requirements. We employ Bagged k-Nearest Neighbors (Bag-kNN), Bagged Decision Tree (Bag-DT), Bagged Naive-Bayes (Bag-NB), Random Forest (RF), Extra Tree (EXTR), Adaptive Boost (AdaB), Gradient Boosting (GraB), and Majority Voting ensemble (MVE) classifiers in this study.

Box-Plot: Classification Techniques. Figure 4 helps show accuracy, precision, recall, and AUC statistics for the various classifiers employed, such as Mean, Median, Min, Max, Q1, and Q3. The model that was trained using the MVE had the best overall performance, with a mean accuracy of 78.29%. In comparison to other classifiers, the GraB and AdaB classifiers performed the worst, with mean accuracy of 71.76% and 71.67%, respectively. The models created with the ensemble classifier have a maximum accuracy of 89.14%, a minimum accuracy of 65.44%, a Q1 accuracy of 73.73%, and a Q3 accuracy of 82.49%. The Bag-kNN classifier performs marginally worse than the ensemble classifier but significantly better than the others.

Friedman Test: Classification Techniques. The Friedman test is also applied to the performance metrics of the various classifiers in order to compare the performance of the models statistically. The test's purpose is to determine if the null hypothesis is true or false. "The requirements classification models constructed using the different classifiers do not have a substantial difference in their prediction ability" is the null hypothesis for this test. The Friedman test

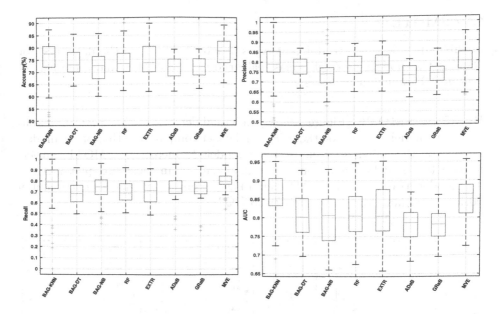

Fig. 4. Box-plot: classification techniques

was performed with degrees of freedom as 7 and a significance threshold of = 0.05. Table 4 shows the mean rank of various classifiers after applying the Friedman test. From Table 4, we can observe that the mean rank of 1.92 and 1.98 of Bag-kNN and ensemble classifier (MVE) is the lowest among all. The GraB classifier with a mean rank of 6.13 is the highest and thus symbolizes that the GraB classifier is the worst performer out of the eight.

Table 4. Friedman test: classification techniques

	BAG-KNN	BAG-DT	BAG-NB	RF	EXTR	ADaB	GRaB	MVE	Rank
BAG-KNN	1.00	0.00	0.00	0.00	0.00	0.00	0.00	0.55	1.92
BAG-DT	0.00	1.00	0.50	0.99	0.55	0.01	0.01	0.00	5.22
BAG-NB	0.00	0.50	1.00	0.53	0.34	0.10	0.04	0.00	5.25
RF	0.00	0.99	0.53	1.00	0.62	0.02	0.01	0.00	5.02
EXTR	0.00	0.55	0.34	0.62	1.00	0.01	0.00	0.00	4.45
ADaB	0.00	0.01	0.10	0.02	0.01	1.00	0.75	0.00	6.03
GRaB	0.00	0.01	0.04	0.01	0.00	0.75	1.00	0.00	6.13
MVE	0.55	0.00	0.00	0.00	0.00	0.00	0.00	1.00	1.98

5.5 SMOTE

In this paper, we use two different types of models based on the data used for training the models. One set is class-balanced using SMOTE, and the other set contains the imbalance classes.

Box-Plot: SMOTE. Figure 5 shows the visual depiction of the predictive ability of the models trained on the balanced dataset compared to that of the models trained on the imbalanced dataset. The models trained using SMOTE outperformed the models trained on the original dataset in most box plot metrics. The models trained with SMOTE had a mean accuracy of 74.44%, maximum of 90.18%, minimum of 50.13%, and 79.13% Q3.

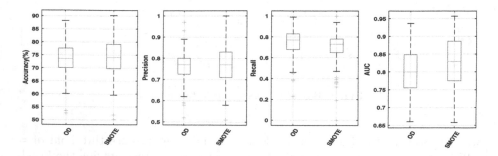

Fig. 5. Box-plot: SMOTE

Friedman Test: SMOTE. Finally, we have also applied Friedman test on the models trained using original data and sampled data. Here, this test was carried out on 0.05 significance level with 1 degrees of freedom. The information computed using this test suggested that the use of sampled data for training models significantly help in improving the performance of the models.

6 Conclusion

Automated classification of functional and non-functional requirements is a crucial task that helps overcome the inconsistencies between the software engineers and user/client demands in significantly less time than manual classification. In this work, various word embedding techniques, class balancing techniques, feature selection techniques, multiple classifiers have been used. The results are expected to help future researchers pick the ideal combination for requirements classification. The key conclusions that we arrived at were as follows:

– The models with features extracted using w2v and TF-IDF performed markedly better than other word embedding techniques.

- The models trained using the Majority Voting Ensemble classifier and bagged k-Nearest Neighbors classifier gave the highest performance out of the eight classifiers used.
- The features selected using the Rank Sum test were superior to any other subset of features used in this study.
- Class balancing using SMOTE helped improve the performance of requirements classification models.

Based on the findings of this experiment, ensemble classifiers are key to more accurate software requirements classification. More work is needed to analyze the best ML techniques to classify the functional and non-functional or quality requirements into their sub-categories, which would provide increased benefits to software developers.

Acknowledgements. This research is funded by TestAIng Solutions Pvt. Ltd.

References

1. Abad, Z.S.H., Karras, O., Ghazi, P., Glinz, M., Ruhe, G., Schneider, K.: What works better? A study of classifying requirements. In: 2017 IEEE 25th International Requirements Engineering Conference (RE), pp. 496–501. IEEE (2017)
2. Cleland-Huang, J., Settimi, R., Zou, X., Solc, P.: Automated classification of non-functional requirements. Requir. Eng. **12**(2), 103–120 (2007)
3. Kumar, L., Sripada, S.K., Sureka, A., Rath, S.K.: Effective fault prediction model developed using least square support vector machine (LSSVM). J. Syst. Softw. **137**, 686–712 (2018)
4. Kumar, L., Sureka, A.: Application of LSSVM and smote on seven open source projects for predicting refactoring at class level. In: 2017 24th Asia-Pacific Software Engineering Conference (APSEC), pp. 90–99. IEEE (2017)
5. Kumar, R., Singh, J., Kaur, A.: An empirical study of bad smell in code on maintenance effort. Int. J. Comput. Sci. Eng. **5**(6), 294–304 (2016)
6. Rahimi, N., Eassa, F., Elrefaei, L.: An ensemble machine learning technique for functional requirement classification. Symmetry **12**(10), 1601 (2020)
7. Rahimi, N., Eassa, F., Elrefaei, L.: One-and two-phase software requirement classification using ensemble deep learning. Entropy **23**(10), 1264 (2021)
8. Tiun, S., Mokhtar, U., Bakar, S., Saad, S.: Classification of functional and non-functional requirement in software requirement using word2vec and fast text. In: Iournal of Physics: Conference Series, vol. 1529, p. 042077. IOP Publishing (2020)

A Novel Approach to Recommendation System Business Workflows: A Case Study for Book E-Commerce Websites

Mounes Zaval[(⊠)], Said Orfan Haidari, Pinar Kosan, and Mehmet S. Aktas

Computer Engineering Department, Yildiz Technical University, Istanbul, Turkey
{mounes.zaval,said.haidari,pinar.kosan}@std.yildiz.edu.tr,
aktas@yildiz.edu.tr

Abstract. Have you ever wondered why a song or a book or a movie becomes so popular that everyone everywhere starts talking about it? If we did not have the technology, we would say that people who love something would start recommending it to their friends and families. We live in the age of technology where there are so many algorithms that can discover the patterns of human interaction and make an excellent guess about someone's opinion about something. These algorithms are building blocks of digital streaming services and E-Commerce websites. These services require as accurate as possible recommendation systems for them to function. While many businesses prefer one type or another of recommendation algorithms, in this study, we developed a hybrid recommendation system for a book E-Commerce website by integrating many popular classical and Deep Neural Network-based recommendation algorithms. Since explicit feedback is unavailable most of the time, all our implementations are on implicit binary feedback. The four algorithms that we were concerned about in this study were the well-known Collaborative filtering algorithms, item-based CF and user-based CF, ALS Matrix Factorization, and Deep Neural Network Based approaches. Consequently, comparing their performances and accuracy, it was not surprising that the Deep Neural Network approach was the most accurate recommender for our E-Commerce website.

Keywords: E-commerce · Deep neural network · Collaborative filtering · Alternating least square · Matrix factorization

1 Introduction

Recommendation engines perform a critical function in mitigating existing overgrowing information overload. Hence, they have been utilized and used by several platforms in many different ways, such as recommending a video on Youtube, a friend on Facebook, a movie on Netflix, or a product to purchase on E-commerce sites.

O. Gervasi et al. (Eds.): ICCSA 2022 Workshops, LNCS 13381, pp. 692–708, 2022.
https://doi.org/10.1007/978-3-031-10548-7_50

One of the most significant barriers to implementing recommendation engines for E-commerce sites is the lack of one user's interactions with the site products-leading to serious difficulties in finding sufficient reliable similar users and the problem of a high data sparsity rate. Hence, in this study, we try to solve the long tail problem and propose a better approach to make better recommendations for less popular items. Traditional recommendation systems, including user-Based Collaborative Filtering, item-based collaborative filtering, and Matrix Factorization-Based recommendation engines, expect actual product ratings to produce good results and have shown poor results when making recommendations based on implicit feedback. Furthermore, they cannot efficiently model user-item interactions when the user-item matrix (Rating Matrix) is highly sparse.

Motivation: There is a need for business workflows for recommendation systems that can allow us to choose different recommendation algorithms as needed. In particular, there is a need for business workflows that could employ not only the classical recommendation algorithms but also deep neural network-based algorithms. Such recommendation system business workflows can be utilized on different E-commerce websites. We are motivated to use this business workflow for a book E-commerce website in this study. There are several methods to extract users' feedback from the website's log files, the most popular method is explicit feedback collecting_when users explicitly rate items_. However, in some cases, there is no explicit way of collecting users' feedback. Therefore, other feedback collecting methodologies like binary feedback (implicit feedback) _based on users' purchases or items click-through, Etc._ are also needed and need to be investigated.

Research Problem: In this paper, we are investigating a novel business workflow that can employ different recommendation algorithms and produce recommendations based on implicit feedback methodology.

Here we list the questions studied under this research problem:

1. What would be the abstract modular software architecture of recommending items on a book E-commerce website?
2. How implicit feedback collecting mechanism can be used in different recommendation algorithms?
3. Which one of the recommendation algorithms would perform better on binary feedback dataset collected from an E-commerce website?

Contribution: In this study, we propose a business workflow that can be used as a recommendation system on E-commerce websites. To understand the usefulness and the benefits of this workflow, we implemented a prototype and did an experimental study to determine the effectiveness of this prototype.

Our experimental results show that among the other recommendation algorithms deep neural network learning approach was the best performer providing better recommendations relatively.

In this study, we also investigated the use of the implicit feedback approach as a feedback collection mechanism; Our results show that this mechanism of gathering users' feedback is also able to produce good results.

Organization of the Paper: We will start by introducing the fundamental concepts a reader should be aware of and then talk about some similar studies in the literature review. Then we will dive in to explain the methodology followed throughout constructing the proposed business workflow architecture for a book E-commerce website's recommendation engine from data flow and modular perspectives. As we finish explaining the methodology, we clarify the used technologies throughout the implementation of the proposed architecture. Furthermore, we report the final performance results for each Recommendation algorithm in the experimental results sections.

2   Fundamental Concepts and Literature Review

2.1   Fundamental Concepts

Collaborative Filtering: The collaborative filtering (CF) technique is one of the most popular recommendation systems out there. CF addresses content-based recommendation's problem of keeping the recommendation in the same circle of what he likes and not trying to predict what the user might like based on other factors. The main idea of collaborative filtering is that two active users show similar behavior (e.g., click-through same items, rate items similarly). Therefore they most likely will share a similar opinion regarding other items [1].

For the sake of giving an example, we assume that a set of users $user_1$, $user_2$, $user_3$, $user_1$ and $user_2$ are the most similar and we want to predict what $user_1$ would rate a specific item (Y), then we seek help from $user_2$ in a way that reflects the most similar user's opinion of an item. Hence, if $user_2$ likes item (Y), then most likely our target user will like the item (Y) too, and vice versa [2].

Collaborative filtering systems encounter several challenges, especially when integrated with big E-commerce companies. Such as [3]:

- **Data Sparsity** Usually, the number of items immensely exceeds the number of users. As a result, a single user cannot interact with all items but with a small set of items, which brings about very high sparsity in the user-item matrix.
- **Scalability** The more users and items we have, the more expensive it becomes to produce CF-based recommendations. Thus, if the number of users and items increases dramatically, then CF systems will suffer from serious scalability issues [4].
- **Gray Sheep** Concerns those whose thoughts are not always on the same line as any other group of users, and hence they do not take advantage of Collaborative Filtering [5].

– **Others** like shilling attacks [6] and Synonymy [7].

For CF systems to provide high-quality recommendations, they must address these challenges in a productive and well-thought manner. The success of a CF system depends on the answer to the question: How **well** does the system handle the environmental challenges?

User-Based CF [8]: Following the same approach explained in the previous section, User-based CF calculates user similarity from a user-item matrix _which is a matrix that draws users' interactions with items_ and then generates recommendations based on this information. The used similarity metric is essential in the process of generating recommendations for active users. It must have some properties, such as considering the actual rating values and properly handling the missing ratings without treating them as negatives. Some well-known similarity metrics are [9]:

1. Pearson Correlation Coefficient Similarity.
2. Log-Likelihood Ratio Similarity.
3. Euclidean Distance Similarity.

And many others. As stated earlier, choosing the appropriate similarity measure is crucial when building a recommendation engine since each similarity metric has a different formula and yields different results. User-item matrix is constructed based on users' past experiences and interactions or ratings of items. User-item matrix is constructed based on users' past experiences and interactions or ratings of items as shown in Table 1.

Table 1. User-Item matrix (rating matrix)

Users\Items	$Item_1$	$Item_2$	$Item_3$
$User_1$	r_{11}		r_{13}
$User_2$	r_{21}	r_{22}	r_{23}
$User_3$		r_{32}	

Where: $r_{i,j} \rightarrow$ Rating of $item_j$ by $user_i$.

Item-Based CF [8]: Item-based collaborative filtering and user-Based collaborative filtering follow the same algorithm with slight differences. Item-based CF is concerned with generating recommendations for active users based on items' similarities rather than users' similarities. Hence, it applies the same calculations but on a different matrix used in user-based CF. Item-user matrix is constructed by taking the matrix transpose of the rating matrix. Item-user matrix is constructed by taking the matrix transpose of the rating matrix as shown in Table 2.

Table 2. Item-User matrix (rating matrix)

Items\Users	User$_1$	User$_2$	User$_3$
Item$_1$	r_{11}	r_{21}	
Item$_2$		r_{22}	r_{32}
Item$_3$	r_{13}	r_{23}	

Where: $r_{i,j} \rightarrow$ Rating of $item_j$ by $user_i$.

Even though item-based and user-based CF are the same theoretically, item-based CF has shown better and more realistic results outperforming user-based CF in the real world. Basically, this is due to users' opinions changing nature over time and having varied tastes. On the other hand, items belong to a small set of genres, and they are much more straightforward.

Matrix Factorization (MF): It has been proven empirically that the most powerful and helpful latent factor models are built on top of MF [10,11]. MF factorizes user-item interactions inferred from the rating matrix and represents these interactions in a shared latent factor space of N dimensions. Assume that p_u and $q_i \rightarrow User_u$ latent vector and $Item_i$ latent vector, then they would be represented in this joint latent factor space by p_u and q_i inner product. Hence, MF can estimate an interaction y_{ui} by[12]:

$$\hat{y_{ui}} = p_u^T q_u = \sum_{i=1}^{N} p_{un} q_{in} \qquad (1)$$

where N is the dimension of the latent factor space. The matrix factorization approach introduces a well-thought solution to the scalability problem, which makes it preferred over other techniques when dealing with large datasets. Additionally, MF can handle and reduce the problem of high sparsity, especially when combined with singular value decomposition (SVD) or principal component analysis (PCA) to reduce dimensionality.

2.2   Literature Review

The attempt to design new hybrid recommendation systems has been studied over the years, as it improves the recommendation results and reduces the uninteresting recommendations. For instance, [13] in the "Hybrid recommender systems for electronic commerce" paper, a hybrid recommendation engine is investigated. They combined both the collaborative filtering recommendation algorithm and the knowledge-based recommendation algorithm _ [14] KBRS uses the acquired knowledge that is inferred from the database about users and items interactions to generate recommendations for the active users attempting to meet the user's requirements._ under one software architecture that provides a recommendation system scheme based on CFRS and KBRS. In 2000, "Hybrid Recommender

Systems: Survey and Experiments" has illustrated several hybridization methods for implementing a hybrid recommendation system [15], including:

1. **Weighted** The final score of a recommended item is calculated based on the recommendation algorithms votes present in the system for this item. The P-Tango system [5] uses such a hybridization approach.
2. **Mixed** Recommendations of all the participated recommendation algorithms are present at the same time. This method is used by the PTV system [16] to produce a recommended television viewing program.
3. **Feature combination** This method is used in integrating content-based and collaborative-based algorithms by considering collaborative information to be simply extra feature data and applying Content-Based approaches to process the enriched dataset [17].

We observe a number of studies in recommendation systems that utilize a variety of approaches, such as rule-based recommendation systems, case-based reasoning-based recommendation systems, and hybrid recommendations systems using collaborative filtering-based algorithms [18–24]. However, in this particular study, we propose a software architecture that follows a specific methodology to produce a successful recommendation system utilizing traditional and deep neural network-based algorithms for a book e-commerce website. There exist studies that focus on analyzing user's browsing behaviour (i.e. click-stream based browsing graph data) to extract knowledge [25–28]. In this study, we focus on user's purchase behaviour on the book e-commerce website.

3 Methodology

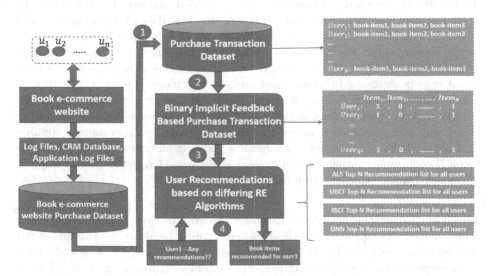

Fig. 1. The proposed business workflow architecture for a book E-commerce website Recommendation Engine _ Data Flow

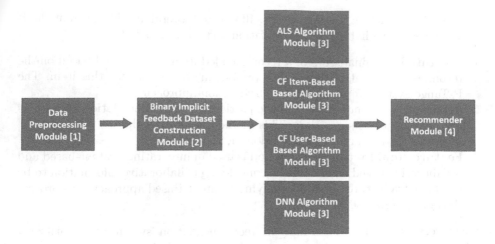

Fig. 2. The proposed business workflow architecture for a book E-commerce website Recommendation Engine _ Modular perspective

This section explains the proposed business workflow methodology followed throughout this study. Figure 1 shows you the data flow extracted from users' interactions in a book website, and Fig. 2 shows you the modular architecture of the software developed in order to produce recommendations; Each number in Fig. 1 refers to the corresponding module in Fig. 2. We are going to explain the business workflow from the modular perspective in detail below:

Data Pre-processing Module: The provided dataset by the book E-commerce website is in raw form. However, for this dataset to be helpful and used as an input to our recommendation algorithms, it should go through the preprocessing stage. the Data Preprocessing module filters out noisy data from the raw dataset. Essentially, we have user interactions from zero to the total number of book items; however, most users have a meager interaction rate with the E-commerce website. For this particular reason, we only want to analyze relatively high interacted users in this study. That is why we picked a threshold in which any user who has interacted (purchased) twenty books or more is counted and considered in our dataset. This module converts the raw data offered by the book E-commerce company into a dataset that can be fed to the Binary Implicit Feedback Dataset Construction Module.

Binary Implicit Feedback Dataset Construction Module: Binary Implicit feedback approach is utilized where explicit feedback information is not accessible or available. Let U and I represent the size of users' sets and items' sets, respectively. We define the user-item interaction matrix $Y \in R^{U \times I}$ from users' binary feedback as:

$$y_{ui} = \begin{cases} 1, & \text{Interaction observed;} \\ 0, & \text{Otherwise.} \end{cases} \tag{2}$$

The developer or the company could define the interaction identity; in our case, if User u purchased Item i, then an interaction happened between them; therefore, the value is one.

Table 3. Binary User-Item matrix

Users\Items	Item$_1$	Item$_2$		Item$_I$
User$_1$	1	0	...	1
User$_2$	1	0	...	1
...	...	...	...	...
...	...	...	...	...
User$_U$	1	0	...	1

As illustrated in Table 3, this would be an output example of this module, where a cell's value is one if the corresponding user did actually purchase the corresponding book item and zero otherwise. And we construct for each user a vector that has a space for all available book items in the book store.

In this context, a zero value does not indicate that $user_u$ dislikes $item_i$; It could mean the user's unawareness of this item. This complicates learning from implicit data because it only gives noisy indications about user preferences. Unobserved entries may be unavailable due to the natural scarcity of negative feedback, while observable entries show users' interest in items.

ALS Algorithm Module: One approach for collaborative filtering which has become popular in recent years is Matrix Factorization. Its potential was first demonstrated in the Netflix Prize competition in 2009. One of the problems that are mainly encountered when using collaborative filtering, contrary to its content-based approaches, is that since they mostly use similarity and neighborhood approaches to recommend items for users, they suffer from a "popularity" problem, which means it primarily recommends popular items since most of the users have given a high rating for the item. Matrix Factorization approaches do not suffer from this problem because they are based on latent factors calculated by the user-item matrix (Fig. 3).

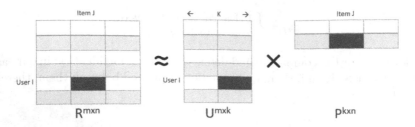

Fig. 3. Matrix factorization [29]

The fundamental concept of Matrix Factorization is illustrated in Fig. 4. The matrix R, which has MxN dimensions, represents our user-item matrix _ where (M, N) denotes the number of (users, items)_ which is decomposed into two MxK and NxK matrices. There are several approaches and implementations of the Matrix Factorization technique for approximating the User-Item relation. Since we are dealing with implicit feedback representing Users-Item interactions using binary values, it is best to use the Alternating Least Square[ALS] approach of matrix factorization [10]. Furthermore, in this study, we are implementing an ALS approach provided in [30] "Collaborative Filtering for Implicit Feedback Datasets."

CF Item-Based Algorithm Module: Despite their apparent problems, classical collaborative filtering approaches are still being used in businesses. Besides being very simple to implement, they are very good at recommending using user interactions.

Since we are using implicit binary feedback for our recommendation system, we also have to choose a good similarity metric to get recommendations. Since Pearson Correlation and Cosine Similarity techniques depend on explicit feedback, we are left with two choices Tanimoto coefficient similarity and Log-Likelihood Similarity, which only account for the presence or absence of the interactions. In our study, we used Log-Likelihood Similarity to calculate users' similarities and limited the recommendations using threshold neighborhood.

CF User-Based Algorithm Module: Item-based and user-based recommenders are both implemented with similar techniques since their fundamental concepts are similarly related to calculating similarity and recommending using any neighborhood method.

Similar to the item-based recommender, we used the Log-Likelihood similarity method for this recommender. Since Log-Likelihood similarity does not consider the ratings given by a user to any items, how does it calculate the similarity between users? To understand this, first, we have to look at Tanimoto coefficient similarity, which is similar to Log Likelihood. Tanimoto coefficient similarity between two users is calculated by dividing the number of items each user has in common, which is their intersection, as shown in Fig. 5, by the sum of the number of items both users have had interaction with, which is their union.

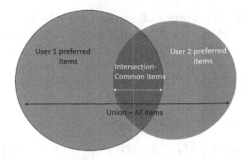

Fig. 4. Tanimoto similarity calculation [29]

Log-Likelihood Similarity calculation is more complex, but its basics are similar to Tanimoto Coefficient Similarity. The only place that they differ is that the Log-Likelihood similarity value shows how unlikely it is that two users' similarity is because of luck.

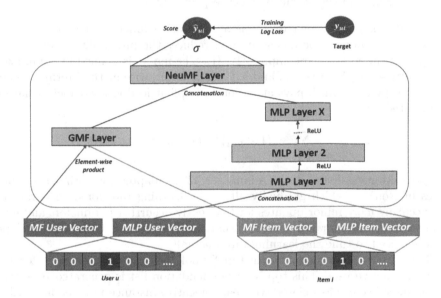

Fig. 5. Deep neural network CF algorithm

Deep Neural Network-based CF Algorithm Module: We are inspired by the deep neural network CF framework that was proposed in the "Neural collaborative filtering" paper published in 2017; Hence we followed the same approach mentioned in the paper [12]. Figure 5 illustrates for us the workflow of the Neural Matrix Factorization algorithm; As it is the product of the fusion of two instantiations of the Neural CF framework _ Generalized MF that models the latent feature interaction linearly and Multi-Layer Perceptron model that employs the non-linearity nature of neural networks to learn the interaction function from data. GMF and MLP models are integrated by concatenating their last hidden layer after learning separate embedding from the sparse user (item) inputs, which enriches the fused NeuMF model with great flexibility.

The formulation of the DNN CF algorithm clarified in Fig. 5 is given as follows [12]:

$$\phi^{GMF} = p_u{}^G \odot q_i{}^G,$$
$$\phi^{MLP} = a_L(W_L{}^T(a_{L-1}(..a_2(W_2{}^T \begin{bmatrix} p_u{}^M \\ q_i{}^M \end{bmatrix} + b_2)..)) + b_L),$$
$$\hat{y}_{ui} = \sigma(h^T) \begin{bmatrix} \phi^{GMF} \\ \phi^{MLP} \end{bmatrix}, \tag{3}$$

where:

1. $(p_u{}^G$ and $p_u{}^M, q_i{}^G$ and $q_i{}^M) \rightarrow$ are (user, item) embeddings for GMF, MLP respectively.
2. $(b_x, a_x$ and $W_x) \rightarrow$ are (bias vector, activation function for the x_{th} layer's perceptron, and the weight matrix) respectively.

This model uses Rectifier (ReLU) as an activation function since it is demonstrated by evidence to be non-saturated, reduces the probability of overfitting, and is well-suited for sparse inputs [12,31]. The model is trained by minimizing the pointwise loss between y_{ui} and $\hat{y}_{ui}$, using a pointwise method termed binary cross-entropy loss, which pays attention to implicit feedback's one-class nature; Formulated by:

$$L = - \sum_{(u,i) \in Y \cup Y^-} (1 - y_{ui}) \log(1 - \hat{y}_{ui}) + y_{ui} \log(\hat{y}_{ui}) \tag{4}$$

Adaptive Moment Estimation (Adam) [12,32] is adapted for optimization purposes in NeuMF, which gradually alters the learning rate for each parameter by executing more minor updates for frequently occurring parameters and more significant updates for infrequently occurring parameters; Thus, the developer does not need to tune the learning rate manually.

The output of this module is the top-N book recommendations items for each individual active user. This top-N recommendation list is generated by sorting the predicted scores associated with each negative instance in ascending order.

Recommender Module: We have the recommendation results for each individual implemented recommendation engine until this point. These recommendations are fed to the Recommender Module to obtain the most relevant ones. As a result, we can generate helpful recommendations for active users, helping them explore book items they most likely will like.

More specifically, in the recommender module, we are merging the results from each recommendation engine based on the hit ratio into one joint list. As we join the results, we assign a weight to each recommendation in the result list based on the corresponding hit ratio score of the source recommender. The score may come from one recommendation engine or two or more recommendation engines. In that case, we take the average hit ratio from these different recommendation engines. Then we rerank the results based on the final hit ratio score and show them to the users. So this way, we can jointly recommend the result from four different recommendation systems.

4 Prototype and Evaluation

4.1 Prototype

This section explains the technologies that enabled us to complete this novel approach for the recommendation system Business Workflows. First of all, we preprocessed and constructed the binary implicit feedback dataset from the data received from the book E-commerce website using python's NumPy and Pandas libraries, converting our data to the form of (user cookie id, book item id, rating) so we can construct a data stack on which we can run all of our recommendation algorithms modules.

With the help of Apache Mahout, we implement both user-based and Item-based collaborative filtering recommendation algorithms employing the great functionality power provided by Mahout. Between Java and Scala programming languages supported by Mahout, Java programming language was our preferred choice. And for implementing Alternating Least Squares (ALS) algorithm, we used Apache Spark, with Python programming language being our choice among supported languages, including Java, Scala, and Python.

Since we followed the "Neural collaborative filtering" paper's approach in constructing our Deep Neural Network Model, we also used their provided code [12,33]. Their source code was written with python version 2.7 as a programming language and Keras V. 1.0.7 with Theano V. 0.8.0 as the backend. Hence, the source code is outdated, allowing us to update it and make it compatible with the latest stable versions _when conducting this study_ of Python, Keras, and Theano.

4.2 Dataset

As stated earlier, we used a database that contains users' behaviors in a book E-commerce website. Table 4 provides some statistics about the dataset before and after preprocessing. The raw dataset is associated with a high noise rate, which prevents extracting the complete interactions as there are many missing user cookie IDs or book item IDs in the raw database.

Table 4. Statistics of the dataset

Dataset	Interactions	Book-items	Users
Before preprocessing	1807669	197261	1327444
After preprocessing	356320	145444	1804

4.3   Test Design

In this particular study, we employed the *leave_one_out* evaluation methodology _which has been used on a large scale in the literature [34–36]_ to measure each recommendation algorithm's performance and understand how good they are. The overall performance of a recommendation list is decided by *HitRatio* (HR) and *NormalizedDiscountedCumulativeGain* (NDCG) [37]. We calculated both measures at 10, 20, 30, 40, and 50 top-N recommendation lists for each user and reported the average score. HR basically detects whether the test item is present on the top-N recommendation list or not. If it is present, NDCG locates the test item position in the list assigning higher scores to hits at the top ranks according to this equation:

$$NDCGscore = \frac{\log(2)}{\log(position + 2)} \tag{5}$$

For example, if the test book-item ID for $user_1$ is 222, and the top-10 recommended books list is [101, 3901, 222, ..., ..., $item_{10}$]; Due to the test item's presence in the recommendation list, the hit value is 1, and therefore the NDCG value would be 0.5.

4.4   Experimental Results

The performance outputs of each recommendation algorithm conducted on our book purchase database are shown in the experimental results. One of this study's purposes was to illustrate how DNN-Based recommendation algorithms perform better than the well-known classical algorithms because of the great flexibility provided by the neural networks allowing us to address several classical recommendation algorithms challenges.

First, we will introduce the classical recommendation algorithms' performance results for HR and NDCG metrics at the top [10, 20, 30, 40, 50] recommendation lists.

Table 5. Classical recommendation algorithm performance

Top-N \Alg.	IBCF	UBCF	ALS	Top-N \Alg.	IBCF	UBCF	ALS
HR @10	0.0055	0.0079	0.0061	NDCG @10	0.0035	0.0043	0.0028
HR @20	0.0071	0.0122	0.0112	NDCG @20	0.0038	0.0055	0.0045
HR @30	0.0082	0.0159	0.0151	NDCG @30	0.0042	0.0062	0.0054
HR @40	0.0094	0.0186	0.0218	NDCG @40	0.0043	0.0068	0.0069
HR @50	0.0114	0.0207	0.0250	NDCG @50	0.0047	0.0071	0.0075

As shown in Table 5, we can observe the low-quality recommendations of the classical recommendation algorithms they produce when they run on top of a highly sparse dataset with binary implicit feedback. The item-based collaborative algorithm was the worst performer. On the other hand, user-based collaborative filtering and Alternating Least squares algorithms compete to show the best results among the classical algorithms, so we notice that for lower values of (N), UBCF is slightly better, but with increasing (N), ALS is showing better results. Now that we reported the average HR and NDCG score performance of the traditional algorithms, we move on to introduce the performance scores of the DNN-Based recommendation algorithm. We set the number of epochs to 20; We report only the performances of the initial model and the best model.

Table 6. DNN-based recommendation algorithm performance

Top-N	Initial HR	Best iteration	Top-N	Initial NDCG	Best iteration
HR @10	0.0006	0.0499	NDCG @10	0.0002	0.0273
HR @20	0.0017	0.0621	NDCG @20	0.0005	0.0302
HR @30	0.0028	0.0676	NDCG @30	0.0007	0.0329
HR @40	0.0028	0.0804	NDCG @40	0.0009	0.0348
HR @50	0.0044	0.0837	NDCG @50	0.0011	0.0409

Table 6 illustrates how well the DNN-Based approach has performed on our sparse dataset. We observe a monotonic increment of the HR and NDCG metrics for the initial model and the best model associated with the increment of N. Consequently, based on what has been shown in the experimental results, we have proven the superiors of the Deep Neural Network approach for generating book recommendations for active users in a book-selling e-commerce website.

Eventually, we create the final recommendation list for the hybrid approach by using the hit ratio as the metric. So, the final result list will favor the results with high ratio hits. Therefore, the hybrid recommender approach will always have highly favored recommended items coming from the available recommendation engines.

5   Conclusion and Future Work

This study designed a novel approach by implementing a hybrid recommendation system for a book e-commerce website by integrating classical collaborative filtering and Deep Neural Network-based methods. Since explicit feedback is often unavailable for items, our data consisted of a preprocessed user-item matrix of binary implicit feedback. Our implemented modules include item-based CF, user-based CF, ALS Matrix Factorization, and Deep Neural Network-based approach. Our item-based and user-based collaborative filtering are implemented in the Mahout framework environment. ALS Matrix factorization is implemented using Apache Spark, and Deep Neural Network is implemented using Keras, Theano, and with the help of the source code from the paper mentioned above. We also evaluated the performances of these recommendation algorithms by calculating the average hit rate and NDCG. We concluded that the Deep Neural Network-based approach had the best result among all other implementations.

In future studies, we will attempt to merge more recommendation algorithms and techniques under the suggested software framework. In addition, multiple tests on several book E-commerce websites will be conducted to investigate the system's performance further.

Acknowledgement. We would like to thank TekhneLogos Company for helping with the dataset and the computational environment.

References

1. Goldberg, K., et al.: EigenTaste: a constant time collaborative filtering algorithm. Inf. Retriev. **4**, 133–151 (2001)
2. Miller, B.N., et al.: PocketLens: toward a personal recommender system. ACM Trans. Office Inf. Syst. **22**(3), 437–476 (2004)
3. Su, X., et al.: A survey of collaborative filtering techniques. Adv. Artif. Intell. **2009**, 2 (2009)
4. Linden, G., et al.: Amazon. com recommendations: item-to-item collaborative filtering. IEEE Internet Comput. **7**(1), 76–80 (2003)
5. Claypool, M., et al.: Combining content-based and collaborative filters in an online newspaper. In: Proceedings of the ACM SIGIR 1999 Workshop on Recommender Systems: Algorithms and Evaluation, Berkeley, California, ACM (1999)
6. Gunes, I., et al.: Shilling attacks against recommender systems: a comprehensive survey. Artif. Intell. Rev. **42**(4), 767–799 (2014)
7. Pandey, A.K., Rajpoot, D.S.: Resolving cold start problem in recommendation system using demographic approach, pp. 213–218 (2016)
8. Papagelis, M., et al.: Qualitative analysis of user-based and item-based prediction algorithms for recommendation agents. Eng. App. Artif. Intell. **18**(7), 781–789 (2005)
9. Bagchi, S.: Performance and quality assessment of similarity measures in collaborative filtering using mahout. Proc. Comput. Sci. **50**, 229–234 (2015)
10. Bokde, D., et al.: Matrix factorization model in collaborative filtering algorithms: a survey. Proc. Comput. Sci. **49**, 136–146 (2015)

11. kumar Bokde, D., et al.: Role of matrix factorization model in collaborative filtering algorithm: a survey. ArXiv abs/1503.07475 (2015)
12. He, X., et al.: Neural collaborative filtering. In: WWW 2017, Republic and Canton of Geneva, CHE, International World Wide Web Conferences Steering Committee, pp. 173–182 (2017)
13. Tran, T., Cohen, R.: Hybrid recommender systems for electronic commerce. In: Proceedings of Knowledge-Based Electronic Markets, Papers from the AAAI Workshop, Technical report WS-00-04, vol. 40. AAAI Press (2000)
14. Burke, R.: Knowledge-based recommender systems. Encycl. Libr. Inf. Syst. **69**, 175–186 (2000)
15. Burke, R.: Hybrid recommender systems: survey and experiments. User Model. User-Adapt. Interact. **12**(4), 331–370 (2002)
16. Smyth, B., Cotter, P.: Personalized tv listings service for the digital tv age. Knowl. Based Syst. **13**, 53–59 (2000)
17. Basu, C., et al.: Recommendation as classification: using social and content-based information in recommendation. In: AAAI/IAAI (1998)
18. Uzun-Per, M., et al.: Scalable recommendation systems based on finding similar items and sequences. Concurr. Comput. Pract. Exp. **2022**, e6841 (2022)
19. Uzun-Per, M., et al.: Big data testing framework for recommendation systems in e-science and e-commerce domains. In: 2021 IEEE International Conference on Big Data (Big Data), pp. 2353–2361. IEEE (2021)
20. Uzun-Per, M., et al.: An approach to recommendation systems using scalable association mining algorithms on big data processing platforms: a case study in airline industry. In: 2021 International Conference on INnovations in Intelligent SysTems and Applications (INISTA), pp. 1–6. IEEE (2021)
21. Tas, K., et al.: On the implicit feedback based data modeling approaches for recommendation systems. In: 2021 International Conference on Electrical, Communication, and Computer Engineering (ICECCE), pp. 1–6. IEEE (2021)
22. Duzen, Z., Aktas, M.S.: An approach to hybrid personalized recommender systems. In: 2016 International Symposium on INnovations in Intelligent SysTems and Applications (INISTA), pp. 1–8. IEEE (2016)
23. Aktas, M.S., et al.: A web based conversational case-based recommender system for ontology aided metadata discovery. In: Fifth IEEE/ACM International Workshop on Grid Computing, pp. 69–75. IEEE (2004)
24. Arpacı, A., Aktaş, M.: Investigation of different approaches for recommendation system. In: ELECO 2018 (2018)
25. Olmezogullari, E., Aktas, M.: Representation of click-stream datasequences for learning user navigational behavior by using embeddings. In: 2020 IEEE International Conference on Big Data (Big Data), pp. 3173–3179. IEEE (2020)
26. Uygun, Y., et al.: On the large-scale graph data processing for user interface testing in big data science projects. In: 2020 IEEE International Conference on Big Data (Big Data), pp. 3173–3179. IEEE (2020)
27. Oz, M., et al.: On the use of generative deep learning approaches for generating hidden test scripts. Int. J. Softw. Eng. Knowl. Eng. IJSEKE. **31**(10), 1447–1468 (2021)
28. Olmezogullari, E., Aktas, M.: Pattern2vec: representation of clickstream data sequences for learning user navigational behavior. Concurr. Comput. Pract. Exp. **34**(9), e6546 (2022)
29. Bokde, D., et al.: Role of matrix factorization model in collaborative filtering algorithm: a survey. arXiv:abs/1503.07475 (2015)

30. Hu, Y., et al.: Collaborative filtering for implicit feedback datasets. In: 2008 Eighth IEEE International Conference on Data Mining, pp. 263–272 (2008)
31. Elkahky, A.M., et al.: A multi-view deep learning approach for cross domain user modeling in recommendation systems. In: Proceedings of the 24th International Conference on World Wide Web. WWW 2015, Republic and Canton of Geneva, CHE, International World Wide Web Conferences Steering Committee, pp. 278–288 (2015)
32. Kingma, D.P., Ba, J.: Adam: A method for stochastic optimization. CoRR abs/1412.6980 (2015)
33. He, X., Liao, L., Zhang, H., Nie, L., Hu, X., Chua, T.S.: Neural collaborative filtering source code. https://github.com/hexiangnan/neural_collaborative_filtering
34. Bayer, I., et al.: A generic coordinate descent framework for learning from implicit feedback. In: Proceedings of the 26th International Conference on World Wide Web. WWW 2017, Republic and Canton of Geneva, CHE, International World Wide Web Conferences Steering Committee, pp. 1341–1350 (2017)
35. He, X., et al.: Fast matrix factorization for online recommendation with implicit feedback. In: Proceedings of the 39th International ACM SIGIR Conference on Research and Development in Information Retrieval. SIGIR 2016, New York, NY, USA, Association for Computing Machinery, pp. 549–558 (2016)
36. Rendle, S., et al.: BPR: Bayesian personalized ranking from implicit feedback. arXiv preprint arXiv:1205.2618 (2012)
37. He, X., et al.: Trirank: Review-aware explainable recommendation by modeling aspects. In: Proceedings of the 24th ACM International on Conference on Information and Knowledge Management. CIKM 2015, New York, NY, USA, Association for Computing Machinery, pp. 1661–1670 (2015)

An Approach to Business Workflow Software Architectures: A Case Study for Bank Account Transaction Type Prediction

Fatma Gizem Çallı[1]($\boxtimes$), Çağdaş Ayyıldız[2], Berke Kaan Açıkgöz[2],
and Mehmet S. Aktas[2]

[1] Software Development Department, Eçözüm Bilgi Teknolojileri A.Ş.,
Istanbul, Turkey
gizem.calli@ecozum.com
[2] Computer Engineering Department, Yildiz Technical University, Istanbul, Turkey
{cagdas.ayyildiz,berke.acikgoz}@std.yildiz.edu.tr, aktas@yildiz.edu.tr

Abstract. Today, practically every bank's computer system can automatically categorize transactions. If someone uses their debit/credit card to buy groceries or clothing, they can see the sort of expense on their user account in seconds. Even though banks provide this level of categorization for individual users, there is no categorization solution for accounting systems. In this article, the main objective is to design and develop a business workflow that can predict bank account transaction types. Various machine learning and deep learning algorithms are used to accomplish this purpose. In the prototype implementation, Support Vector Machines, Random Forest, Long Short-Term Memory Networks, and Frequent Pattern Growth algorithms are used, and the prediction successes of these techniques are analyzed.

Keywords: Electronic bank transaction categorization · Electronic bank transaction prediction · Association mining rules · Deep learning · Machine learning · LSTM · FP-Growth

1 Introduction

People generally use cash to buy and sell products and services, as well as to keep their savings. The use of cash as a medium of exchange has fallen dramatically in recent years. People are increasingly turning to electronic transaction methods, such as debit cards and digital payments. As an example, only 23% of all payments in 2019 were made using cash [1]. This increase in banks' online money transfers has dramatically increased the data volume of banks.

Banks categorize the transfer types for their customers. Although these categories are very diverse, the definition of the type of transaction is usually chosen by the customer performing the transfer. During this selection, most customers do not care much about the type of transaction to complete the transaction as soon as possible and fill this section with incorrect or unnecessary information. The fact that most customers carry out their transactions in this way reduces the value of the data held by the banks and makes it incomprehensible.

Motivation: The banks offer expense categorization to individual users. However, there are no solutions for the accounting categorization for enterprises. Bank account transaction types for enterprises consist of many variable categories. These categories facilitate the periodic summarization for an accountant in the enterprise. There are categories such as Electronic Funds Transfer (EFT), Wire Transfer, bank giro credit, pos machine transactions, etc. Our motivation in this research project is to categorize bank account transactions into specified categories.

Research Questions: A business process is introduced within the scope of this research paper to predict different types of bank account transactions. The prototype application of this business process was developed and the success of this application is calculated. In this context, the following research questions were examined:

- How should be the business process implemented to predict the type or category of bank money transfer?
  What should be the correct embedding approach to model bank account transaction types?
  Which approaches (classical machine learning algorithm, deep learning algorithms, association rule mining algorithms) will give more successful prediction results in bank account transaction type prediction?

Contribution: The goal of this article is to propose a business workflow to process and estimate the bank account transaction type using the created models. A prototype application is created to demonstrate the effectiveness of the suggested business workflow. The results acquired from the developed prototype application is tested to determine whether it accurately categorizes account transaction. Within the scope of this research, the estimation of bank account transaction types was studied with three different approaches;

- Machine Learning Algorithms
- Deep Learning Algorithms
- Association Rule Mining Algorithms

In line with this research, an experimental study was conducted to successful different artificial intelligence approaches predict the category account transaction. The results show that deep learning algorithms other methods.

Paper Structure: The structure of this article is organized as chapter II, the basic concepts of machine learning, deep learning, association mining, and then the literature on big data architectures are presented. provides the methodology and describes the proposed model. In type, evaluation and experimental results are given. In Sect. 5, are evaluated and future studies are mentioned.

2 Fundamental Concepts and Literature Review

2.1 Fundamental Concepts

Machine Learning: Machine learning uses mathematical models to assist a computer in learning without being given explicit instructions. This is a subcategory of artificial intelligence. In machine learning, algorithms are used to find patterns in data. These patterns are also used to create a data model that predicts the outcome. Machine learning results improve with more data and experience, just as people do with more practice.

Because of its adaptability, machine learning is an excellent option in scenarios where data, requests or tasks are constantly changing or when it is impossible to code a solution effectively [4].

Deep Learning: Deep learning is a type of machine learning that employs artificial neural networks to assist digital systems in learning from unstructured, unlabeled data and making decisions.

Machine learning, in general, teaches AI systems to learn by analyzing data, finding patterns, generating recommendations, and adapting. Deep learning allows digital systems to learn from examples rather than just following predefined rules, and then it uses that knowledge to act, behave, and perform like people.

Deep learning software is used to evaluate vast and complicated data sets, conduct complex and non-linear tasks, and reply to a text, voice, or pictures more quickly and accurately than humans by data scientists and developers.

Companies in healthcare, transportation, technology, and other industries invest in deep learning to speed innovation, open new possibilities, and stay ahead of their competition as data volumes expand. As consequence of cheaper and more powerful computers, deep learning becomes incredibly valuable [3].

Association Rules: Association Rules are used to find relations between items in an item set [9–11]. Analyzing connections of customers' purchasing habits is a real-life example of association rule mining. "If X and Y exist, then Z must exist," is how the rule mining is usually described. For the purchasing habits example mentioned before, one can describe the association rules as "if a customer bought X and Y then this customer is inclined to buying Z". Association Rule Mining methods generally use two fundamental formulas: Support and Confidence. The ratio of a subset of all possible transactions to all transactions completed is shown by support and the ratio of items that can be seen if the given condition is correct is shown by confidence.

Most association rule mining algorithms use minimum support and minimum confidence values to remove some unnecessary rules. These values should be determined in the algorithm's parameter. The algorithm used in this paper is described further down.

2.2   Literature Review

While there are no studies in the field of accounting that categorize bank transactions, there are some classification and categorization studies in electronic banking. Adam Wamai Egesa's work in financial transaction analysis was achieved 90% and 84% success in Support Vector Machine (SVM) and Naive Bayes (NB) algorithms, respectively. In the same study, it is seen that one of the success factors is the n-gram data representation method [2]. In another study conducted with the same concept, short text classification was applied on Banking Transaction Descriptions by using Specialized Labeled Corpus [5]. In this study, the performances of SVM as a Machine Learning algorithm and different word n-gram features were compared according to various train test split ratios. As a result of this comparison, SVM and ALL-IN-1 model [6] produced the most successful result with 95.05% precision.

Within the scope of machine learning, there are also similar studies like credit card transactions fraud detection in electronic banking. Some of the methods used in these studies are Random Forest (RF) and Long Short-Term Memory (LSTM) networks. Since 97.67% success was achieved in a similar study with RF [7], the RF algorithm was also included in this study. In equivalent research on fraud detection in credit card transactions, Bénard Wiese's study showed that LSTM produces more successful results than SVM and Feed Forwarding Neural Network (FFNN) [8].

Association rules are used mainly to list other actions that people can take due to reviewing their previous efforts. However, this listing and analysis process takes too long for systems with big data. Programming frameworks such as MapReduce and Spark are often used to manipulate data in such systems [14–16].

FP-Growth algorithm is one of the most widely used algorithms for deleting repeating patterns and generating rules today [16]. But such algorithms are slow in terms of working speed. The FP-Growth algorithm can run in parallel on distributed machines [17]. In the Parallel FP-Growth (PFP) algorithm, the MapReduce approach divides large processing loads into parts, and each machine connected to the algorithm runs on a different processing group. In this way, while contributing to progress, the workload per machine is reduced on the one hand. This strategy, however, does not account for load balancing. The BPFP method separates the total task into equal subtasks by removing the mining unit's duty [18].

Data pre-processing steps in big data processing platforms have been the subject of research [21,22]. Studies on big data processing libraries for data mining were observed [23]. In the business and science domains, we also observe workflows for various purposes [24,25]. In the e-commerce field, there have been studies on supervised learning business workflows for predicting purchase intent [24]. This study also uses big data processing libraries for data pre-processing and data mining algorithms and differs from previous works as it introduces a business workflow for bank transaction type prediction.

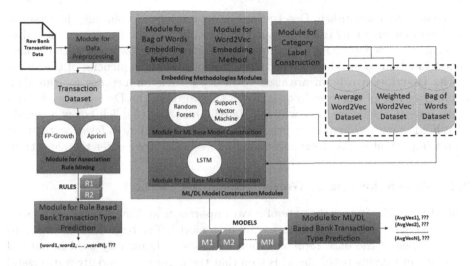

Fig. 1. A system architecture that can predict bank transaction type

3   Methodology

As part of this study, first and foremost, some bank transaction information of Eçözüm Bilgi Teknolojileri A.S. customers were collected in the form of an excel file.

The architecture of the methodology proposed in this study is as shown in Fig. 1. The architecture's main goal is to analyze customer account transaction data and extract useful information from it using Machine Learning, Deep Learning and, Association Rule Mining methods.

In this proposed model, the bank account transactions that customers performed is going to be predicted. Within the context of this study, a prototype is created to illustrate the usability of the suggested architecture. In Sect. 4, the prototype application is briefly explained. In addition, the performance and scalability issues of the application are addressed in Sect. 5. The following sections go over the data analysis and classification processes in detail.

3.1   Module for Data Preprocessing

The initial version of the data consists of 32 columns and 100,000 rows of transaction information. Due to hardware-based computational issues, the sample size is reduced accordingly at this level. Description1, Description2, and Category Name are three columns that were considered useful in the data set. The Description1 and Description2 columns contain the customer and bank's description while performing the transaction. The column Category Name is the transfer type specified by the customer. The values of these columns are the categories specified by the accountants of enterprises.

To analyze the words in Description1 and Description2 columns, the Description1 and Description2 columns were combined into a specific column named as Description. The letters in this column were converted to lowercase with the lowercase function to avoid case-sensitivity problems. The frequencies of the words in the Description column are used to indicate their importance for the algorithm. Because of this, the frequencies of the words in the Description columns in all rows in the entire data was calculated, and those that fell below a certain threshold value were removed from the data. This eliminates fewer words that aren't important in the decision-making phase before they enter the algorithm.

3.2 Module for Bag of Words Embedding Method

One of the main factors that are of great importance and increase the success is how the data is represented before training a model. The bag-of-words (n-gram) method, one of the data representation methods, is frequently used in natural language processing problems. It is seen that the n-gram method gives successful results in similar problems where the sequential or combined probability of the words in the data is essential. Within the project's scope, each Description line is divided into separate tokens from n=1 to n=n from the beginning of the line, according to the maximum length of transaction. E.g., Suppose there is a bank transaction "eft from account A to account B". In the suggested method, the data representation of the original data is produced by n-gram sequences that were obtained separately as "eft", "eft account", "eft account A", "eft account A account ", "eft account A account B".

3.3 Module for Word2Vec Embedding Method

To make the data more meaningful, the data types were converted from word to vector after calculating the frequencies of the words contained in the data. In this way, a sequence is created where each word is represented by a set of 128 vectors. The word vectors which were in the same sentences are combined and the averages of created vectors are calculated. The mean vector was created in two ways to make different comparisons while averaging: Weighted Vector Average and Equally Weighted Vector Average. The function of this module is illustrated in Fig. 2.

The weights of the words were calculated using the frequency values of the words in the Weighted Vector Average. In the Equally Weighted Vector Average, the weights of all words were accepted as 1.

3.4 Module for Category Label Construction

During the construction of the category labels, it is observed that the same category names were repeated for reasons such as extra punctuation marks or English/Turkish characters which can be used interchangeably. For these repetitions not to be processed as different categories by the algorithm, and not to

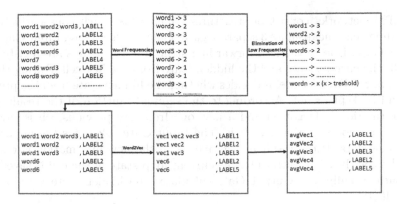

Fig. 2. Module for Word2Vec Embedding Method

reduce the success of the training results, some required operations are applied to the category name list. All letters are converted to lowercase, punctuation is cleaned, similar characters in Turkish/English are mapped and singularized, and finally, words in categories containing more than one word are concatenated with an underscore. In this way, the category names are cleaned and can be expressed with a single vector. As a result of these processes, the number of categories is reduced from the count of 173 to 162.

3.5 Modules for ML/DL Model Construction

Two different learning methods are used for training to predict categories using the data set: machine learning and deep learning.

Module for ML-Based Model Construction: In this project, Support Vector Machines (SVM) and Random Forest (RF) ML algorithms are used to predict transaction types. SVM is appropriate for the data set because it outperforms other classification algorithms based on training results when the data set size is large. SVM also has the advantage of being memory efficient.

Random Forest is a decision tree algorithm that was created to address the problem of overfitting in commonly used decision tree algorithms. The Random forest algorithm works similarly to a typical decision tree algorithm. Random Forest differs in that it employs multiple decision trees and accepts the most common output as the label. The label is determined by taking the average of the obtained results.

Module for DL-Based Model Construction: As a Deep Learning Based Model, Long Short-Term Memory (LSTM) networks are used to make category estimation. LSTM which is a type of Recurrent Neural Network (RNN) has been applied in this project due to its success in the problems requiring sequential estimation [13].

LSTM networks consist of structures called cells. Each consecutively feed forwarding cells encapsulate 3 separate gates called Forget Gate, Input Gate, and Output Gate. Due to the feed forwarding structure, two states are registered in the cell: the current state and the hidden state from the last cell. During the cell stream, in the Forget Gate, it decides whether the hidden state from the previous loop will be kept or not. According to the sigmoid function, if the result is "0" the information is forgotten and a new one from the previous cell is saved. If it is "1", the loop continues as it is. The Input Gate calculates the importance of the new data. If the result is negative (−1), the new information is removed from the cell. If it is positive (1), the current loop state of the cell is saved with new data. Finally, the Output Gate calculates the hidden state value for the next cell [19].

Within the project's scope, a model is designed with 100 Embedding Layer, 100 LSTM Layer, and 162 Dense Layer and trained with the bank account transaction data set. The results are shown in the Experimental Results section according to Accuracy and F1-Score values.

3.6   Module for Association Rule Mining

Methods like Association Rule Mining are used to extract meaningful relationships from data. As one of the Association Rule Mining algorithms, FP-Growth Algorithm is implemented in this module. As a result of the algorithm, Association Rules are generated.

FP-Growth Algorithm: The FP-Growth Algorithm is frequently used in Association Rule Mining as an enhanced version of the Apriori Algorithm. The FP-Growth Algorithm aims to reduce the high disk I/O and computational costs encountered in Apriori [11,12]. Instead of accessing the data at each step, the frequency and association information of the data is kept in the tree structure called FP-Growth Tree by providing access to data set two times. First of all, the frequency of each item is calculated. Based on the specified minimum support value, the Fp-Growth Tree is created by the items that are placed in descending order from the tree's root according to their frequency.

The list of routes for each item in the tree is saved as the Conditional Pattern Base, starting with the items with the lowest frequency, and the most used patterns for each item in this list are placed in the Conditional Pattern Frequency tree with their frequency values. Finally, the list of the rules is extracted from the Conditional Pattern Frequency tree. These are association rules developed for the provided data set using the FP-Growth Algorithm [20].

3.7   Module for Rule Based Bank Transaction Type Prediction

The 'Diger' label appears frequently in the data set used for this research project. This is a generic tag that has no bearing on inference. Using the association rules algorithm, it is attempted to predict whether the transactions labelled as

'Diger' have meaningful values. Association rules are produced with the help of Fp-Growth algorithm. The purpose of the obtained association rules is to categorize the data whose Category Name is 'Diger' in the data set if it complies with the rules. This estimation model is used to estimate rates on the test data set.

3.8   Module for ML/DL Based Bank Transaction Type Prediction

The models that can make the ideal predictions are obtained after the training. The success rates of these models' predictions are provided. When the data from the data set with the Category Name column of 'Diger' is given into the same models, the previously unknown transaction type becomes predictable.

4   Prototype and Evaluation

4.1   Prototype

This section explains how the technologies in this study are used. Python 3 is preferred as the software language because it works fast and is easy to use. The code is written using the Anaconda toolkit's Jupyter Notebook. Jupyter Notebook is a development environment that allows you to keep your code in different notebooks and run and analyze it in parts.

The transaction data received from Eçözüm Bilgi Teknolojileri A.Ş. is converted from excel to CSV format. For data in CSV format, there are ready-to-read commands such as 'read_csv(data)' in the Pandas library and 'read.csv(data)' in the Apache Spark library. Furthermore, reading and writing operations on CSV files are faster than those on XLSX files. A DataFrame containing the edited versions of the preprocessed data is created and saved using the Pandas library. Apache Spark is used to run and evaluate big data analytics operations across distributed systems.

The Spark MLlib which is a collection of machine learning algorithms is used in Spark. Association Rule Mining algorithms were implemented in Spark using this library.

4.2   Data Set

A data set containing customer bank account transaction information is used. This data set was obtained from Eçözüm Bilgi Teknolojileri A.S., a company that can report e-collection, bank integrations, virtual and physical POS transactions, as well as develops open banking technologies. The transfer information of 100,000 transactions was sufficient, considering the server's operating speed and the complexity analysis of the algorithms. The data set used includes 32 columns and 100,000 rows of transaction data. There are 68,281 rows in the data set, with the 'Category Name' column being 'Diger'. There are 173 different category types in the remaining 31,719 lines.

4.3   Test Design

In this study, Machine Learning, Deep Learning, and Association Rule Mining approaches are applied to distributed networks using Apache Spark. Random Forest (RF) and Support Vector Machines (SVM), as well as Long Short Term Memory (LSTM) and Frequent Pattern (FP) Growth algorithms, are used in Bank Account Transaction Type Prediction.

It was decided to focus on the data size to be used for training in order to make the training of the models more efficient. The data set is divided into two parts: a training set of 80% and a test set of 20%, with 80.000 in the training set and 20.000 in the test set.

RF and SVM algorithms in Python's Sklearn library are used within the scope of machine learning. Average Word2Vec embedding and Weighted Word2Vec embedding are the two types of vectors available for RF and SVM algorithms. To speed up reading and writing operations from the file, the data frame obtained during the conversion of words to vectors is saved as parquet file. The Sklearn library's "model selection" subheading is used to achieve the desired model training functions. The Accuracy and F1 Score values of these models are calculated. These values represent the success rates of the models.

Within the context of deep learning, the LSTM model is trained with the batch size 64 parameter. In the model creation, prediction, and evaluation stages, Python's Tensorflow Keras, SckitLearn, and nltk libraries are used.

The efficient FP-Growth Python library is used to apply the FP-Growth algorithm to the data set in order to determine the association rules, as mentioned in the Methodology section. This library provides the opportunity to save a Dataframe with the details of the rules it generates. The results acquired are used to develop the estimating module.

The algorithms were run on an Intel XEON x5650 processor with 8 GB of RAM in a server. This server is provided by Eçözüm Bilgi Teknolojileri A.S. to ensure that company information is not leaked.

The next section explains how to compare the outcomes of the algorithms and calculate the efficiency.

4.4   Experimental Results

This section presents deep learning and machine learning training along with testing results. The accuracy and F1-Score metrics are used to comprehensively summarize these results.

Accuracy Tests for Machine Learning Algorithms: Figure 3 shows the accuracy of the tested machine learning algorithms, while Fig. 4 shows the F1-Score comparison.

The RF and SVM values shown in the figure are the versions of the Weighted Word2Vec data set, as mentioned in the Sect. 3. Random Forest and SVM algorithms have additional "AVG" versions, as shown in the figure. The models are trained using the Average Word2Vec data set in "AVG" versions.

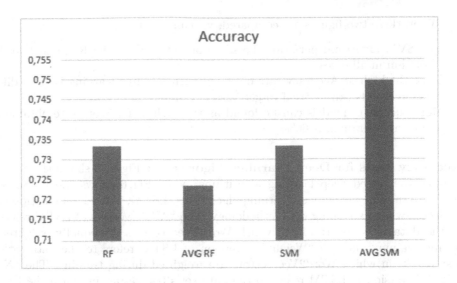

Fig. 3. Accuracy rates of ML algorithms

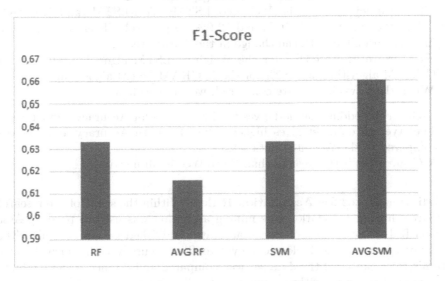

Fig. 4. F1-score rates of ML algorithms

The Random Forest and SVM algorithms both have accuracy rates of 73.3%. On this basis, it can be concluded that both algorithms are capable of training the desired model. When it comes to the "AVG" versions, AVG-RF has a 72.3% accuracy rate, while AVG-SVM has a 75% accuracy rate. While the rate of Random Forest decreases as the feature vector changes, the rate of SVM increases.

F1-Score rates of the Random Forest and SVM algorithms are 63.3%. The F1-Score rate is 61.6% for AVG-RF algorithm and 66% for AVG-SVM algorithm.

When these two figures are compared, we can conclude:

- The SVM algorithm performs the same or better than the Random Forest algorithm in all cases.
- Since the highest Accuracy rate obtained with machine learning is 75%, different methods can be tried to get better results.
- More successful models can be found as the highest F1-Score rate obtained by machine learning is 66%.

Accuracy Tests for Deep Learning Algorithms: Figure 5 shows the accuracy of the tested deep learning algorithms, while Fig. 6 shows the F1-Score comparison. One of the deep learning algorithms, LSTM, is used, as mentioned in Sect. 3 when explaining the methodology. The "AVG" version of LSTM refers to the data set's test result, in which Word2Vec vectors are equally weighted during training and the "Weighted" version of LSTM refers to the data set's test result, in which Word2Vec vectors are weighted during training. The "N-GRAM" version of LSTM refers to the data set's test result, in which the Bag of Words Data set was used in the training phase.

The accuracy rate of the Weighted LSTM, AVG-LSTM, and N-GRAM-LSTM methods are 73.2%, 76%, and 82.9%, respectively. There appears to be an increase in LSTM with the change in the feature vector.

F1-Score rates are 63.6% for the Weighted LSTM algorithm, 70% for the AVG-LSTM algorithm, and 82% for the N-GRAM-LSTM algorithm.

When these two figures are compared, we can conclude:

- N-Gram embedding method gives the best values for Accuracy and F1-Score.
- The Average data set gives higher values for both Accuracy and F1-Score compared to the Weighted data set.
- N-Gram gives better results than Word2Vec in all metrics.

Prediction Rates for Association Rules: Within the scope of the research, FP-Growth from association rule mining algorithm was used to produce Association Rule. There can be no accuracy rate established because the algorithm does not represent a scalable accuracy rate. The accuracy with which the algorithm's rules can label the data set was compared and deemed a success factor in determining the algorithm's success rate. The support and confidence values were set as 0.01 for support and 0.6 for confidence.

In this part, the experimental results for the FP-Growth algorithm are explained in detail. The data set is split into Train and Test data with 80% and 20% ratios, respectively. Different minimum confidence and minimum support values were tried, but 0.06 minimum confidence and 0.01 minimum support values produced the most reasonable result. In this part of the study, 43.6% of the test value could not be assigned to a category, 28.4% was correctly classified, and 27.9% was incorrectly classified.

Since the results show that the Association Rule Mining algorithm is successful in general, FP-Growth requires more data to create reliable rules.

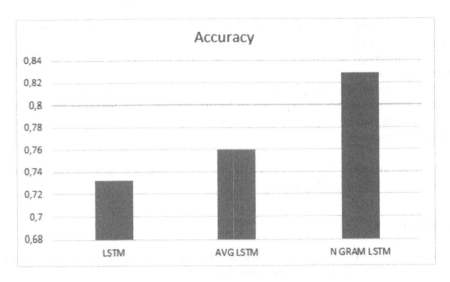

Fig. 5. Accuracy rates of DL algorithms

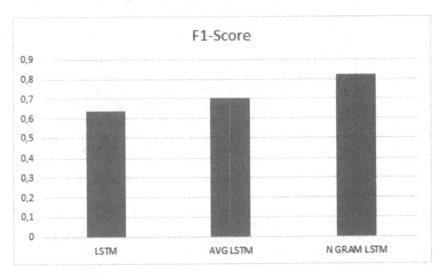

Fig. 6. F1-score rates of DL algorithms

5   Conclusion and Future Work

A software architecture proposal was made as part of this study to determine and make sense of the uncertain data encountered in the banking sector. A prototype application was designed to test the proposed architecture. The proposed architecture uses Random Forest and SVM machine learning algorithms, LSTM deep learning algorithm, FP-Growth association mining algorithm.

Author Index